ISBN 978-1-5282-2418-5
PIBN 10900215

English
Français
Deutsche
Italiano
Español
Português

www.forgottenbooks.com

Mythology Photography **Fiction**
Fishing Christianity **Art** Cooking
Essays Buddhism Freemasonry
Medicine **Biology** Music **Ancient
Egypt** Evolution Carpentry Physics
Dance Geology **Mathematics** Fitness
Shakespeare **Folklore** Yoga Marketing
Confidence Immortality Biographies
Poetry **Psychology** Witchcraft
Electronics Chemistry History **Law**
Accounting **Philosophy** Anthropology
Alchemy Drama Quantum Mechanics
Atheism Sexual Health **Ancient History**
Entrepreneurship Languages Sport
Paleontology Needlework Islam
Metaphysics Investment Archaeology
Parenting Statistics Criminology
Motivational

Occasional Paper 158   1958

THE ELUSIVE FORMULA OF BEST FIT:
A COMPREHENSIVE NEW MACHINE PROGRAM

L. R. GROSENBAUGH

SOUTHERN FOREST EXPERIMENT STATION
PHILIP A. BRIEGLEB, DIRECTOR,
Forest Service, U. S. Department of Agriculture

THE ELUSIVE FORMULA OF BEST FIT:
A COMPREHENSIVE NEW MACHINE PROGRAM

L. R. Grosenbaugh
Southern Forest Experiment Station

Do you need to fit formulas (or regressions) to data?

For any set of data, how would you like a look at all the least-squares formulas which predict Y using every possible linear combination of 9 or fewer variables? A new electronic machine program now lets you do this cheaply and easily, even though you have no background in mathematics or machines. In addition, the program output for each of the hundreds of formulas includes a value which is useful in comparing reliability or efficiency. Before now, such a capability has existed in theory only--the cost by previously existing machine programs was far too high even for the most inquisitive expert.

What does this mean to you?

Suppose that in managing forest land or carrying out a forest research project you have collected data similar to those shown in figure 1. Maybe Y represents individual sample-tree volumes or plot growth, while X_1, X_2, etc., represent associated measurements such as d. b. h. , height, taper, distribution parameters, or functions such as their squares, reciprocals, or logarithms, or joint functions of several of these. Perhaps Y is site index or available soil moisture and the X's are soil or stand variables. Or Y may be cost or value, and the X's may be items thought to influence cost or value. No matter-- your problem is to find a formula that will satisfactorily predict Y when only the X's are known, and to discard any column of X's that does not appreciably improve the prediction.

In the past, people have almost never been willing to spend the time and money involved in calculating and comparing the reliabilities of the hundreds of possible formulas which might be fitted by least squares to observations of a dependent variable and 9 or fewer inde‐

Figure 1.— Raw or coded data.

Y		X_1	X_2	X_3	X_4	X_c	X_6	X_7	X_8	X_9	
9		0	0	0	0	0	0	0	0	0	
23		0	1	0	0	1	0	0	0	1	
17		0	2	0	0	4	0	0	0	8	
5		0	3	0	0	9	0	0	0	27	
8		0	4	0	0	16	0	0	0	64	
9		1	0	0	1	0	0	0	0	0	
8		1	1	1	1	1	1	1	1	1	
5		1	2	2	1	4	2	4	4	8	
15		1	3	3	1	9	3	9	9	27	
2		1	4	4	1	16	4	16	16	64	
3		2	0	0	4	0	0	0	0	0	
3		2	1	2	4	1	4	2	4	1	
7		2	2	4	4	4	8	8	16	8	
4		2	3	6	4	9	12	18	36	27	
9		2	4	8	4	16	16	32	64	64	
7		3	0	0	9	0	0	0	0	0	
11		3	1	3	9	1	9	3	9	1	
7		3	2	6	9	4	18	12	36	8	
4		3	3	9	9	9	27	27	81	27	
18		3	4	12	9	16	36	48	144	64	
9		4	0	0	16	0	0	0	0	0	
5		4	1	4	16	1	16	4	16	1	
11		4	2	8	16	4	32	16	64	8	
14		4	3	12	16	9	48	36	144	27	
23		4	4	16	16	16	64	64	256	64	
7		5	0	0	25	0	0	0	0	0	
18		5	1	5	25	1	25	5	25	1	
13		5	2	10	25	4	50	20	100	8	
19		5	3	15	25	9	75	45	225	27	
29		5	4	20	25	16	100	80	400	64	
Totals 322		75	60	150	275	180	550	450	1650	600	
Number of sets of observations 30											

Figure 2

SOUTHERN FOREST EXPERIMENT STATION 704 REGRESSION PROGRAM OUTPUT   LRG 11- 5-57

IDENTITY NUMBER ITEM	SUM OF SQUARES	0+5	1+6	2+7	3+8	4+9
MEANS		2 10733333	1 25000000	1 20000000	1 50000000	1 91666666
NUMBER PER MEAN		30	30	30	30	30
MEANS		1 60000000	2 18333333	2 15000000	2 55000000	2 20000000
NUMBER PER MEAN		30	30	30	30	30
MAXIMUM MATRIX*SP AND SS						
0 TOTAL =		4 13498667	3 10500000	2 83000000	3 64700000	3 75633335
		3 34900000	4 34096667	4 25730000	5 12909000	4 14510000
1			2 87500000	00000000	3 17500000	3 43750000
		00000000	3 87500000	3 52500000	4 26250000	00000000
2			2 60000000	3 15000000	00000000	
		3 24000000	3 55000000	3 60000000	4 22000000	3 92400000
3				3 90000000	3 87500000	
		3 60000000	4 40000000	4 32500000	5 14250000	4 23100000
4						4 23741667
		00000000	4 47483334	4 26250000	5 14245000	00000000
5						
		4 10440000	4 22000000	4 26100000	4 95700000	4 42000000
6			5 19286667	5 14250000	5 67650000	4 84700000
7				5 12720000	5 54900000	5 10500000
8					6 25981600	5 38500000
9						5 17340000

REGRESSIONS

1		4 102024	2 104401	1-408865	2 139181	1-620519	782138
3 variables			1-713348	1 100537	1 191710	-258930	819440
2 variables 2		3 962228	2 114234	1-408863	1 687096	1-620522	782134
			1-221685	1 100537	1 191711	-258932	
3		3 985202	2 121683	1-667796	2 104657	1-102658	1 130000
			1-627040	-1-303573	622449		819443

Intervening Regressions Omitted

496		3 124417	1 856667		527778		
							-1 555555
497		3 468972	1 727055			766042	
							-1-183712
498		3 362362	1 613954				318568
							-1 836794
499		3 121644	1 916594				
			-1-918866				105936
500		3 602949	1 753291				
				178285			-2-340677
501		3 572682	1 829024				
					266332		-1-775941
502		3 672362	1 845724				
2 variables						-1 568725	-1-425946
1 variable 503		3 126000	1 773333	1 120000			
504		3 114817	1 796667		1 138333		
505		3 465121	1 713889			718889	
506		3 240944	1 781313				318568
507		3 116668	1 872759				
			334291				
508		3 602791	1 749221				
				176789			
509		3 520466	1 769914				
					202280		
510		☀ 3 651415	1 795792				
						-1 504621	
511		3 121419	1 905975				
							-1 836794

pendent variables. Even with the latest electronic machines, only a few of the possible formulas have usually been derived and analyzed, because of the expense of specifying hundreds of variations and then setting up individual machine inputs and programs for each.

But a new day has dawned. Now you can just send your pencil or ink data sheets (like fig. 1) or punched cards to some agency having both an IBM 704 Electronic Data Processing Machine and the Southern Forest Experiment Station's 704 Regression Program. Cost estimates will probably lie between $50 and $250, depending on the number of observations and variables, and whether you submit data sheets or punched cards. The program will completely and automatically handle up to 500 observations of Y (fig. 1 has only 30), along with observations of as many as 9 associated columns of X's (as in fig. 1). All observations should be rounded or coded so that decimals are eliminated and the number of digits does not exceed four. A supplementary program handling more than 500 observations is being developed by the Southern Forest Experiment Station and should be ready shortly, although costs will run somewhat higher.

What will you get for this relatively modest cost? See figure 2, which is only a small part of the actual output generated by the data in figure 1 (the complete program output involved 28 sheets). Briefly, the outlay buys mean Y and all mean X's; the sums of squares and cross-products of deviations from these means; the variation in Y removed by every possible formula involving one or more columns of X (up to 9 columns), and the coefficients needed in each such formula. With (m) columns of X, there will be (2^m-1) possible formulas, and they will have a total of $(m)(2^{m-1})$ coefficients plus (2^m-1) constants. For the maximum of 9 columns of X's the complete program output will furnish information concerning all of the 511 possible different formulas involving these variables, and there will be a total of 2,304 formula coefficients. There will be 1 nine-variable formula, 9 eight-variable formulas, 36 sevens, 84 sixes, 126 fives, 126 fours, 84 threes, 36 twos, and 9 ones. A table of binomial coefficients will tell you how many of each kind of formula there will be if you start with fewer than 9 columns of X's.

Figure 2 may still look like gibberish because the "floating decimal point" notation is unfamiliar. Actually, it's simple. Only the main groups of 6 or 8 digits are real quantities--the single-digit prefixes are merely instructions as to where the decimal point belongs. Where no number precedes a group of 6 or 8 digits, the decimal point is placed immediately in front of the group. Where the prefix 1 precedes the main group, the decimal point is moved one position to the right; where the prefix 2 precedes, the point is moved two positions to the right, etc. Where –1 precedes, one zero is prefixed to the group and the decimal point is moved one place to the left (i. e. , placed to the left of the zero). Where –2 precedes, two zeros are prefixed to the group and the decimal point is placed to the left of both zeros. Where no algebraic sign is printed in front of a group, plus is understood. Any minus sign is always specifically indicated. To illustrate, 2 146532 means 14. 6532; 1 437986 means 4. 37986; –2 –529431 means –. 00529431; 764327 means . 764327; –464789 means –. 464789.

It would have been nice if figure 2 could have had column headings stretching horizontally from 0 through 9, after the "SUM OF SQUARES" heading. The printing machine wasn't wide enough, though, so it had to break the line after X_4 and start X_5 under the first column, or mean Y (here denoted by the 0 heading). Hence, the first numbered column-head is 0 + 5.

Now let's look at figure 2 item by item. The first double row of numbers indicates that mean Y is 10. 733333, mean X_1 is 2. 5000000, etc. , and that each number is the mean of 30 observations. The mean of X_5 is 6. 0000000, with 30 observations indicated beneath it. Note that this starts a second double row directly under mean Y. The column-head 0 + 5 indicates that the upper mean will be Y and the lower mean will be X_5. Then X_6, X_7, X_8, X_9 follow horizontally after X_5. In each case, the column-head indicates what kinds of X will be found in the upper and lower double rows (i. e. , 1 + 6, 2 + 7, 3 + 8, 4 + 9).

Now we get to the part of the results subheaded "MAXIMUM MATRIX, SP and SS." All of these values are sums of squares or cross-products of deviations from some mean X's or mean Y. The particular combination is denoted by the dual column number, by the number of the double row, and by the position of the digits in the upper or lower part of the row. For example, the first entry is 1349. 8667 in the upper part of row 0 under column 0 + 5. (The upper position in a row means that the first digit in the dual column-head is appropriate.) Therefore, its descriptive location is 00, which means it represents the sums of squares of deviations of Y from mean Y--often called the total sum of squares for Y. All other figures in row 0 involve cross-products of Y deviations with X deviations indicated by column-heads. In the lower part of row 3 under column 4 + 9 (descriptive location is 39), we find 2310. 0000, or the sum of cross-products of deviations from mean X_3 and deviations from mean X_9. Note that the lower position in a row means that the second digit in the dual column-head is appropriate.

These figures will be helpful if you later want an inverse matrix (c-multipliers) for a few selected formulas to be calculated locally by existing programs on less expensive machines (the IBM 704 costs about $700 an hour to operate, and is too expensive for relatively routine calculations). Currently, matrix inversion (fifth- to tenth-order matrices) costs only from $30 to $35 on machines such as the IBM 650.

And now for the meat in the coconut. Each consecutive numbered double row below the subheading "REGRESSIONS" gives vital statistics about a single formula involving prediction of Y by some particular combination of the various kinds of X's. Entries in the first column to the right of the row number (the column headed "SUM OF SQUARES") are sums of squares attributable to various regressions, and any one divided by the total sum of squares (1349.8667) mentioned above gives the square of the multiple correlation coefficient (R^2) for the particular formula specified by the remainder of the double row. It is not necessary to perform this division unless you wish to make certain statistical tests or statements. However, you can readily choose the best 8-variable formula, the best 7-variable formula, etc., by merely selecting the line in each particular class which has the largest sum of squares shown in this "SUM OF SQUARES" column. As an example, figure 2 shows that asterisked regression 510 is the best of the 9 single-variable regressions; its "SUM OF SQUARES" attributable to regression (651.415) is the largest in the single-variable series 503-511.

The adjoining figures shown in double rows under columns headed 0 + 5, 1 + 6, 2 + 7, 3 + 8, and 4 + 9 are the coefficients appropriate to that particular formula, with the 0, 1, 2, 3, 4 referring to the upper position and the 5, 6, 7, 8, 9 referring to the lower position in the row. In each double row, the upper quantity shown in the 0 column is a constant. All other quantities are coefficients for X_1 through X_9. Thus, if a double row has figures appearing under 8 heads besides "SUM OF SQUARES" and "Zero" (which represents a constant), a formula is specified which depends on 8 variables to predict Y. As an example, regression # 3 is interpreted as:

$$Y = +12.1663 \quad - 6.67796X_1 + 10.4657X_2 - 1.02658X_3 + 1.30000X_4$$
$$-6.27040X_5 - .0303573X_6 + .622449X_7 \qquad + .819443X_9$$

For regression # 3, the sum of squared residuals (or the sum of squares of the differences between formula-predicted values for Y and the actually observed values of Y) is 1349.8667 minus 985.202, or 364.665. If desirable, the squared multiple correlation coefficient R^2 could be found as $\frac{985.202}{1349.8667}$ = .730. The statistical "degrees of freedom" appropriate to both the sum of squared residuals and to R^2 is the total number of observed sets of values (30 in this case) minus the number of coefficients used in the formula (including the constant in the "Zero" column). In the above example, degrees of freedom would be (30-9) or 21 dfs. The sum of squared residuals divided by the degrees of freedom gives the mean squared residual (or the squared standard error of estimate for the formula). In this case, the mean squared residual would be

$$\frac{364.665}{21} = 17.365 \text{ with 21 degrees of freedom.}$$

With the above explanation, it is possible to explore different sequences for taking variables into account. These techniques are well known and will not be discussed here. However, comparison of the mean squared residual with the improvement in variation progressively accounted for by the best 1-, 2-, 3-, 4-, 5-, 6-, 7-, 8-, or 9-variable formulas will often suffice to decide upon a cutoff point.

Foresters will find this program immediately helpful in converting volume tables to formulas for forest inventory punched-card operations, and in analyzing stand growth or soil-site relationships. It will also be useful wherever else multiple regression techniques are appropriate. It is far cheaper than manual or piece-meal machine calculation of the same data, and it will secure more comprehensive, convenient, and reliable information far more quickly, cheaply, and with less skilled technical knowledge than will any other existing package program the author has been able to locate or devise.

Biometrical Background

Although complex formulas fitted by least squares (i.e., multiple regressions) have gained wide favor in recent years, their use has been limited by many persons' unfamiliarity with data-processing techniques and by the expense of screening out the less efficient combinations of variables where the so-called independent variables are intercorrelated (as they usually are). The interpretation of a conventional partial correlation analysis is clouded by any intercorrelation among independent variables. In other words, estimates of the importance of a given independent variable fluctuate as the variable is grouped with different combinations of other independent variables. Hence, the path or order of fitting affects the apparent importance of any independent variable in a prediction formula. The regression analyses described in most publications deal with a single path or order of fitting, and ignore other possible sequences because of the magnitude of computational labor.

After wrestling with this problem for a number of
author reluctantly decided that no known existing machine
adequate for the job, and that even such excellent equipme
Type 650 Electronic Data Processing Machine did not hav
or the speed to allow development of the needed program
operational cost.

Consequently, he constructed the synthetic sample
signed to allow a number of cross checks) illustrated in fi
D. B. DeLury's 1950 Values and Integrals of the Orthogor
nomials up to n = 26 (page 9), and then worked out the spe
for the program output illustrated by figure 2. Consultati
eral programming agencies finally resulted in a contract
Bureau Corporation, a subsidiary of IBM, to develop a pr
the IBM 704 according to detailed Southern Forest Experi
specifications and example.

The most efficient computational approach seemed
version of the maximum matrix of sums of squares and cr
of deviations to a maximum matrix of simple correlation
From this, a matrix of appropriate simple correlation co
(r_{ij}), always including the Y-correlations, could be cons
each of the 511 possible regressions. Elements (C'_{ij}) of
matrix for each of these correlation-coefficient matrices
puted by the modified Jordan elimination method. Then fo
regression,

$$b_{oj} = -\frac{C'_{oj}}{C'_{oo}} \sqrt{\frac{SS_{oo}}{SS_{jj}}} \text{ , with } o \text{ denoting the depei}$$

with j successively denoting each independent variable pr
given regression, and with SS denoting the sum of square
from the mean. The general procedure is outlined on pag
C. H. Goulden's 1952 Methods of Statistical Analysis. T
of sums of squares attributable to regression and a check
ficients for selected regressions are illustrated on page
Miss Carol Hadek of The Service Bureau Corporation bro
specified mathematical processes into a staggering serie
step machine orders permanently recorded on magnetic t

The program should be widely useful in non-forestry fields. Furthermore, similar programs can be developed in the same format to handle many more than 9 independent variables. It is hoped that other agencies will find it profitable to finance such program extensions, but the existing program will serve in the most commonly encountered forestry situations. The program outlined above, with input at the limiting maxima, is solved by the IBM 704 in about 11 minutes of actual operation. With such potentiality, there seems little need to overheat desk calculators for months on end, or to be satisfied with a single sequence of fit, as has been almost universal practice in the past.

OCCASIONAL PAPER 159

CLIMBING

SOUTHERN

PINES

SAFELY

E. Bayne Snyder
and Harry Rossoll

SOUTHERN FOREST EXPERIMENT STATION
PHILIP A. BRIEGLEB, DIRECTOR
Forest Service, U. S. Department of Agriculture
1958

CONTRIBUTORS

The following experienced climbers are largely responsible for the recommendations and points in this guide to safe climbing:

C.L. Brown, *Texas Forest Service*

T.E. Campbell, *A.J. Hodges Industries, Incorporated*

F.C. Cech, *International Paper Company*

R.E. Goddard, *Texas Forest Service*

T.O. Perry, *University of Florida*

B.J. Zobel, *North Carolina State College*

J.C. Barber, K.W. Dorman, R.W. Johansen, and J.F. Kraus, *Southeastern Forest Experiment Station, U.S. Forest Service*

H.B. Ainsworth, R.M. Allen, R.M. Echols, J.E. Evans, B.W. Henry, F.F. Jewell, S.L. Mallett, W.S. Mauldin, B.A. Redmond, N.B. Saucier, N.M. Scarbrough, P.C. Wakeley, and R.B. Yates, *Southern Forest Experiment Station, U.S. Forest Service*

CLIMBING SOUTHERN PINES
SAFELY

E. BAYNE SNYDER
Southern Institute of Forest Genetics
Southern Forest Experiment Station

HARRY ROSSOLL
Southern Region, U.S. Forest Service

INTRODUCTION

The tree-climbing practices described in this booklet are recommended to tree breeders and cone collectors for combining safety with efficiency. They apply to climbing with sectional ladders and are subject to revision as experience enlarges. These recommendations cannot prevail against the inherent dangers of tree climbing unless they are studied and practiced. Workers can avoid personal injury and set a good example by never putting undue stress on themselves, the equipment, or the tree. Action should be steady and deliberate instead of rapid, so that there is time to detect and evaluate hidden decay in the tree, and other hazards discussed herein.

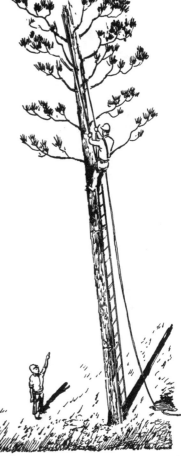

1

PERSONAL CLOTHING

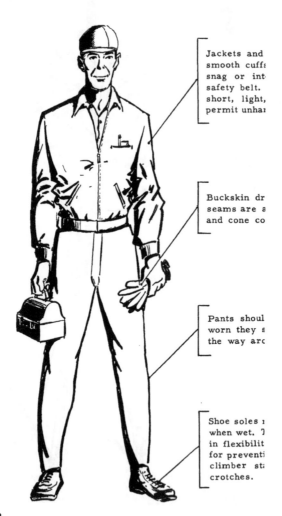

Jackets and
smooth cuff₁
snag or int₁
safety belt.
short, light,
permit unha₁

Buckskin dr
seams are a
and cone co

Pants shoul
worn they s
the way aro

Shoe soles ₁
when wet. ₁
in flexibilit
for preventi
climber sta
crotches.

2

SSIGNED EQUIPMENT

When in use, the safety harness and tree belt should be inspected daily by both the worker and his partner and twice a month by the safety officer or his designate. If visible flaws or more than superficial checks appear in the belt when the grain side is bent double, the equipment must be replaced. Hang the belts away from sharp tools and otherwise treat them with extreme care in storage, transport, and use. Clean them periodically with saddle soap.

VOID USING ROPE TO TOW TRUCKS!

Hard hats or caps must be worn by helpers on the ground and are advised for all cone collectors.

Eye shields should be worn. They will protect the eyes against tools, loose debris, and the saw-like barbs of needles. Some workers object to the feeling of these shields while others claim their prescription glasses fog when the shields are being worn. Antifog chemicals are available. Eyeglasses offer some protection, but do not prevent the eyes from being wounded from the side. Several different types of shields are available and workers should try hard to get accustomed to one of them.

Rope should be of 1/2-inch manila or manila reinforced with nylon. A safe load is no more than one-eighth the minimum breaking strength. Lengths may vary up to 150 feet or more according to the size of the trees. New ropes should be hung in large coils for several months before being used, to minimize effects of original twist. Ropes in use must be inspected daily by both the worker and his partner and twice a month by the safety officer or his designate. Inspection includes separation of strands to see if inside yarns are bright and unbroken. If weaknesses are seen, the rope must be trimmed or discarded. Avoid using the climbing rope for such duties as pulling trucks out of ditches. Testing its strength by subjecting it to strain may weaken it dangerously. Keep it away from fire, acids, sharp tools, etc. If it becomes wet, hang it loosely where there is air circulation. Transport the rope in a coil.

3

Swedish ladders have stiff joints when new or after a period of storage. They should not be used until they are filed and sanded, so as to slide apart easily. Chain snaps must be attached to the chains before the ladder is used. Kicking or hammering ladder brackets damages the bracket rivets and must be avoided.

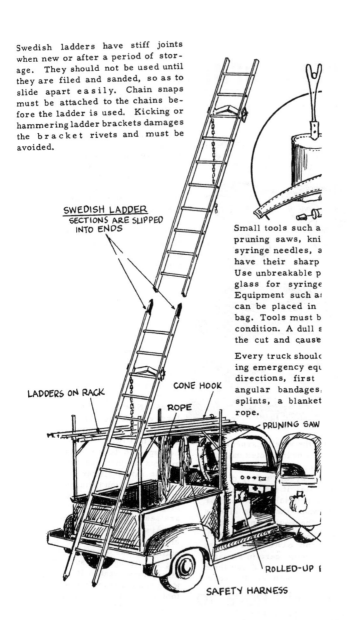

SWEDISH LADDER
SECTIONS ARE SLIPPED
INTO ENDS

Small tools such a
pruning saws, kni
syringe needles, a
have their sharp
Use unbreakable p
glass for syringe
Equipment such a
can be placed in
bag. Tools must b
condition. A dull s
the cut and cause

Every truck shoul
ing emergency equ
directions, first
angular bandages
splints, a blanket
rope.

PRUNING SAW

LADDERS ON RACK   CONE HOOK

ROPE

ROLLED-UP

SAFETY HARNESS

WEATHER AND TREE CONDITIONS

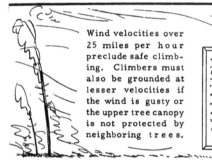

Wind velocities over 25 miles per hour preclude safe climbing. Climbers must also be grounded at lesser velocities if the wind is gusty or the upper tree canopy is not protected by neighboring trees.

Daylight is mandatory since even simple operations are hazardous and difficult before daylight and after dark. Do not climb in dim light.

Temperatures below 36° render climbing unsafe. Fingers become numb and branches brittle. Climbing should not be undertaken below 40° if there is much wind.

TREE TOP STEM 3" TO 4" IN DIAMETER UNSAFE

A tree top with a stem less than 3 to 4 inches in diameter at the point where the worker attaches his safety belt is likely to be unsafe, depending on the wind and the weight of the climber. Give a wider margin of safety by not going so high-- not only for your own sake but for the heavier man who may need to rework the tree in a wind.

Moisture creates slippery surfaces. Shoes may become unexpectedly slippery from wet grass in the early morning. Knots slip if ropes are wet. No climbing should be done in the rain.

WATCH SLIPPERY SHOES FROM WET GRASS

Power lines and electrical storms are especially dangerous. Trees near power or other lines should not be climbed lest the metal ladders and other equipment cause the worker to be electrocuted. Lightning storms move fast and tall breeding trees are frequently hit. If lightning is in the neighborhood, climb down and get away from the tree as quickly as possible.

GET AWAY FROM TREE AS QUICKLY AS

TREE FLAWS
DANGER SIGNS

1. Tree cankers
2. Dead limbs
3. Internal decay
4. Loose bark
5. Tops formerly broken
6. Oblique branch unions

Tree flaws are numerous, but must be detected before climbing is begun. Extreme care must be exercised in examining rust-cankered trees before climbing: the cankers should not exceed one-third the circumference at any one spot. Climbing above high cankers is taboo. Check also for hard-to-see internal decay. Loose bark can make the hand slip from large branches. Care must be taken in trees whose tops have formerly broken out, since the new tops are all the more apt to break. Poor or oblique branch unions and stems with sudden decreases in diameter are similarly prone to breakage. Evaluate the hazards and pass up dangerous trees!

NG TECHNIQUES

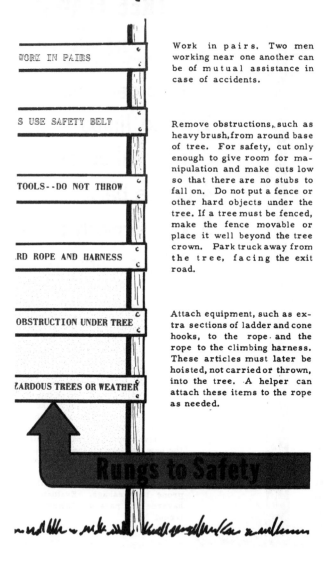

WORK IN PAIRS

S USE SAFETY BELT

TOOLS--DO NOT THROW

RD ROPE AND HARNESS

OBSTRUCTION UNDER TREE

ZARDOUS TREES OR WEATHER

Rungs to Safety

Work in pairs. Two men working near one another can be of mutual assistance in case of accidents.

Remove obstructions, such as heavy brush, from around base of tree. For safety, cut only enough to give room for manipulation and make cuts low so that there are no stubs to fall on. Do not put a fence or other hard objects under the tree. If a tree must be fenced, make the fence movable or place it well beyond the tree crown. Park truck away from the tree, facing the exit road.

Attach equipment, such as extra sections of ladder and cone hooks, to the rope and the rope to the climbing harness. These articles must later be hoisted, not carried or thrown, into the tree. A helper can attach these items to the rope as needed.

In erecting the ladder, it is safest if only two sections at a time are pushed up from the ground and thereafter only one section hoisted at a time. The top section should extend close to or into the crown and between the limbs. Placing the base of the ladder so that the top section will fit between limbs requires careful study.

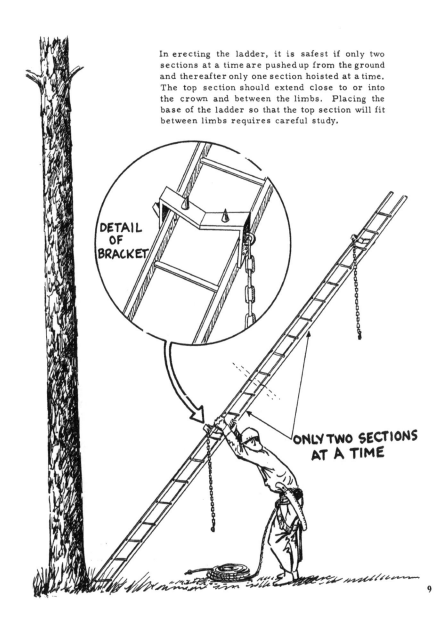

DETAIL OF BRACKET

ONLY TWO SECTIONS AT A TIME

ENCIRCLE TREE WITH SAFETY B

Befor
ground
with sa
just be
slack.
more
worn a
rather
waist.
the bel
as we
Climbe
their s
becaus
"snap,
they w
Such e
fatal a
the gr
fasten
quent
you c

BE SURE BI
SNAPS CON
INTO "D"

SAFETY
BELT

Look as well as listen !

Fasten the chain of the first ladder section around the tree. It is essential that the chain be taut. This manipulation is sometimes strenuous. Push on the right side of ladder with the left arm and the right foot or knee in a rocking motion while pulling back on the chain to get it in the slot at the correct link. If the slot still comes near the middle of a link, the procedure must be repeated after twisting the chain to shorten it the required amount. As a precaution against the link slipping out of the slot the chain should be knotted around the bracket and itself. The chain's loose end should then be passed between the ladder and the tree and wrapped around the other side of the ladder and bracket to take up the free-end slack, after which it can be snapped on itself. The chain of each ladder section must be fastened as the climber comes to it.

PUSH AGAINST RIGHT SIDE OF LADDER WITH LEFT ARM

PULL CHAIN TIGHTLY

PUSH AGAINST LADDER WITH RIGHT LEG

PRUNE ALL STUBS

Prune all dead branches and stubs as you proceed up the tree. Cuts should be flush lest belts or clothing catch on the stubs. It may be necessary to stand on the top of one ladder section and prune branches that are preventing erection of the next section, but avoid positions where large pruned limbs can fall on you. The final ladder section should extend close to or into the crown. Stretching from the ladder to the crown and pulling yourself up is both dangerous and fatiguing. Branches directly above the top section should be pruned higher than necessary to put the ladder up since yet more clearance is needed to take the ladder down. Use only a hand saw (equipped with a scabbard) for pruning.

11

Before transferring to the crown, carefully inspect the limbs. <u>Do not be fooled by dead limbs</u> which are camouflaged by living ones. Cut all dead limbs when you first see them to prevent the possibility of accidentally using them another time. Trusting a dead limb is possibly the greatest single climbing risk.

After dead limbs have been removed, brace feet and hold firmly to the ladder or tree with one hand. Unfasten safety belt with other hand, sling end of belt over shoulder, and fasten to the D-ring of the safety harness. Dangling belts are a hazard.

Trusting a dead limb is possibly the greatest single climbing risk! DON'T DO IT!

RIGHT

POSSIBLE SLIPS!

WRONG

INSTALL POLE STEP

Climbing in the crown requires continued alertness for dead limbs. Whenever possible, distribute the body weight on several live limbs rather than on a single one. If a long reach is necessary within a crown, toss a rope or belt over a limb above as an aid in pulling yourself up. Better yet, install a pole step in trees to be climbed repeatedly. Step in the crotch rather than out on the limb.

NOT LIKE THIS!

LIKE THIS

← USE ROPE OR BELT AS AID IN PULLING UP TO HIGHER POSITION

13

As soon as he has reached his work position the climber must secure himself to the tree with his safety belt. The belt must always be passed around the trunk over a limb on the opposite side of the tree. Usually work is started at the top of the tree. If the stem is thin here, the climber should remain in a vertical position. The belt may be shortened by wrapping it around the thin stem twice. Working with the back to the wind will help alleviate the lean of a thin stem. At a lower work position the sturdier stem will permit extension of the belt, so that the climber can lean out on it from the vertical. Fatigue will then be less because the weight is shared by the harness and the feet. The climber must refasten the belt at each lower work position.

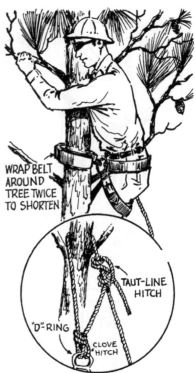

WRAP BELT AROUND TREE TWICE TO SHORTEN

TAUT-LINE HITCH

"D" RING

CLOVE HITCH

IF YOU WISH TO DESCEND, HOLD KNOT.
TO STOP, LET GO!

If there are many work positions or if the outside of the crown is hard to reach, a climbing rope is more efficient than the belt. The belt must be used, however, when tieing and testing the rope. Use a taut-line hitch with the rope secured to the D-ring of the safety harness with a clove hitch (see the bulletin by Thompson, listed on page 17). Before disconnecting the belt and swinging free, make sure the rope has a figure-eight knot at the ground end, is not entangled, and does not extend into a roadway. Unfasten the hitch only when on the ground or secured with a safety belt.

14

A hook, fashioned from no. 6 wire and attached to a no. 9 wire about 6 feet long, is used to pull in limbs. Each end should be bent into a very small loop, to minimize injury if a worker is struck. Colored tape on the wire makes the hook easier to see on the ground.

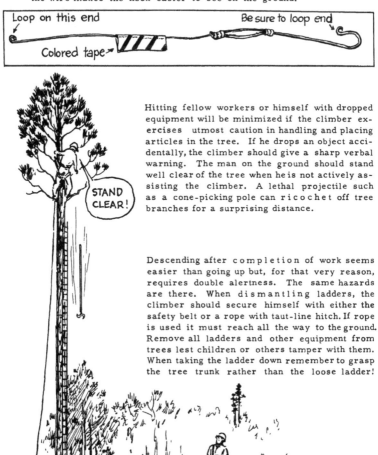

Hitting fellow workers or himself with dropped equipment will be minimized if the climber exercises utmost caution in handling and placing articles in the tree. If he drops an object accidentally, the climber should give a sharp verbal warning. The man on the ground should stand well clear of the tree when he is not actively assisting the climber. A lethal projectile such as a cone-picking pole can ricochet off tree branches for a surprising distance.

Descending after completion of work seems easier than going up but, for that very reason, requires double alertness. The same hazards are there. When dismantling ladders, the climber should secure himself with either the safety belt or a rope with taut-line hitch. If rope is used it must reach all the way to the ground. Remove all ladders and other equipment from trees lest children or others tamper with them. When taking the ladder down remember to grasp the tree trunk rather than the loose ladder!

SUPERVISORY RESPONSIBILITI

Yearly examinations by a physician
tory for all climbers. Workers must
if they have an incapacity, either t
persistent, that might endanger th
helpers. A man who has been w
office is a risk until he toughens u
may rarely be called on to use h
strength, emergencies must be anti
first he should be limited to part-tii
At no time should a man be drivei
endurance.

Red Cross first-aid courses shoulc
of all climbers.

Safety meetings for all climbers
before pollinating and cone-collec
and at other times deemed nece
safety officer. The meetings shoul
procedures and first aid by mean;
demonstrations. It is important th:
or accidents be analyzed.

New men should climb only when trained in
safety and first aid. During their first season
they should always be paired with experienced
personnel.

SOME SOURCES*
OF CLIMBING EQUIPMENT

Wikstrand and Berg cone-picking ladders, Model WI-BE, 10-foot sections. Sandvik Saw and Tool Division, Sandvik Steel, Inc., 47 Warren Street, New York 7, New York.

Saf-I-Flex plastic eyeshield. United States Safety Service Company, Kansas City 6, Missouri.

Model T safety cap. Mine Safety Appliance Company, 1345 Spring St., N.W. Atlanta, Georgia.

Safety strap (2 inches by 5 feet 10 inches, with snaps) and tree harness. A.M. Leonard and Sons, Inc., Piqua, Ohio.

---

*This list is not exhaustive. Inclusion of a firm or product does not constitute endorsement by the U.S. Forest Service, nor does omission indicate dissatisfaction or discrimination. Cordage, ladders, and safety devices are also obtainable from a number of retail suppliers of forestry equipment.

REFERENCES
FOR TREE CLIMBERS

Dorman, K.W., Schopmeyer, C.S., and Snow, A.G., Jr. 1944. *Top bracing and guying in breeding of southern pines.* Jour. Forestry 42: 140-141, illus.

Eversole, K.R. 1954. *Using the climbing rope and saddle in forestry.* Jour. Forestry 52: 285-286, illus.

Miles, E.E., and Hoekstra, P.E. 1954. *Tree climbing safety hint.* Jour. Forestry 52: 526-527, illus.

Perry, T.O. 1954. *Controlled pollination of pine species in North America.* Jour. Forestry 52: 666-671, illus. [Lists suppliers.]

Thompson, A.R. 1955. *Rope knots and climbing.* U.S. Dept. Int. Tree Pres. Bul. 7 (rev.), 20 pp., illus.

———1956. *Safety for tree workers.* U.S. Dept. Int. Tree Pres. Bul. 2 (rev.), 33 pp., illus.

U.S. Forest Service. 1958. *Health and safety code.* 363 pp., illus. [Especially sections 5.25, 6.23, 6.62, 7.39, 8.24.]

Occasional Paper 160   1958

POINT-SAMPLING AND LINE-SAMPLING:
PROBABILITY THEORY, GEOMETRIC IMPLICATIONS, SYNTHESIS

L. R. GROSENBAUGH

SOUTHERN FOREST EXPERIMENT STATION

PHILIP A. BRIEGLEB, DIRECTOR

Forest Service U. S. Department of Agriculture

CONTENTS

POINT-SAMPLING AND LINE-SAMPLING:
PROBABILITY THEORY, GEOMETRIC IMPLICATIONS, SYNTHESIS

L.R. Grosenbaugh

Southern Forest Experiment Station

Foresters concerned with measuring tree populations on definite areas have long employed two well-known methods of representative sampling. In list or enumerative sampling the entire tree population is tallied with a known proportion being randomly selected and measured for volume or other variables. In area sampling all trees on randomly located plots or strips comprising a known proportion of the total area are selected and measured for volume or other variables. List or enumerative sampling is commonly used in timber sales employing sample-tree measurement, and area sampling in timber reconnaissance. Each method, in its simplest valid form, operates to give every tree in the studied population an equal chance of being selected. A class of trees, therefore, can expect to be sampled in proportion to the frequency of trees in that class, and the frequency of a single tree is one.

Modifications of the above two techniques are usually designed to avoid sampling an identical proportion of trees in every class, since many classes are of slight interest but great frequency. These modifications involve the use either of different sampling fractions for different tree classes, or--what amounts to the same thing--different plot or strip sizes for different tree classes. Such stratification and use of several different sampling fractions or plot sizes is the simplest valid case of sampling where individual trees are not given an equal opportunity of being selected. Within strata the sampling fraction or plot size is constant, and most foresters are familiar with the calculation of appropriate blow-up factors for different sampling fractions or plot sizes.

Few foresters, however, appear to be acquainted with the underlying concept of "probability sampling", especially p. p. s. sampling (6)[1](p. p. s. denotes probability proportional to size). Familiarity with this concept is necessary to comprehend all the implications and potentialities of point-sampling and line-sampling. It may be worth while to give a brief explanation of probability sampling and to show how point- and line-sampling of trees are types of probability sampling.

---

[1] Underscored numbers in parentheses refer to Literature Cited, p. 34.

PROBABILITY THEORY
GENERAL

Suppose that a tree population on a tract of land whose area is (A) is comprised of (M) trees, and that each has a different probability (P_i) of being selected by a single random sample. Suppose further that (n) such random samples have selected (m) sample trees (with replacement) and that a dimension or quantity (Y_i) associated with each sample tree will be measured (as will its P_i). The variable (Y_i) might be frequency (in which case each $Y_i = 1$), diameter, basal area, volume, height, value, growth, or some other quantity. An unbiased sample-based estimate of the total value of (Y) for the population (i. e., $\overset{M}{\Sigma} Y_i$) would be $\overset{m}{\Sigma} \frac{Y_i}{nP_i}$ if (m) sample trees were selected by (n) equivalent samples and measured for (Y_i) (with replacement). It is apparent that nP_i is merely the expected number of times that the $i \underline{\text{th}}$ tree will be drawn by n equivalent samples.

There are two special cases of this theory which are simple and familiar to all foresters. If each of the (M) trees in the population has an equal chance of being included in a sample of (m) trees, then each $(nP_i) = \frac{m}{M}$, and the estimate simplifies to $\frac{M}{m} \overset{m}{\Sigma} Y_i$. Similarly, if a tract of area (A) contains (Na) acres, and if all (m) trees occupying (n) randomly located plots or strips, each of identical acreage (a), were measured for (Y_i), then each tree on the area (A) would have an equal chance $\frac{a}{Na}$ of being selected in any given sample plot, and each $(nP_i) = \frac{na}{Na} = \frac{n}{N}$. The estimate of total (Y) on the area then becomes $\overset{m}{\Sigma} \frac{Y_i}{nP_i} = \frac{N}{n} \overset{m}{\Sigma} Y_i$. If the estimate of total (Y) is divided by (Na) to place it on a per-acre basis, it becomes $\frac{1}{na} \overset{m}{\Sigma} Y_i$. The same result can be demonstrated by regarding the center of each tree as surrounded by a circle or rectangle of constant size, with the tree being selected as a sample tree whenever a random sample point or line falls inside the circle or rectangle belonging to the tree. The "blow-up factors" $\frac{M}{m}$, $\frac{N}{n}$, and $\frac{1}{na}$ appropriate to a constant sampling fraction or a constant plot size are well known.

POINT-SAMPLING

Bitterlich (2) first employed the horizontal angle-gauge for estimating basal area density of trees per unit of land area by counting those trees whose d. b. h. subtended angles appearing larger than the horizontal angle-gauge; he did not visualize the implications of probability sampling which permitted sampling tree variables such as frequency, volume, height, and growth. Hirata (7) first employed the vertical angle-gauge and counted qualifying trees to estimate mean squared height.

Grosenbaugh (3, 4, 5) first recognized that any angle-gauge is actually a tool for selecting sample trees with probability proportional to some element of size, and postulated the theory of point-sampling to obtain unbiased estimates of frequency, volume, growth, value, height, etc. per acre from measurements of such p. p. s. sample trees.

Horizontal point-sampling theory postulates that the vertex of a constant angle whose sides are exactly tangent to a circular tree cross section will generate a huge imaginary ring on a level plane around the tree if the vertex is pivoted about tree center (cf. fig. 1A). Vertical point-sampling postulates that the vertex of a constant vertical angle pivoted about a vertical segment of a tree will generate a huge imaginary ring on a level plane around the tree (cf. fig. 2A).

A Circular geometry of horizontal angle-gauge

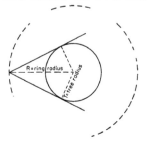

Imaginary ring generated by vertex of horizontal angle-gauge pivoting around a circular tree cross section. Ring radius is always equal to tree radius times a constant. The constant $(K = \frac{R}{r})$ depends on the size of the gauge-angle

B. Horizontal point-sampling

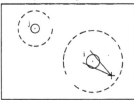

A sample point (+) randomly located within a level, rectangular tract of land has selected the ith tree as a sample tree for measurement, with probability of selection (P_i) equal to $\left(\frac{K^2(\text{tree basal area})}{\text{tract area}}\right)$. Horizontal angle-gauge with vertex at sample point (+) tells observer point lies inside imaginary ring of ith tree (because tree d.b.h appears to more than subtend angle-gauge), and outside the imaginary ring of the jth tree

C. Horizontal line-sampling

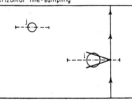

A sample line ($\updownarrow$) randomly located within and parallel to a side of a level rectangular tract of land has selected the ith tree as a sample tree for measurement, with probability of selection (P_i) equal to $\left(\frac{K(\text{tree diameter})(\text{line length})}{\text{tract area}}\right)$. Horizontal angle-gauge with vertex on sample line and with bisector perpendicular to line and passing through center of ith tree tells observer that projection of ith tree radius is intersected by line (because tree d b h appears to more than subtend angle-gauge) The line does not sample the projection of radius of the jth tree.

Figure 1.--*Horizontal point-sampling and line-sampling.*

Ring radius will be a gauge-determined constant (K) multiplied by tr·
if a horizontal gauge is used, or it will be a gauge-determined constant (Q) :
by tree height if a vertical gauge is used. Laying out these imaginary rings
ground with an angle-gauge (as in fig. 1B and 2B) is not necessary, howevei
the vertex of the angle-gauge at the sample point is known to be inside the r
ever the tree diameter or height appears larger than the gauge, and outside
it appears smaller. Hence, an angle-gauge with its vertex at a sample poin·
used to identify all sample trees within whose rings the sample point lies. /
seen from figures 1B and 2B, trees of different sizes have different chances
a sampling point fall within their rings. With the horizontal gauge, the prob·
proportional to the square of d. b. h. (i.e., to tree basal area); with the verti·
to the square of tree height.

If D_i = d. b. h. is the horizontally gauged tree dimension, the expecte
of times that the $_i\underline{\text{th}}$ tree inside a tract of area (A) will selected by (n) rando
samples (with replacement if selected) is $nP_i = \left(\dfrac{nK^2D_i^2}{A}\right)\left(\dfrac{\pi}{4}\right) = \dfrac{nK^2B_i}{A}$, where B
tree basal area measured in the same units as land area (A), and where K =
horizontal gauge-angle. Where (Y_i) is any desired variable associated with
dividual tree (such as frequency, diameter, height, basal area, volume, val
growth, or other quantity), the unbiased estimate of $\overset{M}{\Sigma}Y_i$ (or the total (Y) foi
trees on the tract) is given by $\overset{m}{\Sigma}\dfrac{Y_i}{nP_i} = \dfrac{A}{nK^2}\overset{m}{\Sigma}\dfrac{Y_i}{B_i}$ where (m) sample trees have
selected by (n) point-samples (with replacement) and where each sample tre
measured as to its (B_i) and (Y_i). Dividing through by tract area (A) reduces
pression to the estimate of Y per unit of land area, thus: $\dfrac{1}{nK^2}\overset{m}{\Sigma}\dfrac{Y_i}{B_i} = \dfrac{4}{n\pi K^2}\overset{m}{\Sigma}\dfrac{Y}{C}$
measurement of (Y_i) or (B_i) is necessary when (Y_i) is chosen identical with
basal area (B_i), since then $\overset{m}{\Sigma}\dfrac{Y_i}{B_i}$ = m, the fundamental count on which Bitterl
published.

If H_i = total tree height is the vertically gauged, point-sampled tree
then $Q^2 = \cot^2$ vertical gauge-angle is used instead of $K^2 = \csc^2 \frac{1}{2}$ horizontal ¡
angle, and πH_i^2 replaces $B_i = \frac{\pi}{4}D_i^2$, so that the estimate of Y per unit of land a:
$\dfrac{1}{n\pi Q^2}\overset{m}{\Sigma}\dfrac{Y_i}{H_i^2}$, with ($Y_i$) being any desired variable, as in horizontal point-sampl
Ordinarily, point-sampling with a vertical angle-gauge will be much less efi
than point-sampling with a horizontal angle-gauge, since tops are frequentl)
and since checking doubtful trees is very expensive.

LINE-SAMPLING

Line-sampling is an extension of point-sampling theory. Strand (8) :
published on the use of line-sampling in forest inventory. It employs rando·
line-segments instead of sample points, and the probability per unit-length ·
that a particular tree will be selected is proportional to tree diameter (hori
gauging) or to tree height (vertical gauging) instead of proportional to the sq
these dimensions as in point-sampling. The angle-gauge is used to select s
trees on both sides of sample line-segments located at random on the tract.
continuous and parallel lines will be used; they are analogous to strips. At
times short discontinuous segments, analogous to rectangular plots, will be
preferred.

A. Circular geometry of vertical angle-gauge

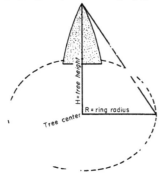

Imaginary ring (in perspective) generated by vertex of vertical angle-gauge pivoting around a vertical tree height Ring radius is always equal to tree height times a constant. The constant $(Q = \frac{R}{H})$ depends on the size of the gauge-angle

B. Vertical point-sampling

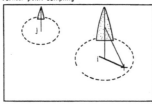

A sample point (+) randomly located within a level, rectangular tract of land has selected the ith tree as a sample tree for measurement, with probability of selection (P_i) equal to $\left(\frac{\pi Q^2 (\text{tree height})^2}{\text{tract area}}\right)$ Vertical angle-gauge with vertex at sample point (+) tells observer that point lies inside the imaginary ring of the ith tree (because tree height more than subtends angle-gauge), and outside the imaginary ring of the jth tree

C. Vertical line-sampling

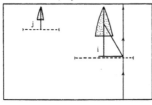

A sample line ($\frac{1}{1}$) randomly located within and parallel to a side of a level rectangular tract of land has selected the ith tree as a sample tree for measurement, with probability of selection (P_i) equal to $\left(\frac{2 Q (\text{tree height})(\text{line length})}{\text{tract area}}\right)$. Vertical angle-gauge with vertex on sample line ($\frac{1}{1}$) held in plane normal to sample line with base level tells observer that i^{th} tree height projected at right angles to sample line will be intersected by line (because tree height appears to more than subtend angle-gauge), and that the jth tree height will not be intersected

Figure 2.--*Vertical point-sampling and line-sampling.*

Any tree with a radius (or height) projection at right angles to and int
ing the sample line-segment is a sample tree (cf. figures 1C and 2C). Criti
gauging of doubtful trees or exact comparisons of distance with tree dimensi
be made perpendicular to the sample line.

If D_i = d. b. h. is the horizontally gauged tree dimension, the expectec
of times that the $_i\underline{\text{th}}$ tree inside a tract of area (A) will be selected by n equiv
randomly located sample line-segments of aggregate length (L) is $nP_i = \dfrac{LKD}{A}$
K = csc ½ horizontal gauge-angle, and where (A) is measured in the square o
units in terms of which both (L) and (D_i) are measured. The unbiased est
of $\overset{M}{\Sigma}Y_i$ (or the total (Y) for all (M) trees on the tract) is given by $\overset{m}{\Sigma}\dfrac{Y_i \cdot}{nP_i} = \dfrac{A}{LK}$
where (m) sample trees have been selected and each has been measured as t
(D_i) and (Y_i), which last might be any desired variable associated with the $_i\underline{\text{th}}$
e. g., frequency, diameter, height, basal area, volume, value, growth. Di
through by tract area (A) reduces the expression to the estimate of Y per uni
area, thus: $\dfrac{1}{LK}\overset{m}{\Sigma}\dfrac{Y_i}{D_i}$. No measurement of (Y_i) or (D_i) is necessary when $(Y_i$
chosen identical with present diameter (D_i), since then $\dfrac{1}{LK}\overset{m}{\Sigma}\dfrac{Y_i}{D_i} = \dfrac{m}{LK}$ where (
merely a tree count (by class if desired). Such line-sampling might be usefc
estimating sum of cull tree diameters per acre to be girdled or poisoned.

If H_i (or length of stem on the $_i\underline{\text{th}}$ tree from breast height to some spe
point such as tree top, pole top, merchantable top) is the vertically gauged t:
dimension in line-sampling, then Q = cot vertical gauge-angle is used (instea
K = csc ½ horizontal gauge-angle) and $(2H_i)$ replaces (D_i); the estimate of Y p
of land area becomes $\dfrac{1}{2LQ}\overset{m}{\Sigma}\dfrac{Y_i}{H_i}$. Then if (Y_i) be chosen identical with (H_i),
length (above breast height) of tree stems per unit of land area can be estim
simply as $\dfrac{m}{2LQ}$, where (m) is merely a sample-tree count (by class desired).
line-sampling might be useful in estimating lineal feet of poles (above breas
per unit of land area.

Of course, where sampling is restricted to only one side of the line,
ceding line-sampling formulae must be doubled.

The foregoing discussion of both point- and line-sampling assumes u
units of measure, but scale factors involving different units such as inches,
chains, and acres can readily be introduced.

Geometric assumptions inplicit in the preceding discussion are:

    (1) Enlarged tree rings or projected radii or heights never extend be
        sampling universe boundaries.
    (2) Effective size of angle-gauge is known, and outcome of comparin
        angle-gauge with tree dimension is unambiguous and consistent.
    (3) Terrain is level.
    (4) Trees are truly vertical.
    (5) Sample trees are visible from points or lines which select them.
    (6) Tree cross sections are truly circular.

The next sections will discuss how contradicting each of these assumptions affects the probability of a given tree's being selected, and how the changed situation in turn must be met either by modifying the size, orientation, or sector swept by the angle-gauge, by adjusting the blow-up factors of individual trees, or by using auxiliary methods. Failure to take the appropriate action will inject a bias into the estimate. That appropriate procedures will prevent appreciable bias even when point-sampling is conducted in a routine manner by cruisers under field conditions has been established by Grosenbaugh and Stover (5). Relative efficiencies of various sampling methods and angle-gauges will depend on local investigations of relative variance and relative costs; indications are that in many situations point-sampling will be more efficient than plot-sampling or line-sampling.

GEOMETRIC IMPLICATIONS

ENLARGED TREE RINGS OR DIMENSIONS PROJECTING BEYOND SAMPLING UNIVERSE BOUNDARIES ("SLOPOVER")

The situation where rings or radii do not overlap (illustrated in figures 1 and 2) is rarely encountered. Usually enlarged tree rings or projected dimensions, be they vertically or horizontally generated, overlap one another. This does absolutely no harm, nor does it affect procedure.

Besides this, two different sample points or lines (located in an unbiased fashion) may each sample the same tree. This again creates no bias. In fact, sampling without replacement of the sampled tree in the tree population (where it may be sampled again) would lead to bias unless unusual procedures were followed.

Enlarged tree rings or dimensions may project beyond the boundary of the tract. With large tracts, this slopover is inconsequential, but theoretically it injects a bias (which may be very large on very small tracts of land) unless special precautions are taken.

The bias arises because random or systematic location of sample points or lines is limited by the tract boundaries, so that the trees with enlarged rings or dimensions projecting beyond the boundary have less chance of being sampled than their size (unadjusted for slopover) would indicate.

If sample points or lines are arbitrarily restrained from falling in the peripheral zone where slopover occurs, an edge-effect bias will result because peripheral trees will not be represented in the sample as heavily as their occurrence in the population warrants.

The best way of eliminating slopover bias is to specify peripheral zones in advance of sampling. Trees with centers in the interior zone will generate whole circles or will project heights or radii on both sides of the tree. Point-sampled trees with centers in peripheral zones will be allowed to generate only half- or quarter-circles away from the outside boundary; line-sampled trees with centers in peripheral zones will be allowed to project heights or radii in only one direction away from the outside boundary. All point-sampled trees are weighted 1, 2, or 4 depending on whether they were allowed to generate whole, half, or quarter circles. All line-sampled trees are weighted 1 or 2 depending on whether they were allowed to project height or radius in 2 directions or only 1 direction.

The practical effect of these geometric limitations on point-samp
when sample points fall within these peripheral zones, normally qualifie
centers in these zones can qualify for tally only if they occur within a 90
outwards sweep of an angle-gauge and have rings overlapping the sample
gardless of whether a sample point is in the interior zone or in a periphe
when it selects a sample tree, the sample tree must be given a weight aj
to its own zone (1, 2, 4). The practical effect of these geometric limitati
sampling is that when sample lines extend into these peripheral zones, r
qualified trees with centers in these zones can qualify for tally only if th
the side of the line nearest the outer boundary. Regardless of whether a
line is in the interior or in a peripheral zone when it selects a sample tr
sample tree must be given a weight appropriate to its own zone (1, 2).

Figure 3A illustrates, for point-sampling, how a rectangular tra
be divided into 8 peripheral zones (4 corner zones, 4 side zones) and an
zone. Peripheral zone width should be a little wider than the radius of t
tree ring expected. Tree A, if selected by a sample point in the interio
be given weight 1. Tree B might be selected by a sample point in the int
but it could also be selected by points in a corner zone or two side zones
case, it would be given weight 1. Tree C could only be tallied from a sa
in the side zone, from which an outward 180° sweep with the angle-gauge
mencing and ending parallel to the outer boundary) would tally the zone,
be given weight 2. Tree D could be tallied from sample points in the int
a corner zone, or either of 2 side zones, but in any case it would be giv

Tree E in Figure 3A could be tallied only from a point in the corr
from which an outward 90° sweep with the angle-gauge (commencing par
outside boundary and ending parallel to the other) would tally the tree; it
given weight 4. Tree F might be similarly selected from a point in the ‹
but it could also be selected from points in two side zones and the interic
all cases, it would be given weight 4.

Trees B and D are illustrations of the fact that sometimes sampl
falling in corner zones will tally some nearby trees with centers in othe
sweep and weights appropriate to the other zones. Trees B and F indica
similar phenomenon is possible in the side zones, and trees F and D illv
similar situation can exist near the edge of the interior zone. In the int
angle-gauge sweep is unlimited, but near the margin of the interior zone
lected trees may lie in a peripheral zone, and will be weighted accordin

It is apparent that non-rectangular, obtuse-, or acute-angled tra
handled by an extension of this technique (with more or fewer peripheral
fractional circles and sweeps involving 30°, 60°, or 120°, etc., and we
as 12, 6, 3, etc.).

Figure 3B demonstrates that the problem of slopover is much sii
line-sampling rectangular tracts than in point-sampling them. Sample l
run parallel to 2 sides, and only two peripheral zones are needed (both ;
zones--there are no corner zones). These side zones are bounded outw
side paralleling the sample line. They should be somewhat wider than t
projected tree height or radius expected, as in point-sampling. Also as
sampling, qualified trees with centers in the interior zone are tallied re
whether the line sampling them lies in the interior zone or a side zone,

A. Technique when point-sampling a rectangular tract; tracts of other shapes are similarly handled, with various fractional circles being used in corner zones.

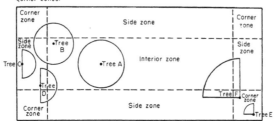

B. Technique when line-sampling a rectangular tract parallel to sides

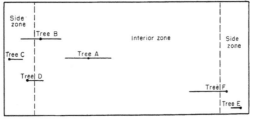

Figure 3.--*Eliminating slopover bias in point-sampling and line-sampling.*

always given weight 1 (fig. 3B, trees A and B). Trees with centers in the side which are otherwise qualified are tallied only if they lie on the outer side of the sample line, and they are always given weight 2, regardless of whether the line sampling them is in the side zone or the interior zone (fig. 3B, trees C, D, E. It will be noted that interior-zone tree B can be tallied from a point in the side : even though it lies inwards from a sample line in the side zone, and it will alwa be given weight 1. Also, trees D and F can be tallied from either interior or si zone, and they will still be given weight 2.

Unfortunately, when non-rectangular tracts are to be line-sampled, th slopover problem becomes much more complex. The simplest way to handle s situations is to subdivide irregularly shaped tracts into smaller rectangular ui that can be line-sampled by judicious delineation of the usual side zones, wi line-samples running parallel to such zones. Peripheral zones inside of the t: but outside of the area included in the various rectangular subdivisions will h to be plot-sampled. This solution, while quite feasible on large tracts, becon awkward on small tracts or tracts where interior angles do not lie between 90 180 degrees. Because of slopover complications, therefore, line-sampling w probably not be very useful on small non-rectangular tracts. Point-sampling, b ever, by use of partial sweeps, is well adapted to tracts of any shape.

The above solutions to the slopover problem were first devised by Grosc baugh (4). Precisely the same slopover bias has long gone unrecognized in circ plot-sampling where random or systematic plot-center location is treated as a p that moves as a continuous variable. Here each tree can be visualized as surro by a circle of constant size (independent of tree size), and the so-called plot cei is merely a sampling-point which selects any trees within whose rings it falls. solution is the same as outlined above; translated into plot terms, it is equivale the use of half- and quarter-plots with straight sides adjacent to and parallel to side boundaries when in peripheral zones (zones should be equal in width to so-c plot radius). Even with triangular or rectangular plots, the same slopover occi plot-center location is treated as a continuous variable. Here, trees can be reg as surrounded by triangles or rectangles of constant size instead of by rings. solution is still the same--use of half- and quarter-plots in the peripheral zone straight sides adjacent to and parallel to outside boundaries.

As has been said, on large areas slopover bias is of small magnitude an been ignored in conventional plot-sampling. However, the solution is relatively simple for those who care to use it. Only in line-sampling of small, non-recta tracts could it become a troublesome procedure.

One last point needs to be mentioned. If tree population outside a tract exactly the same as that inside a tract, no slopover problem exists. Points in peripheral zones merely tally all qualifying trees in a 360° sweep, whether insi tract or outside, and give all trees equal weight. However, equating off-tract to on-tract trees is often an unwarranted assumption, and trees outside the tra should ordinarily always be excluded from an estimate.

DETERMINING EFFECTIVE ANGLE-GAUGE SIZE, CHECKING DOUBTFUL TREES, CALCULATING CONVENIENT GAUGE CONSTANTS

Regardless of the angle supposedly represented by an angle-gauge, each pective user should carefully ascertain for his own eyes the distance from the a vertex to a target of known width when the target exactly coincides with the optical projection of the angle--a process called "calibration". The ratio of this distance (when coincidence is deemed perfect) to the width of target is called the calibration distance factor (X) if the target is perpendicular to the bisector of the angle along which distance is measured. It is called the vertical distance factor (Q) if the target is perpendicular to one side of the angle along which distance is measured. Calibration factors for a given angle-gauge may vary slightly with individuals, because of physiological and psychological differences.

Figures 4A and B illustrate the two types of calibration. The first, which ascertains X, is convenient for calibrating horizontal angle-gauges. The second, which ascertains Q, is convenient for vertical angle-gauges. Q may be directly measured in a vertical or a horizontal plane or it may be indirectly calculated from X, since $Q = X - \frac{1}{4X}$. If the horizontal gauge-angle is called θ, then $X = \frac{1}{2} \cot\frac{\theta}{2}$; if the vertical gauge-angle is called ϕ, then $Q = \cot\phi$.

There is still a third factor (K) which was used earlier in figure 1A to explain horizontal point-sampling and line-sampling. It is the radial enlargement factor, the ratio of imaginary ring radius to tree radius, $K = \csc\frac{\theta}{2}$. These three basic ratios, undistorted by scale differences, are related to each other and to gauge-angle in the following way: $K^2 = 4X^2 + 1 = (Q + \sqrt{Q^2 + 1})^2 + 1 = \frac{1}{\text{haversin } \theta}$.

These scale-free calibration values of X (converted to K or Q), coupled with the basic formulae given on pages 3-6 are sufficient to allow estimation of Y per unit of land area (where Y is tree frequency, diameter, height, basal area, volume, value, growth, etc.) from horizontal or vertical point-sampled or line-sampled tree measurements. Whenever the "tally" or "non-tally" status of a possible sample tree is doubtful even after optical gauging, a check should be made of the distance from angle vertex to heart center of tree (in a level plane). All "tally" trees must be closer to the angle vertex than K times tree radius in horizontal gauging, or than Q times tree height above breast height in vertical gauging.

A. Technique for calibrating horizontal gauge-angle θ in terms of calibration distance required to find X.

B. Technique for calibrating vertical gauge-angle ϕ in terms of calibration distance required to find Q.

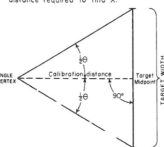
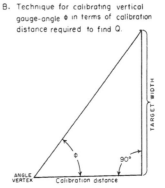

Figure 4.--*Angle-gauge calibration.*

Two instrumental peculiarities must be taken into account in calibra
doubtful tree check. If a magnifying stadia-type angle-gauge is used, the v
the angle will occur one focal length in front of the objective lens, and this
point from which distances should be measured in calibration or doubtful tr
it is also the point which should be kept above the sample-point or sample l

If a hand-held wedge-prism is used as a horizontal angle-gauge, it s
be positioned so that the knife-edge of the prism is vertical and so that the p
bisecting the prism-wedge is parallel to a vertically edged target. When or
edge viewed directly over the top of the prism appears to coincide exactly v
deflected ray from the other target edge (with prism positioned as above), t
ray of the deflected beam makes the same angle leaving the rear glass surfs
did when entering the front glass surface. This horizontal deflection is the
gauge-angle, with vertex at the intersection of the prism-wedge bisector an
perpendicular bisector of the target. If the prism is thus positioned, any r
of the prism in the plane of the prism-wedge bisector will <u>reduce</u> the horizo
component of target-edge deflection; any rotation of the prism in either the
the target bisector or a level plane will <u>increase</u> the horizontal component.
advantage of this (an action analogous to "swinging" a hand-held sextant so :
ensure measuring the minimum angle between horizon and lower limb of su
a check on proper hand-held positioning of prism.

It should be noted that deflections in prism-diopters, as usually mea
by manufacturers of prisms, assume that one prism surface (rather than pi
sector) will be parallel to target and that the exit ray of the deflected beam
perpendicular to one or the other glass surface. This means that so-called
deflections will always be slightly greater than minimum deflections determ
in the preceding paragraph. Figures 5A and B illustrate the different positi
the prism for calibration in terms of minimum deflection (exit and entrance
making equal angles with prism surface) as compared with normal deflectio
ray perpendicular to one or the other prism surface). Hand-held prisms ca
consistently used only if calibrated in terms of minimum deflection, but te
instruments should utilize normally oriented and calibrated prisms in their
The relationship between minimum and normal deflections of a wedge-prisn
complex one, depending on prism-angle, type of glass, and Snell's Law of I

Let d = minimum deflection-angle.
D' = deflection-angle with exit ray normal to glass surface neare
D = deflection-angle with exit ray normal to glass surface neare
P = wedge-angle of prism (i.e., angle between glass surfaces)
G = ratio of $\dfrac{\text{refractive index of glass}}{\text{refractive index of air}}$ (commonly, 1.523 for crov
glass and sodium light).
Then d = [2 arcsin (G sin $\frac{P}{2}$)] - P
D' = arcsin [G sin(P - arcsin $\frac{\sin P}{G}$)]
D = [arcsin (G sin P)] -P

When normal calibration is employed, the ratio of target width to ca
distance that is found directly is Q(<u>not</u> X), and when prisms so calibrated a
horizontal angle-gauges, Q must be converted to X or K, or else used in ap
formulae (fig. 6).

A "Minimum" calibration for use as hand-held horizontal angle-gauge
(prism oriented to establish minimum deflection angle d)

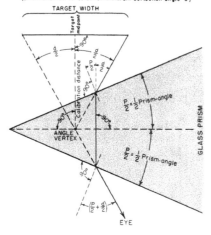

Deflection angle (d) has vertex on prism-bisector, has entrance angle equal to exit angle$(\frac{P}{2}+\frac{d}{2}$ in each case), with deflection-angle bisector perpendicular to prism-angle bisector

B "Normal" calibration for use in telescopic angle-gauge
(prism oriented to establish deflection-angle D or D' with exit ray normal to a prism-face; D > D' > d for a given prism, but D' is only slightly larger than d)

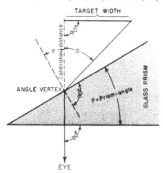

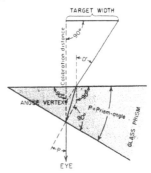

Deflection-angle (D) has vertex on prism-face farthest from eye, has entrance angle (P + D), zero exit angle, with exit ray perpendicular to prism-face nearest to eye

Deflection angle (D') has vertex somewhere in prism interior, has entrance angle (D'), exit angle (P), with exit ray perpendicular to prism-face farthest from eye.

Figure 5.--*Wedge-prism calibration.*

- 13 -

HORIZONTAL ANGLE-GAUGE
IDENTITIES

CONSTANT	IDENTITIES
Calibration Distance Factor (X)	$X = \frac{1}{2}\sqrt{K^2-1} = \frac{1}{2}\left(Q+\sqrt{Q^2+1}\right) = \frac{1}{2}\sqrt{(24\,HDF)^2-1} = \frac{1}{2}\sqrt{\frac{7{,}986{,}573}{HPF}-1} = \frac{1}{2}\sqrt{\left(\frac{7920}{HLF}\right)^2-1} = \frac{1}{2}\sqrt{\frac{1+\cos\theta}{1-\cos\theta}} = \frac{1}{2}\cot\frac{\theta}{2}$
Radial Enlargement Factor (K)	$2\sqrt{X^2+\tfrac{1}{4}} = K = \sqrt{Q+\sqrt{Q^2+1}+1} = 24\,HDF = \sqrt{\frac{7{,}986{,}573}{HPF}} = \frac{7920}{HLF} = \sqrt{\frac{1}{\text{hav}\,\theta}} = \csc\frac{\theta}{2}$
Gauge-Angle Cotangent (Q)	$X-\frac{1}{4X} = \frac{K^2-2}{2(K^2-1)} = Q = \frac{(24\,HDF)^2-2}{2\sqrt{(24\,HDF)^2-1}} = \frac{\frac{7{,}986{,}573}{HPF}-2}{2\sqrt{\frac{7{,}986{,}573}{HPF}-1}} = \frac{\left(\frac{7920}{HLF}\right)^2-2}{2\sqrt{\left(\frac{7920}{HLF}\right)^2-1}} = \cot\theta = \cot\frac{\theta}{2}-\tan\frac{\theta}{2}$
Horizontal Distance Factor (HDF) (maximum allowable distance in feet per inch of tree diameter)	$\frac{\sqrt{X^2+\tfrac{1}{4}}}{12} = \frac{K}{24} = \frac{\sqrt{Q+\sqrt{Q^2+1}+1}}{24} = HDF = \frac{117.7522}{\sqrt{HPF}} = \frac{330}{HLF} = \frac{1}{24}\sqrt{\frac{1}{\text{hav}\,\theta}} = \frac{\csc\frac{\theta}{2}}{24}$
Horizontal Point Factor (HPF) (per-acre blowup factor for ratio sum with denominators being squares of tree diameters in square inches)	$\frac{1{,}996{,}645}{X^2+\tfrac{1}{4}} = \frac{7{,}986{,}573}{K^2} = \frac{7{,}986{,}573}{Q+\sqrt{Q^2+1}+1} = \frac{13{,}865.6}{(HDF)^2} = HPF = \frac{(HLF)^2}{7.85398} = 7{,}986{,}573\,\text{hav}\,\theta = 7{,}986{,}573\,\sin^2\frac{\theta}{2}$
Horizontal Line Factor (HLF) (per-acre blowup factor for ratio sum with denominators being tree diameters in inches & with line length in chains)	$\frac{3{,}960}{\sqrt{X^2+\tfrac{1}{4}}} = \frac{7{,}920}{K} = \frac{7{,}920}{\sqrt{Q+\sqrt{Q^2+1}+1}} = \frac{330}{HDF} = \frac{\sqrt{HPF}}{.356825} = HLF = 7{,}920\sqrt{\text{hav}\,\theta} = 7{,}920\,\sin\frac{\theta}{2}$
Horizontal Gauge-Angle (θ)	$\text{arccot}\left(X-\frac{1}{4X}\right) = \arccos\frac{K^2-2}{K^2} = \text{arc cot } Q = \arccos\left[1-\frac{2}{(24\,HDF)^2}\right] = \arccos\left[1-\frac{2\,HPF}{7{,}986{,}573}\right] = \arccos\left[1-2\left(\frac{HLF}{7920}\right)^2\right] = \theta = 2\left(\frac{\theta}{2}\right)$
Horizontal Gauge Half-angle $\left(\frac{\theta}{2}\right)$	$\text{arccot } 2X = \text{arccsc } K = \text{arccot}\left(Q+\sqrt{Q^2+1}\right) = \text{arccsc}(24\,HDF) = \text{arccsc}\sqrt{\frac{7{,}986{,}573}{HPF}} = \text{arccsc}\frac{7{,}920}{HLF} = \frac{1}{2}\theta = \frac{\theta}{2}$

When it is desired to compare reliability of different angle-gauges, observers, or calibration procedures, the appropriate quantities to compare are coefficients of variation of $\frac{1}{K^2}$ (for horizontal point-sampling), $\frac{1}{K}$ (for horizontal line-sampling), $\frac{1}{Q^2}$ (for vertical point-sampling), or $\frac{1}{Q}$ (for vertical line-sampling). In general, optics with magnification and good light-gathering or light-transmitting capacity will have much lower coefficients of variation than those without. As long as no bias is involved, instrumental variation will be reflected in point-to-point field tally variation, and re_ quires no special consideration.

Although the above discussion covers all that is needful in the matter of cali_ bration theory, for convenience it is usually desirable to derive some additional con_ stants so as to eliminate need for introducing scale factors, π, reciprocals, squares, square roots, and halves.

In addition to X, K, and Q, which are scale-free constants appropriate to a given gauge, it is desirable to have a horizontal distance factor (HDF). When HDF is multiplied by tree diameter in inches, the product establishes the maximum distance in feet allowed between sample point or line and heart center of horizontally gauged questionable sample trees. This constant was formerly called plot radius factor (3) but that term is inappropriate now that lines may also be involved. Doubtful trees should be checked to avoid bias. Distance checks must be perpendicular to the line in line-sampling.

Q may be used directly in vertical gauging as a vertical distance factor which, when multiplied by tree height in feet, sets the maximum distance in feet allowed between sample point (or line) and heart center of vertically gauged questionable sample trees.

Finally, blowup factors or multipliers are needed to convert horizontal or vertical line- or point-sample sums of ratios to a per-acre basis. The horizontal point factor (HPF) assumes that the denominators of the ratios will be the squares of tree diameters in square inches. This constant is called basal area factor (3) when the denominators of the ratios are tree basal areas in square feet. The horizontal line factor (HLF) assumes that the denominators of the ratios will be tree diameters in inches and that line length will be measured in chains (66 feet each). The vertical point factor (VPF) assumes that the denominators of the ratios will be the squares of tree vertical heights in square feet. The vertical line factor (VLF) assumes that the denominators of the ratios will be tree vertical heights in feet, and that line length will be measured in chains.

Formulae for each of these constants in terms of each other are given in Figure 6. Although the introduced scale-factors are for British-American units of measure, scale factors for metric units could be similarly handled.

People may wish to convert a basal area factor for a given gauge to the HLF appropriate to the same gauge in line-sampling. This can be calculated as $12 \sqrt{10}$ Basal Area Factor. Thus, a 104.18-minute angle-gauge has a Basal Area Factor of 10 and an HLF of 120 when trees are sampled on both sides of the line, with tree diameters in inches being used to convert volume tables to ratios of volume divided by diameter.

Similarly, it is convenient to know that 183.346 times Basal
gives HPF, and that .005454154 times HPF gives Basal Area Facto
convenient for machine computations involving slope, elliptical tree
Area Factor is more convenient for mental or manual computation
complications.

SLOPING TERRAIN

All theory previously discussed has assumed that trees wer
from a level plane. When trees rise vertically from an inclined pl;
mountains, there are two ways of preventing slope from biasing poi
line-sampling estimates.

The first approach is best in horizontal line-sampling or po
where punched cards and automatic data-processing machines are t
lation. It involves using a constant angle-gauge to project a circula
radius in line-sampling) of exactly the same magnitude on the inclii
have been projected on the level plane, and to appropriately modify
(P_i) associated with any tree sampled on such inclined plane. This
uring slope dihedrals in horizontal point-sampling, or measuring ii
line-of-sight perpendicular to sample line in horizontal line-sampli
use of a simple and foolproof constant HDF in checking doubtful tre
of slope.

A similar approach can be used in pseudo-vertical angle-ga
the height gauged is the imaginary perpendicular dropped from tree
clined plane which passes through breast height on the tree and is p
sloping terrain; the point where this imaginary perpendicular pierc
plane (instead of tree center) is taken as ring center or height origi
angle always is kept normal to the inclined plane (rather than verti
a level plane). These complications in constant pseudo-vertical an
usually render it less desirable than the slope-adjusted vertical an;
cussed in the next paragraph.

The second approach (and generally the best in vertical line
point-sampling) is to have a slope-actuated instrumental adjustmen
angle so that, for any inclined line-of-sight, the probability (P_i) of
is the same as would have been given by the unadjusted angle on a l
such instrumental adjustment, the HDF or Q for checking doubtful
as the inclination of line-of-sight varies. This is inconvenient, an
gauging is it deemed preferable to the constant-angle technique dii

Constant gauge-angle techniques will be discussed first.

In horizontal point-sampling with a constant gauge-angle on
10 percent, the HPF should be multiplied by the secant of the slope
mean plane of the terrain around the point (balancing out hummock;
slopes). This generally means measuring the slope perpendicular
through the point. A constant unadjusted HDF is then used for all

In horizontal line-sampling with a constant gauge-angle on
10 percent, the HLF should be multiplied by the secant of the slope
to the given sample line segment. A constant unadjusted HDF is u

- 16 -

l trees. Constant-angle point-sampling is probably a more efficient technique r precise estimates in hilly country.

In pseudo-vertical line-sampling or point-sampling with a gauge which is ormal to and makes a constant angle with the inclined plane, exactly the same pro_ :dure is followed as above, except that the gauged height is the imaginary perpen_ cular to the inclined plane discussed earlier, and except that its foot is used in_ ead of tree center in checking doubtful trees. Of course, if estimates of vertical ee height or squared vertical tree height per acre are desired when the imaginary :rpendicular to the inclined plane has actually been gauged, appropriate allowance ust be made. In the case of pseudo-vertical point-sampling, the simple count of ees must be multiplied by the <u>cubed</u> secant of the slope dihedral (to correct the [uare of imaginary height as well as the probability). In the case of pseudo-vertical 1e-sampling, the simple count must be multiplied by the product of secant of the ope dihedral times secant of slope measured in direction perpendicular to sample 1e.

One possible alternative in vertical point-sampling would be to use a gauge at is normal to and makes a constant angle with a level plane through the angle :rtex (roughly, the eye of the observer). This would be equivalent to surrounding ich tree with a constant right cone whose vertex is at tree tip, and whose surface :fines an ellipse when cut by an inclined plane parallel to the terrain and passing rough breast height of the tree. The area of such an ellipse, as projected on a vel plane, can be calculated and compared with the area of a circular cross section such a cone levelly sectioned through breast height on the tree. The ratio of the tter area to the former would be the appropriate correction factor to apply to the PF. However, the calculation of this adjusted VPF would be complex, the calcu- tion of adjusted VDF for checking doubtful trees would be very complex, and the itical distance separating "tally" from "non-tally" trees in an <u>uphill</u> direction from e observer would be indeterminate (or infinite) if terrain and cone had nearly the me slope. Such a vertical gauging procedure on sloping terrain would be quite im- actical.

Slope-adjusted gauge-angle techniques will be discussed next.

For all horizontal line-sampling or point-sampling with slope-compensated uges, the gauge-angle adjusted for inclined line-of-sight should be 2 arccsc

ic $\frac{\theta}{2}$ sec S], where θ is unadjusted horizontal gauge-angle and S is angle of inclin- on of line-of-sight to a given tree. This is a simple angular contraction that can performed mechanically (through rotation), geometrically, or graphically by rious types of instruments. The HDF used to check doubtful trees must also be rrected by multiplication by the secant of the angle of inclination of the line-of- ;ht to the particular tree, which complicates field work. However, HLF and HPF main constant for a given slope-compensated gauge regardless of slope.

For all vertical line-sampling or point-sampling with slope-compensated iges, the adjusted, truly vertical gauge-angle (which gauges the angle between e top and a level plane containing gauge-angle vertex) should be arctan n $\phi \pm$ tan S]. Here ϕ is unadjusted vertical gauge-angle and S is angle of in- nation of line-of-sight to breast height on a given tree; plus is used when gauging iill and minus when gauging downhill. The VDF used to check doubtful trees will Q for the unadjusted gauge multiplied by the secant of the angle of inclination of

line-of-sight to breast height on a given tree. For such a slope-compens
angle, the VPF or VLF used to convert ratio sums to a per-acre basis re
stant, regardless of slope. Checks of doubtful trees are always expensiv
vertical gauging, but the instrumental slope compensation described in th
is probably simpler than the pseudo-vertical constant-angle technique des
earlier.

LEANING TREES

All previous discussion has assumed that trees did not lean (i. e.,
were truly vertical). Lean has little effect on constant-angle horizontal g
breast height. The gauge should be slightly rotated about the line-of-sigh
pensate for the cross-level component of lean. Doubtful-tree checks will
from angle vertex to tree heart center at breast height, of course. If a s
compensating, gravity-actuated instrument is used, it will rarely be feas
compensate for cross-level, so in addition to doubtful trees, the user sho
leaners that appear to barely qualify (using the appropriate Horizontal Di
corrected for inclined line-of-sight). Such checks are intolerably slow o:
if gauged diameter is not readily accessible, which is one reason that gau
breast height is commonly adopted. Of course, if a leaning tree has beer
selected by a horizontal angle-gauge and if height is one of the variables t
measured, the usual conversion of vertically assessed height to tree slan
needed; it can be done by multiplying by secant of angle made by tree axi:
level plane.

Leaning trees cause much greater complications in vertical angle
Not only is the quantity gauged affected by lean, but the point to which che
measurements must be made is translated a considerable distance from h
of tree at breast height. With a slope-compensated vertical angle-gauge,
gauged is the imaginary vertical distance (i. e., perpendicular to a level l
tree tip to intersection with inclined plane parallel to terrain and passing
angle vertex. Any vertically gauged height estimates will be in terms of
this imaginary vertical above the inclined plane, which excludes stem bel
height. Hence, estimates of true height (above breast height) per acre in
line-sampling should use the secant of the angle of lean (from level) inste
counting each tallied tree as 1, and in vertical point-sampling the square
should be used instead of 1. The intersection of the imaginary vertical w
clined plane replaces heart-center of tree as check point or ring-center.

It is impractical to use a constant vertical angle-gauge where tre
though the theory involves merely a slight modification of the constant ps
angle technique discussed on page 17.

Such non-linear complications as sweep or spiral are handled ana
lean (i. e., using an imaginary perpendicular). The real problem there i
some function relating the curved height to the imaginary vertical height
to the secant of angle of lean where straight trees are involved).

INVISIBLE, MASKED, SKIPPED,
OR DOUBLE-COUNTED SAMPLE TREES

Any factor that prevents identification of qualifying trees or that c
confusion of stems will inject a bias into point- or line-sampling estimat

Dense brush or undergrowth can make trees invisible except at very close range, large stems can mask smaller stems behind them, and very numerous quali_fying trees can confuse the observer so that he skips some stems or double-counts others from a single point (the same tree, however, may be validly tallied from two points without bias). The theoretical cure for all of these potential sources of bias is to adopt a gauge-angle large enough to ensure that no tree can qualify farther than it can be detected under woods conditions, and also large enough so that the total number of sample trees qualifying at a point or along a line-segment of given length will be too few to cause frequent confusion in count or close angular juxtaposition of sample trees. Under United States conditions, these requirements are usually met by horizontal gauge-angles within the range 100 to 300 minutes. It is impossible to select vertical gauge-angles that will ensure visibility of tree top in dense stands, especially of hardwoods, but convenient angles in the neighborhood of 60° are probably about the best compromise possible.

After a gauge-angle has been intelligently selected, precautions are still necessary to avoid bias from missing qualified trees. The observer should bodily move from side to side perpendicular to line-of-sight to each nearby tree so as to peer behind each for hidden trees. Any tree thus discovered may be gauged from a point moved from the original sampling point along a line perpendicular to the line-of-sight to the hidden tree (actually, the movement should be along the arc of the circle around the hidden tree through the sample point). In line-sampling, hidden trees often can be detected during progress along the line before or after they become hidden.

Exact gauging of hidden or partially hidden trees at breast height or tree tip is not always possible from a sample point or line, but exact gauging is rarely necessary. If the upper stem qualifies with a horizontal gauge, it is certain that the stem would qualify at breast height unless the tree leans toward the observer. If any height below the vertical gauging point on the upper stem qualifies, the gauging point would qualify. Lastly, if a height or circular cross section qualifies from any point along a sample line, it is sure to qualify when viewed along a perpendicular to the sample line (this is not true of horizontally line-sampled elliptical cross sections--a case discussed later).

When a tree cannot be gauged by orthodox procedures or by any of the preceding shortcuts, it must be treated as a doubtful tree. Then both the distance to tree heart center and the questionable dimension of the tree must be measured; if the tree is to qualify, its distance must be less than the product of tree dimension times HDF or Q, with a slope correction if appropriate.

The above precautions will eliminate any possible bias from failure to detect sample trees.

ELLIPTICAL TREE CROSS SECTIONS

The foregoing exposition of point-sampling and line-sampling theory has assumed that all trees have circular cross sections. Although plot-sampling and strip-sampling usually make the same assumption, the consequences of non-circularity can be somewhat more serious in point-sampling or line-sampling than in plot-sampling or strip-sampling. As far as is known, this paper for the first time works out the applicable theory, explores the consequences, and proposes remedies.

- 19 -

The discussion will be limited to the implications of el
sections, since most tree departures from circularity approxi
gauges cannot be employed except on circular or elliptical sha
angle-gauging is only affected by elliptical trees to the same e
or strip-sampling, subsequent discussion will be concerned o₁
angle-gauging.

The obvious implication of elliptical tree cross sectio₁
sampling is that calculation of individual tree basal area (and
fined as $2 \sqrt{\frac{\text{tree basal area}}{\pi}}$) will be biased unless tree basal a
$\frac{\pi Dd}{4}$ and d.b.h. as $\sqrt{Dd}$ where D is the major diameter (i.e.,
the minor diameter (i.e., the minimum) of the elliptical cross
other expressions (equivalent when D = d) are commonly used
quadratic approximation of Dd is $\frac{D^2+d^2}{2}$; the circumferential a
ameter tape is used) is $(\frac{\text{circumference}}{\pi})^2$; the arithmetic appr₍
maximum and minimum are averaged) is $(\frac{D+d}{2})^2$. But the squ
(Dd) is the only unbiased estimate, and in this day of electroni
machines, there is little excuse for not using it.

A table showing the ratio of calculated ellipse area to t
area indicates the magnitude of bias involved in the preceding
$\frac{d}{D} = \frac{10}{10}$(circle), $\frac{9}{10}$, $\frac{5}{10}$, $\frac{0}{10}$ (line):

Ratio of $\frac{\text{Calculated ellipse area}}{\text{True ellipse area}}$ for variously flatten

Calculated area	Elliptical $\frac{d}{D}$		
	$\frac{10}{10}$	$\frac{9}{10}$	.
	- - - - - Ratios of are₍		
Quadratic estimate	1.0000	1.0056	1.2
Circumferential estimate	1.0000	1.0052	1.1
Arithmetic estimate	1.0000	1.0028	1.1
Geometric estimate	1.0000	1.0000	1.C

It is apparent that although bias is negligible in most c
1, it can be quite serious in the most extreme instances likel₍
$\left\{\frac{d}{D} = 4\right\}$. It is infinitely large in the limiting situation $\left\{\frac{d}{D} = 0\right\}$ w₁
course, be encountered in a tree population. Ellipses flatten₍
common among tree populations, while those flattened so that
extremely rare.

So much for the way in which elliptical tree cross sec
tree measurements of diameter and basal area in any type of
point-sampling or line-sampling they have an additional effect
large as or larger than the one just described. In practice, both

the same direction and usually cause estimates to be too high. Avoiding both types of bias is simple where field parties use calipers, record both major and minor di_ ameters, and have data processed electronically.

Earlier discussion has assumed that a horizontal angle-gauge pivoted about a tree will generate a circle whose area is always K^2 times tree basal area where $K = \csc \frac{1}{2}$ horizontal gauge-angle. Unfortunately, when the tree cross section is elliptical, the shape generated by the pivoted angle-gauge is not elliptical, nor is its area K^2 times the tree's true elliptical basal area.

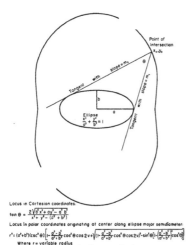

Locus in Cartesian coordinates
$$\tan \theta = \frac{2\sqrt{b^2 x^2 + a^2 y^2 - a^2 b^2}}{x^2 + y^2 - (a^2 + b^2)}$$

Locus in polar coordinates originating at center along ellipse major semidiameter:
$$r^2 = (a^2 + b^2)(\csc^2 \theta)\left[i - \frac{a^2 - b^2}{a^2 + b^2}\cos^2\theta \cos 2\nu + \sqrt{\left(i - \frac{a^2 - b^2}{a^2 + b^2}\cos^2\theta \cos 2\nu\right)^2 - \sin^2\theta\left(i - \left(\frac{a^2 - b^2}{a^2 + b^2}\right)^2 \cos^2\theta\right)}\right]$$
Where r = variable radius
v = variable angle made with major semidiameter

Figure 7.--*Locus of vertex of constant angle with sides tangent to an ellipse.*

Consider a tree's cross section to be the ellipse in figure 7, which has the form $\frac{X^2}{a^2} + \frac{Y^2}{b^2} = 1$ in Cartesian coordinates with origin at center. Next consider the constant gauge-angle θ (less than or equal to 90°, to simplify sign) with variable vertex X_0, Y_0, and with sides having slopes m_1 and m_2 each tangent to the ellipse. In analytic geometry,

$$m_1 = \frac{X_0 Y_0 + \sqrt{b^2 X_0^2 + a^2 Y_0^2 - a^2 b^2}}{X_0^2 - a^2}$$

$$m_2 = \frac{X_0 Y_0 - \sqrt{b^2 X_0^2 + a^2 Y_0^2 - a^2 b^2}}{X_0^2 - a^2}$$

$$\tan \theta = \frac{m_1 - m_2}{1 + m_1 m_2} = \frac{2\sqrt{b^2 X_0^2 + a^2 Y_0^2 - a^2 b^2}}{X_0^2 + Y_0^2 - (a^2 + b^2)}$$

With subscripts suppressed, the locus of the vertex of a constant angle θ whose sides are tangent to an ellipse whose major and minor semi-diameters are a and b is:

$$\tan \theta = \frac{2\sqrt{b^2 X^2 + a^2 Y^2 - a^2 b^2}}{X^2 + Y^2 - (a^2 + b^2)}$$

Figure 7 shows that the shape of the locus is definitely not elliptical. It also gives the equation of the locus transformed into polar coordinates, which are desirable in plotting and in calculations of area or mean diameter. From one or the other of the equations, 4 special loci may be easily deduced. When a = b, the locus is a circle. When b = 0, the locus is the external circumference of two intersecting circles (the limiting third case illustrated in figure 8). When $\theta = 90^\circ$, the locus is a circle (the so-called director circle of a given ellipse). When $\theta = 0^\circ$ or 180°, the locus is an ellipse (limiting cases approached when θ is very small or very large). Henceforth, the locus of the gauge-angle vertex will be referred to as the "shape."

Figure 8 shows how the ratio of shape area to tree ellipse area increases as the tree ellipse flattens. It also indicates that although the algebraic expression for shape area cannot be integrated for the general case, quadrature discloses that it

- 21 -

can be closely approximated in all likely cases by $\frac{\pi(a^2+b^2)}{1-\cos\theta} = \frac{K^2\pi(\frac{D^2+d^2}{2})}{4}$, $K^2 = \csc^2(\frac{\theta}{2})$.

Table 1.--Ratio of $\frac{true\ shape\ area}{(K^2)(calculated\ ellipse\ area)}$ for various angle-gauges pivoted about various ellipses

Type of shape area calculation	Horizontal gauge-angle = θ	Elliptical $\frac{d}{D}$			
		$\frac{10}{10}$	$\frac{9}{10}$	$\frac{5}{10}$	$\frac{0}{10}$
		- - - - Ratio of areas - - - -			
Quadratic or $K^2\pi(\frac{D^2+d^2}{2})/4$	90°	1.0000	1.0000	1.0000	1.0000
	45°	1.0000	1.0006	1.0199	1.0651
	228.842'	1.0000	1.0000	1.0002	1.0011
	104.142'	1.0000	1.0000	1.0000	1.0002
Circumferential or $K^2\pi(\frac{Circum.}{\pi})^2$	90°	1.0000	1.0003	1.0514	1.2337
	45°	1.0000	1.0009	1.0723	1.3140
	228.842'	1.0000	1.0003	1.0516	1.2351
	104.142'	1.0000	1.0003	1.0514	1.2339
Arithmetic or $K^2\pi(\frac{D+d}{2})^2/4$	90°	1.0000	1.0028	1.1111	2.0000
	45°	1.0000	1.0033	1.1333	2.1303
	228.842'	1.0000	1.0028	1.1114	2.0022
	104.142'	1.0000	1.0028	1.1112	2.0004
Geometric or $K^2\pi\ Dd/4$	90°	1.0000	1.0056	1.2500	Infinity
	45°	1.0000	1.0061	1.2749	Infinity
	228.842'	1.0000	1.0056	1.2503	Infinity
	104.142'	1.0000	1.0056	1.2501	Infinity

Where D = major diameter of tree elliptical cross section
d = minor diameter
$$K^2 = \frac{1}{haversin\ \theta} = \frac{2}{1-\cos\theta} = (\cot\theta + \sqrt{\cot^2\theta+1})^2 + 1 = \csc^2(\tfrac{\theta}{2})$$

θ	Cot θ	Basal-area factor	Horizontal point factor
90°	0	21,780.	3,993,286
45°	1	6,379.2	1,169,607
228.842'	15	48.24	8,844.3
104.142'	33	9.99	1,832.2

Table 1 empl·
rature to assess ma⟨
and direction of bia⟨
in approximating th⟨
rocal of true shape⟨
the reciprocal of va⟨
calculated shape ar⟨
volving the 4 expre⟨
used earlier to esti⟨
area of an ellipse. ⟨
seen, the quadratic⟨
mation given above⟨
nearly bias-free es⟨
shape areas genera⟨
angle-gauge apt to⟨
any tree ellipse apt⟨
countered. Assum⟨
shape area is K^2 ti⟨
true elliptical tree⟨
will result in overe⟨
of frequency, basal⟨
volume. The bias c⟨
high as 25 percent⟨
very small gauge-a⟨
minor axis is only .⟨
large as major axi⟨

Line-sampling probability depends on unweighted average shape dia⟨ (roughly a function of the unweighted average of all shape diameters taken a⟨ equiangular intervals through 90°) instead of on shape area (roughly a funct⟨ unweighted average of all squared shape diameters), as in point-sampling.

The unweighted average diameter of an ellipse is $\frac{4}{\pi}\int_0^{\frac{\pi}{4}} r\ dv = D\left(\frac{2\frac{d}{D}}{\pi}\right)\int_0$ where r and v are respectively linear and angular variables in polar coordi⟨ $e^2 = \frac{a^2-b^2}{a^2}$. This integral has been tabled (often it is called the complete ell⟨ tegral K) and it is better approximated by $\sqrt{Dd}$ than by the square root of a⟨ other 3 approximations whose bias in estimating elliptical area was compa⟨

As before, functions which are good estimators of elliptical parame⟨ be very poor for estimating shape parameters. Figure 9 shows that the ra⟨ weighted mean shape diameter to unweighted mean ellipse diameter increa⟨ ellipse flattens. The appropriate function for calculating unweighted mean⟨ diameter is also given in figure 9. Although the algebraic expression cann⟨ tegrated for the general case, quadrature discloses that the integral can be⟨ approximated by $2\sqrt{\frac{a^2+b^2}{1-\cos\theta}} = K\sqrt{\frac{D^2+d^2}{2}}$.

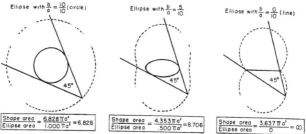

Different shapes are generated by pivoting fixed angle (45°) around various ellipses that range from a circle to a line.

$$\text{Shape-area} = 2\int_0^{\frac{\pi}{2}} r^2 dv = 2(a^2+b^2)(\csc^2\theta)\int_0^{\frac{\pi}{2}}\left[1-M\cos^2\theta\cos 2v+\sqrt{(1-M\cos^2\theta\cos 2v)^2-\sin^2\theta(1-M^2\cos^2\theta)}\right]dv$$

where r = variable radius } in polar coordinate system originating at center along major semidiameter of ellipse.
v = variable angle }

θ = fixed horizontal angle (angle illustrated is 45°)

a and b = major and minor semidiameters, respectively, of given ellipse

$$M = \frac{a^2-b^2}{a^2+b^2}$$

The random point will sample an ellipse only when the point falls within the shape-area around the ellipse.

Probability of such sampling is proportional to shape area $= 2\int_0^{\frac{\pi}{2}} r^2 dv \doteq \frac{\pi(a^2+b^2)}{1-\cos\theta}$

Although this integral cannot be directly evaluated except in special cases, quadrature indicates that the approximation is quite close where $1 \geq \frac{b}{a} \geq \frac{5}{10}$, which includes all tree cross sections usually encountered (see Table I).

↑Figure 8.--*How elliptical trees affect probability in horizontal point-sampling.*

↓Figure 9.--*How elliptical trees affect probability in horizontal line-sampling.*

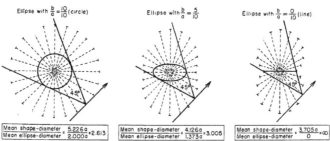

Different shapes are generated by pivoting fixed angle (45°) around various ellipses that range from a circle to a line.

$$\text{Mean shape-diameter} = \frac{4}{\pi}\int_0^{\frac{\pi}{2}} r\, dv = \frac{4}{\pi}\sqrt{(a^2+b^2)(\csc^2\theta)}\int_0^{\frac{\pi}{2}}\sqrt{1-M\cos^2\theta\cos 2v+\sqrt{(1-M\cos^2\theta\cos 2v)^2-\sin^2\theta(1-M^2\cos^2\theta)}}\,dv$$

where r = variable radius } in polar coordinate system originating at center along major semidiameter of ellipse
v = variable angle }

θ = fixed horizontal angle (angle illustrated is 45°)

a and b = major and minor semidiameters, respectively, of given ellipse

$$M = \frac{a^2-b^2}{a^2+b^2}$$

The randomly directed line will sample an ellipse only when the line intersects a shape-diameter perpendicular to the line

Probability of such sampling is proportional to mean shape-diameter $= \frac{4}{\pi}\int_0^{\frac{\pi}{2}} r\, dv \doteq 2\sqrt{\frac{a^2+b^2}{1-\cos\theta}}$

Although this integral cannot be directly evaluated except in special cases, quadrature indicates that the approximation is quite close where $1 \geq \frac{b}{a} \geq \frac{5}{10}$, which includes all tree cross sections usually encountered (see table 2)

Table 2.--Ratio of $\frac{true\ unweighted\ average\ shape\ diameter}{(K)(calculated\ average\ ellipse\ diameter)}$ for various angle-gauges pivoted about various ellipses

Type of shape diameter calculation	Horizontal gauge-angle = θ	Elliptical $\frac{d}{D}$			
		$\frac{10}{10}$	$\frac{9}{10}$	$\frac{5}{10}$	$\frac{0}{10}$
		- - - Ratio of average diameters - - -			
Quadratic or $K\sqrt{\frac{D^2+d^2}{2}}$	90°	1.0000	1.0000	1.0000	1.0000
	45°	1.0000	.9999	.9987	1.0026
	228.842'	1.0000	.9993	.9755	.9043
	104.142'	1.0000	.9993	.9753	.9018
Circumferential or $K(\frac{Circum.}{\pi})$	90°	1.0000	1.0001	1.0254	1.1107
	45°	1.0000	1.0001	1.0240	1.1136
	228.842'	1.0000	.9995	1.0002	1.0044
	104.142'	1.0000	.9995	1.0000	1.0016
Arithmetic or $K(\frac{D+d}{2})$	90°	1.0000	1.0014	1.0541	1.4142
	45°	1.0000	1.0013	1.0527	1.4180
	228.842'	1.0000	1.0007	1.0282	1.2788
	104.142'	1.0000	1.0007	1.0280	1.2753
Geometric or $K\sqrt{Dd}$	90°	1.0000	1.0028	1.1180	Infinity
	45°	1.0000	1.0027	1.1166	Infinity
	228.842'	1.0000	1.0021	1.0906	Infinity
	104.142'	1.0000	1.0021	1.0904	Infinity

where D = major diameter of tree elliptical cross section
d = minor diameter

$$K = \sqrt{\frac{1}{haversin\,\theta}} = \sqrt{\frac{2}{1-\cos\theta}} = \sqrt{(\cot\theta + \sqrt{\cot^2\theta + 1})^2 + 1} = \csc\frac{\theta}{2}$$

θ	Cot θ	Horizontal line factor
90°	0	5600.3
45°	1	3030.9
228.842'	15	263.56
104.142'	33	119.96

Table 2 uses qu
to assess the magni
direction of bias inv
approximating the re
of true unweighted a
shape diameter by th
rocal of variously ca
shape diameters invo
square root of the 4 a
mations used earlier
the area of an ellipse.
seen, the quadratic a
mation given above r
relatively bias-free e
for shape diameters
by any angle-gauge a
used on any tree ellip
be encountered. Wi
range of the small an
commonly employed,
cumferential approxi
slightly better, but r
use of a diameter tap
itself may involve con
bias in the direct esti
elliptical tree basal a
is a high bias implic
suming that unweighte

shape diameter is $K\sqrt{Dd}$. Such an assumption could cause line-sampling to
timate frequency, basal area, or volume by as much as 10 percent even wi
gauge-angles where they sample ellipses whose minor axis is only half of th
axis.

In summary, if a single average measurement of elliptical tree diam
as $\sqrt{\frac{D^2+d^2}{2}}$, $\frac{Circumference}{\pi}$; $\frac{D+d}{2}$, or $\sqrt{Dd}$) is used as though the tree v
lar, bias from use of erroneous individual tree probability may be superpos
in individual-tree basal area calculation. The resultant relative bias in con
the elliptical sample trees to estimates of basal area per unit of land area v
product of the appropriate entry from the text table on page 20 times the ap
entry from table 1 if point-sampling.

For example, estimating basal area with a diameter tape where $\frac{d}{D} =$
tree has been horizontally point-sampled with a 104-minute angle-gauge wo
in erroneously multiplying the correct basal area contribution of that tree b
(1.0514) = 1.25. This means that the basal area contributed by this tree to
timate would be 25 percent too high.

The remedy where precise estimates are desired is to caliper and r
imum and minimum elliptical diameters. Then electronic machines can cal
area as $\frac{\pi Dd}{4}$ and diameter as $\sqrt{Dd}$, with adjusted probability divisor (P_i) be
lated as $\frac{\pi K^2(\frac{D^2+d^2}{2})}{4}$ if point-sampling or $LK\sqrt{\frac{D^2+d^2}{2}}$ if line-sampling (whe

- 24 -

ample line, and K is Radial Enlargement Factor appropriate to the angle-gauge).
s it can be seen that elliptical trees horizontally point-sampled should contribute
$\dfrac{D}{d}\Big)(\dfrac{1}{K^2})$ instead of $\dfrac{1}{K^2}$ to basal area estimates per unit of land area.

The elliptical tree in the paragraph above (where $\dfrac{d}{D}$ =½) should count only
$\dfrac{}{2})(\dfrac{1}{K^2}) = \dfrac{.8}{K^2}$ instead of $\dfrac{1}{K^2}$. This would remove the 25 percent high bias noted when
neter-tape measurement alone was used. Similarly, elliptical trees horizontally
-sampled should be counted $\sqrt{\dfrac{2}{\frac{d}{D}+\frac{D}{d}}}$ instead of 1 in estimating diameter per unit
a of land. Where volume, etc., rather than basal area is being estimated, it
ild be that volume appropriate to a tree whose d.b.h. is $\sqrt{Dd}$, and the adjusted
ability divisor (P_i) will take care of the rest.

Actually, if $\dfrac{d}{D} = \dfrac{9}{10}$, the use of a diameter tape on elliptical trees horizontally
it-sampled or line-sampled with a 104-minute gauge will result in a combined high
of only about ½ of 1 percent, which is quite tolerable in ordinary work, especially
n it is considered that only a small part of the sample trees will be much more
itical. In precise work processed electronically, the bias should be eliminated by
irding and properly using D and d.

One last implication in horizontally gauging the cross sections of elliptical
s should be noted. In horizontal point-sampling, the point can fall anywhere in-
the shape and select the generating tree. Hence, in checking doubtful trees the
ance from point to tree heart center should be compared with the product of HDF
is tree diameter (calculated as $\sqrt{\dfrac{D^2+d^2}{2}}$). This will in effect establish an imagi-
circular shape with the same area as the imaginary non-circular shape, and no
will result. A less desirable alternative is to use the product of HDF times
bered tree diameter perpendicular to the line-of-sight. This product, however,
lves the same bias as assuming that shape area is K^2 times the true basal area
ie elliptical tree.

Similarly, in line-sampling elliptical trees, any check of doubtful trees should
loy as a criterion the product of HDF times tree diameter (either determined by
ieter tape or calculated as $\sqrt{\dfrac{D^2+d^2}{2}}$). Although this criterion may include some
tical trees that the point or line would not qualify, it will exclude an equal number
h point or line would qualify, so it is unbiased. A sample line passing through
wo bulges of a shape but missing the cordate cleft poses a minor problem. How-
, the criterion should be rigorously applied perpendicular to the sample line, re-
less of whether or not the tree appears to qualify from some inappropriate point
ie sample line.

SYNTHESIS

PRECISE ESTIMATES

From the foregoing, it is apparent that vertical angle-gauging is not adapted
ecise work. Tree tips or points on the upper stem are frequently masked, they

are inaccessible for doubtful-tree checks, and the complications introd
are intolerable in precise work. Application to less precise work will
subsequently.

Line-sampling has much less application in precise work than p
for the same reasons that plot-sampling superseded strip-sampling yea)
ever, horizontal line-sampling can be done precisely, since d. b. h. of
to doubtful trees can be cheaply and quickly measured. Procedures fo)
are analogous to those of point-sampling, except that slope corrections
measurements perpendicular to the sample line, and slopover bias is s
troublesome on non-rectangular tracts. Applications to less precise w
considered in a subsequent section.

Horizontal point-sampling is by far the most useful precise ang
nique. A procedure for precise estimates is recommended below; it ta
account all possible biases previously discussed and therefore assume:
sample points in unbiased manner within tract to be sampled; caliperin
ing maximum (D) and minimum (d) for each sample tree; measuring slo
through sampling points, usually perpendicular to contour; using a con:
angle-gauge with optical magnification, unadjusted for slope but proper
on the level by the user; defining peripheral zones and using partial sw
and appropriate tree weights where slopover bias might be important; i
auxiliary tree variables such as form class, total or merchantable hei$
volume is directly calculable as a function of $\sqrt{Dd}$ and auxiliary variable
tables, if used, should be expressed as regression surfaces depending o
variables); checking distance to doubtfully gauged trees against the una
zontal Distance Factor times $\sqrt{\dfrac{D^2 + d^2}{2}}$; selecting gauge-angle and using
to detect all qualified sample trees; tilting horizontal angle-gauge by th
level component of leaning trees; employing electronic data-processing
tree cards (all computations will be done automatically and practically
with figures blown up to a per-acre basis and punched on the individual

On these assumptions, the mensurational field record for a san
appear as follows (omitting all but the most pertinent figures):

D	d	H	F	HPF	Slope	Slopover	Shape
17.0	15.1	66	.80	1833	1.02	2	25$

not e:
in f

This field record indicates use of a 104. 18-minute horizontal ar
(HPF = 1833) with Horizontal Distance Factor 2.75 for check of doubtf(
(substituting 1833 into the appropriate formulae in fig. 6). It also indi
secant of slope perpendicular to contour was 1.02 (so slope must have
17.4 and 22.5 percent). The center of the sample tree lay in a "side z
boundary where slopover might have occurred, hence tree was allowed
only a half circle away from the tract boundary, and slopover factor w
shape area divisor, calculated electronically by a data-processing m

be $\frac{(17.0)^2 + (15.1)^2}{2}$ = 258. 5. The effective d. b. h. is machine-calculated as $\sqrt{Dd}$ =

$\sqrt{(17.0)(15.1)}$ = $\sqrt{256.7}$ = 16. 0 inches. Elliptical basal area in square feet is machine-calculated as . 005454 Dd = 1. 400 sq. ft. Tree volume will be machine-calculated as some function of Dd, H, and F, where H is merchantable height in feet to a specified top and F is Girard form class (or $\frac{\text{d.i.b. at 17.3 ft.}}{\text{d. b. h. o. b.}}$).

Other variables could of course be used, and heights for several different products could be recorded (or lengths of stem could be classified as to product suitability, grade, etc.). A regression surface can be readily fitted to any volume table now by machine techniques. Growth is also readily handled as an individual-tree variable. The multiplier that will blow up sample frequency (1), sample basal area (1. 400 sq. ft.), sample volume (say 288 board feet scaled by International log rule with 1/4-inch kerf), sample growth, etc. to a per-acre basis is:

$$\frac{\text{(HPF)(Slope Factor)(Slopover Factor)}}{\text{(Shape Divisor)}} = \frac{(1833)(1.02)(2)}{(258.5)} = 14.46$$

The machine will compute this automatically and multiply it by every desired individual-tree variable to put each quantity on a per-acre basis. The per-acre quantities that might be punched out on the tree card are:

        (14. 46)(1)   = 14. 46 trees per acre
        (14. 46)(16. 0) = 231. 3 inches of diameter per acre
        (14. 46)(66)   = 954   lineal feet of merchantable height per acre
        (14. 46)(1. 400) = 20. 24 sq. ft. of basal area per acre
        (14. 46)(288)   = 4164   board feet of sawtimber per acre

The above recommendations involve an extremely simple and foolproof field procedure, with a constant horizontal gauge-angle unaffected by slope and with a constant HDF. This latter can be incorporated into a 100-foot tape graduated so that each mark reads the smallest diameter--to tenths of inches--qualifying at that distance. This coupled with a double-entry table of $\sqrt{\frac{D^2 + d^2}{2}}$ for D and d in tenths of inches, will make field checks of doubtful trees quite simple. A single slope factor at a point applies to all trees tallied therefrom. Adjustments for slope, slopover, and elliptical tree cross sections are automatically made by machine in the blowup factor. Volumes are regression-computed by machine. Machines adapted to such inventory are IBM 650, 704, 705, 709, or similar electronic devices.

Had the same tree been line-sampled with the same angle-gauge, HLF = 120 would replace HPF = 1833, the Slope Factor would have been measured perpendicular to line-of-sight to each tree (instead of perpendicular to contour), slopover factor would have been 2 (the same as before, in this case), and shape divisor would have been $\sqrt{258.5}$ = 16. 1 instead of 258. 5. The same HDF = 2. 75 would be used to check doubtful trees in line-sampling as in plot-sampling.

As a last step, whenever tree variables (blown up as above in either point-sampling or line-sampling) have been sorted and tabulated for any physical stratum or population, the totals and subtotals must be divided by the pertinent number of points or length of line involved (in chains) to reduce figures to an acre basis. They must then be multiplied by stratum or tract acreage to get population totals.

The sampling error of estimates based on points or line
clusive of whatever volume-table errors may be involved) can t
as the variance of frequency, basal area, volume, or growth es
(or quantities proportional to them) among randomly located po
ments. Variance of the calibration factor used to blow up samp
at a point is reflected in the variation among point-sampling es
calibration was bias-free. This point seems to have been misu
Calibration-factor variance is also reflected by variance among
sampling.

Precise estimates of various components of tree growth
obtained either from periodic remeasurement of each tree initi
permanent sample point or line, or from a single measurement
core from each tree selected by a temporary sample point or li
of course, be employed to resolve doubts as to sample-tree qua

Use of permanent sample points or lines involves select
identifiable sample trees whose subsequent harvest, death, or
served periodically. With such an installation, periodic measu
change in initial stand per acre can be analyzed into 3 major co
unsalvaged mortality, and growth of surviving trees initially at
A fourth component--ingrowth of trees initially less than 4-1
initially nonexistent--can be estimated, if desired, by coring s
qualifying at time of remeasurement and then measuring and tal
having a breast-height age equal to or less than the growth peri
a small permanent plot (milacre or less) could be used to estim
nating subsequent to initial tally. Trees originating subsequent
not contribute much volume to ingrowth into merchantable size
10-year period, however, and could be ignored if only merchan
were of interest.

Below is an illustration of point-sampling growth analys
tally at a single permanent point where a 104.18-minute gauge
(i.e., Basal Area Factor is 10) has been used. The permanent
shows all trees initially tallied and measured; their subsequent
harvest, survival) and remeasurement if surviving after 10 yea
measurement (at same time as survivor remeasurement) of nev
younger than 10 years of age at breast height (determined from

D.b.h.		Basal area				Vo
Initial	After 10 years	Initial	After 10 years	Difference	Initial	A 10
- Inches -		- - Square feet - -			- - Cub	
4.0	6.0	.0873	.1963	+ .1090	0.0	
10.0	12.0	.5455	.7854	+ .2399	12.0	
10.0	.0 (dead)	.5455	.0	- .5455	12.0	
20.0	.0 (cut)	2.1817	.0	-2.1817	75.0	
.0	1.0	.0	.0055	+ .0055	.0	
.0	6.0	.0	.1963	+ .1963	.0	

N. B. : Newly qualifying trees more than 10 years of age
10-year growth period would be recorded separat

- 28 -

The use of electronic data-processing machines readily allows differences
h tree with initial d. b. h. greater than zero to be multiplied by $\frac{1833}{(\text{initial d.b.h.})^2}$,
erences for each tree with initial d. b. h. equal to zero to be multiplied
$\frac{1833}{\text{ninal d. b. h.)}^2}$. In case elliptical biases were to be eliminated, the ap_
te shape divisors would replace (d. b. h. $)^2$ as denominators of these fractions.
and slopover were involved, the fractions would, of course, be multiplied
,ppropriate factors. Each fraction, corrected for shape, slope, or slop_
actually the <u>number</u> of trees represented by each sample tree.

Any sample tree with zero <u>initial</u> diameter represents ingrowth originating
,ent to initial tally. Any sample tree with zero <u>terminal</u> diameter repre_
,ortality or harvest cut, with a code to distinguish them. Any sample tree
,ther initial nor terminal diameter equal to zero represents survivor growth.
se, segregation of so-called ingrowth into or out of various size classes
od, sawlogs, etc.) could easily be achieved. A good rule of thumb to use
,g newly qualifying trees at remeasurement time is to core only those
than 10 inches in d. b. h. to ascertain age.

From the above periodic remeasurement of sample trees selected by a
ent point, the 4 major components of net change in basal area and volume
e over a 10-year period are readily available:

SUBTRACT					ADD			
Subsequent mortality		Subsequent harvest		Terminal d. b. h. (inches)	Survivor growth		Ingrowth	
Basal area	Volume	Basal area	Volume		Basal area	Volume	Basal area	Volume
Sq. ft.	Cu. ft.	Sq. ft.	Cu. ft.		Sq. ft.	Cu. ft.	Sq. ft.	Cu. ft.
..	...	..	...	6.0	12.49	343.7	..	...
..	...	..	...	12.0	4.40	128.3	..	...
10.00	220.0	..	...	...	...	...	..	...
..	...	10.00	343.5	...	...	...	..	...
				1.0	...	...	10.00	...
				6.0	...	...	10.00	152.8
10.00	220.0	10.00	343.5	Totals	16.89	472.0	20.00	152.8

,f a 1 percent per year simple annual growth rate (or some locally more
timate) is assumed for the slower growing mortality and harvest components
,d to cease growth in midperiod), the harvest and mortality totals should be
,d by multiplication by $1 + (5)(.01) = 1.05$. Hence, the basal-area estimates
-year period would be 10.5 sq. ft. per acre mortality, 10.5 sq. ft. per acre
16.89 sq. ft. per acre survivor growth, and 20 sq. ft. per acre ingrowth--
s growth being 37.89 sq. ft. per acre, from which 10.5 sq. ft. of mortality
5 sq. ft. of harvest must be deducted to get the net gain in growing stock
, over the 10-year period. A similar calculation can be carried out for cubic
,oard feet, and frequency, of course, is directly available as
$\frac{\text{HPF}}{\text{,r terminal d. b. h.)}^2}$

t will frequently be desirable to express these change components as simple
,ercents of initial or terminal stand. The simple annual percents can then
,d to a much larger sample derived from supplementary temporary points
ies, tree class, and diameter or height class if desired)

- 29 -

If permanent points are used for a <u>second</u> growth period, the newly c
ing trees <u>older</u> than 10 years at breast height at the start of the second peric
be included in the new sample, as well as the newly qualifying ingrowth tree:
years of age or younger (which in the second growth period are no longer cl;
ingrowth from the zero d. b. h. class, but will become survivors, harvest, o
mortality). The second growth-period calculations are then based on tree di
measured at the start of the second growth period, just as though there had
been a first growth-period.

Use of temporary sample points or lines, coupled with coring all tall
trees, will furnish estimates of growth of surviving trees and ingrowth (to a:
class from trees originating at any time). Harvest and unsalvaged mortality
be obtained by auxiliary techniques familiar to all users of growth technique:
ing stand projection. Obviously, if temporary points and coring are used fo:
mating survivor growth and ingrowth, the factor by which basal area and vol
ferences should be multiplied is $\dfrac{1833}{(\text{current d. b. h.})^2}$ throughout (properly corre
shape, slope, slopover, etc.).

Although the preceding discussions bring together in usable form all
necessary to obtain precise and unbiased estimates of tree frequency, basal
volume, or growth on a per-acre basis by means of point-sampling or line-s
it might be helpful to compare plot-sampling, line-sampling, and point-sam
a specific situation. For simplicity, each tree will be assumed to have 1 of
diameters (6. 0 inches, 12. 0 inches, 18. 0 inches). Actually, the distributior
in diameter would be spread over a continuum, but this is immaterial to the
of the example.

The 3 diameters will have the following basal areas in square feet: 6.
$\frac{\pi}{16}$ sq. ft.; 12. 0 inches, $\frac{4\pi}{16}$ sq. ft.; 18. 0 inches, $\frac{9\pi}{16}$ sq. ft. Assume that the
stand of trees of the above 3 sizes exists on a specified acre:

Tree D (inches)	Frequency per acre	Diameter per acre	Basal area per acre
	Number of trees	Inches	Sq. ft.
6. 0	96	576 (=48 x 12)	18. 8 (= 6π)
12. 0	64	768 (=64 x 12)	50. 3 (=16π)
18. 0	16	288 (=24 x 12)	28. 3 (= 9π)
	176	1632 (=136x12)	97. 4 (=31π)

The expectation (or average) for a single plot-sample, line-sample,
sample is compared below for a one-tenth-acre plot, a one-chain line-samp
a 104. 18-minute angle-gauge being used on both sides of the line), and a sin
sample (with a 104. 18-minute angle-gauge being used on a full 360° sweep):

Tree D (inches)	Expected tally for--		
	One-tenth-acre plot sample	104.18-minute line-sample	104.18-minute point-sample
	- - - - - Number of trees - - - - -		
6. 0	9. 6	4. 8	1. 88
12. 0	6. 4	6. 4	5. 03
18. 0·	1. 6	2. 4	2. 83
Total	17. 6	13. 6	9. 74

Note that number of trees tallied by one-tenth-acre plot, multiplied by 10, gives frequencies per acre; that number of trees tallied by one-chain line-sample, multiplied by 10, gives aggregate diameter in feet per acre, or multiplied by 120 (= HLF), gives aggregate diameter in inches per acre; and that number of trees tallied by point-sample, multiplied by 10 (=BAF), gives aggregate basal area in square feet per acre, or multiplied by 1833 (= HPF), gives aggregate squared diameter per acre. Further note that line-sampling with a 104.18-minute angle-gauge tallied fewer trees smaller than 12 inches than did one-tenth-acre plot-sampling, and that point-sampling with a 104.18-minute angle-gauge tallied fewer trees smaller than 15.28 inches than did line-sampling, and fewer trees smaller than 13.54 inches than did one-tenth-acre plot-sampling.

It is now apparent that frequency per acre can be estimated by multiplying each tree in the plot-sample by 10, or by multiplying each tree in the line-sample by $\frac{120}{D}$, or by multiplying each tree in the point-sample by $\frac{1833}{D^2}$, where D is measured in inches. If D is measured in feet and if basal area replaces D^2, both numerators will become 10. Thus, HLF (= 120) and HPF (= 1833) are analogs of plot blowup factor, except that an appropriate function of D must also be employed. Slope, slopover, and shape would, of course, modify the factors actually used.

Line-samplers will find additional convenient HLF's to be 165 and 330 (with HDF's of 2 and 1, respectively). These will involve prisms of about 4 and 8 diopter strength, respectively.

LESS PRECISE ESTIMATES

Some less precise adaptations of point- and line-sampling technique are worthy of note. Bell and Alexander (1) have gauged tree diameter at the top of a 16-foot log instead of at breast height. This approach has advantages when used with volume tables entered with first-log diameter, and when half-sweeps gauge only trees on the downhill side of the point. However, it does not appear to be a convenient dimension for ordinary use. The top of the first 16-foot log is expensive to locate, a gauge adjustment is always needed before it can be gauged, and a check on doubtful trees is exorbitantly expensive.

Hirata (7) has point-sampled total height above breast height with a vertical angle-gauge counting all qualifying trees, then counting all trees on small circular plots concentric about each sampling point. Without any tree measurements, an unbiased estimate of quadratic mean tree height in feet $\left(\sqrt{\frac{\Sigma H_i^2}{M}}\right)$ is calculated as 4-1/2 feet plus the product of plot radius (in feet) times tan vertical gauge-angle times square root of the ratio of sum of point-sample counts to sum of plot-sample counts. Since quadratic mean tree height has few uses, it seems unlikely that the technique is of more than theoretical interest, especially in view of the difficulty of detecting all qualified tree tops, and the expense of checking doubtful trees.

Besides Hirata's quadratic mean height technique, several other combinations of point- or line-sampling with plot-sampling are feasible and do not require any tree measurements.

Quadratic mean tree diameter in inches ($\sqrt{\frac{\sum D_i^2}{M}}$) can be estim
horizontally point-sampled tree count and the concentric plot-sample
will be plot diameter in inches times sin 1/2 horizontal gauge-angle t
root of ratio of point-sample count to plot-sample count.

Arithmetic mean tree diameter in inches ($\frac{\sum\limits^{M} D_i}{M}$) can be estima
horizontally line-sampled tree count (samples on both sides) and the t
the strip-sample bisected by the line. It will be strip width in inches
horizontal gauge-angle times the ratio of line-sample count to strip-s

Arithmetic mean tree height in feet can similarly be estimated
vertically line-sampled tree count (with samples taken on both sides c
a tree count on the strip-sample bisected by the line. It will be 4-1/2
product of one-half strip width in feet times tan vertical gauge-angle
of vertical line-sample count to strip-sample count.

Although convenient gauge-angles, plot radii, and strip widths
calculated, it is not believed that the above substitutes will be as effic
sampling or plot-sampling with direct measurement of the desired va
cept under unusual circumstances.

Another combination technique, requiring direct measurement
only, is that of Strand (8). He employed a short segment of line to se
of sample trees--one set selected by a horizontal line-sample with pr
portional to diameter, and another by a vertical line-sample with prol
portional to total height above breast height. If samples are taken on
the line, mean basal area per unit land area is then estimated by the
of the horizontally line-sampled trees times .785398 times sin 1/2 ho
angle, all divided by line-segment length (using common units of mea
by 43,560 to convert to per-acre basis). Total basal area times heig
height) per unit of land area is estimated by the sum of squared diame
vertically line-sampled trees times .392699 times tan vertical gauge
divided by line-segment length in common units of measure; multiply
convert to per-acre basis. Obviously, convenient angles and line-sej
can be chosen to simplify calculations, and basal area times tree hei
height can be readily added to the second estimate. Dividing the secc
the first will give an estimate of mean height (weighted by basal area
trees are selected on only one side of line, the above formulae must l
by 2. This combination technique has the same disadvantage of all ve
without expensive check of doubtful vertical gauging, it is subject to l
each line-sampled tree must be visited for diameter measurement, i
that horizontal point-sampling with measurement of height from a cot
where it is easily visible (and with the usual d. b. h. measurement) we
more efficient or less subject to bias.

Nevertheless vertical line-sampling may have merit in estim
(above breast height) per unit of land area for pole estimates by pole
correlating ground-samples with aerial photo-interpretation in terms
of tree height per unit area of land. From page 6, it may be seen t
angle-gauge tree count on both sides of a sample line (without any di
measurement) will allow an estimate of lineal feet (above breast heig
land area--it is merely the sum of counted trees in a given class tim

tangent vertical gauge-angle, all divided by line-segment length in common units of measure; multiply by 43, 560 to convert to per-acre basis. Even here, the expense of checking doubtful trees and the crude approximation needed to allow for the omitted lengths between stump and breast height probably make   point-sampling preferable if accuracy is desired.

The most useful crude application of horizontal line-sampling will probably be to get the sum of cull tree diameters per unit of land area in need of girdling or poisoning,for costs of such work are closely correlated with circumference or sum of diameters per unit of land area. As hás been explained on page 6, this can be obtained by simply counting horizontally gauged cull trees on both sides of the sample line. The sum of diameters per unit of land area will be the tree count times 1/2 gauge-angle, all divided by line length (all measurements in common units). If tree diameters are desired in inches (1/12 foot), if desired unit of land area is an acre (43, 560 square feet), and if line length is measured in chains (66 feet each), the above formula should be multiplied by 7920.

Probably the most useful crude applications of horizontal point-sampling are included in the diagnostic tally devised by Grosenbaugh (4). These include the original tree count for basal area earlier devised by Bitterlich (2). Convenient tables of gauge-angles, calibration distance factors, basal area factors, horizontal distance factors (called plot radius factors), and slope correction factors may be found in (4).

LITERATURE CITED

(1) Bell, J.F., and Alexander, L.B. 1957. *Application of the variable plot me: sampling forest stands.* Ore. State Board Forestry Res. Note 30, 22pp.

(2) Bitterlich, W. 1948. *Die Winkelzählprobe.* Allgemeine Forst- und Holzwirt: Zeitung 59(1/2): 4-5.

(3) Grosenbaugh, L.R. 1952. *Plotless timber estimates--new, fast, easy.* Jour. 50: 32-37, illus.

(4) _____. 1955. *Better diagnosis and prescription in southern forest mai* U.S. Forest Serv. South. Forest Expt. Sta. Occas. Paper 145, 27 pp.

(5) _____ and Stover, W.S. 1957. *Point-sampling compared with plot-samp southeast Texas.* Forest Sci. 3: 2-14.

(6) Hansen, M.H., Hurwitz, W.N., and Madow, W.G. 1953. *Sample survey methods* 2 vols., illus. N.Y. and London (Esp. vol. 1, pp. 341-342.)

(7) Hirata, T. 1955. *Height estimation through Bitterlich's method.-vertical* sampling [in Japanese]. Japanese Jour. Forestry 37: 479-480.

(8) Strand, L. 1957. *"Relaskopisk" hoyde- og kubikkmassebestemmelse.* Norsk Ski 3: 535-538, illus.

Occasional Paper 161

HOW

TO

PREPARE

GULFCOAST

SANDHILLS

FOR

PLANTING

PINES

Frank W. Woods
John T. Cassady
Harry Rossoll

Southern Forest Experiment Station
Philip A. Briegleb, Director
Forest Service, U.S. Dept. of Agriculture
1958

GROW MERCHANTABLE TREES

Tree growing capacity is wasted on

crub oaks and wire grass

Of course, you will wish to preserve some scrub-oak patches to provide a variety of cover and food for game. Elsewhere, it will pay to...

SWAP YOUR SCRUB OAKS FOR
MERCHANTABLE PINE TIMBER !

Experiments ha\
that scrub oaks ;
grass must be el
before pine c
grown.

The sandhills ‹
nough rain but
don't hold mois

The water table
deep that roots
penetrate to it.

12"

OAK AND WIREGRASS ROO
CENTRATED IN THE UPPER l

After summer showers this mat of roots quickly takes up moisture that pine seedlings need. →

4

RESEARCH WORKERS OF THE U.S. FOREST SERVICE'S CHIPOLA EXPERIMENTAL FOREST HAVE FOUND THAT REMOVING THE OAKS AND GRASS CONSERVES SOIL MOISTURE AT CRITICAL TIMES.

NO VEGETATION REMOVED

ALL OAKS & GRASS REMOVED

In planting experiments, pines survived best where soil moisture was most abundant.

NO VEGETATION REMOVED

ALL OAKS & GRASS REMOVED

METHODS OF CLEARING LAND

EARLY TESTS SHOWED THAT NEITHER FIRE NOR CHEMICALS DO A GOOD
JOB OF CLEARING SANDHILLS. HEAVY MACHINERY IS NEEDED. PINES
GROW BEST ON SITES PREPARED WITH A TANDEM CHOPPER

EQUIPMENT

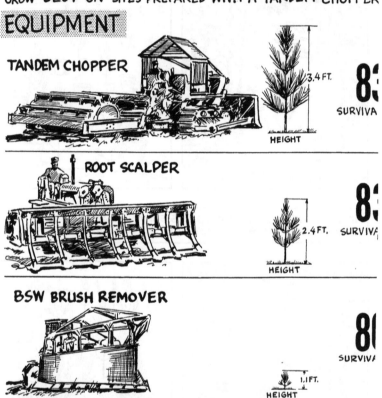

TANDEM CHOPPER

3.4 FT.

HEIGHT

83

SURVIVAL

ROOT SCALPER

2.4 FT.

HEIGHT

83

SURVIVAL

BSW BRUSH REMOVER

1.1 FT.

HEIGHT

80

SURVIVAL

NO TREATMENT

1.1 FT.

HEIGHT

58

SURVIVAL

THIS 22,000-POUND TANDEM CHOPPER PROVED BEST

RECOMMENDED TREATMENT

1. BURN
2. CHOP
3. RECHOP

Planted pines grew much faster on areas that were cleared with the heavy double-drum chopper-- probably because this machine chopped all plant debris into the ground and did not remove topsoil. The very best site treatment consists of burning the ground litter about May 1, allowing 6 to 8 weeks for oaks to sprout and chopping about June 15, then chopping once more in August or September.

Heavy machinery is essential. Ordinary farm equipment is much too light to destroy scrub oaks.

CONSULT YOUR LOCAL FORESTER BEFORE BURNING

WHEN TO CLEAR LAND

OPERATIONS SHOULD START AFTER LEAVES ARE FULLY EXPANDED. LATE APRIL OR EARLY MAY FOR WEST FLORIDA.

Resprouting vigor is low at this time because the food reserves, which are stored in the roots, are scarce.

IMPORTANT: TWO CHOPPING OPERATIONS ARE ESSENTIAL

6 TO 8 WEEKS SHOULD LAPSE BETWEEN OPERATIONS

Oak stumps and root collars should be allowed to resprout and use reserved foods between clearing operations. This saps their vigor and makes them easy to kill with the second chopping.

WHEN TO PLANT

Pines should be planted the first winter after sites are prepared. Weeds and sprouts invade and multiply on cleared areas and seriously compete with pines planted in later years.

Don't delay!

HARRY ROSSOLL

MACHINE PLANTING IS CHEAPEST

WHAT TO PLANT

SLASH PINE

Slash pine has produced the best all-round survival and growth in sand-hills planting tests. No other species can be recommended whole-heartedly at this time. Sand pine, longleaf, and loblolly are showing promise, though, and positive advice for planting these species on cleared sandhills should be available in a few years.

Slash pine, age 13, on sandhills site

YOU ARE INVITED TO VISIT THE CHIPOLA EXPERIMENTAL FOREST,
WHERE FOREST SCIENTISTS CONDUCTED MUCH OF THE RESEARCH THAT
LED TO THIS REPORT. THE FOREST IS 36 MILES SOUTH OF MARIANNA, FLORIDA

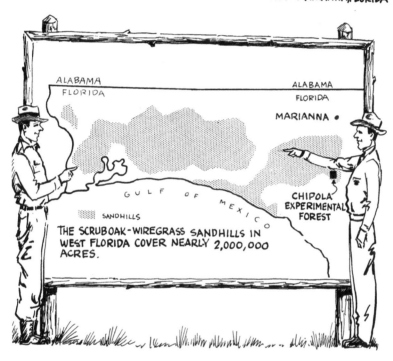

ESEARCH ON WEST FLORIDA'S SANDHILL PROBLEMS IS MADE POS-
IBLE BY COOPERATION. SPECIAL THANKS ARE DUE:

The Florida Board of Forestry - Hardaway Contracting Co.-
International Paper Co.-St. Joe Paper Co.- University of
Florida Agricultural Experiment Station, and many other
State and industrial organizations

Remember — only you can
PREVENT FOREST FIRES!

SOUTHERN
FOREST
EXPERIMENT
STATION

IN COOPERATION WITH

FLORIDA
BOARD
OF
FORESTRY

ccasional Paper 162

1958

CATTLE GRAZING
N LONGLEAF PINE FORESTS
OF SOUTH MISSISSIPPI

L. F. SMITH
R. S. CAMPBELL
CLYDE L. BLOUNT

SOUTHERN FOREST EXPERIMENT STATION
PHILIP A. BRIEGLEB, DIRECTOR
Forest Service U. S. Department of Agriculture

CONTENTS

CATTLE GRAZING IN LONGLEAF PINE FORESTS
OF SOUTH MISSISSIPPI

By

L.F. Smith, R.S. Campbell, and Clyde L. Blount[1]

The forest range has long been an important source of inexpensive forage for livestock on the Gulf Coastal Plain of south Mississippi and adjacent States. Mild winters and ample rainfall have made possible yearlong grazing by cattle with little supplemental feed or herd management. Open-range grazing, however, is accompanied by low animal productivity, inefficient utilization of the forage, and frequent damage to timber. This type of cattle grazing no doubt reached its greatest development on cutover, poorly stocked longleaf-slash pinelands.

During the past 40 years, there has been a gradual improvement in cattle breeding and management on many farms located on the better soils of the area. These farms have cultivated fields suitable for limited production of hay, and pasture for winter feeding and grazing. But some 70 percent of the area is still timberland, and forest range thus remains an important source of forage.

Increased worth of both range cattle and young timber has in recent years stimulated interest in improved practices for grazing cattle and growing timber on the same land. The problems of such integrated land-use include 1.--improvement in yearlong herd management, 2.--supplemental pastures or feeding, 3.--efficient utilization of the native forage, 4.--protection and management of timber stands, 5.--economic use of the reduced amount of forage under moderate to well-stocked pine stands of merchantable age.

---

[1] L.F. Smith and R.S. Campbell are members of the Southern Forest Experiment Station, Forest Service, U.S. Department of Agriculture. Clyde L. Blount is a member of the South Mississippi Branch, Mississippi Agricultural Experiment Station.

The authors are deeply indebted to the agencies and coworkers who helped make the study possible. The South Mississippi Branch of the Mississippi Agricultural Experiment Station supplied the cattle, and John B. Gill and other members of the Branch staff provided weight records on the stock, Marvin Gieger, of the Chemistry Department, Mississippi Agricultural Experiment Station, supervised the chemical analyses of the forage samples. Horace D. Smith, of the Southern Forest Experiment Station, assisted in managing the herds while they grazed on the McNeill Experimental Forest, and took many of the forage measurements.

Several of these problems were studied from 1947 to 1953 on the McNeill Experimental Forest, a 1,210-acre tract of second-growth longleaf pineland in Pearl River County, Mississippi. The results here reported deal with the amount and nutrient value of forage under various pine stands and densities, and with cattle gains during two grazing seasons: spring and spring-summer. Such information is basic to improved management and effective use of native forage on second-growth longleaf pinelands. The findings are mainly applicable to the upland longleaf pine type in south Mississippi and southeast Louisiana, but also are pertinent to south Alabama and southwest Louisiana.

STUDY AREA AND PROCEDURE

About 80 percent of the McNeill Experimental Forest is gently rolling upland, and 20 percent is in stream bottoms or moist sites. Average elevation is about 230 feet. The longtime average annual rainfall is approximately 60 inches, but during 1947-1953 the annual average was 66 inches.

A previous experiment, from 1923 to 1933, measured the effects of grazing and annual burning on young longleaf pine stands and on native forage in two areas of approximately 160 acres each (9)[2].

In 1947, two additional 160-acre areas were fenced, making a total of 4 pastures available for grazing studies (fig. 1). Pasture E, which was burned annually in the 1923-33 study, and Pasture F, which remained unburned during 1923-33, were rather well stocked with longleaf pine. On the two new pastures, A and C, the timber stand was more open than on E and F. Two ungrazed areas of 160 acres each (B and D) were reserved for observations of timber and forage development.

The second-growth pine stands are managed primarily for high-quality sawlogs under an even-aged silvicultural system. The first thinnings were started in 1947, when the average age was about 35 years. Periodic thinnings are scheduled at 3, 5, and 8 years in the different 40-acre compartments. These thinnings gradually open up the stands by removing the smaller and poorer trees for logs, poles, and pulpwood.

To increase the natural longleaf reproduction in the larger openings, prescribed burns were made to improve the seedbed and to control the brown-spot disease. Other silvicultural measures included deadening of unmerchantable upland hardwoods and cutting merchantable dogwood to release young pines. In general, these treatments temporarily

---

[2] Underscored numbers in parentheses refer to Literature Cited, page 25.

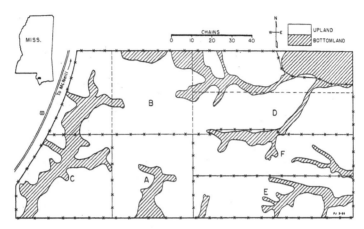

Figure 1. -- The experimental area.

provided more growing space for forage, but were soon offset by the
expanding crowns of the remaining pines.

Each winter, a firebreak about one chain wide was burned inside
the boundaries of the experimental forest. These protection fires provided a small acreage of fresh burns for cattle grazing.

In 1950, 1951, and 1952, small thin yearling steers were purchased locally each spring for the study pastures and sold in the fall.
They were of mixed breeds, with native stock predominating (fig. 2).
Before being placed in the pastures, all animals were vaccinated and
treated for internal parasites. The steers were grouped to provide approximately the same average weight per animal in each pasture. During
the study, each animal was weighed at 28-day intervals. Cattle numbers
were adjusted to allow for variations in the grazing capacity of the different pastures.

The study compared a grazing season of 4 months with one of 7
months. The short season, extending from about April 1 to July 31,
was intended to coincide with the main period of rapid grass growth
through the early leaf and full leaf stages. The long season, from about
April 1 to October 31, included the total growing period of the principal
forage plants through the mature green leaf stage. The purpose of the
short season was to test the feasibility of utilizing the forage while it is

Figure 2.--A group of steers in a moderately stocked longleaf stand in pasture A.

most palatable and nutritious, then moving the animals to improved pastures for the remainder of the summer to maintain a high level of gains.

In 1953 and 1954, two small herds of breeding cows were furnished by a local farmer for supplemental tests with this class of stock.

In 1947, 1948, and 1949, the amount and quality of forage was measured on ungrazed sample plots 3.1 feet square (2). Burned and unburned range was sampled under pine stands of three densities: fully stocked, moderately stocked, and open. The object was to test the effects of burning and tree density on forage growth and nutrient content.

From 1949 to 1952, inventories of the forage were made in selected pastures in July and September, near the end of each of the two grazing seasons.

Samples of the plants preferred by cattle were obtained by observing the animals periodically in two pastures during the 3 years and collecting samples of the plants they ate. The Mississippi Agricultural Experiment Station made chemical analyses of the samples.

THE FORAGE

The forage plants on the experimental pastures are fairly typical of those on longleaf lands in south Mississippi. Although more than 50 species of grass are present, a few provide most of the forage.

Little bluestem[3] and slender bluestem are the most important. Other common species are Elliott, paintbrush, and yellowsedge bluestems, several panicums, pineywoods dropseed, threeawn, Florida paspalum, bearded skeletongrass, and carpetgrass. In the lowland types, panicums, sedges, rushes, and switch cane provide considerable forage.

Several native legumes and other weeds, including tick clover, common lespedeza, swamp sunflower, and goldaster, were grazed in the spring. Browse plants such as southern waxmyrtle, sweetleaf, and blueberry furnished some forage in the early leaf stages in spring.

Under the close grazing during the early experiment, grass density decreased in the burned pasture from 62 percent in 1923 to 21 percent in 1933, and dropped from 79 to 22 percent in the unburned (9). Little bluestem and slender bluestem decreased in both pastures, while carpetgrass and other grasses increased.

Between 1933 and 1949, the experimental forest was grazed lightly. Only parts of the area were burned, and at irregular intervals. As a consequence, when the forage inventory was taken in 1949 grass density had increased to 28 percent. The little bluestem had increased from about one-fourth of the grass stand to more than half (table 1).

Table 1.--Proportions of the principal grasses in Pastures E and F, in 1924, 1933, and 1949 1/

Species	E--burned annually 1924-33			F--unburned 1924-33		
	1924	1933	1949	1924	1933	1949
	- - - - - - Percent - - - - - - -					
Little bluestem	41	23	58	38	26	55
Slender bluestem	25	21	11	35	17	16
Carpetgrass	4	10	5	1	10	2
Other grasses	30	46	25	26	47	27

1/ Pasture E was called Pasture B in the 1923-33 experiment, while Pasture F was named Pasture A in the earlier study (9).

[3] See page 24 for common and botanical names of range plants mentioned in this publication.

Slender bluestem had decreased somewhat, carpetgrass was greatly reduced, and other grasses had declined from barely half to about one-fourth of the stand. Thus, under light grazing from 1933 to 1949, little bluestem again became the dominant grass in the pastures.

Effects of Timber Density and Stand
on Grass Production

In the three-year period 1947 to 1949, grass yields were measured on 10 plots each in open, moderate, and dense pine stands to determine the effect of timber density on the amount and quality of forage (figures 3 and 4). In open stands having about 30 pines per acre four inches d. b. h. or larger, the average annual yield of green grass (air-dry weight) was 850 pounds per acre. In moderate stands with about 225 trees per acre, grass production was 450 pounds per acre. In dense stands having about 300 trees per acre, the yield was 400 pounds per acre annually.

Much of the forage that did grow in the dense stands was so mixed with pine needles that the cattle would not use it. In 1947, the dense pine stands averaged 6, 850 pounds of needle litter per acre on unburned areas,

Figure 3. -- Timber density largely determined the quantity of forage produced. The cattle found little grass under this dense unthinned pole stand in pasture E.

grasses provided ample forage.

the moderate stands had 3,755 pounds of litter, and the open stands had
very little. These results show that as the pines grow and occupy more
space, grass yields are greatly reduced by severe competition from trees
and by smothering from litter.

The effect of timber density on grass growth is corroborated by
data from pasture forage inventories between 1949 and 1952 (table 2). In
longleaf pine pole stands, well-stocked areas produced the least grass,

Table 2. --Green grass (air-dry) per acre in July on unburned plots,
1949-1952

| Year | Longleaf pine | | | | Slash pine | Slash pine-bottomland hardwoods |
| | Pole stocking | | | Reproduction | | |
	Good	Medium	Poor			
	- - - - - - - - Pounds - - - - - - - -					
1949	494	821	1,136	1,033	1,328	500
1950	355	735	1,190	995	1,320	500
1951	169	387	619	615	690	609
1952	112	262	480	442	376	139
Average	282	551	856	771	929	414

to a low during the dry year 1952. These annual fluctuations
production have an important bearing on grazing capacity.

Effects of Rainfall on Grass Production

Rainfall has a major influence on grass growth, both
individual season and from year to year. Figure 5 shows gr
duction in open unburned McNeill stands in relation to seaso.

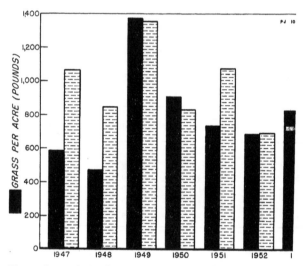

Figure 5.--Relation between seasonal rainfall, April throug
and maximum annual grass production in open, unburned pir
McNeill Experimental Forest, 1947 to 1953.

Average maximum grass growth for the seven years was 799 pounds per acre. The lowest production was 474 pounds per acre in 1948, about 40 percent below average. The highest was 1,375 pounds per acre in 1949, some 72 percent above average, and almost three times that of the poorest year.

These differences in forage production between years are largely caused by variations from normal rainfall during the spring and summer months. For the 7 years of the study, monthly average rainfall in inches during the growing season was:

March	9.15	July	6.79
April	6.29	August	5.35
May	4.08	September	6.45
June	5.75	October	1.39

In most years, there is enough rain in March and April to give the grass a good start. In May, however, rainfall was less than 4 inches in five of the seven years, so that the rate of grass growth slowed down perceptibly. For example, in 1950 the grass yield in April was 688 pounds per acre, partly because the panicums made good early growth. But in May, when only 2.03 inches of rain fell, the panicums largely dried up and only 438 pounds of green herbage per acre was measured.

When rainfall was well distributed, bluestems usually made good growth through June, July, and August, with slender bluestem putting up flowerstalks in late July, and the coarse-leaved bluestems following in August and September. In October, a month of low rainfall, green grass production decreased. In brief, April through August appears to be the critical period for rainfall. Rainfall for these months is compared with maximum annual grass production in figure 5.

The cumulative seasonal curve of grass production in open unburned pine stands is shown by the heavily inked curve in figure 6. About 70 percent of the year's production was reached by June, and 85 percent by July. This corresponds with Cassady's findings in central Louisiana that about 70 percent of the grass, and by far the most nutritious part, is produced during the first half of the growing season (4).

Figure 6 also compares the average grass-production curve with that of 1949, the highest year, and that for 1948, the year with lowest production. In every year except 1949, short droughts reduced or halted grass growth. Growth losses early in the season were not fully recovered even when rainfall in later months was adequate. For example, in the poorest year, 1948, below-average rainfall held down grass growth so greatly in April, May, and June that ample rain during the hot months of

- 9 -

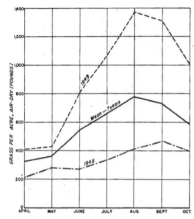

Figure 6.--Cumulative grass production in open, unburned pine stands, 1947-53.

July, August, and September could not overcome the deficit. Maximum production for the year was not reached until September, and was only 474 pounds per acre.

The net effect of good seasonal rainfall is reflected not only in high grass production, but also in a succession of green grasses that provides a longer season of good grazing than would a single species. Any temporary drought, particularly from April through July, reduces total production and disrupts the succession of species.

Forage inventories were made in the grazed pastures and in ungrazed pasture B in September 1949, before grazing began, and in July 1950, 1951, and 1952. Additional inventories were made in the long-season pastures C and E during October of 1951 and 1952. Green grass production (air-dry) in pounds per acre by pastures and years is shown in table 3.

Table 3.--Grass production (air-dry) per acre, 1949-1952

Month and year	Short-season pastures		Long-season pastures		Ungrazed pasture B	All pastures
	A	F	C	E		
	- - - - - - - - - - Pounds - - - - - - - - - - - - -					
September 1949	1,119	794	704	729	948	865
July 1950	902	591	531	528	673	649
July 1951	538	360	363	340	445	412
October 1951	...	...	382	352	...	...
July 1952	378	210	182	182	236	239
October 1952	...	...	371	264	...	...
Average (July-September)	734	489	445	445	576	541

ion from year to year in the pastures was very simi_
reported for the special seasonal forage-production
was highest in 1949 in all pastures, and lowest in 1952.
for all five pastures in 1952 was only 28 percent of
average in all pastures for the four years was 541
or only 63 percent of that in 1949.

GRAZING IN THE PASTURES

Cattle Diet and Forage Utilization

vhich are by far the most abundant kind of range plants
pi, made up about 93 percent of the season-long steer
nental ranges from 1950 through 1952 (table 4). Grass_
ited barely one percent, weeds (broad-leaved herbs or
ind browse 3 percent. The bluestem grasses alone con-
s of the average diet. The larger, coarse-leaved blue-
iinstays of the steer diet, averaging 66 percent for the
ı of 31 percent in March and a high of 89 percent in July.
-leaved bluestems (mainly slender bluestem) averaged
liet for the season, but made up 34 percent when fresh
ind 30 percent in September.

diet, 1950-1952

March	April	May	June	July	August	September	October	Average
- - - - - - - - -Percent- - - - - - - - -
31	78	45	61	89	80	65	80	66
8	2	34	27	4	10	30	3	15
36	10	15	10	6	8	3	14	12
75	90	94	98	99	98	98	97	93
3	1	0	0	0	0	0	0	1
5	6	4	2	1	2	1	2	3
17	3	2	(1/)	0	0	1	1	3
100	100	100	100	100	100	100	100	100

ses contributed at particular seasons of the year. The
ızed eagerly in March, when the bluestems were just
Carpetgrass, dropseed, and paspalums were a small
·ce of green forage.

ilants, mainly sedges, were grazed in March and
ı thereafter.

Several succulent weeds supplemented the grasses, especially in spring and early summer.

When the steers were placed on the range in March, they immediately ate considerable browse, such as sweetleaf, blackberry, sumac, and blueberry. Browse made up 17 percent of the diet in March, but rapidly dropped off to a negligible amount by June.

Knowledge of the kinds and amounts of the various plants grazed by cattle is essential in planning good range management. Equally important is an understanding of the factors influencing the utilization of a pasture as a whole, and the distribution of utilization within a pasture. Overall pasture utilization is largely the result of the amount of forage produced for the season or year and the kind and number of animals grazed.

The four grazed pastures were only lightly to moderately utilized during the three years they were stocked with steers. With high forage production and low animal numbers (36 steers) in 1950, average utilization for the four pastures in July was estimated at 11 percent. In the two succeeding years, when forage growth was less and animal numbers had been increased (48 steers), estimated utilization in July averaged 17 percent in 1951 and 16 percent in 1952. Among the individual pastures, the lowest utilization was 10 percent in A and E in 1950, and the highest was 26 percent in E in October 1951 (table 5). Proper use was considered to be about 40 to 50 percent.

Within the individual pastures, distribution of animals, and therefore utilization, was influenced by location of water supplies, roads, fence lines, and salt; and by reseeding, fertilization, and burning.

Table 5.--Utilization of grass herbage by steers, 1950-1952

Year and month	Short-season pastures				Long-season pastures				Average for all pastures
	A		F		C		E		
	Average	Burned[1]	Average	Burned[1]	Average	Burned[1]	Average	Burned[1]	
	- - - - - - - - - - - - Percent - - - - - - - - - - - -								
1950									
July	10	...	12	...	12	92	10	66	11
November	...	...	...	...	13	83	10	23	12
1951									
July	14	...	19	...	19	54	15	37	17
October	...	...	...	...	23	48	26	43	24
1952									
July	17	84	17	88	15	81	13	...	16
October	...	...	...	...	24	64	25	...	25

1/ Utilization in "burned" column represents cattle grazing on firebreaks and other small areas prescribe-burned the year before grazing started.

In 1950, pasture A was unburned. Estimated utilization in July averaged 10 percent, but varied from 0 to 27 percent in the uplands and ranged up to 35 percent on limited spots near water holes in the bottom. land. Utilization was recorded for the 15 to 20 feet adjacent to each of several objects as follows:

Object	Utilization (percent)
Logging roads	15 to 25
Fence lines	15 to 20
Salt box	20
Pine stumps	20 to 25
Deadened hardwoods	20 to 25

A fertilized and seeded area was closely grazed, but adjacent native forage was utilized only about 20 percent.

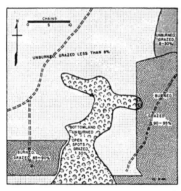

Figure 7.--Utilization map of Pasture A, July 1952, showing estimated utilization zones after 4 months of grazing by 16 steers.

The tremendous effect of burning on utilization is shown in table 5. Most areas of fresh burn were utilized 50 to 90 percent. Figure 7 shows the utilization, in July 1952, of Pasture A, parts of which were prescribe-burned in February 1952. The grasses on the burned areas were utilized 85 to 95 percent. Unburned uplands were generally grazed less than 10 percent; many areas were ungrazed. Spots in the bottomland were grazed up to 30 percent. Roads, salt boxes, and nearness to the swamp had comparatively little effect on utilization and then no more than a few yards away.

Nutrient Value of Forage

Analyses of ungrazed native grasses showed that nutrient values were highest in the early leaf stages--that is, during the period of most rapid growth. In the spring, crude protein ranged from 8 to 13 percent in grasses growing under the different kinds of pine stands. In early summer, when grasses reached the full leaf stage, protein content in these ungrazed grasses dropped to about 6 percent and remained at low levels for the rest of the season. Except in spring, protein values were below the minimum 8 to 9 percent required by beef breeding animals (7).

Chemical analyses of cattle diet samples for 1951 and 1952 (table 6) showed a high of 9.02 percent crude protein in March. After the grasses reached full leaf, they were less palatable and cattle preferred the regrowth on areas previously grazed closely in the spring. Cattle diet samples of new growth on areas previously grazed showed 8.42 percent protein in May to 6.58 percent in September. The higher nutrient content of new growth on previously grazed areas probably explains the patchy utilization characteristic of forest ranges.

Table 6. --Analyses of cattle-diet samples for 1950 and 1951 (moisture-free basis, average for two years)

Month	Crude protein	Phosphorus	Calcium	Total ash
	- - - - - Percent - - - - - -			
March	9.02	(1/)	0.42	9.94
April	7.96	0.11	.37	6.92
May	8.42	.12	.40	7.70
June	6.85	.10	.34	6.09
July	7.28	.10	.33	6.99
August	(1/)	(1/)	(1/)	(1/)
September	6.58	.10	.42	7.03
October	(1/)	(1/)	(1/)	(1/)
November	4.88	.06	.38	7.11

1/ No samples taken.

Several native weeds and legumes had a higher protein value, but were less abundant than grasses and were grazed mainly in their immature stages.

In early leaf stages, phosphorus values in ungrazed native grasses ranged from 0.15 to 0.20 percent. However, the cattle diet samples showed only 0.10 to 0.12 percent phosphorus from April to September. To compensate in part for the low phosphorus content of the forage, mineral supplements of salt and bone meal were provided in all pastures during the study.

Calcium content of ungrazed grasses ranged from 0.22 to 0.40 percent, moisture-free. In the cattle diet samples, calcium varied from 0.33 to 0.42 percent. It apparently was adequate for cattle throughout both the short and long grazing seasons.

Protein and phosphorus values were higher on burned than on unburned range, but the differences were too small to affect grazing values. Neither did differences in forage nutrients under the different rates of timber stocking appear significant in cattle nutrition.

Analyses of similar forest range forage in central Louisiana indicated that energy values are deficient during much of the year (3). It appears that the range forage provides adequate total energy for cattle breeding herds only when animals can secure a fill of grass in the young-leaf and early full-leaf stages. Protein and mineral deficiencies in Louisiana were very similar to those at McNeill.

Grazing Capacity

Grazing capacity is the number of grown cattle that can safely graze a range unit for the proper season each year over a period of years. It is based on utilization of the better forage plants at a degree that will assure their continued productivity (about 40 to 50 percent utilization of the current year's growth of little bluestem). To allow for year-to-year variations in forage production, a practical rate of stocking must be considerably under the maximum year and somewhat over the poorest year.

At McNeill, the 4 grazed pastures showed a maximum grass production (air-dry) of 865 pounds per acre in 1949, and a minimum of 240 pounds per acre in the very dry summer of 1952. Average production for the 4 years was 541 pounds per acre, of which not more than half, or about 270 pounds, could be removed without injury to the plants. As insurance against running short of forage in a dry year, many stockmen also allow a safety margin of about 25 percent of the average usable forage. With such an allowance, about 200 pounds of forage per acre annually were available for grazing at McNeill.

The small 350-400 pound steers used in the study consumed 8 to 10 pounds of grass (air-dry basis) apiece each day. This is about half the estimated requirement of 18 pounds for grown cattle averaging 700 pounds on range in central Louisiana (3). It is calculated that the McNeill pastures, averaging 200 pounds of usable forage per acre, would have a grazing capacity for mature range cattle of about 11 cow-days per acre (200 ÷ 18). This would amount to 11 acres per cow for a 4-month season (120 days ÷ 11), or 19 acres per cow for a 7-month season (210 days ÷ 11).

Small steers, similar to those used in the experi...
only about half the acreage needed for grown sto

Based on the forage production shown in ta
grazing capacity for each timber stand classificat

	One m (acr
Longleaf pine	
Poles, good stocking	4.
Poles, moderate stocking	2.
Poles, poor stocking	1.
Reproduction	1.
Slash pine	1.
Slash pine-bottomland hardwoods	3.

These estimated capacities should be help
or farmer interested in determining the approxim
forest range. For the 7-month season on the gra
this works out as follows

	Total (acres)
Longleaf pine	
Poles, good stocking	270
Poles, moderate stocking	76
Poles, poor stocking	94
Reproduction	75
Slash pine	14
Slash pine-bottomland hardwoods	117
Total	646

The above tabulation, calculated by types
capacity of 33 head for 7 months on the 646 ac

Where a part of the range is burned, of co
centrate on the burned area and grazing capacity
mainly on the burned portion, at least for the spr

For the 1949-53 experiment in mainly second-growth pole stands of long-leaf pine, the estimated capacity was 19 acres per cow for a 7-month season. The average stocking during the 1923-33 experiment in open and young longleaf stands was about 9 acres per cow for a 7.5-month season, varying from 5 to 10 acres in different years. Undoubtedly, there was overgrazing in some years.

Effect of Cattle Grazing on Timber

Since the McNeill tract is now being managed primarily for timber, the influence of cattle grazing on tree reproduction and growth is of major importance.

From 1923 to 1933, the survival of longleaf pine seedlings that came in during the course of the experiment ranked from highest to lowest, as follows, under the various land treatments: 1. -- unburned and ungrazed, 2. --unburned and grazed, 3. --burned annually and ungrazed, and 4. --burned annually and grazed. By 1933, survival of seedlings from the heavy 1924 seed crop was 43 percent on unburned and ungrazed areas, as against 5 percent or less on the other three land treatments. It was concluded that browsing by cattle probably injured a few of the smaller seedlings, but that on the whole the injury was negligible except under heavy grazing or on carpetgrass areas (all carpetgrass areas were closely grazed regardless of stocking).

Under the light grazing from 1950 to 1954, there was no appreciable damage to pine reproduction. The youngest longleaf seedlings were two years old when grazing began in 1950. During the spring and summer grazing periods, no browsing of pines was observed.

A recent report on longleaf pinelands in central Louisiana recommends that, if cattle are permitted to graze in young longleaf pine stands, the size and distribution of the herd should be controlled to prevent heavy grazing (5). The seedling stand should be examined frequently, during winter and early spring especially, to see if there is serious damage, and if corrective action is needed.

Cattle browsed the foliage of several hardwood species in early spring on the McNeill Forest, but all of the species grazed, except yellow-poplar, were considered to be of low quality for pinelands. It was found necessary to protect natural or planted yellow-poplar seedlings completely, by fencing out cattle until the trees were past the sapling stage.

Cattle Gains

The small native steers averaged 350 pounds when turned into the pastures. For the early part of the season, they gained about 1 pound per head per day, but thereafter gains were smaller as the nutrient content of the grasses declined. In the 3-year grazing period, steers gained an average of 82 pounds each in the short-season pastures and 115 pounds in the long-season pastures (table 7). But because the cattle-days of grazing were greater in the short-season pastures, the total gains averaged 353 pounds per year more than in the long-season pastures. In the 3-year period, annual weight gains averaged 7.2 pounds per acre in the short-season pastures and 5.3 pounds in the long-season pastures. Total gains averaged 1,198 pounds per year in the short-season pastures and 845 pounds in the long-season pastures.

Table 7. --Average gains, per steer, 1950-1952 [1]

Year	Short-season pastures			Long-season pastures			Average all pastures
	A	F	Average	C	E	Average	
	-	-	- - - - - Pounds - - - - - - - -				
1950	87	100	92	134	118	126	104
1951	73	75	74	101	152	127	92
1952	87	74	81	103	89	96	86
Average	82	81	82	111	120	115	93

[1] In 1950, pasture A was stocked with 14 head, pasture F with 10 head, and pastures C and E with 6 head each. In 1951 and 1952, pasture A had 18 head, F 14 head, and pastures C and E 8 head each.

In 1925-33, 3-year-old steers grazed an average of 217 days from April through November, with average stocking at 9 acres per head. The animals were larger, the forest stands were younger and more open, and steer gains somewhat higher than in the present study (fig. 8). The 1925-33 seasonal steer gains averaged 119 pounds per head on burned range as compared with 92 pounds per head on unburned range. In both studies, maximum cattle gains were made in the spring, when the forage was growing most rapidly. The rate of gain declined in summer as the forage matured and hot weather and flies hampered grazing.

In the earlier study, the cattle usually lost weight in August in both burned and unburned pastures, probably because fresh forage was scarce during this time on the closely grazed ranges. Thereafter they made fair gains in September and October, but all lost weight in November. Probably it was the lighter grazing in the 1950-52 study that permitted the steers to gain throughout the summer.

- 18 -

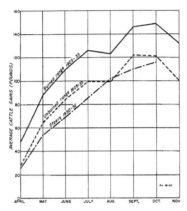

Figure 8. --Cumulative steer gains, 1925-1933 and 1950-1952.

In 1953 and 1954, a local farmer furnished animals to stock two of the study pastures. On April 7, 1953, 7 native cows with 7 calves were placed in Pasture A, and 5 cows, 4 calves, and 3 two-year-old heifers in Pasture C. At the end of 5 months, the cows in Pasture A averaged gains of 31 pounds, and the calves had gained 158 pounds per head. In Pasture C, cows gained 29 pounds, calves 136 pounds, and heifers 68 pounds.

In 1954, 12 cows and a bull were grazed in Pasture A. Pasture E was stocked with 12 yearling heifers. Grazing began April 5 and the cattle were removed July 21, at the end of 107 days of grazing. Two cows and one heifer bogged down and died. At the start, cows averaged 532 pounds and the heifers 350 pounds. Average gains were 121 pounds per head for cows and 56 pounds for heifers. Cow gains include the weights of 4 calves that were born on the range.

Cattle gains by pastures, years, and class of stock are shown in table 8. The class of stock seemed to have little influence on the total

Table 8. --Total cattle gains in short-season and long-season pastures

Year	Class of stock	Short-season pastures		Long-season pastures	
		A	F	C	E
		- - - - - - Pounds- - - - -			
1950	Steers	1,220	996	804	710
1951	Steers	1,318	1,053	811	1,215
1952	Steers	1,564	1,035	820	710
1953	Mixed	1,320	(1/)	895	(1/)
1954	Mixed	1,330	(1/)	(1/)	2/620
Average		1,350	1,028	832	814

1/ Not stocked.
2/ Cattle in Pasture E during 1954 were heifers.

- 19 -

advanced in 1950, but fell off moderately in 1951. In
pronounced drop during the grazing season.

In the first year gross returns were large eno
costs, including handling stock and other expenses, a
substantial profit. In 1951 returns were somewhat le
and in 1952 the sharp price decline caused a substanti

Table 9. --Costs and returns from steers, 1950-1952

Item	1950		1951	
	Short season	Long season	Short season	Long season
	- - - - - - -Dollars - -
Purchase price per cwt.	20.79	20.73	29.31	29.31
Selling price per cwt.	25.50	21.24	22.38	23.12
Purchase cost per steer	74.00	74.00	94.39	94.39
Selling price per steer	114.24	102.59	88.62	103.69
Gain or loss	40.24	28.59	-5.77	9.30

1/ Other direct costs, including handling, commissioi
and medicines, varied from about $8.00 to $12.00 per
values above do not include shrinkage due to hauling 1

Because stocker quality cattle normally declii
spring and fall, steers do not appear to be as promis
forest grazing as a breeding herd. With a breeding l

using forest range can depend upon the sale of calves for annual income. Moreover he need not make cash expenditures for replacements in the herd. Of course, supplemental feed or pasture should be provided to keep the herd thrifty during the fall and winter, and other good manage_ ment practices should be applied (1).

In a south Georgia study, with a high winter maintenance level of grazing on Bermudagrass pasture and hay, cows grazed on range in spring and summer and produced a 75-percent calf crop. Calves aver_ aged 413 pounds at weaning (8). This is in contrast to the 57 percent calf crop and weaned-calf weight of 273 pounds from cows maintained at minimum levels in fall and winter.

In the early phases of a study in central Louisiana, a herd of common range cattle was given just enough cottonseed cake to keep the animals alive during winter. Beef production was low, with calf crops averaging about 50 percent and calves seldom weighing more than 300 pounds in the fall.

Beginning in 1954, one herd was fed adequate supplements on the range and other improved management practices were put into effect (6). Phosphorus was kept before the animals all year. Protein was fed as soon as the range forage dropped below minimum require_ ment for this nutrient, usually from November to May.

The animals responded rapidly; beef production more than doubled. In 1956 and 1957 calf crops averaged 85 percent, and calves weighed 453 pounds at 7 months of age[4]. The feed cost was $17.46 per cow or $20.63 per calf. The calves sold in August at an average price of $81.57, leaving $60.94 per calf for range and handling costs, interest on the investment, and profit to the owner.

RECOMMENDED RANGE AND
HERD MANAGEMENT PRACTICES

Since steers were grazed in the spring and summer on the forest range and sold at the end of each grazing season, little information was obtained on yearlong-herd management. However, the Louisiana studies indicate that the following measures are essential to the successful man_ agement of beef cattle on forest range:

---

[4] Data by Don A. Duncan and L.B. Whitaker, on file at Southern Forest Experiment Station.

Fence forest ranges to facilitate adequate supervision of the
   herds.
Provide salt, minerals, and water throughout the grazing
   season.
Treat animals periodically for parasites and diseases.
Use improved beef breeds and control the breeding season
   to make efficient use of forage.

Although burning to remove old grass and litter improves grazing,
it is not essential for satisfactory utilization of the forest range in this
territory. Where burning is done for forestry purposes, small burns are
undesirable because cattle will concentrate on the burned area and over-
graze it.

Adequate yearlong nutrition may be provided cattle herds on
forest land either by feeding supplements on the range in fall and winter
or by giving the animals other pasture or feed during this period. The
McNeill results show that, if the first alternative is used, stock normally
should be removed from the range about October 1 and placed on improved pastures until about March 15. Where cultivated fields are available, fall and winter pastures of oats, crimson clover, ryegrass, or other
forage plants · provide winter feed.

SUMMARY

Forest range is an important source of inexpensive forage for
livestock on the Gulf Coastal Plain of south Mississippi and adjacent
States. This study, on the McNeill Experimental Forest in Pearl River ·
County, Mississippi, provides information about the amount and nutrient
value of native forage under various stands and densities of second-
growth longleaf pine. In 1947, when the study began, the pines were about
35 years old.

Four pastures, each of about 160 acres, were fenced. Two were.
rather well stocked with pine and two had only a moderate stand. Two
of the pastures were grazed for 4 months (April 1 to July 31), and two
for 7 months (April 1 to October 31). In 1950, 1951, and 1952, small, ·
thin yearling steers were grazed; while in 1953 and 1954 supplemental
tests were made with breeding cows. The short-season pastures were
stocked with about twice as many animals as the long-season pastures,
considering the forage available.

Bluestem grasses made up the bulk of the forage on the experimental areas, along with panicums, dropseed, threeawn, paspalums,
carpetgrass, and certain palatable weeds and shrubs. In an earlier ex-

periment under rather heavy grazing, average grass density decreased from 70 percent in 1923 to 21 percent in 1933, and the valuable little blue. stem lost ground to other grasses. By 1949, under light grazing and only periodic burning, the grass density increased to 28 percent and little blue. stem regained its dominance.

As the pines grew and occupied more space, grass yields were reduced by competition from trees and by smothering from accumulated litter. Open pine stands produced an average of 850 pounds of green grass (air-dry) per acre annually during the three years 1947-1949, moderate stands produced 450 pounds, and dense stands grew 400 pounds.

Rainfall influenced grass production both seasonally and from year to year. Rainfall for the April-August period was roughly correlated with maximum grass growth during 1947-1953. About 70 percent of each year's grass production was reached by June and 85 percent by July.

Bluestem grasses contributed 81 percent of the average seasonal diet of steers, other grasses 13 percent, weeds 3 percent, and browse 3 percent (although browse was as high as 17 percent in March).

The experimental areas were lightly to moderately grazed during the study. Utilization averaged from 10 to 25 percent, but was somewhat greater in the immediate vicinity of logging roads, salt boxes, tree stumps, girdled trees, and water holes. On fresh burns, from 50 to 95 percent of the growth was utilized.

Chemical analyses of plant samples representing cattle diets varied from an adequate 9.02 percent crude protein in March to a below-maintenance low of 6.58 percent in September. New growth in spring and on previously grazed areas during summer had higher protein than older, more mature herbage. Calcium content apparently was adequate for animals needs, but phosphorus was not.

Grazing capacity for the experimental range was estimated at about 11 acres per cow for a 4-month season or 19 acres per cow for a 7-month season.

The experimental steers averaged 350 pounds in weight when placed on the pastures in March. Steers in the 4-month pastures gained an average of 82 pounds apiece, while those in the 7-month pastures gained 115 pounds.

Grazing damage to pine reproduction was negligible under the light to moderate grazing in this study, except on a few very localized areas where cattle concentrated and browsed or trampled some seedlings. However, it was necessary to fence out planted areas of yellow-poplar to prevent serious browsing of this species.

It is recommended that forest range grazing in this timber type be limited to spring and summer months, and that cattle be carried on low-cost pasture or other feed in winter.

COMMON RANGE FORAGE PLANTS
ON THE MCNEILL PASTURES

Grasses

Andropogon scoparius	Little bluestem
A. elliottii	Elliott bluestem
A. virginicus	Yellowsedge bluestem
A. tener	Slender bluestem
A. ternarius	Paintbrush bluestem
Aristida purpurascens	Arrowfeather threeawn
Arundinaria tecta	Switch cane
Axonopus affinis	Carpetgrass
Gymnopogon ambiguus	Bearded skeletongrass
Panicum spp.	Panic grasses
Panicum virgatum	Switch grass
Paspalum floridanum	Florida paspalum
Sorghastrum nutans	Indian grass
Sporobolus gracilis	Pineywoods dropseed

Weeds

Helianthus radula	Swamp sunflower
Desmodium ciliare	Littleleaf tick clover
Lespedeza striata	Common lespedeza
Chrysopsis aspera	Grassleaf goldaster

Shrubs

Callicarpa americana	French mulberry
Myrica cerifera	Southern waxmyrtle
Cornus florida	Dogwood
Rubus allegheniensis	Blackberry
Symplocos tinctoria	Sweetleaf
Vaccinium spp.	Blueberry

- 24 -

LITERATURE CITED

l, R. S., and Cassady, J. T.
. Grazing values for cattle on pine forest ranges in Louisiana.
La. Bul. 452, 31 pp.

and Cassady, J. T.
. Forage weight inventories on southern forest ranges. U. S.
Forest Serv. South. Forest Expt. Sta., Occas. Paper
139, 18 pp.

Epps, E. A., Jr., Moreland, C. C., and others.
. Nutritive values of native plants on forest range in central
Louisiana. La. Bul. 488, 18 pp.

. J. T.
. Herbage production on bluestem range in central Louisiana.
Jour. Range Mangt. 6: 38-43.

and Whitaker, L. B.
. Supplemental feeding and management of beef cattle on forest
range in Louisiana. Proc. Soc. Amer. Foresters 1956:
52-54.

Hopkins, Walt, and Whitaker, L. B.
. Cattle grazing damage to pine seedlings. U. S. Forest Serv.
South. Forest Expt. Sta., Occas. Paper 141, 14 pp.

H. R., Gerlaugh, Paul, and Madsen, L. L.
Recommended nutrient allowances for beef cattle. Nat. Res.
Council, 37 pp. Rev.

. K., and Southwell, B. L.
Supplemental feeding of range cattle in wiregrass-pine
ranges of Georgia. Soc. Amer. Foresters Proc. 1956:
58-61.

:rg, W. G., Greene, S. W., and Reed, H. R.
Effects of fire and cattle grazing on longleaf pine lands, as
studied at McNeill, Mississippi. U. S. Dept. Agr. Tech.
Bul. 683, 52 pp.

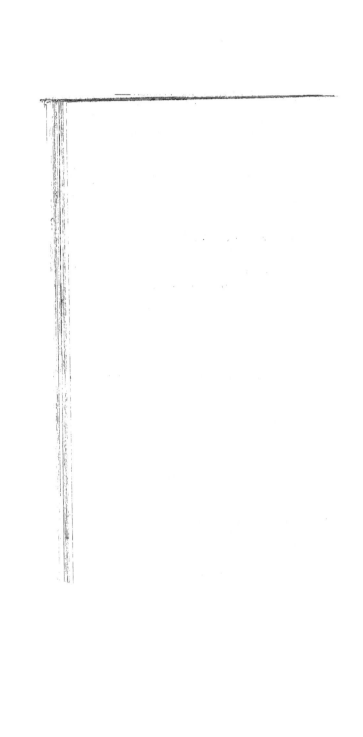

MANAGING A SMALL FOREST
IN EAST TEXAS

CARTER B. GIBBS

OCCASIONAL

SOUTHERN FOREST EX

FOREST S

U. S. DEPT. OF

This paper is based on work conducted at the East Texas Research Center, which is maintained at Nacogdoches, Texas, by the Southern Forest Experiment Station in cooperation with Stephen F. Austin State College.

Research at this center is concentrated on the 2,500-acre Stephen F. Austin Experimental Forest in Nacogdoches County and on the nearby Kurth Tract. Here specialists are making basic studies in soils, plant physiology, entomology, forest management, fire, and regeneration. Some work is also under way at the San Jacinto Experimental Forest in Walker County and elsewhere in east Texas.

Cover: *Stephen F. Austin Farm Forest.*

MANAGING A SMALL FOREST IN EAST TEXAS

Carter B. Gibbs
Southern Forest Experiment Station

America's demand for timber is increasing. The U. S. Forest Service estimates that the market for wood will double before the century is out. Much of the timber to supply the mills of the future will come from small tracts, for more than half the nation's forested area is in holdings of less than 5,000 acres. Today's small-tract owner has a better opportunity than ever before to make money by growing trees.

Most small woodlands are p r o d u c i n g only a fraction of their potential income--and those in east Texas are no exception. To gain information that would aid forest managers in this region, a tract on the Stephen F. Austin Experimental Forest was designated as a farm forest in 1947. It contains 67 acres. In size it is thus very close to the 65-acre average for the forested portions of small landownerships in east Texas.

Prior to 1947 the experimental tract had been cut heavily at least three times. Each cut had removed the best timber. The first cut had been in the 1890's, the second about 1915, and the last in the late 1930's. In 1947 the average acre had 3,300 board feet (International 1/4-inch rule) of rough pine and 2,612 of low-quality hardwood. Though this stocking was a little heavier than average, the tract shared the problems common to the region's small forests. Low-quality hardwoods were occupying sites that should have been growing pines. Desirable trees were small in size and few in number. Many areas needed seeding or planting. Cattle grazing had to be controlled.

The objectives of management were threefold:

To apply the kind of forestry that would be practical for most owners

To determine the costs and returns

To demonstrate the possibilities of getting an annual income while rebuilding the forest.

What Was Done

To concentrate each year's operations, the tract was divided into five compartments of about 13 acres each (fig. 1). One compartment is harvested every year, so that the entire forest is worked over in 5 years. The 1957 harvest marked the end of the second 5-year cutting period.

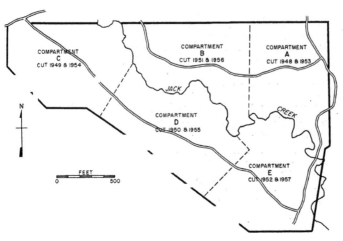

Figure 1.--*Compartments of the Stephen F. Austin Farm Forest.*

Each time a compartment is due for a cut, all pines in it are inventoried to determine how much the stand has grown since the previous cut. One-half to two-thirds of the growth is harvested; the rest is left to build up the stand.

Trees marked for cutting may occur singly or in small groups. A stand is never cleared off completely, though small openings may be made here and there. In marking pines to sell, the principle is "Take the worst first." Most of the trees that were damaged by insects, disease, or fire, or those that were coarse-limbed or otherwise of poor form, were removed in the first cut. In the second cycle, the bulk of the volume came from thinning and from harvest of large mature pines.

Most of the 67 acres are moderately dry uplands capable of growing good pines but unsuited to the production of quality hardwoods. For this reason, all upland hardwoods that would make a sawlog or crosstie were sold as soon as possible. A small amount of promising hardwood was retained on favorable branch-bottom soil.

A tie operator went over the entire tract in 1947, removing all hardwoods suitable for his purposes. After that, the initial cut on each compartment included all salable hardwood sawlogs. In addition, unmerchantable hardwoods that were overtopping natural or planted pines were deadened. Those 8 inches or above were girdled with an ax or the Little Beaver power girdler. Smaller hardwoods sprout prolifically when girdled or felled, but the Little Tree Injector, loaded with 2, 4, 5-T, has been very effective in killing both tops and roots.

Hardwoods suitable for wildlife food and dens are retained.

Wildfires have been strictly controlled with the cooperation of the Texas Forest Service, and cattle grazing has been held to safe limits. Pine sites infested with small hardwoods were prescribe-burned to prepare them for seeding or planting. Fire will not be used at all when the forest becomes fully stocked to all sizes of pines, because small pines are very susceptible to fire damage.

Marking a tree for harvest. Poor-risk and inferior trees are marked first, and then the rest of the harvest is taken from large, high-quality timber.

The Little Tree Injector with a silvicide like 2,4,5-T is a safe and effective method of killing undesirable hardwoods. Results are best when hardwoods are treated in spring or early summer.

Results of Management

Pine growth on the forest ranged from 106 to 220 board feet per acre annually. It varied from compartment to compartment (table 1), being influenced not only by the pine stocking but also by the density of competing hardwoods.

In 1947 the pine volume on the entire tract was 222, 894 board feet. By 1957 it had increased to 243, 552 board feet. This increase of 20, 658 board feet, plus 92, 875 board feet that were harvested (table 2), brings the total growth to 113, 533 board feet for the ten years of management.

- 3 -

Table 1.--Growth per acre, by compartments

Compartment	Volume after first cut	Volume 5 years later	Annual growth
	Board feet	Board feet	Board feet
A	3,827	4,803	195
B	2,619	3,317	140
C	3,702	4,803	220
D	2,574	3,105	106
E	3,076	3,697	124

Table 2.--Products harvested, 1947-1957

Year	Pine logs, Int. 1/4-inch rule	Hardwood logs, Int. 1/4-inch rule	Hardwood ties	Pine pulpwood	Pine posts
	Board feet	Board feet	No.	Cords	No.
1947	...	...	883	...	...
1948	6,903	6,410	...	3.63	...
1949	7,044	1,023	...	...	124
1950	7,231	7,104	...	...	...
1951	12,397	5,529	...	...	...
1952	8,375	6,547	...	...	285
1953	11,108	1,109	...	2.50	...
1954	11,673	3,527	...	4.00	...
1955	13,300	...	...	6.50	...
1956	8,800	...	...	...	...
1957	6,044	...	...	...	...
Total	92,875	31,249	883	16.63	409

Thinning shortleaf pines for pulpwood.

All timber was sold as stumpage. In addition to the pine logs, the sales included hardwood sawlogs and ties and some pine pulpwood and fenceposts. The annual harvests rarely amounted to more than a half-dozen truckloads. In the past, small sales have often been difficult to make. Now they are much easier, especially if the tract is near a good road and the offering includes a reasonable amount of pine.

As table 3 shows, the gross returns from stumpage sales have been nearly $2,800, or $4.15 per

Table 3.--Ten-year costs and returns [1]

Stumpage sales		
92,875 bd. ft. of pine at $25 per M	$2,321.88	
31,249 bd. ft. of hardwood at $3 per M	93.75	
883 hardwood crossties	295.68	
16.63 cords of pine pulpwood at $3 per cord	49.89	
409 posts at $0.04 each	16.36	
Cash receipts		$2,777.56
Costs		
Taxes, 67 acres at $0.15 per acre, 10 years	$100.50	
Hardwood control, 171.1 hrs. at $1.00 per hr.	171.10	
Planting, 124.1 hrs. at $1.00 per hr.	124.10	
Burning, 53.8 hrs. at $1.00 per hr.	53.80	
Town ant control, 3.0 hrs. at $1.00 per hr.	3.00	
Scaling, 32.0 hrs. at $1.00 per hr.	32.00	
Marking, 91.0 hrs. at $1.20 per hr.	109.20	
Supplies--fuel, seedlings, axes, etc.	45.14	
Total expenditure		$638.84
Net cash return per acre per year		$4.15

[1] Labor costs and stumpage prices are based on estimated rates for the 10-year period.

acre annually. Pine logs brought 8 times as much per thousand board feet as hardwood logs. With ties included, the harvests contained as much hardwood as pine, yet the income from the hardwoods was less than $400. The quality of the hardwoods could be improved under management on most of the tract, but pines are much more profitable.

From these gross returns must be subtracted the costs of managing the forest. Most of the outlays were for labor. Three and one-half man-days per year were devoted to controlling undesirable hardwoods and planting pine. Marking and scaling the harvests, controlled burning, and related activities took another 2-1/2 man-days annually. Taxes and supplies

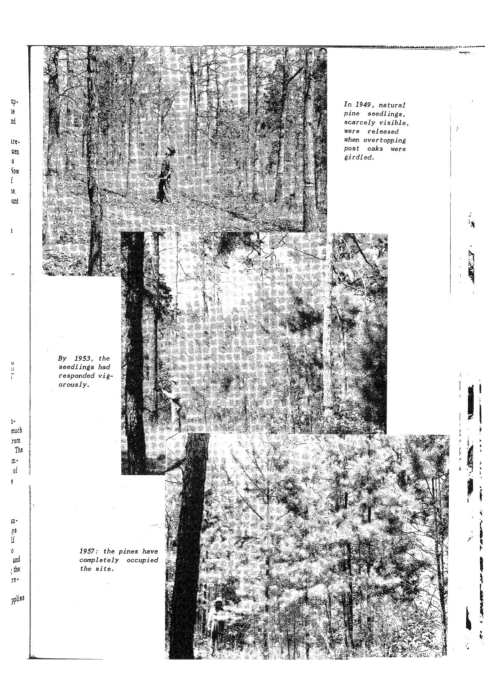

In 1949, natural pine seedlings, scarcely visible, were released when overtopping post oaks were girdled.

By 1953, the seedlings had responded vigorously.

1957: the pines have completely occupied the site.

were additional expenses (table 3). The average for all costs was 95 cents per acre annually. Net yearly cash returns from management thus have been $3.20 per acre.

These net returns do not fully measure the benefits from management. The increase in pine growing stock is worth about 80 cents per acre annually, so that the total net returns have been about $4.00 per acre each year.

While management improved the growth prospects of the existing pines, a combination of poor seed crops and hot, dry summers prevented adequate pine reseeding. To supplement natural seeding, 8,900 pines were planted during the 10 years, but many of these also died of drought. Seedlings and saplings were sparse in 1947, and,while some young pines did become established, the forest still is seriously lacking in small trees. Figure 2 shows the changes in number of sawtimber pines between 1948 and 1957.

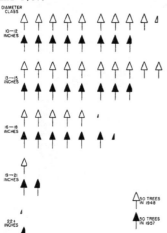

Figure 2.--*Distribution of pine trees, by diameter classes, 1948 and 1957.*

The unbalanced distribution of tree sizes is sure to be temporary. Improved methods of controlling hardwoods and brush have increased the success of recent plantings. Sooner or later, too, the return of normal weather will improve the natural seed catch.

Lightning and Ips beetles have killed a few trees, but in general the stand is healthy. Town ants have occasionally destroyed seedlings, but their colonies have been controlled with methyl bromide.

Recommendations to Landowners

Ten years of management have transformed a wild woodland into a managed forest, and at a modest cost in time and money. Timber stocking has been improved in volume and quality. This does not mean, however, that every small forest has to be managed by exactly the same methods as were used here.

The study was begun on the assumption that the owner of a small forest would want an annual income and that he would have to stretch his investment in labor and supplies over the years. Not all landowners need to operate under these restrictions.

For one thing, annual harvests are not always the most efficient. Cuts of entire small holdings at intervals of 3 to 5 years are larger in volume and hence can often be marketed more advantageously.

The upland portions of nearly all east Texas forests are dominated by low-grade hardwoods--as the experimental forest was in 1947. The sooner that the hardwoods are removed and replaced with pines, the more rewarding will be the investment. If the owner lives on his land, he can do much of the work himself. Non-resident owners will usually profit by contracting the hardwood-control job. Tree farmers who have completed this phase of management are almost unanimous in saying that the best time to tackle the hardwoods is in the first year or two.

Planting a few pine seedlings each year can sweeten future harvests. In east Texas, pines should be planted between December 1 and March 1. They must be released from overtopping hardwoods immediately.

In these early tasks, as well as in the more complicated decisions that will have to be made later, most owners will benefit from a forester's advice. The Texas Forest Service, besides assisting in fire protection, will, on request, provide technical guidance on individual tracts. Several lumber and pulp companies also offer free management assistance. Non-resident owners, especially, may be interested in hiring a consulting forester to manage their tracts.

Tree seedlings for planting are available at cost from nurseries of the Texas Forest Service. The Agricultural Stabilization and Conservation Program includes payments for planting trees and improving young pine stands; information about the program can be had from the county ACP committees.

The various kinds of assistance just described, the application of new forestry methods developed by research, and the rising demand for wood have eased many problems that formerly beset the managers of small forests. The owner who will make the most of today's opportunities has an excellent chance for earning money in the timber markets of tomorrow.

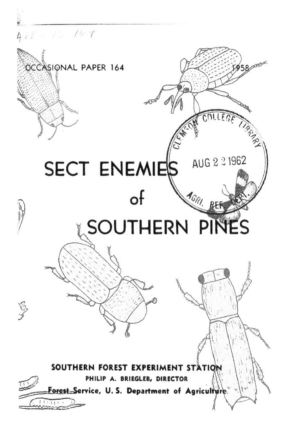

OCCASIONAL PAPER 164   1958

SECT ENEMIES

of

SOUTHERN PINES

SOUTHERN FOREST EXPERIMENT STATION
PHILIP A. BRIEGLEB, DIRECTOR
Forest Service, U. S. Department of Agriculture

CAUTION!

THE INSECTICIDES MENTIONED IN THIS
PUBLICATION ARE POISONS. USE THEM
ACCORDING TO THE SAFETY INSTRUC-
TIONS ON THE CONTAINER. AVOID IN-
HALING THE DUSTS OR SPRAYS. IF YOU
CONTAMINATE YOUR SKIN WITH CON-
CENTRATED INSECTICIDES, WASH IM-
MEDIATELY WITH SOAP AND WARM WATER.
AVOID WEARING CONTAMINATED CLOTHING.

METHYL BROMIDE, AS RECOMMENDED FOR
THE CONTROL OF THE TEXAS LEAF-
CUTTING ANT, IS A POISONOUS GAS.
DO NOT STORE METHYL BROMIDE IN
BUILDINGS WHERE PEOPLE LIVE OR
WORK, AND DO NOT INHALE THE GAS.
IT IS BEST TO USE A PREPARATION
CONTAINING A SMALL AMOUNT OF CHLORO-
PICRIN (TEAR GAS) TO SERVE AS A
WARNING AGENT, SINCE METHYL BROMIDE
ALONE HAS VERY-LITTLE ODOR.

INSECT ENEMIES OF SOUTHERN PINES

William H. Bennett
Charles W. Chellman
William R. Holt

Southern Forest Experiment Station

This publication brings together information on the identification, habits, and control of the most common insect enemies of southern pines. With very slight changes, it is a combination of Numbers 10, 19, and 21 of the SOUTHERN FOREST PEST RE-PORTER. It is intended as an identification aid and reference for woods workers, forest managers, and others interested in protecting forests from insect damage.

Some of the insects discussed are usually not considered serious. Generalizations about the importance of an insect, however, may be short-lived. Occasionally, large populations of a so-called minor insect build up in limited areas or on individual trees. Or there is always the possibility that a small, widespread insect population may develop into a serious menace to vast forest areas within a short period. The black turpentine beetle, currently the most troublesome insect enemy of southern pines, was once of little significance.

Reports of any unusual insect conditions will be gratefully received at the Southern Forest Experiment Station.

PINE INSECTS OF THE SOUTH

	INSECT	SYMPTOMS	PAGE
BARK BEETLES	**Southern Pine Beetle** Bores under bark and girdles trees of various sizes. Usually attacks middle of trunk and spreads up and down. Out of control, it can kill millions of dollars worth of green timber.	Small, reddish to white pitch-tubes on bark. Sometimes just boring dust. S-shaped and criss-crossed tunnels engraved in inner bark. Beetles brown to black, about 1/8-inch long; rounded hind end; minute notch on front of head when viewed from above.	4
	Ips Engraver Beetles Bore under bark and girdle trees of small and commercial size. Not as spectacular as the southern pine beetle but present all the time and do considerable damage.	Small, reddish to white pitch-tubes on bark of trunk. Sometimes just red boring dust in cracks of bark and on ground. Y- or H-shaped tunnels, almost straight and parallel with wood grain, on inside bark. Beetles light to dark brown or black, 1/4-inch long or less; hind end cut-off and shovel-shaped.	7
	Black Turpentine Beetle Girdles inner bark of stumps and butts of large trees. Following logging, fires, etc., the insect may increase and kill trees, especially trees that have been scarred, turpentine-faced, or otherwise damaged.	Large, sugar-like pitch-tubes on stumps and lower trunk. Hard particles of resin at tree base. Tunnels on inner bark are more or less shapeless, and contain considerable pitch; larvae feed in groups and eat out whole patches of inner bark. Beetles brown to black, about 1/4 to 1/3-inch long.	10
WOOD BORERS	**Southern Pine Sawyer** Round-headed borer tunnels in dead and dying trees and fresh-cut logs. The tunnels cause severe defects in lumber.	Pencil-size and larger holes in sapwood and heartwood, with coarse excelsior-like frass. Funnel-shaped holes in bark where eggs have been deposited.	14
	Turpentine Borer Flat-headed borer in fire-scarred and turpentined trees. Degrades lumber and weakens stems so that they may break from wind or ice.	Elliptical emergence holes on fire scars and particularly in turpentine faces. Larval tunnels filled with tightly packed fine frass and resin. Trees broken off about breast high during high winds.	16
	Ambrosia Beetles Pin-hole borers in dying trees, logs, and unseasoned lumber. Make small holes in the wood and introduce a dark stain.	Pin-hole damage and black stain in lumber. Piles of fluffy white boring dust on ground and in bark crevices of infested trees and logs.	18
ROOT, TWIG, AND EXTERNAL BARK FEEDERS	**Nantucket Pine Tip Moth** Bud and shoot destroyer of seedlings and saplings. Causes the trees to become bushy and stunted. Growth loss may be severe.	Underdeveloped buds and dead shoots hollowed out. White crust of resin near bud. Small, yellowish to brown larvae or pupae inside bud or shoot. Moth about 1/4-inch long, reddish-brown with silver-gray markings. Flies around foliage at dusk during summer.	20
	Bark Weevils External bark feeders and girdlers of seedlings. Most destructive during the spring following fall or winter cutting.	Planted or natural seedlings with bark girdled externally above or below ground line. Weevils dark brown to black, 1/4- to 1/2-inch long; prominent beak; feed at night and in cloudy weather; commonly breed in stump roots.	22
	White Grubs Root feeders on nursery seedlings and young plantation stock.	Foliage of seedlings fading and dying. Roots girdled or chewed off. Adults (May beetles) attracted to lights; feed on foliage of hardwoods.	24

Red-headed Pine Sawfly — Needle chewer. Trees are weakened and occasionally killed by repeated defoliation. Growth loss may be severe.	Needles chewed to short stubs; manure pellets on ground. Masses of worm-like larvae feed together; red-brown heads, yellow bodies with black spots, about an inch in length; many small legs.	26
Loblolly Pine Sawfly — Needle chewer. Prefers loblolly pine. Defoliates pines from March to May, causing heavy growth losses.	Needles chewed and trees defoliated, manure pellets on ground. Groups of worm-like larvae up to about an inch in length; red-brown heads; bodies dull green and gray striped; many small legs on body. Difficult to see on foliage.	26
Black-headed Pine Sawfly — Needle chewer.	Larvae same as above except with black heads and black spots along sides of green and gray striped body.	26
Pine Webworm — Defoliates seedlings in nurseries and young plantations.	Seedlings have masses of silk webbing mixed with excrement pellets.	28
Texas Leaf-Cutting Ant — Defoliates seedlings during winter. Serious problem in parts of Louisiana and Texas.	Needles, bark,and buds removed from natural and planted seedlings. Large red-brown ants live in towns made up of many conspicuous mounds.	30
Pine Colaspis Beetle — Feeds on needles of natural and planted re-production and larger trees.	Needles appear as if singed by fire and are highly reflective at night. Symptoms most noticeable in June and July.	33
Pine Needle Miner — Burrows and feeds within needles. Probably causes growth loss.	Conspicuous browning and yellowing of needles. Partly hollowed needles with excrement particles and minute holes.	34
Pine Pitch Midge — Alaska twigs and lives in glob of resin. Common but of little economic importance.	Small masses of semi-fluid resin containing yellowish-orange larvae with occasional swelling of plant tissue. Twigs sometimes swell under the pitch glob.	34
Scale Insects — Suck sap from needles and twigs. Occasionally become very numerous, reducing tree vigor and killing young pines.	Scale-like insects covering needles or twigs. Fading or browning foliage in severe infestation with honeydew present.	34
Aphids — Suck sap from needles, bark, roots. Cause growth loss and malformation of infested parts.	Soft-bodied plant lice on foliage or bark. Honeydew present.	34
Spider Mites — Suck sap from needles and twigs. Sometimes kill ornamental conifers.	Spotty, pale-green and brown foliage. Fine webbing with cast skins and eggs or mites on needles or twigs.	35

LEAF FEEDERS

MISCELLANEOUS INSECTS

SOUTHERN PINE BEETLE

Dendroctonus frontalis

Importance. --The southern pine beetle is considered to be the most destructive forest insect in the South. It attacks pines of all sizes and can kill apparently vigorous trees. It is especially dangerous following prolonged drouth, but sometimes reaches epidemic status without obvious reason.

The beetle carries with it a blue-stain fungus that hastens the death of trees and lowers their lumber value.

Habits. --The beetle is about 1/8-inch long, brown or black. Its hind end is rounded, in contrast to the chopped-off posterior of Ips beetles (below). When the beetle is viewed from above with a hand lens, a minute notch may be seen on the front of the head.

Side view of hind end of southern pine beetle (greatly enlarged).

Side view of hind end of Ips beetle (greatly enlarged).

The beetles construct S-shaped, criss-crossed tunnels in the inner bark and kill the tree by girdling it and introducing a blue-stain fungus. Eggs are deposited in niches along the tunnels and larvae soon develop from them. Larvae usually feed within the bark, where they change to pupae and finally transform to beetles. In warm weather the life cycle is completed in 30 to 40 days. There may be 5 or 6 generations a year.

The beetle kills trees in groups that vary in size from a few trees to many thousands. Population trends are violent and hard to predict. Buildups are fast and often without apparent reason. When the epidemic has run its course, the insects sometimes disappear as rapidly as they came; in some years it is almost impossible to find any beetles at all,

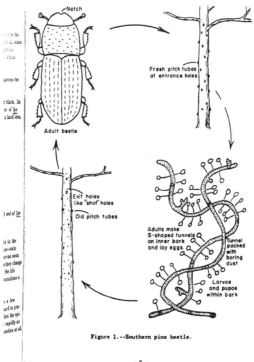

Notch

Adult beetle

Fresh pitch tubes
at entrance holes

Exit holes
like "shot" holes
Old pitch tubes

Adults make
S-shaped tunnels
on inner bark
and lay eggs

Tunnel
packed
with
boring
dust

Larvae
and pupae
within bark

Figure 1.--Southern pine beetle.

Signs of attack. --The earliest signs of infestation are numerous white, yellow, or sometimes red-brown pitch tubes, about as large as a wad of gum, scattered over the bark of the main stem. In trees of low vigor, pitch tubes may be lacking but reddish boring dust will be seen in bark crevices and in spider webs on the bark and at the base of the trees.

New broods often leave the trees when the foliage is only slightly faded or yellow. When the crowns turn red, the beetles have usually left (except during winter).

Control. --When beetle populations are rising, control measures should be applied immediately and pushed forward vigorously. Salvage logging will check beetle populations only if the infested trees are cut and taken to the mill before the beetles have left. Slabs of infested bark knocked off in felling and skidding should be destroyed.

Where rapid salvage logging is impractical, the infested trees should be immediately cut and sprayed with benzene hexachloride (BHC). Only pines with living broods within them should be treated. These are usually green-topped or slightly faded trees.

The recommended spray for controlling the southern pine beetle is 0.25 percent gamma isomer benzene hexachloride in No. 2 diesel oil. This may be prepared as follows:

Stir one gallon of benzene hexachloride concentrate (containing about one pound of gamma isomer per gallon) into about 50 gallons of No. 2 diesel oil. The spray costs about 20 cents per gallon.

BHC concentrate can be purchased in 5-gallon containers and 53-gallon drums. One gallon of the spray mixture will treat about 100 square feet of bark surface. All surfaces should be covered thoroughly--until drops begin to form and run off. Logs should be turned so that the underside can be sprayed.

IPS ENGRAVER BEETLES

Ips avulsus, Ips grandicollis, and Ips calligraphus

Importance. --The 3 common species of Ips beetles kill sapling and larger pines that have been weakened by drouth, fire, hail, ice storms, or other causes. They can almost always be found in lightning-struck trees. Logging slash, fresh-cut logs, and fire-scorched trees are especially attractive to them.

Infested trees are typically scattered through the forest, but the beetles may kill clumps of trees when conditions are in their favor. Cumulative damage is very high, and is accentuated by the fact that the beetles carry a blue-stain fungus that degrades the lumber cut from infested trees.

Habits. --All three species girdle the cambial region, but they are unlike in size and they sometimes show a preference for different parts of the tree. Young adults are yellow, older ones nearly black.

Ips avulsus, the smallest species, is not quite 1/8-inch long. It attacks the crowns and frequently the trunks of trees of all sizes. Populations normally build up in fresh logging slash and spread to crowns of nearby timber when logging ceases or when the standing trees have been weakened by drouth or some other disturbance. They sometimes kill one branch at a time but when abundant may suddenly attack the entire crown. When they are particularly active, they may make stands more susceptible to other Ips beetles and the southern pine beetle. This species has recently displayed signs of unusual aggressiveness. Landowners should take pains not to overlook it. Its presence in the crowns may not be noticeable except to an experienced spotter or with the aid of binoculars.

Ips grandicollis is medium-sized (about 3/16-inch long). It commonly attacks the middle and upper trunk. Ips calligraphus, almost 1/4-inch long, generally prefers the lower trunk. Both species, however, may be found on any part of the trunk and larger branches.

The three species may work together in the same tree, their tunnels overlapping, or they may work independently or in succession. They may also become associated with southern pine beetles and the black turpentine beetle. There may be 4 or 5 generations per year.

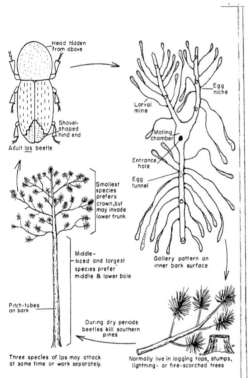

Head hidden from above

Shovel-shaped hind end

Adult Ips beetle

Egg niche

Larval mine

Mating chamber

Entrance hole

Egg tunnel

Gallery pattern on inner bark surface

Smallest species prefers crown, but may invade lower trunk.

Middle-sized and largest species prefer middle & lower bole

Pitch-tubes on bark

During dry periods beetles kill southern pines

Three species of Ips may attack at some time or work separately.

Normally live in logging tops, stumps, lightning- or fire-scorched trees

Figure 2.--*Ips* engraver beetle.

Signs of attack. --Trees infested with Ips will usually have numerous pink or red-brown (sometimes whitish) pitch-tubes, about the size of
a wad of gum, on the bark of the branches or trunk. In trees of low
vigor, however, pitch-tubes may be lacking, and the earliest signs of
attack will be reddish boring dust in bark crevices and in spider webs at
the base of the tree.

If the crowns alone are infested, pitch-tubes will be difficult to
see and the foliage may be only a trifle faded when the broods are ready
to leave. Sometimes the crowns turn yellow or red, limb by limb.

The egg tunnels, engraved on the inner bark and the surface of
the wood, are more or less straight. They are typically Y- or H-shaped
and run parallel to the grain of the wood. The egg tunnels are generally
free of boring dust. Larval feeding mines--wavy, somewhat indistinct,
and filled with boring dust--lead from the egg tunnels.

Control. --When beetle trees are widely scattered, control is
generally too expensive to be practical. However, if the attack seems to
be getting out of hand, currently infested trees should be salvaged before
the beetles have left, and the slabs should be burned at the sawmill. Where
early salvage is impossible, the trees should be felled and the tops, trunks,
and stumps sprayed. This "cut-spray" treatment costs $1.20 to $2.50 or
more per tree, depending upon the size and accessibility of the trees and
the concentration of the outbreak. When logging in a drouth year or on
poor sites, it is generally a good precaution to avoid intermittent cutting
and to burn or spray the tops and slash immediately.

The BHC formulation recommended for the southern pine beetle
will also control Ips.

The general strategy in control is to keep ahead of the insect by
treating only trees that have broods in them. Usually crowns are still
green or faded when broods are ready to leave. By the time the foliage
has turned red, beetles have usually, though not always, left. Do not
make the mistake of treating vacated red-tops and overlooking nearby infested green-tops.

Where drouth is the primary cause of unusual Ips beetle activity,
soaking rains will generally stop the infestation.

BLACK TURPENTINE BEETLE

Dendroctonus terebrans

Importance. --Formerly considered of little importance, the black turpentine beetle has in recent years become a serious forest pest capable of killing the best trees in a stand. It is especially prevalent following fires, heavy cutting, drouths, windstorms,and other disturbances to the forest. The beetle has also become a major problem in naval stores areas. Turpentined trees with virgin faces installed with a broad axe and intensively worked trees in dense stands are particularly susceptible to attack. The increased use of mechanized equipment may have something to do with the insect's new importance in logging areas, since heavy vehicles not only damage the residual trees but compact the soil and injure the roots.

Habits. --The adults are dark-brown or black beetles 1/4- to 1/3-inch long. They bore into the cambial region and lay eggs there. The larvae, creamy white grubs up to 1/3-inch long, feed in groups on the cambium, side by side, and eat out large patches between bark and wood. When the attack is light the tree usually recovers. When beetle broods are numerous they girdle the cambium and the tree slowly dies. At least 2-1/2 months are required to complete the life cycle of the beetle. Usually there are about 2 generations a year, but broods overlap.

The adult beetles are attracted by fresh resin and skinned or severely scorched bark. Populations may build up in fresh stumps and then spread to living trees. The beetle appears to prefer trees on low, flat, normally wet or poorly drained sites, especially during drouths. It is also common along woods roads and trails.

Signs of attack. --The most obvious signs of attack are conspicuous pitch-tubes on the lower trunk and stumps. The tubes are large--sometimes about the size of a walnut--and white to reddish in color. Older tubes have a sugar-like texture. Granular pieces of hard, whitish resin will be found on the ground below the pitch-tubes. The tunnels and irregular excavations beneath the bark are packed with sticky resin and red boring dust. When ambrosia beetles have entered the tree, their whitish boring dust will also be seen around the base.

Crown foliage color is not a satisfactory clue to the activities of this pest, because heavy populations may develop in an area before the trees are killed.

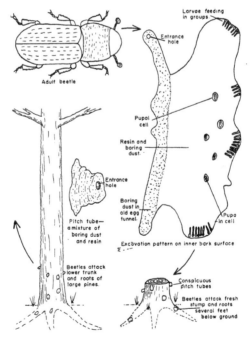

Adult beetle

Larvae feeding in groups

Entrance hole

Pupal cell

Resin and boring dust.

Entrance hole

Boring dust in old egg tunnel.

Pupa in cell

Pitch tube—a mixture of boring dust and resin

Excavation pattern on inner bark surface

Beetles attack lower trunk and roots of large pines.

Conspicuous pitch tubes

Beetles attack fresh stump and roots several feet below ground

Figure 3.--Black turpentine beetle.

Control. --Buildup to outbreak proportions is comparatively slow, and if stands are watched carefully, many attacks can be headed off. Unusual disturbances to the stand should be avoided, so far as possible. Logging should be done in such a way as to minimize injury to the remaining trees. If logging is carried on when outbreaks are likely, the green stumps and areas of skinned bark on remaining trees should immediately be sprayed with BHC. Spraying is especially useful where heavy logging equipment is used on poorly drained soils or where precutting of polewood is done a few months before crop trees are removed.

Seed trees or other valuable trees in outbreak areas can be protected by spraying the lower 4 feet of the trunk and exposed roots with BHC, a single treatment will last 6 months or more.

If many trees are being killed or if large numbers of active pitch-tubes indicate a rising population, control measures must be taken. Where the dying trees are too scattered to be salvaged, or when salvage cutting cannot be done immediately, the only recourse is to spray the stumps and infested butts of attacked trees with BHC.

Where salvage is feasible, the dead or dying trees should be cut and milled as soon as possible, the slabs from the butt logs should be burned in the millyard. Stumps and the butts of all remaining infested trees should be sprayed with BHC.

When trees are being marked for salvage, those having the white dust of ambrosia beetles around the base may be considered doomed to die. Lightly infested trees can often be saved by prompt spraying. Much sympathy is due the forester who has to decide which trees to cut and which to try to save. His task is somewhat easier if several salvage cuttings are possible within the year; then light marking can be used in the hope that many infested trees will recover. Where only one salvage cut can be made, heavy marking of infested trees may be necessary.

Sprays to be used on the turpentine beetle should contain two to four times the amount of BHC recommended for the southern pine beetle. The cost will be 10 to 30 or more cents per stump or butt, depending on the bark roughness, diameter, accessibility, and concentration of trees to be sprayed.

Before treatment, debris and litter should be scraped from around the base of the tree or stump, so that the spray can penetrate the vicinity of the larger roots. All surfaces of infested bark, including the crevices, should be sprayed to the point of run-off. A second pass is then made around the tree or stump, directing the spray at the basal

- 12 -

6 inches to add more insecticide to the soil. In thick-barked pines, especially slash pine in ponds and draws, it is usually necessary to scrape moss and loose bark off the lower trunk of the tree. Spraying should not be done during or after a rain when the bark is wet.

In naval stores timber, spotting can be facilitated by providing the chippers and dippers with marking tape or narrow strips of white cloth each 36 inches long. When an attacked tree is found, the tape or strip is fastened around the trunk at eye level or higher. These marked trees can be easily located for spraying after they have been reported in a general area.

When infested turpentine-faced trees have been sprayed, chipping should be avoided for the next two periods. This is recommended so that the trees may have a better opportunity to recover from the beetle attack and the spray. If possible, trees with numerous attacks should not be chipped for the remainder of the season.

As long as beetles are active in the area, trees should be repeatedly inspected and sprayed when necessary to keep the population low. This is quite easy in naval stores timber, where the important job of spotting newly attacked trees can be accomplished in the normal course of chipping and dipping operations.

SOUTHERN PINE SAWYER

Monochamus titillator

Importance. --Larvae of the southern pine sawyer tunnel through
the sapwood and heartwood of green logs and dead or dying pines, de-
grading the lumber and opening the way for decay fungi. The insect is
particularly destructive to windthrown and fire-killed timber and to logs
left in the woods or held in storage during the warm months.

Habits. --The larvae are legless, somewhat flattened white grubs
up to two inches long. The thoracic or front segments of the body are
slightly wider than the abdominal segments. The adult is a beetle,
mottled greyish-brown, 3/4 to 1-1/4 inches long. The antennae are
sometimes two or three times as long as the body.

The female beetles cut funnel-shaped pits in the bark surface and
deposit eggs in the phloem. Upon hatching, the larvae feed in the cambium
and sapwood and later tunnel deep into the sapwood and heartwood.
Eventually they return almost to the surface and construct a pupal cell.
Following transformation, the adults chew a hole to the surface and
emerge. Two or three generations a year are produced in the South.

Signs of attack. --The earliest signs of attack are the funnel-shaped
egg niches in the bark. Beneath the bark, dense, brownish frass and coarse-
shredded, excelsior-like wood shavings are present. Circular pencil-
size holes in the wood and bark are a sign that adults have emerged.

Control. --Rapid salvage and utilization of dead and dying trees or
green logs will reduce losses. If the beetle populations are large and logs
must be stored, damage may be prevented by promptly spraying the bark
with benzene hexachloride (BHC) in fuel oil.

The recommended spray is prepared by stirring one gallon of BHC
concentrate (containing one pound of gamma isomer per gallon) into 49
gallons of No. 2 fuel oil. The finished spray costs approximately 20 cents
per gallon. The concentrate can be purchased in 1, 5, and 55-gallon
containers.

One gallon of the finished spray will treat about 100 square feet of
bark surface. All surfaces should be covered thoroughly--until drops
begin to form and run off. Logs should be turned so that the under sides
can be sprayed.

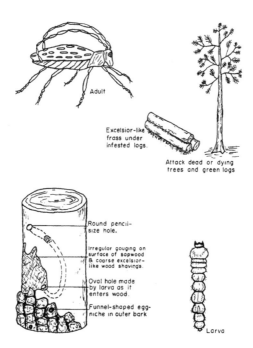

Adult

Excelsior-like
frass under
infested logs.

Attack dead or dying
trees and green logs

Round pencil-
size hole.

Irregular gouging on
surface of sapwood
& coarse excelsior-
like wood shavings.

Oval hole made
by larva as it
enters wood.

Funnel-shaped egg-
niche in outer bark

Larva

Figure 4.--Southern pine sawyer.

TURPENTINE BORER

Buprestis apricans

Importance. --Larvae of the turpentine borer attack the basal portion of pines that have been turpentined, fire-scarred, or injured mechanically. Larval boring may weaken the trees so that they break off in windstorms. When infestations are severe, 3 to 6 feet of the butt log may become unfit for lumber. Sound, healthy trees are seldom attacked.

Habits. --The legless larvae are elongated white grubs up to 1-1/2 inches long. They appear flat-headed because the thoracic or front segments of the body are distinctly wider than the abdominal segments. The beetle is grayish-bronze with a greenish metallic luster, 1-1/4 inches long.

The female lays eggs in checks in drywood of turpentined trees or trees that have been fire-scarred or otherwise injured. The larvae mine extensively in the sapwood and heartwood. The life cycle is completed in approximately 3-1/2 years.

Signs of attack. --Often the earliest signs of this beetle are elliptical emergence holes in dry turpentine faces or fire scars, or tunnels in trees broken off by wind. When infested trees are sawn into lumber, larval tunnels filled with fine, tightly-packed boring dust and resin are exposed.

Control. --The turpentine borer has been a major pest in the naval stores region. However, although many worked-out trees still remain in the forest as breeding places for this insect, modern naval stores practices, and particularly the prompt harvest of worked-out trees, have virtually eliminated severe infestations. Prescribed burning to decrease wildfire hazards and to reduce the number of charred, cracked faces on trees worked for naval stores has also helped.

Occasionally, tree trunks will require spraying to protect them, and the recommended spray is BHC in No. 2 fuel oil. It is prepared by stirring two gallons of BHC concentrate (containing one pound of gamma isomer per gallon) into 48 gallons of the fuel oil. The finished spray costs approximately 24 cents per gallon. One gallon of the finished spray will treat about 100 square feet of surface. All surfaces subject to attack should be covered thoroughly--until drops begin to form and run off.

- 16 -

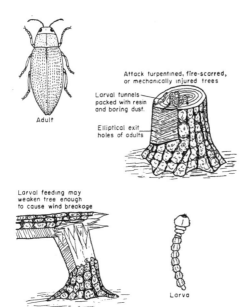

Adult

Attack turpentined, fire-scarred,
or mechanically injured trees

Larval tunnels
packed with resin
and boring dust.

Elliptical exit
holes of adults

Larval feeding may
weaken tree enough
to cause wind breakage

Larva

Figure 5.--Turpentine borer.

AMBROSIA BEETLES

Platypus spp.

Importance. --Ambrosia beetles of the Platypus group attack weakened, dying, or freshly cut pines and unseasoned pine lumber. They degrade the wood by boring small holes and introducing a black stain.

Habits. --The adults are reddish-brown, elongated beetles, approximately 1/4 inch in length . The beetles bore into the sapwood and heartwood of logs or lumber, making pin-size holes that usually are darkly stained by an ambrosia fungus upon which the adults and larvae feed. The female lays eggs in small clusters in the tunnel, and the developing larvae excavate small cells extending from the tunnel parallel with the grain of the wood. There are several generations each year.

Signs of attack. --Small piles of yellowish-white fluffy boring dust accumulate around the base or in bark crevices of infested trees, stumps, and logs. In lumber the characteristic pin-size holes surrounded by black stain may be observed extending into the wood.

Control. --Prompt utilization of dead and dying trees and rapid seasoning of lumber will reduce or eliminate losses. Where these courses are impractical, green logs may be protected for several months by spraying with BHC in No. 2 fuel oil, mixed in the same proportion as recommended for the turpentine borer.

Green lumber may be protected by dipping it in a water emulsion prepared by mixing two quarts of BHC emulsifiable concentrate (containing one pound of the gamma isomer per gallon) with 50 gallons of water.

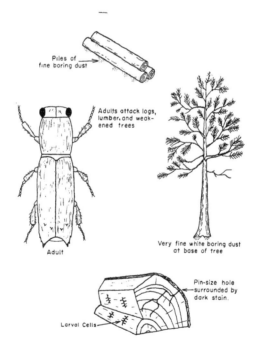

Piles of fine boring dust

Adults attack logs, lumber, and weakened trees

Very fine white boring dust at base of tree

Adult

Pin-size hole surrounded by dark stain.

Larval Cells

Figure 6.--Ambrosia beetle.

NANTUCKET PINE TIP MOTH

Rhyacionia frustrana

Importance.--The larvae of the tip moth kill buds and twigs of young planted and natural loblolly and shortleaf pines. Vigorous seedlings may grow fast enough to overcome the effects of the insect, but severe and repeated setbacks may result in stunted, deformed trees of little value, especially on poor sites.

Habits.--The adults are about 1/4-inch long, copper-colored with silvery markings on their wings. They are active from February until late fall, but are not often seen unless disturbed. Eggs are laid on the needles and twigs. The larvae are yellowish to pale brown, worm-like, and up to 1/3-inch long. They feed within the buds and twigs and later change into brown, capsule-like pupae about 1/4-inch long.

Signs of attack.--Terminals and branches of infested pines have many brown, dead, hollow buds and stunted twigs. A crust of hard, whitish resin can be seen between the buds, needles, and twigs; and the insides of dead buds and twigs contain granular, brown, manure particles.

Control.--The insect is so widespread that few young stands are free of it. Control is difficult at all times, treated areas often becoming re-infested. Severely infested plantations can often be pulled through by thoroughly spraying the foliage with DDT when the moths appear in February or March. Since moths are difficult to find on the trees, it is suggested that infested branch tips be caged outdoors during the late winter, and moth emergence   used as a guide to proper timing. The spray is prepared by stirring 1 gallon of 25 percent DDT emulsifiable concentrate or 4 pounds of 50 percent DDT wettable powder in 50 gallons of water. Spraying in early spring will destroy most of the existing population and permit the trees to make a spurt of growth that will lessen damage from attacks later in the season. A second spraying at the next flight period of the moths, usually in early June, is often advisable. Treatment for 3 or 4 successive years may be needed.

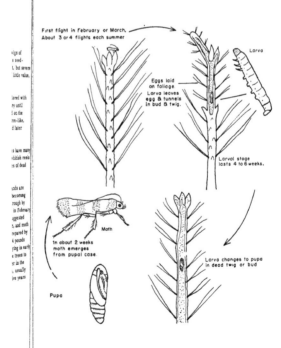

First flight in February or March.
About 3 or 4 flights each summer

Larva

Eggs laid
on foliage.
Larva leaves
egg & tunnels
in bud & twig.

Larval stage
lasts 4 to 6 weeks.

Moth

In about 2 weeks
moth emerges
from pupal case.

Pupa

Larva changes to pupa
in dead twig or bud

Figure 7.--Nantucket pine tip moth.

WEEVILS

Hylobius pales
Pachylobius picivorus

Importance. --Adult weevils girdle pine seedlings planted or growing naturally in areas where older pines have recently been cut or killed
by fire, bark beetles, or other causes. The pales weevil is a pest in most
of the eastern U.S., but is becoming more apparent and increasingly important in the South as a result of more widespread clear-cutting and
planting practices. A related species, Pachylobius picivorus, closely re-
sembles the pales weevil and is apparently of equal importance in the South.

Habits. --The weevils are attracted to freshly cut pine stumps and
scorched pine trees in the spring and fall and chew the tender bark of seedlings in the vicinity. They lay eggs in the root bark of stumps and scorched
trees and infrequently beneath the bark of logs and slash. The larvae
develop under the bark, and when the new adults emerge they feed on
nearby seedlings.

The adults are brown to black, 1/4- to 1/3-inch long, with a prominent snout. The grubs are creamy white and about 1/4- to 1/3-inch long.
They make oval chip cocoons of finely shredded wood beneath the bark.

Signs of attack. --The weevils may eat patches of bark, or they may
girdle the stem completely by removing most of the bark. Attacked seedlings wither and die. Heaviest feeding is in the spring and early summer
and sometimes in the fall.

Control. --Weevil damage is most likely to be severe when planting
follows immediately after fall or winter cutting or severe burning. Areas
cut during the spring and early summer can be planted the following winter
without much danger of serious loss.

Preliminary tests indicate that where weevil populations are heavy,
damage can be greatly reduced by dipping the tops of planting stock in a
2-percent emulsion of aldrin, dieldrin, or heptachlor.

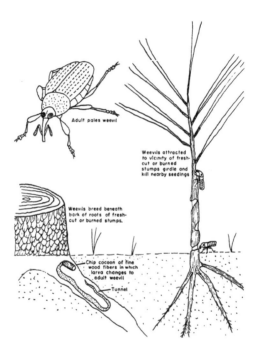

Adult pales weevil

Weevils attracted
to vicinity of fresh-
cut or burned
stumps girdle and
kill nearby seedings

Weevils breed beneath
bark of roots of fresh-
cut or burned stumps.

Chip cocoon of fine
wood fibers in which
larva changes to
adult weevil

Tunnel

Figure 8.--Pales weevil.

WHITE GRUBS

Phyllophaga species

Importance. --White grubs, the larvae of the common May or June beetle, are among the worst insect pests of pine nurseries. They also damage young pine plantations and natural regeneration in old fields or sod-land. It seems likely that grubs cause some of the mortality laid to drouth or vegetative competition.

Habits. --Beetles appear in spring and early summer and most species feed on hardwood foliage. Females lay their eggs in the soil, and the larvae feed on roots of pine seedlings, grasses, and other plants. Grubs reach an inch or more in length. The life cycle varies from 1 to 3 years, depending on the species.

Signs of attack. --Attacked seedlings wither and turn yellow or brown. Since the grubs destroy most of the roots, the dying trees can easily be pulled from the soil. The grubs can usually be found beneath the soil surface near dying or recently killed seedlings. Large numbers of beetles attracted to lights in the spring may indicate trouble later the same year or the year following.

Control. --Infested nursery beds should be treated, before sowing, with the equivalent of 10 pounds of actual chlordane per acre. Dusts, wettable powders, and emulsifiables have all been used with good results. To insure that the insecticide will penetrate the soil, it should be applied just before a rain or wet down promptly with the nursery sprinklers and worked into the soil.

Before seedlings are planted, especially in grasslands, the soil should be sampled for grubs. In grub-infested areas, planting should be avoided. Valuable planted seedlings may be protected by treating the infested soil with chlordane.

Preliminary tests are being made in the use of aldrin, heptachlor, and other chemicals as protective root dips for seedlings.

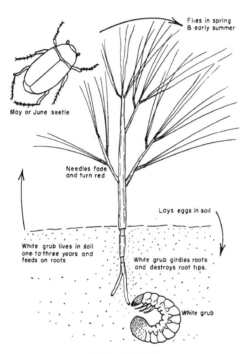

Flies in spring
& early summer

May or June beetle

Needles fade
and turn red

Lays eggs in soil

White grub lives in soil
one to three years and
feeds on roots

White grub girdles roots
and destroys root tips.

White grub

Figure 9.--White grubs.

PINE SAWFLIES

Neodiprion species

Importance. --At least three species of sawflies attack southern pines: the redheaded pine sawfly (Neodiprion lecontei), the loblolly pine sawfly (N. taedae linearis), and a little-known black-headed species, N. exitans. All have caterpillar-like larvae that chew the needles of pines of all sizes. Severe infestations will stunt or malform young trees and sometimes kill them. Larger trees suffer severe growth loss.

Habits. --The habits of all three species are similar. The adult female cuts slits in pine needles and deposits an egg in each slit. The larvae usually feed in clusters. When full grown they are almost an inch long and hairless; their color differs with the species. When they are fully developed, they make shiny-brown, oval cocoons about 1/3-inch long. The cocoons are usually in the soil or on it, less frequently in bark crevices or in the foliage. There may be one to several generations each year, depending upon the species.

Signs of attack. --The larvae themselves, their cocoons or excrement pellets under the tree, or the chewed needles and needle stubs are obvious signs of attack.

Control. --If defoliation is severe enough to warrant, infestations can be controlled by spraying with DDT, preferably when the larvae are young and more easily killed.

For aerial applications or truck-mounted mist blowers, dissolve 1 pound of technical DDT in a suitable solvent and dilute with fuel oil to make 1 gallon of insecticide: apply at the rate of 1 gallon per acre.

For garden or knapsack sprayers, mix 50-percent DDT wettable powder in water at the rate of 1 pound of powder to 50 gallons of water, and thoroughly spray all infested foliage. The mixture must be constantly agitated to prevent the DDT from settling out.

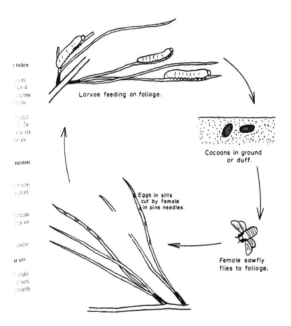

Larvae feeding on foliage.

Cocoons in ground
or duff.

Eggs in slits
cut by female
in pine needles.

Female sawfly
flies to foliage.

Figure 10.--Pine sawflies.

PINE WEBWORM

Tetralopha robustella

Importance. --Infestations of pine webworms are usually light and scattered, but sometimes young pines in nurseries and plantations are defoliated and killed.

Habits. --The full-size larva is a caterpillar approximately 4/5-inch long. The head is tan with darker markings, and the body light brown with dark longitudinal stripes running down each side. The adult is a moth with a wingspread of approximately one inch. The forewing usually is grey in the middle portion and darker at the base and tip.

Eggs are laid on seedlings or small trees between May and September. The caterpillars live in silken webs surrounded by masses of excrement pellets. They feed on the needles. Normally each web contains one or two larvae, but occasionally twenty-five or more may be found. After it completes feeding, the caterpillar drops to the ground and makes an oval pupal cell slightly below the soil surface. Generally, two generations are produced each year in the South.

Signs of attack. --Defoliation and masses of silk webbing surrounding pellets of excrement are the most common signs of attack. Occasionally dead defoliated seedlings may be present.

Control. --When populations are high or when valuable nursery stock becomes infested, chemical control may be necessary. Mix 50 percent DDT wettable powder in water at the rate of 1 pound of powder to 25 gallons of water, and thoroughly spray all infested foliage. The mixture must be constantly agitated to prevent the DDT from settling out. The finished spray costs approximately 2 cents per gallon. Fifty percent DDT wettable powder can be purchased in 4-pound and 50-pound containers.

As DDT may aggravate mite troubles it is well to include a miticide or to watch seedlings and be ready to spray if mites become a problem.

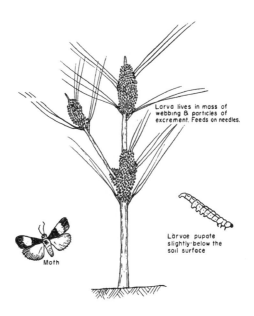

Larva lives in mass of webbing & particles of excrement. Feeds on needles.

Larvae pupate slightly·below the soil surface

Moth

Figure 11. -Pine webworm.

TEXAS LEAF-CUTTING ANT

Atta texana

Importance.--The Texas leaf-cutting ant, or town ant, is one of the worst enemies of pine seedlings in east Texas and west-central Louisiana. Where ant towns are numerous, they must be eradicated before pines can be established. The ants strip the needles and leaves from a variety of plants, including pine and hardwood trees and many field crops. Large trees may be defoliated within several days, and small plants within a few hours. Pines are damaged most severely during the winter when other green plants are scarce. Trees of sapling size or larger usually survive, but seedling stands are often wiped out.

Habits.--The ants cut the leaves or needles into fragments and carry them below ground to make the "soil" for growing a fungus that is the only known food of these insects.

Texas leaf-cutting ants can defoliate pine seedlings very rapidly. The ants carry the needles over their heads.

During their foraging, the ants clear trails that resemble miniature highways. They file along these trails, carrying leaf or needle fragments like tiny parasols. Defoliation by these ants appears very much like the work of several other leaf-chewing insects, particularly sawflies. Usually the injured trees are within sight of one of the colonies, or the ants themselves may be seen cutting the needles. Bits of the needles are left about the base of the trees and along the trails, which often extend several hundred feet out from the colony. During late fall and winter the fresh mounds of subsoil in the towns are very conspicuous.

The nest is made up of a large number of circular or semi-circular mounds, each with a funnel-like opening. A colony, or town, may cover from several square feet to a quarter of an acre or more, depending upon its age.

Typical mounds of the Texas leaf-cutting ant.

In May and June, winged ants swarm and mate, and the females (queens) establish new nests. Upon leaving her home colony each female carries in her mouth a small amount of fungus, which she cultures and subsequently uses to feed her young.

Side view of a Texas leaf-cutting worker

The activities of the ants are influenced by the temperature. They forage during mild days in winter, and mostly at night in the summertime. The workers are inactive on cold, wet, or cloudy days, particularly in the morning hours.

The distribution of the ants is apparently limited by soil type. Most colonies are on sandy soil. A deep sandy surface soil underlain by a layer of clay seems to be preferred. On sloping ground, most colonies occur on southern and western exposures.

Control. --When signs of the ants are found on areas to be planted or seeded to pine, a systematic effort must be made to locate all nearby colonies. Scouting is easiest during the fall and early winter, when the mounds are not hidden by vegetation. As they are located, colonies should be marked with a stake or other device to guide the control crews to them.

Fumigation with methyl bromide is the most effective control devised so far. At warm temperatures and atmospheric pressure, methyl bromide is a colorless gas, poisonous to humans as well as to ants but neither combustible nor explosive. Being about 3-1/2 times heavier than air, it penetrates into the underground chambers of the colony. It may be obtained liquified under pressure in one-pound cans.

The best time to apply the gas is in late fall or early winter, on cool, wet, or cloudy mornings, when the ants tend to remain underground. In general, applications during warm months have been unsatisfactory, probably because the colonies are less centralized and there is more chance of the gas failing to reach all the chambers and galleries.

The methyl bromide is applied with a special device consisting of a valve and a piece of flexible tubing attached to the can:

1. Insert about two feet of the tubing into one of the central openings to the colony. The mound may have to be cleared away to facilitate access to the hole.

2. Lightly tamp some soil around the tube and press on the packed soil with one foot, taking care not to pinch the tube. This will prevent the tube from whipping out of the hole when the valve is opened and the pressure in the can is released.

3. Hold the inverted can with one hand, open the valve with the other, and allow the gas to escape into the colony. The can may either be discharged entirely into one hole or divided among two to four holes of the same colony.

A one-pound can of gas usually is enough to kill the ants in a colony of average size--that is, one occupying about 600 square feet of surface soil. Larger colonies, or average colonies on loose, porous soils, may require two pounds of gas. If the colony is on a hillside, the gas should be applied to one of the uppermost openings rather than to a central hole.

Colonies should be checked two to four weeks after treatment. Any sign of ant life indicates that another fumigation is necessary.

PINE COLASPIS BEETLE

Colaspis pini

Importance. -- Feeding by the pine colaspis beetle produces a spectacular browning of the needles similar to that caused by fire. The beetle is not known to kill pines and apparently has slight effect on their growth. Infestations occur sporadically throughout the South.

Habits. -- The beetles are oval-shaped, one-fourth inch long, with brown stripes and minute greenish jewel-like specks over the body. From May to early July they feed on the one-year-old needles of young pines and occasionally on needles of larger trees. At times several hundred acres of natural and planted saplings may be attacked, but infestations usually are spotty, with the affected trees occurring singly or in groups throughout the area. One generation is produced each year.

Signs of attack. -- The earliest evidence of attack is the presence of small drops of resin on the needles. At night the resin drops are highly reflective and appear to be luminescent when a light is flashed on them. The foliage later becomes discolored, and an examination will reveal irregular saw-like edges along the needles, particularly those in the upper half of the crown. By late summer new growth again makes the trees look normal.

Control. -- Colaspis beetles may reach alarming populations in an area one year and then appear elsewhere the next. Chemical control usually is not justified in the forests, but ornamental trees can readily be protected with a DDT spray. The spray should be applied when the first symptoms of beetle activity appear in late May or early June.

To prepare the spray, stir one pound of 50 percent DDT wettable powder into 50 gallons of water, and keep the mixture well agitated while it is being applied. The finished spray costs approximately those 1 cent per gallon. Fifty percent DDT wettable powder can be purchased in 4-pound and 50-pound containers. A 10 percent DDT dust may be used instead of the spray.

DDT may aggravate mite troubles. It is advisable to include a miticide or to watch foliage and be ready to spray if mites become a problem.

OTHER PINE INSECTS

Pine needle miner (Exoteleia sp.). --The larvae burrow into the needles of longleaf and other pines, leaving the outer part of the needles dead and semi-transparent. When infested trees are observed from a distance, the foliage looks brown or yellow. The larvae are light brown with black heads and are approximately 3/16-inch long. The adult is a brownish-yellow moth with silvery scales. Damage to pines is presently considered of minor importance, although some growth loss may be expected.

Pine pitch midge (Retinodiplosis sp.). --The midge is a delicate fly usually less than 1/4-inch in length. The orange, legless larvae occur singly or in groups in small globs of resin exuding from swellings on branches or twigs of pines. In some years they are common and some twigs may be killed. They probably cause little damage, however.

Scale insects (Coccidae). --Scales are soft, waxy insects that suck sap from plant tissues. The adult females hardly resemble insects, as they are scale-like and do not move. The newly hatched young are micro-scopic and are known as crawlers. They move about over the needles and twigs.

The pine needle scale (Phenacaspis) is a white, elongate scale about 1/8-inch in length. It occurs on the needles. The pine bark scale (Toumeyella) is a brown species about the size of a pea, and usually occur in crowded masses on the twigs and branches.

Heavily infested pines become pale-green or yellow and covered with a sticky "honeydew" excreted by the insects. A black, sooty mold often grows over the honeydew and increases the unsightliness of the foliage. Occasionally small plantation trees are killed.

Control is generally not recommended under forest conditions. On ornamental pines, scales may be destroyed by spraying with malathion, following directions of the manufacturer. The spray is most effective when the insects are in the crawler stage.

Aphids (Aphidae). --Aphids or plant lice are light green or brown soft-bodied insects, varying in size from 1/16- to 1/4-inch. Both winged and wingless forms occur. The aphids suck sap from the needles, bark, and sometimes the roots. Usually infestations attract attention because of the dropping of sticky honeydew as the aphids feed. Very little is known of the overall effects on forest trees by large and frequent aphid

- 34 -

populations. Undoubtedly they cause growth loss and some malformation of infested parts.

Chemical control is generally unnecessary or impractical under forest conditions. Where shade trees and ornamental pines are heavily infested, a spray of 25 percent malathion emulsifiable concentrate diluted at the rate of one pint per 100 gallons of water will be satisfactory.

Spider mites (Tetranychidae). --Mites are not insects but animals related to ticks and spiders. There are many species.

Mites are among the most persistent of plant-feeding pests; they cause foliage to fade and later turn brown. Damage is most severe during hot, dry weather. When infestations are heavy, mites can be found all over the needles and twigs, running over the fine webbing they spin. Though they are very small, their presence may be easily determined by jarring them off the foliage onto a sheet of white paper. If living mites are absent, their cast skins, egg shells, and webbing usually can be found on infested plants.

Infested pines growing under forest conditions may appear rusty brown, but usually recover following soaking rains. Mites may be removed from ornamental trees or shrubs by thoroughly and repeatedly washing the plants with a strong stream of water. Several of the newer chemicals used in mite control are malathion, aramite, kelthane, and DN-111.

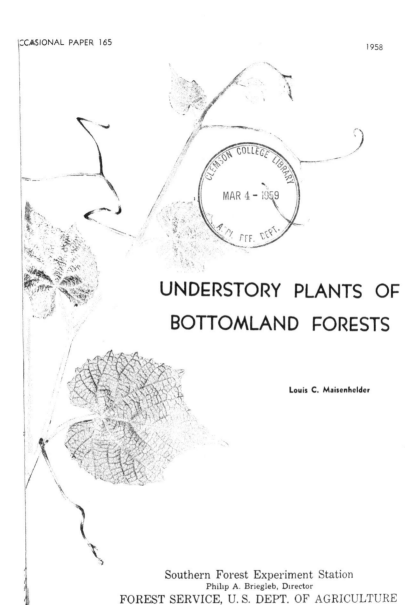

UNDERSTORY PLANTS OF
BOTTOMLAND FORESTS

Louis C. Maisenhelder

Southern Forest Experiment Station
Philip A. Briegleb, Director
FOREST SERVICE, U. S. DEPT. OF AGRICULTURE

CONTENTS

UNDERSTORY PLANTS OF BOTTOMLAND FORESTS

Louis C. Maisenhelder[1]
Southern Forest Experiment Station

The purpose of this manual is to provide foresters and land-owners with a quick and simple means of identifying some of the more conspicuous minor plants in the a l l u v i a l bottoms of major southern rivers. It is written particularly for the Delta of the Mississippi River, but applies at least in part to the bottoms of the larger streams along the Gulf and Atlantic Coasts from the Carolinas to Texas, as well as to some areas outside the bottomlands.

The species described are those considered by the author to be important in forest management or otherwise conspicuous enough to draw attention. Opinions as to what species should have been included will naturally differ, and it is probable that future revisions will add to the coverage.

Grasses are d e s c r i b e d first, then forbs, and finally woody plants--vines, shrubs, and small trees. With most species, identifi-cation should be possible from the pictures alone, but short written de-scriptions have also been provided. The range over the eastern United States is given to aid users outside the Delta bottomlands. Within the Delta, the description of the sites on which the species most commonly occur will be helpful in identification.

A glossary defines such botanical terms as seemed necessary to use. Latin and common names for woody plants follow Little's Check List of Native and Naturalized Trees of the United States. Those for all other plants are from Fernald's eighth edition of Gray's Manual of Botany. These and additional publications that were consulted are listed on page 40, but are not otherwise cited.

The author wishes to thank several individuals who assisted with this publication. Dr. W. L. Giles, Superintendent of the Delta Branch of the Mississippi Agricultural Experiment Station, made local identi-fications of many of the plants, and suggested improvements in the text. Miss Jane W. Roller, U. S. Forest Service, identified all the plants. Dr. J. R. Swallen, U. S. National Museum, and Dr. E. L. Little, Jr., U. S. Forest Service, verified the grasses and woody material, respectively. Dr. S. F. Blake, U. S. Agricultural Research Service, checked the c o m p o s i t e s, and Dr. F. A. McClure, U. S. National Museum, checked the Arundinaria.

---

[1] Stationed at the Delta Research Center, Stoneville, Mississippi. This Center is maintained by the Southern Forest Experiment Station in cooperation with the Missis-sippi Agricultural Experiment Station and the Southern Hardwood Forest Research Group.

GIANT CANE

Family Gramineae
Arundinaria gigantea

Leaf

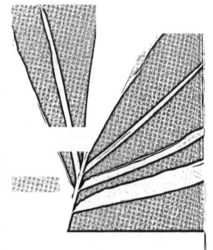

Description.--The outstanding characteristics of giant cane are the bamboo-like stems (often used as fishing poles) and the presence of green leaves and twigs the year around on branches of the main stem.

This grass of the bamboo tribe grows in small groups, thickets, or extensive canebrakes. It sprouts from heavily grazed crowns or underground stems. Above-ground stems grow 4 to 30 feet tall. The stems are canes up to 3/4 inch in diameter, with distinct joints 3 to 5 inches or more apart. The parallel-veined leaves occur in fan-shaped clusters of 3 or more at the end of small branches. They are 4 to 11 inches long and 1/2 to 1-1/2 inches wide, tapering to a sharp point. Flowers appear at infrequent intervals on individual plants, the leafless flower stalk arising from the underground stems. The flowering period usually continues for about a year. Flowering stems apparently die after seeding. A smaller and similar species, *Arundinaria tecta,* called switch-cane, growing only 2 to 13 feet tall, may also be encountered.

Growth habit

Site preference and range. --Giant cane grows on the lighter soils such as sandy and silt loams. It prefers a moist but well-drained site, and is found on river banks and the borders of sloughs and swamps. It ranges from Florida west to Texas, and north to Maryland and the southern parts of Ohio, Indiana, Illinois, and Missouri.

Importance in forest management. -- In the understory of established forest stands it does little damage and is good forage for livestock and wildlife. In openings, dense canebrakes may prevent tree reproduction, but in light concentrations the cane frequently acts as a nurse crop. Heavy grazing, repeated burning, or cultivation will control the cane but cannot be used if the desired forest tree reproduction is already present.

- 2 -

Leaf

JOHNSON-GRASS

Family Gramineae
Sorgum halepense

Description. -- Johnson-grass is among the tallest of the bottomland grasses.

This perennial reaches a height of 9 to 10 feet. It spreads by underground stems that send up shoots, so that it grows in clumps. The light green leaves are 15 to 20 inches long and 4/10 to 8/10 of an inch broad. The flower stalk is 15 to 20 inches long. The flowers are borne in small spikes which, in west-central Mississippi, appear from July through September.

Site preference and range. -- Johnson-grass grows on any soils except coarse sands and is prevalent in alluvial bottomlands. It is found on practically all sites except those inundated for part of the growing season. It ranges from Florida through Texas to California, north to southern New England, New York, West Virginia, Ohio, Indiana, Illinois, and Iowa.

Importance in forest management. -- In plantations or on areas to be restocked naturally it is one of the worst weeds encountered, for it begins growth early in the spring and quickly overtops planted seedlings or cuttings and reproduction starting from seed. In an established stand the shade of the tree crowns usually prevents its development. Its value as forage should be recognized where grazing is permitted in mature or near-mature timber stands.

The persistence of the underground stems makes control difficult. Repeated disking or mowing, where possible, can eradicate it in several seasons. The cost of preparing planting sites can often be reduced by growing row crops for several years before planting the trees. The repeated cultivation helps to eradicate the grass. Another possibility is to fallow the land for a year and then plow it several times after midsummer so as to expose the underground roots to the sun.

COCKLEBUR

Family Compositae
Xanthium pensylvanicum

Leaves

Fruit

Description.--The most noticeable feature of cocklebur is its small prickly burs which, in the autumn, adhere to the clothing of persons and coats of animals coming in contact with the plant.

It is a coarse weedy annual with branching stems. Height ranges from 1 to 6 feet. The leaves are roughly heart-shaped and have three lobes. They are 4 to 6 inches long, 2 to 4 inches wide, and are arranged alternately on the stem. The flowers are borne in the leaf axils and are not showy. In west-central Mississippi they appear in midsummer. The fruit is a rough bur, ovoid in shape and covered with prickles having hooked tips. It is 1/2 to 3/4 of an inch long and slightly less than 1/2-inch in diameter.

Site preference and range.-- Cocklebur is most frequently found on rich, moist soils of almost any kind except the coarser sands. Along the Mississippi River levees it is one of the most common plants in the borrow pits. Elsewhere it grows on low areas of waste or cultivated land and roadsides. It ranges from the West Indies to Florida and Mexico, and north to southern Canada, Michigan, Wisconsin, Minnesota, and Nebraska.

Importance in forest management.-- Cocklebur does no harm in established stands but interferes with tree seedlings on open areas. Thick stands on the river fronts often prevent cottonwood and willow seed from reaching mineral soil and shade out seedlings that do start.

Control in forest plantations is probably best obtained by disking between rows until the trees outgrow the cocklebur plants. Fire can be used to destroy the plants and seed on areas in need of restocking, but the weed is most prevalent where flooding is frequent, and a new supply of seed may be brought in before trees become established.

- 4 -

Seeds

Growth habit

stem, are lanceolate to linear in shape and light green in color. They are from 4 to 8 inches long and 1 to 2 inches wide. The leaf adjacent to the flower is heart-shaped and folded together to form an enclosure for the blossom. The **flowers**, which are blue and about 1/2-inch across, bloom all summer. The **fruit** is a small capsule containing three to several seeds that ripen throughout the summer.

Site preference and range.--Dayflower is found most often on heavy clay soils in damp, fertile woods and along watercourses. On the floodplains of the Mississippi River and its tributaries the presence of this plant is a fair indication that the site is under standing water at some time during the year. It occurs from New York south to Florida and west to Michigan, Kansas, and Texas.

Importance in forest management.-- This plant is troublesome chiefly on areas in need of restocking. The thick mass of underground stems interferes with the root development of tree seedlings, and the dense, low shade of the plants prevents germination of tree seeds or smothers the seedlings. The very wet sites complicate the problem of control; at present no recommendations can be made.

- 5 -

YELLOW DOCK

Family Polygonaceae
Rumex crispus

Young plant

Description.--Yellow dock is one of the commonest weeds in the bottomlands. It is a perennial that grows from 3 to 5 feet tall and has a deep taproot. The stems arise from the taproot and from last year's basal rosette of leaves. The alternate, simple leaves are dark green with wavy-curled margins. They vary from 3 to 12 inches long but are only 1/2 to 2 inches wide. The light green **flowers** appear during late spring in west-central Mississippi. They are borne on a single stalk, where they are interspersed with leaves except toward the tip. The fruit is a valve 1/10 to 1/5 inch in diameter bearing a single achene; it is brown when mature. Other species of dock may be encountered but all are similar in form and growth habit.

Site preference and range.--Because of its deep root system, dock readily adapts itself to a variety of soils and sites. It is most common on the heavier clays and moist to wet sites on cultivated land, abandoned fields, and open places in the woods. It ranges throughout central and eastern United States.

Importance in forest management.-- The shade produced by clumps of these plants prevents the germination of seed and the development of very young seedlings. Once the trees are 5 or 6 feet tall, they soon shade out the dock.

This weed sprouts vigorously from the root. Repeated disking will keep it down in plantations. Eradication by digging is sometimes practiced in agricultural lands but is hardly economical in silvicultural practice. Fairly good results have been obtained by applying 2,4-D spray or dust to the stem at ground level and to the newly forming leaves.

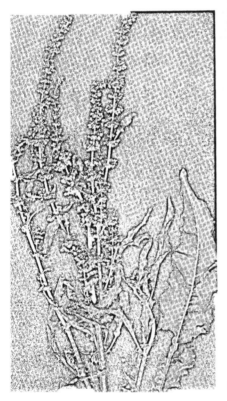

Fruiting branch

Description.--Goldenrod is most conspicuous for its yellow flowers.

There are many species, all similar in appearance to the one pictured here. This coarse-textured perennial is 2 to 6 feet tall. The stems are grayish and covered with numerous short hairs. The leaves, 2 to 5 inches long and 4/10 to 8/10 inch wide, are medium-green on top and lighter, almost gray, on the underside. They are sessile, and are crowded along the stem. Bright yellow flowers, appearing between August and November in west-central Mississippi, are borne in irregular compound heads. The fruit is an inconspicuous achene.

Site preference and range.--Goldenrod occurs on a wide variety of soils and on both dry and moist sites. It develops best in woods clearings, abandoned fields, and on roadsides, seldom being found in shady places. Its range is from Florida to Texas, and north to Canada.

Importance in forest management.-- Goldenrod interferes with tree reproduction, but is not important after trees reach heights of six feet or more. Becoming established in mid-summer, it develops in thickets and often outgrows and shades out tree seedlings.

Disking controls it in young plantations but no method is known for areas of natural regeneration. Chemical control has not been satisfactory, for the chemicals must be applied late in the season, when they also damage or kill the trees.

Stem with fruit and flowers

STINGING NETTLE

Family Euphorbiaceae
Tragia urticifolia

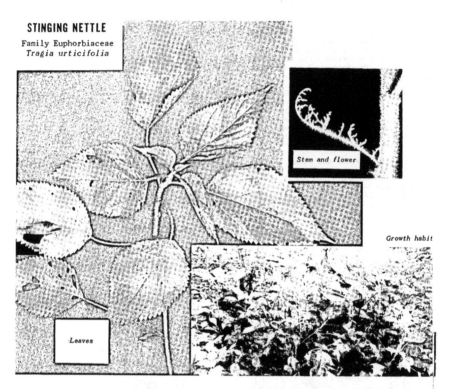

Stem and flower

Growth habit

Leaves

Description.--Stinging nettle, locally called bull nettle, is known for the stiff, stinging hairs that cover the stem and leaves.

This perennial herb grows in clumps and attains a height of 2 to 4 feet. The dark green leaves are ovate-lanceolate, coarsely cut-toothed, and 5 to 6 inches long by 2 to 3 inches wide. Small, inconspicuous, greenish-white flowers are borne on stalks 2 to 3 inches long. In west-central Mississippi they appear from June to September. The fruit is a capsule 2/10 to 4/10 inch wide.

Site preference and range.-- Stinging nettle grows on the lighter textured sandy soils. It prefers well-drained to dry sites like the ridges, drainage course banks, and high flats in the Mississippi River bottomlands. Its range is from Florida to Arizona, north to Virginia, Missouri, Kansas, and Colorado.

Importance in forest management.-- Except for the discomfort experienced by persons who touch its stinging hairs, nettle does little harm in established stands. When growing in dense clumps on areas in need of re-stocking, it may prevent tree species from becoming established.

No specific controls have been tried, but repeated cultivation, until the trees outgrow the competition, should prove effective.

*Flowering branch
with fruit*

Description.--Its clusters of dark purple berries are poke's most noticeable feature.

This stout perennial herb, often called pokeweed, grows 6 to 10 feet tall. At maturity the rind of the stem is a rich purple. It has a rather unpleasant odor and a very large poisonous root often 4 to 6 inches in diameter. The young leafy sprouts are used as greens. The leaves are alternate, lanceolate, and entire, and are 3 to 5 inches long by 1 to 2 inches wide. The white or pinkish flowers, on elongated stalks opposite the leaves, appear from July to September in west-central Mississippi. The fruit is a berry 3/10 to 4/10 of an inch in diameter, containing 5 to 12 seeds.

Site preference and range.--Poke will grow in all kinds of soil if light is abundant. It prefers low moist sites and often develops after overflow waters have receded. Its range is from Florida to Texas, and north to Canada.

Importance in forest management.-- On areas in need of regeneration poke often forms dense stands that produce heavy low shade and considerable root competition for desirable tree reproduction. Trees an inch or more in d.b.h. or 4 to 6 feet tall are rarely affected. Repeated cultivation, until the trees outgrow the weed, is the most effective control.

- 9 -

Description.--This herbaceous perennial has leaves resembling in miniature those of the mimosa tree.

Height varies from 1 to 8 feet. The very delicate leaves, 2 to 3 inches long, are twice pinnate with 6 to 15 pairs of pinnae and 20 to 30 pairs of leaflets on each pinna. Small, greenish-white, inconspicuous flowers appear from June through August. The fruit is a legume 1/2 to 1 inch long and 1/8 to 3/16 of an inch wide. The numerous pods, each containing 2 to 6 seeds, are borne in dense globose heads.

Site preference and range.--Prairie-mimosa prefers moist but not extremely wet sites on alluvial soils of almost any type except the coarser sands. It grows principally in openings where there is an abundance of light. It is associated with a wide variety of herbaceous plants and vines. It ranges from Alabama to Texas, north to North Dakota, and east through Minnesota, Illinois, and Ohio.

Importance in forest management.--Although prairie-mimosa is not usually troublesome by itself, the complex with which it is often associated produces a low shade that interferes with natural reproduction. When vines are present, they climb over the other plants, forming a mat that often deforms young trees.

Control by disking is probably the most practical method.

Growth habit

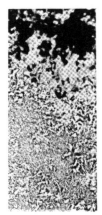

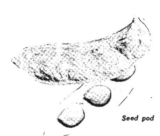

Seed pod

- 10 -

COMMON RAGWEED

Family Compositae
Ambrosia artemisiifolia

Flowering stem

Description. - -Ragweed is probably best known for its pollen, which is an important cause of hay-fever.

It is a very common late-summer annual which attains heights of 2/3 to 8 feet. It is much branched, with dull green leaves mostly alternate and pinnately lobed. The greenish flowers, which appear in late summer in west-central Mississippi, are inconspicuous and borne in the leaf axils. When mature, the seed-bearing stems are about 2 to 3 inches long. The fruit is an ovoid achene about 1/10 to 2/10 of an inch long. Several species in the genus are markedly similar.

Site preference and range. - -Ragweed seems to have no particular soil preference but is not usually found on the wetter sites. It requires considerable light and seeds in on abandoned fields and open areas in the woods, and along logging roads. Considering all species, its range includes the entire eastern United States.

Importance in forest management. -- Ragweed does little harm in fully stocked forests. Sparse stands may act as a nurse-crop for tree seedlings. When it grows densely, however, it shades out reproduction; it has caused considerable mortality in first-year cottonwood plantations established from cuttings.

Cultivation can control the weed, but may have to be repeated several times, for the seed is transported by water and reinfestation can easily occur. Eradication in stands of natural reproduction is not practical.

SUMPWEED

Family Compositae
Iva ciliata

Description.--This plant is a coarse, rough, hairy annual 1 to 6 feet tall. The leaves are thick, ovate, pointed, coarsely toothed, and downy on the underside. They vary from 1-1/2 to 4 inches long and 1/2 to 1-1/4 inches in width. The greenish-white flowers, which appear from July to October in west-central Mississippi, are crowded on spikes 1-1/2 to 1-3/4 inches long in the leaf axils. The fruit is a small achene.

Site preference and range.--Sumpweed grows on all but the sandiest soils. It prefers moist sites. In the Mississippi River bottomlands it is very abundant on the alluvial soils in borrow pits and other open places along the levees and in the woods. Its range is from Indiana to Nebraska, south to Louisiana, Texas, and New Mexico.

Importance in forest management.-- On open areas thick stands of sumpweed may shade out young reproduction and the almost solid cover of leaves prevents much of the seed of light-seeded species, such as cottonwood or willow, from reaching the ground. Once the trees have asserted dominance no further damage is done.

Cultivation will keep sumpweed out of plantations, but controls for use in stands of natural regeneration are unknown.

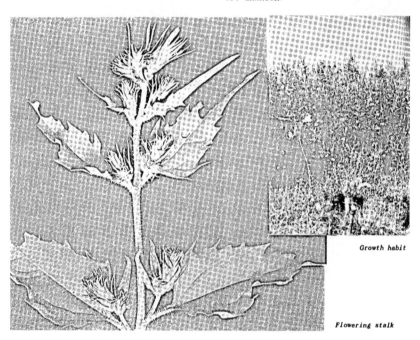

Growth habit

Flowering stalk

BLACKBERRY

Family Rosaceae
Rubus sp.

Stem and leaves

Description.--The blackberries are ll known for the strong prickles on eir canes, and for their fruit.

The genus çontains a large number species that are difficult to disnguish, but since positive identication is rarely necessary in forest nagement, separation into two sily recognized groups is adequate. ese groups are (1) blackberries, ants with erect stems; and (2) dewrries, plants with stems that trail the ground.Blackberries have erect, out, ridged **canes** 4 to 8 feet tall. ey are perennial, and new canes are oduced each year by the rootstocks. e canes, leaf petioles, and in some ecies the mid-rib of the leaves are med with sharp prickles. The comund **leaves** are alternate and 3 to 5 ches long and wide, the leaflets ually having finely serrate margins. ey are prominently veined,dark green ove and lighter green to grayish beath.The **flowers** are white and numers, appearing from May through June west-central Mississippi. The **fruit** a collection of black drupelets rying in size with the species.

Site preference and range.--Blackberries are found on all but the wettest sites. They prefer moist but well-drained situations with an abundance of light, and are common in old fields and openings in the woods. They are one of the first plants to become established on burned-over areas. Considering all species, blackberries are found throughout the eastern United States.

Importance in forest management.--Although blackberry briars frequently form dense thickets they are probably less of a hindrance to tree reproduction than most other weeds. Their shade, while insufficient to inhibit the growth of tree seedlings, reduces soil temperatures and helps to conserve moisture. When other vines climb into and over the briars, however, competition with tree seedlings may become a problem. In plantations, briars can be controlled by disking. Before they are destroyed, "briar patches" should always be checked to be certain they do not contain advanced tree reproduction.

DEWBERRY

Family Rosaceae
Rubus sp.

Leaves

Description.--In contrast to blackberries, dewberries have trailing or low-arching vines.

Their slender, tough canes are usually tip-rooting. They are perennial and new canes are produced each year. The first-year canes and usually the older ones have hairy bristles along the stem and on the leaf petioles between the numerous strong prickles. The compound leaves have five somewhat evergreen leaflets 1-1/2 to 3 inches long and 1/2 to 1 inch wide. The white flowers are numerous and appear during April and May in west-central Mississippi. The fruit is a collection of black drupelets about 1/2 to 3/4 of an inch long. The genus contains many species, but species identification is rarely important in forest management.

Site preference and range.--Dewberries occur on a variety of soils, usually on well-drained sites. In the Mississippi River bottomlands they flourish in the batture (lands lying between the levees and the river), growing either in full light or under the high shade of somewhat open stands of timber. They range from Florida to Texas and north to Maryland, Missouri, and Oklahoma.

Importance in forest management.--Except when they climb over other plants dewberries rarely form dense thickets. They are thus usually less of a hindrance to tree reproduction than most other weeds, and they sometimes act as a nurse crop for tree seedlings. They are reported to provide good grazing for cattle and wildlife.

Control, although rarely necessary, is probably easiest to obtain by disking.

Flowers

Berries

- 14 -

GRAPE

Family Vitaceae
Vitis sp.

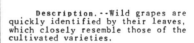

Description.--Wild grapes are quickly identified by their leaves, which closely resemble those of the cultivated varieties.

The grapes are chiefly perennial vines that climb by the coiling of naked-tipped tendrils. The graybark or pigeon grape is used here as an example, but other species bear a strong family resemblance. The **bark** of the main stem and branches shreds off after the first year. The **leaves** are 2-1/4 to 5-3/4 inches broad, ovate, with prolonged tips, either unlobed or with short shoulders. Wool-like hair, covers the upper and lower surfaces. **Flower** clusters, 2 to 6 inches long, appear in June and early July in west-central Mississippi. The **fruit** is a blackish berry 2/10 to 4/10 inch in diameter, containing seeds 1/10 to 2/10 inch long.

Site preference and range.--Grapes are found on almost any soil but usually prefer moist sites along rivers and sloughs and in alluvial bottoms. Their range is the entire eastern United States, with the graybark grape occurring from Florida to eastern Texas, and north to south-eastern Virginia, southern Ohio, Illinois, and Nebraska.

Importance in forest management.--Trees of sapling size or larger are frequently deformed or broken by the weight of grapevines. The tops of older trees, when burdened with vines, are badly damaged in sleet storms accompanied by wind. Young vines sometimes form a dense canopy by climbing over low shrubs, to the detriment of tree reproduction. Grapes are a valuable cattle and wildlife food and this utility may at times exceed the damage they do in timber stands.

Control of larger vines can be accomplished by cutting with an ax and applying a 2,4,5-T solution to prevent sprouting.

Stem, leaves, and tendrils

Growth habit

COMMON GREENBRIER

Family Liliaceae
Smilax rotundifolia

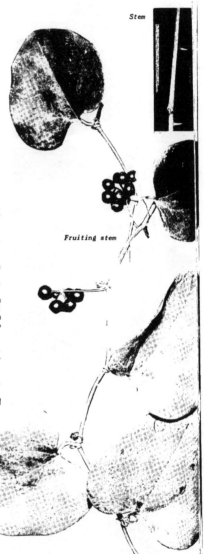

Stem

Fruiting stem

Description.--The greenbrier (or smilax) is notable for its tough, green, climbing stem, usually with stout flattened prickles.

This perennial woody vine, of which there are several species,climbs by means of tendrils and frequently reaches high into the crowns of trees. The vines arise from long slender underground stems. The leaves are ovate to nearly round, bright shiny green on both sides and 1-3/4 to 4 inches long and wide.The flower stalks are about 1 inch long and the inconspicuous greenish to bronze flowers appear from late April to June in west-central Mississippi. The fruit usually is a blue-black berry about 2/10 of an inch in diameter, with 2 seeds. It is borne in small clusters.In one species it is brilliant red.

Site preference and range.--Though greenbrier grows on all soils, it prefers well-drained but moist sites. In the Mississippi River bottomlands it is common on the flats and ridges both in the woods and in recently cleared or abandoned fields. Its range is from Florida to eastern Texas, and north to Canada.

Importance in forest management.-- This vine does its greatest damage by deforming or breaking seedling, sapling, or pole-size trees. The vines also twist about the trunks of larger trees, killing them or greatly reducing the quality of the logs. On old fields, these vines often form rather dense thickets which greatly reduce the accessibility of the area. Cattle and wildlife graze on the new growth in the spring. No practical controls are known.

- 16 -

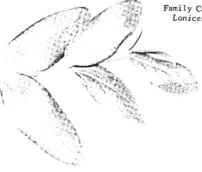

Fruiting branch

Description.--Its very fragrant, early spring flowers are the outstanding feature of Japanese honeysuckle.

This perennial high-twining or trailing vine has short-petioled, entire, ovate or oblong green leaves varying from 1 to 2 inches long by 1/2 to 3/4 inch wide. The new flowers are white or white tinged with purple, turning yellow with age, and 1 to 1-1/2 inches long. The fruit is a several-seeded black berry about 1/4 inch in diameter.

Site preference and range.--Honeysuckle is found on light soils with good drainage but abundant moisture. In the Mississippi River bottomlands it frequently occurs on the ridges and high flats. It ranges throughout the eastern United States.

Importance in forest management.-- This plant is a pernicious weed both in the open and in timber stands. It climbs into larger trees and spreads over the low-growing plants, smothering and strangling them. Trees up to six inches d.b.h. have been killed. Tree reproduction is deformed or killed and new seedlings are unable to get started. No entirely satisfactory control has been found. Foliage sprays with 2,4-D and 2,4,5-T have some promise, but at least two applications are needed and the cost is high. Small patches of honeysuckle have been controlled by mulching with a 2-inch layer of sawdust.

In the spring livestock and wild-

Family Polygonaceae
Brunnichia cirrhosa

Description.--Ladies'-eardrops, also called redvine, is a climbing vine with a woody stem up to 3/4 of an inch in diameter at the base. It climbs by means of tendrils from the ends of the branches. The alternate **leaves** are simple, ovate, entire, and from 2 to 4 inches long by 3/4 to 2 inches wide. The inconspicuous greenish **flowers** are borne in clusters crowded on axillary or terminal stalks; there are 2 to 5 flowers in a cluster. The **fruit** is a small achene.

Site preference and range.--This plant grows on all except the very sandy soils. It prefers moist sites, being very common along river and slough margins and on the low flats in the backwater area of the lower Mississippi River valley. Its range is from Florida to Texas, and north to South Carolina, western Kentucky, southern Illinois, and Oklahoma.

Importance in forest management.--It is very tolerant of shade and persists but does not flourish under fully stocked stands. When given sufficient light, it climbs over other weeds and shrubs, forming dense mats that interfere with tree reproduction.

Repeated cultivation until the trees outgrow the competition controls the vine in plantations, but no practical method is known for areas being restocked naturally.

Growth habit

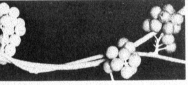

Fruiting stem

Description. -This perennial woody vine has triangular to heart-shaped leaves and red berries.

It wraps itself around any available vegetation and climbs to considerable heights in trees and shrubs. The leaves are oval, heart-shaped or arrow-like, and downy beneath. They are 2 to 3 inches long and 1-1/2 to 2 inches wide. Inconspicuous greenish flowers appear in July and August in west-central Mississippi. The fruit is a red drupe about 1/4 inch in diameter.

Site preference and range. --Red-berried moonseed grows on almost any soil or site. In the Mississippi River bottomlands it is most prevalent on the heavier, well-drained soils which have ample moisture during the growing season. Its range is from Florida to Texas, and north to southeastern Virginia, southern Illinois, and southeastern Kansas.

Importance in forest management. --This vine is most damaging in young stands when climbing in and over reproduction or saplings, which it sometimes breaks or deforms. When wrapped around the stems it may kill by cutting through the cambium layer. It rarely, if ever, prevents the establishment of tree reproduction. If the stems are numerous they interfere with travel through the woods. Control is difficult except where disking is possible. A closed tree canopy usually holds the vine in check.

Fruit

Leaf variations

MORNING-GLORY

Family Convolvulaceae
Ipomoea sp.

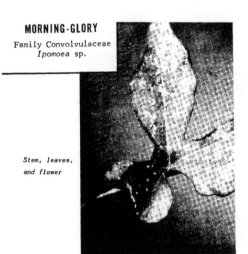

*Stem, leaves,
and flower*

Leaf variation

Description.--The morning glories are notable for their bright, trumpet-shaped blossoms, the color varying with the species.

These vines comprise a large and complex genus, but since the species resemble each other in growth habits, appearance, and importance in the forest it is unnecessary to distinguish them here. They are twining annuals that climb over any low ground cover. Quite frequently they form dense mats by intertwining with other vegetation. The **leaves** are generally heart-shaped and 1-1/2 to 2 inches long and wide. The **flowers** are short-stemmed and only about 1-1/2 inches long but very showy. They appear from July to October in west-central Mississippi.

Site preference and range.--Morning glories are restricted to the lighter and better drained soils such as sandy or silt loams. They are most common in cultivated or abandoned fields, along roadsides, or in openings in the woods where light is abundant. The range including all species covers the entire eastern United States.

Fruiting branch

PEPPER-VINE

Family Vitaceae
Ampelopsis arborea

Description.--Pepper-vine, often
called buckvine, is one of the worst
weeds in the bottomlands. This vine
has a woody stem with close bark. It
grows either erect and bushy or climbing over other plants. The **leaves** are
alternate, twice pinnate, and 3 to 5
inches long, with individual pinnae 1
to 1-1/4 inches long. They have cut-
toothed margins and are a shiny dark
green when mature. New growth is frequently reddish. Tendrils or flower
stalks, where present, appear opposite
the leaves. The inconspicuous, light
green **flowers** bloom from June to August
in west-central Mississippi. The **fruit**
is a black, spherical berry 1/4 to 3/8
of an inch in diameter and is borne in
a spreading head.

Site preference and range.--
Pepper-vine grows on a variety of soils
but is more common and usually develops
best on the heavier soils. In alluvial
areas it prefers the low flats and the
margins of small watercourses, but it
will also grow on rather dry ridges.
It ranges from Florida to Texas and
north to eastern Maryland, southern
Illinois, Missouri, and Oklahoma.

Importance in forest management.--
Pepper-vine is very tolerant of shade
and survives for years under stands
having a closed crown canopy. When
openings occur its growth is greatly
stimulated, and it forms dense, nearly
impenetrable, waist-deep tangles of
stems in which tree seedlings can
rarely develop.

Elimination of established pepper-
vine areas is difficult. Clearing with
a bulldozer followed by disking to
keep down the sprouts has been the
most successful method, though rather
costly. Chemical treatment has been
unsatisfactory and burning causes prolific sprouting.

Stem with leaves and tendrils

- 21 -

POISON IVY

Ripe fruit

Family Anacardiaceae
Rhus radicans

Description.--Poison ivy is a slender shrub or climbing vine with shiny, attractive leaves, each with three leaflets resembling those of boxelder.

It is characteristically a vine and climbs by means of aerial roots. Older stems are woody, brownish-gray to dark brown; they frequently grow to three inches or more in diameter. When without other plants on which to climb, poison ivy may stand upright or trail over the ground. The leaves are 3 to 12 inches long and compound, with 3 leaflets whose margins may be entire or variously toothed. The leaf surface varies from smooth and shiny to somewhat hairy and dull. Arrangement on the stem is alternate. The small greenish-white flowers, appearing in June-July in west-central Mississippi, are clustered and rather inconspicuous. The fruit is a gray-white fleshy drupe almost spherical and about 1/4 inch in diameter.

Site preference and range.--Poison ivy grows in almost all soils and on practically all sites except those inundated for a major portion of the year. In alluvial bottomlands as many as 70 thousand stems per acre have been recorded. It is commonly found in thickets, open woods, rocky areas, and in fence rows where the seed is deposited by birds. It ranges throughout the eastern United States.

Importance in forest management.--Where this plant occurs in extremely heavy concentrations on the ground, young trees may be crowded or shaded out, but such damage is not usual. More often small trees are deformed or broken down by the weight of the vines in their crowns. The tops of older trees, when burdened with vines, are badly damaged in sleet storms accompanied by wind. The skin irritation resulting from contact with the sap is another serious objection to the plant. Widespread control is probably impractical in the woods. On planting areas, disking will keep it in check. Spraying the foliage with a 32.5 percent solution of ammonium sulfamate kills the vine but also affects tree reproduction. Vines in large trees can be cut with an ax and treated with chemicals to prevent sprouting.

Growth habit

- 22 -

Description.--Supple-jack, some-times called rattan-vine, has shiny leaves with prominent parallel veins.

This perennial high-climbing vine twines about the trunks and crowns of trees and shrubs. The upper stem de-velops many fine, supple branches. After the first year the stems become woody and dark green, the older ones bearing prominent white streaks. The parallel-veined leaves are alternate, oblong-ovate, with a slightly wavy margin. They are 2-1/2 to 3 inches long by 1 to 1-1/4 inches wide. The small greenish-white flowers are in-conspicuous; they appear in May in west-central Mississippi. The fruit is a blue drupe about 3/10 of an inch long. The leaves, flowers, and fruit are often high in trees.

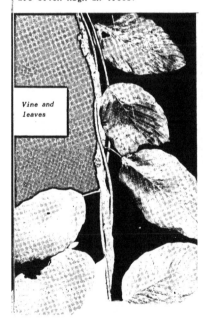

Vine and leaves

Site preference and range.-- Supple-jack occurs on all except very sandy soils, but prefers moist to wet sites. It tolerates shade and thrives even under fully stocked stands. Its range is from Florida to Texas, and north to Virginia, Tennessee, and southern Missouri.

Importance in forest management.-- By twisting around and strangling the trees on which it climbs, this vine either kills them or greatly reduces the quality of the logs. Older vines may be cut, and possibly treated with chemicals to prevent sprouting.

TRUMPET-CREEPER

Family Bignoniaceae
Campsis radicans

Flowering branch

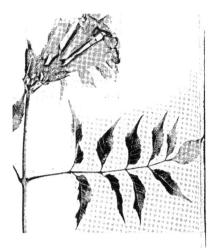

Description.--The most noticeable features of trumpet-creeper, sometimes called cow-itch, are the bright orange funnel-shaped flowers in summer and the large seed pods in the fall

This perennial, woody vine climbs to considerable heights by means of aerial rootlets. It also pushes out over low plants to form dense masses. It is frequently confused with pepper-vine and patches of either vine or combinations of the two are locally called buckvine areas. The pinnately compound **leaves** are opposite, light green, and from 3 to 6 inches long. There are 9 to 11 ovate, pointed, slightly toothed **leaflets** 1-1/4 to 2 inches in length by 1/2 to 3/4 inch wide. The conspicuous orange to scarlet **flowers**, 2-1/4 to 3 inches long, appear from June through September in west-central Mississippi. The fruit is a large dry pod 4 to 8 inches long by 3/4 inch in diameter and containing many large flat-winged seeds.

Fruit

Site preference and range.-- Trumpet-creeper grows on any soil but is most common on those of heavier texture. In the Mississippi River bottomlands it is almost universally present on the better-drained flats and moist ridges but not in the sloughs or other very wet locations. Its range is from Florida to Texas, and north to southern Iowa and New Jersey.

Importance in forest management.-- Trumpet-creeper survives but does not flourish under fully stocked timber stands. With abundant light--as in old fields or openings in the woods caused by heavy cutting or repeated fires-- this vine by itself or intertwined with other vegetation forms dense mats through which it is almost impossible for natural or planted tree seedlings to force their way.

Elimination of established trumpet-creeper thickets is difficult. Clearing with a bulldozer and then disking repeatedly to keep down sprouts has been the most successful method, though rather costly. Chemical treatment has been unsatisfactory and burning causes prolific sprouting.

Growth habit

WILD BEAN

Family Leguminosae
Apios americana

Description. --The wild bean or groundnut is conspicuous for its attractive purplish or mauve flowers.

It is a perennial vine that twines about and climbs over low plants and bushes. Tuberous enlargements at regular intervals make the roots resemble a string of beads. The compound leaves are light green, 6 to 7 inches long. There are 3 to 9 ovate-lanceolate leaflets 1-3/4 to 3 inches long by 3/4 to 1-1/2 inches wide. The flowers are crowded on a stalk 1-1/4 to 6-1/2 inches long; they appear from July through September in west-central Mississippi. The fruit is a straight or slightly curved, many-seeded legume about 1 inch long.

Site preference and range. --Wild bean grows on practically all types of soil except dry sands, but it prefers well-drained sites with abundant moisture. In the bottomlands it occurs on the better drained portions of flats and on ridges. Its range is from the Gulf Coast to Canada, and as far west as Colorado.

Importance in forest management. --It does little damage in well-stocked forests. In abandoned fields or open areas it forms a dense mat by intertwining with other ground cover. Such mats frequently prevent seedlings from getting started and deform or break small trees.

No practical controls are known for use in areas of natural reproduction. In plantations repeated cultivation until the trees outgrow the competition is often worthwhile.

em

COMMON BUTTONBUSH

Family Rubiaceae
Cephalanthus occidentalis

Description.--The outstanding features of buttonbush are its prominent white flowers borne in spherical heads and its occurrence on very wet sites.

This plant, though usually a shrub not over 15 to 20 feet tall, occasionally attains tree form with heights of 40 to 50 feet and diameters as large as 1 foot. The **trunk** may be free of limbs for 15 or 20 feet before dividing into a spreading crown. The **bark** of large trees is gray-brown to nearly black and deeply fissured into broad flat ridges. The prominently veined, dark-green **leaves** are opposite or in whorls of three, with lighter under surfaces. They are 4 to 6 inches long and 2 to 4 inches wide. Small white **flowers** are massed in globose clusters 1 to 1-1/2 inches in diameter. Late June through July is blossoming time in west-central Mississippi. The **fruit** ripens in late autumn in heads 5/8 to 3/4 inch in diameter.

Site preference and range.-- Buttonbush grows well on heavy soils in wet sites. Its most common habitat is the margin of river-bottoms, swamps, ponds, and drainage ditches. It is widespread over the eastern United States.

Importance in forest management.-- Under established stands this shrub is held in check by the overhead shade. In openings, especially after fires, it often forms a dense mat 3 to 3-1/2 feet deep that shades out most reproduction and deforms whatever seedlings may push up through it. Fire does not kill it, for it sprouts prolifically. Chemicals such as 2,4-D and 2,4,5-T have likewise been unsuccessful. If the sites are not too wet, the best control probably is thorough disking before natural seeding or planting, followed by cultivation of plantations during the first season to keep down sprouts.

Branch with leaves and flowers.

Seed

Mature fruit

Growth habit

- 26 -

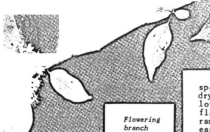

ROUGHLEAF DOGWOOD

Family Cornaceae
Cornus drummondii

Flowering branch

Site preference and range.--This species is found on rather poor or dry sites. It is widely distributed on low ridges and the better-drained flats of alluvial bottomlands. The range of this tree is throughout the eastern United States.

Importance in forest management.-- As an understory tree roughleaf dogwood does little damage in established stands, and can be left as a source of food for wildlife. Reproduction is rather sparse, but in open areas on suitable sites it can easily take over to the exclusion of commercially important trees.

Control measures include disking to destroy young dogwoods, and cutting and chemically treating larger ones.

Description.--Although usually a small tree, roughleaf dogwood sometimes attains heights of 40 to 50 feet and diameters of 8 to 10 inches on the most favorable bottomland sites.

The **trunk** is short and the branches form a narrow, irregular, open head. New branches are light green in their first year, changing later to light reddish brown and finally to light gray-brown. The **bark** is divided by shallow fissures into narrow ridges with closely appressed dark red-brown scales. The **leaves** are opposite, 3 to 4 inches long and 1-1/2 to 2 inches wide; the tip is prolonged. They are dark green, roughened above by short white hairs, and pale below. The midrib is thin and 4 to 6 pairs of veins run roughly parallel with the edge of the leaf. The white **flowers** appear when the leaves are nearly fully grown, usually in mid-May in west-central Mississippi. Flower clusters are 1-1/2 to 2-3/4 inches wide with individual flowers about 3/8 inch across. The **fruit** is a small white drupe that is 1/4 inch in diameter and contains 1 or 2 seeds.

Growth habit

Flower

This shrub usually varies from 3 to 15 feet tall but frequently reaches tree size, 30 feet tall and 2 feet in diameter, in the South. The pinnately compound **leaves** are 4 to 10 inches long with 5 to 11 non-hairy leaflets 2 to 4 inches in length. Leaflets are finely saw-toothed on the edges, dull green on the upper surface and lighter below. Leaf arrangement is opposite. The broad clusters of small, fragrant **flowers** are 4 to 6 inches across and bloom from early June through August in west-central Mississippi. The **fruit** is a purplish-black, fleshy, berry-like drupe about 3/16 inch in diameter, containing 3 or 4 small seed-like nutlets.

Site preference and range. -- American elder occurs on a variety of soils and sites but is most common on moist to wet, fairly well-drained sites in the bottomlands. It ranges throughout the eastern United States and beyond.

Importance in forest management. -- It reproduces readily and, because of its spreading growth, prevents the development of tree seedlings. Where tree reproduction is desired, elder plants should be frilled and treated with chemicals. Otherwise they can be left for their aesthetic value and the usefulness of their fruit to wildlife.

Growth habit

Ripe fruit

- 28 -

Leaves

Flowering branch

Description.--The hawthorns are conspicuous for their usually scaly bark and their attractive white flower clusters in early spring.

There are several species, both shrubs and trees. All are very difficult to distinguish but none are commercially important. Usually they have crooked, thorny branches. The **bark** is light tan to cinnamon colored and scaly. The dark yellow-green **leaves** are alternate, simple, serrate, and 1-1/2 to 3-1/2 inches long by 3/4 to 1-1/2 inches wide. The **flowers** appear in April in west-central Mississippi. The **fruit** is a pome with 1 to 5 bony nutlets, usually 1-seeded.

Site preference and range.--Hawthorn occurs on almost all soils but in the alluvial bottomlands is limited to the well-drained flats and ridges. It is very tolerant of shade and is scattered in the understory, but may make a thicket in openings. Its range covers the eastern United States.

Importance in forest management.--Hawthorn flowers have aesthetic value, and the fruits provide food for wildlife Where they are interfering with tree regeneration young hawthorn thickets can be bulldozed, and trees can be frilled and treated with chemicals.

AMERICAN HOLLY

Family Aquifoliaceae
Ilex opaca

Leaves

Branch with fruit

Description. --Shiny, evergreen leaves and the bright red berries it bears in the winter distinguish the American holly.

This tree is usually short-boled and confined to the understory of timber stands, but it often reaches diameters of 2 to 3 feet and heights of 50 feet or even 100 feet. It has a narrow pyramidal head formed by short slender branches. The limited supply of **wood** goes into specialty uses and the fruit-bearing branches are in demand for Christmas decorations. The **bark** is about 1/2 inch thick, light gray, and with small wart-like growths. The evergreen leaves are elliptic with undulating margins bearing small spines about 2/10 inch long. They are yellow-green and about 2 to 4 inches long with a prominent midrib and veins. The small, white staminate and pistillate **flowers** are borne on separate trees. The **fruit** is a globose red drupe 3/8 inch in diameter.

Site preference and range. --Holly is usually found on sands or sandy loams and on moist sites in the alluvial bottomlands. Elsewhere it occurs principally in minor stream bottoms. Its range is throughout the eastern United States, excluding the New England States north of Massachusetts.

Importance in forest management. -- In some areas holly occupies space that could be used by species of greater commercial value. Because of its tolerance for shade it readily becomes established in the understory and may interfere with other reproduction as the overstory is removed. Since holly has an important aesthetic value, however, it should be spared wherever possible. It can be killed by applying 2,4,5-T solution in a frill.

*Flowering
branch*

*Fruiting
stem*

inches long by 1/4 to 5/8 inch wide
and marked with minute dots. The
flowers are in erect cylindrical
clusters 4 to 6 inches long and bloom
in May and June in west-central Mississippi. The **fruit** is a 1- to 2-seeded
pod about 1/4 inch long.

Site preference and range.--False
indigo generally favors the heavier
soils in moist sites. In the Mississippi River bottomlands it is very
common in the batture lands around
borrow pits and the smaller drainage
courses. It ranges from northern
Florida to Louisiana, and north through
the Central States.

Importance in forest management.--
It forms rather large, dense thickets
that interfere with tree reproduction,
but no attempts at control have been
reported. Methods other than disking
or bulldozing would be expensive because of the many small stems.

Description.--False indigo, sometimes locally called leadplant, is conspicuous in the spring for its spikes
of small purple flowers with golden
stamens.

This shrub grows 12 to 15 feet
tall. Its branches and leaves are
covered with short gray hairs. The
leaves resemble those of black locust.
They are 4 to 7 inches long and pinnately compound, with 13 to 30 leaflets. The **leaflets** are 1/2 to 1-1/4

PALMETTO

Family Palmae
Sabal minor

Growth habit

Leaf blade

Description.--Palmetto is easily recognized by its broad fan-shaped leaves.

This plant is an evergreen perennial. On dry sites it is "stemless "--that is, the stem remains buried in the ground. On most alluvial soils it produces a trunk that is normally 2 to 3 feet high and sometimes reaches 6 to 8 feet. The green, nearly round **leaves** are 1 to 3 feet wide with petioles up to 3 feet long; they have 32 to 50 segments. The small, whitish, very numerous **flowers** appear on stalks up to 10 feet tall from May to July in west-central Mississippi. The **fruit** is a black globose drupe about 1/3 of an inch in diameter and mostly one-seeded.

Site preference and range.--Palmetto grows on any soil. It occurs on dry sandy sites in the pine lands but makes the largest trunk growth in the shade on alluvial soils that are swampy or subject to some flooding. It may invade pastures and even cottonfields. Its range is from Georgia to Texas, and north to South Carolina and eastern Arkansas.

Importance in forest management.--Though this plant is much browsed by cattle and wildlife, it frequently forms dense thickets that interfere with the natural restocking of woodland areas.

Applying kerosene to the growing tip has been reported as a successful control measure. Disking eliminates it temporarily but sprouting is prolific and many of the chopped-up pieces of stem root to form new plants. Repeated disking is necessary in plantations until the trees outgrow the competition.

- 32 -

PLANERTREE

Family Ulmaceae
Planera aquatica

*Flowering branch
with young leaves*

Site preference and range.--
Planertree grows on the heavier clays
and prefers sites covered with water
for a portion of the year. In the Mississippi River bottomlands it is widely distributed in swamps, deep sloughs,
and low, poorly drained flats. It ranges
from northern Florida to Texas, and
north to North Carolina, Kentucky, and
southeastern Missouri.

Importance in forest management.--
Because of its spreading crown, the
planertree interferes with the growth
and reproduction of commercially important species. It can be controlled
either by bulldozing or with 2,4,5-T
in frills.

Description.--The most conspicuous
characteristic of the planertree is
its leaves, which are miniature copies
of those of the American elm.

Growth habit

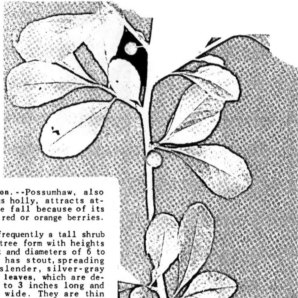

Fruiting stem

Description.--Possumhaw, also called deciduous holly, attracts attention in late fall because of its abundant bright red or orange berries.

It is most frequently a tall shrub but may attain tree form with heights of 20 to 30 feet and diameters of 6 to 10 inches. It has stout, spreading branches and slender, silver-gray branchlets. The **leaves,** which are deciduous, are 2 to 3 inches long and 1/3 to 1 inch wide. They are thin early in the season, but become thick and firm when mature. The inconspicuous **flowers** appear in April and May in west-central Mississippi and are crowded at the end of the lateral branches of the previous season. Occasionally they occur solitarily on the branches of the current year. The red or orange **fruit** is globose and about 1/4 inch in diameter. It frequently persists until after the new leaves appear in the spring.

Site preference and range.-- Possumhaw generally grows on the heavier soils in low, moist locations such as the flats of alluvial areas and along the borders of streams and swamps. Its range is throughout southern United States and as far west as Oklahoma.

Importance in forest management.-- Possumhaw varies in growth habit from individual trees and small clumps to extensive thickets that crowd out the reproduction of desirable species of trees.

It can be controlled with an ax or by applying a basal spray of 2,4,5-T in diesel fuel--the chemical reduces sprouting after treatment. As the fruit is eaten by birds, it may be desirable to leave trees where they do not interfere with forest management.

Seed pod

Description.--The eastern redbud--sometimes called Judas-tree--is conspicuous for the pink flowers it bears in early spring.

It is a small understory tree, rarely growing more than 40 to 50 feet tall. The trunk separates into stout branches at 10 to 20 feet above the ground, so that the tree often develops a wide, flat crown.

The new branches are brown and shiny during their first season, changing to grayish-brown later. The **bark** of the trunk is reddish-brown, with deep longitudinal fissures that divide it into narrow plates. The heart-shaped glossy green **leaves** are 3 to 5 inches long and wide. The **flowers**, which range from light pink to purplish, appear in clusters along the branches, usually just before the leaves unfold. Late March is blossoming time in west-central Mississippi.

The **fruit** is a many-seeded red-brown pod about 3 inches long. In the South the pod is fully grown by late May, but often persists until early winter, or even longer. When ripe, seeds are brown and about 1/4 inch long.

Site preference and range.--In the bottomlands this tree prefers the less frequently flooded slack-water areas and the Brown Loam bluffs. It occurs in uplands and bottomlands throughout most of the eastern United States. In the South it is found throughout Tennessee and Arkansas, in all but the coastal fringe of Alabama and Mississippi, in northern Louisiana, and in eastern Oklahoma and Texas.

Importance in forest management.--In established stands it can usually be left for its aesthetic value. Where reproduction of commercially important species is desired, its spreading crown, in combination with other low shade, may be a serious handicap. It should then be frilled and perhaps also treated with chemicals.

Fruiting branch with leaves

Flowers

- 35 -

SMOOTH SUMAC

Family Anacardiaceae
Rhus glabra

Growth habit

Fruiting branch

Description.--Smooth sumac is most conspicuous for the large red-brown fruit clusters it bears in late summer.

The species described here is the most common in the bottomlands, but several others are found, all similar in appearance. This small shrub has smooth stems and grows from 2 to 10 feet tall. The **leaves** are pinnately compound and from 18 to 24 inches long. There are 11 to 31 leaflets from 2 to 6 inches long and with serrated edges. The upper surface is yellow-green and the underside distinctly whitish. The **flowers** are mostly of a single sex, white to greenish-white. Those developing into fruit are usually more compact than the others. They appear in June to July in west-central Mississippi. The **fruit**, a small globular dry drupe covered with crimson hairs, is borne in dense panicles 6 to 8 inches long and 2 to 3 inches wide.

Site preference and range.--Sumac grows on all but the heavier clay soils and prefers well-drained and dry sites. In the Mississippi River bottomlands it occurs along river, creek, and drainage ditch banks as well as on the better drained flats and ridges, where in abandoned fields or woods openings it frequently forms thickets. It is found in almost every State in the Union.

Importance in forest management.--Sumac is troublesome in forest management mainly because it occupies space that could be used more profitably by other species. It rarely is a hindrance to tree reproduction except when it occurs in dense thickets. The most practical control is to bulldoze areas of young sumac, and frill and treat larger plants with chemicals to prevent sprouting.

Fruit

- 36

Branch and leaves

Growth habit

Description.--The most conspicuous characteristic of swamp-privet is the wide-spreading and often drooping habit of its crown.

It is a small tree, usually 10 to 20 feet tall. Occasionally it reaches 50 feet in height, with a short trunk 8 to 10 inches in diameter. Its slender branches are light brown, becoming darker in the second year. The deciduous leaves are opposite and elliptic, yellow-green on the upper surface and lighter below. They vary from 2-1/2 to 4-1/2 inches long by 1 to 1-1/2 inches wide. The **flowers,** which appear before the leaves in April and May, are inconspicuous; the pistillate ones occur in several-flowered clusters about 3/4 to 1-1/4 inches long. The **fruit** is a dark purplish drupe 1 to 1-1/4 inches long which falls as soon as ripe in June and July.

Site preference and range.--This tree occurs on the heavier soils and the wetter sites along river banks, shallow sloughs, ponds, and swamps. On the low, wet flats in the Mississippi River bottomlands it frequently forms dense, nearly pure, stands referred to as privet flats. Its range is from Florida to Texas, and north to South Carolina and the southern portion of the Central States.

Importance in forest management.-- Swamp-privet shades out new growth and overtops and crowds out advanced reproduction. It must be eliminated before commercially important species can replace it. It can be controlled either by bulldozing or by spraying the basal portion of the trunk with 2,4,5-T. Where natural regeneration cannot be relied on, these treatments must be followed by planting with desirable species suited to the site.

Flowering branch

Achene. A small dry and hard 1-locular 1-seeded indehiscent fruit, like the individual fruits of *Ranunculus.*

Alternate. Said of leaves, etc.--not opposite to each other on the axis, but borne at regular intervals at different levels.

Annual. Of only one year's duration. Winter-annual, a plant from autumn-sown seed which blooms and fruits in the following spring.

Appressed. Lying close and flat against.

Axil. The angle formed between any two organs.

Axillary. In or related to the axis.

Berry. A pulpy fruit with immersed seeds, as the grape, cranberry, etc.; loosely extended to cover other fleshy fruits, such as the strawberry (ripened receptacle), raspberry (coherent drupelets).

Blade. The expanded portion of a leaf.

Cambium. A layer, usually regarded as one cell thick, of persistent meristematic tissue (referring to vascular and cork cambia); or a persistent meristematic layer which gives rise to secondary wood and secondary phloem (vascular cambium).

Capsule. A dry dehiscent fruit composed of more than one carpel.

Catkin. A dry scaly spike, usually unisexual, such as the flower of willows, birches, etc.

Compound. Composed of 2 or more similar parts united into one whole. **Compound** leaf, one divided into separate leaflets.

Deciduous. Not persistent; not evergreen.

Drupe. A fleshy or pulpy fruit with the inner portion of the pericarp (1-locular and 1-seeded, or sometimes several-locular) hard or stony.

Drupelet. A diminutive drupe, as in a raspberry or blackberry.

Entire. Without toothing or division.

Forb. Any herb other than grass.

Globose. Globular; spherical.

Herb. A plant with no persistent woody stem above ground; also plants used in seasoning or in medicine.

Herbaceous. Having the characters of an herb; leaf-like in color and texture.

- 38

Staminate. Having the pollen-bearing organs of the flower.

Tendril. A slender clasping or twining cauline or foliar outgrowth.

Tree. Perennial woody plant with an evident trunk.

Undulate. With a wavy surface margin, repand.

Valve. One of the pieces into which a capsule splits; the partially detached lid of an anther.

Veins. Threads of fibrovascular tissue in a leaf or other organ, especially those which branch (as distinguished from nerves).

Vine. Any plant whose stem requires support, and which climbs by tendrils or other means or which trails or creeps along the ground. Also the stem of such a plant.

REFERENCES

Bailey, L.H.
    1935. *The standard cyclopedia of horticulture.* Reissued with corrections. 3,639 pp., illus. New York.

————and Bailey, E.Z.
    1930. *Hortus.* 652 pp., illus. New York.

Bomhard, M.L.
    1950. *Palm trees in the United States.* U.S. Dept. Agr. Agr. Inform. Bul. 22, 26 pp., illus.

Brown, C.A.
    1945. *Louisiana trees and shrubs.* La. Forestry Comn. Bul. 1, 262 pp., illus.

Fernald, M.L.
    1950. *Gray's manual of botany.* Ed.8, 1,632 pp., illus. New York, Cincinnati [etc.].

Langdon, O.G., Bomhard, M.L., and Cassady, J.T.
    1952. *Field book of forage plants on longleaf pine-bluestem ranges.* U.S. Forest Serv. South. Forest Expt. Sta. Occas. Paper 127, 117 pp., illus. [Processed.]

Little, E.L., Jr.
    1953. *Check list of native and naturalized trees of the United States (including Alaska).* U.S. Dept. Agr. Agr. Handb. 41, 472 pp.

Putnam, J.A.
    1951. *Management of bottomland hardwoods.* U.S. Forest Serv. South. Forest Expt. Sta. Occas. Paper 116, 60 pp. [Processed.]

————and Bull, Henry
    1932. *The trees of the bottomlands of the Mississippi River Delta region.* U.S. Forest Serv. South. Forest Expt. Sta. Occas. Paper 27, 207 pp., illus. [Processed.]

Sargent, C.S.
    1926. *Manual of the trees of North America (exclusive of Mexico).* Ed. 2, 910 pp., illus. Boston and New York.

Van Dersal, W.R.
    1938. *Native woody plants of the United States, their erosion-control and wildlife values.* U.S. Dept. Agr. Misc. Pub. 303, 362 pp., illus.

Occasional Paper 166   1958

SOIL-MOISTURE CONSTANTS AND THEIR VARIATION

WALTER M. BROADFOOT and HUBERT D. BURKE

SOUTHERN FOREST EXPERIMENT STATION
PHILIP A. BRIEGLEB, DIRECTOR
Forest Service U.S. Department of Agriculture

CONTENTS

SOIL-MOISTURE CONSTANTS AND THEIR VARIATION

Walter M. Broadfoot and Hubert D. Burke
Southern Forest Experiment Station

"Constants" like field capacity, liquid limit, moisture equivalent, and wilting point are used by most students and workers in soil moisture. These constants may be equilibrium points or other values that describe soil moisture. Their values under specific soil and cover conditions have been discussed at length in the literature, but few general analyses and comparisons are available.

During the past several years the Vicksburg Research Center[1] of the Southern Forest Experiment Station has been accumulating information on effects that physical properties have on soil hydrology. The work has included an extensive review of literature in addition to field studies on many sites throughout the United States, Alaska, and Puerto Rico. Values were secured for most recognized constants.

This paper summarizes the data gathered in the library and the field. The authors believe that it may be a useful reference for other researchers. For students, it may illustrate the fact that soil-moisture constants, far from being fixed, vary considerably with the physical condition of the soil.

Some explanation is due of the procedure followed in compiling the information, together with some precautions as to its use. The data are from 901 samples of surface soil and 400 samples of subsoil. Data from published sources were combined with those obtained in studies at the Vicksburg Research Center.

This procedure raised some difficulties, one being that of citing sources. Because data from published sources lost their identity upon being tabulated, no attempt was made to cite references for specific observations. All published sources, however, are included in the bibliography (p. 23). Published material was accepted at face value, as it was assumed that procedures used in obtaining it were standard though not necessarily identical.

Most surface soil samples were from depths of 0 to 6 inches, but some samples were as much as 36 inches deep. Thick layers, when reported in the literature as surface soils, were assumed to be uniform in

---

[1] Maintained at Vicksburg, Mississippi, by the Southern Forest Experiment Station, Forest Service, U. S. Department of Agriculture, in cooperation with the Waterways Experiment Station, Corps of Engineers, U.S. Army.

moisture values and other properties. Subsoil samples were those indicated in published material as being from the B horizon or below, or (especially in the sampling at Vicksburg) from depths greater than 6 inches.

The number of observations, although seemingly large, provided too little data for some comparisons. Consequently only the most commonly used constants are represented. Values for the sandy clay and silt textural classes often had to be omitted entirely.

The first values to be discussed are those relating moisture to soil texture, land use, and aeration. Later sections discuss ways of predicting bulk density, and "wet" and "dry" values from other soil properties. Finally, results from four methods of estimating available water are tabulated and briefly discussed. The tables generally include the number of observations on which the average value is based, the average value for the relation, and the standard deviation of the mean.

EXPLANATION OF TERMS AND SYMBOLS

The following symbols and definitions have been adhered to through- this report. For the most part they follow general practice, but the soil perties that were used in the regression analyses are represented by two ıbols. The first is the abbreviation that appears in many of the charts tables (as S, BD), the second designates the property in the regression lysis (as X_1, X_2).

atmosphere moisture (0.1-atm). Moisture ɔntent of a soil that has been saturated ʌd then brought to equilibrium at pres- ure of 0.1 atmosphere.

atmosphere moisture (1/3-atm). Moisture ontent of a soil that has been satu- ated and then brought to equilibrium at pressure of 1/3 atmosphere.

tmospheres moisture (15-atm). Moisture ontent of a wetted soil after reaching quilibrium at a pressure of 15 atmos- heres.

m moisture (60-cm). Moisture content of n undisturbed soil core that has been aturated and then brought to equilibri- m at 60 cm of water tension.

lable water capacity, calculated by one f these methods:
0-cm value minus 15-atm value
/3-atm value minus 15-atm value
ield capacity minus wilting point
ield maximum minus field minimum.

pores (BP) (X_4). That pore volume re- ɪorted in the literature as big pores, on-capillary pores, or readily drained ɪores; or that volume obtained by sub- ʌracting the 60-cm water-tension value rom the total pore volume of a sample.

density (BD) (X_5). Ratio of the weight ɪf dry soil to the volume it occupied n the field, expressed as grams per ubic centimeter.

nage capacity (DC) (X_7). That volume f a sample representing the difference n total pore volume and volume of water eld at 1/3-atmosphere pressure.

d capacity (FC). Field moisture content f well-drained soils approximately two ays after saturation.

d maximum (F max) (X_8). Maximum re- urring average moisture content of a ɔil *in situ*.

d minimum (F min) (X_9). Minimum re- urring moisture content of a soil *in itu*.

Field moisture index (FMI) (X_{10}). Field maximum moisture content minus the field minimum moisture content.

Liquid limit (LL) (X_{12}). Moisture content in percent by weight at which a soil will barely flow under an applied force.

Moisture equivalent (ME). Moisture content of a soil subjected to a force of ap- proximately 1,000 x gravity.

Organic matter (OM) (X_3). Organic content expressed as percent by weight.

Plastic limit (PL) (X_{11}). Moisture content in percent by weight at or above which a soil will puddle if handled or worked.

Saturation (0-5 cm). Moisture content of a soil core that has been saturated and then brought to 0-5 cm of water tension.

Saturation percentage. Moisture content of a sample of soil that has been brought to saturation by adding water while stirring.

Soil separates
Clay (C) (X_2). Percent by weight.
Sand (S) (X_1). Percent by weight.
Silt (Si) (X_6). Percent by weight.

Soil .texture classes
Clay loam (CL)
Loam (L)
Loamy sand (LS)
Sandy clay (SC)
Sandy clay loam (SCL)
Sandy loam (SL)
Silt loam (SiL)
Silty clay (SiC)
Silty clay loam (SiCL)

Total pore volume. Percent by volume of total pore space of a sample as calcu- lated from bulk density and specific gravity for soils with less than 10 per- cent organic matter, or the value as reported in the literature references.

Water-holding capacity. Moisture content of a soil core or disturbed column of soil after it has drained following saturation.

Wilting point (WP). Moisture content of a soil when plants growing in it wilt permanently.

SOIL-MOISTURE CONSTANTS AND TEXTURAL RELATIONSHIPS

Average values of mechanical composition were calculated for each texture class defined by the Soil Survey Manual of the U.S. Department of Agriculture (Agriculture Handbook 18). Results are shown in figure 1. Most averages were well centered within the class, except that the clay soils were somewhat lower than average in clay content and higher in silt.

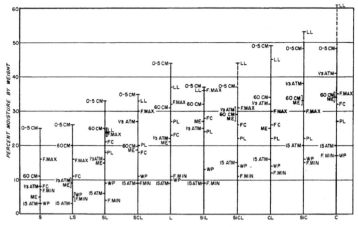

Figure 1.--*Average textural composition of the samples used in relating soil-moisture constants to texture.*

Soil-moisture constants vary considerably with change of texture. Table 1 and figure 2 summarize the relative moisture values of the most common textural classes, as arranged in approximate order of grain size. In general, values averaged lower for the sandy soils.

Field maximums in the sand, loamy sand, and sandy loam classes were more closely approached by the 60-centimeter values than by the

Figure 2.--*Moisture values of various textural classes of surface and subsoils.*

- 4 -

Table 1.--Moisture constants, by weight, for various textural classes

Soil-moisture constant	Soil textural class									
	S	LS	SL	SCL	L	SiL	SiCL	CL	SiC	C
0-5 cm										
N[1]	19	10	10	2	21	104	13	8	8	8
$\bar{X}$[2]	25	26	33	35	44	37	37	49	48	48
s[3]	5.2	7.4	9.7	18.4	15.7	11.6	14.3	16.6	20.1	15.1
F max										
N	4	2	32	5	30	92	16	8	5	16
$\bar{X}$	16	16	24	30	32	36	31	30	30	35
s	3.7	2.8	10.1	8.0	8.7	12.5	4.8	6.1	9.9	8.4
60-cm										
N	9	3	14	4	33	111	19	7	7	11
$\bar{X}$	11	20	25	20	31	32	29	34	33	34
s	7.4	5.0	7.4	4.0	10.9	10.6	5.4	9.3	7.3	6.5
0.1-atm.										
N	15	10	5	2	13	59	2	7	3	4
$\bar{X}$	7	12	20	30	26	35	47	40	49	35
s	2.1	5.2	6.6	10.6	8.2	11.5	12.7	10.2	6.0	7.9
FC										
N	2	9	40	3	12	29	13	11	...	56
$\bar{X}$	8	11	21	18	23	28	26	26	...	32
s	2.8	3.2	5.9	2.6	3.0	7.4	2.6	5.0	...	4.8
1/3-atm.										
N	12	10	26	2	24	102	16	11	6	19
$\bar{X}$	8	9	16	27	22	25	29	32	38	41
s	1.9	4.5	6.0	12.7	5.7	7.7	5.9	7.3	8.4	12.3
ME										
N	28	29	131	14	103	186	53	32	15	83
$\bar{X}$	5	9	15	19	21	27	29	25	33	34
s	3.2	4.9	5.2	6.2	5.0	6.9	4.2	5.5	5.8	8.9
15-atm.										
N	23	17	51	8	52	162	27	21	9	47
$\bar{X}$	3	3	6	9	9	9	15	16	20	20
s	1.8	1.9	2.9	2.6	4.6	3.6	2.4	4.4	9.6	5.7
WP										
N	7	19	38	3	33	46	33	20	4	64
$\bar{X}$	3	5	9	11	10	13	14	14	16	17
s	3.1	2.5	3.4	5.0	3.7	4.9	3.1	4.2	2.8	2.9
F min										
N	4	2	21	5	25	88	22	10	9	14
$\bar{X}$	7	5	4	9	11	9	11	12	15	17
s	.6	.0	2.9	5.0	6.4	3.5	2.7	2.2	2.6	4.7
LL										
N	...	...	14	4	25	119	27	9	10	17
$\bar{X}$	...	...	24	33	37	36	.44	45	53	61
s	...	...	4.6	6.2	10.7	8.8	6.7	6.8	9.9	15.1
PL										
N	...	...	14	4	25	118	26	8	10	15
$\bar{X}$	...	...	18	20	27	24	22	22	22	27
s	...	...	4.2	4.5	8.8	5.6	2.5	2.1	5.9	5.7

[1] Number of samples.
[2] Mean.
[3] Standard deviation.

- 5 -

moisture-equivalent and 1/3-atmosphere values. In fine soils the 1/3-atmosphere and moisture-equivalent values were about as high as the 60-centimeter readings, possibly because they were determined from disturbed or bulk samples whereas the 60-centimeter values were from undisturbed soil cores.[2]

In coarse soils, the 15-atmosphere and wilting-point values were as small as 3 percent by weight. In the fine soils, there was a definite and consistent tendency for 15-atmosphere values to be higher than other "dry end" constants. In all fine soils, wilting point and field minimum were very close together.

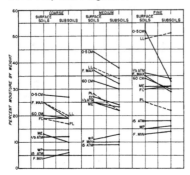

Figure 3.--*Average moisture constants, by weight, for coarse, medium, and fine soils.*

Additional examination was made with moisture values grouped by coarse, medium, and fine textural classes. The grouping of the twelve classes was as follows: (1) coarse, consisting of sand, loamy sand, and sandy loam; (2) medium, consisting of loam, silt loam, sandy clay loam, sandy clay, and silt; (3) fine, consisting of silty clay loam, clay loam, silty clay, and clay. Values are shown on a percent-by-weight basis in table 2 and figure 3. Both surface and subsoil data for each of the three groups are given. To facilitate comparison, the moisture values in figure 3 for surface and subsoils are shown connected by lines.

For coarse-textured soils, moisture content at field capacity and 60-centimeter tension were about equal (approximately 20 percent) for both surface and subsoils. Field-maximum values were about 5 percent higher than the 60-centimeter and field-capacity values in the surface layers but were about equal to them in the subsoils. Moisture-equivalent and 1/3-atmosphere values were considerably lower than field capacity in the coarse-textured soils. The moisture content at which these soils puddled was only slightly less than field-capacity or 60-centimeter water tension.

In the medium textural group, field capacity, 1/3-atmosphere moisture, moisture equivalent, and plastic limit are closely bunched at about 26 percent in the surface soils and 23 percent in the subsoils. The 60-centimeter moisture constant is higher by 6 to 7 percent in both surface and subsoils.

---

[2] Broadfoot, W.M. *Core vs. bulk samples in soil-moisture tension analysis.* In SOME FIELD, LABORATORY, AND OFFICE PROCEDURES FOR SOIL-MOISTURE MEASUREMENT. U.S. Forest Serv. South. Forest Expt. Sta. Occas. Paper 135, pp. 22-25. 1954.

ble 2.--Moisture constants, by weight, of coarse, medium, and fine soils

COARSE TEXTURE

extural compo-sition and isture constant	Surface soils			Subsoils			All soils		
	Samples	Mean	Standard deviation	Samples	Mean	Standard deviation	Samples	Mean	Standard deviation
	No.	- Percent -		No.	- Percent -		No.	- Percent -	
id	94	68	13.0	42	71	12.9	136	69	12.9
:	80	23	11.1	41	20	10.9	121	22	11.1
iy	96	9	5.0	42	9	4.5	138	9	4.9
	10	25	4.4	4	20	2.1	14	24	4.6
	10	19	4.9	4	17	1.4	14	18	4.2
; cm	30	28	8.7	9	27	3.3	39	28	7.7
nax	26	25	11.1	12	19	4.0	38	23	9.8
-cm	17	20	8.2	9	19	12.0	26	20	9.4
-atm	25	11	6.6	5	8	3.1	30	11	6.3
	41	19	6.8	10	19	7.8	51	19	6.9
-atm	37	12	6.6	11	12	5.8	48	12	6.4
:	151	13	6.1	37	10	4.9	188	12	6.0
atm	72	5	2.5	19	5	2.5	91	5	2.5
'	51	7	3.6	13	7	5.0*	64	7	3.9
nin	17	4	1.6	10	6	3.7	27	5	2.6

MEDIUM TEXTURE

	Surface soils			Subsoils			All soils		
id	158	28	14.7	138	26	15.0	296	27	14.8
t	154	56	14.7	138	55	16.1	292	56	15.4
iy	160	16	6.2	138	19	6.2	298	17	6.3
	64	38	9.6	86	34	8.5	150	36	9.1
	63	28	6.2	86	22	5.2	149	25	6.3
; cm	78	44	11.2	50	38	13.4	128	42	12.4
nax	71	37	12.2	59	32	10.8	130	35	11.8
-cm	76	33	10.8	74	30	10.7	150	32	10.8
-atm	51	35	10.6	24	30	13.8	75	33	11.8
:	34	27	7.2	12	24	5.5	46	26	6.9
-atm	83	25	8.0	47	23	6.7	130	24	7.6
:	225	25	7.2	89	22	5.3	314	24	6.9
-atm	135	9	3.9	92	9	3.4	227	9	3.8
'	56	11	4.9	34	13	4.3	90	12	4.7
nin	66	10	5.4	54	10	3.7	120	10	4.7

FINE TEXTURE

	Surface soils			Subsoils			All soils		
id	49	17	11.6	69	15	11.9	118	16	11.7
t	47	42	14.6	68	48	14.4	115	45	14.6
iy	54	41	11.6	70	37	8.5	124	39	10.1
	20	49	11.2	43	51	12.8	63	50	12.2
	18	25	5.7	41	22	3.9	59	23	4.7
; cm	21	52	17.2	16	33	6.5	37	44	16.5
nax	23	35	6.7	22	29	6.4	45	32	7.2
-cm	18	34	7.2	26	30	6.1	44	32	6.8
-atm	14	43	9.5	2	31	5.7	16	41	9.9
	67	30	5.6	13	31	3.9	80	30	5.4
-atm	27	36	11.2	25	34	9.6	52	35	10.4
:	132	31	8.3	51	31	6.3	183	31	7.8
-atm	49	18	6.1	53	18	4.3	104	18	5.2
'	90	15	3.3	31	16	4.2	121	16	3.6
nin	29	13	4.0	26	14	3.8	55	13	3.9

The plastic limit for the fine-textured soils occurred about midway between field capacity and wilting point, or when approximately 50 percent of available water was present.

Wilting-point, field-minimum, and 15-atmosphere values are about 5 percent for the coarse-textured soils, 10 percent for medium-textured soils, and 15 percent for fine-textured soils. The field-minimum and wilting-point values are less than the 15-atmosphere value in the fine soils.

Soil moisture in percent by volume is shown in table 3 and figure 4. The values are similar to those calculated on a weight basis, but are not necessarily from the same set of samples.

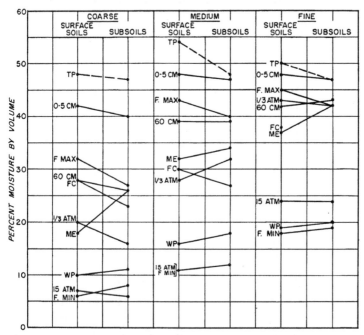

Figure 4.--*Average moisture constants, by volume, for coarse, medium, and fine soils.*

Table 3. --Moisture constants, by volume, of coarse, medium, and fine soils

COARSE TEXTURE

Total pore volume and moisture constant	Surface soils			Subsoils			All soils		
	Samples	Mean	Standard deviation	Samples	Mean	Standard deviation	Samples	Mean	Standard deviation
	No.	- Percent -		No.	- Percent -		No.	- Percent -	
Total pores	79	48	7.0	20	47	6.2	99	47	6.8
0-5 cm	14	42	5.2	8	40	3.7	22	41	4.8
F max	26	32	9.6	12	27	8.8	38	30	9.5
60-cm	14	28	9.9	9	26	13.7	23	27	11.2
0.1-atm	7	20	10.8	4	12	5.9	11	17	9.9
FC	14	28	7.7	5	23	2.4	19	26	7.0
1/3-atm	17	20	9.1	10	16	6.8	27	19	8.4
ME	46	18	7.1	2	26	7.8	48	18	7.2
15-atm	28	7	3.2	14	6	3.4	42	7	3.2
WP	12	10	3.4	3	11	.7	15	11	3.0
F min	16	6	2.1	10	8	3.6	26	7	2.9

MEDIUM TEXTURE

Total pore volume and moisture constant	Surface soils			Subsoils			All soils		
	Samples	Mean	Standard deviation	Samples	Mean	Standard deviation	Samples	Mean	Standard deviation
Total pores	195	54	6.4	124	48	7.6	319	51	7.4
0-5 cm	50	48	7.4	50	47	8.6	100	47	8.0
F max	69	43	6.8	59	40	7.2	128	42	7.1
60-cm	74	39	7.1	74	39	6.6	148	39	6.8
0.1-atm	24	33	7.1	24	36	9.1	48	34	8.2
FC	21	30	6.5	9	27	3.9	30	29	6.0
1/3-atm	48	28	7.4	44	32	5.7	92	30	6.9
ME	98	32	5.5	22	34	6.0	120	38	5.6
15-atm	86	11	3.9	86	12	4.5	172	12	4.3
WP	25	16	6.1	18	18	4.5	43	17	5.5
F min	55	11	5.4	54	12	5.1	109	12	5.2

FINE TEXTURE

Total pore volume and moisture constant	Surface soils			Subsoils			All soils		
	Samples	Mean	Standard deviation	Samples	Mean	Standard deviation	Samples	Mean	Standard deviation
Total pores	50	50	6.0	52	47	6.0	102	48	6.2
0-5 cm	8	48	6.7	16	47	7.3	24	48	7.0
F max	20	45	4.0	22	42	7.0	42	43	5.9
60-cm	12	42	5.5	26	43	7.2	38	43	6.7
0.1-atm	1	51	.0	2	42	6.4	3	45	6.7
FC	4	38	11.3	...	...	...	4	38	11.3
1/3-atm	9	43	16.6	15	42	7.1	24	43	11.3
ME	30	37	7.0	12	42	6.9	42	38	7.3
15-atm	16	24	6.8	36	24	6.5	52	24	6.5
WP	17	19	4.2	7	20	1.4	24	20	3.1
F min	19	18	4.6	17	19	7.7	36	18	6.2

SOIL-MOISTURE CONSTANTS
AS RELATED TO LAND USE AND AERATION

Data representing known land-use conditions were grouped into three categories: forest, old field, and pasture.

The forest category was comprised of all soils supporting a moderately well-stocked stand of trees, whether or not the soils were virgin. Some of the samples were from 10- to 15-year-old pine plantations on abandoned farm land. These sites were classed as forest because only the surface layer was sampled, and it was felt that the trees had had enough time to influence this layer.

The old-field category included only former cultivated fields that had herbaceous cover at the time of sampling and were not grazed. Grazed old fields, as well as grazed woodland, were included in the pasture category.

The surface soils under forest had better structure than either the old-field or pasture soils (table 4, figure 5).

Table 4. --Porosity and moisture constants, by volume, for surface soils under different land uses

Total porosity and moisture constant	Forest			Old field			Pasture		
	Samples	Mean	Standard deviation	Samples	Mean	Standard deviation	Samples	Mean	Standard deviation
	No.	- Percent -		No.	- Percent -		No.	- Percent -	
Total pores	67	56	8	72	50	7	47	51	6
0-5 cm	22	47	9	13	45	4	23	46	6
F max	24	36	9	33	41	6	25	43	8
60-cm	33	36	8	21	37	5	33	41	6
1/3-atm	22	22	8	20	32	10	19	28	8
ME	25	24	10	30	32	8	12	36	4
15-atm	38	8	4	52	15	8	34	14	6
F min	22	8	4	25	13	6	23	12	6

Total pore volume was 56 percent in the forest soils, 50 percent in the old fields, and 51 percent in the pasture soils. Inclusion of the grazed woodland soils in the pasture category probably increased the average porosity to that of old fields.

At field maximum and 60-centimeter tension, which represent wet condition or water-holding capacity, soils in all three categories were close together, but the forest soils had the most space for further absorption of water (as indicated in figure 5 by the difference between the 60-cm and 0-5 cm value--roughly the volume of big pores). The additional space amounted to about 11 percentage points, that is, 0.11 inch of water per inch of soil under forests as compared to about 0.08 inch in old field and 0.05 inch in

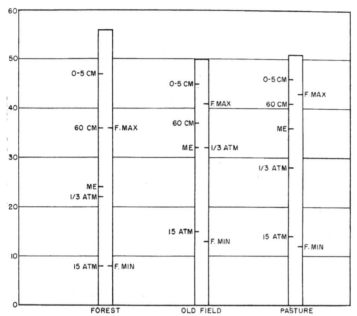

igure 5.--*Average moisture constants of surface soils in forests, old fields, and pastures. otal pore volume is indicated by the height of the bars.*

astures. This comparison would indicate that, in the surface 12 inches, ne forest soils could absorb about 1/2-inch more rain than the pasture and ld-field soils.

The degree of soil aeration, as measured by the amount of big pores, s an important criterion in estimating plant-soil-water relationships. On ell-drained sites, soils with considerable volume of big pores empty uickly after saturation and permit entry of air. Another commonly used ndex of aeration is drainage capacity. The relationships of big-pore olume and drainage capacity to soil texture and land use are shown in ables 5 and 6. Both properties seem well correlated with texture. Surface oils had consistently more big-pore volume and higher drainage capacity nan subsoils.

The influence of land use is also apparent, in that forest soils have ubstantially more big pores and greater drainage capacity than old-field or asture soils. Cultivation and trampling by livestock are probably re-ponsible for the differences.

- 11 -

Table 5. --Average volume of big pores, by textural groups and land-use categories

Textural group and land use	Surface soils			Subsoils			All soils		
	Samples	Mean	Standard deviation	Samples	Mean	Standard deviation	Samples	Mean	Standard deviation
	No.	- Percent -		No.	- Percent -		No.	- Percent -	
Textural group									
Sand	5	30	8	4	31	6	9	30	7
Loamy sand	5	17	12	1	9	0	6	16	11
Sandy loam	27	16	9	6	14	7	33	16	9
Average for coarse soils	37	18	10	11	20	11	48	18	10
Sandy clay loam	3	22	6	4	22	13	7	22	10
Loam	25	19	8	16	11	6	41	16	8.
Silt loam	102	17	9	64	9	6	166	14	9
Silt	4	11	11	3	16	12	7	13	11
Sandy clay	1	24	0	1	10	0	2	17	10
Average for medium soils	135	17	9	88	10	7	223	15	9
Silty clay loam	12	12	5	21	8	12	33	9	5
Clay loam	3	6	11	2	9	4	5	7	8
Silty clay	5	10	7	2	4	4	7	8	7
Clay	3	23	14	10	5	5	13	9	11
Average for fine soils	23	12	8	35	6	4	58	9	7
Land use									
Forest	45	19	9	...	...	...	...	...	...
Old field	21	13	7	...	...	...	...	...	...
Pasture	33	9	6	...	...	...	...	...	...

Table 6. --Average drainage capacity, by volume, for textural groups and land-use categories

Textural group and land use	Surface soils			Subsoils			All soils		
	Samples	Mean	Standard deviation	Samples	Mean	Standard deviation	Samples	Mean	Standard deviation
	No.	- Percent -		No.	- Percent -		No.	- Percent -	
Textural group									
Sand	4	35	9	2	37	3	6	36	7
Loamy sand	2	34	7	1	32	0	3	33	5
Sandy loam	26	31	13	9	30	8	35	31	12
Average for coarse soils	32	32	12	12	31	7	44	32	11
Sandy clay loam	1	13	0	1	9	0	2	11	3
Loam	9	27	13	6	25	15	15	26	13
Silt loam	39	26	12	38	18	13	77	22	13
Average for medium soils	50	25	13	46	20	14	95	23	13
Silty clay loam	8	10	6	9	6	4	17	8	5
Clay loam	2	18	1	2	10	5	4	14	5
Clay	2	6	8	3	3	-6	5	4	6
Average for fine soils	14	10	6	15	6	5	29	8	6
Land use									
Forest	45	35	3	...	...	...	...	...	...
Old field	50	19	3	...	...	...	...	...	...
Pasture	31	21	8	...	...	...	...	...	...

ESTIMATION OF BULK DENSITY FROM SOIL PROPERTIES

It is often necessary to express moisture content in inches of water per unit depth of soil. If the bulk density is known, the volumetric moisture content can be calculated by multiplying bulk density by moisture content calculated on a weight basis. The product, multiplied by the depth of soil, expresses moisture as the rainfall equivalent in area-inches.

Owing to its great variation, bulk density is not easy to determine in the field. The swelling and shrinking of soils with addition and loss of water causes some differences, but structure probably accounts for more. Texture, organic content, occurrence of natural hardpans, and disturbances are also influential. In view of the importance of bulk density in soil-moisture studies, and the difficulties involved in its determination, an analysis was made to ascertain if it could be estimated from certain soil properties.

Average bulk-density values by textural class and land use are shown in table 7. There is a consistent increase in bulk density from surface soils to subsoil layers in all textural classes, except silt and sandy clay (these two classes were among those with fewest samples). In general, bulk density was lowest in the silt loams, loams, and other soils of medium texture, higher in the fine-textured soils, and highest in the sandy soils. The average was 1.28 for 319 samples of medium-textured soil, 1.37 for 100 samples of fine texture, and 1.38 for 95 samples of coarse or sandy soil. Standard deviation was slightly less than 0.2 gram per cubic centimeter.

Table 7.--Average soil bulk density, for textural classes and land-use categories

Textural group and land use	Surface soils			Subsoils			All soils		
	Samples	Mean	Standard deviation	Samples	Mean	Standard deviation	Samples	Mean	Standard deviation
	No.	Grams per cc		No.	Grams per cc		No.	Grams per cc	
Textural group									
Sand	8	1.40	0.11	4	1.49	0.04	12	1.43	0.09
Loamy sand	9	1.32	.52	3	1.44	.11	12	1.35	.16
Sandy loam	60	1.36	.21	11	1.42	.18	71	1.36	.20
Average for coarse soils	77	1.36	.20	18	1.44	.15	95	1.38	.19
Sandy clay loam	5	1.35	.15	4	1.36	.29	9	1.36	.21
Loam	45	1.24	.19	27	1.38	.17	72	1.29	.19
Silt loam	138	1.20	.20	89	1.39	.12	227	1.27	.22
Silt	5	1.29	.08	3	1.11	.36	8	1.22	.22
Sandy clay	2	1.50	.27	1	1.49	.00	3	1.50	.19
Average for medium soils	195	1.22	.20	124	1.38	.21	319	1.28	.22
Silty clay loam	23	1.30	.13	26	1.38	.13	49	1.34	.14
Clay loam	9	1.40	.18	6	1.50	.14	15	1.44	.17
Silty clay	5	1.31	.10	2	1.46	.12	7	1.35	.12
Clay	12	1.28	.20	17	1.44	.19	29	1.38	.21
Average for fine soils	49	1.31	.16	51	1.42	.15	100	1.37	.16
Land use									
Forest	67	1.12	.22	...	...	...	...	...	...
Old field	72	1.31	.18	...	...	...	...	...	...
Pasture	47	1.27	.17	...	...	...	...	...	...

Bulk density averaged 1.12 for the surface layers under forest cover, 1.27 for soils under pasture, and 1.31 for old-field soils with herbaceous cover. A substantial number of the samples in the pasture category were from grazed woodlands; the relatively high organic content of these samples probably lowered the bulk-density values for the category.

Single and multiple regressions and correlation coefficients were calculated to relate bulk density to various other soil properties (table 8). Of the factors chosen for analysis only clay content failed to show a highly significant relationship. All significant single correlations except for sand content were negative.

Table 8.--Bulk-density relationships, for surface and subsoil samples combined

Equations [1]	Samples	Independent variable	Mean		Correlation coefficient	Standard deviation from regression
			X	Y		
	No.					
$Y = 1.29 + .0015X_1$	345	S	30	1.33	+.18**	0.184
$Y = 1.46 - .0029X_6$	326	Si	50	1.32	-.31**	.177
$Y = 1.29 + .0015X_2$	326	C	20	1.32	+.10	.185
$Y = 1.47 - .0658X_3$	337	OM	2.64	1.29	-.69**	.149
$Y = 1.78 - .0196X_{11}$	170	PL	24	1.30	-.65**	.157
$Y = 1.44 + .001X_1 + .001X_2 - .010X_3$	...	...	...	...	+.75**	.138
$Y = 1.47 + .001X_1 - .100X_3$	...	...	...	...	+.75**	.138

[1] Y is predicted value.
**Significant at 1-percent level.

Organic content had the highest degree of correlation. Bulk density decreased by .0658 gm per cc. for each increase of one percent in organic matter content. A multiple regression involving sand and organic-matter content improved the prediction. Addition of clay to these other variables had no influence.

Here and in other comparisons, the variables chosen for analysis were those the authors deemed most likely to be related. If more extended analysis had been possible, other variables or combinations might have shown significance.

ESTIMATION OF "WET" MOISTURE CONSTANTS

　　　　Moisture held by a core of soil at 0 to 5 cm of water tension ap_
proximates the wettest condition of the soil, and when expressed as volume
is a measure of total pore space. The 60-centimeter water tension and
1/3-atmosphere pressure are often taken as the upper limit of available
soil moisture, or as a moisture content equivalent to the field capacity.
These three constants at the "wet end" of the soil-moisture range were
analyzed as to their relationships with several other properties. Results
are summarized in tables 9, 10, and 11.

Table 9.--Saturation (0-5 cm) relationships, for surface and subsoil samples combined;
moisture expressed as percent by volume

Equations [1]	Samples	Independent variable	Mean X	Mean Y	Correlation coefficient	Standard deviation from regression
	No.					
$Y = 49 - .077X_1$	132	S	30	47	-.22*	8
$Y = 42 + .086X_6$	132	Si	54	47	+.21*	8
$Y = 46 + .067X_2$	132	C	16	47	+.09	8
$Y = 42 + 2.099X_3$	132	OM	2.11	47	+.41**	7
$Y = 74 - 21.245X_5$	132	BD	1.27	47	-.59**	7
$Y = 48 - .141X_4$	132	BP	13	47	-.16	8
$Y = 30 + .413X_8$	116	F max	40	47	+.44**	8
$Y = 30 + .688X_{11}$	108	PL	25	48	+.64**	6
$Y = 36 + .315X_{12}$	108	LL	37	48	+.45**	7
$Y = 40 - .052X_1 + .055X_2 + 2.038X_3$	...	...	...	...	+.43**	7
$Y = 77 - .052X_1 - .136X_2 + .281X_3 - 21.16X_5$	...	...	...	...	+.60**	6

1/ Y is predicted value.
* Significant at 5-percent level.
**Significant at 1-percent level.

Table 10.--60-cm relationships, for surface and subsoil samples combined; moisture expressed
as percent by volume

Equations [1]	Samples	Independent variable	Mean X	Mean Y	Correlation coefficient	Standard deviation from regression
	No.					
$Y = 45 - .212X_1$	192	S	30	39	-.54**	7
$Y = 29 + .191X_6$	192	Si	52	39	+.44**	7
$Y = 35 + .216X_2$	192	C	18	39	+.30**	8
$Y = 36 + 1.409X_3$	192	OM	1.97	39	+.26**	8
$Y = 52 - 10.203X_5$	192	BD	1.30	39	-.25**	8
$Y = 46 - .563X_4$	192	BP	12	39	-.61**	7
$Y = 19 + .517X_8$	134	F max	39	39	+.59**	6
$Y = 29 + .461X_{11}$	116	PL	26	40	+.48**	6
$Y = 32 + .219X_{12}$	116	LL	38	40	+.37**	7
$Y = 53 - .275X_1 - .090X_6 + 1.182X_3 - 3.014X_5$	...	...	...	...	+.59**	7
$Y = 45 - .314X_1 - .064X_6 + .922X_3 + .324X_4$	...	...	...	...	+.43**	8
$Y = 64 - .194X_1 - .055X_3 - 15.061X_5$	...	...	...	...	+.59**	7
$Y = 44 - .110X_1 + 2.801X_3 - .584X_4$	...	...	...	...	+.81**	5
$Y = 46 - .268X_1 - .076X_6 + 1.446X_3$	...	...	...	...	+.59**	7
$Y = 42 - .210X_1 + 1.352X_3$	...	...	...	...	+.59**	7
$Y = 48 - .140X_1 - .432X_4$	...	...	...	...	+.47**	6

1/ Y is predicted value.
**Significant at 1-percent level.

Table 11.--1/3-atm relationships, for surface and subsoil samples combined; moisture expressed as percent by volume

Equations [1]	Samples	Independent variable	Mean		Correlation coefficient	Standard deviation from regression
			X	Y		
	No.					
$Y = 38 - .312X_1$	126	S	32	28	-.64**	8
$Y = 20 + .148X_6$	126	Si	53	28	+.26**	11
$Y = 16 + .745X_2$	126	C	16	28	+.79**	7
$Y = 28 + .193X_3$	118	OM	2.15	28	+.03	11
$Y = 16 + 9.556X_5$	135	BD	1.30	29	+.18*	11
$Y = 44 - .674X_7$	135	DC	22	29	-.81**	7
$Y = 28 + .130X_{11}$	107	PL	24	31	+.09	10
$Y = 14 - .167X_1 + .580X_2 + .130X_3 + 7.248X_5$	...	...	...	...	+.85**	6

[1] Y is predicted value.
* Significant at 5-percent level.
**Significant at 1-percent level.

In the regressions with sand content, the correlation coefficient was lowest for the 0-5 centimeter values and highest for the 1/3-atmosphere constants. The correlation coefficient of the silt factor was highest for the 60-centimeter constant. The clay factor was non-significant at 0-5 centimeters but highly significant in the 60-centimeter and 1/3-atmosphere comparisons. The correlations for sand content were negative, while those for silt and clay were positive.

The relationships with soil organic matter were highly significant at 0-5 centimeter and 60-centimeter tensions but non-significant at 1/3-atmosphere pressure. These relations were positive. Highly significant negative relationships were found between bulk density and 0-5 centimeter and 60-centimeter tensions; the relation with 1/3-atmosphere pressure was significant and positive.

There was a highly significant positive correlation between 0-5 cm tension and field maximum, plastic limit, and liquid limit. The relationship between 0-5 cm tension and big pores was non-significant, but when moisture tension was increased to 60-cm the correlation became highly significant. An interesting point in the correlation between field maximum and 60-cm tension was that the mean values of the 134 samples were 39 percent by volume for each variable. The relationships between plastic limit and 0-5 cm tension and 60-cm tension were significant at the one-percent level, but plastic limit was not significantly related to 1/3-atmosphere tension.

Several combinations of soil variables were used in multiple regressions in an attempt to reduce the standard deviations. For the 0-5 cm or saturation constant, a combination of the effects of sand, clay, and organic matter failed to reduce the standard deviation below that of organic matter alone. Adding one more variable, bulk density, reduced the standard deviation slightly.

The multiple regression with the highest degree of significance for the 60-centimeter relationships was a combination of sand content, organic matter, and big pores. The standard deviation from the regression was 5 percent, less than any of the single-factor deviations.

A multiple regression of 1/3-atmosphere moisture on 4 independent variables--sand, clay, organic matter, and bulk density--was slightly better than any single regression.

In a further test of these relationships, thirty samples, representing the entire textural range and a variety of parent materials, were selected at random from a large group of southern soils for which 0-5 and 60-centimeter moisture had been determined. The mean difference of these 30 determined values from the estimated values was computed (table 12). Here again, 0-5 cm moisture (saturation) was estimated with fair accuracy from bulk density alone. Moisture content at 60-centimeter tension was best estimated from sand, among the single variables; but the estimate was improved when sand, organic matter, and bulk density were used in conjunction.

Table 12.--Differences, in percent by volume, between estimated and actual values of saturation and 60-cm moisture

Methods of estimation	Average estimated values		Mean differences from actual values	
	Saturation	60-cm.	Saturation	60-cm.
Textural group mean	45.3	36.2	6.6	5.6
Sand	45.4	35.2	6.7	4.8
Silt	...	34.4	...	6.8
Clay	47.3	...	8.0	...
Organic matter	45.8	37.9	7.4	8.9
Bulk density	42.1	35.5	3.9	7.8
Plastic limit	44.9	37.9	5.2	5.4
Sand, clay, organic matter, bulk density	40.2	...	4.4	...
Sand, organic matter, bulk density	...	32.7	...	4.5
Sand, organic matter, big pores	...	37.9	...	5.7
Average	41.7	33.8	...	...

While scarcity of data prevented the inclusion of moisture equivalent in the regressions, the relationship between this value and 1/3-atmosphere is suggested in figures 2 and 3.

ESTIMATION OF 15-ATMOSPHERE CONSTANT

Moisture content of the soil at 15-atmospheres tension is widely used to delineate the lower limit of water available for plant growth. Because of the general utility of this value, an attempt was made to develop equations to predict it from various other soil properties, singly and in combination. The properties used in the analysis were field minimum moisture, bulk density, and percentages of sand, silt, clay, and organic matter.

The close relationship between 15-atmosphere values and wilting-point is generally recognized. Lack of data prevented regression analysis of these two values, but available information is summarized in figure 6. In this chart, 15-atmosphere values average about the same as those for wilting point in coarse and medium soils but go slightly higher in the fine-textured soils. For most texture classes wilting-point values were above those for field minimum.

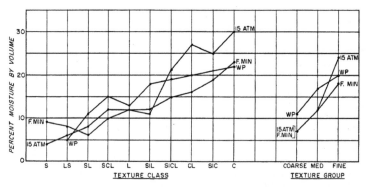

Figure 6.--*Variation of three "dry" moisture constants with soil texture.*

The relationships of 15-atmosphere moisture and silt, organic matter, and bulk density were not significant (table 13). Those for sand and clay content, and for field minimum, were highly significant. The smallest standard deviation from regression was 4 percent by volume for the clay variable. Two multiple regressions did not reduce the standard error of estimate below that for the single regression on clay.

A separate correlation was attempted between 15-atmosphere moisture and liquid limit. Here the 15-atmosphere value, as well as liquid limit, was expressed as percent by weight, rather than by volume. Though liquid limit is not a "dry end" constant, it approximates saturation

- 18 -

Table 13. --15-atm relationships, for surface and subsoil samples combined; moisture in percent by volume

Equations [1]	Samples	Independent variable	Mean		Correlation coefficient	Standard deviation from regression
			X	Y		
	No.					
$Y = 18 - .145X_1$	241	S	31	13	-.43**	7
$Y = 15 - .029X_6$	241	Si	50	13	-.08	7
$Y = 4 + .483X_2$	246	C	19	14	+.84**	4
$Y = 12 + .543X_3$	236	OM	1.96	13	+.11	7
$Y = 12 + 1.276X_5$	241	BD	1.33	13	+.03	7
$Y = 4 + .815X_9$	130	F min	12	14	+.73**	5
$Y = -7 + .265X_1 + .504X_2 + 1.121X_3 - 068X_5$	...	...	...	...	+.68**	5
$Y = 2 + .463X_2 + 1.115X_3$	...	...	...	...	+.84**	4

[1] Y is predicted value.
**Significant at 1-percent level.

percentage, which in turn has been useful as an indication of water-holding capacity and texture[3]. The regression equation was $Y = -2.0 + .36X_{12}$ where Y is 15-atmosphere moisture and X_{12} is liquid limit. The correlation coefficient, +.85, was significant at the one-percent level. The standard deviation of the regression was 2.9

---

[3] Wilcox, L.V.
   1951. *A method for calculating the saturation percentage from the weight of a known volume of saturated soil paste.* Soil Sci. 72: 233-237, illus.

ESTIMATION OF AVAILABLE WATER CAPACITY

Data on available water capacity, as calculated by various methods, were tabulated to indicate the relationship of this constant to soil texture and land use. An attempt was also made to estimate available water capacity from other soil properties.

Four methods of calculating available water capacity were used:

(1) Determining the field moisture index, or the difference between field maximum and field minimum.
(2) Subtracting the water held at 15-atmospheres pressure from the water retained at 60-centimeters tension.
(3) Subtracting the 15-atmosphere value from the 1/3-atmosphere value.
(4) Subtracting wilting point from the field capacity.

Table 14 shows average values for each textural class and land-use category. Both in surface and subsoil, medium-textured soils tended to be highest in available water capacity and coarse-textured soils lowest.

In general, the first method of determination--field maximum less field minimum--gave the highest values. Capacities obtained by subtracting 15-atmosphere from 60-centimeter values usually were next highest.

In determinations by the first two methods, medium-textured soils tended to have the greatest water capacity, and coarse-textured soils the least. These relationships did not follow this pattern in the 1/3- and 15-atmosphere comparisons, nor in the field capacity-wilting point determinations. The authors attributed these differences to seemingly high wilting-points for some samples from medium soils, and to high 1/3-atmosphere values for some fine soils. The high 1/3-atmosphere values were from sieved or disturbed material. There was no explanation for the high wilting-point values, except perhaps the authors' predilections.

Samples of known bulk density were used to compute available water capacity on a volumetric basis. The values in table 15 are presented as inches of available water capacity per inch of soil for each textural class, so that they can be used to derive water capacity for any depth of soil. In figure 7, these data are averaged by texture groups. This chart and table 15 illustrate the same general moisture-capacity trends noted in table 14.

The capacities obtained by subtracting 15-atmosphere values from 60-centimeter values were correlated with several soil properties. This method was chosen because the authors believed that the 60-centimeter determination closely approximated the upper limit of available water for all textural classes. The best estimate of available water capacity was obtained from silt content and field moisture index (table 16). Highly significant correlations were also obtained with clay, bulk density, field maximum, field minimum, plastic limit, and liquid limit.

Table 14. --<u>Average available water capacity, percent by weight, as determined by 4 methods</u>

FIELD MAXIMUM MINUS FIELD MINIMUM

Textural group and land use	Surface soils			Subsoils			All soils		
	Samples	Mean	Standard deviation	Samples	Mean	Standard deviation	Samples	Mean	Standard deviation
	No.	- Percent -		No.	- Percent -		No.	- Percent -	
Textural group									
Sand	2	12	2	2	7	1	4	10	3
Loamy sand	1	13	0	1	9	0	2	11	3
Sandy loam	18	19	9	7	15	3	25	18	8
Average for coarse soils	21	18	9	10	13	4	31	16	8
Sandy clay loam	1	25	0	3	19	4	4	20	4
Loam	11	26	7	10	17	5	21	21	8
Silt loam	42	28	11	40	23	9	82	26	10
Average for medium soils	55	28	10	54	22	10	109	25	10
Silty clay loam	9	20	4	5	18	4	14	19	4
Clay loam	4	22	4	2	8	1	6	18	8
Silty clay	2	20	2	2	14	5	4	17	5
Clay	4	19	8	7	14	5	11	16	6
Average for fine soils	19	20	5	16	14	5	35	18	5
Land use									
Forest	21	28	9	...	...	...	...	...	...
Old field	25	29	6	...	...	...	...	...	...
Pasture	23	31	6	...	...	...	...	...	...

60-CENTIMETERS TENSION MINUS 15 ATMOSPHERES

Textural group and land use	Surface soils			Subsoils			All soils		
Textural group									
Sand	4	11	8	4	7	3	8	9	6
Loamy soils	2	18	6	1	18	0	3	18	4
Sandy loam	9	16	5	4	22	6	13	18	6
Average for coarse soils	15	15	6	9	15	9	24	15	7
Sandy clay loam	...	...	...	4	12	4	4	12	4
Loam	17	22	7	15	19	7	32	21	7
Silt loam	57	25	9	54	21	9	111	23	9
Average for medium soils	75	25	8	74	20	9	149	23	9
Silty clay loam	4	16	3	14	14	4	18	14	4
Clay loam	3	16	7	2	10	6	5	14	6
Silty clay	5	17	7	2	11	1	7	15	6
Clay	1	8	0	7	14	7	8	13	7
Average for fine soils	13	16	6	25	13	5	38	14	5
Land use									
Forest	36	26	6	...	...	...	...	...	...
Old field	21	27	5	...	...	...	...	...	...
Pasture	33	27	7	...	...	...	...	...	...

1/3-ATMOSPHERE TENSION MINUS 15 ATMOSPHERES

Textural group and land use	Surface soils			Subsoils			All soils		
Textural group									
Sand	11	4	3	2	2	1	13	4	3
Loamy sand	8	4	3	1	2	0	9	4	3
Sandy loam	16	10	6	8	10	4	24	10	5
Average for coarse soils	35	7	5	11	8	5	46	7	5
Sandy clay loam	1	21	0	1	9	0	2	15	8
Loam	16	12	3	7	10	2	23	11	3
Silt loam	63	16	7	38	14	4	101	15	6
Average for medium soils	81	15	6	47	13	5	128	15	6
Silty clay loam	5	16	7	9	13	2	14	14	4
Clay loam	6	14	5	3	11	4	9	13	5
Silty clay	5	17	9	1	12	0	6	16	8
Clay	7	21	8	12	18	8	19	19	8
Average for fine soils	23	17	7	25	15	6	48	16	7
Land use									
Forest	23	13	7	...	...	...	...	...	...
Old field	33	19	6	...	...	...	...	...	...
Pasture	19	13	4	...	...	...	...	...	...

FIELD CAPACITY MINUS WILTING POINT

Textural group and land use	Surface soils			Subsoils			All soils		
Textural group									
Sand	2	6	2	...	...	...	2	6	2
Loamy sand	7	7	2	2	8	0	9	7	2
Sandy loam	10	11	2	5	10	4	15	11	3
Average for coarse soils	19	9	3	7	9	4	26	9	3
Sandy clay loam	1	12	0	1	6	0	2	9	4
Loam	4	13	2	5	13	2	9	13	2
Silt loam	1	17	0	1	15	0	2	16	1
Average for medium soils	6	14	3	8	12	4	14	13	3
Silty clay loam	9	13	2	2	18	2	11	14	2
Clay loam	8	14	4	2	14	8	10	14	4
Silty clay	...	...	...	...	...	...	...	...	...
Clay	39	16	3	9	11	3	48	15	4
Average for fine soils	56	15	4	13	13	4	69	15	4

Table 15.--Available water capacity in inches per inch of soil

Soil texture	Field moisture index		60-cm minus 15-atm		1/3-atm minus 15-atm		Field capacity minus wilting point	
	Surface	Subsoil	Surface	Subsoil	Surface	Subsoil	Surface	Subsoil
Sand	0.16	0.10	0.15	0.10	0.08	0.03	...	...
Loamy sand	.21	.14	.27	.27	.05	.04	0.09	0.10
Sandy loam	.25	.20	.22	.29	.15	.12	.20	.16
Sandy clay loam	.29	.23	...	.16	...	.13	.18	.16
Loam	.29	.21	.26	.25	.12	.12	.16	.17
Silt loam	.32	.28	.30	.27	.19	.19	.16	...
Sandy clay	...	...	...	...	.27	...	...	.08
Silt	.30	.40	.34	.34	...	.20	...	...
Silty clay loam	.28	.25	.21	.20	.18	.18	...	...
Clay loam	.28	.14	.22	.15	.10	.12	.18	...
Silty clay	.26	.20	.21	.17	.18	.17	...	...
Clay	.25	.20	.12	.21	.37	.18	.23	...

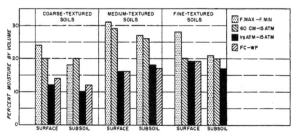

Figure 7.--*Available water capacities, by four methods of determination.*

Table 16.--Available water capacity relationships (60-cm minus 15-atm), for surface and subsoil samples combined; moisture expressed as percent by volume

Equations [1]	Samples	Independent variable	Mean		Correlation coefficient	Standard deviation from regression
			X	Y		
	No.					
Y = 28 − .072X₁	120	S	31	26	−.20*	7
Y = 16 + .189X₆	120	Si	52	26	+.51**	6
Y = 31 − .300X₂	120	C	17	26	−.48**	7
Y = 25 + .523X₃	120	OM	2.10	26	+.11	8
Y = 39 − 10.326X₅	120	BD	1.26	26	−.30**	7
Y = 28 − .136X₄	120	BP	14	26	−.16	7
Y = 17 + .229X₈	120	F max	39	26	+.26**	7
Y = 31 − .445X₉	120	F min	12	26	−.38**	7
Y = 12 + .524X₁₀	120	FMI	27	26	+.56**	6
Y = 18 + .298X₁₁	105	PL	26	26	+.28**	7
Y = 33 − .184X₁₂	105	LL	38	26	−.29**	7

1/ Y is predicted value.
* Significant at 5-percent level.
**Significant at 1-percent level.

BIBLIOGRAPHY

Aldrich, D.G., and Martin, J.P.
1952. EFFECT OF FUMIGATION ON SOME
CHEMICAL PROPERTIES OF SOILS.
Soil Sci. 73: 149-159, illus.

Allyn, R.B., and Work, R.A.
1941. THE AVAILAMETER AND ITS USE IN
SOIL MOISTURE CONTROL. II. CALI-
BRATION METHODS. Soil Sci. 51:
391-406, illus.

Anderson, M.A., and Browning, G.M.
1949. SOME PHYSICAL AND CHEMICAL
PROPERTIES OF SIX VIRGIN AND SIX
CULTIVATED IOWA SOILS. Soil Sci.
Soc. Amer. Proc. 14: 370-374.

Ashcroft, Gaylen, and Taylor, S.A.
1953. SOIL MOISTURE TENSION AS A MEAS-
URE OF WATER REMOVAL RATE FROM
SOIL AND ITS RELATION TO WEATHER
FACTORS. Soil Sci. Soc. Amer.
Proc. 17: 171-174.

Ayers, A.D.
1952. SEED GERMINATION AS AFFECTED BY
SOIL MOISTURE AND SALINITY. Agron.
Jour. 44: 82-84, illus.

Bhaumik, H.D., and Clark, F.E.
1947. SOIL MOISTURE TENSION AND MICRO-
BIOLOGICAL ACTIVITY. Soil Sci.
Soc. Amer. Proc. 12: 234-238,
illus.

Biswell, H.H.
1935. EFFECTS OF ENVIRONMENT UPON THE
ROOT HABITS OF CERTAIN DECIDUOUS
FOREST TREES. Bot. Gaz. 96: 676-
708, illus.

Blake, G.R., and Corey, A.T.
1951. LOW-PRESSURE CONTROL FOR MOISTURE-
RELEASE STUDIES. Soil Sci. 72:
327-331, illus.

Bodman, G.B., and Day, P.R.
1943. FREEZING POINTS OF A GROUP OF
CALIFORNIA SOILS AND THEIR EX-
TRACTED CLAYS. Soil Sci. 55:
225-246, illus.
————and Rubin, J.
1948. SOIL PUDDLING. Soil Sci. Soc.
Amer. Proc. 13: 27-36, illus.

Bouyoucos, G.J., and Mick, A.H.
1947. IMPROVEMENTS IN THE PLASTER OF
PARIS ABSORPTION BLOCK ELECTRICAL
RESISTANCE METHOD FOR MEASURING
SOIL MOISTURE UNDER FIELD CON-
DITIONS. Soil Sci. 63: 455-465,
illus.

Broadfoot, W.M.
1951. SOIL REHABILITATION UNDER EASTERN
REDCEDAR AND LOBLOLLY PINE. Jour.
Forestry 49: 780-781.
————
1954. CORE VS. BULK SAMPLES IN SOIL-
MOISTURE TENSION ANALYSIS. In
Some Field, Laboratory, and
Office Procedures for Soil-
Moisture Measurement. U.S. Forest
Serv. South. Forest Expt. Sta.
Occas. Paper 135: 22-25.
[Processed.]
————and Raney, W.A.
1954. PROPERTIES AFFECTING WATER RE-
LATIONS AND MANAGEMENT OF 14
MISSISSIPPI SOILS. Miss. Agr.
Expt. Sta. Bul. 521, 18 pp.,
illus.

Brown, D.A.
1953. CATION EXCHANGE IN SOILS THROUGH
THE MOISTURE RANGE, SATURATION TO
THE WILTING PERCENTAGE. Soil Sci.
Soc. Amer. Proc. 17: 92-96, illus.

Browning, G.M.
1941. RELATION OF FIELD CAPACITY TO
MOISTURE EQUIVALENT IN SOILS OF
WEST VIRGINIA. Soil Sci. 52:
445-450, illus.
————and Milam, F.M.
1941. A COMPARISON OF THE BRIGGS-McLANE
AND THE GOLDBECK-JACKSON CENTRI-
FUGE METHODS FOR DETERMINING THE
MOISTURE EQUIVALENT OF SOILS.
Soil Sci. 51: 273-278.
———— and Sudds, R.H.
1942. SOME PHYSICAL AND CHEMICAL PROP-
TIES OF THE PRINCIPAL ORCHARD
SOILS IN THE EASTERN PANHANDLE OF
WEST VIRGINIA. West Va. Agr.
Expt. Sta. Bul. 303, 56 pp.,
illus.

Campbell, R.B.
1952. FREEZING POINT OF WATER IN PUD-
DLED AND UNPUDDLED SOILS AT DIF-
FERENT SOIL MOISTURE TENSION
VALUES. Soil Sci. 73: 221-229,
illus.

Carlson, C.A., and Pierce, R.S.
1955. THE FIELD MAXIMUM MOISTURE CON-
TENT. Soil Sci. Soc. Amer. Proc.
19: 81-83, illus.
————Reinhart, K.G., and Horton, J.S.
1956. PREDICTING MOISTURE IN THE SURFACE
FOOT OF SOIL. Soil Sci. Soc. Amer.
Proc. 20: 412-415, illus.

Chandler, R.F., Jr.
1940. THE INFLUENCE OF GRAZING UPON CERTAIN SOIL AND CLIMATIC CONDITIONS IN FARM WOODLANDS. Jour. Amer. Soc. Agron. 32: 216-230, illus.

Chang, Chia Wei.
1941. AN EXPERIMENTAL STUDY ON THE DEVELOPMENT OF ADOBE STRUCTURES IN SOILS. Soil Sci. 52: 213-227, illus.

Colman, E.A., and Hendrix, T.M.
1949. THE FIBERGLAS ELECTRICAL SOIL-MOISTURE INSTRUMENT. Soil Sci. 67: 425-438, illus.

Corey, A.T., and Blake, G.R.
1953. MOISTURE AVAILABLE TO VARIOUS CROPS IN SOME NEW JERSEY SOILS. Soil Sci. Soc. Amer. Proc. 17: 314-317, illus.

Cykler, J.F.
1946. EFFECT OF VARIATIONS IN AVAILABLE SOIL WATER ON YIELD AND QUALITY OF POTATOES. Agr. Engin. 27: 363-366, illus.

Decker, G.J.
1953. APPLICATION OF THE SOIL MOISTURE CHARACTERISTIC CURVE. Agr. Engin. 34: 96-97, 102, illus.

Dennis, E.J., and Chesnin, Leon.
1953. THE AVAILABILITY OF PHOSPHORUS TO ALFALFA IN THE HORIZONS OF FOUR EASTERN NEBRASKA SOILS. Soil Sci. Soc. Amer. Proc. 17: 49-52.

Diebold, C.H.
1953. SIMPLE SOIL TEST TELLS WHEN TO IRRIGATE. What's New in Crops and Soils 5: 14-15, illus.

Dortignac, E.J.
1950. A SIMPLE VOLUME-WEIGHT SAMPLER AND PROCEDURE. Soil Sci. 69: 95-105, illus.

Dreibelbis, F.R., and Post, F.A.
1940. STUDIES ON SOIL MOISTURE RELATIONSHIPS AT THE NORTH APPALACHIAN EXPERIMENTAL WATERSHED. Soil Sci. Soc. Amer. Proc. 5: 377-385, illus.

Dyal, R.S., and Drosdoff, Matthew.
1943. PHYSICAL AND CHEMICAL PROPERTIES OF SOME IMPORTANT SOILS OF THE SOUTHEAST USED FOR THE PRODUCTION OF TUNG OIL. Soil Sci. Soc. Amer. Proc. 8: 317-322.

Feustel, I.C., and Byers, H.G.
1936. THE COMPARATIVE MOISTURE-ABSORBING AND MOISTURE-RETAINING CAPACITIES OF PEAT AND SOIL MIXTURES. U.S. Dept. Agr. Tech. Bul. 532, 25 pp., illus.

Frahm, E.E.
1948. CHEMICAL AND PHYSICAL CHARACTERISTICS OF BOWDOIN CLAY FROM THE MILK RIVER VALLEY OF MONTANA. Soil Sci. Soc. Amer. Proc. 13: 455-460, illus.

Free, G.R., Browning, G.M., and Musgrave, G.W.
1940. RELATIVE INFILTRATION AND RELATED PHYSICAL CHARACTERISTICS OF CERTAIN SOILS. U.S. Dept. Agr. Tech. Bul. 729, 51 pp., illus.

Gaiser, R.N.
1952. READILY AVAILABLE WATER IN FOREST SOILS. Soil Sci. Soc. Amer. Proc. 16: 334-338, illus.

Garey, C.L., and McHenry, J.R.
1947. DEPENDENCE OF CERTAIN PHYSICAL AND CHEMICAL MEASUREMENTS IN A SOIL PROFILE ON THE TYPE OF WATER-STABLE AGGREGATE. Soil Sci. Soc. Amer. Proc. 12: 44-49, illus.

Haise, H.R.
1948. FLOW PATTERN STUDIES IN IRRIGATED COARSE-TEXTURED SOILS. Soil Sci. Soc. Amer. Proc. 13: 83-89, illus.

Hanson, W.J., and Nex, R.W.
1953. DIFFUSION OF ETHYLENE DIBROMIDE IN SOILS. Soil Sci. 76: 209-214, illus.

Harradine, F.F.
1949. THE VARIABILITY OF SOIL PROPERTIES IN RELATION TO STAGE OF PROFILE DEVELOPMENT. Soil Sci. Soc. Amer. Proc. 14: 302-311, illus.

Harris, H.L., and Drew, W.B.
1943. ON THE ESTABLISHMENT AND GROWTH OF CERTAIN LEGUMES ON ERODED AND UNERODED SITES. Ecol. 24: 135-148, illus.

Hedrick, R.M., and Mowry, D.T.
1952. EFFECT OF SYNTHETIC POLYELECTROLYTES ON AGGREGATION, AERATION, AND WATER RELATIONSHIPS OF SOIL. Soil Sci. 73: 427-441, illus.

Hendrickson, A.H., and Veihmeyer, F.J.
1931. INFLUENCE OF DRY SOIL ON ROOT EXTENSION. Plant Physiol. 6: 567-576, illus.

_____and Veihmeyer, F.J.
1945. PERMANENT WILTING PERCENTAGES OF SOILS OBTAINED FROM FIELD AND LABORATORY TRIALS. Plant Physiol. 20: 517-539, illus.

Hoover,M.D.,Olson,D.F.,Jr., and Greene,G.E.
1953. SOIL MOISTURE UNDER A YOUNG LOB-
LOLLY PINE PLANTATION. Soil Sci.
Soc. Amer. Proc. 17: 147-150,
illus.
Hunter, J.R., and Erickson, A.E.
1952. RELATION OF SEED GERMINATION TO
SOIL MOISTURE TENSION. Agron.
Jour. 44: 107-109, illus.
Jamison, V.C.
1953. CHANGES IN AIR-WATER RELATION-
SHIPS DUE TO STRUCTURAL IMPROVE-
MENT OF SOILS. Soil Sci. 76:
143-151, illus.
_____and Reed, I.F.
1949. DURABLE ASBESTOS TENSION TABLES.
Soil Sci. 67: 311-318, illus.
Klute, A., and Jacob, W.C.
1949. PHYSICAL PROPERTIES OF SASSAFRAS
SILT LOAM AS AFFECTED BY LONG-
TIME ORGANIC MATTER ADDITIONS.
Soil Sci. Soc. Amer. Proc. 14:
24-28, illus.
Lecompte, S.B., Jr.
1952. AN INSTRUMENT FOR MEASURING SOIL
MOISTURE. N. J. Hort. News 33:
2563, 2568, 2572, illus.
Laws, W.D., and Evans, D.D.
1949. THE EFFECTS OF LONG-TIME CULTI-
VATION ON SOME PHYSICAL AND
CHEMICAL PROPERTIES OF TWO
RENDZINA SOILS. Soil Sci. Soc.
Amer. Proc. 14: 15-19, illus.
Legg, J.O., and Beacher, R.L.
1952. THE POTASSIUM SUPPLYING POWER OF
REPRESENTATIVE ARKANSAS SOILS.
Soil Sci. Soc. Amer. Proc. 16:
210-214, illus.
Lewis, M.R.
1937. RATE OF FLOW OF CAPILLARY MOISTURE.
U.S. Dept. Agr. Tech. Bul. 579,
29 pp., illus.
Lunt, H.A.
1948. THE FOREST SOILS OF CONNECTICUT.
Conn. Agr. Expt. Sta. Bul. 523,
93 pp., illus.
_____
1950. LIMING AND TWENTY YEARS OF LITTER
RAKING AND BURNING UNDER RED (AND
WHITE) PINE. Soil Sci. Soc. Amer.
Proc. 15: 381-390, illus.
Lutz, H.J.
1940. DISTURBANCE OF FOREST SOIL RE-
SULTING FROM THE UPROOTING OF
TREES. Yale Univ. Forestry Bul.
45, 37 pp., illus.

Lutz, H.J.
1944. DETERMINATION OF CERTAIN PHYSICAL
PROPERTIES OF FOREST SOILS. I:
METHODS UTILIZING SAMPLES COL-
LECTED IN METAL CYLINDERS. Soil
Sci. 57: 475-487.
_____
1944. DETERMINATION OF CERTAIN PHYSICAL
PROPERTIES OF FOREST SOILS. II:
METHODS UTILIZING LOOSE SAMPLES
COLLECTED FROM PITS. Soil Sci. 58:
325-333.
McGinnies, W.G., and Arnold, J.F.
1939. RELATIVE WATER REQUIREMENTS OF
ARIZONA RANGE PLANTS. Univ. Ariz.
Tech. Bul. 80, 246 pp., illus.
McHenry, J.R., and Rhoades, H.F.
1942. INFLUENCE OF CALCIUM CARBONATE
CONTENT AND EXCHANGEABLE SODIUM-
CALCIUM RATIO ON CONSISTENCY
CONSTANTS, RESIDUAL SHRINKAGE,
MOISTURE EQUIVALENT, AND HYGRO-
SCOPIC COEFFICIENT OF SOILS.
Soil Sci. Soc. Amer. Proc. 7:
42-47, illus.
Martin, J.P., and Chapman, H.D.
1951. VOLATILIZATION OF AMMONIA FROM
SURFACE-FERTILIZED SOILS. Soil
Sci. 71: 25-34.
Middleton, H.E.
1930. PROPERTIES OF SOILS WHICH IN-
FLUENCE SOIL EROSION. U.S. Dept.
Agr. Tech. Bul. 178, 16 pp.
_____ Slater, C.S., and Byers, H.G.
1934. THE PHYSICAL AND CHEMICAL CHARAC-
TERISTICS OF THE SOILS FROM THE
EROSION EXPERIMENT STATIONS--
SECOND REPORT. U.S. Dept. Agr.
Tech. Bul. 430, 62 pp., illus.
Miller, R.D., and Richard, F.
1952. HYDRAULIC GRADIENTS DURING IN-
FILTRATION IN SOILS. Soil Sci.
Soc. Amer. Proc. 16: 33-38, illus.
Moore, R.E.
1940. THE RELATION OF SOIL TEMPERATURE
TO SOIL MOISTURE: PRESSURE PO-
TENTIAL, RETENTION, AND INFIL-
TRATION RATE. Soil Sci. Soc. Amer.
Proc. 5: 61-64, illus.
Morgan, M.F., and Street, O.E.
1939. SEASONAL WATER AND NITRATE LEACH-
INGS IN RELATION TO SOIL AND
SOURCE OF FERTILIZER NITROGEN.
Conn. Agr. Expt. Sta. Bul. 429,
43 pp.

Moser, U.S., and Olson, R.V.
    1953. SULPHUR OXIDATION IN FOUR SOILS AS INFLUENCED BY SOIL MOISTURE TENSION AND SULPHUR BACTERIA. Soil Sci. 76: 251-257, illus.

Neller, J.R., and Kelley, W.H.
    1949. WOOD WASTE LIGNINS TO PRODUCE SOIL ORGANIC MATTER OF A STABLE NATURE. Soil Sci. Soc. Amer. Proc. 14: 212-215.

Nijhawan, S.D., and Olmstead, L.B.
    1947. THE EFFECT OF SAMPLE PRETREATMENT UPON SOIL AGGREGATION IN WET-SIEVE ANALYSIS. Soil Sci. Soc. Amer. Proc. 12: 50-53.

Oskamp, Joseph.
    1938. SOILS IN RELATION TO FRUIT GROWING IN NEW YORK. PART XII: TREE BEHAVIOR ON IMPORTANT SOIL PROFILES IN THE PERU, PLATTSBURG, AND CROWN POINT AREAS IN CLINTON AND ESSEX COUNTIES. Cornell Univ. Agr. Expt. Sta. Bul. 705, 27 pp.

Pearson, G.A.
    1931. FOREST TYPES IN THE SOUTHWEST AS DETERMINED BY CLIMATE AND SOIL. U.S. Dept. Agr. Tech. Bul. 247, 143 pp., illus.

Peele, T.C., and Beale, O.W.
    1950. RELATION OF MOISTURE EQUIVALENT TO FIELD CAPACITY AND MOISTURE RETAINED AT 15 ATMOSPHERES PRESSURE TO THE WILTING PERCENTAGE. Agron. Jour. 42: 604-607, illus.

—————— Beale, O.W., and Lesesne, F.F.
    1948. IRRIGATION REQUIREMENTS OF SOUTH CAROLINA SOILS. Agr. Engin. 29: 157-158, 161.

Peters, D.B., Hagan, R.M., and Bodman, G.B.
    1953. AVAILABLE MOISTURE CAPACITIES OF SOILS AS AFFECTED BY ADDITIONS OF POLYELECTROLYTE SOIL CONDITIONERS. Soil Sci. 75: 467-471.

Pillsbury, A.F.
    1947. FACTORS INFLUENCING INFILTRATION RATES INTO YOLO LOAM. Soil Sci. 64: 171-181, illus.

Powers, W.L., Jones, J.S., and Ruzek, C.V.
    1939. COMPOSITION, RATING, AND CONSERVATION OF WILLAMETTE VALLEY SOILS. Ore. Agr. Expt. Sta. Bul. 365, 38 pp., illus.

Rader, L.F., Jr., White, L.M., and Whittaker, C.W.
    1943. THE SALT INDEX--A MEASURE OF THE EFFECT OF FERTILIZERS ON THE CONCENTRATION OF THE SOIL SOLUTION. Soil Sci. 55: 201-218.

Reisenauer, H.M., and Colwell, W.E.
    1950. SOME FACTORS AFFECTING THE ABSORPTION OF CHLORINE BY TOBACCO. Soil Sci. Soc. Amer. Proc. 15: 222-229, illus.

Reitemeier, R.F.
    1946. EFFECT OF MOISTURE CONTENT ON THE DISSOLVED AND EXCHANGEABLE IONS OF SOILS OF ARID REGIONS. Soil Sci. 61: 195-214, illus.

—————— and Richards, L.A.
    1944. RELIABILITY OF THE PRESSURE-MEMBRANE METHOD FOR EXTRACTION OF SOIL SOLUTION. Soil Sci. 57: 119-135, illus.

Reuther, Walter, and Crawford, C.L.
    1947. EFFECT OF CERTAIN SOIL AND IRRIGATION TREATMENTS ON CITRUS CHLOROSIS IN A CALCAREOUS SOIL. II: SOIL ATMOSPHERE STUDIES. Soil Sci. 63: 227-240, illus.

Richards, L.A.
    1941. A PRESSURE-MEMBRANE EXTRACTION APPARATUS FOR SOIL SOLUTION. Soil Sci. 51: 377-386, illus.

—————— and Fireman, Milton.
    1943. PRESSURE-PLATE APPARATUS FOR MEASURING MOISTURE SORPTION AND TRANSMISSION BY SOILS. Soil Sci. 56: 395-404, illus.

—————— and Weaver, L.R.
    1943. FIFTEEN-ATMOSPHERE PERCENTAGE AS RELATED TO THE PERMANENT WILTING PERCENTAGE. Soil Sci. 56: 331-339, illus.

—————— Campbell, R.B., and Healton, L.H.
    1949. SOME FREEZING POINT DEPRESSION MEASUREMENTS ON CORES OF SOIL IN WHICH COTTON AND SUNFLOWER PLANTS WERE WILTED. Soil Sci. Soc. Amer. Proc. 14: 47-50, illus.

Robertson, L.S., and Kohnke, Helmut.
    1946. THE pF AT THE WILTING POINT OF SEVERAL INDIANA SOILS. Soil Sci. Soc. Amer. Proc. 11: 50-52, illus.

Roe, H.B., and Park, J.K.
    1944. A STUDY OF THE CENTRIFUGE MOISTURE EQUIVALENT AS AN INDEX OF THE HYDRAULIC PERMEABILITY OF SATURATED SOILS. Agr. Engin. 25: 381-385, illus.

Russell, M.B., Klute, A., and Jacob, W.C.
    1952. FURTHER STUDIES ON THE EFFECT OF LONG-TIME ORGANIC MATTER ADDITIONS ON THE PHYSICAL PROPERTIES OF SASSAFRAS SILT LOAM. Soil Sci. Soc. Amer. Proc. 16: 156-159, illus.

Sherwood, L.V., and Engibous, J.C.
1953. STATUS REPORT ON SOIL CONDITION-
ING CHEMICALS. II. Soil Sci. Soc.
Amer. Proc. 17: 9-16, illus.
Shockley, D.R.
1955. CAPACITY OF SOIL TO HOLD MOISTURE.
Agr. Engin. 36: 109-112, illus.
Slater, C.S., and Bryant, J.C.
1946. COMPARISON OF FOUR METHODS OF
SOIL MOISTURE MEASUREMENT. Soil
Sci. 61: 131-155, illus.
Smith, H.W., and Rhoades, H.F.
1942. VARIATIONS IN THE BUTLER SOIL
SERIES IN NEBRASKA. Soil Sci. Soc.
Amer. Proc. 7: 460-465, illus.
Smith, R.M., and Browning, D.R.
1946. OCCURRENCE, NATURE, AND LAND-USE
SIGNIFICANCE OF "SILTPAN" SUB-
SOILS IN WEST VIRGINIA. Soil Sci.
62: 307-317, illus.
_____ and Browning, D.R.
1947. SOIL MOISTURE TENSION AND PORE
SPACE RELATIONS FOR SEVERAL SOILS
IN THE RANGE OF THE "FIELD
CAPACITY." Soil Sci. Soc. Amer.
Proc. 12: 17-21, illus.
Smith, W.O.
1944. THE EFFECT OF SOIL PHYSICAL
CONDITIONS ON MOISTURE CONSTANTS
IN THE UPPER CAPILLARY RANGE.
Soil Sci. 58: 1-16, illus.
Stephenson, R.E., and Schuster, C.E.
1941. LABORATORY, GREENHOUSE, AND FIELD
METHODS OF STUDYING FERTILIZER
NEEDS OF ORCHARD SOILS. Soil Sci.
52: 137-153.
Stone, J.T., and Garrison, C.S.
1940. RELATIONSHIP BETWEEN ORGANIC
MATTER CONTENT AND MOISTURE CON-
STANTS OF SOILS. Soil Sci. 50:
253-256.
Tharp, W.H., and Young, V.H.
1939. RELATION OF SOIL MOISTURE TO
FUSARIUM WILT OF COTTON. Jour.
Agr. Res. 58: 47-61, illus.
U.S. Bureau of Reclamation.
1948. LAND CLASSIFICATION REPORT,
WELTON-MOHAWK DIVISION, GILA
PROJECT, ARIZONA. U.S. Dept. Int.
[Processed.]
U.S. Forest Service and U.S. Army Engineers
Waterways Experiment Station.
1954. THE DEVELOPMENT OF METHODS FOR
PREDICTING SOIL MOISTURE CONTENT.
FORECASTING TRAFFICABILITY OF
SOILS, REPORT NO. 3. Technical
Memorandum 3-331, 2 vols. and
appendix.

Van Bavel, C.H.M., and Wilson, T.V.
1952. EVAPOTRANSPIRATION ESTIMATES AS
CRITERIA FOR DETERMINING TIME OF
IRRIGATION. Agr. Engin. 33:
417-418, 420, illus.
Veihmeyer, F.J., and Hendrickson, A.H.
1948. SOIL DENSITY AND ROOT PENETRATION.
Soil Sci. 65: 487-493.
_____ and Johnston, C.N.
1944. SOIL-MOISTURE RECORDS FROM BURNED
AND UNBURNED PLOTS IN CERTAIN
GRAZING AREAS OF CALIFORNIA.
Trans. Amer. Geophys. Union 25:
72-88, illus.
Volk, G.M.
1950. FACTORS DETERMINING EFFICIENCY
OF CYANAMID AND URAMON FOR WEED
CONTROL IN TOBACCO PLANTBEDS.
Soil Sci. 69: 377-390, illus.
Weaver, J.E., Hongen, V.H., and Weldon, M.D.
1935. RELATION OF ROOT DISTRIBUTION TO
ORGANIC MATTER IN PRAIRIE SOIL.
Bot. Gaz. 96: 389-420, illus.
Whitney, R.S., and Gardner, Robert.
1943. THE EFFECT OF CARBON DIOXIDE ON
SOIL REACTION. Soil Sci. 55:
127-141, illus.
Wilson, H.A., Riecken, F.F., and Browning, G.M.
1946. SOIL PROFILE CHARACTERISTICS IN
RELATION TO DRAINAGE AND LEVEL
TERRACES. Soil Sci. Soc. Amer.
Proc. 11: 110-118, illus.
Winterkorn, H.F.
1943. THE CONDITION OF WATER IN POROUS
SYSTEMS. Soil Sci. 56: 109-115,
illus.
Woodruff, C.M.
1940. SOIL MOISTURE AND PLANT GROWTH IN
RELATION TO pF. Soil Sci. Soc.
Amer. Proc. 5: 36-41, illus.
Work, R.A., and Lewis, M.R.
1934. MOISTURE EQUIVALENT, FIELD CA-
PACITY AND PERMANENT WILTING
PERCENTAGE AND THEIR RATIOS IN
HEAVY SOILS. Agr. Engin. 15:
355-362, illus.
Zwerman, P.J., Page, J.B., and Yoder, R.E.
1953. SOIL STRUCTURAL STABILITY OF
BROOKSTON CLAY AS A FACTOR IN
SUGAR BEET YIELDS. Soil Sci. Soc.
Amer. Proc. 17: 159-164, illus.

Occasional Paper 167 1959

SOIL-MOISTURE TRENDS
UNDER VARYING DENSITIES OF OAK OVERSTORY

PAUL T. KOSHI

SOUTHERN FOREST EXPERIMENT STATION
PHILIP A. BRIEGLEB, DIRECTOR
Forest Service, U.S. Department of Agriculture

Typical post oak stands, averaging 65 square feet of basal area per acre, were thinned, left undisturbed, or clearcut prior to observation of soil-moisture trends. The stand pictured here was subsequently thinned to 26 square feet of basal area per acre.

SOIL-MOISTURE TRENDS UNDER VARYING DENSITIES OF OAK OVERSTORY[1]

Paul T. Koshi
Southern Forest Experiment Station[2]

Plant growth, including the growth of forests, is profoundly affected by intricate interactions between the soil, the soil moisture, and the plants themselves. Understanding of so complex a relationship can be acquired only a little at a time as studies can be conducted in various soil types and different cover conditions.

Phases of these relationships were studied on one important soil type near College Station, Texas, in oak stands that had been thinned to three levels of basal area in a forage-production study. Electrical-resistance units were used to measure soil-moisture content in three soil horizons from May 1953 to August 1954. Laboratory determinations of physical soil characteristics afforded a basis for interpreting soil-moisture trends and for possible application of the data to other situations.

STUDY AREA

The study area is in southern Robertson County, Texas, 20 miles northeast of College Station. The site had not been burned or excessively grazed for 10 to 15 years. It is fairly representative of some 4,450,000 acres of woodland in the East Texas Post Oak Belt.

The study was conducted on four 1-acre plots located within four adjacent 5-acre blocks.

Vegetation

The vegetation of the area is typical of an upland site of the Post Oak Belt. Dominant trees are post oak (Quercus stellata Wangenh.) and blackjack oak (Q. marilandica Muenchh.), with winged elm (Ulmus alata Michx.), gum bumelia (Bumelia lanuginosa (Michx.) Pers.) and black hickory (Carya texana Buckl.) as associated species. Basal area averaged 65 square feet per acre on unthinned plots but had been reduced in 1951-52 to 26 square feet on the thinned plots and to zero on the clearcut areas. By 1954 growth on residual trees in the thinned stands had doubled (5)[3], probably reflecting a considerable expansion of root systems.

[1] This study was conducted in partial fulfillment of the requirements for the Ph.D degree at A & M College of Texas, College Station, Texas. The author wishes to acknowledge the aid of Dr. Robert A. Darrow and Wayne G. McCully in planning and conducting the studies, and the cooperation of Mr. Frank Seale in making the land available.

[2] East Texas Research Center, maintained at Nacogdoches, Texas, by the Southern Forest Experiment Station in cooperation with Stephen F. Austin State College.

[3] Underscored numbers in parentheses refer to Literature Cited, p. 11.

The chief understory shrubs were yaupon (Ilex vomitoria Ait.),
French mulberry (Callicarpa americana L.), tree sparkleberry (Vaccinium
arboreum Marsh.), and hawthorn (Crataegus spp.).

Grasses constituted 95 percent or more of the herbaceous cover.
Little bluestem (Andropogon scoparius Michx.) comprised 70 to 85 percent
of the forage in 1951 and 1952.[4] Oven-dry forage in 1951 prior to treatment ranged from 385 to 545 pounds per acre. Reduction in overstory
densities greatly stimulated forage growth in 1953 and 1954[5] (6), production in 1954 measuring 209, 484, and 1,106 pounds per acre respectively
on the undisturbed, thinned, and clearcut areas.

Other perennial grasses making up the herbaceous cover consisted
of paintbrush bluestem (A. ternarius Michx.), yellowsedge bluestem (A.
virginicus L.), paspalums (Paspalum spp.), panicums (Panicum spp.),
Indiangrass (Sorghastrum nutans (L.) Nash.), tall dropseed (Sporobolus
asper Kunth), brownseed paspalum (P. plicatulum Michx.), purpletop
(Tridens flavus Hitchc.), longleaf uniola (Uniola sessiliflora Poir.),
beaked panicum (P. anceps Michx.). Increases in paspalums and panicums
were observed in 1953 and 1954.

Topography and Soils

The topography is gently rolling with an easterly exposure. The
soils are Susquehanna-like or of the Susquehanna series of the Red and
Yellow Podzolic group, having a gray sandy surface soil that averages
about 6 inches in depth. The clay subsoils range in color from red to
yellow, with conspicuous mottling at lower depths. They are massive and
sticky when wet, become very hard upon drying, and swell and shrink considerably. After a substantial rain, the upper profile remains water-
logged for several days, indicating a very slowly permeable subsoil.

Physical properties of the soil were determined on four replications of the three oak treatments (table 1) 24 to 26 months after
the oaks had been cut. Soils on cleared sites showed very significantly[6]
higher bulk density at 0 to 6 inches, very significantly lower percentage of total aggregates at 6 to 12 inches, and significantly higher noncapillary and lower capillary pore space at 12 to 24 inches than those
on thinned sites. Differences from the unthinned sites were similar
except for noncapillary pore space, which was not significant. In
other respects, the soil physical factors did not differ significantly.

---

[4] Koshi, P.T. An evaluation of forage production under various densities of oak woodland. Master's thesis, A & M College of Texas, College Station, Texas, 62 pp. 1953.

[5] Koshi, P.T. An evaluation of forage production, vegetational composition, tree growth,
and physical characteristics of soils under varying densities of oak woodland overstory.
Ph.D. dissertation, A & M College of Texas, College Station, Texas, 116 pp. 1957.

[6] Where differences are described as significant, the 5-percent level of significance by
analysis of variance is implied. Highly or very significant implies the 1-percent
level.

Table 1.--Physical properties of soils

Soil layer and oak treatment	Textural class	Analysis			Total aggregation	Pore space			Bulk density
		Sand	Silt	Clay		Noncap-illary	Capil-lary	Total	
		- - Percent - - -			Percent	- - Percent - - -			Grams per cc
0- to 6-inch layer									
Oaks undisturbed	Sandy loam	71.4	21.1	7.5	(1)	12.0	29.4	41.4	1.45
Oaks thinned	Sandy loam	69.6	23.1	7.3	(1)	11.0	31.9	42.9	1.43
Oaks clearcut	Sandy loam	69.1	23.5	7.4	(1)	11.4	28.3	39.7	1.52**
6- to 12-inch layer									
Oaks undisturbed	Clay	35.8	11.4	52.8	39.1	10.2	38.3	48.5	1.41
Oaks thinned	Clay	34.7	10.7	54.6	46.6	9.5	38.4	47.9	1.42
Oaks clearcut	Clay	40.4	12.6	47.0	31.8**	10.6	38.1	48.7	1.37
12- to 24-inch layer									
Oaks undisturbed	Clay	31.9	9.1	59.0	31.8	8.8	41.9	50.7	1.42
Oaks thinned	Clay	35.6	11.2	53.2	37.6	7.4*	40.3	47.7	1.46
Oaks clearcut	Clay	37.0	11.9	51.1	22.8*	9.3	36.3*	45.6	1.49

[1] Not determined for surface soils, which were primarily of single-grain structure.

* Difference from comparable statistics for other treatments significant at 0.05 level.

**Difference from comparable statistics for other treatments significant at 0.01 level.

It is not certain whether the differences in soils were inherent in the sites, or developed after treatment. They may have resulted from compaction due to heavier grazing (cattle were attracted by more abundant forage in the disturbed plots), and to changes in water regime within the soil.

Important equilibrium points of the moisture-tension curves are presented in Table 2. Soils under the three oak treatments had quite similar waterholding capacities. The upper 24 inches of the profile was estimated to hold 8.4 to 9.0 inches of water at field capacity

Table 2.--Average soil-water contents, by soil horizon and oak treatment, at indicated tension values

Profile horizon (inches)	Saturation (0.00 atm.)		Field capacity (0.04 atm.)		Permanent wilting point (15.00 atm.)		Available water-holding capacity (between 0.04 and 15.00 atm.)	
	Percent	Inches	Percent	Inches	Percent	Inches	Percent	Inches
0- to 6-inch layer								
Oaks undisturbed	28.9	2.5	20.6	1.8	1.8	0.2	18.8	1.6
Oaks thinned	30.2	2.6	22.4	1.9	1.9	.2	20.5	1.7
Oaks clearcut	26.0	2.4	18.6	1.7	1.8	.2	16.8	1.5
6- to 12-inch layer								
Oaks undisturbed	35.2	3.0	27.7	2.3	20.8	1.7	6.9	.6
Oaks thinned	34.0	2.9	24.8	2.3	20.8	1.8	4.0	.5
Oaks clearcut	36.1	3.0	28.2	2.3	17.9	1.5	10.3	.8
12- to 24-inch layer								
Oaks undisturbed	36.0	6.1	28.5	4.8	21.9	3.7	6.6	1.1
Oaks thinned	32.9	5.8	28.1	4.8	20.3	3.6	7.8	1.2
Oaks clearcut	30.4	5.4	24.5	4.4	19.5	3.5	5.0	.9
Total profile horizon								
Oaks undisturbed	...	11.6	...	8.9	...	5.6	...	3.3
Oaks thinned	...	11.3	...	9.0	...	5.6	...	3.4
Oaks clearcut	...	10.8	...	8.4	...	5.2	...	3.2

(0.04 atm. tension), and 5.2 to 5.6 inches at approximate wilting point
(15 atm. tension), leaving an indicated 3.2 to 3.4 inches available to
plants. The high clay content of the subsoils undoubtedly accounted for
the high amount of water held at permanent wilting point, and the low
amounts of available water.

The moisture content at saturation (0.00 atm. tension) was significantly higher under the undisturbed stands than on the clearcut sites but
not significantly different from that for the thinned site at 12 to 24
inches. This difference affects temporary waterholding capacity, but may
not greatly alter the amount available to plants.

Weather

The normal precipitation for College Station, Texas, is 38.94 inches
annually. There was an excess of 5.67 inches in 1953, whereas 1954 was
11.04 inches below normal. Precipitation was well distributed during 1953.
In 1954 only 0.14 inch fell in June and in August, while February and March
had less than 1 inch each.

Mean maximum temperature during July and August, when soil moisture
is expected to be at a critically low level, was 93.2°F in 1953, 96.5°F in
1954.

PROCEDURE FOR STUDYING FIELD MOISTURE

Soil-moisture measurements were made on two plots of each of the
three oak treatments. Soil-moisture units of the Colman electrical-
resistance type, equipped with thermistors (1), were installed at three
selected depths: 2 inches above, 2 inches below, and 12 inches below
the top of the subsoil. In calculations of moisture content of the soil
profile, these locations were assumed to reflect conditions in the 0- to
6-, 6- to 12-, and 12- to 24-inch levels, respectively.

The moisture units were installed centrally in openings in the
stand; these openings were at least 15 to 20 feet in diameter. At one
opening in each plot, two units were buried at each depth. In two
other openings, single units were installed at each depth. Readings
from the four units at each level on each plot were averaged. Measurements
were made weekly or biweekly from May to November 1953 and from March to
August 1954, and monthly from December 1953 through February 1954.

The relationship between soil-moisture content and electrical
resistance of the Colman units was determined by laboratory calibration
from composite soil samples for each depth. Approximately 1 kilogram
of soil was packed with a test unit in a quart container to approximate
field conditions. Resistance readings and weights were taken at 24-hour
intervals after saturation until the soils were dry. Two dry-down cycles
were employed in the calibration procedure.

The resistance readings obtained in the calibration and field measurements were corrected to 60°F. with the aid of tables supplied by the Vicksburg Research Center of the Southern Forest Experiment Station. Moisture percentages determined in this manner were converted to inches of water by methods outlined by Land and Carreker (8) and Reinhart (9).

Soil-moisture trends were evaluated principally by graphic analysis.

RESULTS

Moisture trends under the oak treatments, together with rainfall at College Station, Texas, are graphed in figures 1 and 2.

Soil Moisture Regime

Total profile.--Throughout the period of observation soils of the cleared plots had more moisture than those of the undisturbed plots, while the thinned plots were intermediate. Differences tended to be greatest at high water contents, and least at times of drought. During July and August 1954, after a prolonged drought, there was little difference in residual moisture among the three treatments.

Differences in total moisture resulted partly from differential net accretion rates after rains, and partly from different depletion trends. After rains in June, September, and October of 1953, accretion in the cleared plots exceeded that on the undisturbed areas; the thinned plots also acquired more water than the undisturbed from the June and October rains. By contrast, after a heavy rain in May 1954 accretion was greatest on the thinned plots, intermediate on the undisturbed, and least on the cleared plots.

Depletion trends were roughly parallel for the three treatments. During three of the five depletion periods the cleared plots lost more moisture than the untreated. The reverse was true for the May-June period of 1953 and the January-April period in 1954. Except for the July-August period in 1953, depletion trends for the thinned plots were more like those for the undisturbed plots than for the cleared plots.

When the cleared plots lost less moisture than the others, their rate of depletion was less. But during summer periods, when more moisture was lost from the cleared plots, rates of loss were similar but cleared plots continued to lose moisture longer. Thus, during May-August 1954, rapid depletion continued more than two weeks later on the cleared areas than on the other treatments.

The undisturbed and thinned plots reached approximately the same minimum--3.2 inches of residual moisture--in August and October 1953 and July-August 1954. The depletion curves also flattened out

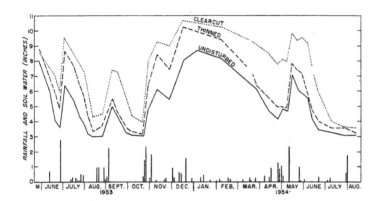

Figure 1.--*Water in upper 24 inches of soil under three densities of oak overstory. Rainfall at College Station, Texas.*

Figure 2.--*Water in various soil horizons under three densities of oak overstory.*

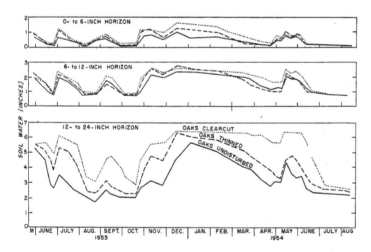

for the cleared plots at about this same moisture content in 1954. These levels are about two inches below the nominal permanent wilting point as determined in the laboratory.

0- to 6-inch depth.--Minimum moisture levels at this depth were close to laboratory determination and nearly identical for all treatments and all depletion periods. After rains, thinned and cleared plots absorbed and retained more moisture in this level than did undisturbed plots.

6- to 12-inch depth.--Here again consistent minima were reached during each depletion period, except that the cleared plots did not fall so near the minimum in April 1954. The leveling-off point (July-August 1954) is nearly an inch below the laboratory-determined permanent wilting point. Accretions and maximum moisture levels on the three treatments were more consistent than at either of the other soil levels.

12- to 24-inch depth.--This portion of the profile contributed most to the determination of total moisture trends, not only because of its greater thickness, but also because the major differences due to treatment appeared most prominently in it.

The cleared plots again contained the most moisture, and the undisturbed plots the least. Moisture on the undisturbed and thinned plots followed trends quite consistent with those of the upper horizons and the total profile. On the cleared plots, however, moisture content increased more rapidly in the fall of 1953, reaching 6.4 inches by December 1953. It remained at this level, with little deviation, until June 1954, but by the second week in July this moisture had been depleted to approximately the same level as for the other two treatments.

Periods of Soil-Moisture Stress

The effect of moisture on tree and forage growth may be closely related to the frequency and duration of droughts.

To identify such periods, it was assumed that plants were adequately watered as long as rapid depletion occurred, and that reduced depletion rates signified that moisture was too low to be readily available to plants. In the light of this assumption, the permanent wilting points determined in the laboratory seemed to be too high for the soil and vegetation under consideration. Periods of soil-moisture stress were determined, therefore, from figures 1 and 2, with the lower limit of available water being taken as the point where drastic reduction in depletion occurred. The results appear in table 3.

Under the undisturbed stand, two periods of soil-moisture deficiency occurred in 1953, for a total duration of 53 days. At 26 square feet of overstory basal area the 1953 stress period was reduced by 10 days, while on the clearcut areas only 4 days of stress occurred.

Table 3.--Duration of soil moisture deficiency for three oak treatments, with flexpoints of depletion curves taken as permanent wilting points

Years	TOTAL PROFILE Oak treatment		
	Undisturbed	Thinned	Clearcut
	Days	Days	Days
1953	53	43	4
1954	53	40	16
Total	106	83	20
	0- TO 6-INCH DEPTH		
1953	54	51	44
1954	76	73	44
Total	130	124	88
	6- TO 12-INCH DEPTH		
1953	42	41	18
1954	36	36	36
Total	78	77	54
	12- TO 24-INCH DEPTH		
1953	66	46	4
1954	53	35	16
Total	119	81	20

In 1954 stress in the undisturbed and thinned stands developed in June and continued for 53 and 40 days respectively to the conclusion of the study on August 13. On the clearcut plots the deficiency level was reached July 28.

On all treatments, stress was most prolonged in the 0- to 6-inch horizon. Stress periods at the 0- to 6- and 6- to 12-inch levels did not vary greatly with treatment, but at the 12- to 24-inch level stress periods were shortest where the overstory had been thinned or removed.

DISCUSSION

Differences in moisture regime revealed in this experiment are believed to be related primarily to differences in vegetation resulting from the overstory treatments. The tree roots extended into and to some extent proliferated through the second foot of soil. The observations of soil moisture suggest that throughout most of the study grass roots were confined chiefly to the upper 12 inches of the soil profile.

Except for the initial measurements, and the low-level measurements in July-August 1954, the moisture content of the soil profile was consistently highest in the cleared plots, intermediate in the thinned plots, and lowest in the undisturbed stands. While there were gross differences in rates of accretion as well as depletion, the frequency of observation was insufficient to establish whether differences in instantaneous accretion rates occurred. Thus the accretion on all treatments in the fall of 1953 was the resultant between water added by rainfall and moisture lost through evapotranspiration prior to measurement. It is entirely possible, therefore, that evapotranspiration from tree leaves might have been sufficient to account for the apparently lower accretion rates on the thinned and undisturbed plots. Also, some precipitation may have been lost from interception.

Maximum total depletion rates varied surprisingly little between treatments. When moisture was abundant, all three stands reached growing-season depletion rates close to 0.2 inch per day. Under all three treatments depletion continued at high rates until soil moisture was virtually exhausted. In conjunction with findings of Veihmeyer and Hendrickson (10), Gaiser (4), Fletcher and McDermott (3), and Zahner (11) these results indicate that, with either tree or grass vegetation, soil moisture may be utilized during the growing season at maximum rates until the wilting point is nearly reached.

In winter, depletion rates were distinctly higher on the wooded than on the cleared plots--approximately 0.04 to 0.05 inch per day, in contrast to 0.01 to 0.02 inch. These differences suggest some absorption of moisture from the soil and perhaps evaporation from stems of hardwood trees.

Differences in moisture content of the profile result primarily from differences in the 12- to 24-inch horizon. In the 0- to 6- and 6- to 12-inch horizons the trends are remarkably uniform for all three oak treatments, but in the 12- to 24-inch horizon the moisture losses on the cleared plots were distinctly less than for the other two treatments. On the cleared plots this horizon was saturated throughout much of the winter and spring of 1954. It did not reach the wilting point until late in the July-August drought of 1954, nearly a month after available moisture at this level had been depleted in the undisturbed plots.

It seems reasonable to conclude that roots of trees withdrew water from all three soil horizons, as reported by Gaiser (4) for the oak forests in Ohio, and that the shallower grass roots drew water primarily from the upper 12 inches. In Efimova's studies (2), herbaceous vegetation extracted moisture rapidly from the surface 1/2 meter, whereas trees utilized moisture uniformly from a depth of 1 meter. It was evident from the present study, however, that under stress, as during the summer of 1954, the grass roots could exhaust the moisture from at least the upper two feet of the profile. In this geographic region any type of vegetation that fully occupies the site is evidently capable of utilizing all of the season's moisture.

The differences in physical properties of the soil two years after cutting may or may not be attributable to treatment effects, since no determinations were made prior to treatment, but some of the variations may reflect inherent soil differences. Cleared plots differed significantly from the undisturbed or thinned plots, or both, in having a lower percent of aggregation at the 6- to 12- and 12- to 18-inch levels, in lower capillary pore space at the 12- to 18-inch level, and higher bulk density at the 0- to 6-inch level. These differences could have been related to the clearing operation and subsequent soil changes.

Compaction of the surface is believed to have resulted from increased trampling by livestock attracted to the improved forage and possibly to reduced incorporated organic matter.

Since the indicated changes are in the direction of poorer internal drainage, some of the differences in depletion rates may reflect different rates of percolation to soil horizons below those measured. Such effects, however, probably could not account for differences in depletion of the observed magnitude.

The prolongation of near-saturated conditions in the 12- to 24-inch horizon on the clearcut plots for nearly six months may affect root development and soil hydrology. The depletion pattern in the 12- to 24-inch horizon under clearcutting definitely indicates lack of root activity. Kramer (7) states that the physiological effect of poor aeration is twofold with respect to absorption of water: the metabolism in the root cells is reduced, and there is an increased resistance of the root to entry and transmission of water. Root penetration may also have been restricted as a result of poorer soil structure.

Detention and retention storage capacities are very limited when profiles are saturated. During the winter, when excessive rains are most frequent, the cleared sites had considerably less capacity for storing additional rainfall than the wooded areas.

SUMMARY AND CONCLUSIONS

From May 1953 to August 1954 a study was made of soil-moisture trends under undisturbed, thinned, and cleared post oak stands on Susquehanna-like soils in Texas.

Throughout most of the test, the moisture content of the upper two feet of the soil profile was highest in the cleared, intermediate in the thinned, and lowest in the undisturbed areas. Most of the difference occurred in the 12- to 24-inch horizon.

Roots of grasses were active chiefly in the upper 12 inches of the soil profile, while the tree roots also withdrew water consistently from the 12- to 24-inch horizon.

Moisture content at 15.0 atmospheres pressure was not an accurate index of wilting point, since rapid depletion continued to considerably lower levels.

Either grass or tree vegetation is capable of withdrawing all available moisture from the entire upper 24 inches of the soil profile. Trees withdrew water from upper and lower horizons simultaneously; grasses tended to exhaust the upper horizons before making substantial withdrawals from the 12- to 24-inch levels.

Maximum daily depletion rates occurred during the growing season and were in the magnitude of 0.2 inch for both grass and tree vegetation. In winter the wooded plots lost moisture at rates of 0.04 to 0.05 inch daily, in contrast to 0.01 to 0.02 inch for the cleared plots.

The number and duration of periods of moisture stress, during which little or no moisture was available in the upper 24 inches of soil, were reduced by thinning and clearing.

ssentially saturated condition of the soils on the cleared
hout the winter season may have limited root development in
4-inch level by reducing soil aeration. The saturated soils
cut plots afforded less opportunity for storage of excessive
d thereby offered less check to runoff and flooding.

LITERATURE CITED

E. A.
(rev, 1952). Manual of instructions for use of the fiberglas
soil-moisture instrument. U. S. Forest Serv. Calif. Forest
and Range Expt. Sta., 20 pp. [Processed.]

A. D.
Changes in the reserve of moisture in the soil under forest
and herbaceous vegetation. Trudy Inst. Lesa. Akad. Nauk.
21:149-169.

, P. W., and McDermott, R. E.
Moisture depletion by forest cover on a seasonally saturated Ozark ridge soil. Soil Sci. Soc. Amer. Proc.
21:547-550.

R. N.
Readily available water in forest soils. Soil Sci. Soc.
Amer. Proc. 16:334-338.

. T.
Diameter growth of post oak best in sparse stands. Jour.
Forestry 55:847.

, T., Darrow, R. A., and McCully, W. G.
Forage production in oak woodland as influenced by removal
of tree cover. Tex. Agr. Expt. Sta. Prog. Rpt. 1661, 4 pp.,
illus. [Processed.]

?. J.
Causes of decreased absorption of water by plants in poorly
aerated media. Amer. Jour. Bot. 27:216-220.

B., and Carreker, J. R.
Results of evapotranspiration and root distribution studies.
Agr. Engin. 34:319-322, illus.

K. G.
Relation of soil bulk density to moisture content as it affects soil-moisture records. In Some field, laboratory, and
office procedures for soil-moisture measurement. U. S.
Forest Serv. South. Forest Expt. Sta. Occas. Paper 135,
pp. 12-21. [Processed.]

10. Veihmeyer, F. J., and Hendrickson, A. H.
     1955. Does transpiration decrease as the soil moisture decreases?
            Trans. Amer. Geophys. Union 36:425-428.

11. Zahner, R.
     1955. Soil water depletion by pine and hardwood stands during
            a dry season. Forest Sci. 1:258-264, illus.

16:168

Occasional Paper 168 1959

INTENSITY OF PREPLANTING SITE PREPARATION
REQUIRED FOR FLORIDA'S SANDHILLS

R. L. SCHEER and F. W. WOODS

SOUTHERN FOREST EXPERIMENT STATION
PHILIP A. BRIEGLEB, DIRECTOR
Forest Service, U. S. Department of Agriculture

10.

11.

INTENSITY OF PREPLANTING SITE PREPARATION
REQUIRED FOR FLORIDA'S SANDHILLS

R.L. Scheer and F.W. Woods
Southern Forest Experiment Station

Two million acres of scrub oak-wiregrass sandhills in west Florida are not producing cash incomes for their owners. However, on a few small sandhill areas planted slash pines (Pinus elliottii Engelm.) and naturally seeded longleaf pines (P. palustris Mill.) have survived and are growing into well-stocked stands. Without exception, these small stands originated on old fields or other cleared sites where the pines did not have to compete with scrub oaks and wiregrass for water and nutrients. All attempts to re-establish pine on this excessively drained soil, without fairly complete site preparation, have been unsuccessful.

Studies of sandhill planting site preparation requirements were started in 1952 on the newly established Chipola Experimental Forest, located in west Florida about halfway between Marianna and Panama City. The research summarized in this paper was concerned essentially with the intensity, rather than the method, of preparation necessary for good survival and growth of planted pines. The results of investigations directly concerned with methods of site preparation are reported elsewhere (2, 6)[1].

THE PROBLEM

The virgin longleaf pine forests of west Florida were rather open woodlands--scattered pine trees interspersed with scrub oaks and wiregrass (2). Longleaf reproduction and advance growth were scant. In the vicinity of the Chipola Experimental Forest, logging was started about 1900 and has continued wherever merchantable timber remains. The pattern of timber removal has been essentially the same over the entire region, with each successive logging taking smaller and smaller residual trees. Only isolated patches of old-growth remain today, most of them being

---

[1] Underscored numbers in parentheses refer to Literature Cited, p. 12.

in the protected Eglin Air Force Reservation, on what was formerly the Choctawhatchee National Forest. Over most of the sandhills no pine is left except scattered, individual longleaf trees--either stunted, flat-topped residuals or second-growth trees.

The vegetative cover which has developed in response to removal of the longleaf pine and the frequent grass fires is characterized by dense stands of turkey oak (Quercus laevis Walt.), bluejack oak (Q. incana Bartr.), and wiregrass (Aristida stricta Michx.). Some areas have from 2,000 to 5,000 individual scrub oak stems per acre. Locally, other species may be important, such as persimmon (Diospyros virginiana L.) and dwarf post oak (Q. stellata var. margaretta (Ashe) Sarg.). In very limited areas, mainly along the coast, sand pine (P. clausa (Chapm.) Vasey) is abundant.

The topography of the sandhills and the parent material of their soils were formed during the most recent glacial (Pleistocene) period. As the northern glaciers increased in size, the oceans crept back from the land; the sandhills of the lower Coastal Plain are the bars, spits, dunes, and other high places left exposed around the shores of the receding ocean. Thus the soils (predominantly of the Lakeland series, deep phase) are extremely sandy.

The climate is generally mild, with extremes of temperature rarely over 100° F. or below 20° F. The annual average rainfall is nearly 60 inches, with a range of about 40 to 80 inches. The monthly distribution is fairly uniform, varying from about 2.0 to 3.0 inches in October and November to about 7.0 to 8.0 inches in July and August. The moisture-retention capacity of the soils is so poor, however, that two weeks without rainfall during late spring and summer can result in drouth.

Vegetation and site factors on the Experimental Forest are very similar to those of large areas in west Florida. Therefore, this research should be applicable to large areas of west Florida and other parts of the southern Coastal Plain where turkey oak and wiregrass are dominant on excessively drained deep sands.

METHODS

In 1952, seven methods of site preparation were tested. These methods, designed to produce different intensities of site preparation, were repeated in another test in 1953. The treatments were:

Bulldozing.--All vegetation and several inches of topsoil were windrowed by a bulldozer. Plots were then either scraped and leveled with a road grader or disk-harrowed with a wheel tractor and harrow. For three growing seasons after pines were planted, oak sprouts were hand-grubbed at least once each season.

Furrowing.--A Mathis-type fireplow was used to make open furrows 4 to 5 inches deep and 4 feet wide, with 2 feet of "spoil" on either side. Furrow centers were approximately 8 feet apart.

Chopping and burning.--Plots were prepared with one trip of a single-drum chopper, weighing approximately 1-1/2 tons, pulled by a bulldozer. The bulldozer knocked down all trees. The chopper cut limbs and twigs less than one inch in diameter, leaving boles and larger limbs uncut. Wiregrass was only slightly disturbed. About two months after chopping, in October, the vegetation was burned with a hot headfire.

Burning.--Plots were burned with a hot headfire in October.

Harrowing.--A heavy-duty bush-and-bog disk harrow was used to prepare the entire plot area. The harrow was 8 feet wide and had six 16-inch serrated disks, set to throw out.

Chemical control of oaks.--All woody stems were treated with foliage sprays (sprouts) or basal sprays of 2,4,5-T. Some larger trees survived, but were killed with Ammate in cups.

No treatment.--This was the check.

All site preparation was done in summer and early fall. Test seedlings were hand-planted the following December and January. On the furrowed plots, seedlings were set in the furrow bottoms.

A randomized block design with four blocks was chosen. Each block contained one large plot (200 by 248 feet) of each site-preparation treatment. These treatment plots were split and planted with pine seedlings for species comparisons. Slash and longleaf pines were planted on the plots prepared in both 1952 and 1953. Sand pine was planted only in 1953. Two 25-tree plantings of each species were established on each major plot of the 1952 treatments; 49-tree plantings of each species were established in the 1953 treatments.

Slash pine gave the best survival of the species tested, regardless of treatment. Average survivals for all site treatments at the end of the first growing season after planting were:

Pine species	1952 treatments	1953 treatments
	(Percent)	(Percent)
Slash	54	79
Longleaf	23	42
Sand		42

Because of its much better survival, slash pine alone was used to evaluate the site preparation methods.

SLASH PINE SURVIVAL AND GROWTH

Plots cleared by bulldozing had the highest survivals at the end of the first growing season and the least mortality thereafter (fig. 1). The complete removal of all scrub oaks and wiregrass enabled the planted pines to make optimum use of available moisture and nutrients. Under all other treatments clearing was incomplete and native vegetation recovered quickly and competed in various degrees for soil moisture. This competition was expressed by the progressive mortality of the pines.

The futility of destroying only the scrub oaks and leaving wiregrass was clearly demonstrated. When oaks alone were killed, wiregrass multiplied and produced a level of competition at least equivalent to that existing before the treatment.

Slash pine survival percentages at the end of the first growing season are tabulated below:

Site treatment	1952 tests	1953 tests
Bulldozing	94	86
Furrowing	66	90
Chopping and burning	54	76
Burning	52	76
Harrowing	45	78
Chemical control of oaks; wiregrass left	38	69
No treatment	34	77

- 4 -

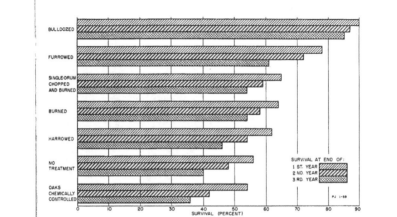

Figure 1.--*Slash pine survivals by site preparation method. Combined data from 1952 and 1953 tests.*

Figure 2.--*Longleaf pine seedling approximately five months after being planted on bulldozed plot. Oak sprouts are almost totally absent and forbs and grasses show extremely poor development.*

Figure 3.--*Furrowed plot (above) and harrowed plot (below), both about 5 months after being planted to pine. The undisturbed native vegetation between the furrows is invading the bared strips. Harrowing left much of the wiregrass and was followed by vigorous sprouting of the oaks.*

Except on the bulldozed plots, pine survival was distinctly higher in the 1953 tests, probably because of a more uniform distribution of rainfall during the spring. Only bulldozing produced high survivals in both years, regardless of weather.

Thus, for first-year survival alone, the degree of site preparation may not be critical if rainfall and soil moisture are adequate. However, later results have shown that pine growth is less and mortality is progressively higher on incompletely prepared sites (fig. 1).

Seedling height growth further confirmed the superiority of bulldozing over less complete methods of site preparation. At the end of the third growing season, average slash pine heights for both tests were as follows:

Treatments	1952 tests (Feet)	1953 tests (Feet)	Average (Feet)
Bulldozing	2.0	1.4	1.7
Chemical control of oaks	1.3	1.6	1.4
Chopping and burning	1.5	1.3	1.4
Burning	1.3	1.3	1.3
Furrowing	1.0	1.4	1.2
Harrowing	1.1	1.4	1.2
No treatment	1.2	1.2	1.2

As with survivals, growth differences between treatments from tests established in 1952 were greater than from tests established in 1953, with its more favorable rainfall. Bulldozed plots produced the most nearly acceptable average height growth in both tests, but even the best height growth was unsatisfactory. Later studies (2, 6) have shown that substantially better growth can be obtained when planting sites are cleared with either a rootrake-scalper or a tandem-drum brush chopper. These machines, while destroying all of the wiregrass and scrub oaks, leave part or all of the topsoil on the site. The bulldozer removes all of it to a windrow.

Figure 5.--Top: plot on which oaks were chemically controlled--
approximately five months after planting. Although oak sprouting
was negligible, the wiregrass flourished. Below: untreated check
plot.

plots. The possible effects of fire in increasing fertility and
decreasing soil moisture also have been recognized by other investigators (4, 5). Fire may be especially valuable in managing
sandhills soils, which are inherently low in fertility.

To obtain information on drouth days (table 2) stacks of
Colman soil-moisture units were installed at depths of 1.5, 4.5,
7.5, and 10.5 inches in two replications each of the bulldozed,
furrowed, chemically controlled, and check plots. Moisture and
temperature determinations were made with all units three times a
week for two years (1). Data from replicated treatments were averaged. Field experience indicated that 2.0 percent is the approximate limit to which soil moisture can fall and still maintain
vital plant processes for an extended period in the soils of the
study area.

Table 2.--Drouth days from May 1 to August 31, 1954 and 1955, and
survival of slash pine after 2 years

Site treatment	Proportion of drouth days, May 1 to August 31 [1]				Pine survival
	0- to 3-in. depth	3- to 6-in. depth	6- to 9-in. depth	9- to 12-in. depth	
	- - - - - - - - - Percent - - - - - - - - - -				
Bulldozing	38	1	4	0	87
Furrowing	39	9	18	8	72
No treat- ment	32	21	21	25	47
Chemical control of oaks	42	26	24	23	42

[1] Percentages based on 119 sampling dates. In this study a
drouth day was defined as a 24-hour period during which the
soil moisture was in the wilting range.

As table 2 shows, pine survival was distinctly higher on
the sites with the fewest drouth days (the 0- to 3-inch depth excepted). The check plot, with totally undisturbed soil, had fewer
drouth days in the 0- to 3-inch soil layer than any other treatment. At lower depths, however, there were fewer drouth days in
both the bulldozed and the furrowed plots. Shading by the foliage
of oaks seems to conserve soil moisture at shallow depths.

- 11 -

Figure 5.--*Top: plot on which oaks were chemically controlled--
approximately five months after planting. Although oak sprouting
was negligible, the wiregrass flourished. Below: untreated check
plot.*

plots. The possible effects of fire in increasing fertility and decreasing soil moisture also have been recognized by other investigators (4, 5). Fire may be especially valuable in managing sandhills soils, which are inherently low in fertility.

To obtain information on drouth days (table 2) stacks of Colman soil-moisture units were installed at depths of 1.5, 4.5, 7.5, and 10.5 inches in two replications each of the bulldozed, furrowed, chemically controlled, and check plots. Moisture and temperature determinations were made with all units three times a week for two years (1). Data from replicated treatments were averaged. Field experience indicated that 2.0 percent is the approximate limit to which soil moisture can fall and still maintain vital plant processes for an extended period in the soils of the study area.

Table 2.--Drouth days from May 1 to August 31, 1954 and 1955, and survival of slash pine after 2 years

Site treatment	Proportion of drouth days, May 1 to August 31 [1]				Pine survival
	0- to 3-in. depth	3- to 6-in. depth	6- to 9-in. depth	9- to 12-in. depth	
	- - - - - - - - - - Percent - - - - - - - - - - - -				
Bulldozing	38	1	4	0	87
Furrowing	39	9	18	8	72
No treatment	32	21	21	25	47
Chemical control of oaks	42	26	24	23	42

[1] Percentages based on 119 sampling dates. In this study a drouth day was defined as a 24-hour period during which the soil moisture was in the wilting range.

As table 2 shows, pine survival was distinctly higher on the sites with the fewest drouth days (the 0- to 3-inch depth excepted). The check plot, with totally undisturbed soil, had fewer drouth days in the 0- to 3-inch soil layer than any other treatment. At lower depths, however, there were fewer drouth days in both the bulldozed and the furrowed plots. Shading by the foliage of oaks seems to conserve soil moisture at shallow depths.

SUMMARY AND CONCLUSIONS

During 1952 and 1953, seven degrees of site preparation were tested on deep sands at the Chipola Experimental Forest in west Florida. The treatments were evaluated by comparing survival and height growth of planted slash pines through the first three growing seasons after planting.

Complete removal of competing vegetation was found necessary for consistently satisfactory survivals. The principal limit to survival is soil moisture, which quickly becomes critical unless rains are frequent. After 14 rainless days, soil moisture was well above the wilting range only on the bulldozed plots. These same plots, during two consecutive growing seasons, also had the least number of drouth days in the 3- to 12-inch soil layer.

Height growth was unsatisfactory on all plots, though generally better under the bulldozing than under the other treatments. Recent studies have shown, however, that improved preparation techniques which destroy the wiregrass and scrub oaks, but leave the topsoil on the site, will yield acceptable growth.

LITERATURE CITED

1. Colman, E. A. 1947 (rev. 1950). Manual of instructions for use of the fiberglas soil-moisture instrument. U. S. Forest Serv. Calif. Forest and Range Expt. Sta. 20 pp., illus. [Processed.]

2. Grelen, H. E. 1959. Mechanical preparation of pine planting sites in Florida sandhills. Weeds 7: 184-188, illus.

3. Harper, R. M. 1914. Geography and vegetation of northern Florida. Sixth Ann. Rept., Fla. Geol. Surv. 451 pp., illus.

4. Heyward, F. 1939. Some moisture relationships of soils from burned and unburned longleaf pine forests. Soil Sci. 47: 313-327.

5. Vlamis, J., Biswell, H. H., and Schultz, A. M. 1956. Seedling growth on burned soil. Calif. Agr. 10: 13.

6. Woods, F. W. 1959. Converting scrub oak sandhills to pine forests in Florida. Jour. Forestry 57: 117-119, illus.

A 13.40/6:169

ASIONAL PAPER 169

ROTECT

ND

ANAGE

OOD

OUTHERN

ARDWOODS

J. S. McKnight

SOUTHERN FOREST EXPERIMENT STATION
Philip A. Briegleb, Director
FOREST SERVICE, U. S. DEPARTMENT OF AGRICULTURE

1959

HARRY
ROSSOLL

Grow Good Hardwoods!

Hardwoods are the trees to grow for the greatest timber values on the bottom-lands of most rivers and small streams of the South. The Brown Loam Bluffs along the eastern edge of the Delta, as well as other uplands with deep rich soil, are also prime hardwood sites. Many swamps grow excellent tupelo, bay, and cypress.

Hardwood stands can be managed to grow better than 500 board feet per acre annually.

Market prospects are good. A volume of almost 8 billion board feet of hardwood is harvested each year in the South. This is about two-thirds of the total production of hardwoods in the United States. The volume of good pine timber is increasing, that of the good hardwoods is decreasing. But pine cannot substitute for the distinctive uses that hardwoods serve. The likelihood of a strong and continuing demand for quality hardwoods means that it will pay landowners to protect and manage hardwoods that are growing on suitable sites.

Illustrations by Harry Rossoll, U. S. Forest Service, Region 8.

WHAT ARE GOOD HARDWOODS?

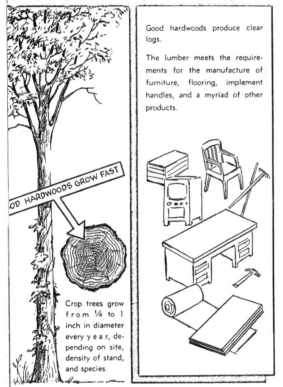

Good hardwoods produce clear logs.

The lumber meets the requirements for the manufacture of furniture, flooring, implement handles, and a myriad of other products.

OD HARDWOODS GROW FAST

Crop trees grow from ¼ to 1 inch in diameter every y e a r, depending on site, density of stand, and species.

MOST HARDWOOD FORESTS CONTAIN MANY SPECIES—NEARLY ALL FIND MARKETS. THOUGH LUMBER AND VENEER LOGS ARE THE MOST VALUABLE PRODUCTS, HARDWOOD STANDS ALSO YIELD PULP-WOOD, TIES, POSTS, PILING, AND CONSTRUCTION LUMBER.

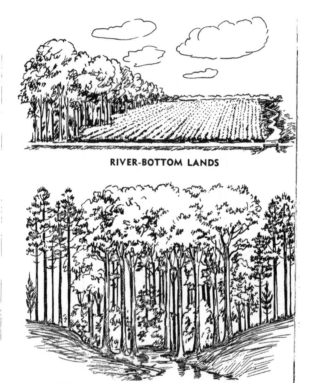

RIVER-BOTTOM LANDS

CREEK AND STREAM BOTTOMS IN PINEY WOODS

DEEP, RICH UPLAND SOILS

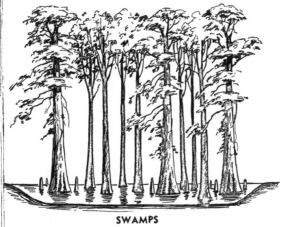

SWAMPS

IF YOU HAVE SUCH FORESTED SITES, THEN . . .

PROTECT—FROM FIRE!

Fire kills the young trees and destroys litter that holds moisture and provides nutrients.

It w o u n d s larger hardwoods, permitting entry of rot that progresses as the tree grows.

EVEN IF FIRE OCCURS ONLY ONCE IN A GENERATION, IT CAN NULLIFY THE EFFORTS OF MANAGEMENT AND REDUCE THE EARNING POWER OF THE FOREST FOR YEARS TO COME DRY AUTUMNS, PARTICULARLY AFTER HEAVY FROST, ARE ORDINARILY THE DANGEROUS PERIODS. UNUSUALLY DRY WINTERS OR EARLY SPRINGS ALSO CALL FOR EXTRA VIGILANCE.

LIVESTOCK OF ALL KINDS—CATTLE, HOGS, SHEEP, GOATS, HORSES, AND MULES—WILL PREVENT DEVELOPMENT OF WELL-FORMED YOUNG TREES AND THUS CUT OFF CONTINUOUS YIELDS FROM A HARDWOOD FOREST.

PROTECT—FROM UNCONTROLLED CUTTING!

IN SOME AREAS WOODCUTTERS HAVE DONE AS MUCH DAMAGE AS FIRE IN ELIMINATING HARDWOODS OF GOOD FORM AND QUALITY. PROPERLY SUPERVISED, FUELWOOD CUTTING CAN IMPROVE THE STAND BY REMOVING WORTHLESS TREES. FOREST OWNERS SHOULD ALSO PREVENT THE CUTTING OF POTENTIAL MONEY TREES FOR FENCE POSTS OR TO "CATCH A COON."

DEADEN CULL TREES

IN MOST HARDWOOD STANDS, PAST FIRES AND CUTTING HAVE LEFT NUMEROUS WEED AND CULL TREES THAT ARE WASTING GROWING SPACE.

HARDWOOD FORESTS USUALLY CONTAIN TREES OF MANY SIZES, SPECIES, AND QUALITIES. UNDER MANAGEMENT, THE FIRST SEVERAL HARVESTS WILL BE AIMED AT REMOVAL OF DAMAGED AND SLOW-GROWING TREES. THE GOAL SHOULD BE TO BUILD UP VOLUME IN STEMS OF BETTER QUALITY AND PREFERRED SPECIES. REMOVAL OF LESS DESIRABLE TREES WILL CREATE OPENINGS IN WHICH SEEDLINGS CAN DEVELOP, AND WILL RELEASE ESTABLISHED TREES FOR FAST GROWTH. (IN THE PICTURE, LINES AT STUMP HEIGHT MARK TREES THAT SHOULD BE CUT.)

IN CROWDED STANDS OF PULPWOOD SIZE, THIN TO GIVE THE
CROWNS OF THE THRIFTIEST TREES ROOM TO EXPAND. BEGIN BY
TAKING OUT THE DAMAGED AND WEAK (USUALLY THE SMALLEST)
TREES.

CONSIDER BEFORE CLEARING

- MANAGED HARDWOODS CAN YIELD STUMPAGE WORTH 5 TO 10 DOLLARS OR MORE PER ACRE ANNUALLY.

- IN MANY SITUATIONS TIMBER GROWING IS MORE PROFITABLE IN THE LONG RUN THAN OTHER LAND USES.

- THE HARDWOOD FORESTS ARE THE PRINCIPAL GAME HABITATS OF THE SOUTH.

- IT IS MUCH MORE DIFFICULT TO RE-ESTABLISH A HARDWOOD FOREST THAN IT IS TO DESTROY IT.

HARDWOOD PLANTING?

MUCH HAS YET TO BE LEARNED ABOUT HARDWOOD PLANTING ON
GOOD SITES, COTTONWOOD CAN BE SUCCESSFULLY PLANTED AS
CUTTINGS. SEEDLINGS OF ASH, YELLOW-POPLAR, RED OAKS, AND
SWEETGUM HAVE SHOWN PROMISE IN WELL-TENDED PLANTATIONS.
SEEK DETAILS BEFORE PLANTING. TRY IT ON A SMALL SCALE FIRST.

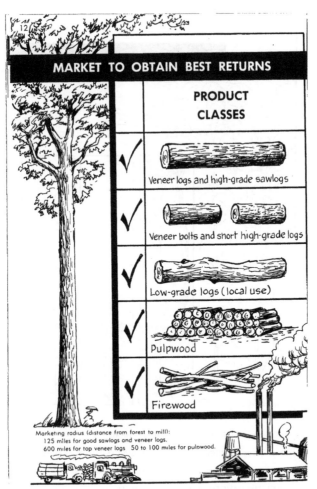

MARKET TO OBTAIN BEST RETURNS

	PRODUCT CLASSES
✓	Veneer logs and high-grade sawlogs
✓	Veneer bolts and short high-grade logs
✓	Low-grade logs (local use)
✓	Pulpwood
✓	Firewood

Marketing radius (distance from forest to mill):
125 miles for good sawlogs and veneer logs.
600 miles for top veneer logs   50 to 100 miles for pulpwood.

Know Your Timber — Investigate all Markets

SOUTHWEST ARKANSAS' SMALL WOODLAND OWNERS

e D. Perry
m Guttenberg

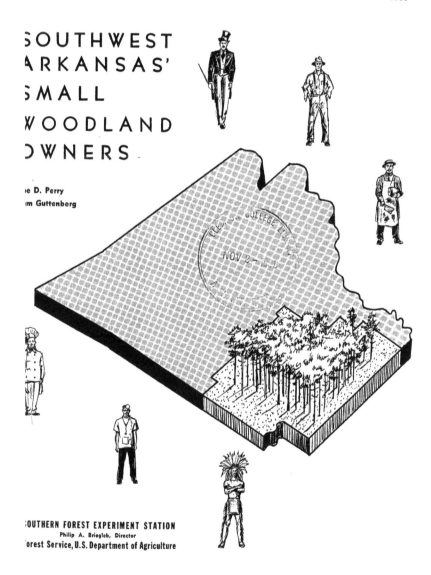

SOUTHERN FOREST EXPERIMENT STATION
Philip A. Briegleb, Director
orest Service, U.S. Department of Agriculture

In Brief

Seventy-eight percent of southwest Arkansas' 8.9 million acres is timberland.

About 3.4 million wooded acres are in tracts of less than 5,000 acres in size, held by 55,000 owners. The average holding is 62 acres.

The individuals who tend to invest in forestry have above-average assets. Instead of contributing their own time, they typically hire labor for forest operations.

Active managers make up less than 10 percent of the owners but hold one-third of the acreage.

Planting open areas to pine and removing undesirable trees are the most popular practices. Sixty percent of those who plant and 84 percent of those who control weed trees receive government payments.

An estimated 7,000 owners in possession of over half a million acres are interested in leasing their tracts to obtain full professional management—a promising approach.

Public and private forestry agencies have stimulated good intentions among two-thirds of the region's landowners. Community leaders are confident that a sizable share of these intentions are ready to be converted to practice.

Agencies wishing to stimulate management on small holdings will probably accomplish most by first concentrating their resources on tracts of more than 99 acres.

Contents

eive

Acknowledgment

Much assistance in the field work of this study was received from John R. Henry and Edmond I. Swensen of the Southern Region, U. S. Forest Service, and William C. Siegel of the Southern Forest Experiment Station.

Southwest Arkansas' Small Woodland Owners

Joe D. Perry and Sam Guttenberg

Southern Forest Experiment Station

Southwest Arkansas is timber country. Seventy-eight percent of the 8.9 million acres in the 20-county region (fig. 1) is forested, and timber-connected industries provide much of the region's employment. Pulp mills in and on the periphery of the area have been expanding, new ones have been built, and more are planned. Some of the South's most modern sawmills have been constructed here. In part, these developments are based on prospects for the larger timber business implicit in a rising gross national product and expanding population.

The eventual size of the forest industry, its stability, and its capacity to provide rewarding employment will be affected by the level of management applied to the region's timberlands. About 3 million acres are held by wood-using industries. These holdings are above the average in current stocking and are being managed for continuous and expanding timber production. Even so, much of the timber to supply the mills will continue to come from the area's small tracts—holdings of less than 5,000 acres, 3.4 million acres in all.

This report is based on a 1958 study of the area's 55,000 small forest owners. Among other things, the object was to determine what the owners are like, how much they own, what they are doing about their timber-growing prospects, and what their needs are.

A CHANGING ECONOMY

Southwest Arkansas is an exporter of people. Between 1940 and 1954 population declined 9 percent, to 387,000. Rural population, how-

Figure 1. *Study area.*

ever, decreased 21 percent; this decline carries implications of an improved ratio of resources to people. Migration has occurred in all age groups, but chiefly among the young workers.

The changing population has been associated with farm abandonment and widespread conversion of farmsteads to rural residences. Those still farming have been acquiring additional acreage. Average farm size increased from 85 acres in 1945 to 116 acres in 1954. In the same period, woodland acreage went from 32 to 52 acres per farm (or, if farms with no woodlands are excluded, from 53 to 75 acres). Still in the same time span, the proportion of farmers working 100 days or more per annum in off-the-farm jobs jumped from 24 to 40 percent. The 1954 census estimated that 51 percent of the region's farmers earned more from off-farm activities than from farming. The agricultural revolution and prospects for further industrial expansion suggest that, definitional changes aside, there will be further gains in farm size and further declines in the rural population.

These trends are having a favorable effect on forest acreage. For the region as a whole, woodland acreage increased 6 percent between 1936 and 1949 and 10 percent between 1949 and 1958. Farming is being progressively confined to the better croplands. Cattle production, which requires less manpower than field crops, is on the increase. In the short period 1950-54, cattle numbers rose from 250,000 to 374,000—this despite a severe drought. In some places, pasture programs are competing with timber growing for use of the land. But various government programs designed to restrict basic crop production have materially aided reforestation in the past few years. The fact that farmers are now specifically included in the Social Security program should ease the pressure to cut small-tract timber prematurely.

THE STUDY

The basis for sampling was the existing Forest Survey grid of points spaced 3 miles apart in cardinal directions and superimposed on aerial photographs. Points 6 miles apart, 392 in the entire region, were examined on aerial photographs to determine their land-use status. Non-forested points were excluded. In effect, the sample was drawn strictly in proportion to forest acreage. The 392 sample points were plotted on county highway maps that showed section, range, and township lines. These maps made it possible to obtain each landowner's name, address, and acreage from county tax records. Frequently the tax assessors and other informed public officials provided additional information.

Any forested point that was found to be on a holding of less than 3 or more than 4,999 acres was excluded from the sample, as were points on public lands. By these criteria, the 392 forested points netted 149 tracts held by 147 small woodland owners.

Though indirect sources provided some information on all 147 owners, diligent efforts were made to contact and personally interview each. The questionnaire for these interviews (see p. 12) was a consolidation of those used in prior ownership studies (5)[1]. As is usual in personal-interview research, there was a varying degree of response. Difficulties also stemmed from the large proportion of absentee owners: only 40 respondents resided on their holdings. Thirty-two respondents lived outside the 20-county area, but distance did not prevent interviewing some respondents as far off as Nashville, Tennessee. When an owner could not be interviewed, his legal representative or someone commissioned to look after the land was contacted instead. As a last resort, a combination of mail contact and telephone interview was used; this approach accounted for 7 of the 147 respondents. Eight owners could not be interviewed at all.

The forested acreage surrounding each qualifying sample point was examined, the number of locations inspected being determined by the size of the tract (table 1). A wedge prism of 3.03 diopters (basal area factor of 10) was used to pick trees to be tallied. Information was taken on species group, tree size, tree class, stocking, and degree of grazing.

Table 1. *Sampling intensity by tract size*

Tract size (acres)	Locations inspected
3 to 9	1 per 2 acres
10 to 99	6 plus 1 for each 10 acres above 10
100 to 499	14 plus 1 for each 20 acres above 100
500 to 4,999	34 plus 1 for each 200 acres above 500

Each of the net sample points represented 23,040 forested acres. When the 23,040 acres was divided by the total regional forest acreage

2

held by the owner on whose tract the sample point fell, the quotient was regarded as representing the number of similar ownerships in the region. Performing this operation for each sample point and summing the quotients provided regional estimates of small woodland owners by category. The most accurate estimates are for total acreage and all owners. Subdividing the data necessarily leads to larger errors of estimate.

THE OWNERS IN BRIEF

The survey disclosed 55,000 small private ownerships in the study area, the total holdings being some 3.4 million forest acres and the average individual holding 62 acres. Table 2 shows that the smallest size class (3-29 acres) includes 52 percent of the owners but only 11 percent of the timberland. The 2 largest size classes, with less than 2 percent of the owners, contain 29 percent of the acreage. Forty-four percent of the respondents own more than one tract within the region, while 11 respondents own 4,470 acres outside.

Table 2. *Small-tract landowners and forest area, by size class, in southwest Arkansas*

Total forest holdings (acres)	Owners	Forest area
	Number	Acres
3-29	28,700	369,000
30-99	19,200	991,000
100-499	6,300	1,083,000
500-2,499	900	783,000
2,500-4,999	100	207,000
Total	55,200	3,433,000

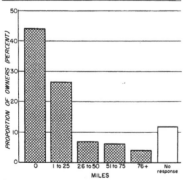

Figure 2. *Distance from owners' residences to their tracts.*

As has been implied, ownership and residence do not necessarily go hand in hand. Only 44 percent of the region's owners reside on their tracts (fig. 2). Seventy percent live within 25 miles of their properties. The average distance from tract to residence is 18 miles, the median 1 mile. Because distance is usually considered a handicap in forest management, it is of interest to note that owners residing more than 75 miles from their tracts have only 1/4 million acres.

What about owners' ages? Nearly half are over 50 years old (fig. 3). Youths are notably scarce; only 4 respondents were less than 31 years of age. The fact that more than 47 percent are over 50 may portend problems for sustained forest-management programs.

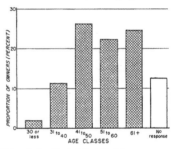

Figure 3. *Landowners by age class.*

The legal forms of ownership and methods by which titles are transferred also favor or hamper timber management. Titles were initially read from the tax records and then verified with the owners. Two-thirds of the tracts are held by individuals (fig. 4). Partnerships are fairly numerous. They commonly are family affairs—husband-wife or father-son. Other partnership arrangements are generally lacking because of the associated financial liability.

Some 2,500 estates control 1/3 million acres. Heirs of half the estates are unable to agree on a definite course of property management. Respondents wishing to manage estate timber bear the burden of winning acceptance for their policies, while needy heirs have an insatiable appetite for liquidation and the sentimental will not agree to any act which would change the "old home place."

3

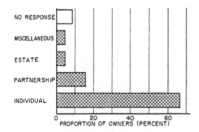

Figure 4. *Legal form of ownership.*

The information on tenure reflects both the regional population changes and the generally aged forest owners. As used here, tenure refers to the number of years the particular tract surrounding the sample point has been in the owner's possession. One-fourth of the owners acquired their tracts in the past 5 years (fig. 5). This rather large turnover in real estate is at least partly related to the decline in the rural population. Those remaining on farmsteads or in the nearby towns have been adding to their land-holdings. Because the average owner is 54 years old, however, it is not surprising to find that almost half of the tracts have been held more than 15 years—time enough to grow a first cut of pine pulpwood.

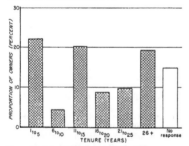

Figure 5. *Ownerships by length of tenure.*

At face value, the tenure statistics are somewhat misleading, because they disregard the means by which the land was acquired. Three-tenths of the tracts were inherited (fig. 6). The

family tenure of many inherited lands is measured in decades rather than years—one case going back 60 years. Gifts of land are an alternative form of inheritance that may become more popular, for tax considerations make it desirable for an owner to give assets away prior to his death. Purchase, however, is the most common form of acquisition, accounting for over 50 percent of the title transfers.

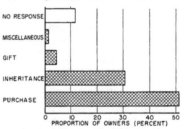

Figure 6. *Ownerships by method of acquisition.*

The large number of tracts acquired recently, and typically by purchase, appears associated with timber sales activity. Over half the owners have sold timber at least once. About one-fourth have had sales in the past 5 years (table 3). Moderately stocked pine tracts in this province can support a cut every 5 years. Frequent cutting is especially desirable when there is opportunity to reduce mortality losses and improve species composition, tree quality, and spacing.

Table 3. *Period since last timber sale*

Years since last timber sale	Proportion of owners
	Percent
0-5	25.7
6-10	15.2
11-and longer	14.3
Haven't cut	32.1
Don't know	.7
No response	12.0
Total	100.0

The active timber markets, widespread employment in timber-connected activities, and both public and private forestry promotion programs have affected owners' attitudes. When asked about intended use of their woodlands, two-thirds of the owners claimed to be primarily interested in growing timber (table 4).

4

Table 4. *Primary land-use intentions*

Present intention	Proportion of owners	Proportion of forest acreage
	Percent	Percent
Timber growing	65.2	69.8
Grazing	6.3	6.7
Residence	4.7	.7
Speculation	4.9	4.7
Other	6.9	10.0
No response	12.0	8.1
Total	100.0	100.0

In terms of intent, grazing is another aspect of land clearing for agriculture. With the advent of blooded stock for beef production, more rather than less forest land will be converted to pasture. As yet, only some 7 percent of small-tract acreage is involved. In terms of forest management, table 4 perhaps signifies more promise than substance. The achievement has largely been in getting people to acknowledge that timber growing is worth while. It takes time for intentions to be converted to practice. But the questionnaire and field examinations make it possible to assess the current forest management status.

MANAGERS VERSUS NON-MANAGERS

A management yardstick is needed. In this study, respondents were classed as managers if they had taken any one of a number of positive steps. These measures included planting, cull timber removal or timber stand improvement (TSI), fire protection, control of grazing,

planned harvesting, and prescribed burning. This standard was adhered to: some purchasers of woodlands with firm management plans were classed as non-managers because they had not done anything as yet.

What distinguishes active managers from non-managers? Managers are somewhat younger, averaging 45 years of age as against 55 for non-managers. Ninety percent of the managers say they intend to grow timber, though so do 71 percent of the non-managers. That some owners have made an investment in forestry without claiming to be timber growers partly reflects the imprecision of interview studies. The greatest apparent difference is in assets.

The managers' holdings average 228 forested acres, in contrast with 46 for non-managers. The relationship between management and tract size appears in virtually all ownership studies, for, as Southern and Miller (4) have noted, "Foresters have found that the type and size of ownership of forested lands exert a major influence on how timber on such holdings is managed." There is at least a rough correlation between total assets and acreage owned—and considerable out-of-pocket investment is required to apply remedial measures to the depleted tracts that are the norm for small woodlands (2).

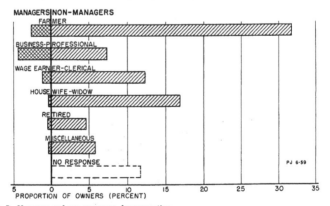

Figure 7. *Managers and non-managers, by occupation.*

5

The occupation class of the owners is another rough yardstick of assets. Investments in forestry have been made by a greater proportion of business and professional people than any other owner group (fig. 7). Farmers, long considered to be in the best position to practice forestry, do not show up well. The data in table 5 suggest the superior financial situation of business and professional people in this area. As the changing rural population implies, agriculture has not generally been a very rewarding occupation. In the better farming areas, the need for increased acreage and for equipment, seed, fertilizer, and other working capital probably takes most, if not all, of the funds available for investment.

Assets aside, the implication of table 5 that one-third of the forest land is being managed must be accepted with caution. The costs of the two most popular measures, tree planting and TSI, are largely recoverable. Thus, 84 percent of the landowners who had improved their stands and 60 percent of those who had planted received government payments for their efforts. Too, all planting stock was and is grown by the Arkansas Forestry Commission and sold at cost. In recent years forest industries have purchased 2,000,000 of these seedlings annually for free distribution to small-tract owners.

Programs that cover entire tracts are notably scarce. In effect, the overwhelming majority of the acreage still receives very little management. Professional skills are required to delineate the needs for regeneration, thinning, harvest cutting, and adjustments in species composition.

Contacts by Professional Foresters

About 6,000 managers or non-managers have

Table 6. *Owners contacted by professional foresters, by proportion of forester groups[1]*

Owner age class	Private foresters		Public forester	Both public and private
	Consulting	Industrial		
	Percent	Percent	Percent	Percent
40 and younger	...	38.3	13.3	1.6
41-50	(2)	6.7	13.3	1.7
51-60	(2)	3.3	10.0	1.7
61 and older	(2)	(2)	6.7	1.7
Total	1.7	48.3	43.3	6.7

[1] Information from 46 respondents representing 6,000 owners.
[2] Less than 1 percent.

been contacted by foresters, and of this number 400 have utilized both public and private foresters. Of owners who sought or welcomed expert assistance, more than 50 percent were less than 41 years old, while those above 60 accounted for only 10 percent (table 6).

Not all respondents were able to recall precisely what agency, act, or individual motivated them to take advantage of professional forestry services. To the extent possible, owners' reflections were allocated to the 5 categories listed in table 7. Demonstrations seem to have had the greatest effect. Among other things, influential demonstrations included tree-farm exhibits and the management activities of lumber

Table 5. *Distribution of small forest ownerships, by management status, owner occupation, and proportion of acreage held*

Owner occupation	Managers		Non-managers	
	Proportion of owners	Proportion of forest acreage	Proportion of owners	Proportion of forest acreage
	Percent	Percent	Percent	Percent
Farmer	2.7	7.4	31.7	18.8
Business-professional	4.3	16.1	7.4	10.7
Wage earner-clerical	1.1	2.0	12.5	9.4
Housewife-widow	.2	2.0	16.8	12.8
Retired	.4	3.3	4.7	3.3
Other	.4	2.7	5.8	3.4
No response	...	...	12.0	8.1
Total owners	9.1	...	90.9	...
Total acreage	...	33.5	...	66.5

and pulp companies. The annual field days of the Southern Forest Experiment Station's research center at Crossett, Arkansas, were also mentioned by respondents. Forestry literature was notably inferior as motivation while contacts with private individuals were very effective. In a word, forestry-inclined neighbors and community leaders were excellent promoters.

Table 7. *Media influencing owner to seek professional forestry services*

Influence	Owners[1]
	Percent
Forester	16.7
Private individual	20.0
Public employee (non-forester)	10.0
Forest literature	5.0
Demonstrations and meetings	48.3
Total	100.0

[1] Information from 46 respondents representing 6,000 owners.

The limited use of professional foresters is partly related to the cost-consciousness of small owners. One-third of the non-users believe

6

they lack sufficient land and timber to justify a forester's services (table 8). These owners hold 19 acres of forest on the average and, all things considered, may have grounds for their opinion. Despite the efforts of public and private agencies, one-eighth of the owners are unaware that services are available. All who used free public forestry services intend to do so again.

Table 8. *Owners' reasons for not utilizing professional forestry services*

Reasons	Proportion of owners[1]
	Percent
Feels he does not have enough land or timber	34.6
Not interested in forestry	29.8
Unaware that services are available	11.9
Hadn't thought about it	6.9
Feels familiar with forestry	3.6
Estate cannot agree	2.2
Other	11.0
Total	100.0

[1] Information from 91 respondents representing 41,900 owners.

Agricultural Conservation Program (ACP)

In this region the Agricultural Stabilization Committee will rebate to owners about 75 percent of the costs of planting 20 acres of trees annually, and of carrying out stand-improvement measures on an equal acreage. The landowner may contract the work to recommended crews or do it himself, but it must pass inspection prior to rebate. Although practically all owners are eligible, the program has not been used by those holding less than 30 acres of woodland.

The regional estimate is some 2,800 recipients of ACP forestry payments; of this number 85 percent hold between 30 and 499 acres. Among non-users it is estimated that 16,500, a surprisingly large number, are unaware that payments are available, while 1,500 lack time for the work, and others complain of red tape. Of the estimated 8,400 owners who object to subsidy programs in general, some have made forestry investments solely with their own resources.

Tree planting popular.—Recent decades have seen a steady increase in the rate of planting trees, chiefly loblolly pine. Almost all plantings have been on abandoned fields and pastures. In several counties, landowners have planted over 4 million seedlings in each of the past few years. The Soil Conservation Service

(SCS) handles most of the seedlings and resolves planting problems, whether the owners are under ACP or not.

The 105,000 acres of plantings summarized in table 9 include only those made during the present owners' tenure. From 1936 through 1957 government payments for planting in Arkansas were made on 44,000 acres, mostly in the Southwest. It seems obvious that the various inducements inspired owners to plant beyond the allotments of the subsidy programs. Most older plantations have been thinned once and will soon yield additional revenue. Some of the stands were established by the Civilian Conservation Corps.

Table 9. *Occupation class of owners with pine plantations[1]*

Occupation class	Proportion of owners	Proportion of acreage planted
	Percent	Percent
Farmer	25.8	15.5
Business-professional	50.5	53.4
Wage earner-clerical	16.3	13.2
Retired	4.6	12.2
Other (includes corporations)	2.8	5.7
Total	100.0	100.0

[1] Information from 36 respondents representing 3,900 owners and 105 thousand acres of plantations.

Owners are proud of their plantations, new or old. One told of how he was talked into letting "the CCC boys" plant an eroded acre; he now wishes that more land had been planted. One SCS Work Unit Conservationist said, "Get a man to plant his first tree, and he will plant for the rest of his days."

Despite the enthusiasm that planting generates, an increase in the pace may be difficult. Respondents complained about the rationing of seedlings. Production in forest nurseries is rising, but SCS personnel feel that demand for service will exceed the capacity of the present staffs. The interviews disclosed that, in recent years, few owners have personally planted trees. Most hire teams chosen from lists supplied by the SCS or the Agricultural Stabilization Committee. These professional planters are trained by SCS personnel and become highly skilled.

Several respondents remarked that it had taken two or three attempts to establish their plantation. Drought was the most common cause of failure but rabbits and livestock were also destructive. Under the ACP, the land-

7

owner is not penalized if unavoidable natural hazards destroy his seedlings.

From the interviews it is estimated that over 23,000 owners believe they have no acreage to plant. In this heavily wooded region, practically all owners have sizable areas on which low-value hardwood stands can profitably be replaced with pine. In fact, the unrecognized bulk of the plantable area requires underplanting of pine combined with hardwood control.

TSI favored too.—Between 1936 and 1957, government payments for the control of worthless hardwoods were made on about 88 thousand acres in Arkansas—again chiefly in the Southwest. In practice, TSI covers three distinct operations. First is the deadening of cull timber on both hardwood and pine sites. Second is the deadening of inferior hardwoods to release natural pine seedlings. Third is the removal of the hardwood overstory from areas underplanted to pine. This last practice is just becoming established in the region, and the limited acreage converted so far is included in the planting reported above. All three types of TSI need to be greatly expanded. On most small tracts, the returns per dollar of investment are likely to be greater than those to be had in planting open areas. The size of the need can be inferred from table 10.

Regardless of management status, the tracts average more than 10 square feet of basal area in cull timber alone. Pine tracts have nearly half their cubic footage in low-value hardwoods. Hardwood tracts are also infested with an over-abundance of low-grade trees. What the survey reveals is a rather primitive level of management, characterized mainly by tree planting on open lands.

TIMBER MARKETING

An effort was made to learn how and under what conditions stumpage is sold. About two-thirds of the owners with recent sales experience appear to have had an adequate idea of their timber's volume and value prior to sale

(table 11). The once-prevalent lump-sum sale apparently is being supplanted by cut-product sales, at least where pulpwood is concerned. Pulpwood buying yards are now found in most timbersheds, and many owners sell stumpage merely by stipulating a unit price: volume is then determined by the scalers at these yards.

Pulp company conservation foresters and other private and public foresters marked tracts for some 3,400 landowners. Though 27 percent of the owners who sold wood in the past decade are classed as timber managers, not many have taken steps to control cutting to promote stand growth and development. As can be deduced from table 10, much of the recent cutting has been in the pine component of mixed stands. In such stands confining the cut chiefly to hardwoods would be more beneficial to the

Table 10. *Respondents' stands*

Management status	Respondents	Size of average tract	Volume per acre		Basal area per acre	
			Hardwood	Softwood	Cull	Total
	Number	Acres	Cubic feet	Cubic feet	Square feet	Square feet
Pine-site tracts						
Managed	38	238	236	242	11	55
Unmanaged	61	102	239	314	11	64
Hardwood-site tracts						
Managed	12	859	469	134	18	71
Unmanaged	26	135	316	38	14	55

owner. On most upland soils in southwest Arkansas, removing hardwoods to favor pine production can increase net returns ten to twenty times.

Table 11. *Timber sales in the past 10 years, by method of sale*[1]

Volume and value	Proportion of owners selling by —	
	Lump sum	Scale of cut products
	Percent	Percent
Known by owner	1.7	63.3
Not known	31.7	3.3
Total	33.4	66.6

[1] Information from 32 respondents representing 6,000 owners.

FOREST INSURANCE, CREDIT, AND TAXATION

Forest insurance.—No forest fire insurance contracts were reported by landowners; the two respondents who had looked into the matter had decided that premiums are too high. Another individual considered his contribution to the State fire-protection fund as insurance. Other respondents, even if they knew that insurance was available (1), felt it unnecessary. But nearly all are fire-conscious. It is a testimonial to decades of public and private fire-prevention activity that not one respondent said that wildfire benefits the forest.

Before much insurance is written its availability will have to be made widely known and premiums reduced. Considerable loss experience, however, will have to be accumulated before rates can reflect actual costs. Forest credit, if it becomes widely used, may make insurance much more attractive to both lenders and borrowers.

Credit.—Few respondents use their woodlands for collateral, though four had obtained short-term loans at 6 or 7 percent. One man borrows repeatedly on timberland to obtain working capital for his sawmill. Five respondents had been able to obtain timberland loans for non-forestry purposes. Some of these loans had been made in the 1930's. Several others had tried to borrow but had been discouraged by the difficulties.

Respondents who reported difficulties in obtaining loans on timberland probably were referring to the era before 1953. In that year, section 24 of the Federal Reserve Act was amended to authorize national banks to make mortgage loans secured by first liens of forest tracts that are properly managed in all respects. The maximum loan is limited to 40 percent of the appraised value of merchantable timber.

Today Federal Land Banks, commercial banks, and insurance companies also make some loans that take into account the earning possibilities of farm woodlots (3). In addition, loans on timber property may be had from State banks in at least 20 States, Arkansas included. But if an owner wishes to borrow for stand-improvement measures or to acquire more forest property, he must use other collateral.

Taxation.—In speaking about timber taxes, respondents confined themselves to the ad valorem issue. Some said "Too high!" but the consensus is that these taxes are a small price to pay for ownership. Several respondents related taxes to the need for making woodlands yield a return on the investment. They pointed out that they will sell the land if taxes or some other expense pre-empt the yield.

No owners, not even the aged, mentioned inheritance taxes on timberland. Nor was the capital-gains aspect of timber income noted.

In short, there is little or no evidence to support the contention that insurance, credit, and taxation are major problems for Arkansas' small-tract owner. Yet these factors are theoretically important. It would appear that concern with them follows, rather than precedes, investment in timber growing.

LEASING ARRANGEMENTS

Leasing is a promising method for bringing full professional management to small wooded tracts. In many respects the production possibilities of these parcels of timberland are worth more to the wood-using industries and consulting foresters than to their owners. Under formal arrangements, the lessor assumes management of the land and usually pays the owner specified amounts for rental and for timber severed. In informal arrangements, a timber products firm gives professional services to the owners on a fee basis and receives the privilege of first refusal on stumpage. Alternatively, consulting foresters may manage the timber and sell stumpage for the landowner on shares.

Formal and informal leasing arrangements have two things in common: the lessor is under pressure to increase timber production and concomitant returns to the lessee, and the landowner is substantially relieved from making forest-management decisions. The survey found four ownerships with leasing arrangements in force.

It is estimated that 7,000 owners are interested in learning more about leasing arrangements. Most of them have little notion of what to expect. However, one respondent experienced in oil leasing expected one dollar per acre per year. The average holding of interested people is 73 acres, the median 40.

The prevailingly small tracts do not necessarily confront the would-be lessor with insuperable problems. For wood-using firms, leasing may provide greater financial returns than promoting management through alternative programs, such as farm forestry. Too, the outlay of the wood-using industries for locating and acquiring small-tract stumpage could be minimized by leasing.

9

Conclusions

Southwest Arkansans, like small-tract owners worldwide, have yet to satisfy foresters' desires for timber production. Current stocking is well below economic limits. Yet the acreage in small ownerships remains vital to the region's timber supply.

Some small-owner problems are all-owner problems. In varying degree, all holdings need improved protection from fire, insects, and diseases. All will benefit from widespread markets for little-used species, logging and milling residues, and "cull" trees. Superior strains of hardwood and pine planting stock and improved timber growing and harvesting techniques will be of value to all owners.

Aggregation is taking care of some of the small-tract problem. Between 1949 and 1958, industrial holdings increased from 2.5 to nearly 3 million acres. In the same time span, growing stock on industrial lands rose roughly 200 cubic feet per acre. It now averages 1,150 cubic feet, about double that on small tracts. Within the category of holdings of 5,000 acres or less fractioning and aggregation are likely to continue. The number of owners may stay constant or increase, but the gross acreage in holdings between 500 and 5,000 acres seems certain to rise.

To infer that the small-ownership problem is self-liquidating might be comforting, but would hardly be realistic for those who value time. This study strongly suggests a wide gap between owners' favorable attitudes and their practice.

No single panacea will serve — not even markets for "cull." Increased seedling production, more demonstrations, larger staffs of service foresters, and expansion of incentive payments would be helpful. On many tracts, however, nothing short of full professional management appears likely to succeed. It takes professional judgment to identify acres to be underplanted, areas to be regenerated naturally, trees to be deadened, and stands to be thinned. When the diagnosis has been made, moreover, the prescription will very likely have to be put into effect by someone other than the landowner. For these reasons, forestry agencies will probably stimulate management most by concentrating their efforts on tracts over 99 acres in size.

Leasing is one of the promising approaches for the 7,300 ownerships in excess of 100 acres (2 million acres in all). In a sense, the lessor has a greater financial stake in timber production than the landowner. He is under pressure to make money for the owner while providing raw material for his plant or deriving income from his services. Under lease wood-using industries can frequently manage intermingled and nearby tracts in conjunction with their own, at less cost to the owner than if he attempted to provide his own forestry services.

Consulting foresters can also aid small owners, often by giving more than advice alone. What is frequently needed are individuals or firms able to contract for all management operations from inventory and regeneration to timber harvesting and marketing.

Regardless of the form of lease or contract, it should provide for management continuity against the day the tract becomes an estate.

What are the prospects for small-tract owners in southwest Arkansas? The economic climate is favorable. Trends in land aggregation, per-capita income, and timber prices are all positive. There is also recognition that the region has economic advantages for timber growing. To benefit from these trends will require sustained and heavy investment during the next two decades. Public and private forestry agencies have stimulated good intentions among two-thirds of the area's landowners. Community leaders are confident that a sizable share of these intentions are ready to be converted to practice. Past accomplishments and future prospects suggest that it would be advantageous for the public, forest industries, and consulting foresters to redouble efforts to inspire landowners to invest in timber management.

Literature Cited

(1) Anon. 1955. Forest insurance available in South. Jour. Forestry 53: 312, 314.

(2) Mignery, A. L. 1956. Factors affecting small-woodland management in Nacogdoches county, Texas. Jour. Forestry 54: 102-105.

(3) Resources for the Future, Inc. 1958. Forest credit in the United States. 164 pp.

(4) Southern, J. H., and Miller, R. L. 1956. Ownership of land in the commercial timber area of southeast Texas, 1955. Texas Agri. Expt. Sta. Prog. Rpt. 1853, 6 pp., illus. [Processed.]

(5) U. S. Forest Service. 1958. Timber resources for America's future. U. S. Dept. Agr. Forest Res. Rpt. 14, 713 pp. (See pp. 287-321.)

Appendix

FOREST SERVICE   Budget Bureau No. 40-57176
U. S. DEPARTMENT OF AGRICULTURE   Approval Expires: 12-31-58

SURVEY OF PRIVATE FOREST LANDOWNERS

1. Name of owner: ....

2. Mail address of owner: ....

3. Ownership sample code number: ....

4. Legal form of ownership (check one): (1) individual ......; (2) partnership ......; (3) corporation ......;

    (4) estate ....

5. Occupation of owner (if more than one, indicate priority):

    Operator of wood-using plant ....(specify type: ....);

    Farmer .... (specify type: ....);

    Other .... (specify: ....).

6. Area of ownership:

    a. Area of ownership in sampling unit .... acres.
    b. Area of forest land in sampling unit .... acres.
    c. Total forest land owned in United States.. acres.
    d. General location of forest land owned outside the sampling unit ....

7. How did you acquire title to the forest land in sampling unit?
    (1) Purchase ......; (2) Inheritance ......; (3) Other ...... (specify ....).

8. Number of years in present ownership ....

9. What is the distance from tract to owner's residence? .... miles.

10. Age of owner .... years.

11. Intent of present use of forest land owned in the sampling unit? (if more than one use, number by priority):

    (1) timber growing ....;   (5) recreation ....;
    (2) timber liquidation ....;   (6) residence ....;
    (3) clearing land for   (7) minerals ....;
        agriculture ....;   (8) speculation ....;
    (4) grazing ....;   (9) other .... (specify ....).

12. Have you followed any forestry practices on any of your properties?

    (1) none ......; (2) planting ......; (3) timber stand improvement ....;
    (4) regeneration cutting ....; (5) fencing out stock ....;
    (6) prescribed burning ....; (7) plowing fire lines ....;
    (8) other .... (specify ....)

13. Do you think it would be profitable to invest your money in any of these forestry practices?
    Yes ....; No ....

    a. IF YES, specify practices ....
    b. IF NO, state reasons ....

14. Have you used a forester on any of your properties?

    (1) none ....; (2) private consulting forester ....; (3) industrial service forester ....;
    (4) State forester ....; (5) SCS forester ....; (6) extension forester ....;
    (7) other .... (specify ....).

    a. IF ANY USED, who or what influenced you to employ them? (if more than one, indicate priority):

(1) county agent ......; (2) CFM service forester ......;
(3) ASC committee man ......; (4) SCS personnel ......;
(5) neighbor's recommendation ......; (6) public forestry literature ......;
(7) private forestry literature ... ; (8) public demonstrations and meetings ......;
(9) private demonstrations and meetings ......; (10) other (specify ....).

b. IF ANY USED, what is your opinion of forestry services provided?

(1) Was service prompt? Yes ......; No ......;
(2) Was cost reasonable? Yes ......; No ......;
(3) Would you use forestry services again if they were free? Yes ......; No ......;
(4) If a nominal charge were made? Yes ......; No ......;
(5) If you would not use foresters again give reasons briefly: _____

c. IF NOT USED, what was the most important reason for not doing so?

(1) not interested in forestry ......; (2) services sought but not located ......; (3) owner unaware that services were available ......; (4) owner disagreed with forester's advice ......; (5) owner believed he knew forestry principles ......; (6) other (specify _____).

15. Have you obtained ACP forestry payments on any of your properties? Yes ......; No ......

a. IF YES, what ACP conservation measures were adopted?

(1) tree planting ......; (2) thinning ......; (3) pruning ......; (4) release of desirable trees ......; (5) site preparation for natural seeding ......; (6) fencing ......; (7) other ...... (specify _____).

b. IF YES, who or what influenced you to obtain ACP payments? (if more than one, indicate priority).

(1) count agent......; (2) CFM service forester ......; (3) ASC committee man ......; (4) SCS personnel ......; (5) neighbor's recommendation ......; (6) public forestry literature ......; (7) private forestry literature ......; (8) public demonstrations and meetings ......; (9) private demonstrations and meetings ......; (10) other ...... (specify _____).

c. IF NO, why were payments not obtained?

(1) not available in locality ......; (2) owner not interested in forestry ......; (3) owner unaware that payments were available ......; (4) too much "red tape" involved in making application ......; (5) lack of time to do the work required ......; (6) owner unsympathetic to subsidy programs ......; (7) other ...... (specify: _____).

16. What area have you planted to trees on your properties? ......acres.

a. From what source did you obtain the planting stock? (if more than one indicate priority).

(1) State forester ......; (2) ASC committee (Soil Bank) ......; (3) ACP ......; (4) SCS ......; (5) forest-industry ......; (6) commercial nursery ......; (7) other ...... (specify: _____).

b. IF YES, who or what influenced you to plant? (if more than one, indicate priority).

(1) county agent ......; (2) CFM service forester ......; (3) ASC committee ......; (4) SCS area advisor ......; (5) neighbor's recommendation ......; (6) public forestry literature ......; (7) private forestry literature ......; (8) public demonstrations and meetings ......; (9) private demonstrations and meetings ......; (10) other (specify _____).

c. IF NO, what was principal reason for not participating in program?

(1) lack of plantable area ......; (2) owner unaware that assistance was available ......; (3) terms of program unsatisfactory ......; (4) lack of time to plant ......; (5) unsympathetic to public aid programs ......; (6) other ...... (specify: _____).

17. Have you tried to borrow funds on the security of any of your forest land and timber? Yes ......; No ......

a. IF YES, was credit sought to:

(1) acquire or manage forest property _____;
(2) other (nonforestry) purposes _____

b. If loan was granted, what were conditions of loan? _____

c. IF NO, was reason:

(1) credit not needed ......; (2) belief that credit was not available ......; (3) terms not satisfactory ......; (4) other ......(specify: _____).

18. Have you tried to insure any of your timber stands against forest fire or other hazards? Yes ......; No ......

a. IF YES, was insurance desired by a lender in connection with a loan on your timber stand Yes ....; No ....

b. IF NO, why did you not apply? ....

19. Have you placed any of your forest properties under long-term lease or other arrangement for forest management? Yes ....; No ....

    a. IF YES, indicate area under lease: .... acres.

    b. IF YES, give name and type of management agency ....

    c. IF NO, would you be interested in having your forest property managed for you by lease or other arrangement? Yes ....; No ....

        (1) If interested, indicate acceptable terms ....
        (2) If not interested, why not ....

20. Do you lease or rent any of your forest land to farmers under terms where the farmer holds the cutting rights? Yes ....; No ....

    a. If yes, how much forest land do you rent to him? .... acres.

21. Do the taxes on your forest land and timber materially affect your forest management decisions? Yes ....; No ....

22. Do you think that uncontrolled wild fires are bad for your timber? Yes ....; No ....; Why? ....

23. When did you last sell timber? 19........

    a. Was a written timber-sale agreement used? Yes ....; No ....

    b. Did you have an accurate estimate of volume and value? Yes ....; No ....

    c. What was the basis of payment?
        (1) lump sum ....; (2) scale of cut products ....;
        (3) other .... (specify ....).

    d. Is home use important? Yes ....; No ....

24. General description of forest cover in sample tract in sampling unit:
        (1) Forest types: ....
        (2) Stand size classes: ....
        (3) Stocking: ....
        (4) Quality of timber: ....
        (5) Average basal area per acre: ....sq. ft.
        (6) Estimated average timber value per acre: $ ....

25. Grazing use of forest area in sampling unit:
        (1) Heavy ....; (2) light ....; (3) none ....

26. Remarks: ....
....

Recorder: ....

Date: ....

OCCASIONAL PAPER 171   1959

GUIDELINES

for

Direct-Seeding

Longleaf Pine

Harold J. Derr

and

W. F. Mann, Jr.

SOUTHERN FOREST EXPERIMENT STATION

PHILIP A. BRIEGLEB, DIRECTOR

FOREST SERVICE, U. S. DEPARTMENT OF AGRICULTURE

Acknowledgments

The direct seeding of longleaf pine has received a large impetus from foresters whose confidence in the species prompted them to make exploratory seeding trials. Their cooperative efforts furnished basic information on the requirements for longleaf seeding in the years before effective repellants were developed. The following persons and organizations merit special recognition:

Charles H. Lewis, Jr., Crosby Chemicals, Inc., DeRidder, Louisiana.

Robert E. Mitchell, Hillyer-Deutsch-Edwards. Inc., Oakdale, Louisiana.

James E. Mixon and staff members of the Louisiana Forestry Commission, Baton Rouge, Louisiana.

William M. Palmer, Jr., Nebo Oil Company, Good Pine, Louisiana.

Hugh S. Redding and staff members of the Kisatchie National Forest, Alexandria, Louisiana.

Cooperation was also furnished by the Director and staff members of the Denver Wildlife Laboratory, Fish and Wildlife Service, U. S. Department of Interior. The assignment of Mr. Brooke Meanley to Alexandria, Louisiana, for bird-repellant investigations from July 1955 to August 1957 expedited the testing of repellent materials and of techniques for their use.

Cover: *Direct seeding is bringing longleaf pine back to many acres of its native range.*

CONTENTS

Figure 1. *The major breakthrough in developing successful seeding techniques for the southern pines was the finding of an effective bird repellant.*

GUIDELINES FOR DIRECT-SEEDING LONGLEAF PINE

Harold J. Derr and W. F. Mann, Jr.

Southern Forest Experiment Station

In the past few years, direct seeding of longleaf pine has moved from the exploratory stage to full operational use. This achievement culminates a dozen years of intensive study of a forest regeneration technique that has long intrigued foresters by its apparent simplicity.

Direct sowing of pine has been especially appealing to owners of the cutover longleaf lands, where seed trees are usually inadequate for natural regeneration, and where planting of this species is unreliable. Wide acceptance of direct seeding as a method of restocking longleaf land promises to keep this valuable species in the pine forests of the South.

Since 1947, when the first direct-seeding test was installed by the Alexandria Research Center, 19 field-plot and pilot-stage studies have been completed. While these dealt with all aspects of the topic, the principal objective was control of seed losses to birds and mammals. After a 1953 study demonstrated that a chemical seed coating would repel birds, progress was rapid. In the past four years, Louisiana landowners have seeded 42,300 acres on 31 separate projects.

Invaluable experience has been gained from the efforts of landowners whose interest prompted many of the earlier exploratory trials. Large-scale seedings furnished a means for evaluating the mass effect of seed predators, and, later, critical repellant testing that was impossible to achieve on small plots.

Direct seeding in essence involves the process of supplying viable seed to prepared forest sites in the proper amounts and at suitable seasons of the year so that germination of the seed in place will result in adequate stocking. Achieving this objective economically requires accurate distribution of seed and protection of seed and seedlings against predators. Each major aspect of longleaf pine direct seeding, from initial planning to management of the stand, is discussed separately in the following sections. As the discussions embody the results of numerous studies and the conclusions from many operational trials, no attempt has been made to document or analyze each study and pilot test.

The research and field trials on which these guidelines are based were completed entirely within the longleaf pine type in central and southwestern Louisiana. Direct seeding can probably be used to regenerate longleaf pine throughout its natural range. However, variations in climatic or biotic conditions may require some modification of the procedures developed in Louisiana. For example, when rodents are a limiting factor, effective chemicals for their control must be included in the seed coating. Where soil conditions are adverse, such as in the Florida sandhills, very intensive site preparation may be essential. Geographic variations in the amount and distribution of rainfall can alter the sowing dates or seedbed treatments recommended for Louisiana conditions. Trials east of the Mississippi River should include local study of the factors affecting seed losses, seed germination, and initial survival. Results from a single test should be interpreted with caution. Variations in the biological factors involved, together with fluctuations in the climatic influences from year to year, will often necessitate several years of testing before the necessary modifications in techniques for a local area are apparent.

A list of references has been provided for readers interested in phases of the subject that are beyond the scope of this paper.

PLANNING FOR LONGLEAF SEEDING

Planning for the direct seeding of longleaf must take cognizance of several basic factors. Adaptability of longleaf to the sites in need of regeneration must be weighed, along with the stringent requirements of this species for intensive management and protection while the stands are young. When it has been decided that longleaf is suitable to the site in question, early planning should be directed toward the protection of seeds and seedlings.

Site Selection

It is tempting to try direct seeding first on sites where planting has failed or appears unlikely to succeed. A sounder policy is to confine initial trials to the better, easier sites and move cautiously to the adverse ones as experience is gained.

Longleaf does well on a wide variety of soils in the Gulf Coastal Plain. Its performance on the drier sites is notable, and some foresters value it also for its ability to survive and grow in areas where the incidence of wildfires makes loblolly or slash pine a risky choice.

In theory, longleaf can be seeded on all sites that it occupied in the virgin stands. In practice, some of these sites may present difficulties.

Many good longleaf sites are dominated by scrub hardwoods. Trials in a few stands of post-size blackjack oak and post oak indicate that such areas can be seeded if complete control of the hardwoods is achieved before or very soon after pine is seeded (fig. 2). Any method that will eradicate the overstory and prevent sprouting from the rootstocks is satisfactory. The practice of delaying hardwood control until there is assurance of first-year pine survival is inadvisable. Though longleaf seedlings will survive for a year under a hardwood canopy, their response to delayed release is slow. By contrast, seedlings released in their first season can develop the vigor they need to get above the heavy growth of herbaceous plants that usually follows complete hardwood control.

Hardwood areas tend to have large populations of seed-eating mammals, particularly rodents, during the germination season. While rodents ordinarily are not a serious threat to November sowing on open land, damaging numbers of them may be encountered on sites with a uniform cover of scrub hardwoods. Seeding on such areas requires the addition to the seed coating of a chemical which will repel or kill persistent seed-eating rodents.

Common to the area that originally supported longleaf are the "flatwoods," broad tracts of sandy or silt-loam soil whose internal drainage is impeded by a shallow hardpan. Surface drainage also is poor, though the flatwoods are not necessarily level. While these lands once supported longleaf, seeding and planting both run considerable risk from unfavorable weather. These sites can be as droughty as sandy ridgetops, for the moisture in the shallow soil above the hardpan is quickly depleted. There is evidence, too, that intensive site preparation such as double disking is ineffective in reducing heavy seedling mortality during severe dry periods in the first summer. On the other hand, these sites tend to flood for extended periods when heavy rains fall during the germination season. Longleaf seed can tolerate brief flooding, but frequent or extended inundation causes germination failures. While seeding on flatwood sites has met with moderate success, it should be recognized that greater risks are involved.

Planning for Protection

Adequate protection of both seed and seedlings is vital. Every seeding project encounters many hazards between the date of sowing and the time when the trees are in active height growth. The most obvious risk—loss of seed to birds, insects, and rodents during the germination period—can be averted by using a repellent seed coating. Post-germination hazards should receive considerable attention during the planning stage, as the heavy mortality of new seedlings can be as disastrous as the total loss of seed.

Fencing is a prerequisite on most sites where livestock roams freely. No matter how it is regenerated, young longleaf cannot tolerate even moderate grazing by cattle, sheep, or goats. Hogs, even in small numbers, are fatal.

Under open-range conditions, fencing raises multitudinous problems. To keep the per-acre cost of a hog-proof fence down, large areas must be enclosed, but if local-use cattle grazing is permitted, light cross fences are usually also required. Land heavily grazed by cattle is best fenced 6 to 8 months prior to seeding, so as to conserve the new stand of grass that develops after the preparatory burn.

Within their ranges, town ants and pocket gophers ("salamanders") can be very destructive on well-drained sites. The ants must be controlled well in advance, for they begin their work as soon as the seeds germinate. Generally some follow-up treatments will also be needed before the seedlings start height growth. Pocket gophers are not a threat until the second or third year after germination, but control before seeding will simplify the task of keeping down populations thereafter.

The probable need for at least one prescribed burn for control of brown-spot needle blight should be considered. If installed in advance of seeding, the firebreaks required for such burning will reduce the hazard of wildfire.

Burns to control brown spot are generally made after the seedlings have passed their third growing season. Reinforcement seeding on areas with inadequate reproduction must be timed so that the fires will not seriously damage the different age classes. Assignment of other species to sites within a longleaf seeding area is inadvisable, especially where the brown-spot hazard is high. Islands of an unburnable species or age class run up the cost of burning, partly because they prevent the use of inexpensive headfires. They also are sources of brown-spot reinfection.

SITE PREPARATION

A light grass rough, such as develops after a burn made 6 to 8 months before seeding, has proved to be the best seedbed on most sites. Fresh burns and disked strips have also been seeded successfully. Each of these site treatments, however, has specific limitations.

A light rough was recommended after it was recognized that old roughs prevent longleaf seed from reaching the mineral soil, and after operational trials had demonstrated that untreated seed on a fresh burn is vulnerable to heavy bird attack. Even with effective bird repellants, a light rough is generally preferable to a fresh burn, as it provides a more favorable microclimate for germination by reducing the drying effect of wind and sun and by accumulating dew. This effect was demonstrated in a 1954 trial of repellant-treated seed on both types of seedbeds. Soil moisture was ample when the 180-acre project was seeded on November 22, but no rain fell for 19 days thereafter. The soil surface within the burned area became so dry that much of the germinating seed failed to root. The tree percent (proportion of seeds that produced seedlings) after 41 days was 23 on the fresh burn and 35 on the light rough.

When soil moisture is not critical, freshly burned seedbeds are satisfactory and may have some advantages. Seeding on a fresh burn is often necessary when unexpected seed becomes available or bad weather interferes with spring burns. Autumn fires, as opposed to spring burns, provide better control of brown spot on areas with infected natural seedlings, greater reduction of rodent populations, later control of hardwood sprouts, and slightly faster juvenile growth of pine seedlings. Fresh burns should not be relied upon completely because in wet seasons they may be difficult to accomplish just prior to seeding. A safe policy is to burn in April or May, and reserve fall burning for special contingencies. Fresh burns are always superior to grass roughs more than one year old. They are not recommended on rolling sites because surface runoff during heavy rains often washes the seed and dislodges seedlings before the radicles have entered the ground.

In preparing sites, the influence of adjoining areas should be considered. When the seedbed burn is made, a buffer area should be burned if possible. Grass roughs older than two years often harbor numerous rodents and other small mammals, but a buffer strip of 5 to 10 chains in width should markedly reduce rodent damage on the periphery of the seeded area.

On dry sites, thorough disking improves first-summer survival by eliminating much of the vegetation that competes with pines for soil moisture. On good sites, disking will promote seedling growth if brown spot is not severe, but it must be complete enough to kill most of the native perennial grasses. The best procedure is to burn in the winter before seeding and then disk twice during late summer. To kill grass roots, initial disking should be done during hot, dry weather. Relatively heavy equipment is needed. The second disking can be done with lighter equipment 3 to 6 weeks after the first. A single disking with light or medium equipment during the fall months just before seeding is of questionable value, for partial control of competing vegetation is of small benefit.

The cost of the heavy treatment that is needed to remove native grasses on open sites can be held down by disking in strips. Disking 8-foot strips, spaced 8 feet apart, will require approximately one-half mile of equipment travel per acre for each disking. Less seed is required than for overall sowing, especially if sowing is confined to disked strips.

The benefits of disking should be weighed against the disadvantages. A large investment in equipment for disking and seeding is needed. Simple broadcast sowing—whether from the ground or the air—has not proved satisfactory on disked sites. So far, good results have been achieved only with mechanical seeders that press the seed into contact with firm soil. This fact limits operations to the capacity of tractor-drawn seeders, and prevents working on heavy soils in wet weather.

Disked soil, like burned sites, dries quickly after a rain. Consequently, light rains, which can sustain germination on a rough, are often ineffective on disked soil. On the other hand, heavy rains can be damaging, especially if the disking impedes natural drainage. The hazard of flooding can be reduced somewhat by elevating or ridging the soil in the final disking. If elevated, disked strips must be run at right angles to the topographic contours to facilitate drainage.

A final consideration is the brown-spot hazard. The intensity of brown-spot infection varies from place to place. Seedlings on some areas have remained free of the disease for five years, while elsewhere two or more control burns have been required to get a stand out of the grass. By exposing mineral soil, disking can increase the rate of infection and necessitate additional burns. On high-hazard areas, the full benefits of disking can be realized only when a brown-spot control spray is used (fig. 3).

SEED PROCUREMENT

Early planning for seed procurement is essential. A landowner has three alternatives. He may either collect and extract his own seed, collect cones and have the seed extracted by a commercial dealer, or buy cleaned seed. All

Figure 3.

These pines were seeded on disked strips and sprayed once for control of the brown-spot disease. They are now in the middle of their fourth growing season.

three methods have merit, and the landowner's choice will depend on the supply of cones in his area, his facilities for drying cones, and the cost of commercial seed. If commercial seed is to be used, it is advisable to place orders at least six months in advance. Usually suppliers will accept orders by June or July if they think that a crop is in prospect.

A major difficulty in longleaf seeding has been the procurement of large quantities of fresh seed for November sowing. Early failures with stored seed of unknown viability led to the assumption that fresh seed was essential.

Recent trials have shown that stored seed can be used if viability is maintained at a high level. In the fall of 1956, approximately 3,000 pounds of one-year-old (1955) seed were sown by 5 Louisiana landowners, along with 5,000 pounds of fresh seed (1956). No important differences were detected in either total germination or rate of germination. On one 450-acre tract, fresh seed yielded 5,100 established seedlings per acre, while stored seed produced 4,600. All sowing was at the rate of 3 pounds of seed per acre. In the fall of 1957, stored seed was used entirely on one 1,800-acre area with satisfactory results. Moisture during the germination period was ample in both years. The performance of stored seed when moisture is critically low has not been tested adequately.

Cold storage of longleaf seed for at least one year is practical. Excellent viability can be maintained at storage temperatures between 0° F. and 32° F. if the moisture content is held between 8 and 10 percent. These conditions can be met by drying the seed in a forced-air cone kiln, then storing it in sealed drums. Failures of earlier trials with stored seed were due

largely to storage at moisture levels of 18 to 20 percent. Studies now under way indicate that 3-year storage may be feasible.

In purchases of seed, whether fresh or stored, minimum standards of quality and purity should be specified. Variations in cone maturity, cone storage, seed-extraction methods, and the equipment for dewinging and cleaning can cause wide variations in different lots from the same seed year.

Unless fresh seed is damaged by improper handling, germination of 75 to 90 percent (sound-seed basis) can be expected. With fresh seed, the general procedure has been to omit a pre-sowing germination test. Stored seed should be thoroughly tested so that adjustment in the sowing rate can be made if the germinative capacity is below 70 percent. To what extent **seed can deteriorate in storage and still be ac-**ceptable has not been determined. Low viability can be partially compensated by increasing the sowing rate, but seed that performs poorly in laboratory tests may do even worse amid the rigors of the field. When viability drops to 50 percent or less, the seed is of questionable value for direct seeding.

Cleaning to 95 percent sound seed is easily attained, and should be specified. Impurities should be held to less than 2 percent by weight. At best, precise sowing of repellant-coated longleaf seed is not easy. Trash and poorly dewinged seed make the job difficult to the point of impossibility, especially when airplanes are used. Empty seeds are an unnecessary burden.

Since 1948, the price of clean seed has ranged from $0.89 to $3.25 per pound, mainly in response to variations in the supply. The price

5

will tend to stabilize as more suppliers enter the market, but short crops are likely to inflate costs until storage facilities are developed and wider experience is gained with stored seed.

The irregularity of generally good longleaf seed years is well known, but abundant cone crops occur nearly every year somewhere within the species' range. To obtain adequate supplies of fresh seed, landowners sometimes draw on distant sources. While it is recognized that geographic races of longleaf pine exist, the hazard of moving seed beyond its distinct geographical zone has not been so clearly demonstrated as for shortleaf and loblolly pine. Georgia seed, used in Louisiana during 1953 and 1954, performed satisfactorily in respect to germination, survival, and juvenile growth. Within the past 10 years, the second-growth stands in southwest Louisiana have produced a collectible cone crop at intervals of about 3 years—in 1948, 1951, 1955, and 1958. To direct-seed longleaf annually with fresh seed means that non-local sources must be relied upon in two years out of three. The alternatives are to develop storage facilities for local seed or to synchronize operations with good local crops, which generally can be predicted a year in advance.

Proper handling of fresh seed is often neglected when large quantities are involved. Longleaf seed can deteriorate rapidly if stored at high temperatures—above 80° F.—or if the moisture content is too high. Moisture content of fresh seed ordinarily ranges from 15 to 25 percent, depending on the method of extraction. While this is excessive for long storage, the seed can be kept for short periods without refrigeration in a cool, well-ventilated room, and if bulking or close stacking is avoided. For storage of more than 7 to 10 days, refrigeration is the safest procedure.

Prolonged bulk storage after the repellent coating has been applied should be avoided (see p. 9).

BIRD AND ANIMAL HAZARDS

Correct evaluation of the bird and mammal hazards is the most difficult aspect of a seeding project. Judging animal populations requires considerable experience. In their early seeding trials, foresters often underestimate the biological hazards on a specific site. Frequent and detailed observations, as well as knowledge of seasonal population cycles, usually are required to detect predators. Birds are particularly difficult to evaluate because the troublesome species such as the meadowlark and blackbird fluctuate widely in their daily activity, and when seasonal migration begins bird numbers increase suddenly. However, either of the two tested chemical repellants—Arasan and anthraquinone—obviate the bird problem in longleaf seeding.

Small mammals are not sensitive to these repellants. Hence, a prospective site should be examined for gross evidence of unusual concentrations of such seedeaters. The offenders include shrews and the common field rodents such as the harvest mouse, white-footed mouse, and the cotton rat. Of the larger animals that are known seedeaters, the cottontail rabbit is the most widely distributed. Raccoons, opossums, and skunks are sometimes troublesome locally.

Much remains to be learned about the ecology of shrews and small rodents that inhabit the longleaf pine type. Trapping records and observations form the basis for the following general statements:

Wide seasonal fluctuations occur on upland sites, with populations usually peaking in late January or February. Apart from these seasonal variations, shrew populations appear to be cyclic, whereas the numbers of small rodents are fairly consistent from year to year.

The October-November population on areas burned in the previous spring is low when compared to that on similar unburned sites, but after the mid-winter population peaks are reached shrews and rodents inhabit all cover conditions, including fresh burns.

All rodents and shrews are voracious seedeaters. The Arasan compounds will deter these animals, but are not effective when populations are heavy. Under such conditions a toxic chemical must be included in the seed coating.

In Louisiana's longleaf type, a catch of 1 or 2 shrews or rodents per 100 trap nights in October and November might be considered normal. A catch of 5 to 10 animals per 100 trap nights indicates an unusually high population for open sites with a light grass rough. By mid-January, 15 to 20 animals frequently can be taken in 100 trap nights.

An alternative to trapping is the seed-spot technique. Small cleared places sown with 50 untreated seeds will serve the purpose. A spot visited by an animal during a night of exposure is treated as a trap catch. Spots should be in transect lines spaced so as to sample adequately the various cover conditions on an area. Locations on the transects should be at least 5 chains apart. Evaluation of results requires some familiarity with the distinction between bird and small-mammal damage to untreated seed. Figure 11, page 15, illustrates typical damage caused by some of the most prevalent predators.

Raccoons, skunks, and opossums usually are not numerous. Normally, cottontail rabbits are not a serious threat. Populations vary from year to year, however, and may reach levels of one animal for two acres on upland sites. When fresh droppings are found on 30 to 40 percent of milacre sample plots, a high population is indicated. If seeding is attempted, very careful observation of seed and seedlings is essential. Hunting is the most practical control for rabbits. Night hunting is very effective, but most states require the approval of game authorities. The effect of chemical seed coatings on rabbits when high populations are encountered has not been determined. Though repelled from taking seed, rabbits may still eat seedlings during the first winter after germination.

CHOICE OF A REPELLANT

Prior to the 1954 season, direct seeding of longleaf pine on an operational scale was a hit or miss proposition. Success or failure hinged on the prevalence of birds during the germination period. Early seeding was resorted to in an attempt to avoid losses to fall migratory birds, and shotgun patrols were employed to scare birds.

In a preliminary test in 1953, Morkit[1] and sublimed synthetic anthraquinone showed considerable promise as bird repellants. A 180-acre pilot test in 1954 demonstrated that Morkit, which contains anthraquinone as the active ingredient, effectively repelled most species of birds common to open sites. Use of repellants expanded rapidly in 1955, and both Morkit and anthraquinone gave excellent bird control on 7,000 acres. Morkit was withdrawn from the American market during the summer of 1956, but preliminary tests of Arasan[2] had indicated this chemical would repel birds and possibly rodents. Consequently, Arasan was used in the 1956 season on seven projects totalling 4,000 acres. It was also employed on approximately 10,000 acres of operational seeding in Louisiana during 1957. In addition, seven intensive small-plot studies confirmed that Arasan is a very effective bird repellant, but revealed that its rodent repellancy was not so great as originally thought.

The present choice of a bird repellant is between Arasan and sublimed synthetic anthraquinone. Either Arasan or Arasan-75 can be used. Other Arasan compounds should not be substituted because some are toxic to the seeds. Both Arasan compounds are equally effective, and at the recommended dosages cost about the same. When used with latex sticker, the wettable Arasan-75 provides a firmer seed coating than the nonwettable Arasan. Because both Arasan formulations irritate skin, eyes, and mucous membranes, they are undesirable for hand seeding, where laborers are constantly exposed to chemical dust from the seed. They can be used for aerial and tractor seeding if workers avoid prolonged exposure or wear protective masks. Anthraquinone, a non-irritating chemical, is recommended for hand seeding even though it is slightly more expensive than the Arasan compounds.

Anthraquinone and Arasan should be applied at the rate of 15 pounds per 100 pounds of seed. Arasan-75, containing a higher concentration of thiram than Arasan[2], can be used at a 10-percent concentration or 10 pounds of Arasan-75 per 100 pounds of seed.

In most cases, endrin should be blended with the bird repellant for protection of the seed against insects, shrews, and rodents. The amount should be varied according to the hazard. For early fall sowing on sites where populations of seed-eating insects or rodents are

---

[1] A proprietary bird repellant developed for agricultural use by German chemists, and suggested for direct seeding trials at Alexandria, Louisiana, by Professor John Kuprionis of Louisiana Polytechnic Institute
[2] The term Arasan includes the 50 percent formulation of thiram (tetramethylthiuramdisulfide) known as Arasan, and also Arasan-75, which is a wettable powder containing 75 percent thiram.

known to be low, 1 pound of Stauffer's Endrin 50W[3] (0.5 pound effective endrin) per 100 pounds of seed provides ample protection. Where populations are high (or unknown), the concentration of Endrin 50W should be 2 pounds per 100 pounds of seed.

Many November seedings in Louisiana have been highly successful without the use of endrin. For this reason, careful consideration should be given to the dosage used. The chemical, sold mainly as an insecticide, is very poisonous to all animal life, including human beings. Under no circumstances should endrin be used alone, because it is not an adequate bird repellant and will endanger birdlife.

If used, endrin should be thoroughly mixed with the bird repellant before it is applied to the seed. Complete mixing of the two chemicals is essential to insure that all seeds have the proper amount of each. This can be done best with regular mixing equipment available at commercial chemical formulating plants. Safety precautions for handling endrin-treated seed are discussed on page 9.

An adhesive is essential for holding the repellant to the seed. Flintkote C-13-HPC asphalt emulsion and Dow Latex 512R have served well under various weather conditions. Asphalt emulsion should be mixed with water in a ratio of 1:3, by volume. Latex can be diluted with water in the ratio of 1:9. With either sticker, about one gallon is needed for 100 pounds of seed.

SEED TREATING TECHNIQUES

Methods improvised in 1954 for coating large quantities of seed with a chemical repellant have been used since then to treat at least 120,000 pounds of longleaf seed. The technique is simple, but requires planning, timing, and facilities for drying seed after treating.

Equipment consists of a mixing drum, a dipping vat and perforated seed basket, scales, and drying facilities. If inclement weather prevents sun drying, well-ventilated sheds or other buildings should be available where the seed can be spread out in thin layers.

Figure 4 illustrates simple but effective home-made equipment. The drum on the right

has the top removed; it holds the sticker, into which the seed is dipped by means of the 20-inch-deep, fine-meshed heavy wire basket. The other drum is for applying the chemical. It has a close-fitting but removable cover and is mounted on an axle so that it tumbles end-over-end when the crank is turned. A single set of baffles is welded inside the drum to help mix the seed and repellant.

Figure 4. *With this simple equipment, made from 2 oil drums, a 3-man crew can treat a ton of seed a day.*

If a blend of Arasan or anthraquinone and endrin is to be used, the first step is to mix these chemicals together thoroughly. This can be accomplished in the tumbling drum or in a small cement mixer. If possible, though, it is best to have the job done in a plant that formulates agricultural insecticides.

The sticker is mixed with water in the dipping drum. If asphalt emulsion is chosen, it should be stirred until all lumps disappear—warm water gives faster action than cold. Latex mixes very quickly with water and no special precautions are needed. Either sticker should be stirred at regular intervals during the treating operation. The actual treating is done by putting 35 to 50 pounds of dewinged seed into the basket and lowering it into the sticker. The seed should be stirred with a wooden paddle. In 1 or 2 minutes, the basket is pulled up and

3 A list of current supply sources and approximate costs of repellants and stickers is available on request.

8

the surplus sticker allowed to drain off for about 30 seconds. Next, the seed is emptied from the basket into the tumbler and a weighed quantity of repellant poured over it and mixed in with the paddle. The cover is then closed tightly and the drum rotated for about two minutes, after which the coated seed is spread out on a canvas to dry.

With either adhesive, it is important to apply the dry repellant while the sticker is wet. If the sticker is given time to set, excessive amounts of the repellant will be lost in the field. The time allowed for draining after a batch is removed from the immersion drum should not exceed ½ minute. When latex is used, a measured quantity can be applied directly to the dry seed in an open rotating mixer. Only the amount required to coat a batch of seed is added. This method is faster and does not require the preparation of surplus material needed for batch immersion. It is satisfactory only for latex, however, as asphalt emulsion does not weather well unless seeds are immersed in it for 1 to 2 minutes.

Aluminum powder, at a rate of about 15 tablespoons per 100 pounds of seed, hastens drying and improves flow characteristics. If used, the powder should be placed in the treating drum after the seed is mixed with the repellant.

A difficulty in local treating is the drying and handling of seed during extended periods of wet weather. Efficient aerial sowing requires 3,000 to 4,000 pounds of seed for a day's operation, and the seed must be dry enough to flow freely through the hopper opening of the plane. A safe procedure on large projects is to schedule seeding for a specific date, then treat during fair weather in the week preceding. If the seed is well dried, it can be stored for short periods in a cool, well-ventilated building. An alternate procedure is to arrange for artificial drying. Forced-air kilns operating at temperatures of 100° F. or less are satisfactory.

Arasan and anthraquinone are effective only when fully exposed on top of the sticker. Slurries, or mixtures of the dry powder with the liquid adhesive, lack full repellancy. Consequently, personnel treating seed or handling large quantities of the treated seed are exposed to considerable chemical dust. It is difficult to avoid, even when working outdoors. Workers should be furnished protective respirators, preferably the type with a face mask covering the eyes. Their clothing should fit closely. All who work with endrin should wear rubber gloves and bathe at the end of the day. These measures prevent discomforting effects from Arasan dust. With endrin, they are essential for safety, for this poison can be absorbed through the skin.

Seeding failures in recent years have been due largely to the improper use of the adhesive. An increase in the concentration of either the asphalt or latex is likely to slow the absorption of moisture by the seed, and thus reduce the rate of germination. Sticker concentrations below the recommended levels will reduce the durability of the coating. Dow latex, as received from the manufacturer, is a suspension of solids that will break down through improper storage and cannot be recovered. Temperatures above 110° F. or below 32° will destroy the suspension, as will storage in metal containers and dilution with very hard water. The thin rubbery coating provided by latex can be rubbed off by prolonged agitation in the mixing drum. Fresh batches of latex or asphalt emulsion should be prepared if treating is interrupted for more than 12 hours, for these preparations appear to lose their effectiveness with time.

A 3-man crew can treat a ton or more of seed per day. The limit on production usually is the amount that can be dried. Labor and materials averaged about $0.15 per pound when treating was done at the rate of 3 man-days per ton. For a typical operation in which Arasan was applied at 15 percent by weight, treating costs were:

	Cost per ton
Labor @ $1.25 per hour	
Seed treating	$ 30.00
Drying and sacking	8.00
Latex sticker—2 gallons @ $3.00	6.00
Arasan—300 pounds @ $0.88	264.00
Total	$308.00
Cost per pound	$0.154

Costs run about the same when asphalt emulsion is substituted for latex and when anthraquinone is used in place of Arasan. These estimates do not include supervision or depreciation.

9

RATE AND SEASON OF SOWING

A sowing rate of three pounds of dewinged seed per acre was adopted in initial studies at Alexandria and has been used in most operational seeding by broadcast methods. With fresh seed of good quality, this rate provides approximately 10,000 viable seeds per acre. The rate on disked strips has been about 1½ pounds per gross acre.

The highest tree percent in trials with untreated seed was about 25, or 2,500 established seedlings per acre. With repellants, a maximum tree percent of 60 has been achieved. However, results from most of the operational trials have ranged between 30 and 50 percent, or 3,000 to 5,000 seedlings per acre. Experience indicates that on good sites minimum initial stocking in the spring following seeding should be at least 2,000 well-distributed seedlings per acre. On poor sites the goal for initial stocking should be higher because first-year mortality will be greater. Intensive site preparation, which lowers the hazard of drought losses in the first summer, reduces the level of initial stocking needed. On disked strips 1,500 seedlings per gross acre seems adequate.

In 1957, exploratory tests of several lower seeding rates achieved an average of about 1,700 seedlings per pound of seed when predators were controlled. These and other results indicate that the rate can be reduced to two pounds per acre on favorable sites. Three pounds are still recommended for adverse sites.

The foregoing recommendations presuppose seed of good quality. Fresh longleaf seed, properly handled and thoroughly cleaned, will have about 3,400 viable seeds per pound, with some variation by year of collection, source, and moisture content. In estimating quality, sufficient weighed samples of a lot should be counted and cut open to provide a numerical estimate of the sound seed in a pound. Germination of fresh sound seed averages about 80 percent, but may range from 70 to 95 percent in a single season. Unless damage in extraction or handling is suspected, fresh seed can be sown without waiting for the results of a germination test, which requires about two weeks. Even if sowing proceeds, however, a sandflat or a screened field-test of the seed may provide a useful record. With stored seed, pre-sowing testing should always be scheduled. Adjust-ments in the rate of sowing can be most readily computed when results are expressed in terms of viable seeds per pound. The test lots should be selected before the repellent coating is applied. With treated seed, laboratory or sandflat tests often underestimate germinative capacity in the field.

Optimum conditions for seeding longleaf in Louisiana usually occur in November. It is inadvisable to sow before the maximum daily temperatures have dropped below 80° F. and the soil has become moist enough to sustain germination. Occasionally, in dry seasons, it is necessary to wait until the first or second week of December, but most operations have been completed during the last two weeks of November.

Spring sowing—in March—has been moderately successful on disked soil. The principal disadvantage of late-season germination is the sensitivity of the very young seedlings to drought. In Louisiana, where damaging early droughts can be expected in about one year out of two, spring germination increases the hazard of severe first-season losses. Spring seeding on disked strips should be completed before maximum daily temperatures during the germination period rise above 80° F. Spring sowing on non-disked sites cannot be recommended except as exploratory trials in areas where early summer droughts are less prevalent than in central Louisiana.

SOWING METHODS

Longleaf seed can be distributed by hand, by tractor-operated machines, or by aircraft. Each method differs somewhat in cost and in the conditions under which it is most effective.

Hand seeding.—For broadcast seeding on small areas, the hand-operated "cyclone" seeder (fig. 5) is very economical. It is especially useful for sowing irregular openings to supplement natural seedfall.

Hand seeding has several limitations. Foremost, perhaps, is the high labor requirement. To sow an acre requires a half-mile of walking. An experienced man can seed about 20 acres of open land per day. On rough terrain or where brush interferes, efficiency is reduced.

Exposure of personnel to dust from the repellant coating restricts hand seeders to small

Figure 6. *Seeding on disked strips requires special tractor-mounted machines that meter the seed at regular intervals and press it into contact with firm soil. (Photo by Louisiana Forestry Commission.)*

proximately 4 feet apart. The obvious limitation of machines that operate in direct contact with the soil is that imposed by wet ground. When soil moisture conditions are suitable, however, the machines are capable of seeding 40 to 60 acres per day.

Another mechanized seeder, developed recently for the sandy coastal soils of Alabama and western Florida, is the H-C Furrow Seeder (fig. 7). It sows a row on an elevated ridge

Figure 7. *This recently developed machine sows pine seed on an elevated ridge within a scalped furrow.*

within a scalped furrow. Site preparation and sowing are done simultaneously. Preliminary trials indicate that the furrow seeder is capable of covering approximately 20 acres per day when rows are spaced 8 feet apart.

The cost of mechanized seeding can be estimated from the amount of equipment travel per acre. Sowing on 8-foot disked strips that are spaced 8 feet apart requires approximately one-half mile of travel per gross acre. Broadcasting with tractor-mounted cyclone seeders also requires about one-half mile per acre, while furrow seeding on 8-foot centers necessitates one mile of equipment travel per acre.

Airplane seeding.—The use of aircraft has expanded rapidly since 1955, when the seed distributor for light agricultural planes was altered to permit close calibration of longleaf seedflow. This modification, described on p. 13, has been used with consistent accuracy on approximately 28,000 acres.

The main advantage of aerial seeding is its speed, which permits taking advantage of optimum germination conditions. Another advantage, a principal one in some cases, is that the type of repellent seed coating is not restricted, provided that seed handlers observe caution when Arasan and endrin are used. Nor are aircraft hampered by rough terrain, hardwood brush, wet ground, or other factors that reduce the efficiency of ground methods.

Aircraft also have limitations. Costly errors in the seeding rate can be made with a plane capable of distributing 3,000 to 4,000 pounds of seed per day. Accurate work requires properly calibrated equipment, careful control of seedflow by the pilot, and a well-supervised ground crew. The cost of aerial seeding may restrict its use on areas of less than 500 acres, or where a convenient landing strip is lacking. Costs of contract sowing (exclusive of flagging) have ranged from $0.50 to $0.88 per acre, depending largely on size of the area to be seeded and distance to a landing strip.

All types of aircraft commonly used for agricultural work can be adapted for direct seeding. The light, single-wing type (fig. 8) is very effective because it can operate from a short dirt runway constructed on the seeding area. Frequent flights with light aircraft carrying 150 pounds of seed provide better control of the

Figure 8. *Light aircraft, operating from improvised landing strips, can economically seed a large acreage in a day. (Photo by Louisiana Forestry Commission.)*

seeding rate than is possible with larger planes. A light plane, working from a landing strip on the seeding area and adequately supported by loading and flagging crews, can seed 1,500 acres per day. Accuracy is comparable to the other methods of broadcast seeding.

CALIBRATING THE SEEDING EQUIPMENT

It is difficult to sow longleaf seed accurately and rapidly at a relatively low rate per acre. The large seed, with its asymmetrical form and soft, easily damaged outer coat, does not flow evenly, nor can it be metered readily with devices designed for smooth, hard-coated seed. The repellent coating increases the difficulty, especially when the treated seed cannot be fully dried before sowing. However, techniques have been developed for controlling the seeding rate with the equipment commonly used.

Weight of untreated seed per acre should be the basis for expressing the rate of seeding. The repellent coating increases the weight of seed 25 to 35 percent, depending upon the chemical and sticker used, the treating method, and the amount of moisture removed in drying the coating. The following data from a 1956 test illustrate the variation within a single treating operation when three different chemicals were used over an asphalt sticker:

Chemical coating	Rate of application	Weight of seed lot Untreated	Treated	Weight increase
	Percent	Pounds		Percent
Morkit	25	336	475	41
Arasan	15	1,320	1,828	38
Arasan-75	15	240	293	22

12

The wide difference in weight increase between the two Arasan treatments was due to a differential in drying rates between large and small seedlots. Differences of such magnitude suggest that the safest procedure is to develop a weight-increase factor for each project. This can be accomplished easily by weighing the untreated seed, then weighing the treated seed as it is bagged for delivery to the field. If the weight-increase factor is 25 percent, 3.75 pounds of treated seed must be sown per acre to achieve a 3-pound rate.

Aircraft equipment has been the most difficult to calibrate accurately. In early trials it was hard to obtain the desired rates, and distribution was seldom uniform. Two sources of error were recognized. First, the long, narrow hopper opening on agricultural aircraft tends to clog or bridge over while the plane is in flight. The second source of error lay in the method of adjusting the sowing rate from seed-trap counts.

In 1955 trials, the seed-release opening was converted from a narrow slot of about 27 by ¾ inches to three adjustable openings 3½ inches long, one at the center and one at each end of the distributor (fig. 9). These openings permit a uniform flow of longleaf seed. The modification is accomplished with a metal plate cut to

Figure 9. *Longleaf seed can be distributed accurately with agricultural aircraft when the hopper release gate is covered with a metal template having three square holes. Metal wedges are added within the hopper to direct seed into the openings.*

fit over the sliding release gate at the bottom of the hopper. Metal wedges over the blanked-off areas direct seedflow toward the three holes in the metal plate.

Calibration entails the adjustment of seedflow to ground speed. Pilots experienced in low-level flying can usually maintain a constant speed and altitude. Therefore, the problem is to determine the hopper opening for the desired rate of seeding. Counting the number of seeds falling into traps or on prepared plots has been unsatisfactory for adjusting aerial equipment, mainly because it is rarely practical to take enough samples. In 1955, when the modified hopper was first tested, area control of seed weight was substituted for control by count. Weight calibration has proved accurate enough so that it is now being used not only for sowing longleaf but also slash and loblolly pine.

The procedure for calibrating aircraft equipment is:

1. Determine the weight of treated seed required per acre.

2. Determine width of the strip that the airplane will seed at each pass. Strip width is influenced by several factors, such as species, airspeed, altitude, and the type of distributor mounted on the plane. At 90 m.p.h. and an altitude of 80 to 100 feet, a plane of the type shown in figure 8 will sow a strip approximately 66 feet wide. The sowing width for other types of equipment can be checked with a trial run over a landing field or other hard-surfaced area. Some overlap should be allowed.

3. Determine the ground speed at which the aircraft will be operated, then calculate the weight of seed to be released per minute. For example, if a plane operates at 90 m.p.h. it will travel 1.5 miles per minute. During one minute of operation over a 66-foot strip it will cover 12 acres $\frac{(66 \text{ feet} \times 7{,}920 \text{ feet})}{43{,}560}$. If the weight of treated seed required per acre is 3.75 pounds, the equipment must be adjusted to flow 45 pounds of seed per minute.

4. With the plane on the ground, select an approximate hopper opening. The pro-

13

cedure is to load the hopper with more seed than required for one minute of operation, place open-net bags over the rear openings of the distributor, and then make a 1-minute flow test with the engine running. Start with the hopper openings at a definite setting, i.e., 1½ inches, then increase or decrease it as the actual flow per minute indicates. Usually three trials will suffice.

5. Fly a measured course over the seeding area to check the weight of seed released per acre. The 1-mile intervals between section lines are convenient for this purpose. Direction of flight should be perpendicular to the wind. On a 1-mile course, and with 66-foot strips, two flights in opposite directions will cover 16 acres. The amount of seed released per acre can be determined from the weight of seed left in the hopper after a 2-flight trial. After the remaining seed is weighed and adjustments are made in the hopper opening, the plane can be loaded for a 4-flight trial. Successive loads should be increased by 16-acre increments until the capacity of the plane's hopper is reached. After the controls have been adjusted as closely as possible, accurate seeding is up to the pilot. He must be able to maintain a uniform ground speed and detect stoppages in seedflow and correct them promptly. Area control of the sowing rate requires a constant check of the acreage covered during the operation. The pilot should be given an accurate map so that he can estimate the distance flown and acreage covered with each load of seed.

The lines that the pilot is to fly are indicated by flagmen on the ground. Ordinarily, flagging is a service provided by the landowner. Three flagmen are usually enough—one at each end of the flight line and one at the middle. More may be needed if the area contains high obstructions, for to maintain accurate flight lines the pilot must be able to see at least two flags after completing a turn, and the flag under the turning plane is usually out of view. When the lines exceed a mile in length, the terminal flags must be large and should be kept in motion while the aircraft is approaching. To avoid lost time or inaccurate seeding,

the pilot should have the opportunity to discuss techniques of low-level flying with the ground crew.

Seed distribution is affected by wind velocity and altitude. Pilots vary in their reaction to wind. One will insist on calm weather for low-level flying, while another will work in moderate cross-winds if they are steady. Calm is desirable, but it is often windy during the longleaf seeding season. Consequently, some aerial seeding has been done in steady winds up to 10 m.p.h. Because of the need to maintain uniform ground speed, the flight lines should be at 90° to the wind direction.

Cross-winds affect the pattern of seed distribution, but not the width of the seeded strip. They have a windrowing effect on the seedfall pattern. Distribution upwind is shortened, while seed released on the downwind side is carried farther than usual. The net effect is alternate strips with relatively high and low seeding rates. A certain amount of windrowing can be tolerated when the alternative is to hold treated seed for an indefinite period while waiting for calm weather. Sowing in gusty winds should be avoided because they accentuate windrowing.

The plane's altitude affects strip width. Aircraft operating at heights of 80 to 100 feet will distribute seed uniformly if a constant altitude is maintained. On rolling terrain, the pilot should endeavor to clear hills by 60 feet, as below this level strip width narrows markedly with decreases in altitude.

The procedure for calibrating aerial equipment can be used for hand-operated and tractor-mounted broadcast seeders. After the seed weight required per acre and the effective strip width have been determined, trial runs are made over a measured course with a known weight of seed in the hopper. A convenient strip width for calibrating hand-operated or tractor-mounted cyclone seeders is 16½ feet. This width permits easy conversion of distance traveled to acres. A mile-long strip is equivalent to two acres. Accurate sowing with hand-operated seeders requires some practice, and operators must check constantly for stoppages.

With mechanical seeders designed for op-

14

Figure 10. *A station on a burned seedbed for detection of seed or seedling predators. Arrows indicate two exposed seed spots. The wire cones protect seed to be used in estimating field germination.*

eration on disked strips, the seeding rate is adjusted to the number of seeds required per 100-foot segment of strip. A rate of one pound (3,400 viable seeds) per gross acre requires about 130 seeds per 100-foot segment when strip centers are 16 feet apart.

DETERMINING SEED AND SEEDLING LOSSES

Even though repellants are used, the seeded area should be systematically observed during the germination period, especially during initial seedings when experience with local predators is not available. The installation illustrated in figure 10 is convenient for detecting major predation. In sufficient numbers on a project area, these stations will provide a good estimate of the species of predators at work, and a fair estimate of their distribution.

The station consists of an identification stake, two exposed seed spots, and one or more screened spots. The exposed spots, about four feet from the stake in opposite directions, should be cleared of vegetation with a shovel

and slightly depressed to prevent seeds from being washed away by rains. Each spot is sown with 25 treated seeds, pressed gently into the soil. The protected spot receives 10 or 15 seeds, depending on size of screen cone, and serves to measure field germination. If a comparison of germination between treated and untreated seed is desired, two screened spots can be used. Hardware cloth with a ¼-inch mesh is well suited for constructing the cones. The number of stations will depend on the size of the seeded area and on the amount of data desired. About 50 stations can be examined per man-day. This number is usually sufficient to detect major depredations on areas up to several thousand acres in size.

Weekly inspections are sufficient. Identification of the animal responsible for losses may be difficult, but unless the seed is removed entirely fragments remaining on the spot often provide ample clues.

Figure 11 illustrates characteristic damage to seed hulls by the common predators. Some

Figure 11. *Characteristic damage to untreated longleaf seed by the principal seed predators in central Louisiana. These hull fragments were obtained from caged predators. (Photo by Brooke Meanley, U. S. Fish & Wildlife Service.)*

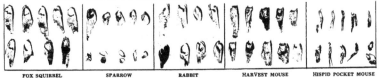

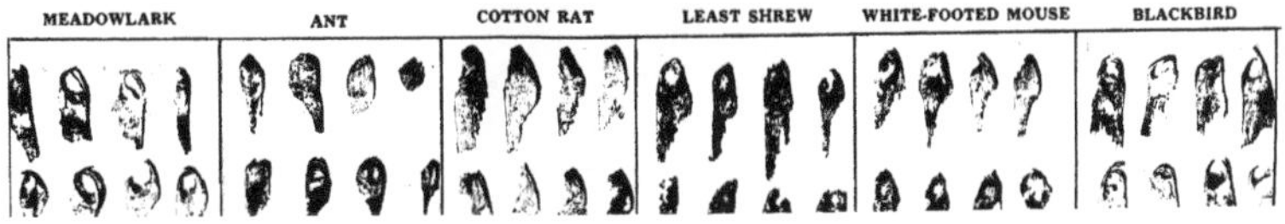

FOX SQUIRREL   SPARROW   RABBIT   HARVEST MOUSE   HISPID POCKET MOUSE

MEADOWLARK   ANT   COTTON RAT   LEAST SHREW   WHITE-FOOTED MOUSE   BLACKBIRD

rodents have a definite method of opening long-leaf seed. The harvest mouse cuts off the small end, while the cotton rat removes an edge of the seed coat. Hispid pocket mice leave long slender fragments, and the fox squirrel opens the seed coat on the flat side. But not all damage is distinctive. Fragments of seed destroyed by meadowlarks resemble those left by rabbits. The white-footed mouse cuts seed hulls in the same way as the least shrew. Except when definite types of damage are found, therefore, a predator usually cannot be identified from a few samples of damaged seed. The principal advantage of an observation station is that it entices animals to a small area. Droppings, tracks, and other indications can then be used for identification along with remnants of seed.

Feeding habits are also clues. Most species of birds are sporadic feeders. Usually they remove from 10 to 50 percent of the seed at each visit. Some small mammals remove the entire seed to places of concealment or to underground burrows, while others eat it in place. Hispid pocket mice usually take every seed on a spot and leave a neat pile of slender fragments. When the population of small mammals is low, observation stations often are undamaged during the 30- to 40-day period required for germination. When undamaged, they can be used to detect post-germination seedling mortality.

Loss of established seedlings during a relatively short period in the winter immediately after germination is a longleaf seeding problem yet unsolved. Identity of all the responsible animals or insects has not been established. Figure 12 illustrates the most frequent type of damage: clipping of the stem about ⅛ inch

above the ground, with the cotyledons either consumed completely or carried off. Occasionally seedlings will be cut at the groundline, or pulled out with the radicle clipped and left on the surface. These losses are difficult to detect unless a representative sample of the seedling stand is pinned soon after germination is complete.

Since 1953, when clipping of this nature was first observed, losses averaging about 25 percent of the catch have been recorded each year. In some years serious damage was confined to 2 or 3 weeks in early January; in others, clipping continued into March. Initially, rabbits were considered to be responsible. Later the short-tailed cricket was recognized as a definite predator. In 1957, observation on study plots where 23 percent of the seedlings were destroyed during the first three weeks of March revealed that a small mammal—rodent or shrew—clips germinated seedlings. Cutworms may also be responsible.

If unusually active, rabbits can easily be recognized by their droppings and crickets by their small earthen mounds. If crickets are feeding on seedlings, fragments of the cotyledons can be found in the upper chamber of their galleries. In the absence of these two predators, shrews or one of the small rodents should be suspected.

Repellent coatings are ineffective against seedling predators, because they avoid the seedcoat entirely, even when it is still attached to the cotyledons. Until practical controls are developed, the seeding rate should be kept high enough to compensate for the post-germination losses.

Figure 12.
Predominant type of seedling loss in the first winter after germination has been clipping of the stem about ⅛ inch above the ground.

16

ESTIMATING INITIAL STOCKING
AND FIRST-YEAR SURVIVAL

The Importance of Initial Stocking

Initial stocking denotes stand density in the spring—May or June—following germination. The level of stocking recorded then will indicate success or failure insofar as germination and the influence of seed and seedling predators are concerned. Stocking estimates after the first growing season also are needed, because first-summer mortality can be high if prolonged droughts occur.

Why estimate initial stocking? This task, requiring several man-days of labor on the average, may seem unnecessary inasmuch as survival after the first season determines whether a stand has been established. Several reasons can be cited. Accurate appraisal of the yield from various rates of seeding requires an estimate of initial stocking. Landowners seeding for the first time need the estimate for assurance, if for no other reason, that the inconspicuous seedlings are actually there. Finally, the extent of summer mortality to be expected in specific site or soil conditions can be derived only from accurate stocking estimates.

Estimating Stocking

For broadcast seeding, the line-plot method is used for estimating stocking both initially and after the first summer. Circular milacre plots are established along transect lines spaced at regular intervals on a base line. The total number of living seedlings on each plot is recorded. Average plot stocking multiplied by 1,000 provides an estimate of stand density per acre. Seedling distribution is expressed as the proportion of sample plots stocked with at least 1 seedling. Eighty percent stocking, for example, implies that 800 of 1,000 possible sample plots per acre have 1 or more seedlings. The two expressions of stocking are related. One estimates tree percent or the yield of seedlings per unit of seed; the other measures the efficiency of seed distribution. Generally, 80-percent plot stocking is achieved with hand or aerial seeding methods when the level of stocking reaches 3,000 per acre.

The number of plots required depends on size of the area, variance between samples, and degree of accuracy desired. For broadcast seed-

ing, the coefficient of variation of the sampled stands has averaged about 100 percent. The number of samples required for a specified limit of error with 67 percent reliability is:

$$N = \left(\frac{\text{coefficient of variation in percent}}{\text{limit of error in percent}} \right)^2$$

An estimate with a standard error of $\pm$ 10 percent would require 100 sample plots. If faulty seeding techniques or other causes have increased the coefficient of variation, a larger sample must be taken for the same degree of accuracy. If seeding rates, seedlots, or sites vary within an area, it is often desirable to segregate the stocking estimate for the area into homogeneous sub-blocks. Sampling intensity must be increased for accurate sub-unit estimates unless wider limits of error are acceptable.

Estimating stocking on disked strips requires a different technique. When only a portion of the gross acreage is seeded, the estimate derived from sample plots on the strips must be adjusted to a gross acreage basis. This adjustment requires a separate estimate of the area in the disked strips. The procedure is to establish, on regular transect lines, sample plots consisting of two adjacent 6.6-foot segments of the disked strip. A location marking the common boundary of the two sub-plots is selected in an unbiased manner. Then the total number of seedlings on each sub-plot is recorded. Finally, the distances from the center of the sampled strip to the center of each adjoining strip are measured at each location. The estimate of seedling density per gross acre is calculated by multiplying the mean stocking per sample location (13.2-foot plot) by

$$\frac{3,300}{\text{average distance between strips}}.$$ For example,

if the mean plot stocking is 10, and the strip centers average 16.5 feet apart, stand density

is $10 \times \dfrac{3,300}{16.5} = 2,000$ seedlings per acre.

Stocking percent based on 1,000 perfectly distributed seedlings per acre is derived by multiplying the percent of stocked sub-plots (6.6-foot segments) by

$$\frac{6.6}{\text{average distance between strips}}.$$

17

It should be noted that stocking percent based on 1,000 seedlings per acre cannot exceed the proportion of milacres actually seeded. Full plot stocking with 16.5-foot intervals between strip centers would be $100 \left(\frac{6.6}{16.5}\right)$ or 40 percent.

Frequently it is convenient to express stocking on the basis of 250 perfectly distributed seedlings per acre. This value for disked strips is calculated by multiplying the proportion of stocked 13.2-foot sample segments by

$$\frac{13.2}{\text{average distance between strips}}$$

First-Year Survival

What is satisfactory stocking? As previously mentioned, the goal for broadcast seeding should be at least 2,000 initial seedlings per acre, and for strip seeding 1,500 per acre. These are approximate values suggested by experience on areas in which first-year mortality has been measured. Requirements will vary with soil types, summer rainfall means, and the degree of protection from controllable losses. On undisked sites, first-summer survival of initially established seedlings has ranged from 25 percent (1952) to 98 percent (1955), but has usually been between 50 and 80 percent. Thus a minimum initial stocking of 2,000 seedlings per acre should provide between 1,000 and 1,600 established seedlings by the end of the first growing season.

Table 1 records initial and first-year stocking for a number of operational seedings. Drought is the chief enemy of longleaf stands in their first year. The hazard is worst in the early half of the season. By July, taproots have generally penetrated to soil layers moist enough to sustain the trees through late-summer dry spells. Once seedlings are in their second or third year, droughts comparable in severity to those occurring in Louisiana during the past 10 years do not seriously affect survival.

In dry years, seedlings on disked strips tend to grow faster, both above and below ground, than those on undisked sites, for disking conserves the moisture in soil layers below 6 inches. In years when survivals of 70 or 80 percent are attained on non-disked sites, however, the performance on disked sites may not be noticeably better. As has been remarked, site preparation by disking should be considered as an insurance against droughts early in the growing season. Seedlings on disked strips have survived a 4-week May-June drought that wiped out natural seedlings in a light grass rough. Early droughts of still longer duration, however, can be fatal regardless of site treatment. When poorly drained "flats" have a tight hardpan within 12 to 18 inches of the surface, limited soil moisture capacity leads to early mortality in droughts even though disking has reduced competition.

Table 1. *Initial and first-year stocking record for 12 selected operational seedings*

Year	Seeded area	Seedbed	Seeding rate per acre	Seed age	Repellant	Stocking per acre		First-year survival
						Initial	First-year	
	Acres		Pounds			— — Number — —		Percent
1951	214	1-year rough	3.36	Fresh	None	1,900	477	25
1951	210	Burn	3.33	Fresh	None	2,260	1,660	73
1952	915	Disked strips	1.70	Fresh	None	972	482	50
1953	260	1-year rough	3.07	Fresh	None	1,930	788	41
1953	182	1-year rough	3.04	Fresh	None	2,530	1,320	52
1954	65	Burn	3.40	Fresh	Morkit	2,840	2,790	98
1954	110	1-year rough	3.40	Fresh	Morkit	3,330	3,270	98
1955	1,110	1-year rough	3.00	Fresh	Morkit	2,558	(1)	....
1955	2,500	Disked strips	1.50	Fresh	Morkit and anthroquinone	1,900	1,200	63
1956	225	1-year rough	3.20	Year old	Arasan	4,600	2,628	57
1956	225	1-year rough	3.20	Fresh	Arasan	5,100	2,914	57
1956	172	1-year rough	2.90	Year old	Arasan	4,180	3,400	81
1956	1,035	1-year rough	2.90	Fresh	Arasan	3,330	1,940	58
1956	216	Burn	2.85	Year old	Arasan	2,658	2,411	91
1956	226	Burn	3.12	Fresh	Arasan	2,373	2,160	91
1957	890	Burn	3.00	Fresh	Arasan	4,146	(1)	....
1957	100	Burn	2.00	Fresh	Arasan-Endrin	3,406	(1)	....

[1] Not recorded.

Proper timing of control treatments for hardwood competition can improve survival. Numerous studies have shown that when hardwoods are deadened during the pines' first growing season, survival in dry years is increased in comparison to that on open sites or under comparable stands of living hardwoods. Too often the early control of woody competition is considered only as a financial risk rather than as a silvicultural necessity for pine regeneration on difficult sites.

Some losses to animals, disease, and fire can be expected after the first year. The magnitude of these losses will depend on the amount of protection and on the skill with which the established stand is managed.

STAND PROTECTION AND MANAGEMENT

After the first growing season, mortality from drought is no longer a major problem. Henceforth, growth and development depend on the adequacy of protection, and on the timeliness of the necessary management or silvicultural treatments. Requirements for protection vary with site quality and cover conditions, brown-spot infection rates, and prevalence of predators like the town ant, pocket gopher, and cotton rat. If protection from hogs and grazing animals is complete, some seedling stands may need no more management than a single (prescribed) burn for brown-spot control after the second or third growing season. Others may require intensive care such as poisoning to control town ants or cotton rats in the second season after germination, or two or more brown-spot control burns.

The prerequisite for effective management is regular and systematic inspection of the stand during the grass stage. Only by thorough periodic examinations can the need for burning be properly evaluated and the presence of predators detected. A useful procedure is to install semi-permanent plots when the initial inventory is undertaken. These plots, if well distributed, can then be used for estimating survival and for periodically appraising stand conditions. An alternate procedure is to schedule periodic inventories to record stand density, seedling damage, and the amount of brown-spot infection.

Healthy longleaf seedlings can withstand the competition of heavy stands of grass, so burning for rough reduction alone is not required (fig. 13). Optimum seedling growth is achieved

Figure 13. *When brown spot is not a problem, longleaf seedlings are capable of vigorous growth in heavy grass roughs. This 4-year-old seedling is beginning active height growth. Prescribed burning solely for rough reduction is not required.*

without burning. During their first two or three years, however, most stands develop brown-spot infections that must be controlled if the seedlings are to emerge from the grass stage in reasonable time. After they reach one-third of an inch in groundline diameter, seedlings can withstand fire with practically no mortality.

Predetermined burning schedules cannot be used in seeded stands because the rate of brown-spot infection varies widely by geographic location and from year to year. The typical infection develops gradually enough so that it can be kept under observation in the regular annual or semi-annual inspections of the stand. Only rarely is a stand in a grass rough severely infected by the end of the first season—fortunately so, as seedlings this young are vulnerable to fire. On the other hand, burning must not be deferred so long that a substantial portion of the seedlings will be in the vulnerable stage of early height growth.

The severity of infection, as recorded in December or January, should be the principal basis for deciding when the first burn is to be made. If, after 2 years, a representative sample of the stand has a low proportion (10 to 20 percent) of the needle tissue killed by the disease, burning can be deferred one year. When second-year needle kill is high (20 to 40 per-

19

cent) fire is needed. These are rough guides. Vigor and size of seedlings, and character of the fuel, also enter into the decision.

Burning for brown-spot control should be done late in the dormant season—in January, or early February. Fast headfires, set on cold days with steady winds, have been used for initial burning with good results. Headfires have several advantages over backfires. They are cheaper, they raise ground surface temperatures less, and they do a better job of destroying the brown-spot pathogen. Headfire burning can also be accomplished when fuel moisture is too high for backfires. Large areas can be treated in a relatively short period of time when burning conditions are stable. Headfires cannot be used under all circumstances. They may not be advisable on areas with accumulations of heavy fuels such as logging slash or hardwood debris. Nor are they satisfactory when the seedling stand is composed of two age classes—a situation found when reinforcement seeding is done in understocked natural stands.

If a second burn is needed when a portion of the stand is in active height growth, backfires are recommended to avoid killing the most vigorous seedlings. Two objectives should be kept in mind when backfiring for brown-spot control. One is to keep surface temperatures low—best accomplished by firing against a steady wind on cold days. The other is to secure a complete burn. Patchy burning can result in a rapid reinfection by brown spot.

Death of vigorous seedlings in the second or third season indicates cotton rat or pocket gopher activity. Both predators are root feeders. They are inconspicuous and can be easily overlooked until they do serious harm. Figure 14 illustrates typical cotton-rat damage on two-year-old seedlings. The rats attack longleaf seedlings at or slightly below groundline, and usually excavate a small depression in the soil. They apparently work from only one position. The damage to seedlings that are one-half-inch in diameter or larger is a half-girdle that usually heals over in the following season. Smaller seedlings often are completely severed. Cotton rats inhabit the heavy grass roughs that develop on seeded areas after the second year. Their presence is revealed by well-defined runways through the grass. They can be controlled

Figure 14. *This seedling was attacked by a cotton rat.*

by placing poisoned grain along runways, or by destroying their cover with fire. Control with poison is necessary only for a heavy attack in the second season when seedlings are small and vulnerable.

While the cotton rat frequents low areas with heavy herbaceous cover, pocket gophers are usually found on well-drained slopes or ridgetops. Generally, their damage is not noted until seedlings reach one-half-inch or more in diameter. Then they feed on the entire taproot, and often pull a portion of the top into their burrows. While characteristic mounds of loose soil often indicate the presence of gophers, serious damage has been observed where no recent mound building was found. Under these conditions control is difficult, simply because the presence of the animal cannot be ascertained. It is advisable to look for gopher infestation after the initial burn for brown-spot control. Poisoned bait placed within their underground burrows is the most practical control.

After the influence of site quality is taken into account, the two principal causes of variation in growth of seeded stands in Louisiana have been the degree of site preparation and the incidence of brown spot. The combination of two intensive treatments—heavy disking and brown-spot control with a fungicidal spray—has produced the fastest early growth.

20

Figures 15 and 16 illustrate extremes in seedling vigor due mainly to local differences in brown-spot infection. The vigorous trees in figure 15 are four years old. They are on a site where the brown-spot hazard was low and burning during the grass stage was not required. The six-year-old stand in figure 16 was seeded in an area where the rate of brown-spot infection has been high for many years. It re- ceived three controlled burns—after the third, fifth, and sixth seasons. Generally, the growth and vigor of young longleaf stands established by direct seeding on unprepared sites will be somewhere between these two extremes. If brown spot can be controlled adequately with a single fire after the second or third season, active height growth can be expected during the fourth year after seeding.

Figure 15. *Four-year-old longleaf established by seeding on a light rough. As brown-spot infection was negligible, no prescribed burns were made.*

Figure 16. *A 6-year-old seeded pine stand in an area where brown spot reduced seedling vigor and necessitated three control burns.*

SELECTED REFERENCES

ANONYMOUS
1959. PLANTING PINES LIKE CORN. Pulpwood Production and Saw Mill Logging 7(1): 6-8, illus.

BRUCE, D.
1951. FIRE RESISTANCE OF LONGLEAF PINE SEEDLINGS. Jour. Forestry 49: 739-740.

——————
1956. YOUNG LONGLEAF DO BEST ON FRESH BURNS. U. S. Forest Serv. South. Forest Expt. Sta. South. Forestry Notes 101. [Processed.]

CASSADY, J. T., HOPKINS, W., and WHITAKER, L. B.
1955. CATTLE GRAZING DAMAGE TO PINE SEEDLINGS. U. S. Forest Serv. South. Forest Expt. Sta. Occas. Paper 141, 14 pp., illus. [Processed.]

DERR, H. J., and COSSITT, F. M.
1955. LONGLEAF PINE DIRECT SEEDING. Jour. Forestry 53: 243-246, illus.

HEBB, E. A.
1957. REGENERATION IN THE SANDHILLS. Jour. Forestry 55: 210-212, illus.

HOLT, W. R.
1957. CONTROLLING THE TEXAS LEAF-CUTTING ANT. U. S. Forest Serv. South. Forest Expt. Sta. South. Forest Pest Rptr. 19, 4pp., illus. [Processed.]

LEWIS, C. H., JR.
1954. DIRECT SEEDING OF LONGLEAF PINE (WITH SPECIAL REFERENCE TO SOWING ON DISKED STRIPS IN VERNON PARISH, LOUISIANA, BY CROSBY CHEMICALS, INC.) Proc. Third Ann. Forestry Symposium, La. State Univ., pp. 1-8. [Processed.]

MANN, W. F., JR.
1957. DIRECT SEEDING THE SOUTHERN PINES. Forest Farmer 17(2): 8-9, illus.

—————— and DERR, H. J.
1955. NOT FOR THE BIRDS. Forests & People 5(3): 32-33, illus.

MANN, W. F., JR., DERR, H. J., and MEANLEY, B.
1956. BIRD REPELLENTS FOR DIRECT SEEDING LONGLEAF PINE. Forests & People 6(3): 16-17, 48.

McCLURKIN, D. C.
1953. SOIL AND CLIMATIC FACTORS RELATED TO THE GROWTH OF LONGLEAF PINE. U. S. Forest Serv. South. Forest Expt. Sta. Occas. Paper 132, 12 pp., illus. [Processed.]

MEANLEY, B., and BLAIR, R. M.
1957. DAMAGE TO LONGLEAF PINE SEEDLINGS BY COTTON RATS. Jour. Forestry 55: 35.

NEFF, J. A., MEANLEY, B., and BRUNTON, R. B.
1957. BASIC SCREENING TESTS WITH CAGED BIRDS AND OTHER RELATED STUDIES WITH CANDIDATE REPELLENT FORMULATIONS, 1955-1957. U. S. Fish and Wildlife Serv. Denver Wildlife Res. Lab., Research on Bird Repellents Prog. Rpt. 3, pt. I, 19 pp., illus. [Processed.]

RUSSELL, T. E., and MEANLEY, B.
1957. LISTEN FOR THE CRICKETS. U. S. Forest Serv. South. Forest Expt. Sta. South. Forestry Notes 110. [Processed.]

SIGGERS, P. V.
1944. THE BROWN SPOT NEEDLE BLIGHT OF PINE SEEDLINGS. U. S. Dept. Agr. Tech. Bul. 870, 36 pp., illus.

TEVIS, L., JR.
1956. SEED SPOT METHOD OF CENSUSING FOREST-RODENTS. Jour. Forestry 54: 180-182.

——————
1957. BEHAVIOR OF A POPULATION OF FOREST MICE WHEN SUBJECTED TO POISON. Jour. Mammalogy 37: 358-370.

UNION BAG-CAMP PAPER CORPORATION, WOODLANDS RESEARCH DEPARTMENT.
1956. PROCEEDINGS, SOUTHEASTERN DIRECT SEEDING CONFERENCE, 66 pp. [Processed.]

WAKELEY, P. C.
1954. PLANTING THE SOUTHERN PINES. U. S. Dept. Agr. Agr. Monog. 18, 233 pp., illus.

Longleaf seed germinates quickly—often starting 3-7 days after sowing, and finishing in 4 weeks. This seedling is just ready to shed its seed coat. (Photo by Elemore Morgan.)

Occasional Paper 172

1959

Composite Aerial
Volume Table
for
Southern Arkansas

Gene Avery
and
David Myhre

SOUTHERN FOREST EXPERIMENT STATION
Philip A. Briegleb, Director
Forest Service, U.S. Department of Agriculture

CONTENTS

LOBLOLLY — SHORTLEAF PINE—HARDWOOD
UPLAND HARDWOOD
BOTTOM-LAND HARDWOOD
NONTYPED; LESS THAN 10% FOREST

Figure 1.—*Generalized forest type map of Arkansas, showing the 20 counties covered by this study.*

ii

Composite Aerial Volume Table for Southern Arkansas

Gene Avery and David Myhre [1]

Aerial photo volume tables are useful for making direct estimates of gross timber volumes, for preparing forest maps based on stand-size classes, for planning extensive forest inventories, and for reducing the intensity or cost of field work in photo-controlled ground cruises (3).[2] The initiation of the third Forest Survey of Arkansas in 1958 presented an opportunity to collect special data to construct and evaluate an aerial stand-volume table for making direct estimates of gross timber volume in the southern part of the State (fig. 1).

In the interests of statistical accuracy, aerial stand-volume tables are ordinarily constructed for a single tree species or a group of similar species. For example, tables have been prepared for upland oaks in Pennsylvania (4), Douglas-fir in Oregon (10), and Rocky Mountain conifers (7). This refinement has obvious advantages when forest types can be reliably differentiated on aerial photographs, but its importance is lessened when stand mixtures cannot be consistently classified.

In southern Arkansas, it was found that southern pines and hardwoods could not be adequately separated on the aerial photographs obtainable from the U. S. Department of Agriculture—9- by 9-inch prints, at a scale of 1:20,000 made from panchromatic film exposed with a minus blue filter. Although pine timber predominates, many stands are composed of pine-hardwood mixtures that exhibit minimal tonal contrast on panchromatic prints. Because of the difficulty of separating these species-groups for making photo measurements, it was decided that a composite table should be compiled for this area. The feasibility of constructing and using an aerial volume table for both pines and hardwoods had been previously demonstrated in northeast Mississippi (2).

CONSTRUCTION PROCEDURE

Every fourth Forest Survey location in each of 20 counties was mechanically selected for analysis. This result was a total of 304 paired point-sample locations[3] arranged on a 6- by 6-mile grid pattern. After elimination of stands that had been cut between the dates of photography and field measurement, 216 locations remained for interpretation.

One-acre circular plots were scribed on the 216 stereo pairs of photographs to exactly encompass the two point-samples at each Forest Survey location. Two photo interpreters measured, on each location, the average total height of the three tallest trees, average diameter of the three largest crowns, and the crown closure percent. The two sets of photo measurements for each location were then averaged for use in the statistical analysis.

[1] The authors, members of the U. S. Forest Service, are currently located at the Southeastern Forest Experiment Station, Asheville, North Carolina, and the Southern Forest Experiment Station, New Orleans, Louisiana, respectively.

[2] Bold face numbers in parentheses refer to Literature Cited, p. 9.

[3] In the Forest Survey of Arkansas sample trees were selected from two points located 117.75 feet apart; they were chosen with a prism having a basal area factor of 10.

Total heights of the three tallest trees were also determined on the ground for each of the 216 locations. These data, along with tree tallies for computing volumes, were obtained by Forest Survey field personnel.

The next step was the selection of those stand variables most valuable for predicting gross cubic volume. A graphical analysis indicated that field-measured tree heights were more closely related to location volumes than any other single variable, including heights measured on aerial photographs. It was therefore decided that the former measurements should be used in the statistical tests, thus eliminating a degree of interpreter bias. Crown closure percent appeared to be the second-best variable and average crown diameter ranked third.

A wide span of values was exhibited by each group of stand measurements. Field heights ranged from 23 to 123 feet, crown closures from 5 to 90 percent, crown diameters from 5 to 28 feet, and gross volumes from 15 to 3,880 cubic feet per acre.

Several additional variables were formulated from combinations of the 3 basic measurements. The 9 chosen for regression analysis[a] are as follows:
1. Height
2. Crown closure percent
3. Height $\times$ crown closure
4. (Height)^2
5. (Height)^2 $\times$ crown closure
6. Height $\times$ (crown closure)^2
7. Crown diameter $\times$ crown closure
8. Crown diameter $\times$ height
9. (Crown diameter)^2 $\times$ height

The objective was to obtain the degree of correlation between these 9 variables and the gross cubic volume per acre as determined from Forest Survey field measurements.

Data were analyzed by the Southern Forest Experiment Station's IBM 704 Regression Program (6). From the 511 regressions computed, this 5-variable equation[b] was selected

---

[a] The term "height" used here refers to the average to ground. Crown closures and crown diameters are p
[b] Multiple correlation coefficient is + 0 834. Standar
[c] The proportion of the forest canopy occupied by tre crown density.

Table 1.—*Composite aerial volume table for southern Arkansas*

Average total height [1] (feet)	Crown closure									
	5 percent	15 percent	25 percent	35 percent	45 percent	55 percent	65 percent	75 percent	85 percent	95 percent
	— — — — — — — Gross cubic feet per acre [2] — — — — — — —									
40	175	215	250	290	325	365	400	440	475	515
45	240	295	345	400	450	505	555	610	660	715
50	330	395	460	525	590	655	720	790	855	920
55	395	490	580	675	765	860	950	1,045	1,140	1,230
60	480	600	715	830	950	1,065	1,180	1,300	1,415	1,530
65	585	725	860	1,000	1,135	1,275	1,410	1,545	1,685	1,820
70	715	865	1,020	1,175	1,330	1,480	1,635	1,790	1,945	2,100
75	860	1,025	1,195	1,360	1,530	1,695	1,865	2,030	2,200	2,365
80	1,020	1,200	1,380	1,555	1,735	1,910	2,090	2,270	2,445	2,625
85	1,205	1,390	1,575	1,760	1,945	2,130	2,315	2,500	2,685	2,870
90	1,410	1,600	1,785	1,975	2,165	2,350	2,540	2,730	2,915	3,105
95	1,635	1,820	2,010	2,200	2,385	2,575	2,765	2,950	3,140	3,330
100	1,875	2,060	2,245	2,430	2,615	2,800	2,985	3,170	3,355	3,540
105	2,140	2,315	2,495	2,675	2,850	3,030	3,210	3,385	3,565	3,745
110	2,420	2,590	2,755	2,925	3,095	3,260	3,430	3,600	3,765	3,935
115	2,725	2,880	3,030	3,185	3,340	3,495	3,650	3,805	3,960	4,115
120	3,045	3,180	3,320	3,455	3,595	3,730	3,870	4,005	4,145	4,280

[1] As the table is based on field measurements of tree heights, photo heights must be adjusted as explained in the following section.

[2] Gross volumes are inside bark and include the merchantable stems of all live trees 5 inches d.b h. and larger from stump to a variable top diameter not smaller than 4 inches i. b.

mates should include only those trees that are taller than 30 feet. Crowns of shorter trees should be ignored, as they presumably represent stems smaller than 5 inches d.b.h.

Height measurements and parallax conversion. — Tree heights can be determined within $\pm$ 5 to 10 feet on aerial photographs from stereoscopic measurements of differential parallax (dP). Two basic types of floating dot instruments are used for this purpose: parallax wedges reading to 0.002-inch dP, and parallax bars reading to 0.01-millimeter dP. Measurements with either device are converted to tree heights by substitution in the parallax formula:

$$ho = \frac{H \times dP}{P + dP}, \text{ where:}$$

ho = height of object
H = height of aircraft above ground datum
P = average photo base length
dP = differential parallax

If object heights are to be determined in feet, the height of the photographing aircraft must also be expressed in feet. Average photo base length (P) and differential parallax (dP) may be expressed either in inches or millimeters, but both must be in the same

units. Solution of the formula is not difficult, but conversion of parallax readings can be simplified by use of special tables. For example, table 2 was prepared for quickly converting parallax-bar readings to tree heights in feet. A similar table is available for converting parallax wedge measurements (8).

To apply table 2, the interpreter must make three determinations:

a. **Differential parallax** of the tree or object, measured with a parallax bar (fig. 2) and recorded to the nearest hundredth of a millimeter. For use with the composite aerial volume table, height measurements should represent an average for 3 to 5 of the tallest trees on the acre.

b. **Average photo base** for the stereo-pair. This corresponds to the average distance between principal and conjugate principal points. It should be measured with an engineer's scale and recorded to the nearest 0.1 inch (conversion to millimeters was accounted for in constructing the table).

c. **Average flying height of aircraft,** determined by multiplying the photo scale denominator by the camera's focal length in feet. For example, if photo scale in the area of measurement is 1:19,000 and camera focal

3

Table 2.—*Parallax-bar height conversion factors* [1]

Average photo base (P)	Average flying height (H) above ground datum in feet							
	2,500	3,000	3,500	4,000	4,500	5,000	5,500	6,000
Inches	— — — — *Object heights (ho) in feet per millimeter* — —							
2.1	46	55	64	74	83	92	101	110
2.2	44	53	62	70	79	88	97	105
2.3	42	50	59	67	76	84	93	101
2.4	40	48	56	65	73	81	89	97
2.5	39	47	54	62	70	78	85	93
2.6	37	45	52	60	67	75	82	90
2.7	36	43	50	57	65	72	79	86
2.8	35	42	49	55	62	69	76	83
2.9	33	40	47	54	60	67	74	80
3.0	32	39	45	52	58	65	71	78
3.1	31	38	44	50	56	63	69	75
3.2	30	36	43	49	55	61	67	73
3.3	29	35	41	47	53	59	65	71
3.4	29	34	40	46	51	57	63	69
3.5	28	33	39	44	50	56	61	67
3.6	27	32	38	43	49	54	60	65
3.7	26	32	37	42	47	53	58	63
3.8	26	31	36	41	46	51	56	62
3.9	25	30	35	40	45	50	55	60
4.0	24	29	34	39	44	49	54	58
4.1	24	29	33	38	43	48	52	57
4.2	23	28	32	37	42	46	51	56
4.3	23	27	32	36	41	45	50	54
4.4	22	27	31	35	40	44	49	53
4.5	22	26	30	35	39	43	48	52

Average photo base (P)	Average flying height (H) above ground datum in feet							
	11,500	12,000	12,500	13,000	13,500	14,000	14,500	15,000
Inches	— — — — *Object heights (ho) in feet per millimeter* — —							
2.1	212	221	230	239	249	258	267	276
2.2	202	211	220	228	237	246	255	264
2.3	194	202	210	219	227	236	244	253
2.4	185	194	202	210	218	226	234	242
2.5	178	186	194	202	209	217	225	256
2.6	172	179	187	194	201	209	216	224
2.7	165	172	180	187	194	201	208	216
2.8	159	166	173	180	187	194	201	208
2.9	154	161	167	174	181	187	194	201
3.0	149	155	162	168	175	181	188	194
3.1	144	151	157	163	169	176	182	188
3.2	140	146	152	158	164	170	176	182
3.3	136	142	147	153	159	165	171	177
3.4	132	137	143	149	154	160	166	172
3.5	128	133	139	145	150	156	161	167
3.6	124	130	135	141	146	152	157	162
3.7	121	126	132	137	142	147	153	158
3.8	118	123	128	133	138	144	149	154
3.9	115	120	125	130	135	140	145	150
4.0	112	117	122	127	132	136	141	146
4.1	109	114	119	124	128	133	138	143
4.2	107	111	116	121	125	130	135	139
4.3	104	109	113	118	123	127	132	136
4.4	102	106	111	115	120	124	129	133
4.5	100	104	108	113	117	121	126	130

[1] To use table, measure parallax difference (dP) of object to nearest hundredth of a millimeter (as 0.41 mm, for example). If average photo base (P) is 3.1 inches and flying height (H)

	Average flying height (H) above ground datum in feet								Average photo base (P)
00	7,500	8,000	8,500	9,000	9,500	10,000	10,500	11,000	
	— — — Object heights (ho) in feet per millimeter — — — —								Inches
29	138	147	157	166	175	184	193	203	2.1
23	132	141	149	158	167	176	185	193	2.2
18	126	135	143	152	160	168	177	185	2.3
13	121·	129	137	145	153	161	169	177	2.4
09	116	124	132	140	147	155	163	171	2.5
04	112	119	127	134	142	149	157	164	2.6
01	108	115	122	129	136	144	151	158	2.7
07	104	111	118	125	132	139	146	153	2.8
04	100	107	114	120	127	134	141	147	2.9
01	97	104	110	117	123	130	136	142	3.0
18	94	100	107	113	119	125	132	138	3.1
15	91	97	103	109	115	122	128	134	3.2
13	88	94	100	106	112	118	124	130	3.3
10	86	92	97	103	109	114	120	126	3.4
8	83	89	95	100	106	111	117	122	3.5
6	81	87	92	97	103	108	114	119	3.6
4	79	84	89	95	100	105	111	116	3.7
2	77	82	87	92	97	103	108	113	3.8
0	75	80	85	90	95	100	105	110	3.9
8	73	78	83	88	93	97	102	107	4.0
7	71	76	81	86	90	95	100	105	4.1
5	70	74	79	84	88	93	97	102	4.2
4	68	73	77	82	86	91	95	100	4.3
2	66	71	75	80	84	89	93	98	4.4
1	65	69	74	78	82	87	91	95	4.5

	Average flying height (H) above ground datum in feet								Average photo base (P)
,000	16,500	17,000	17,500	18,000	18,500	19,000	19,500	20,000	
	— — — Object heights (ho) in feet per millimeter — — — —								Inches
	304	313	322	331	341	350	359	368	2.1
	290	299	308	316	325	334	343	352	2.2
9	278	286	295	303	311	320	328	337	2.3
8	266	274	282	290	298	306	315	323	2.4
8	256	264	271	279	287	295	302	310	2.5
9	246	254	261	269	276	284	291	298	2.6
0	237	244	251	259	266	273	280	287	2.7
2	229	236	243	250	257	264	270	277	2.8
4	221	228	234	241	248	254	261	268	2.9
7	214	220	227	233	240	246	253	259	3.0
1	207	213	220	226	232	238	245	251	3.1
4	200	207	213	219	225	231	237	243	3.2
9	195	200	206	212	218	224	230	236	3.3
3	189	194	200	206	212	217	223	229	3.4
8	184	189	195	200	206	211	217	222	3.5
3	179	184	189	195	200	206	211	216	3.6
8	174	179	184	189	195	200	205	211	3.7
4	169	174	179	185	190	195	200	205	3.8
0	165	170	175	180	185	190	195	200	3.9
6	161	166	171	175	180	185	190	195	4.0
2	157	162	167	171	176	181	186	190	4.1
9	153	158	162	167	172	176	181	186	4.2
5	150	154	159	163	168	172	177	181	4.3
2	·146	151	155	160	164	168	173	177	4.4
9	143	147	152	156	160	165	169	173	4.5

000 feet, the conversion factor of 188 is multiplied by 0.41 for an object height of 77 feet. near interpolations may be made in the table for determining conversion factors not shown.

length is six inches, H = 19,000 × 0.5 or 9,500 feet.

Thus, if P = 3.2 inches and H = 9,500 feet, the conversion factor of 115 is read from table 2 and multiplied by dP (as 0.44 mm, for example) for a height of 51 feet.

Table 2 may be safely applied only when dP is small with relation to P. With ordinary 9- by 9-inch aerial photos and an average overlap of 60 percent, the ratio of dP to P is 1:100 or smaller. If the ratio becomes as large as 1:50, however, values should be substituted directly in the parallax formula.

The range of photo base lengths used in compiling this table (2.1 to 4.5 inches) was chosen on the assumption that the table would be used with 7- by 7-, 7- by 9-, or 9- by 9-inch aerial prints having an average forward overlap of 50 to 70 percent. The range of flying heights above ground (2,500 to 20,000 feet) covers photo scales from 1:2,500 to 1:40,000, assuming use of cameras with 12- and 6-inch focal lengths, respectively.

Individual adjustments of photo heights.— The composite aerial volume table (table 1) was based on field-measured tree heights. As individuals may differ widely in determining heights on aerial photos, each interpreter should make his own corrections for converting photo heights to actual tree heights. This can be done as follows:

Select 15 or more trees within the area to be interpreted, and determine their total heights by ground measurement. These sample trees should span a wide range of heights and be readily identifiable on the aerial photographs.

Measure each sample tree at least three times to determine its average photo height. On cross-section paper, plot field heights over photo heights, and fit a line to the plotted points by either the graphical or least squares method.

Use the graph to correct all subsequent photo height determinations prior to entering the aerial volume table.

Figure 2.—*Abrams parallax bar used for making stereoscopic determinations of tree heights. Differential parallax readings in millimeters can be converted to feet by reference to table 2.*

6

DIRECT ESTIMATES OF GROSS VOLUME

The accuracy of aerial timber estimates depends on the scale and quality of available photography, the ability of photo interpreters to make required stand measurements, and the statistical reliability of the aerial volume table. Even when these circumstances are favorable, individual location volumes can rarely be determined with precision. However, reliable estimates of average volume per acre may be obtained by interpreting large numbers of locations.

Field check 1.—One hundred additional Survey locations in southern Arkansas were selected for evaluation by two interpreters. Each man made independent determinations of cubic volume for the 100 locations by entering the composite aerial volume table. Neither interpreter had participated in the collection of field data, and actual volumes were unknown. Photo and field comparisons of average volume per acre are presented in table 3.

Estimates by both interpreters showed good agreement with average field volumes. On the first 50 locations, the maximum interpreter error was minus 16 percent; for the second group, the greatest deviation was plus 17 percent. For each interpreter, negative differences on the first 50 locations were compensated by higher readings on the second set of 50 measurements. When the 100-location averages were used for comparison, interpreter errors decreased to less than 3 percent of the average field volume per acre.

Comparison for individual locations were much more erratic than the checks of average volumes. Photo estimates occasionally differed by 75 to 90 percent from field values. Such variations were not unexpected, however, as the standard error of estimates for the composite table was 437 cubic feet, or about 45

percent of the mean field volume. Some disagreements between individual estimates can be attributed to the fact that photo measurements were made on 1-acre circular plots, while field volumes were determined from 2 point-samples spaced 117.75 feet apart at each ground location.

Field check 2.—To further evaluate the composite aerial volume table, two 160-acre tracts in southern Arkansas were chosen for a comparison of photo and field cruises on small ownerships. Tract 1 had a predominant forest cover of loblolly-shortleaf pines and tract 2 was in a stand of mixed pines and upland hardwoods. A transparent template was used to locate 32 one-acre plots on 1:15,840 infrared photographs of each tract. These circular sample areas were mechanically spaced at 5- by 10-chain intervals. Two interpreters determined the volume of each plot by use of table 1. Average per-acre volumes were then multiplied by tract areas to obtain estimates of total gross volume for each tract. As in the previous test, field volumes were determined by point-sampling (5). Tree tallies were made at 80 points systematically located within each tract. A wedge prism having a basal area factor of 10 square feet per acre was used to select sample trees for measurement.

Photo and field estimates of total cubic volume for the 2 tracts are summarized in table 4. The relatively small interpreter errors again demonstrate the feasibility of aerial timber cruising. All photo estimates were within 12 percent of field values. This improvement in interpreter accuracy over the previous check (table 3) is partly due to the fact that the forest on the two 160-acre tracts was relatively homogeneous and even-aged, while the 100 Forest Survey locations encompassed a much wider range of stand-size classes.

Table 3.—*Comparison of average volumes from 100 Forest Survey locations with photo estimates by two interpreters*

Number of locations [1]	Average field volume per acre	Interpreter A		Interpreter B	
		Volume per acre	Error [2]	Volume per acre	Error [2]
	Cubic feet	Cubic feet	Percent	Cubic feet	Percent
1-50	1,544	1,297	−16.0	1,430	− 7.4
51-100	1,101	1,288	+17.0	1,254	+13.9
All 100	1,323	1,293	− 2.3	1,342	+ 1.4

[1] Randomly selected from 20 counties in southern Arkansas.
[2] Difference between photo and field volume expressed as a percent of field volume.

Another factor was the availability of better aerial photographs for the small tracts. Infrared prints at a scale of 1:15,840 were supplied by The Crossett Company for this check, while the previous analysis required the use of 1:20,000 panchromatic photographs.

Ordinarily, it is inadvisable to rely strictly on aerial-photo determinations. Prior to computation of total tract volumes, 5 to 10 percent of the photo plots should be field-checked to derive local per-acre correction factors (1). Such corrections not only improve the reliability of the final estimate, but also increase its acceptability to persons unfamiliar with aerial cruising techniques.

Aerial timber cruising cannot be expected to replace ground work for obtaining detailed breakdowns of tree species, diameter classes, growth, cull, and mortality. Thus, airphoto and field techniques are ordinarily not mutually exclusive alternatives. Instead, the advantages of both methods are logically combined in a forest inventory design that has greater efficiency than either approach considered singly (3).

As aerial volume tables are occasionally applicable outside the areas for which they were originally constructed, the authors would be interested in hearing from users of the composite table, particularly those in east Texas, north Louisiana, and central Mississippi. Applications in these areas should be feasible, provided local adjustments are derived by field checks.

Table 4.—Comparison of photo and field volumes for two 160-acre forest tracts in southern Arkansas

Tract	Total field volume [1]	Interpreter A		Interpreter B	
		Volume [1]	Error [2]	Volume [1]	Error [2]
	Cubic feet	Cubic feet	Percent	Cubic feet	Percent
Mixed loblolly-shortleaf pines	336,480	361,600	+ 7.5	376,000	+11.7
Mixed pines and hardwoods	342,720	305,600	−10.8	311,200	− 9.2

[1] Tract volumes may be converted to rough cords by dividing by 79
[2] Difference between photo and field volumes expressed as a percent of field volume.

LITERATURE CITED

1) AVERY, GENE
   1957. FORESTER'S GUIDE TO AERIAL PHOTO INTER-
   PRETATION. U. S. Forest Serv. South.
   Forest Expt. Sta. Occas. Paper 156, 41 pp.,
   illus. [Processed.]

2) ———
   1958. COMPOSITE AERIAL VOLUME TABLE FOR
   SOUTHERN PINES AND HARDWOODS. Jour.
   Forestry 56: 741-745, illus.

3) BICKFORD, C. ALLEN
   1953. INCREASING THE EFFICIENCY OF AIRPHOTO
   FOREST SURVEYS BY BETTER DEFINITION OF
   CLASSES. U. S. Forest Serv. Northeast.
   Forest Expt. Sta. Sta. Paper 58, 9 pp.
   [Processed.]

4) GINGRICH, S. F., and MEYER, H. A.
   1955. CONSTRUCTION OF AN AERIAL STAND VOLUME
   TABLE FOR UPLAND OAK. Forest Sci. 1:140-
   147, illus.

5) GROSENBAUGH, L. R.
   1952. PLOTLESS TIMBER ESTIMATES—NEW, FAST,
   EASY. Jour. Forestry 50: 32-37, illus.

6) GROSENBAUGH, L. R.
   1958. THE ELUSIVE FORMULA OF BEST FIT: A COM-
   PREHENSIVE NEW MACHINE PROGRAM. U. S.
   Forest Serv. South. Forest Expt. Sta.
   Occas. Paper 158, 9 pp., illus. [Processed.]

7) MOESSNER, K. E.
   1957. PRELIMINARY AERIAL VOLUME TABLES FOR
   CONIFER STANDS IN THE ROCKY MOUNTAINS.
   U. S. Forest Serv. Intermountain Forest
   and Range Expt. Sta. Res. Paper 41, 17
   pp., illus. [Processed.]

8) ——— and ROGERS, E. J.
   1957. PARALLAX WEDGE PROCEDURES IN FOREST
   SURVEYS. U. S. Forest Serv. Intermountain
   Forest and Range Expt. Sta. Misc. Pub.
   15, 22 pp., illus. [Processed.]

9) ——— BRUNSON, D. F., and JENSEN, C. E.
   1951. AERIAL VOLUME TABLES FOR HARDWOOD
   STANDS IN THE CENTRAL STATES. U. S.
   Forest Serv. Central States Forest Expt.
   Sta. Tech. Paper 122, 15 pp., illus. [Pro-
   cessed.]

10) POPE, R. B.
    1950. AERIAL PHOTO VOLUME TABLES. Photogram.
    Engin. 16: 325-327.

REST DEVELOPMENT OPPORTUNITIES

in

NORTH CENTRAL MISSISSIPPI

* * * *

Herbert S. Sternitzke

Southern Forest Experiment Station

Philip A. Briegleb, Director

FOREST SERVICE, U. S. DEPT. OF AGRICULTURE

1959

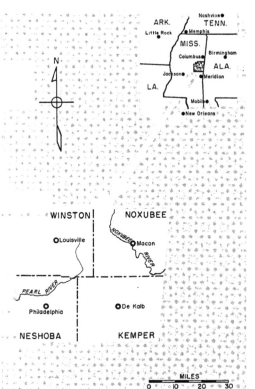

Figure 1.—*North central Mississippi counties.*

TIMBER: KEY TO A VIGOROUS LOCAL ECONOMY

This study shows how development of the forests could greatly strengthen the local economy of four counties in north central Mississippi—Kemper, Neshoba, Noxubee, and Winston. The conclusions and recommendations may also be widely applicable in neighboring counties that share similar timberland problems and opportunities.

Lack of resources to sustain current levels of population is perhaps the key problem in this 4-county area (fig. 1). Developing the full productive capacity of the forests would not only increase the generally low income of the predominantly rural population, but would also enable the area to provide a better livelihood for an even greater population.

Urgent need for cash frequently creates heavy pressure on landowners to liquidate timber as soon as the minimum salable volume develops. Such harvesting methods, repeated a few times, reduce timber income to a mere fraction of a dollar per acre annually. In turn, poor and infrequent timber returns discourage investment in forest management.

It takes time and money to rebuild depleted timber stands. And in this area depletion has progressed so far that the cost of remedial action exceeds the funds available to most individual landowners. The problem is further complicated by the large number of woodland owners—some 9,100—and the small size of individual tracts. Thus, broad-scale public and private measures may be needed to assist landowners in rehabilitating their stands. Expansion of markets and local industry is also needed to permit use of more low-grade material, as well as to expand employment opportunities.

Though the forest betterment task is sizeable, the effort is well worth making. North central Mississippi lies in one of the Nation's inherently most productive forest zones. Despite heavy timber use and slowness to appreciate the possibilities of trees as a crop, much economic activity, directly or indirectly, still arises from the forests.

A higher sustained level of ·forest management in the area is eminently in the public interest. Locally this would mean increased payrolls and income. Additionally, the well-documented present and future need of the Nation for timber puts a premium on high levels of forest productivity to supply expanding markets. After a very thorough appraisal of prospective timber needs, the Forest Service

estimates that the Nation will require at least 30 percent more wood by 1975, and almost twice the present volume by the turn of the century. Only with full development of potentially productive forest lands, such as those in the area under consideration, can these needs be met.

NORTH CENTRAL MISSISSIPPI: THE SETTING [1]

Recent population statistics in north central Mississippi largely indicate emigration—the flight of workers toward the more rewarding employment they hope to find elsewhere. Population declined 15 percent between 1940 and 1950 and another 15 percent—to 71 thousand—between 1950 and 1958.

Associated with population changes have been notable shifts in land use. Number of farms dropped from 15.5 thousand in 1940 to 11.4 thousand in 1954. At the same time, average farm size rose to 104 acres, a 42-percent increase. In addition to consolidating their holdings, farmers have been releasing from cultivation acreage that is eroded or in other ways submarginal. On farms reporting woodlands, forested area rose from 46 to 76 acres between 1939 and 1954.

Field crops still provide most of the farmer's cash receipts. Nearly half the farms are essentially cotton-growing enterprises, and many of the others raise some cotton. Value of farm products sold in 1954, according to the latest Census of Agriculture, totaled some $13.5 million, a 26-percent increase since 1949. Of 1954 product value, more than $8 million was attributable to field crops, chiefly cotton; livestock and livestock products accounted for nearly $5 million; and forest products cut on farms (including standing timber) amounted to $0.5 million.

Farm income is being increasingly supplemented by outside employment. Proportion of farmers reporting off-farm work of 100 days or more totaled 7 percent in 1939, 16 percent in 1949, and 22 percent in 1954. Nearly one-third of the farm families received more than half of their 1954 income from other sources than farm products.

[1] Statistical material in this section is drawn largely from the following sources: (1) Various reports on population, agriculture, and manufactures issued by the Bureau of the Census, U. S. Department of Commerce. (2) County Business Patterns, First Quarter, 1956. U. S. Department of Commerce; U. S. Department of Health, Education, and Welfare. 1958. (3) Estimated Population Trends in Mississippi 1950-58. Agricultural Experiment Station, Mississippi State University. 1959. (4) Personal Income in Mississippi Counties. Bureau of Business Research, University of Mississippi. 1957 (5) Income Structure of Mississippi Counties. Bureau of Business Research, University of Mississippi. 1957.

← *Reversion of farmland to forest exceeds land clearing in north central Mississippi.*

Growth of non-farm employment is in many respects a healthy development. Much of the increase in income from off-farm work no doubt goes into needed capital improvements that raise the productivity and income of labor in agriculture.

Manufacturing—particularly in forest-based enterprises—contributes significantly to non-farm employment. In the first quarter of 1956, for example, over half of the 2,600 manufacturing employees covered by old-age and survivor insurance worked in lumber and other wood-products industries. About two-thirds of the 80 manufacturing establishments reported by the 1954 census were lumber and wood-products firms; most of the remainder were small food-products establishments, such as milk-processing plants. In this year, total value created by manufacturing was $11 million, of which some $6 million might be attributed to forest-based industries.

More illuminating than total values, however, are per-capita income estimates developed by the University of Mississippi Bureau of Business Research. Estimated 1954 income ranged from $394 in Kemper County to $589 in Winston County; the regional average was about $540. (While the incomes of land-owning families may be better than average, they are still likely to be relatively low.) No county had a per-capita income as high as the State average of $850 (fig. 2). Of civilian participation income, [1] some 32 percent was attributable to

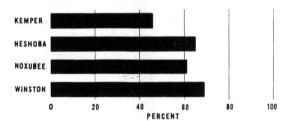

Figure 2.—*Per-capita income in north central Mississippi counties relative to State average.*

[1] Civilian participation income includes wage and salary disbursements, proprietors' income, and other labor income but excludes property income, transfer payments, and pay of military personnel.

⟵   *The D. L. Fair Lumber Company at Louisville provides year-round employment for hundreds of local residents.*

5

farming, 16 percent to manufacturing, 27 percent to trades and services, 15 percent to government, and 10 percent to miscellaneous sources. Though the Bureau did not separate the component directly and indirectly attributable to timber products, it is estimated to be more than one-third of the total. This includes the values from timber products arising in trades, services, transportation, government, and the like, as well as the direct returns.

More favorable adjustment of people to resources might seem implicit in recent economic trends. But there is room to doubt that the decline in population is necessarily favorable. Dr. Harald Pedersen, formerly Professor of Sociology at Mississippi State College, has shown that it is chiefly Mississippi's young people who migrate. In effect, the 4 counties have been investing heavily in the rearing and education of youths for productive adulthood elsewhere. Though some migration may be desirable, the community needs to retain its share of these potential leaders.

It bears stressing that low income is not solely a problem in forestry. It is also a problem in agriculture, industry, and indeed, of the whole regional economy. To expand employment and investment opportunities, therefore, is not a small order. Economic development, which is subject to public and private business policies on a broad front, must have as its goal the raising of incomes—through the medium of all resources including forests.

THE FOREST RESOURCE

North central Mississippi is extensively wooded. Nearly six out of every ten acres of land bear forest growth. The proportion of forest land varies somewhat from one county to the other. It is highest, 69 percent, in Kemper County; lowest, 48 percent, in Noxubee. The forests are characterized by young timber—that is, second-growth stands that have arisen since the original timber was cut over. Loblolly and shortleaf pines in varying mixture with hardwoods, mainly upland oaks and hickory, dominate most of the forest area. Along waterways, such as the Pearl River and its tributaries, are stands of pure hardwoods—chiefly bottom-land oaks and gum.

Forest Area Is Increasing.—Land clearing for agriculture, urban expansion, and other uses during the past two decades has been over-

---

← *The bottom lands along the Pearl River and other local waterways are well suited to growing industrial hardwoods.*

7

shadowed by reversion of farmlands to forest. In 1935, forests occupied 882,300 acres; in 1947, 940,500 acres; and in 1957, 990,500 acres. Today woodlands cover 59 percent of the land. [3]

The trend toward conversion of farmlands to forest, at a rate in excess of localized land clearing, has been heaviest in the eastern part of the region (Kemper and Noxubee Counties). Here, forest area has increased 21 percent since 1935; in the two western counties it has risen some 4 percent.

In these 4 counties, the net result of the shifting land-use pattern is that present forest area is 12 percent greater than in 1935, when the initial forest survey was made. At this rate, forest area is extending at an average of nearly 5,000 acres annually.

More Pine Timber.—Growing stock—which includes sound, well-formed trees at least 5.0 inches in diameter—totals 536 million cubic feet in north central Mississippi, or about 540 cubic feet (nearly 8 cords) per acre. Softwood, virtually all southern pine, makes up 241 million; hardwood, 295 million. The trees large enough for sawtimber contain 1.7 billion board feet, [4] of which nearly three-fifths is pine (fig. 3).

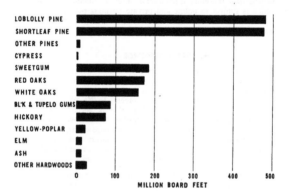

Figure 3.—*Sawtimber volume by species.*

[3] County statistics on forest area, as well as other items of forest inventory, will be found on page 38
[4] All board-foot volumes in this report, unless otherwise indicated, are International 1/4-inch log rule, which approximates green-chain lumber scale.

8

Recent trends in growing stock are noteworthy. Softwood has increased 8 percent since the forest inventory of 1947. This is a reversal of earlier regional trends. The improvement, however, is strongly localized. Softwood volume has increased some 40 percent in Neshoba and Winston Counties, where the timber had been heavily logged by 1947. It has declined 12 percent in Kemper and Noxubee Counties. The upward trend in the western counties largely reflects expansion in pine management programs since World War II.

Hardwood inventory has declined 24 percent since 1947. The shrinkage is due partly to cultural operations aimed at reducing growing space occupied by unwanted hardwoods on areas more valuable for pine; partly to the sixfold increase in hardwood pulpwood production. It needs to be emphasized that hardwood pulpwood is generally cut from soft-textured species—sweetgum, for example—which reach their best development on the minor stream bottoms. The firm-textured species such as oak and hickory, which make up most of the upland hardwood volume, are little used for pulping.

Relative to its suitability for standard factory lumber, 16 percent of the hardwood sawlog material in the bottom lands and 11 percent in the uplands is of Grade 2 or higher—that is, logs clear enough to yield a substantial proportion of No. 1 Common and better lumber. The rest is in lower grade logs, which are generally less marketable. Of the volume below Grade 2, however, over half is in logs that are capable of yielding practical proportions of clear cuttings. Much of the pine grades low, too, and while this tends to limit returns to the timber grower and increase unit-costs of harvesting and processing to the timber operator, it does not ordinarily prevent profitable cutting.

Growth Now Exceeds Cut.—Essential to analysis of the forest resource is appraisal of the timber growth and the volume cut. Especially important in such an appraisal is the relationship of the growth and cut of sawtimber-size trees, which make up most of the annual harvest. Even pulpwood is taken largely from sawtimber trees.

Projection of growth rates from central Mississippi, within which the 4-county area lies, indicates that current net annual growth on growing stock totals 47 million cubic feet, of which the sawtimber component is 164 million board feet. Two-thirds of the sawtimber growth is pine. Softwood sawtimber growth is at least double the cut throughout the 4 counties. Growth of hardwood sawtimber in the 4 counties exceeds the cut by a much smaller margin—roughly a fifth. Moreover, the surplus of hardwood sawtimber growth is limited to Neshoba and Winston Counties. In Kemper and Noxubee, the annual cut of hardwood sawtimber exceeds the net growth.

There is little quantitative information on which to appraise the quality of the present hardwood growth. But as only a quarter of the hardwood sawtimber inventory is in trees more than 16 inches in diameter, it is apparent that most of the current growth is on trees that are still too small to yield much knot-free material for such uses as factory lumber and veneer. Furthermore, it is likely that the larger, better-formed hardwoods are being cut most heavily.

Except for quality hardwoods, however, the current situation with respect to growth and utilization of timber appears encouraging.

Timber Yields Can Be Doubled.—The forest soils of north central Mississippi have the capacity to produce a far greater volume of wood than they are currently growing. It can be reasonably assumed that with application of basic forestry practices on all commercial forest land, net annual growth in the 4-county area might eventually be raised from nearly 0.7 cord per acre to at least 1 cord. Under more intensive management potential yield might be raised to double the current growth. Over limited areas, even higher yields may be anticipated. On the Land Utilization Project between Ackerman and Louisville, for example, a loblolly pine plantation produced some 29 cords in about 16 years, or 1.8 cords per acre annually. An increased level of growth would, in the long run, enable the area to support much more forest industry than it now does. Essential to such forward movement is the planting of idle forest land and the removal from timber stands of those trees (principally cull hardwoods) that have little or no utility.

Planting southern pines is the surest and quickest way of rebuilding depleted stands on upland sites with inadequate seed sources. As one phase of the recent forest inventory, therefore, information was gathered on the area in need of pine planting.

The pine sites in the 4-county area—that is, forested uplands better adapted to growing pine than industrial hardwoods—total about 737 thousand acres, of which 416 thousand are in Kemper and Noxubee Counties, and 321 thousand in Neshoba and Winston. Some 280 thousand acres of the total have both inadequate pine stocking and an inadequate seed source. For full stocking of pine these acres will require planting or interplanting. Of the remaining 457 thousand acres regarded as pine sites, 288 thousand have at least 50 percent

---

The inherent productivity of north central Mississippi's forest soils is attested by this stand of southern pine on the Henson Estate.

11

stocking of pine, and 169 thousand have enough seed trees to assure eventual natural restocking to pine.

In both the Neshoba-Winston and Kemper-Noxubee areas the proportion of pinelands that require planting is about the same, namely 38 percent. The area in need of such treatment is about 159 thousand acres in Kemper and Noxubee and 121 thousand acres in Neshoba and Winston. These estimates do not include fields that are no longer in cultivation but have not yet reverted to forest and on which planting may also be desirable for erosion control, watershed protection, or other reasons.

The survey revealed, too, that 610 thousand acres of pine sites have a hardwood problem in the sense that 20 percent or more of each acre is occupied by hardwoods. Generally speaking, the hardwoods on these sites are less desirable than pine. Most of them grow slowly, have short boles, and are apt to be limby or defective in one way or another. Such trees are hard to sell, and when they do find a buyer they bring much less than pine timber does. When freed from these competing hardwoods, young pines grow rapidly. Deadening (or selling whenever possible) such trees is one of the best investments that a forest landowner can make. Needs for hardwood control loom somewhat larger in the Kemper-Noxubee area (359 thousand acres) than in Neshoba and Winston Counties (251 thousand acres). Some 201 thousand of these 610 thousand acres are already adequately stocked with pine seedlings. Treating them first—before the young pines succumb to hardwood competition—will yield the earliest returns.

Of the 254 thousand acres in the 4-county area considered suitable for growing industrial hardwoods, such as the Pearl and Noxubee River bottoms, the survey found some 94 thousand acres noticeably encumbered with cull trees. That is, a sixth or more of these encumbered acres is dominated by culls—trees that are unmerchantable now or prospectively because of rot, defect, or species. Removal of this material would release established growing stock and create openings for reproduction.

Future timber yields could also be increased by strengthening and extending public fire-control facilities, and improving arrangements for detecting and taking prompt action against insect outbreaks.

Full and immediate attention to these remedial measures—that is, planting, timber stand improvement, and protection—would probably come close to doubling timber yields within the next two decades, if timber harvesting is carried out conservatively.

The volume of timber cut annually for industrial use declined from 25.5 million cubic feet in 1946 to 23.5 in 1956. Partly because of the recent recession, the industrial cut is estimated to have dipped to about 21.1 million cubic feet in 1958. Softwood has consistently made up the bulk of the industrial wood and at the time of the latest inventory comprised nearly three-fifths of the cut.

Lumber Is Main Product.—Lumber has long been, and still is, the dominant forest product of the 4-county area. Cutting by large sawmills removed virtually all of the old growth prior to World War II. Immediately after the war the housing boom greatly expanded markets for all species of lumber, largely produced by portable mills. Since then, the number of sawmills has contracted sharply. In 1946, 144 sawmills were operating in the 4 counties. A canvass in March of this year found only 40. [1]

The fewer number of sawmills is partially reflected in timber harvest trends. The cut of sawlogs dropped 37 percent during the decade between the two most recent forest surveys. Softwood sawlog cut declined 25 percent, hardwood, 48 percent. The 1958 cut of sawlogs, over 50 million board feet, was 51 percent of the total 4-county cut of industrial wood (fig. 4).

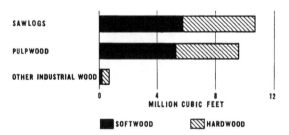

Figure 4.—*Cut of industrial wood in north central Mississippi, 1958.*

[1] A 1959 listing of primary wood-using establishments in north central Mississippi will be found on pages 39-40

13

A recent innovation at the larger sawmills is the use of mechanical log barkers and chipping equipment for making bark-free pulp chips. Such equipment permits fuller log use and thus enhances profit margins. Currently, five sawmills in north central Mississippi are shipping chipped slabs and edgings to pulp mills. Formerly these coarse residues were largely regarded as unavoidable waste.

Pulpwood Output Is Expanding.—Most notable of timber harvesting trends is the spectacular growth in pulpwood cutting. Pulpwood accounted for 9 percent of the industrial timber cut in north central Mississippi in 1946, for 28 percent in 1956, and for 45 percent in 1958. The rate of increase in the 4-county area has been double that of the State as a whole.

In response to the tremendous expansion of the pulp and paper industry both in and around Mississippi, pulpwood production in the 4 counties rose from 35,000 cords in 1946 to 95,000 cords in 1956. Output in 1958 reached an all-time high of more than 123,000 cords, of which two-thirds were pine (fig. 5).

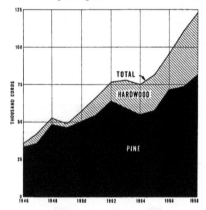

Figure 5.—*Round pulpwood production in north central Mississippi, 1946-58.*

At the A. DeWeese Lumber Company in Philadelphia, bark-free logs yield pulp chips as well as lumber. ⟶

14

Eight pulp and paper companies draw bolts and chips from the area. The wood is hauled distances ranging from 15 to nearly 200 miles. Although no pulp mills are located within the 4 counties, strong competition for wood is offered by the several surrounding mills. Competition is certain to heighten in the near future as mills under construction or announced by two more companies go into production at Counce, Tennessee, and Columbus, Mississippi.

Specialties Are Locally Important.—Industrial wood other than lumber and pulpwood—poles, piling, posts, veneer, handle-stock, and the like—makes up about 4 percent of the annual timber cut, or some 0.8 million cubic feet. Six specialty plants are currently operating in the 4 counties—a package-veneer mill at Macon, hardwood dimension mills at Louisville and Philadelphia, and wood-preserving plants at Louisville, Macon, and Philadelphia (fig. 6).

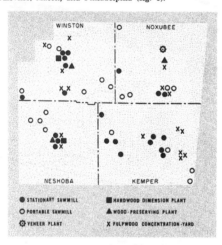

Figure 6—*Location of primary forest-products plants and woodyards in north central Mississippi counties.*

Sawmill residues, such as slabs and edgings, provide pulp chips by the carload. →

16

m the

nding
mills
into

r than
k, and
some
rating
limen-
plants

odyards

Although the trend of future cutting in the area cannot be ascertained with certainty, general directions can be indicated. There does not appear to be any reasonable basis for concluding that the total harvest will increase markedly in the immediate future. As discussed earlier, regional hardwood volume declined heavily between the latest two forest surveys. Prolonged increases in the total hardwood cut, therefore, would further deplete the marketable hardwood inventory. As for softwoods, it has been indicated that volume has increased over the past decade. But the historic turn for the better took place at a relatively low level of productivity. Current softwood inventory exceeds the 1947 stand, but is still well below the volume tallied during the initial forest survey of 1935. Sharp increases in softwood cutting in the near future, therefore, would tend to reverse the current favorable trend. Too, on those properties where softwood volume is increasing, much of the timber is being reserved to improve stocking and thus build up future timber growth.

Projection of cutting trends for major products, however, suggests that during the next few years pulpwood is likely to make up a greater proportion of the volume that is harvested. Also, industrial wood may soon make up practically all of the hardwood cut, for rural residents are continuing shifting to nonwood fuels for cooking and heating. Some of the estimated 5 million board feet of hardwood sawtimber trees channelled into fuelwood and miscellaneous domestic uses in 1958 were no doubt suited for industrial usage.

PEOPLE AND FORESTS

Owners of Small Tracts Predominate.—A good deal of the timber situation traces back to private landowners, over 9,000, who hold nine-tenths of the land. Specifically, wood-using industries such as lumber and pulp companies own some 17 percent of the forest land, farmers 53 percent, and other private owners—businessmen, professional people, wage earners, and the like—about 22 percent.

Contrasts in average pine stocking are somewhat indicative of relative forest management efforts among the several broad classes of private ownership. It was noted earlier that north central Mississippi is essentially a pine-producing region—that is, three out of every four forest acres are more valuable in pine than hardwood. Efforts at

Soft-textured hardwoods, like sweetgum, are converted into package veneer by the General Box Company at Macon. ⟶

18

controlling hardwood encroachment and improving pine volume have been most effective on forest-industry holdings, which are largely under supervision of professional foresters. On these holdings, for example, growing stock averages 880 cubic feet per acre, of which some three-fifths is pine. On private nonindustrial holdings, other than farmer-held, growing stock averages about 420 cubic feet per acre, half pine. Farmers' woodlands average nearly 470 cubic feet per acre, but only a third is softwood (fig. 7).

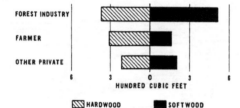

Figure 7.—*Average volume per acre in north central Mississippi, by type of ownership.*

Most of the private nonindustrial forest is in ownerships of less than 5,000 acres. To supplement data regularly collected as one phase of the forest survey, a special study of small woodland owners in the area was undertaken. Respondents were selected from owners on whose lands the Southern Forest Survey maintains permanent timber-sampling points, which are systematically located throughout the area.

It was found that small-tract owners are about equally divided between farmers and nonfarmers. The median forest acreage held by these owners is about 130. Nearly half of the owners reported gross annual incomes of less than $5,000.

Over 40 percent of the respondents had made some kind of forestry effort—planting trees, for example, or deadening cull hardwoods. Though the effort was often limited, at least in terms of acres, it is indicative of an awakening interest in forest improvement.

Loblolly pine planted in 1940 by Marshall Rivers of Neshoba County. The stand has already been thinned twice for pulpwood; the next cutting is scheduled for about 1964. ⟶

20

An encouraging number of small-tract owners—about one in four —had availed themselves of some professional forestry assistance. Indeed, most of these owners had made use of professional help on more than one occasion. For those who actively seek it, competent professional guidance is locally obtainable. The Mississippi Forestry Commission maintains a forestry staff at Philadelphia. Technical assistance is also available from the Soil Conservation Service and the State Extension Service. At least three pulp companies and two other wood-using concerns have foresters who will provide some technical help without charge. One of the latter concerns supports a comprehensive management program for interested timber owners, presently numbering about 100 in the 4-county area.

But what about the bulk of the small-tract respondents—the ones who have not yet availed themselves of professional guidance? A few believe they lack enough acreage to justify management. About one in six also indicated that they are simply "not interested in forestry." Many of these respondents—some 40 percent—strongly implied that they know enough about the woods so that they do not need professional help; in view of the resource trends discussed earlier, this seems highly improbable. Rather, it may be assumed that these owners do not have a fully adequate concept of what forest management involves and are unaware of the yields that may be realized through skillful application of scientific forestry principles. In brief, many landowners apparently do not recognize that there is a way of managing their forest land that is superior to their present methods. This suggests a big job ahead in informing landowners about the value of forestry before they may be willing to accept help, even if freely offered.

Aside from various technical-assistance programs, the other major public activity affecting forestry relative to small landowners is the Agricultural Conservation Program (ACP). Beginning in 1936 Congress authorized this cost-sharing program of soil-building and water-conserving practices.

In the 4-county area the ACP will share with landowners up to 65 percent of the cost of planting trees, or of carrying out timber stand improvement (TSI) measures such as girdling cull hardwoods. Current maximum per-acre rebates reported by local ACP offices are: $6.40 for TSI; $7.50 for machine planting; and $9.00 for hand planting.

About a quarter of the small-tract respondents had received ACP forestry payments, mostly for tree planting. Of those receiving pay-

22

ments, the majority had also made use of a forester at one time or another. It is likely that these owners initially availed themselves of ACP payments upon the forester's recommendation. Among non-users, about 20 percent were unaware that payments are available. An even larger number, almost 40 percent, reported a lack of time to do the required work. The latter response also suggests lack of program knowledge. Little time is actually required on the owner's part—even the field work may be contracted. For the majority of non-users, therefore, responses might be reasonably interpreted as reflecting inadequate knowledge regarding ACP benefits and eligibility, relative to its forestry aspects. Again, it reinforces the earlier conclusion as to the magnitude of the educational task that needs doing among woodland owners. Though both timber industries and public agencies offer forestry guidance to local landowners, efforts in this direction should be substantially bettered.

Forest Development: How Much Will It Cost?—Under the Agricultural Conservation Program, landowners in the 4 counties planted trees on 1,444 acres in 1958 and did initial stand-improvement work on 4,390 acres. While no data are available on the total acreage in the 4-county area on which such measures were carried out, it is conservatively estimated to be at least double or perhaps even triple the above figures. This added acreage would include public lands, forest industry holdings, and other nonindustrial holdings on which no ACP payments were received for the work done.

Information provided by local industrial and public foresters suggests that average costs for planting in the 4 counties are $15 per acre, and for TSI, $5.[*] Based on the acreages in need of such treatment as revealed by field surveys,[†] and assuming the above average costs, an approximation of total required expenditure is $4,200,000 for forest planting, plus $3,520,000 for initial improvement of timber stands.

These estimates do not include additional fire, insect, and disease prevention and control measures that may be required under more intensive management. These activities are largely directed by the Mississippi Forestry Commission.

Of the protection measures, installation of public fire-control facilities in Neshoba, Noxubee, and Winston Counties is a necessary first step to forest development. For the 12-month period preceding July 1, 1959, it is estimated that about 1.7 percent of the forest area

[*] Costs are based upon use of experienced woods crews. Reported range of TSI costs are $1 to $8 per acre, depending on stand conditions. Planting costs include seedlings furnished by the Mississippi Forestry Commission at $4.80 per thousand.
[†] See detailed discussion in earlier section titled, "Timber yields can be doubled."

was burned in these counties. In Kemper County, where the forests are under protection of the Mississippi Forestry Commission, scarcely 0.3 percent of the forest acreage burned over during the same period. That the area burned in the other 3 counties was not even greater is mainly attributable to a number of industrial landowners who made their fire-fighting facilities available to others.

Institution of county fire control requires local approval of landowners, as they are assessed protection costs of 2 cents per acre annually for timberland and uncultivatable land. Voters in Winston and Neshoba Counties recently approved county forest fire protection, but funds have not yet been locally allocated for installation of facilities. In protected counties, local funds are supplemented with State and Federal monies. Total fire-protection expenditures generally average 12 to 14 cents per acre for the initial year in protected counties, and 6 to 9 cents thereafter.

It is evident that a sizeable capital outlay will be necessary to upgrade the resource. Of the $7.7 million indicated for planting and TSI, it is presumed that $1.2 million will be expended on lands of public agencies and wood-using industries.

In essence, the above total is predicated upon spending about $8 per acre on the typical woodland for planting and release of seedlings from worthless overtopping hardwoods. Naturally, additional costs will be incurred over a period of years for such items as cruising, marking, supervision, management plans, and protection. The added costs for out-of-pocket expenses and labor might average as much as a dollar per acre annually. What returns might landowners expect from investment in intensive management?

It can be assumed that the average forest holding will be retained in individual or family ownership for a considerable time. Thus, land costs and taxes do not enter into appraisal of management opportunities—only the extra costs of growing timber and the returns therefrom. Costs and returns will of course vary somewhat with size of holding, differences in initial stocking, and site quality. But at least one indication of anticipated returns is suggested by a study tract maintained by the Forest Service in southern Arkansas, an area similar in productive capacity to north central Mississippi. This tract is the oldest intensively managed area in the Midsouth for which detailed records are available. When management began the tract

Too much of north central Mississippi's future payroll still goes up in smoke. This promising young pine plantation was killed by wildfire in July 1959. →

24

contained about 2 MBF (Doyle rule) of pine per acre, as well as numerous low-value hardwoods. Over a 15-year period, stumpage sales have paid all management expenses and returned $4 per acre annually (adjusted to a current price basis). In addition, the timber stand has been markedly improved in structure. The growing stock has increased in worth by over $6 per acre per year. These values would represent an annual compound rate of return of approximately 6 percent from investment in the management program. In terms of future opportunities, the latter estimate is probably conservative. In appraising management possibilities, landowners must also consider future changes in dollar values, wood demand, and timber growing techniques. The net effect of such changes could well be a relative gain in timber receipts as against timber growing costs.

ACP Aids Forest Betterment.—By reducing owner's out-of-pocket expenses, the ACP is instrumental in speeding forest improvement. ACP funds totaling $33,690, or 7 percent of total ACP allocation, were paid out by the 4 counties in 1958 for tree planting and timber stand improvement. In the same year, neighboring Lafayette County used 49 percent of its total ACP allocation for forestry practices. If the 4 north central counties had apportioned their total allocation similarly, $225,145 would have been available for cost sharing of approved forest treatments.

Tree planting has received further impetus during the past few years from the Soil Bank Conservation Reserve Program, a part of the Agricultural Act of 1956. This program established a system of cost-sharing, annual land payments, and technical guidance to enable farmers to undertake practices—tree planting, for example—that conserve soil, water, and wildlife on land withdrawn from cultivated crops. In 1958 about 1,150 acres in the 4 counties were planted to pine under this program, and nearly $12,000 was paid out to help participating farmers defray the costs. Additionally, these participants are receiving an annual land rental of $9.50 per acre for ten years from date of planting. Unless the authority is extended, new Soil Bank planting contracts will not be accepted after 1960.

MARKETING OF FOREST PRODUCTS

Markets Are Varied.—Demand for timber is heavy and outlets numerous in north central Mississippi. The lumber and pulpwood industries provide the principal markets. These industries, together with a few manufacturers of other products such as poles, veneer, and

Released from overtopping hardwood, these young pines on the Chris Allen tract near Philadelphia are now grow- ing rapidly. ⟶

handle-stock, utilize about 90 percent of the timber harvest. The rest goes into fuelwood and other domestic uses.

Lumber varies widely in species, grade, seasoning, degree of manufacture, and value. Marketing methods, therefore, vary according to the operations necessary to assemble, prepare, and sort the material for use. Rough unseasoned mill-run lumber from small sawmills may be sold directly to local users for farm repairs and construction, uses in which requirements are not exacting. To reach national markets, rough lumber usually must be further seasoned, graded, sorted, and sometimes planed. Since the small mill is generally equipped only for rough sawing, the lumber passes from it to concentration yards and large mills that provide the necessary skills, equipment, and finances. From these agencies, it goes through channels leading to the ultimate user or, particularly with hardwood, to furniture and similar industries for further manufacture.

Few sawmills have precise specifications for their raw timber needs. Ten inches in diameter at breast height might be taken as a rough minimum tree diameter for pine sawtimber. Quality, though seldom a barrier to utilization of pines, nevertheless influences the prices paid for stumpage. Prices are also affected by accessibility and competition. Common pine stumpage sells for about $30 to $35 per MBF (Doyle rule), while better material may bring $40 or more per MBF.

Commercial hardwood mill operators will accept some logs as small as 10 inches in diameter and 8 feet in length, provided that defects are few. But preferred logs are at least 12 inches in diameter and 12 or 14 feet in length. With few exceptions, therefore, a marketable hardwood sawtimber tree must be at least 15 inches in diameter and have a butt log capable of yielding clear cuttings. Opportunities for sale of low-grade hardwood sawtimber—that is, small logs, or large, knotty logs usable only for rough construction lumber—are more limited. In the current market, better quality hardwood suitable for factory lumber may bring from $12 to $20 per MBF (Doyle rule) on the stump. Hardwood that runs heavily to logs of minimum merchantability may bring scarcely $8 per MBF (Doyle rule) stumpage, when a buyer can be found.

Pulpwood demand is sizable in the 4 counties. It is certain to increase in view of announced industry expansion. Eight pulp companies are currently competing for local wood. Wood deliveries to

Mechanized concentration yards speed wood deliveries to pulp mills. ⟶

pulp mills are coordinated through a system of mechanized wood-yards and rail sidings at 16 strategic locations. Cordage is shipped to Alabama and Louisiana, as well as to mills within the State.

Pulpwood is cut into 5-foot lengths, with stated maximum diameters of 18 inches and minimum diameters of 4 inches. The standard cord is the accepted unit of measure, and prices are adjusted for differences in length of bolts. Pine cordage presently brings some $5 on the stump. Hardwood, largely soft-textured species like gum, is about half the price of pine. Delivered at local wood-yards, pulpwood is worth about $13 per cord for pine, $9 for hardwood.

Local outlets for products other than sawlogs and pulpwood are offered by hardwood dimension mills at Louisville and Philadelphia, which utilize hickory and gum; a package-veneer plant at Macon that accepts soft-textured hardwoods; and several plants using preservatives to treat wood products, such as pine poles, posts, and piling. Specifications for hardwood dimension and veneer approximate those for better-quality factory logs, but shorter lengths are utilized. Poles are generally marketed under specifications developed by the American Standards Association; piling under specifications of the American Society for Testing Materials. [1]

Prices for specialties are generally quoted at local delivery points for rough-cut products measured in standard units. Knot-free gum blocks (9 inches and up in diameter) for furniture stock, for example, currently bring about $22 per cord; clear hickory logs (12 inches and up in diameter) for dimension use, about $55 per MBF (Doyle rule); package-veneer logs (9 inches and up in diameter) are worth about $50 per MBF (Doyle rule). Common pine posts (7 feet long, 3 to 5 inches in diameter) average some 14 cents apiece. Pine poles for distribution lines in the widely used ASA Class-5, 35-foot length, presently bring at least $5 each. Piling, production of which is largely a special-order business, may bring about 25 cents per lineal foot.

Most Owners Sell Stumpage.—Because of the large number of forest owners and the small size of the average forest holding, the stumpage market is a composite of many small local transactions. The timber owner entering such a market is often hampered by lack of experience and information.

[1] For specifications of poles and piling see Southern Forest Experiment Station Occasional Paper 153.

The American Creosote Works at Louisville ships southern pine poles to national markets. →

Timber from most sellers enters the market in the form of stumpage, but some sell cut products. Interested landowners can usually arrange to have local contractors, for example, cut and haul logs for about $20 per MBF (Doyle rule). Logs are generally scaled at the mill yard by the buyer and paid for at a prearranged price per unit of measure. The usual practice in such transactions is for the buyer to make out two checks—one to the contractor for his fee, another to the seller for the residual amount.

With timber demand strong in the 4 counties, even small volumes are marketable. Stumpage sales of 50 cords of pulpwood or 20,000 board feet of sawlogs are not uncommon. Even smaller amounts are salable, especially where the landowner performs or contracts the cutting.

Improving Markets.—The factor that overshadows all other aspects of the marketing system is that timber owners are not realizing the potential production of their forest land. Narrowing the gap between what foresters know about timber growing and what the average landowner practices will require more technical assistance to landowners.

It would be helpful if information on forest products markets could be kept current by service agencies. Advantages of selling timber by measurement should be stressed, and known methods of measuring and grading widely demonstrated.

Full use of the available resource also calls for putting each tree harvested, and each part of each tree, into the highest use it can satisfy. If some of the added returns possible from improved utilization accrue to landowners, their incentives for growing timber will be increased. A recent study of hardwood logging operations by the Carbondale (Illinois) Research Center of the Forest Service illustrates the added returns possible from better utilization.[9] It was found that if the trees studied had been bucked for optimum grade, the timber operator's profit margin would have been increased about $6.50 per MBF. The study disclosed that major reasons for loss of quality and volume were: woods crews were not familiar with log grades, trees were cut with stumps higher than standard or were jump-butted unnecessarily, and merchantable top material was left lying in the woods.

---

[9] Increase your profit in the woods. U. S. Forest Serv., Cen States For. Expt. Sta. Tech. Paper 151. 1956

Small sawmills offer outlets for locally grown stumpage. ⟶

32

In putting timber to its most profitable use, sellers frequently have the option of selling pine stumpage as sawtimber or pulpwood. A study by the Southeastern Forest Experiment Station has shown that comparative prices between these products may be determined by comparing two ratios, one of which is a characteristic of the timber to be sold and the other a market condition. [*] The first is the ratio of cords/MBF; the second is the ratio of price per MBF to that of pulpwood per cord. If the price ratio is greater than the volume ratio, a sawtimber sale is more attractive to the seller, and if the price ratio is less, a pulpwood sale is preferred. Thus, in a stand where the trees to be sold have a ratio of cordwood volume to board-foot volume of 3 cords for each thousand board feet of sawtimber, it is apparent that when pulpwood is selling for $5 per cord, an equivalent sawtimber bid above $15 would be more attractive. Where the small quantities of cordwood in the tops of sawtimber trees can be marketed for pulpwood, borderline cases can best be decided in the favor of sawtimber. In the case of more limited markets—poles and piling, for example— sellers with timber that may qualify for these products should contact buyers, learn their specifications, and then look over their timber again. If there are a sufficient number of trees that qualify, it will usually be most profitable to sell the trees in such markets.

Efforts to attract secondary wood-using industries that can remanufacture local lumber into consumer goods might well be intensified. Timber growth plus the dwindling fuelwood demand is making more and more low-grade hardwood available for industrial use. Local plants might make parts for furniture and fabricated products. Small furniture plants, for example, could use local lumber in conjunction with quality material shipped in from other areas. Plants using small hardwood dimension stock might produce chair rounds, play pens, toys, and other items. If all avenues to more effective utilization of surplus hardwoods are fully explored, the market situation will be greatly helped. This would in turn stimulate the practice of forestry.

---

[*] Comparative stumpage prices. U S. Forest Serv., Southeastern For. Expt. Sta., Sta. Paper 16. 1952

Southern hardwoods can be used for furniture and fabricated products. ➔

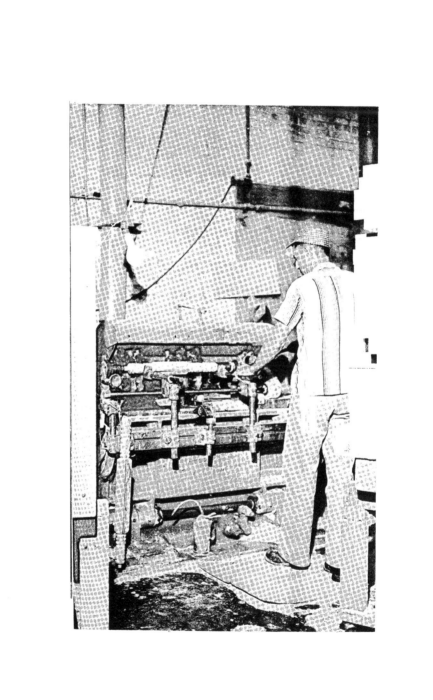

SUMMARY

Forest resources can be the basis of a flourishing local economy. Translating the capability into reality depends partly upon over-all public and private forestry programs. To increase the tempo of forestry efforts will require better ways of adapting systems of forest management to the needs of small landowners with limited capital, more efficient methods of timber utilization and marketing, and outlets for material currently unmerchantable.

What needs to be done within the 4 counties to realize the potential benefits? It is clear that more effort must go into rehabilitation of forest resources. To carry out prescribed land treatments on many small tracts in the 4 counties will require professional management, together with financial assistance in one form or another.

Land treatments recommended are to:

Plant pines on 280,000 acres of forest land that are now inadequately stocked with pine and do not have enough seed trees to assure eventual natural restocking.

Undertake timber stand improvement on 610,000 acres of forest land that is more valuable for pine than hardwood.

Remove cull timber on 94,000 acres of forest land that is best suited to growing industrial hardwood.

Install public fire-control facilities in Neshoba, Noxubee, and Winston Counties.

Harvest all timber in such a way as to put the forests in condition for high, continuous yields of wood crops.

Some of the benefits of forest development will be immediate and tangible. Thus, the proposed restoration work would provide at least 500 thousand man-days of local employment. An increase in forest land values is another likely benefit. Lands supporting small, defective timber would increase sharply in market value with planting and timber stand improvement—and this before a single post or stick of pulpwood is cut.

These immediate benefits would be incidental to, and small in comparison with, the ramified effects of expansion of basic industries. Some idea of these ultimate effects may be secured from factors derived by the New Jersey Development Council. According to the Council, 4,000 new jobs in a basic industry add 28,000 people to the local population. Taxable evaluation expands by $50 million, 660 new stores and shops open for business, and there are another 6,400

36

cars on the road. Whether or not the New Jersey estimates apply precisely to the 4 counties, it seems likely that the population decline would be reversed, and a larger population would enjoy a higher per-capita income and better community services than at present.

How rapidly the forest potential is achieved hinges upon the intensity of developmental efforts; future changes in the timber supply and demand situation; and the period required to produce salable wood of desired species, size, and quality on the many acres of understocked forest land. In large measure, the capital needs for forest development may have to come from outside the area, but much of the leadership should come from within. The outlook for future timber markets is excellent and the area has outstanding natural and economic advantages for producing quality timber. The costliest alternative will be delay or inaction.

APPENDIX

Forest Statistics [11]

Table 1.—*Land area and commercial forest by county*

County	All land	Commercial forest	
	Thousand acres	Thousand acres	Percent
Kemper	484.5	332.3	68.6
Neshoba	363.5	199.6	54.9
Noxubee	444.8	214.4	48.2
Winston	387.8	244.2	63.0
All counties	1,680.6	990.5	58.9

Table 2.—*Growing stock volume [1] by county*

County	Total	Softwood	Hardwood
	— — — Million cubic feet — — —		
Kemper	143.9	69.3	74.6
Neshoba	135.4	56.2	79.2
Noxubee	102.8	52.6	50.2
Winston	154.2	62.8	91.4
All counties	536.3	240.9	295.4

[1] Includes sound, well-formed trees at least 5.0 inches in diameter at breast height.

Table 3.—*Sawtimber volume [1] by county*

County	Total	Softwood	Hardwood
	— — — Million board feet [2] — — —		
Kemper	380.2	255.6	124.6
Neshoba	471.2	220.2	251.0
Noxubee	342.7	233.0	109.7
Winston	524.2	261.3	262.9
All counties	1,718.3	970.1	748.2

[1] Includes softwoods at least 9.0 inches in diameter at breast height; hardwoods, 11.0 inches.
[2] International ¼-inch rule.

Table 4.—*Sawtimber volume by tree diameter and county*

County	All diameter classes	Softwood		Hardwood	
		9.0-14.9 inches	15.0 inches and up	11.0-14.9 inches	15.0 inches and up
		— — — — Million board feet [1] — — — —			
Kemper	380.2	160.5	95.1	82.7	41.9
Neshoba	471.2	184.4	35.8	150.5	100.5
Noxubee	342.7	155.3	77.7	69.9	39.8
Winston	524.2	181.3	80.0	136.3	126.6
All counties	1,718.3	681.5	288.6	439.4	308.8

[1] International ¼-inch rule.

[11] Statistics given here are taken from most recently published data of the Forest Service. Statistical analysis indicates the sampling error to which the estimates may be liable two chances out of three are plus or minus 1.3 percent for the estimate of total forest area, 5.3 percent for total cubic volume, and 7.3 percent for total board-foot volume.

Primary Forest-Products Establishments
In Kemper County

Type of establishment	Name of owner or company	Location [1]
Stationary sawmill	Monroe Dean	Moscow
Stationary sawmill	D. L. Fair Lumber Co.	De Kalb
Stationary sawmill	J. A. McDade	Electric Mills
Stationary sawmill	J. E. McDonald	Preston
Stationary sawmill	Barnett Company	Moscow
Stationary sawmill	T. E. Darnell	Moscow
Stationary sawmill	Fisher Brothers Lumber Co.	De Kalb
Stationary sawmill	R. L. Ishee	Porterville
Stationary sawmill	Robert Ridgon	Porterville
Portable sawmill	Pat Griffin	Porterville
Portable sawmill	W. N. Johnson	De Kalb
Portable sawmill	Earle Lee Steadman	Preston
Portable sawmill	Nolan Martin	Porterville
Pulpwood concentration-yard	Richton Tie & Timber Co.	Porterville
Pulpwood concentration-yard	Shubuta Tie & Timber Co.	Scooba
Pulpwood concentration-yard	Culpepper Woodyard	De Kalb
Pulpwood concentration-yard	O. W. Hall	Porterville
Pulpwood concentration-yard	W. E. Batty	Scooba
Pulpwood concentration-yard	Fred Rogers	Porterville

[1] Indicates community nearest to the establishment. Location of portable sawmills is as of March 1959.

Primary Forest-Products Establishments
In Neshoba County

Type of establishment	Name of owner or company	Location [1]
Stationary sawmill	A. DeWeese Lumber Co.	Philadelphia
Stationary sawmill	Molpus Lumber Co.	Philadelphia
Stationary sawmill	Deemer Lumber Co.	Philadelphia
Portable sawmill	R. L. Ferguson	Arlington
Portable sawmill	Sam Marshal	Arlington
Portable sawmill	Paul Woods	Arlington
Portable sawmill	Harold Willis	Philadelphia
Wood-preserving plant	A. DeWeese Lumber Co.	Philadelphia
Hardwood dimension mill	A. DeWeese Lumber Co.	Philadelphia
Pulpwood concentration-yard	Richton Tie & Timber Co.	Philadelphia
Pulpwood concentration-yard	P. L. Jordson & Sons	Philadelphia

[1] Indicates community nearest to the establishment. Location of portable sawmills is as of March 1959.

Primary Forest-Products Establishments
In Noxubee County

Type of establishment	Name of owner or company	Location [1]
Stationary sawmill	O. B. Persons Lumber Co.	Shuqualak
Stationary sawmill	J. L. Jenigen	Mashulaville
Stationary sawmill	R. E. Prince	Shuqualak
Portable sawmill	E. S. Kelly	Shuqualak
Portable sawmill	Quenton Pierce	Shuqualak
Portable sawmill	Bill Hayne	Brookville
Portable sawmill	Emmitt Butler	Gholson
Portable sawmill	W. P. Beasley	Gholson
Veneer plant	General Box Company	Macon
Wood-preserving plant	Woody Jones Creosote Plant	Macon
Pulpwood concentration-yard	Shubuta Tie & Timber Co.	Shuqualak
Pulpwood concentration-yard	Kelly's Woodyard	Shuqualak
Pulpwood concentration-yard	R. N. Henley	Macon

[1] Indicates community nearest to the establishment. Location of portable sawmills is as of March 1959.

Primary Forest-Products Establishments
In Winston County

Type of establishment	Name of owner or company	Location [1]
Stationary sawmill	D. L. Fair Lumber Co.	Louisville
Stationary sawmill	Barrier & Neeks	Noxapater
Stationary sawmill	Odie Commer	Plattsburg
Stationary sawmill	Ross Burton	Louisville
Stationary sawmill	Sanford Brothers	Louisville
Stationary sawmill	Bill Rieves	Louisville
Portable sawmill	F. W. Vowell	Vowell
Portable sawmill	Arthur Davis	Louisville
Portable sawmill	William Rhodes, Jr.	Louisville
Portable sawmill	Sam Tripplet	Fern Springs
Portable sawmill	W. E. Robertson	Noxapater
Portable sawmill	Howard Hurt	Fern Springs
Wood-preserving plant	American Creosote Works, Inc.	Louisville
Handle-stock plant	B. E. Watson & Sons	Louisville
Pulpwood concentration-yard	H. B. Maxey	Noxapater
Pulpwood concentration-yard	J. D. Wilks Woodyard	Louisville
Pulpwood concentration-yard	John Carter	Noxapater
Pulpwood concentration-yard	Jimmie Lampley	Louisville
Pulpwood concentration-yard	C. B. Ray	High Point

[1] Indicates community nearest to the establishment. Location of portable sawmills is as of March 1959.

OCCASIONAL PAPER 173

Southern Forest Experiment Station
Philip A. Briegleb, Director
FOREST SERVICE, U. S. DEPT. OF AGRICULTURE

1959

the
truth
about
tessie
terebrans

William H. Bennett
&
H. Eugene Ostmark

Meet TESSIE TEREBRANS, the black
turpentine beetle. She's only half
the length of your fingernail, but
she's quite a gal!

You

The

to
any

...he delights in
...e fragrance
...f fresh
...esin...

...so she
...an't stay
...wa... from
...ogg...rs who
...re cutting
...that
...ELICIOUS
...pine.

3

She's also attracted
by loggers who
damage trees
by skinning and
bruising the bark.

4

and who crush tree roots

...with heavy machinery

on low, poorly drained sites,

5

... and who leave those

T
  A
    L
      L

tasty stumps for her to make her home.

But Tessie is
fickle and
unpredictable.

She may be happy
sticking to
her stumps...

or she just
may try to
invade LIVING
TREES !!

Foresters and loggers often seem determined to help Tessie make up her mind to be BAD !!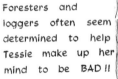

They log in the same stand repeatedly --maybe cutting poles and pilings first...

 then sawlogs...

and last, pulpwood.

8

By timing these cuts
just right, they make
fresh living places for
each new generation
of Tessie's children.

Tremendous hordes
build up in stumps,
and finally overflow
into nearby LIVING TREES!

IF all of the
trees are healthy
and vigorous,
chances are that
they will just "pitch"
Tessie and her brood back out...

BUT...
when trees have been weakened
by repeated logging traffic,
they don't stand a chance!

When Tessie sets up housekeeping,
be it in a fresh stump or
in the lower trunk of a live pine,
she advertises herself
by making HUGE pitch tubes.

When these pitch tubes appear on living trees the forester knows that EXTRA fast measures are needed.

EXTRA
BHC STOPS TESSIE

Lightly infested trees saved by timely spraying.

Benzene hexachloride can be dangerous to men, too.

ckpack pumps
ve effective

Stumps also must be sprayed

EVER give Tessie ...

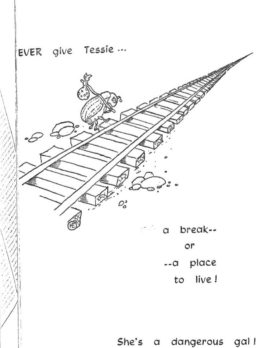

a break--
or
--a place
to live!

She's a dangerous gal!

Learn   MORE ..

about   stopping   Tessie.

Get   a   free   copy   of —

**INSECT ENEMIES OF
SOUTHERN PINES**

from

Southern Forest Experiment Station
2026 St.Charles Avenue
New Orleans 13, Louisiana

1959

occasional paper 174 —

SOUTHERN FOREST EXPERIMENT STATION
Philip A. Briegleb, Director
Forest Service, U.S. Department of Agriculture

SELECTIVE
CONTROL
of
CULL
HARDWOODS
in
EAST
TEXAS

George K. Stephenson
Carter B. Gibbs

Southern Forest Experiment Station
Philip A. Briegleb, Director
FOREST SERVICE
U. S. Department of Agriculture

CONTENTS

SELECTIVE CONTROL OF

CULL HARDWOODS

IN EAST TEXAS

George K. Stephenson
and
Carter B. Gibbs

The four southern pines, short-
af, longleaf, loblolly, and slash, make
） the primary forest crop of east Texas
ıd adjoining parts of Louisiana, Ar-
ınsas, and Oklahoma. They grow well
ı a wide range of soils, reach mer-
ıantable sizes early, and bring high
ʑerage prices. Except on bottom lands
ıd some other sites where hardwoods
ʳe best adapted, pine is the foresters'
ıoice for timber production.

That choice must be followed up
ʳ positive action if pine is to be main-
ined on most upland sites in this area.
ardwoods,tolerant of shade and able to
ﾟrout from roots or rootcollars when
ﾟove-ground parts are killed, develop
ıder pine stands and take over prompt-
when the pines are harvested. Though
ﾟmetimes useful for game food, they
ıve little commercial value, and pro-
ıce only inferior trees on dry upland
tes. Throughout the pine forests of
e West Gulf region, therefore, some
ʲgree of hardwood control is essential
 profitable management of the pine
ﾟecies.

Approaches to hardwood control
ıve included broadcast methods, such
 prescribed burning and aerial spray-
g,and the treatment of individual trees.
ıch approach has advantages and limi-

Nacogdoches Research Center, maintained in
öperation with Stephen F. Austin State College,
ʈogdoches, Texas.

tations, each is particularly suited to
some circumstances, and sometimes
both may be needed.

Broadcast methods produce relatively uniform results over the area
treated. They are selective only to the
extent that the treatment or material
affects certain classes of stems more
than others. Thus prescribed fire is
chiefly effective on small stems, and
shows little species selectivity, while
aerial spraying with silvicides takes out
the large overstory trees, and may be
quite selective as to species. With
broadcast methods, there is little opportunity to save individual trees that
may have potential value for wildlife
food or timber.

Individual-tree treatments can be
as selective as the skill of the operator
or the intensity of supervision permits.
Thus they permit economies by limiting
treatment to undesirable trees actually
affecting desirable stems, and they afford opportunity for considering each
tree on its merits as a competitor for
growing space and as a potential pro-
ducer of timber or wildlife forage. During the past ten years, the Nacogdoches
Research Center of the Southern Forest
Experiment Station has devoted considerable time to development of selective methods.

The earliest study in this field, installed in 1947, is still in progress. It was designed to compare the effects on pine growth from four intensities of hardwood control. Ax girdling or cutting was used except for one treatment in which sprouting was minimized by application of Ammate in groundline notches on trees under 8 inches in diameter. After 8 growing seasons, the treatments had had little effect on growth of pine trees above 10 inches in diameter at breast height, but had resulted in sizable, though not quite significant,

increases in volume of trees from 5 to 9 inches d.b.h., and in numbers of trees in the 2-, 3-, and 4-inch diameter classes. The treatments which removed the most overtopping hardwoods were the most effective. The Ammate treatment prevented resprouting and was especially notable for increasing the numbers of pine stems in the 2- to 4-inch classes. In a few more years, when these small trees develop appreciable volumes, there will be demonstrable benefits from some or all of the test treatments.

Figure 1.--*Although stunted and suppressed before they were released by the girdling of overstory oaks in 1947, these pines were reaching merchantable size by 1959.*

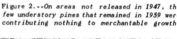

Figure 2.--*On areas not released in 1947, th few understory pines that remained in 1959 wer contributing nothing to merchantable growth*

Another finding of this study em-
asized one of the hard facts of forestry
the western limit of the pine belt.
ne of the treatments resulted in es-
blishment of new pine reproduction.
or seed crops, trashy seedbeds, and
mmer droughts delayed seeding or
lled each new crop of seedlings until
leased areas were reoccupied by
ush. In Texas, where competition for
il moisture is intense, pine stems on
e ground are precious assets, very
uch worth saving. So the Nacogdoches
nter began to concentrate on methods
at might help salvage a maximum of
e fortuitous advance reproduction still
ive in our upland stands.

POWER GIRDLING

A newly marketed power girdler
was tested in 1954.[2] This machine, consisting of a rotary cutting head powered
through a flexible shaft by a light gaso-
line engine carried on the operator's
back, offered possibilities of reducing
the manpower requirements and the accident hazards of ax work. It was found
(fig. 4) that under east Texas conditions
a man could treat about three times as
many trees with the power girdler as
with the ax. For example, to girdle 600
diameter inches per acre with the machine required 66 minutes, while the
same amount of ax girdling took 3.5
hours. The advantages of the girdler
were widely recognized and its use gave
a considerable impetus to hardwood
control in Texas and throughout the
South.

Figure 3.--*A gasoline-powered
girdling machine enables woods
workers to treat trees at three
times the speed of a man with an
ax. The rotary cutter-head is
driven through a flexible shaft.*

Harrington, T.A. 1955. More power to girdling.
rest Farmer 14(8): 12, 16-17, illus.

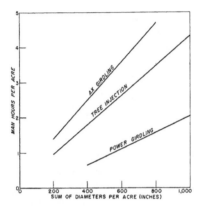

Figure 4.--*Labor required for girdling and injecting undesirable hardwoods in east Texas.*

Since the girdle made by the machine was shallow, trees died more slowly than after ax work, and on occasional stems, callus growth bridged the girdles, permitting the tree to survive. A survey[3] in 1955, covering some 6,000 trees treated by various methods, showed that bridging had occurred on 2.8 percent of the power-girdled trees, with an additional 4.9 percent showing callus growth short of bridging. This survey, 4 to 30 months after treatment, also showed (fig. 5) crowns killed on 35 percent of the power-girdled trees, as compared to 68 percent of those girdled with a double ax cut, and 44 percent of those receiving single ax frills. Only 11 percent of the power-girdled crowns were apparently unaffected, however, and eventual crown-kill of these trees is expected to approach 90 percent. This difference in promptness of kill was also revealed in a designed test on post oak and sweetgum, where two seasons after

[3] Mignery, A.L. 1956. What gives with girdling? Southern Lumberman 193(2417): 214-215, illus.

Loblolly pines planted within 24 hours after silicide applications suffered no ill effects, and their survival was as good as those planted two months later.[6] Obviously the pines were sufficiently tolerant of 2, 4, 5-T to make this chemical a good candidate for use in selective hardwood removal. With this assurance, which has been confirmed by subsequent observations, work was concentrated on various selective applications of 2, 4, 5-T.

This chemical was tested as a supplement to girdling, in the hope that it would give quicker and more complete top-kill as well as sprout control. Because transportation of large quantities of liquid in the woods is laborious and expensive, applications of the concentrated propylene glycol butyl ether ester were tried, as well as the recommended 1-to-50 dilution in diesel oil. The concentrate (4 pounds acid equivalent per gallon) was applied as a fine spray from a squeeze bottle; the dilute solution was brushed on, in each case the equivalent of approximately 1 cc of concentrate per tree. These chemicals were applied in April 1955 to ax and power girdles on sweetgums and post oaks in three test areas--a total of 240 trees. In a companion test, sweetgums were machine-girdled and given the chemical treatments in January, July, and November.

Both concentrations accelerated top-kill (fig. 6), increasing from 85 to 99 the percentage of treated trees dead above the girdle after two years;[7] the difference is statistically significant. Only the dilute treatment, however, effectively reduced sprouting. For the April applications, the average percent of trees dead without sprouts was 42 without chemical and 56 with the concentrate, but the differences were not statistically significant. The dilute

2, 4, 5-T increased the non-sprouting mortality to 87 percent, a highly significant increase. With both chemical treatments, power and ax girdles resulted in practically identical percents of trees killed and not sprouting. The seasonal test produced high percentages of top-kill from girdles at all seasons, but sprouting was much less frequent after growing-season treatment.

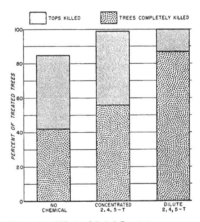

Figure 6.--*Effect of 2,4,5-T, at two concentrations, on sweetgum and post oak in east Texas.*

Two other studies have emphasized this seasonal variation in the effectiveness of 2, 4, 5-T as a sprout suppressor. In one,[8] where spring applications of dilute 2, 4, 5-T suppressed sprouts from post oak and sweetgum stumps more effectively than the same amount of chemical in concentrate form, winter treatments were ineffective. In the other,[9] December applications of a 23.5-pound ahg solution in diesel oil on

[6] Harrington, T.A. 1955. 2,4,5-T basal spray on hardwoods does not harm loblolly planted next day. U.S. Forest Serv. South. Forest Expt. Sta. South. Forestry Notes 95.

[7] Stransky, J.J. 1959. Concentrated or diluted 2,4,5-T as a supplement to girdling? Jour. Forestry 57: 432-434, illus.

[8] Davis, J.R. 1958. Diluted 2,4,5-T more lethal than undiluted in east Texas. Jour. Forestry 56: 516.

[9] Davis, J.R. 1958. Basal spray with 2,4,5-T for winter hardwood control in east Texas. Jour. Forestry 56: 349.

fresh stumps of small hardwoods delayed sprouting, only 37 percent of treated stumps having sprouted the following April as compared with 92 percent of untreated stumps. By the following spring, however, 97 percent of the treated stumps had sprouts. This is in strong contrast to the effectiveness of the same solution applied as a basal spray on standing trees, 93 percent of which died, though many retained their leaves through the first season. Only 5 percent of these trees sprouted.

It was concluded that where control of sprouting is important, basal spraying is most effective for small trees, while either ax- or machine-girdling should be supplemented by dilute 2,4,5-T. Best results can be expected from treatment during the growing season. Spraying with 2,4,5-T concentrate, though it hastened top-kill, did not effectively suppress sprouts.

There is need for further testing to determine whether some intermediate concentration of 2,4,5-T can be effective without being too bulky for use with a power girdler.

BASAL SPRAYS

After the tests with oaks and gums, basal spray with 2,4,5-T was tried on hawthorn and ironwood, which are pests on some of the best sites. A propylene glycol butyl ether ester in a 23.5 ahg dilution with diesel oil was applied in December, both as a basal spray and painted on cut stumps. For comparison, a slushy paste of Ammate in water was put on other cut stumps (table 1). Top-kill from basal spray was 100 percent for ironwood and 91 percent for hawthorn, and after two years none of the trees had sprouted.[10] The 2,4,5-T treatment on stumps suppressed sprouts on ironwood (2 percent sprouted), but not on hawthorn (45 percent sprouted). The

[10]Mignery, A.L. 1956. Basal spray controls ironwood and hawthorn. Texas Forest News 35(4): 10.

Figure 7.--*Spraying the basal 18 inches of the trunk with 2,4,5-T in diesel oil killed oaks, sweetgum, hawthorn, and ironwood. Sprouting was negligible.*

ere may be further opportunity for onomy in the use of rather dilute solutions. Lest there be a temptation to tend this surmise too far, it might be ded that no kill whatever was secured en one of the men accidentally sprayed group of trees with pure diesel oil.

INJECTION OF SILVICIDES

Another approach to economy in plication of silvicide came with the velopment of improved versions of the Cornell tool.[11] These tools deposit emical inside the bark at the ground-e. Essential parts are a pipe that ntains the chemical and has a cutting ade at its end, plus a device for re-asing appropriate amounts of liquid o the wounds made by the blade. The ade is jabbed into the tree just above e root collar. Wounds must be closely

spaced, preferably overlapping, since there is little lateral translocation of chemical.

In an early Texas test with such an injecting tool, the silvicide was a propylene glycol butyl ether ester of 2, 4, 5-T in a 36-pound ahg concentration in diesel oil. An experienced laborer treated the small hardwoods on 22 acres of experimental plots--a total of 5, 609 stems, mostly oaks, ranging from 1 to 7 inches in diameter, and averaging 2.1 inches.

The job required 2.12 man-hours and 0.87 gallon of the chemical solution per acre. The solution cost $1.31 per gallon. Thus with labor at $1.00 per hour, the cost of treating 255 small hardwoods was $3.26 per acre--$2.12 for labor and $1.14 for chemical. The job required considerably less labor than would have been required to cut or girdle these trees, but considerably more than power girdling. Since the alternate methods would have required

Cope, J.A., and Spaeth, J.N. 1931. The kill-g of trees with sodium arsenite. Jour. Forestry 775-783, illus.

chemical follow-up to control sprouts, the injector treatment is competitive in cost where complete control is important.

When the test was reported in 1955,[12] the Nacogdoches Center was hopeful, but uncertain, about the ultimate effectiveness of tree injection. Subsequent observations on these plots and on many other areas indicate a high degree of effectiveness and almost complete absence of sprouting. Most of such failures as occur result from improper treatment--usually spacing injections too far apart. A few species, though, are consistently resistant to all but growing-season treatment.

Figure 8.--*Injection of 2,4,5-T in cuts is an effective way to kill weed trees. The instrument holds about 7 pints of silvicide. A valve meters a predetermined amount into the cut through a hole in the cutting blade.*

The Texas National Forests cooperated in a study involving 480 sweetgum and oak trees, to test the effectiveness of iso-octyl ester of 2,4,5-T, which was available at 60 percent of the cost of the propylene glycol butyl ether ester. Four concentrations, 40, 20, 13.3, and 8 pound ahg in diesel oil, were applied as in a standard injector operation.

The 40-pound ahg concentration was 100 percent effective on both species the 20-pound dosage killed 82 percent of the oaks but only 50 percent of the sweetgums (fig. 9). The lighter dosages were correspondingly less effective. Sprouting was negligible on top-killed trees of both species. The iso-octyl ester appears to be effective in concentrations comparable to those recommended for other low-volatile esters, and is being used extensively.

[12] Davis, J.R., and Duke, W.B. 1955. Quick, Bunyan, the needle! South. Lumberman 191(2393): 171-172, illus.

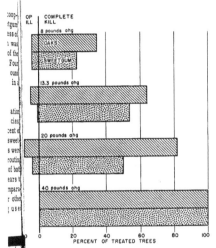

Figure 9.--*Effect of iso-octyl ester of 2,4,5-T, applied by tree injector.*

high concentrations, whereas the esters are not effective unless diluted. Further tests of the 2,4-D amine are desirable to determine an optimum dosage (perhaps about 1.0 ml.). A modified injector which can accurately meter these small quantities should be developed.

SUMMARY

Because reduced competition is essential to pine regeneration in east Texas, hardwood control is destined to play an increasingly important role in the forestry of the area. Where wide areas are to be reproduced, there will be need for the broadcast methods, including prescribed fire, aerial sprays, and machine clearing. For smaller areas, and the many stands with salvageable understories of desirable species, methods for deadening individual trees will find a place.

A test of 2,4-D amine was completed in 1958. The object was to determine if this material could be used full strength, thus greatly reducing the volume of fluid to be handled. Post oaks and sweetgums were wounded at the base with an empty tree injector, cuts being spaced approximately on three-inch centers as in normal treatment with this tool. Measured quantities of 2,4-D amine were then applied to each cut, half the trees receiving 0.5 ml. per cut, the remainder receiving 2.0 ml. (fig. 10).

After two growing seasons, the lighter dosage had top-killed 96 percent of the oak and 81 percent of the sweetgum, and the heavier dosage had top-killed 99 percent of the oak and 100 percent of the sweetgum. Sixteen percent of the gums sprouted, but there were no sprouts on the oaks. These results seem to confirm conclusions from other areas that amines of the phenoxy herbicides can be used in

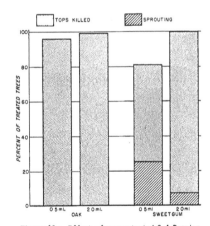

Figure 10.--*Effect of concentrated 2,4-D amine, applied by tree injector.*

- 9 -

Ax and machine girdling without chemicals are useful where sizable pines are to be released, but do not control sprouting. More and more, chemical methods that control both top and root are being recognized as essential for control of stand composition. Ammate is corrosive to metal and somewhat messy to handle, but nevertheless a good chemical--safe, effective, and reasonably cheap. The phenoxy silvicides offer possibilities of some economies and greater convenience. They can be effective as supplements to girdling, as basal sprays, and when injected beneath the bark. At present, tree injection seems to offer the best possibility for economical treatment of the troublesome small

1959

Guide
for

EVALUATING
SWEETGUM
SITES

W. M. Broadfoot
R. M. Krinard

SOUTHERN FOREST EXPERIMENT STATION
Philip A. Briegleb, Director
FOREST SERVICE
U. S. DEPARTMENT OF AGRICULTURE

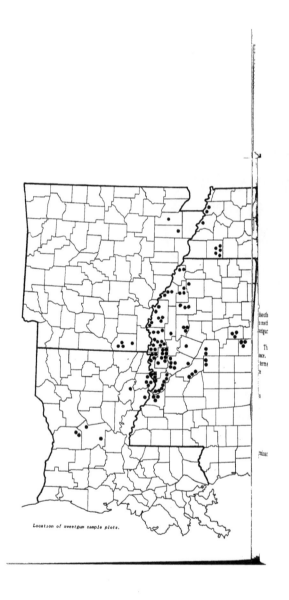

Location of sweetgum sample plots.

Guide for

EVALUATING SWEETGUM SITES

W. M. Broadfoot
R. M. Krinard

Studies at the Stoneville Research Center[1] have established 3 practical methods of estimating the ability of
Midsouth soils to grow sweetgum (Liquidambar styraciflua).
The methods were developed from data collected from 104
sweetgum plots in the area mapped on the opposite page.

The choice of method is a matter of individual preference. All three methods give site potential (site index)
in terms of the height, in feet, that a free-growing forest
tree will have reached at the age of 50 years.

In one study, the total height of trees at age 50 years
was related to 37 chemical and physical properties of the
soil. The two properties that proved most closely related,
clay content and amount of exchangeable potassium, form
the basis for evaluating sweetgum sites in the first method.

The second method provides rapid on-the-spot classification of sites by observation of surface drainage and determination of soil texture, internal drainage, and presence
or absence of hardpan. This method is applicable only in
the lower Mississippi Valley.

A third method requires that soils be mapped or otherwise identified by standardized series and phase, after which
sweetgum site index can be read from a table.

[1]Maintained at Stoneville, Mississippi, by the Southern Forest Experiment Station in cooperation with the Mississippi Agricultural Experiment
Station and the Southern Hardwood Forest Research Group.

Method I

To apply the first method, two or more representativ[e] bulk soil samples should be collected from each site in th[e] area for which sweetgum growth potential is to be de[-] termined. For example, a broad flat with heavy clay so[il] would require separate sampling from a ridge with sand[y] soil. Samples should be from a depth of 36 to 48 inche[s] and are preferably taken with a bucket-type soil auger. Th[e] samples from each site can be composited and mixed, an[d] about 1 pint saved for laboratory analysis.

The samples may then be either turned over to [a] soils laboratory for determination of clay content an[d] pounds of exchangeable potassium per acre, or prepare[d] for these analyses if suitable laboratory facilities exis[t] locally. For local analysis, the samples should be air dried and sieved through a 2-mm screen and then put in [a] clean, pint-sized ice cream carton. Instructions for de[-] termining clay and exchangeable potassium by standar[d] procedures usually can be obtained from State experimen[t] stations.

When clay and potassium content have been determine[d] from the sample, the site index can be read from table 1[.] The range of sites that may be encountered in this metho[d] are shown in figure 1.

Figure 1.--*Range of sweetgum site indexes as determined from amount of clay and potassium in the soil.*

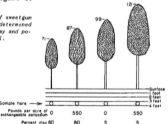

- 2 -

Table 1.—Height of sweetgum at age 50 years, as determined from clay and potassium contents at 36- to 48-inch soil depth[1]

Clay (percent)	Exchangeable potassium, in pounds per acre											
	0	50	100	150	200	250	300	350	400	450	500	550
	- - - - - - - - - - - - - -Feet- - - - - - - - - - -											
5	99	101	103	105	107	109	110	112	114	117	119	121
10	97	99	100	102	104	106	108	110	112	114	116	118
15	95	97	98	100	102	104	106	108	110	111	114	116
20	93	95	96	98	100	102	104	105	107	109	111	113
25	91	93	94	96	98	99	101	103	105	107	109	111
30	89	91	92	94	95	97	99	101	103	104	106	108
35	87	89	90	92	94	95	97	99	100	102	104	106
40	85	87	88	90	91	93	95	96	98	100	102	104
45	83	85	86	88	90	91	93	94	96	98	100	101
50	82	83	85	86	87	89	91	92	94	96	97	99
55	80	81	83	84	86	87	89	90	92	94	95	97
60	78	79	81	82	84	85	87	88	90	92	93	95
65	76	78	79	81	82	83	85	86	88	90	91	93
70	75	76	77	79	80	82	83	85	86	88	89	91
75	73	74	76	77	79	80	81	83	84	86	87	89
80	71	73	74	75	77	78	79	81	82	84	85	87

[1]Standard error of estimate for Delta and combined soils, 8 percent; for non-Delta soils, 9 percent.

Method II

This procedure, as yet applicable only in the Mississippi River flood plain, requires use of a soil auger or spade the first 2 feet of soil to determine texture, internal rainage, and presence of hardpan. A fourth site factor, inerent moisture condition, can be established by observation. After the four components have been determined, site index an be read from figure 2 or keyed out in table 2.

Texture: Classify texture in the surface 2 feet as fine, medium, or coarse. Clays (buckshot and gumbo) are classed as fine, sandy soils as coarse, and all the rest as medium.

- 3 -

Internal drainage: If there is no distinct gray or reddish-brown mottling within the surface 2 feet, classify the site as moderately to well drained. If there is distinct mottling, classify internal drainage as moderate to poor.

Hardpan: If a firm or compact zone is present in the upper 2 feet, classify the site as having a pan.

Inherent moisture condition: If the site is on a slope or ridge, or is otherwise situated so that floodwater or heavy rains drain off, classify it as dry. If it is level, or situated so that it is subject to flooding, classify as moist. Generally no other classification of inherent moisture is necessary, but sometimes such factors as nearness of root zone to mean low water in rivers, streams, or lakes may have to be considered.

Table 2.--*Site index for sweetgum for soils derived from alluvium on the Mississippi River flood plain*[1]

Soil-site description	Site index
I. Fine texture	
A. Moderate to good internal drainage	100
B. Moderate to poor internal drainage	
1. Without pan	
a. Inherently moist	85
b. Inherently dry	95
2. With pan	70
II. Medium texture	
A. Moderate to good internal drainage	
1. Without pan	
a. Inherently moist	110
b. Inherently dry	105
2. With pan	90
B. Moderate to poor internal drainage	
1. Without pan	
a. Inherently moist	95
b. Inherently dry	105
2. With pan	75
III. Coarse texture	
A. Moderate to good internal drainage	
a. Inherently moist	100
b. Inherently dry (not a sweetgum site)	

[1] Key not applicable to soils outside the Mississippi River flood plain--as loess and Coastal Plain alluvium. Sites not indexed are either nonexistent or are not recommended for sweetgum.

- 4 -

Soils of fine texture

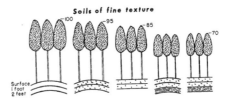

Soils of medium texture

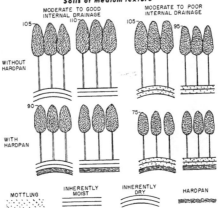

Figure 2.--Height of sweetgum at 50 years on fine and medium soils derived from alluvium on the Mississippi River flood plain.

Method III

The third method requires identification of the [soil] series and its local phase. Identification can be made in [the] field by any locally competent soil scientist. Standard s[oil] surveys have been made in many counties, and the result[ing] maps will serve as the quickest means of identifying [the] soil.

With soil series and phase determined, sweetgum s[ite] index can be roughly classified from table 3. It should [be] remembered that sites may vary considerably withi[n] series and phase.

Figure 3.--*Site index for sweetgum averaged 104 feet on recent natural-levee soils (left), and 90 feet on slack-water soils (right).*

- 6 -

Table 3.--*Site index of sweetgum by soil series and phase*

Series and phase	Site index
Soils of recent natural levees	
Robinsonville, sloping phase	109
Commerce	105
Mhoon, level phase	100
Soils of old natural levees	
Bosket, level phase	101
Dundee	98
Forestdale	97
Sloping phase	103
Level phase	85
Soils of slack-water areas	
Bowdre, sloping phase	97
Sharkey	86
Sloping phase	89
Level phase	83
Alligator	93
Sloping phase	97
Level phase	87
Bottom-land soils from loess	
Vicksburg, sloping phase	97
Collins	105
Falaya	101
Waverly	94
Bottoms from mixed loess and Coastal Plain material	
Ina	100
Beechy	95
Alluvial soils with Permian Red Bed influence	
Perry	90
Yahola	90
Soils from Coastal Plain alluvium	
Bibb	85
Chastain	95
Urbo	95
Terrace soils	
Brittain	95
Lintonia, moist	110
Olivier	95
Calhoun	75
Carroll	70
Hatchie	90
Scipio	95
Soils developed in loess	
Memphis, moist, moderate erosion	80
Loring, moist, no erosion	95
Lexington, moist, moderate erosion	85

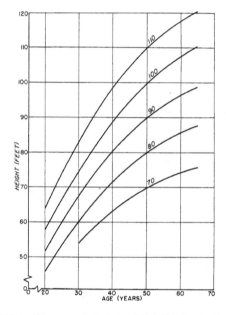

Figure 4.--*These curves indicate the expectable heights of sweetgum &*
on sites of various quality. They can be used to check the site ev-
ations made by methods I, II, and III. To make such a check requires m
urement of the heights of dominant and codominant trees in well-sto-
stands that have had no modifying influence or treatment. For exam
trees 80 feet tall at age 40 would signify a site index of 90.

OCCASIONAL PAPER 177

1960

WEIGHT-SCALING

SOUTHERN PINE

SAW LOGS

Sam Guttenberg

Donald Fassnacht, William C. Siegel

SOUTHERN FOREST
EXPERIMENT STATION
Philip A. Briegleb, Director

●

FOREST SERVICE

●

U. S. DEPARTMENT
OF AGRICULTURE

Acknowledgment

The Woodlands Department of the Olin Mathieson Chemical Corporation made this research possible by providing timber, log-handling and milling facilities, manpower, and photography.

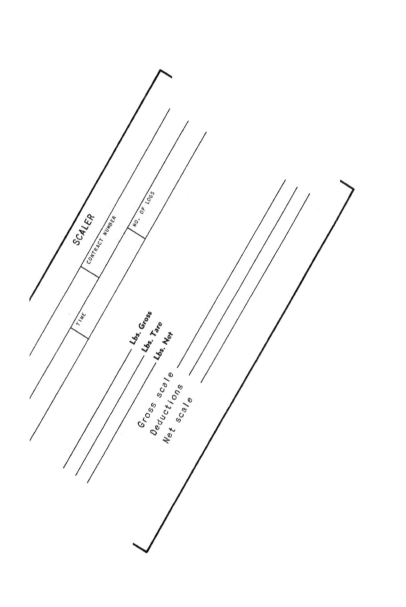

SCALER

CONTRACT NUMBER

NO. OF LOGS

TIME

Lbs. Gross
Lbs. Tare
Lbs. Net

Gross scale
Deductions
Net scale

Figure 1.—Errors and hazards of conventional
ing are lessened if logs are scal-
weight.

WEIGHT-SCALING

SOUTHERN PINE

SAW LOGS

Sam Guttenberg

Donald Fassnacht, William C. Siegel

SCALING BY WEIGHT promises equal accuracy and greater day-to-day consistency in predicting lumber yields from southern pine saw logs than scaling by traditional log-rule methods. In a study with loblolly and shortleaf pine saw logs, the log-to-lumber prediction was closer when based on the weight of the logs than when derived from values of the Doyle, Scribner Decimal C, or International rules. When weighing is done by truckloads rather than by individual logs, relative accuracy can be further enhanced, and substantial savings in time and money can be realized.

The precision of the weight-yield relationships developed for the mill under study suggests the suitability of weight-scaling in the southern pine region. While individual mills will have to develop factors for their local conditions, several potential advantages of weight-scaling seem to assure its future:

A single objective measurement that can supplant scaling by timber growers, loggers, haulers, and mill men.

The elimination of stick scaling's log-by-log computations and opportunities for error.

Shorter truck turnaround time at the mill.

Feasibility of uncontested spot payment for delivered logs.

A stimulus for delivery of green logs, free from stain.

Lessening of the risk of physical injury to scalers.

FIELD METHODS

A total of 203 pine saw logs were chosen from the forests of southern Arkansas and northern Louisiana (fig. 2). The object was to obtain representation of each diameter class from 6 to 20 inches (table 1). Lengths varied from 12 to 20 feet, and both shortleaf and loblolly were represented. None had rot or sweep enough to require downgrading by the *Interim Pine Log Grades* (9).[1] The exclusion of defective logs appeared justified by the Forest Survey's findings that only 3 percent of the area's gross pine volume is defective.

The following factors were measured at the mill yard, before the logs were more than 5 days from the stump:

Diameter—Minimum and maximum diameters were taken at the small end of each log, to the nearest 0.01 foot, inside bark.

Length—The longest and shortest log faces were taped to the nearest 0.01 foot.

Figure 2.—*Log sources.*

Table 1.—*The log sample*

Diameter class, D b (inches)	Length 12 feet	14 feet	16 feet	18 feet	20 feet	All logs	Butt logs
	— — — — — — Number of logs — — — — — —						
6	5	.	7	1	...	13	2
8	10	9	8	2	.	29	7
10	3	8	15	1	4	31	4
12	2	5	12	4	7	30	8
14	1	10	7	9	3	30	6
16		3	13	7	7	30	16
18	1	5	3	4	7	20	10
20 +	1	1	8	6	4	20	12
Totals	23	41	73	34	32	203	65

Weight—Each log was weighed twice, to the nearest 10 pounds. At every tenth log the scales were calibrated with 1,000 pounds of standard 50-pound check weights.

Lumber yield—Each log was sawn to 4/4 boards, except that an 8/4 center piece was used to control log identity through the mill. Each board was scaled and graded in terms of finished lumber.

Moisture percent—A wafer was taken one foot from each end of the 8/4 center piece and green weight determined immediately.

Specific gravity—Additional wafers were cut adjacent to the moisture content samples. The ratio of green volume to oven-dry weight was determined in a laboratory.

All factors measured twice were averaged and the mean values used in the analyses.

SINGLE-LOG ESTIMATES

From weights and lumber yields of the individual logs, a factor was developed for predicting lumber tally from logs of various weights. A condensed set of values, based on this factor, is found in Table 2.

Table 2.—*Lumber yield from southern pine logs of various weights*

Log weight (pounds)	Predicted green lumber yield [1]
	Board feet
200	9
600	51
1,000	94
1,400	138
1,800	184
2,000	207
2,200	231
2,600	278
3,000	328

[1] $\text{Board feet} = \dfrac{\text{Weight}}{9.88} + \dfrac{(\text{Weight})^2}{254,362} - 10.96$

[1] Bold-face numbers in parentheses refer to Literature Cited, p. 6.

How did weight-scaling with this factor compare with standard log-rule scaling? Figure 3 provides a visual comparison. Charts for weight and for three log rules are drawn to the same proportions. The diagonals represent exact agreement between estimated and actual lumber yields. The dots represent the 203 study logs. If all dots fell on the diagonals, the prediction would be perfect.

The patterns in Figure 3 indicate that a weight factor can compare favorably with precise log-rule scaling. Since sawing is rarely done to standard log-rule specifications and

the weight estimator is based on actual yield of the 203 logs, this was not unexpected.

The popular Doyle rule behaves normally. Lumber yield is substantially underestimated: very few points appear to the right of the diagonal. The arched dot pattern illustrates the variation in overrun with log size. The dots in the Scribner chart cluster around the diagonal but not so closely as those in the weight diagram. International-rule predictions fall chiefly below the diagonal—signifying underrun. This rule requires production of 4- and 6-foot boards, but the mill preferred to manufacture pulp chips instead of shorts.

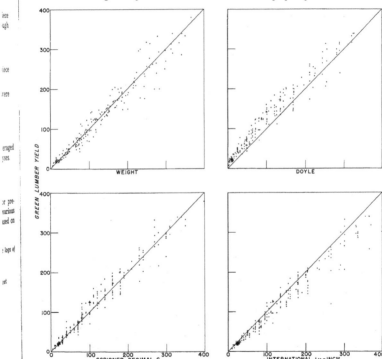

Figure 3.—*Comparison of weight-scaling with standard log-rule scaling. All values are in board feet.*

The charts indicate that weight is a good predictor of lumber outturn. A statistical analysis summarized on page 6, was designed to answer the question, "Can weight alone account for the single or combined effects of such variables as diameter, length, moisture content, or specific gravity in predicting lumber yield?"

The analysis indicated that for practical purposes weight alone will do the job. Adding the effects of moisture content and specific gravity improved the prediction made from weight alone, but the gain was very small and does not justify the cost of taking the measurements.

Differences in the moisture content of trees from season to season have sometimes been thought to complicate weight-scaling. While the present test offered no evidence on this point, the U. S. Forest Products Laboratory (7) has found no significant seasonal moisture differences. Recently, Dr. R. M. Echols of the Southern Institute of Forest Genetics sampled living southern pines throughout the year. Though he found sizable differences in moisture content between trees, the seasonal moisture differences within any one tree were negligible.

Because of its susceptibility to rapid changes in moisture content, outer bark may also seem an important source of weight variation. King and Taras, however, report that usually 10 percent or less of saw-log weight is bark (4, 10). When local weight factors are developed, sampling loads or logs over a period of several months substantially accounts for the variation in bark moisture.

TRUCKLOAD ESTIMATES

As most industrial weight-scaling will be done in truckload lots, a weight factor was computed for this purpose. Yearlong scaling records indicated that the typical single-axle logging trucks were carrying loads of 20 to 35 logs. Simulated loads ranging from 20 to 33 logs were therefore drawn randomly from the data. Weights of the loads varied from 22,000 to 43,100 pounds and volumes from 2,089 to 4,361 board feet.

The calculated truckload weight factor is shown as the solid line in Figure 4. It represents the average relationship between lumber yield and load weight. The clustering of dots

Valid local factors for truckload lots can be developed in a variety of ways. The single-log approach used in this study takes fewer logs than do truckload appraisals, but requires year-long scale records from which to reconstruct representative loads.

A rough-and-ready factor can be had by selecting about 50 loads at random over a period of months and dividing the gross yield (either in company scale or green-chain tally) by the gross weight. If records are kept by individual loads, mathematical analysis of the data becomes possible. Among other things, such analysis can determine the reliability of the factor at different load weights, the number of loads that must be sampled to achieve specified accuracy standards, and the variation in log or load characteristics that might affect the factor.

After the yield factor has been determined, occasional checks will be desirable. Log trim allowance should also be measured periodically. Mills whose average log size tends to be fairly stable can utilize a single weight per MBF.

When individual sources of supply show considerable variation in log size, value factors can be adjusted to the number of logs per ton—in the same fashion that log diameter is used.

Under today's conditions, firms sawing more than 5 million board feet annually can benefit from measuring logs by weight. Equipment, installation, and housing will cost from $8,000 to $12,000. This assumes a 34- by 10-foot drive-on model with 30-ton capacity—a suitable size for most mills. It would have a direct-reading dial and unit for printing gross, tare, and net weight on cards. Depending upon the mill's annual cut, savings over conventional scaling and bookkeeping alone should recover costs in 2 to 5 years. Mills that receive considerable timber in logs longer than 20 feet will probably need scales of 50 to 60 tons' capacity.

Firms converting to weight estimation will find an educational program helpful in speeding acceptance. Initial reaction of loggers, haulers, and timber growers to weight-trading is likely to reflect human resistance to change. The Wells-Griffin Lumber Company of Georgia (1) has made a successful conversion to weight. To retain good will it began by offering to scale as well as weigh loads for any contractor who desired a comparison.

The overrun from the Doyle rule is still a favored control device of mill managers, though shifts in average log size between accounting periods affect the percent of overrun. In conversion to weight-scaling, the advantages of the device can be retained by adjusting locally derived mill-tally weight factors for whatever overrun percent is desired.

Present and Future Uses

By recording the weight of loads assigned to storage, truckload weight factors can be used for inventory control. When inventory of depleted piles is required, weighing offers considerable savings over scaling. Moisture changes during fall and winter storage can be ignored. Cuno and Lindgren (2, 5, 6) found that during 2 to 3 months of fall or winter storage, moisture loss in southern pine pulpwood bolts was negligible. They also established that loss declined as bolt diameter increased. Thus, saw logs would lose even less moisture in storage. Within the plant, logs can be sorted by weight into broad diameter classes to feed different sides of a mill or gangsaws. Material more suitable for chipping than sawing also could probably be classified by weight.

Both research and management are increasingly aware of the advantages of describing timber stands and yields in tons per acre. Weight-scaling will facilitate the trend toward managing timber by the ton. For this reason, as well as for the more immediate benefits already noted, it is likely to become common practice in the South.

5

LITERATURE CITED

(1) Cline, C. 1958. Wood Tick Trail. Pulpwood Prod. 6(3): 27-28, 30-32, 34.

(2) Cuno, J. B. 1939. Production of loblolly pine pulpwood in the mid-Atlantic region. South. Pulp and Paper Jour. 1(4): 13-16 and 1(6): 9-15, 26.

(3) Grosenbaugh, L. R. 1958. The elusive formula of best fit: a comprehensive new machine program. U. S. Forest Serv. South. Forest Expt. Sta. Occas. Paper 158, 9 pp., illus.

(4) King, W. W. 1952. Survey of sawmill residues in east Texas. Texas Forest Serv. Tech. Rpt. 3, 59 pp., illus.

(5) Lindgren, R. M. 1951. Deterioration of southern pine pulpwood during storage. Forest Prod. Res. Soc. Proc. 5: 169-181.

(6) ————1953. Deterioration losses in stored southern pine pulpwood. TAPPI 36: 260-263.

(7) Peck, E. C. 1959. The sap or moisture in wood. U. S. Forest Serv. Forest Products Lab. Rpt. D768 (rev.) 14 pp., illus.

(8) Schumacher, F. X. 1946. Volume-weight ratios of pine logs in the Virginia-North Carolina Coastal Plain. Jour. Forestry 44: 583-586.

(9) Southern Forest Experiment Station, et al. 1953. Interim log grades for southern pine. 18 pp.

(10) Taras, M. A. 1956. Buying pulpwood by weight as compared with volume measure. U. S. Forest Serv. Southeast. Forest Expt. Sta. Sta. Paper 74, 11 pp., illus.

APPENDIX

The Southern Forest Experiment Station's 704 regression program (3) was used to obtain the solutions to all 255 possible equations involving the 8 variables in the single-log analysis:

X_1 = Weight
X_2 = $(X_1)^2$
X_3 = Length
X_4 = $(X_2)(X_3)$
X_5 = $(X_1)(X_3)$
X_6 = Specific gravity
X_7 = (X_6) (moisture percent)
X_8 = Scaling diameter

As Table 3 indicates, the biggest relative gain in precision was achieved by adding log moisture percent and specific gravity to weight. Though additive effects were had from various functions and combinations of log weight,

length, and diameter, their practical significance was nil.

Table 3.—Regressions with highest R^2 for each level

Variables	R^2	S. E. Board feet
X_1, X_2, X_4, X_5, X_6, X_7, X_8	0.970	15.47
X_1, X_3, X_4, X_5, X_6, X_8	.970	15.63
X_2, X_5, X_6, X_7, X_8	.969	15.70
X_2, X_3, X_6, X_8	.967	16.18
X_1, X_6, X_7	.966	16.35
X_1, X_7	.964	16.91
X_1	.956	18.60

Because the yield from heavy logs varied more widely than that from lighter ones, a final regression was fitted to the data on the assumption that the variance was proportional to log weight. The equation is:

$$Y = \frac{Weight}{9.88} + \frac{(Weight)^2}{254,362} - 10.96$$

$R^2 = .980$

6

sional Paper 178

Field Guide for

EVALUATING

COTTONWOOD

SITES

W. M. Broadfoot

RN FOREST EXPERIMENT STATION
Phillip A. Briegleb, Director
FOREST SERVICE
. DEPARTMENT OF AGRICULTURE

1960

Field Guide for

EVALUATING
COTTONWOOD
SITES

W. M. Broadfoot

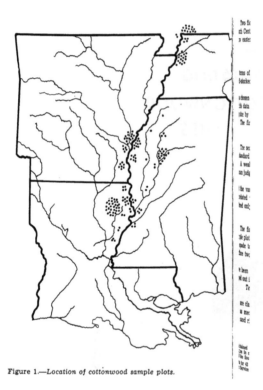

Figure 1.—Location of cottonwood sample plots.

Two field methods have been developed at the Stoneville Research Center[1] for estimating the capability of Midsouth soils to grow eastern cottonwood (*Populus deltoides* Bartr.). Data for establishing the procedures were collected from 155 plots[2] at the locations indicated in Figure 1.

The methods give site index—that is, tree-growing potential—in terms of the height, in feet, that free-growing cottonwoods in well-stocked forest stands will reach at the age of 30 years. While 50 years is the customary age for expressing site index, 30 years was chosen because it is close to the average for the stands from which data were secured and because most cottonwood trees are log size by 30 years.

The first method provides a fast field classification of sites from determinations of soil texture, internal drainage, and inherent moisture conditions.

The second method requires the soil to be identified according to standard soil series and phase.

A weakness of both methods is that they rely heavily upon human judgment. Attempts have been made to predict cottonwood site index from soil variables that can be objectively measured, but the variables initially tested did not prove to be very well correlated with site index. The present subjective methods are offered only until more objective measures can be developed.

METHOD I

The first method is applicable only in the area where the sample plots were measured (fig. 1). It requires use of a soil auger or spade to determine the texture and internal drainage in the surface two feet of soil. The inherent moisture condition of the site can be obtained by observation. After these three components have been established, site index can be read from Figure 2 or keyed out in Table 1.

Texture.—Classify texture of the surface 2 feet as fine, medium, or coarse. Clays (buckshot and gumbo) are classed as fine, sandy soils as coarse, and all the rest as medium. Excessively drained and exceptionally dry sand ridges should be excluded from the coarse class, as they are not recommended for growing cottonwood.

[1] Maintained at Stoneville, Mississippi, by the Southern Forest Experiment Station in cooperation with the Mississippi Agricultural Experiment Station and the Southern Hardwood Forest Research Group.
[2] Data for 43 plots in northeast Louisiana were furnished by the Soil Conservation Service, U. S. Department of Agriculture.

Internal drainage.—If there is no distinct gray or reddish-brown mottling within the surface 2 feet, classify the site as well drained. If mottling is distinct, classify internal drainage as poor.

Inherent moisture condition.—If the site is on a slope or ridge, or is otherwise situated so that floodwaters or heavy rains drain off, classify it as dry. If it is level, or situated so that it is subject to flooding, classify as moist. Generally, no other classification of inherent moisture is necessary, but sometimes factors like nearness of root zone to mean low water in rivers, reservoirs, streams, or lakes may have to be considered.

Table 1.—*Field key for estimating cottonwood site index*[1]

Soil-site description	Site index
	Feet
I. Fine texture	
A. Good internal drainage	
1. Inherently moist	110-119
2. Inherently dry	100-109
B. Poor internal drainage	
1. Inherently moist	90-99
2. Inherently dry	<90
II. Medium texture	
A. Good internal drainage	
1. Inherently moist	120+
2. Inherently dry	110-119
B. Poor internal drainage	
1. Inherently moist	100-109
2. Inherently dry	90-99
III. Coarse texture	
A. Good internal drainage	
1. Inherently moist	110-119
2. Inherently dry[2]	100-109

[1] Key not applicable to soils outside the Mississippi River flood plain—as loess or Coastal Plain alluvium. Sites not indexed are either nonexistent or are not recommended for cottonwood.
[2] Sand ridges are excluded from this class, as they are too dry for cottonwood.

2

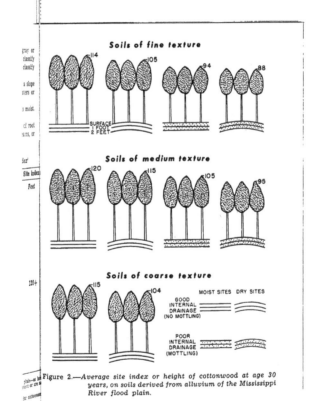

Figure 2.—*Average site index or height of cottonwood at age 30 years, on soils derived from alluvium of the Mississippi River flood plain.*

3

METHOD II

The second method requires identifying the soil series and its local phase (moist or dry). Identification can be made in the field by any locally competent soil scientist. The quickest way of identifying the soil is from standard soil survey maps, but not all counties have been mapped. Standard soil maps will not show inherent moisture phases, but will show slopes and phases that can be translated into moist or dry phases by the procedure outlined in Method I.

With soil series and phase determined, the estimate of cottonwood site index can be obtained from Table 2.

Table 2.—*Site index of cottonwood, at age 30 years, by soil series and phase*

Soil series	Site index	
	Moist phase	Dry phase
	Feet	*Feet*
Soils of recent natural levees		
(Mississippi River alluvium)		
Commerce	122	118
Robinsonville	115	105
Crevasse	114	104
Mhoon	114	103
Soils of old natural levees		
(Mississippi River alluvium)		
Dundee	. . .	93
Forestdale	. . .	90
Soils of slack-water areas		
(Mississippi River alluvium)		
Bowdre	115	94
Tunica	110	. . .
Sharkey	91	90
Alligator	88	80
Bottom-land soils from loess		
Collins	122	110
Falaya	109	93
Waverly	97	. . .
Arkansas River soils		
Pulaski	113	. . .
Norwood	109	. . .
Perry	95	. . .

4

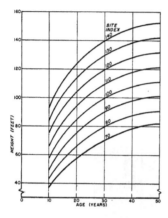

Figure 4.—*These curves indicate the expectable height of cotton wood trees on sites of various quality. They can be used to check the evaluations made by either method. Making a check requires measuring the heights of dominant and codominant trees in well-stocked stands that have had no modifying influence or treatment. For example, trees 100 feet tall at age 20 would signify a site index of 115.*

The curves are based on stem analyses of trees on a wide range of sites; the analyses involved cutting, sectioning, and counting annual rings of tree stems at intervals of 8 feet from a 1-foot stump to the top. The data from the sections were substantiated by plotting tree height over age for the study plots and for several young plantations. Smooth curves were then drawn by eye. These curves apply only to cottonwood in the Midsouth through age 50 years.

6

Occasional Paper 179

1960

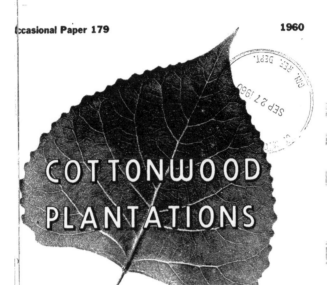

COTTONWOOD PLANTATIONS

for

SOUTHERN BOTTOM LANDS

Louis C. Maisenhelder

SOUTHERN FOREST EXPERIMENT STATION
Philip A. Briegleb, Director
FOREST SERVICE
U.S. DEPARTMENT OF AGRICULTURE

Cottonwood planting is rapidly becoming a standard land-management technique for the bottom lands of large southern rivers. One reason for the quickening interest is that cottonwood can be grown on land unsuited for other crops. Even sites densely covered with vines may be planted profitably, and the species' tolerance of flooding and silting enables it to do well on batture and other low sites. Several large timber-using firms have started reforestation programs. Their experience, coupled with research, is steadily enhancing cottonwood planting as a business venture.

COTTONWOOD
PLANTATIONS
for
SOUTHERN
BOTTOM LANDS

Louis C. Maisenhelder [1]

Because of its value, rapid growth, and natural preference for bottom-land sites, eastern cottonwood *(Populus deltoides* Bartr.) is an excellent tree to grow in plantations along the Mississippi River and on the flood plains of other large southern rivers.

The present cottonwood plantations in the Yazoo-Mississippi Delta are mostly experimental, but a few companies and individual landholders have planted a considerable acreage for commercial purposes. Interest is increasing as landowners recognize that by planting this fast-growing forest crop they can put certain types of submarginal agricultural land, as well as odd corners and ditch banks, on a pay-

ing basis. In addition, a large acreage of heavily cutover and burned-over forest, most of it with a dense growth of weeds, vines, and undesirable tree sprouts, lacks a seed source but can be reclaimed by planting cottonwood. The larger openings on cutover land are also good cottonwood sites if planted before vines and brush come in.

This bulletin summarizes the results of 18 years of research with cottonwood culture at Stoneville, Mississippi [2]. How to grow cottonwood profitably in plantations is now known, though future research and practical application are needed to improve the methods.

RANGE AND USES OF COTTONWOOD

While cottonwood grows naturally as far north as Canada, and as far east and west as Georgia and Kansas, it attains best commercial development on the alluvial bottom lands of the Mississippi River and its tributaries from southern Missouri to the cypress swamps in Louisiana. Here large, pure stands are found on the river

islands and the batture lands (the areas between the river and its levees which are unprotected from flooding). Young stands on such lands are commonly mixed with willow, but the faster-growing cottonwood gradually dominates and kills out its associate, so that large cottonwoods

[1] Stationed at the Stoneville Research Center, Stoneville, Mississippi. The Stoneville Research Center is maintained by the Southern Forest Experiment Station in cooperation with the Mississippi Agricultural Experiment Station and the Southern Hardwood Forest Research Group.

[2] It supersedes Bulletin 485 of the Mississippi Agricultural Experiment Station, **Planting and Growing Cottonwood on Bottomlands**, by Louis C. Maisenhelder, 1951.

are generally found in pure stands. Scattered individuals or small groups also occur in other hardwood forests throughout the bottom lands.

The wood is light in both color and weight, generally straight-grained, and soft but tough. It has good nailing properties and surfaces well except for pieces containing gelatinous tissue, or tension wood, which occurs mostly in crooked or leaning stems. Smoothed surfaces take glue, finishes, and printing well, and the dried wood is notably free from taste and odor. The logs generally yield high proportions of upper-grade lumber and veneer. Cottonwood has long ranked high as a source of both ground and soda pulp, and the improved chemical processes for hardwoods are likely to increase the demand for it.

One or another of these characteristics adapts cottonwood to a large variety of industrial uses. The primary raw-material forms are package and commercial veneer, factory lumber, and pulpwood. For shipping containers it is pre-eminent as both sawed stock and veneer and for all types of use but the heaviest and roughest. It is particularly appreciated for all sorts of food, grocery, and produce containers from beverage bottle crates to berry baskets. As commercial veneer, it is especially well adapted to use as core stock but also appears in common furniture panels, partitions, and drawer bottoms.

The lumber provides the best of wagon-box or truck-body boards, parts for light-colored bedroom and enameled kitchen furniture and trim, sawed core stock, and numerous specialties such as drawing boards. The cordwood is a favorite for the highest class of book and magazine paper and for all types of wallboard. It shows unusual promise for newsprint.

Cottonwood is one of the least durable of woods, is inclined to shrink excessively in drying, and warps considerably if not cured carefully. In common with most hardwoods, therefore, it has not generally been regarded as an appropriate source of construction lumber. Nevertheless, if kept clear of the ground and free of permanent or frequent moistening, it tolerates normal weathering exceptionally well. If skillfully cured before installation, it stays put and takes paint readily. It has been used successfully as subflooring, sheathing, and siding.

Annual production of cottonwood lumber in the South in recent years has averaged about 90 million board feet. Most of this comes from the Delta regions of Mississippi, Arkansas, and Louisiana. Cottonwood ranks fifth nationally among hardwood veneer species in the amount consumed.

GROWTH RATE

Cottonwood usually matures in about 45 years, but some stands continue rapid growth for a longer period. In natural stands on the better sites, it often grows 2/3 to 1 inch in diameter and 4 to 5 feet in height annually up to about 25 years of age Planted trees do better than this. At Stoneville, trees planted as cuttings have increased 10 feet in height during their third growing season. The best first-year growth from cuttings has been 19.0 feet in height for a single tree and 13 5 feet for a stand. Trees up to 25 or 30 years of age grow only a little slower. Well-stocked natural stands in the Mississippi Valley contain trees that average 20 inches d.b.h.

(diameter at breast height, 4½ feet above ground) and 120 feet tall at 35 years of age. Growth usually begins to decline sharply at about this age, so that at least part of the trees should be harvested.

In the fall of 1947 a commercial logging removed about 60 percent of the volume from a 55-year-old stand whose diameter growth had declined noticeably 10 years before. Cutting was on a tree-selection basis, and took mostly trees of poor to medium vigor. The release given the remaining cottonwoods of good vigor stimulated their diameter growth, even though many were 30 inches d.b.h. or over (fig. 1).

—2—

Figure 1.—*A 55-year-old unmanaged cottonwood stand on batture land. A commercial timber sale has just removed about one-third of the total sawtimber volume of 36,000 board feet per acre (Doyle rule). The remaining trees, which will be cut some 10 years hence, range from 20 to 32 inches in diameter and are still increasing rapidly in volume and value. Managed plantations on comparable sites can be expected to do as well or better.*

The trees, which were on a good batture site, had grown 3.2 inches in diameter in the decade preceding the cut. Two years afterwards they were growing at the rate of 4.8 inches in 10 years—an increase of 50 percent.

Growth rate varies with site, the moister locations ordinarily producing the better growth. In one plantation, 6-year-old trees on a ridge averaged 2.6 inches d.b.h. and 22 feet in height. In the same plantation but on a gentle slope from the ridge to swamp—a moister location than the ridge—trees averaged 4.1 inches d.b.h. and 31 feet high. Similar variations can be expected in most areas.

In well-stocked natural stands, cotton-wood prunes itself very well and produces a long, straight trunk that is generally clear of limbs for at least 50 feet when mature. In plantations, where original spacing is usually wider than in young natural stands, artificial pruning may be necessary to obtain comparable stem form.[1] Natural stands on good sites have yielded about 24 cords of pulpwood at 10 years and 50 cords at 15 years. The volume in board feet per acre, Doyle rule, has been estimated at 5,700 at 20 years, 10,700 at 25 years, 19,200 at 30 years, and 27,500 at 35 years. Most natural stands, especially over large areas, are not fully stocked and therefore do not attain these yields, but in Iowa plantations 30 to 40 years old with high survival and uniform spacing seem to be producing at comparable rates.

Johnson, R. L. **Pruning Cottonwood.** South. Lumberman 198(2473): 28-29, illus. 1959.

—3—

NATURAL REPRODUCTION

Cottonwood reproduces naturally from seed only under exacting conditions. Bare soil that remains saturated but not flooded for long periods during seedfall is essential. Natural reproduction occurs principally on sand bars and other accretion lands along the larger rivers. Here, growing conditions are optimum, and extensive pure stands or mixtures with willow result. Less extensive stands occur on protected sites along water courses, drainage ditches, and borrow pits. Old fields occasionally seed to cottonwood during years of frequent rainfall.

The site must remain moist and free from vegetation that would overtop the seedlings during the first growing season. Cottonwood will stand silting if only a short length of the stem is covered. It is, however, extremely intolerant of shade and will not develop even under very sparse stands of trees. Adequate natural reproduction is almost never seen on land from which mature cottonwood has been harvested, for seedlings that start are soon killed by the shade from residual trees and from the heavy ground cover that develops after cutting. Where cottonwood is found in mixed hardwood stands, it has originated in openings.

PLANTING AND CULTIVATING

Hardwood trees require more care than pine if successful plantations are to be established, and they will not do well if untended. This fact is usually not appreciated by the novice tree planter, and failure to provide the proper care is one of the major reasons for the small number of acceptable plantings.

For farmers, the care of the cottonwood plantation during the first year will at times coincide with the peak of work on field crops, but it must be given the proper priority in the farm program. The trees will not tolerate being neglected in favor of cotton and beans.

CHOICE OF PLANTING SITE

In the Mississippi Delta cottonwood does best on moist, well-drained fine sandy loam or silts in the batture (fig. 2),

Figure 2.—
A 5-year-old cottonwood plantation on a good sandy loam site. Dominant trees average about 40 feet tall and 5 inches in diameter. The largest tree is 45 feet tall and 8.4 inches in diameter. The trees have been pruned.

but it also thrives on the heavier clays of gentle slopes bordering swamps or sloughs. The heavy clay "buckshot" soils which dry out and crack in the late summer are less favorable, but planting can succeed if the best practices are carefully followed and if the first summer is not unusually dry. Growth on such soils is relatively slow (fig. 3).

Heavy clay that has lost all its organic matter by exhaustive cropping and has become stiff and waxy at the surface will not grow cottonwood. Tests have shown that cottonwood is unable to obtain water from these soils when they still contain 30 percent moisture and feel damp to the touch. A stunted, sparse growth of weeds on a field which has been abandoned for several seasons is usually an indication of these conditions. Ten years of weed growth were needed on one such old field to restore enough organic matter to the soil so that green ash and soft and cedar elms were able to seed in naturally. Such areas might be made suitable for cottonwood by plowing under leguminous cover crops for several years, thus building up the organic content of the soil; but this practice has not been tested. Irrigation during dry periods is also being tried.

Most other bottom-land sites in the Mississippi Delta seem satisfactory for cottonwood unless they are extremely dry in the late summer and fall, or are under water during the growing season.

One land condition which may or may not require planting is the "brush patch," in which annual weeds, briars, vines, and shrubs form a dense ground cover. Where this is the only vegetation, planting is needed. Often, however, close examination discloses tree sprouts and seedlings, usually of other species than cottonwood. If not too heavy, the briars and weeds act as a nurse crop for the trees and are usually more beneficial than harmful. If as many as 700 to 1,000 good seedlings per acre (one to each 40 or 60 square feet) of desirable species are found, planting is unnecessary and a suitable stand will usually develop without aid.

Ridges of coarse sand (former sandbars), common in the batture, are unsuitable for cottonwood. These can usually be recognized by their complete lack of any tree growth; in fact, when the water table falls in summer they commonly become so dry that they support only a sparse stand of grass. A few borings with a soil

Figure 3.—
These cottonwoods were planted on a dry ridge of heavy clay soil. After 15 years they average only 45 feet tall and 5 inches in diameter.

auger will identify this condition. Swampy areas where floods or backwaters are likely to submerge the small trees completely for several days during the growing season also are entirely unsuitable. Cottonwood does not grow well on poorly drained sites.

In general, cottonwood does not survive or grow as well in the small bottoms of upland hardwood or pine areas as it does on the flood plain of large rivers. Often the non-Delta soils are shallow, dry, or impervious and change from very wet to very dry in a short time. As it is often difficult to evaluate a site from its appearance,' the best course is to try small-scale planting a year before undertaking a big job on a new area.

For erosion-control work, cottonwoods can serve as living dams (fig. 4) in moist gully bottoms of the eroding bluffs along the eastern edge of the Delta. For this purpose, trees are often planted 6 inches apart in the row, with 18 to 24 inches between rows. The rows are set at right angles to the water course, so as to slow the washing of soil. The fact that it is one of the few trees that endures silting-in around the stem adds to cottonwood's utility for this purpose.

Figure 4 —Cottonwood used as a living dam to control erosion in the brown loam bluffs of Mississippi.

SITE PREPARATION

Before being planted, all sites should be cleared of existing vegetation. Planting cottonwood without site preparation and subsequent cultivation is almost always futile. Weeds and vines kill many of the trees and greatly reduce the vigor and growth of survivors. Even if survival is occasionally good, vigor is likely to be poor.

Where the ground cover is annual weeds and vines, clearing can be done by disking alone. Cross-cultivation with a disk harrow or a heavy bush and bog disk is effective. Very thick sods are among the most difficult sites to prepare for planting, and sometimes require 4 diskings. If vines, shrubs, and undesirable trees are abundant, as in areas covered with button-bush or in pure boxelder stands, bulldozing prior to disking is recommended. Bulldozing should remove as little of the topsoil as possible.

Whatever method is used, the ground should be left level to facilitate later machine cultivation. To avoid forming large clods, which are easily rolled onto the small trees during cultivation, it is best to work the planting site in the fall, before it has been soaked by winter rains.

Usually the most practical procedure is to clear the entire planting area, but where this is too costly, planting can be done on cleared strips about 10 feet in width, and with the debris windrowed between them. Spacing between rows necessarily exceeds the customary 10 feet. Difficulty of cultivation (chiefly hand work) may offset some of the savings from partial clearing.

New developments in strip cultivation are likely. The Chicago Mill and Lumber Company has established a plantation near Greenville, Mississippi, on narrow strips cleared at one pass with a bulldozer that scraped off a heavy cover of vines and annual weeds. Rooted trees 6 to 8 feet tall were planted, and no cultivating was done (fig. 5).

Underplanting cottonwood cuttings in stands of low-grade trees has failed ever

' Broadfoot, W M **Field Guide for Evaluating Cottonwood Sites.** U. S. Forest Service, Southern Forest Experiment Station Occasional Paper 178, 6 pages, illus. 1960

Figure 5.—*One-year-old rooted trees just after they were planted on a 9-foot strip cleared with a bulldozer. Spacing is 20 by 20 feet.*

when the overstory trees were frilled and treated with chemicals at the time of planting. Cultivation was impossible, and falling limbs of deadened trees deformed most of the cottonwoods that survived the competition with grass and brush.

Planting in furrows made with a middle-buster plow stimulates growth on the drier sites, but increases the difficulty of machine cultivation. A better practice, suitable on any site with a sandy loam soil free from tree roots, is to use a tractor-drawn subsoil plow to break through the compact layers of soil and open a narrow slit in which to plant the trees. Subsoiling simplifies the planting job and facilitates penetration of moisture to the roots. All the benefits of furrowing are obtained and, because the ground is left flat, cultivation by any method is possible. Sub-soiling or furrowing operations are in addition to disking. Cross-disking an acre of land with a wheel tractor and a two-row disk harrow requires 1.1 hours Subsoiling one acre with a wheel tractor takes 0.6 hour.

To clear sites on which the trees can

be easily uprooted by a bulldozer requires 2 to 3 hours per acre.

Special site preparation usually is not needed on areas logged in late summer or during the fall and winter just prior to planting, for logging scarifies the ground. Earlier logging will be followed by a crop of weeds which must be removed; a bush and bog disk will do the job. If the openings created by logging are less than ¼-acre in size, it is probably best not to attempt planting.

Less satisfactory practices.—Several additional site preparation practices have been tested. They are not recommended for general use but may be adaptable to special situations.

Two fire-line plows failed to clear strips wide enough to permit machine cultivation. The Ranger's Pal plow was too light to make a satisfactory furrow in heavy stands of pepper-vine and trumpet-creeper. A heavier hydraulically controlled plow that made a furrow about 3 feet wide seemed satisfactory at the time of plowing, but by the end of the first growing season vine sprouts from along the edges of the furrow had closed in over most of the planted cottonwood and were seriously restricting growth.

A self-propelled rotary tiller has done a good job of preparing planting strips in heavy vine stands but would not be suitable where trees are 3 inches or more in diameter. Such equipment is not as generally available to landowners as are disks and bulldozers, and is expensive.

SPACING

How far apart should cottonwoods be planted? Spacings ranging from 6 by 10 to 10 by 10 feet (providing from 60 to 100 square feet of growing space per tree) are most satisfactory for the production of both pulpwood and sawlogs. At such spacing the trees will possibly require pruning, but should have room enough to reach pulpwood size before the first thinning becomes necessary. These spacings are also convenient for machine cultivation.

At spacings of 6 by 6 and 4 by 10 feet, survival as well as height and diameter growth are less than in wider spacings. Spacing wider than 10 by 10 feet may cause understocked stands unless adequate care is taken to insure high survival; furthermore, the quality of the trees may be inferior because early natural pruning may not occur. The cultivation method to be used will also influence the choice of spacing. In general, present recommendations for spacing are:

On sites where at least three-fourths of the cuttings can be expected to survive and grow vigorously, space 10 by 10 feet.

On drier and less productive land, where not more than two-thirds of the cuttings can be expected to grow vigorously, make rows 10 feet apart and set trees 6 to 8 feet apart in the row.

TIME OF PLANTING

While planting may be done at any time between the first severe frost in fall and the opening of buds in spring, February

While supplies of elite trees are being developed, the cottonwood grower can immediately improve the stock he plants by taking his cuttings from trees of better than average height and diameter growth. The stricter the selection, the better will be the results. The investment required to establish and care for a cottonwood plantation is high, and only the best planting stock should be used.

Where only a few thousand cuttings are desired, they can usually be obtained cheaply along drainage ditches or in highway borrow pits on the safe side of the levee. Larger quantities rarely occur except on bars along the Mississippi and other large rivers, and such sites may be difficult of access during January and February, when the collecting must be done. The establishment of cutting nurseries, therefore, appears desirable where a large planting program is planned. Instructions for setting up such nurseries are given later in this publication.

Planting stock can be harvested either by pulling seedlings up by the roots or by cutting them off about an inch above the ground. Cutting is the fastest and cheapest and has the further advantage that the rootstock left in the ground will send up sprouts which can be harvested year after year. Thus, well-located natural stands can serve as nurseries.

For successful planting, seedlings and cuttings must be dormant. The succulent green tissue of rapid growth may persist for a short time after the first fall frost, but the buds and current season's wood must have stopped growing and be hardened before cuttings are made.

After being harvested, the cottonwood switches must be cut to the proper length for planting—twenty-inch lengths are suitable for most areas. Twenty-five-inch lengths help prevent complete submergence on sites subject to shallow flooding during the growing season and are also recommended for deep planting on dry sites.

All lateral branches should be trimmed off flush with the main stem; large laterals may be made into cuttings. Cuttings should range from ⅜ to ¾ inch in diameter at the small end. Sizes smaller than this dry out excessively after planting and contain too little stored food to give the tree a good start. Cuttings larger than ¾ inch are hard to handle and plant, though once in the ground their survival and growth are good. Crooked sections of stem should be discarded, since they cannot be pushed into the ground easily and will usually be planted improperly. On cuttings that include some root, the taproot should be cut back to 15 inches or less, until it is stiff enough to insert in the planting hole, and the larger side roots should be pruned sufficiently to permit this insertion.

Cuttings can be mass-produced by laying several switches at a time on a block and chopping them all off at once at right angles to the axis of the stem. Chopping must not smash or split the ends, since this can cause failure to sprout. For ease in handling and counting, cuttings should be tied in bundles of 100 with all the butt ends pointing in the same direction.

Costs of making cuttings.—In a nursery, cutting sufficient full-length sprouts with a machete to yield a thousand 20-inch cuttings and bunching them for transportation takes about ¾ man-hour. Trimming the laterals and cutting shoots to length has taken 4 man-hours of additional work. Counting and bundling has taken 1¼ hours more. In one trial a small circular power saw produced cuttings as rapidly as a machete and without splitting the ends. Practical experience will reduce production time and costs.

Storing cuttings.—For a few days of storage during the planting season, the butt ends of cuttings and the roots of seedlings may be placed in water (ditches or stump holes) or heeled into moist soil. Cuttings require less care than rooted seedlings, but should not be exposed to the sun or wind. Covering them with wet burlap sacks is good practice.

When planting will be done after the start of the normal growing season, the buds must be prevented from opening. A cold storage locker where the temperature can be maintained between 28° F. and 32° F. will be necessary. Cold air must be

on disked areas where the ground is free of roots this is best done with a subsoil plow set for a depth of 15 inches. The plow should have a small point, for if the slit it makes is too wide the soil may not settle properly about the cuttings.

When cross-cultivation is planned, it is best to mark the rows in both directions, but otherwise the spacing in the row can be determined by pacing the distance as the planting is done. The cross-marking can be accomplished with ordinary farm row-marking equipment. If planting strips

are used, the trees are merely set in the middle of the strip. On rough woods areas, uneven spacing between rows and between trees within the row will often be necessary to avoid holes, stumps, down trees, and other debris.

Where subsoiling is impractical, cuttings can be set in holes punched with an iron rod like that illustrated in Figure 7. Such a rod is easy and cheap to make, and quick to use. It should have a step 15 inches from one end for pushing it into hard ground. The upper end should form

Figure 7.—*Four steps in planting a cottonwood cutting· A—Starting the planting rod into the ground. B—Pushing rod down to the step (15 inches). C—Putting a 20-inch cutting in the hole. D—Closing the hole by a kick of the heel.*

a handle, preferably L-shaped, and the lower end should be pointed. A ⅝-inch rod is preferable for most seedlings and sprout cuttings, but a ⅜-inch rod is best for the smaller cuttings made from the tops of seedlings.

There must be contact between the planted tree and the soil. Cuttings must be pushed all the way down to the bottom of the hole. Shallow planting results in poor survival and slow height growth. The top of the hole should be closed by a kick of the heel. If the soil is very wet and soft, the cuttings may sometimes be pushed in 15 inches, so that no rod is needed. In the drier soils, it is undesirable to plant without a rod or to use a rod of smaller diameter than the cuttings, for the bark may be stripped off or the cutting broken as it is forced into the ground.

Mattocks or wedge-shaped pine planting bars are slower than a rod, especially in wet clay soils, and do not improve survival or growth.

The cost of planting varies with the efficiency of the crew and the size of the job. Fairly well-trained men on a small job took 5½ man-hours to plant an acre of 20-inch cuttings at 6- by 10-foot spacing (726 trees). With a less experienced crew and more brush, 6 man-hours were required to plant an acre at 10- by 10-foot spacing (436 trees).

CULTIVATION

From the very earliest attempts to grow cottonwood, it has been apparent that this tree is most intolerant of competition from weeds and vines. Heavy mats of trumpet-creeper and pepper-vine, often called buckvine, are probably the worst ground cover, but heavy grass sods also reduce survival greatly and are very difficult to control.

During the plantation's first year, cultivation is absolutely essential. It not only controls weeds but also conserves soil moisture and incorporates organic matter. Growth of the trees is directly related to the thoroughness of the cultivation. Failure to cultivate whenever it is required always results in reduced height and vigor and almost as frequently causes total

cause the trees do not emerge from this band of weeds as easily as from the narrow ring left by cross-disking.

From results obtained in the nursery it would appear that cultivating with a machine that straddles the row of trees, though somewhat more costly than other methods, is a most advantageous way to control weeds and stimulate general vigor and height growth. One-way straddle cultivation is especially suited to narrow planting strips; cross-cultivation is possible at any spacing that permits passage of a tractor. When the trees become too tall to pass without damage beneath the machine, hand-hoeing, disking, or mowing must be resorted to. The method is not adaptable where roots and stumps are numerous.

Hand hoeing with ordinary cotton-chopping hoes to clear an area 5 feet in diameter around each tree is the most expensive method, although a successful one. It is very useful as a supplement to machine work or in treating small areas when labor is cheap and plentiful. It is the only alternative on rough woods sites where machinery cannot be used.

Crops like corn or beans can often be planted between the tree rows for several years, until the shade becomes too dense. The tree rows should be about 9 feet apart, with cuttings 6 to 8 feet apart in the row, to make a 6- by 9-foot or 8- by 9-foot spacing. The trees will be cultivated as the

crop is worked, and will thus provide an immediate cash return with little extra outlay of money or labor. In a plantation on a well-prepared abandoned field, weeds between rows were controlled by a broadcast sowing of soybeans. Tree spacing was 6 by 11 feet, to permit harvesting the beans with a combine. In the first year, two straddle cultivations kept down weeds in narrow strips on each side of the tree rows (fig. 8). In the second year no beans were sown, and after a single disking the trees were safely ahead of all competition.

Several other methods of weed control have been tested and found unsatisfactory.

Flame cultivation with a machine used in cotton culture killed 20 percent of the cuttings by destroying the cambium layer. Even if less lethal flame techniques should be worked out, special machines of more rugged construction than the cotton cultivators would be needed on rough sites.

Sterilizing the soil by scattering white arsenic on top of the ground controlled annual weeds fairly well during the first year, but the deeper rooted vines and brush survived and soon overtopped the cuttings. The possibility of poisoning humans, livestock, and wildlife is a further drawback to this method.

When strips were prepared with the Mathis fireline plow but not cultivated after planting, the vines were controlled but annual weeds soon overtopped the seedlings.

Figure 8.—*Six-week-old soybeans growing between first-year trees spaced 6 by 11 feet.*

Costs.—The costs of cultivation will vary with the locality and the method, size, and type of operation, but the requirements in Table 1 are typical under many conditions.

Table 1.—*Typical requirements per acre for cultivating cottonwood plantations*[1]

Method	Man- or machine-hours
Hand hoeing alone	32.00
Hand hoeing to supplement machine work in plantations disked one way	25.00
Cross-disking between rows	.72
Disking between rows, one way only	.36
Cultivating astraddle the planting strip	1.00

[1] Six- by ten-foot spacing for all methods except cross-disking, where spacing is taken as 10 by 10 feet.

Use of 5-foot square patches of building paper as a mulch to keep down weeds was prohibitively expensive, and the vegetation around the patches and some which came up through breaks in the paper seriously retarded tree growth.

Pre-planting control of weeds with chemicals has not been found feasible so far.

FERTILIZATION

Fertilizing cottonwood cuttings with ammonium nitrate gives varying results, depending upon the amount of rain during the growing season. In wet years almost any combination of fertilization and cultivation is satisfactory, but during dry seasons the weeds are stimulated more than the trees, thus increasing the need for cultivation. When used at planting time, the nitrate should be applied at the rate of 2 ounces per tree. To prevent damaging the roots, it should be distributed in a ring on the surface of the ground around each cutting, but at least 6 inches away from the cutting itself.

With good moisture conditions, hoeing combined with fertilization has produced survivals of 75 to 95 percent and individual trees 10 to 12 feet high in a single season. Under adverse conditions mortality has been very heavy.

Since fertilizing costs about $4 per acre (726 trees) and depends for success on the

—14

GROWING NURSERY STOCK

A nursery for growing cottonwood planting stock will pay for itself whenever a few thousand cuttings are needed annually for several years. It should be established on moist sandy loam in an accessible location. Exceptionally fertile soil should be avoided as root systems are likely to grow so large in 2 years that most of the shoots will be above maximum size for cuttings. Less fertile soils yield more crops before the shoots become so large that the nursery must be replanted.

CUTTING NURSERIES

The nursery may be started from seed, but it is much easier and more economical to use cuttings of the same specifications as for field planting.

Especially for a nursery, cuttings should be taken from none but the most vigorous 1- to 3-year-old seedlings, since the trees to be grown will have the characteristics of the parent. The most vigorous seedlings are usually the tallest, and their stems are dark green rather than dull brown.

To obtain the highest grade of growing stock, only the best 20 percent or less of the switches in natural stands should be selected for use as cuttings. Work is now under way to demonstrate the superiority of selected stock and, in time, certified better-than-average cuttings should be available from state and commercial nurseries.

Cuttings should be set in the nursery at a spacing of 1 foot by 3 feet, or about 14,500 per acre (fig. 9). The 3 feet be-

tween rows allows for economical tillage with either a 4-row cotton cultivator or smaller 1-row equipment.

Five or six cultivations with standard straddle-row cotton cultivators are advisable during the first year. These should begin about April 1 and be repeated every 10 days until June 1. After this, the trees will be too tall for straddle cultivation, and their shade will retard weeds. A small amount of hand hoeing is frequently desirable to control late-summer weeds. Two or three cultivations are usually adequate the second season; after that the sprouts will outgrow everything except possibly Johnson grass, but sod should never be permitted to form. The nursery must also be protected from fire and grazing throughout its lifetime.

With average site and weather, annual per-acre production will be approximately 25,000 twenty-inch cuttings—enough to plant 57 acres at 10- by 10-foot spacing. From three to six annual harvests, the number depending on the fertility of the soil, can be made from the same rootstocks before the sprouts become too large in diameter for economical use. After the first year, branches from some of the main stems of sprouts will yield ¾-inch cuttings.

The cost of establishing a 1-acre nursery and maintaining it for 6 years (at 1960 wage scales) would be about $135—chiefly for labor. Thus the nursery charges (exclusive of harvesting, trimming, bundling, storage, and transportation) against the approximately 150,000 cuttings yielded are 90 cents per thousand.

Figure 9.—
One-year-old cottonwood sprouts on two-year-old rootstocks in a nursery started from cuttings. Spacing is 1 foot by 3 feet.

NURSERY STOCK FROM SEED

Raising cottonwood nursery stock from seed is an exacting operation not recommended for general use. It will, however, be necessary to employ this method in any tree-breeding work directed toward the development of elite strains. The requirements for propagation in the nursery also indicate the conditions which must exist if successful natural regeneration is sought.

Seed collection.—In the central portion of the Yazoo-Mississippi Delta cottonwood seed generally matures and falls from about the first of May until late July, with dissemination at its peak in late May. Abundant crops are produced every year. Seed may be safely collected after the first of May, and frequently collection is possible from a few late-maturing trees in June. A good rule is to collect after the pods have started to turn brown and the first pods have begun to open.

The best seed-bearers are large, open-grown trees. Usually little seed can be had from trees less than 10 inches in diameter at breast height or less than 10 years old. Seed is borne only by female trees. Male trees usually have red flowers, and female trees yellow flowers.

The green pods or capsules are most easily gathered from tops of trees felled by loggers. A large tree may yield over a bushel of pods, from which several pounds of seed can be extracted. A pound of seed, clean enough for sowing, contains about one-half million seeds.

If stored in bulk following collection, the unopened green pods will heat; they should therefore be spread out in thin layers to cure or dry at ordinary room temperatures. After 2 or 3 days most of the pods will still be closed but sufficiently dry to be easily opened. They may be air-dried for a week with little or no loss of seed viability, and 3 weeks of moist cold storage (at about 40° F.) is possible.

Crushing or rubbing the pods against a coarse screen releases the seed, and to some extent loosens it from the cottony matrix. Parts of the pods will fall through the screen with the seed and its cotton. This mixture is known as "unclean seed."

—16

Constant, ample moisture for at least 3 days is required for germination and initial establishment. If an overhead sprinkling system is available, the beds should be wet before planting and kept continuously moist. Equally good results may be obtained by irrigation (fig. 10), in which case the beds are first thoroughly soaked by flooding and then drained just enough to expose the surface on which the seeds are sown, preferably broadcast. Sufficient water is used to keep the alleys full, thus maintaining a saturated bed. This method is especially suitable for a small nursery, but requires a level site. The young seedlings should not be submerged, for development is then checked and more mortality will occur, especially on hot, sunny days.

Germination occurs within 12 to 24 hours after sowing. The seedling develops very slowly at first, but accelerates steadily and rapidly after about 3 weeks of growth.

Shades or screens help to conserve and maintain uniform surface moisture, but are necessary only if sufficient moisture cannot otherwise be maintained. Half-shade provided by a screen made of laths stapled to wire is suitable.

If the beds are overstocked, the seedlings should be thinned when about 4 weeks old to approximately 20 trees per square foot. Subsequent culture is the same as for most other tree species. The beds will need several weedings, especially when the seedlings are small. This involves hand-picking if the seeds were broadcast, but on drill-sown plots may be largely done with a hoe. The trees should be watered generously during the summer.

Figure 10.—One-month-old cottonwood raised from seed in a nursery. Note arrangement of rows on the narrow bed and method of flooding the alleys to keep beds continuously moist.

—17—

PROTECTING THE PLANTATION

Cottonwood plantations must be guarded against fire, grazing, and insects. They should also be closely examined for disease and other kinds of damage.

FIRE

Even a very light burn will kill seedlings and young trees. Larger trees are a little more resistant but those that do survive become badly scarred and soon develop serious butt rot. Even one fire of moderate intensity can kill trees 6 to 10 inches in d.b.h. (fig. 11). All this emphasizes the need for fire protection in natural stands of cottonwood as well as in plantations. Where natural firebreaks like roads, trails, and sloughs do not break up the area into blocks of approximately 40 acres, 15-foot firelines should be plowed. Firelines should also be made around the boundaries of the stand or plantation.

Figure 11.—*One year after a summer fire ran through a 12-year-old cottonwood plantation. Left.—As the leafless branches indicate, nearly every tree is dead. Average tree d b h. was 6 5 inches and average height was 53 feet. The stand will be a total loss, since it is below merchantable size. Right.—Bark at the base of this fire-killed tree is loose, and wood-rotting fungi are fruiting all along the bole. Rapid decay makes prompt salvage necessary if fire-killed trees are of merchantable size.*

GRAZING

Cattle and other livestock seriously damage small cottonwoods by trampling and browsing at all seasons of the year. Where deer are numerous, they are likely to strip young trees of their bark in winter and of their early leaves in spring, when other deer food is scarce. Both livestock and deer kill many trees and cause others to be weakened or to have multiple sprouts. Livestock should be fenced out before cottonwood is planted. Deer damage to fruit trees has been controlled by spraying the trees with repellents, but these preparations do not appear to have been tested on cottonwood.

RODENTS

Rabbits may gnaw the bark of small trees in winter, sometimes completely girdling them. Usually the trees sprout again, but often with reduced vigor; at best one or more seasons' growth is lost.

Repellents have been partially effective, but except where heavy damage is expected it is doubtful if their expense is warranted. An effective rodent repellent can be made by stirring 5 pounds of liquid asphalt paint into 3-1/3 quarts of water and adding 3-1/3 pounds of copper carbonate, plus enough water to make up 4 gallons. This mixture is sprayed on the cuttings after they are planted.

INSECTS

About a dozen different insects have been observed to attack cottonwood in nurseries, plantations, and natural stands, but only a few have so far proven serious. Boring in the stems and twigs and defoliation are the two chief types of damage.

Most harmful is the cottonwood twig borer (*Gypsonoma haimbachiana*) that attacks the growing branch tips and prevents the twigs from elongating normally (fig. 12). Terminal tips are often killed,

Figure 12.—*Left: Twig borers killed the young branch tips on this 1-year-old cottonwood and produced a stunted, bushy plant. Right: This tall, straight tree is also 1 year old, but was not attacked by borers.*

and the tree becomes bushy and stunted. The caterpillar that does the damage is whitish with a brown head, and about ¼-inch long when full grown. The adult is a grey moth.

The damage is most easily recognized by the short distance between leaf scars, the orange-brown interior of damaged twigs, and exit holes near the leaf scars. The insect is important in both nurseries and plantations. Definite controls have not yet been proven, but in two years of tests dipping half the length of the cutting at planting in a systemic poison, 44 percent Thimet-carbon dust, has been successful. As soon as the material is marketed, its use on all new plantations should be beneficial. The present treatment is effective for only one year, but some way of protecting the trees in following years is being sought.

The cottonwood root and stem borer (Paranthrene dollii) is a clear-wing moth. The adult has a brown body and dark wings; wingspread is about 1½ inches. The larvae make tunnels as much as 6 inches long in the pith and wood of young root crowns and lower stems. An important indication of attack is the hole that is kept open to the outside for the escape of the adult moth. The caterpillar is white or pinkish, has a brown head, and is about 1 inch long when fully grown.

Figure 13.—*Both adults and larvae of the cotto culent young tissue of cottonwoo*

nursery, and all refuse from the production of cuttings, should likewise be destroyed. All cuttings gathered for planting should be examined to exclude and destroy those containing borers.

DISEASE

No important disease has as yet been observed on cottonwood plantings. The poplar canker *(Cytospora* sp.) frequently kills some of the less vigorous and weakened young trees. It is most noticeable on the poorer sites where growth is slow. The trees usually die in late fall or winter; the inner bark on the main stem is attacked and killed first. This canker is very common, and the causal fungus lives either on dead wood or live wood of low vitality. The only remedy seems to be to avoid the poorest sites and to cultivate or release trees before growth is seriously retarded.

A rust fungus of the genus *Melampsora* sometimes defoliates cottonwoods of all ages. The rust forms yellow spores on the lower side of the leaves, and dead leather-colored patches on the top. Slight evidences of this disease are noticeable almost every year, and sometimes trees are almost defoliated. In the Mississippi Delta intermittent loss of leaves does not kill the trees, but slows their growth. In climates with more severe winters it is reported to kill many trees. Trees defoliated in midsummer sometimes put on new leaves the same season. There is no satisfactory control, but damage is seldom severe enough to endanger a plantation.

RETURNS

stands under proven practices. Two types of site are considered—abandoned cropland and areas of rundown woods and worthless brush. Chiefly because of the difficulty of site preparation, wooded areas are likely to require at least double the investment necessary on old fields. As will be seen, their extra cost does not rule out woods plantations as good investments, though it suggests that, where there is choice, the easier sites should be planted first.

Table 2.—*Costs per acre of establishing a cottonwood plantation at 10- by 10-foot spacing (436 trees per acre)*

Operation	On abandoned agricultural land	On wooded land[1]
	Dollars	*Dollars*
Site preparation		
Bulldozing	...	18.80
Debris reduction	...	1.75
Crossdisking entire area	2.50	2.50
Total	2.50	23.05
Planting stock		
Raising cuttings in nursery	.40	.40
Harvesting and preparing cuttings	1.35	1.35
Total	1.75	1.75
Planting		
Subsoiling and row marking	1.50	...
Setting trees	2.00	3.50
Total	3.50	3.50
First-year cultivation		
2 crossdiskings with wheel tractor	4.75	...
4 crossdiskings with wheel tractor	...	9.50
1 supplemental hoeing	6.00	6.00
Total	10.75	15.50
Grand total	18.50	43.80

[1] Costs on woods sites are from: Moore, H. 1958. Planting cottonwood cuttings. Proc. Seventh Annual Forestry Symposium, La. State Univ., pp. 10-15.

Yields of mature cottonwood plantations have not yet been determined in the Yazoo-Mississippi Delta. The estimates in Table 3 are from unthinned, fully stocked natural stands as documented by Williamson.[2] The volumes shown as removed prior to the final harvest represent a cutting of only those trees that would otherwise die of overcrowding as the stand grows. The pulpwood volume includes both the amount in pulpwood-size trees and topwood from larger trees.

The table assumes that the trees will average 17 inches d.b.h. at age 30; volume per acre, including that removed before then, should be about 19 thousand board feet plus 45 cords of pulpwood. The stand might be harvested at age 30, but as the trees would still be growing rapidly the table also considers the possibility of holding them to age 42. By then they would average 23 inches in d.b.h., and would have produced 33.5 thousand board feet per acre, of which about 60 percent would be in veneer logs, plus 59 cords of pulpwood. Possibly these estimates are less than the growth attainable in well-managed plantations on good sites.

The dollar values in the table were calculated on the assumption that stumpage will be worth $2 per cord for pulpwood, $20 per MBF for saw logs, and $3_ per MBF for veneer logs.

[2] Williamson, A. W. Cottonwood in the Mississippi Valley. U S Dept Agr Bul 24, 62 pp., illus. 1913

Table 3.— *Estimated volumes and values per acre, of 10- by 10-foot cottonwood plantings*

30-year rotation

Cut-ting age (years)	Volume removed				Volume left	
	Pulp-wood	Saw-timber	Veneer logs	Stumpage value	Saw-timber trees	Topwood and pulpwood trees[1]
	Cords	MBF	MBF	Dollars	MBF	Cords
12	7.4	0.0	0.0	14.80	0.2	0.2[2]
18	8.4	.0	.0	16.80	4.1	12.0
25	4.8	.0	.0	9.60	10.7	14.6
30	24.4	11.5	7.7	509.80	.0	.0
35	...	...	...	...	...	...
42	...	...	...	...	...	...

42-year rotation

12	7.4	.0	.0	14.80	.2	.2
18	8.4	.0	.0	16.80	4.1	12.0
25	4.8	.0	.0	9.60	10.7	14.6
30	4.6	.6	.0	21.20	19.2	20.5
35	4.7	1.4	2.0	97.40	27.5	27.5
42	29.5	11.8	17.7	826.00	.0	.0

[1] Includes only pulpwood-size trees (7-14 inches d b.h.) and topwood in larger trees. A cord was assumed to equal 90 cubic feet. Topwood was computed as 1 cord per thousand board feet of logs cut.
[2] Plus 319 trees below pulpwood size.

Table 4 estimates rates of return on money invested in cottonwood plantations growing at the rate suggested by Table 3. The estimates are for 3 kinds of site and 2 methods of computation. If their land is already paid for or if the area to be planted is a small part of other holdings, property owners will probably choose the computational method that excludes land cost and taxes. Commercial operators who are acquiring land for planting should use the first method; here, land cost was estimated at $15 per acre, taxes at 50 cents per acre annually on lands protected from flooding and 5 cents on unprotected, and 5 cents per acre for controlling or preventing grazing and fire.

As standard procedures were followed

in computing the compound rates of return, the table can be used to compare cottonwood planting with other investment opportunities. Comparisons should be on an after-tax basis because timber revenue can be reported as capital gain.

Whichever way land costs are computed, the returns in Table 4 compare well with those obtainable from other kinds of investment. The 42-year rotation, though showing a slightly lower rate of return than the 30-year, yields more than twice as much veneer log volume, a factor most desirable for many growers.

Finally, the forecasted rates of return are likely to prove conservative for reasons other than those connected with the

Table 4.—*Estimated rates of return on money invested in cottonwood planting*

	On submarginal agricultural land		On run-down wooded land			
			Protected by levee		Unprotected	
	Age 30	Age 42	Age 30	Age 42	Age 30	Age 42
	— — — — — — Percent — — — — — —					
Including land cost and taxes	9.9	8.9	7.8	7.3	8.1	7.6
Excluding land cost and taxes	13.0	11.4	9.4	8.5	9.4	8.5

estimates of volume growth. Research and industrial experience promise to diminish costs of establishing plantations. Use of cottonwood timber is increasing, yet less than 3 percent of the timber in the Mississippi River Delta is of this species. The acreage that could be put to growing cot-

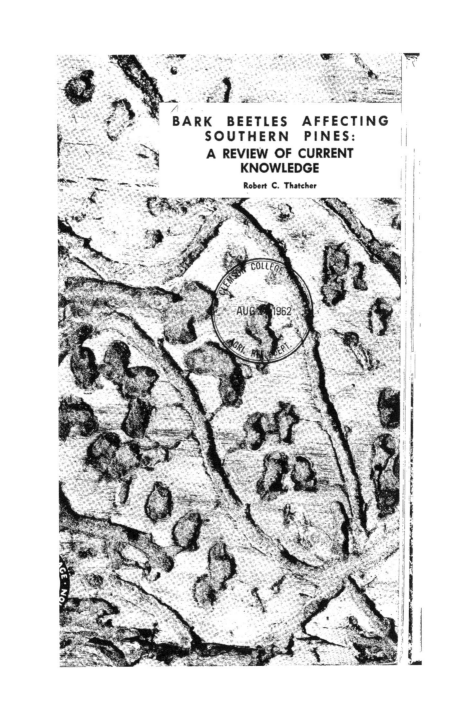

BARK BEETLES AFFECTING
SOUTHERN PINES:
A REVIEW OF CURRENT
KNOWLEDGE

Robert C. Thatcher

FOREWORD

Bark beetles are generally considered the most destructive insects affecting southern pines. They have received considerable attention from entomologists and foresters, but much of the accumulated knowledge is not readily available in publications. Thatcher has performed a valuable service by assembling, organizing, summarizing, and interpreting information from many sources.

This compilation and analysis of existing knowledge shows the need for much additional research. Some facets of the broad problem are pointed out, and work on these will undoubtedly suggest many more. It is hoped that this paper will stimulate other entomologists to undertake studies that will contribute to eventual solution of the bark beetle problem.

Bark-beetle control methods now in use are little more than stop-gaps that may keep losses from becoming catastrophic. Very little is definitely known about the physical and biological conditions that permit outbreaks to develop or cause them to diminish. Such information can only be obtained by painstaking study of each insect, its natural enemies, and the physical and biotic factors that affect its host trees.

Entomologists, foresters, students, and others will find this a useful reference.

L. W. Orr

Contents

BARK BEETLES AFFECTING SOUTHERN PINES:
A REVIEW OF CURRENT KNOWLEDGE

Robert C. Thatcher
Southern Forest Experiment Station [1]

Bark beetles are the most destructive insects of southern pine forests, annually killing millions of board feet of sawtimber 'and large volumes of pulpwood.

Five species are responsible for most of the loss—the southern pine beetle *(Dendroctonus frontalis* Zimm.), the three southern *Ips* engraver beetles *(Ips calligraphus* Germ., *Ips grandicollis* Eichh., and *Ips avulsus* Eichh.), and the black turpentine beetle *(Dendroctonus terebrans* (Oliv.)).

The southern pine beetle causes the most spectacular damage by epidemic attacks which destroy large volumes of pine in localized areas at infrequent intervals of time. The southern *Ips* beetles and black turpentine beetle, on the other hand, are widely dispersed, seldom killing more than a few trees in one location except during very adverse weather. Over the years, however, they probably destroy more timber than does the southern pine beetle *(60, 68).*[2]

Pine bark beetles are found in a wide variety of environments over the South, and the species differ greatly in their life histories and their effects on the host trees. Weakened or dying trees, rather than healthy green ones, may be considered their normal environment. In such material they are generally innocuous, though they may hasten deterioration. It is their ability to leave their normal hosts and destroy apparently healthy trees that makes them important to foresters and entomologists.

All species of pine native to the southern states *(11, 12, 15, 53, 55, 56, 66, 92)* are attacked. In northerly parts of the bark beetles' range *(59, 79) Picea* and other species of *Pinus* also are hosts.

Table 1 summarizes the outbreaks that have been recorded in the southern region since 1882. Although the early reports often indicated only the gross area affected, the table nevertheless gives some indication of the damage from the more serious outbreaks. Since 1950 there has been an attempt to record endemic as well as epidemic losses, but scattered attacks, primarily by *Ips* and black turpentine beetles, are still generally overlooked. Perhaps the best estimate of total damage is in the U.S. Forest Service's TIMBER RESOURCES FOR AMERICA'S FUTURE *(124).* On the basis of data from Federal, State, and private foresters, the compilers estimated that bark beetles caused more than 400 million board feet of mortality and growth loss in southern pine forests during 1952. That was not a year of heavy beetle activity; losses would be much greater during epidemic years.

SPECIES CHARACTERISTICS

The outstanding biological characteristic of the bark beetle is the secluded life of all stages. The beetles spend most of their lives in the cambium and inner bark of their hosts. Construction of egg galleries by the adults and subsequent mining by larvae girdle the tree. This girdling, plus the introduction of associated fungi, kills the host tree.

Mature adults of all species are cylindrical, ranging from reddish-brown to black in color and from 1 to 8 mm. in length. Antennae are capitate. Larvae have white bodies and brown head capsules, and are legless. *Dendroctonus* adults can be distinguished from *Ips* by their rounded elytral declivity, as contrasted with the concave declivity of *Ips*.

[1] Nacogdoches Research Center, maintained in cooperation with Stephen F. Austin State College, Nacogdoches, Texas.
[2] Italic numbers in parentheses refer to Literature Cited, page 21.

Table 1.—*Recorded pine bark beetle outbreaks in the South*

SOUTHERN PINE BEETLE

Date	General location	Volume loss or area of infestation	Reference source
1882-85	Texas		(53)
1890-92	Central Atlantic States	75,000 sq. mi.	(53)
1902-05	North Carolina, Georgia		(26)
1907-08	Virginia		(26)
1910-12	Entire South		(26, 58)
1913-16	Tennessee, Virginia	200 sq. mi.	(26)
1920	Entire South	117,000 MBF	(1)
1922-24	Entire South		(26)
1926	Texas		(¹)
1929	North Carolina, Virginia		(87)
1931-32	Entire South		(21)
1937-38	Virginia		(40)
1939	Texas		(¹)
1949-51	Texas	200,000 MBF	(61)
1952-55	Alabama	4,330 MBF	(110, 112)
	Mississippi	75,000 MBF	(110)
1957-58	South Atlantic	53,200 MBF	
	Coastal States	138,600 cords	(72)
	Louisiana		(116)
	Mississippi	1,204 MBF	(118)
	Texas		(120)
1958-	Texas	10,000 MBF	(²)

IPS BEETLES

Date	General location	Volume loss or area of infestation	Reference source
1922-24	Entire South	100,000 MBF	(85)
1925	Florida		(21)
1931-32	Entire South		(21)
1949-51	Florida	20,850 MBF on 74,000 acres	(69)
1952-55	Alabama	1,000 MBF	(112)
	Arkansas	27,750 MBF	
	Mississippi	25,000 MBF	(110)
	Texas	4,507 MBF	(³)
	South Atlantic	502,400 MBF	
	Coastal States	728,300 cords	(72)
1956	Arkansas, Louisiana, Oklahoma, Texas	100,000 MBF	(³)

BLACK TURPENTINE BEETLE

Date	General location	Volume loss or area of infestation	Reference source
1949-51	Louisiana	3,000 MBF, 14,000 cords on 125,000 acres	(65)
1952-55	Louisiana	1,000 MBF	(112)
	Mississippi	75 MBF	(112)
	Texas	263 MBF	(⁴)
	South Atlantic Coastal States	107,000 MBF, 31,200 cords	(72)
1956	Texas	98 MBF	
1957-58	Louisiana	2,000 MBF	(119)
	Texas	105 MBF	(⁴)

¹ Personal communication with Kirby Lumber Corporation, Silsbee, Texas.
² Personal communication with Texas Forest Service.
³ Personal communication with Kirby Lumber Corporation, Silsbee, Texas, Champion Paper and Fibre Company, Huntsville, Texas, and Texas National Forests, Lufkin, Texas, and estimates by Southern Forest Experiment Station.
⁴ Personal communication with Champion Paper and Fibre Company, Huntsville, Texas, and Texas National Forests, Lufkin, Texas.

The earliest signs that a tree is under attack are white, yellow, or reddish-brown pitch tubes on the bark, or reddish boring dust or white resinous particles (in the case of the black turpentine beetle) in the bark crevices or on foliage of understory plants. Such particles can often be seen in spider webs near the base of the trees.

Later, as the broods develop, foliage becomes discolored, bark sloughs from the upper stem (southern pine beetle and *Ips* beetles), and white boring dust from ambrosia beetles may accumulate around the base of the tree. The foliage of trees infested by southern pine or *Ips* beetles may turn pale green to yellow in 2 to 3 weeks and brownish to red in 4 to 6 weeks during warm months (11, 12, 66). With the black turpentine beetle, fading usually begins 4 to 8 or even 12 months after initial attacks (98, 99, 102). Crowns discolor uniformly on trees infested by all beetles except *Ips avulsus*, which normally causes discoloring from the top down.

Occasionally the workings of associated insects are confused with those of the bark beetles. Some general features that distinguish bark-beetle attacks from those of wood borers, ambrosia beetles, and other associates are listed in Table 2.

Table 2.—*Features that distinguish workings of southern pine bark beetles from those of associated insects*

Southern pine bark beetles	Wood borers	Pinhole borers	Other associated insects [1]
Distinct pitch tube or fine reddish boring dust or white resinous boring particles created by entering adults.	Adults do not enter through bark.	Attack associated with dead portions of tree; small holes through bark; fine white or yellowish boring particles.	No pitch tubes and few boring particles.
Characteristic egg galleries cut by adults in cambium-phloem.	Eggs in niche cut in outer bark or placed in bark crevice; no egg gallery.	Distinct egg gallery cut in outer sapwood and stained black by ambrosial fungi.	Few construct egg galleries.
Egg galleries of *D. frontalis* and *D. terebrans* tightly packed with fine boring dust; galleries of *Ips* usually clean.		No boring particles in egg gallery; ambrosial fungus on gallery walls.	Egg galleries of secondary bark beetles with or without boring dust depending on species; termite galleries with cement-like deposit.
Larval mines generally perpendicular to egg gallery; located in cambium-phloem or cambium-phloem-middle bark; packed with fine boring dust.	Initial larval mines meander in cambium-phloem and surface of sapwood; subsequent mining in sapwood for several species.	Larvae usually develop and feed on ambrosial fungi in adult galleries.	Location and orientation of larval mining varies by species or is lacking.
Pupation in individual cells in cambium-phloem or phloem-middle bark.	Pupation in frass-plugged mine in sapwood, or in frass-surrounded cell immediately below bark.	Pupation in sapwood cells.	Pupation in sapwood, beneath or in bark.
Emergence of adults creates shothole effect in bark.	Emergence through relatively large, scattered, circular or oval holes.	Emergence frequently after bark has sloughed off.	Emergence holes less numerous and of size varying with species.

[1] Secondary bark beetles, scavengers, predators, wood feeders other than borers.

3

Southern Pine Beetle

Because beetles are hard to find readily except during epidemics, and no methods for maintaining laboratory populations have been developed, the southern pine beetle is difficult to study. Its frequent scarcity is illustrated by Blackman's failure to find specimens during 7 months of collecting in Mississippi during 1922 *(15)*. Nevertheless, a fairly complete idea of its normal life history, and some of its biological characteristics, can be constructed from work done by Hopkins from 1890-1910, by Blackman and Snyder in the early 1900's, by MacAndrews, Beal, St. George, and others in the 1920's and 1930's, and by Fronk, Osgood, and others since 1945.

Adults range from 2.2 to 4.2 mm. in length (table 3). The front of the adult head has a distinct longitudinal groove bordered by a nar-

Table 3.—*Comparative characteristics for southern pine bark beetles*

Characteristics	Ips			Dendroctonus	
	avulsus	*grandicollis*	*calligraphus*	*frontalis*	*terebrans*
Adult length (mm.)	2.1-2.6	3.0-3.8	4.0-6.0	2.2-4.2	5.0-8.0
Adult width (mm.)	.8-1.0	1.1-1.4			
Adult color	Reddish-brown to black	Reddish-brown	Reddish-brown to black	Brown or black	Dark-brown to black
Teeth on elytral declivity	4	5	6	None	None
Elytral declivity	Moderately excavated	Strongly excavated	Deeply excavated	Convex	Convex
Portion of tree usually attacked	Limbs and tops under 6 inches in diameter	Upper trunk, limbs of larger trees	Trunk	Middle and lower trunk	Base of trunk, or stump
Pitch tubes	Frequently none	Small, pink or red-brown	Small, pink or red-brown	Small, white, yellow or red-brown	Large, white to deep pink
Boring particles	Fine, red-brown	Fine, red-brown	Fine, red-brown	Fine, red-brown	Coarse, white or red resinous particles
Egg gallery—shape	Irregular, longitudinal	H- or I-shaped	H- or I-shaped	S-shaped	Simple or branched longitudinal
Egg gallery—location	Phloem, cambium	Phloem, cambium	Phloem, cambium	Phloem, cambium	Phloem, cambium
Manner of egg deposition	Individual egg niches	Individual egg niches	Individual egg niches	Individual egg niches	Eggs deposited in masses
Larval mines—location	Cambium-phloem	Cambium-phloem	Cambium-phloem	Cambium-phloem to outer bark	Cambium-phloem-middle bark
Larval feeding habit	Individual mines	Individual mines	Individual mines	Individual mines	Gregarious feeding
Pupal cell—location	Phloem and inner bark	Phloem and inner bark	Phloem and inner bark	Inner bark	Phloem and inner bark
Adult emergence habit	Several emerge through 1 hole	Several emerge through 1 hole	Several emerge through 1 hole	Individual exit holes	Several emerge through 1 hole
Days required for one complete generation	18-25	20-30	25-30	30-54	75-120
Generations per year	10 or more	6 or more	6 or more	3 to 5 or more	2 or more

row elevation on each side. The elytral declivity is convex. The sexes may be differentiated by the presence of a transverse elevation on the anterior area of the pronotum of the female (16).

The insect is monogamous. It completes its life cycle within the bark of the host in 30 to 54 days. In the Deep South, activity often continues throughout the year.

First attacks on a tree usually occur on the mid-stem and are marked by whitish pitch tubes and red boring dust. If resin flow is abundant, initial burrows may be confined to the outer and middle layers of bark for some distance before they penetrate the inner bark. Initially attacking beetles are often "pitched out"—repelled by an excessive resin flow— but successive attacks usually overcome the host. Thereafter, or in the absence of a heavy resin flow during preliminary attacks, the beetles bore directly through the bark and the female constructs a small nuptial chamber in the phloem (52, 66). The exact role of resin in overcoming early beetle attacks and the relation of multiple attacks to subsequent resin flow are inadequately understood. The rate at which gallery construction proceeds is apparently influenced by the amount of resin the adults encounter in the phloem-cambial area (66).

Following fertilization by the male in the nuptial chamber, the female begins to excavate the egg gallery diagonally across the grain of the wood. Most mining is in the cambium and phloem, but the surface of the sapwood is etched faintly. The direction of the mining eventually is reversed, thus creating a typical S-shaped or serpentine pattern. The male follows the female and removes the boring particles (35). When the beetles have excavated one or two inches of egg gallery, they construct a secondary opening radially to the bark surface and fill the main entrance and gallery to that point with borings. This process of making new openings to the surface and filling in the previous gallery is repeated at intervals of one-half to one or more inches as long as egg gallery excavation proceeds (52).

Hopkins (52) reported that the female begins to deposit individual, pearly white eggs in small cavities in each side of the gallery about the time the first secondary opening is formed. Niches containing eggs usually are one-eighth to one or more inches apart. Eggs are held in place by fine, tightly packed borings. Each female deposits about 20 eggs (75).

Eggs normally hatch in 3 to 9 days (35). By pushing against the egg-securing material, the tiny larvae are able to bite into and enter the phloem. Tunnels constructed by early stage larvae are thread-like and visible when the inner bark is exposed. As the larvae develop, their tunnels are considerably enlarged and are usually concealed within the inner bark. Fronk indicates that there are four larval instars, the larval stage usually lasting 25 to 38 days. Completed larval mines are comparatively short, 5 to 20 mm. long (66).

Prior to pupation, the larva extends an oval feeding area outward into the middle bark and parallel with the cambium. Usually the cell is large enough to break through the inner bark, although pupation may occur at various levels within the bark, apparently depending upon bark thickness. The pupal stage usually lasts 8 to 11 days.

Each adult constructs its own emergence hole, either directly from the pupal cell or— following a brief period of feeding—from a lateral gallery in the outer bark (12). Parent adults frequently leave the host tree while their broods are still in the larval stage. They may reattack the same tree or fly to new trees as do some of the western bark beetles. Brood adults may emerge over a period of 10 to 32 days, depending in part upon the time elapsed between the laying of the first and last eggs (66). A complete generation may develop in 30 to 54 days. Four complete generations and a partial fifth have been reported in West Virginia (55) and Virginia (35), and 3 to 5 in western North Carolina (11). Six or more generations appear possible in the lower South.

Early in the season, broods occur in all attacked trees except defoliated ones. During middle and late summer, most of the brood is gone from trees with yellow foliage and emergence is complete from red-topped trees. In southwest Mississippi and east Texas, broods emerge during late summer, prior to any apparent crown fading. Trees attacked in fall may remain green until spring. MacAndrews (66) found that, in western North Carolina, trees with yellow foliage contained the insect in the larval stage; those with sorrel foliage, larvae and pupae; and those with brown foliage, mature pupae and adults. This correlation

5

varies with season, probably with latitude and elevation, and with amount of blue stain.

Emerging broods may attack immediately adjacent trees or fly to stands some distance away. Trees under 15 years of age or 2 inches in diameter are rarely attacked, but outbreaks may develop in a wide variety of stands and sites *(7, 25, 55, 66)*. Spot kills of one-eighth to several hundred acres are characterized by a central area of defoliated trees, a surrounding zone of red-topped trees, and a perimeter of trees that have fading crowns or are still green, though infested. Infestations may extend in finger-like projections from the periphery.

Hopkins *(52)* and MacAndrews *(66)* report that the southern pine beetle exhibits a swarming habit. This observation is partially confirmed by the great numbers found on and around host trees during initial attack. Hopkins wrote that the beetles fly by night as well as by day, and that at times great swarms rise high in the air and are carried long distances by wind. Detailed information on this feature of the beetle's behavior is lacking.

Study of dispersal habits has been unsuccessful. Recent attempts to determine flight habits by releasing beetles treated with radioactive iridium failed for lack of a satisfactory technique for handling the insects between collection and release *(121)*.

The beetle overwinters in all stages of development, usually in single trees widely scattered around the periphery of active spot kills. Lack of crown discoloration often hinders detection until after broods have emerged.

Large and sudden population fluctuations characterize the southern pine beetle. Hopkins *(54)* believed that increases may be associated with varieties of the typical form which are able to extend their range into new areas or attack trees that would normally be resistant. Other workers feel that population increases are caused by environmental influences which have detrimental effects upon the host *(25, 26, 41, 42, 71)*. Fungus disease, parasitic nematodes, excessive rainfall, or low temperatures have been suggested as causes for sudden beetle declines *(8, 26, 33, 39, 52)*.

Observations by Lee *(62, 111)* indicate that, where populations are increasing, the beetles attack scattered groups of pines in young, dense stands. When an epidemic has developed, all age classes and densities are vulnerable. Where the population is declining, attacks are confined to scattered trees but under a wide variety of stand conditions. Lee also reported that infestations frequently occur in slow-growing stands.

Attempts to induce attack on standing trees or caged bolts have been extensive, varied, and never fully successful, though they have produced much useful information. In early experiments in the Southeast, effects of drought were simulated by trenching around pine trees and covering the soil with canvas. Data were taken on subsequent growth, sap density of the phloem and leaves, soil-moisture and temperature relationships, and susceptibility of trees to attack *(66, 90, 106)*. These and subsequent studies indicated that some abnormal physiological condition resulting from drought is essential for brood development *(25, 26)*; that beetles introduce blue stain spores into trees and create conditions favorable to stain development *(18, 19, 78)*; that the rapid death of trees may be directly attributed to blue stain fungi and yeasts, rather than to girdling of the inner bark *(18, 77)*; that the wood beneath beetle galleries dries from the outer ring toward the center of the trunk; that the blue stain fungus *Ceratocystis minor* (Hedgc.) Hunt [2] is closely associated with stoppage of conduction and drying of wood *(20)*; and that broods may be adversely affected by excessive moisture and extreme low temperatures *(8, 10, 29, 91)*.

The early studies suggested that some type of mechanical injury which would affect moisture content of the host would create conditions favorable for the beetle. In subsequent studies *(13, 29, 66, 86, 90, 91)* girdling, salting, scorching, and lodging generally failed to induce attack. Caging beetles on trees was unsuccessful because of difficulties in handling the insects. Caging infested bark on uninfested trees or logs induced emerging beetles to attack the new material. Trap-tree experiments indicated that growth retardation plus basal or mid-stem circumferential bark-stripping invited attack. Watering of trees, or complete defoliation by fire, caused heavy mortality of newly established broods, but pruning or topping had very little effect. Large tops, slash, and logs served as breeding sites where beetles were not nu-

---

[2] *C. minor* (Hedgc.) Hunt was previously described as **Ceratostomella pini** Rumbold.

merous enough to carry on their development in green trees.

During 1954-1958, several workers attempted to rear the insect under artificial conditions. Unsuccessful efforts included electrical "shocking" of bolts and introduction of blue stain fungi prior to exposure (103). Osgood and Carter, after testing several techniques for rearing, concluded that poor development and low emergence were not correlated with degree of attack but with high moisture content in the wood and bark which caused heavy larval mortality (82). Texas studies in 1958 and 1959 also resulted in poor brood development despite rather heavy attack, but were inconclusive regarding the role of host moisture content.

IPS Engraver Beetles

The three *Ips* species differ in detail, but are so similar in habits and life histories that they can be considered together. They have not been intensively studied and research may reveal behavioral patterns of use in control.

The posterior end of the adult's elytra is diagonally truncate and somewhat concave, and the exterior margins are lined with teeth. *I. avulsus* is 2.1 to 2.6 mm. long and has four teeth on each wing cover; *grandicollis*, 3.0 to 3.9 mm. long, has five; and *calligraphus*, 4.0 to 6.0 mm. long, has six (table 3). The males have coarser sculpture and greater development of the declivital teeth than do the females (16).

Ips prefer recently killed trees and slash, but are capable of breeding in trunks and limbs of apparently healthy trees (2). Infestations in green timber are usually sporadic and of short duration. Spot or group kills in pulpwood- or pole-size pines, or less often in mature stands, characterize outbreaks. As with the southern pine beetle, broods may develop rapidly enough in the summer to emerge shortly after or even before crowns begin to fade.

Season of activity corresponds with that of the southern pine beetle. Near the Gulf Coast, new attacks occur and established broods frequently become active during mild periods in winter.

Ips avulsus prefers stems less than 6 inches in diameter or the tops and branches of recently felled trees, and occasionally attacks tops of apparently healthy trees. When weather is adverse to tree growth, as during the severe drought in east Texas in 1956, *avulsus* may become a primary attacker, infesting the entire stems of large trees. Under other circumstances, it is a secondary invader of trees attacked by other insects or dying from other causes. *Ips grandicollis* prefers the stems of saplings or the upper stems and limbs of larger trees, though it may burrow in limbs less than 1 inch in diameter or in stumps of recently cut trees. *I. calligraphus*, the largest of the three southern species, occupies larger stems, usually above 6 inches in diameter. Chittenden (24) considered *I. grandicollis* as potentially very destructive to live timber.

Ips are polygamous. Three to 5 females and 1 male usually occupy each gallery. In all 3 species the male attacks first, boring a hole through the outer bark and constructing a small irregular nuptial chamber in the phloem. He initiates a series of egg galleries which are completed when the females arrive. These galleries radiate in all directions from the nuptial chamber through the phloem but eventually tend to run parallel with the grain of the wood to form a rough H or I shape. In the Gulf States, galleries of all 3 species are usually visible in the exposed inner bark surface. Haliburton reported that, in North Carolina, *avulsus* larval galleries are usually concealed within the inner bark (37).

As the females continue the excavations, they deposit eggs individually in small niches at irregular intervals on both sides of the galleries and secure them with plugs of frass. A *calligraphus* female may lay 100 fertile eggs in one gallery (37); comparable data for the other two species are not available. The larvae of all three species tunnel through the phloem until fully grown, when they hollow out cells in the inner bark and pupate. Number of larval instars is undetermined.

Callow or young adults feed beneath the bark before emerging. Several may emerge from a single hole (11). Limited observations indicate that *calligraphus* may complete a generation in 25 days (66), *grandicollis* in 20-25 days, and *avulsus* in 18-25 days. *Ips avulsus* may, therefore, have 10 or more generations a year, the two larger species 6 or more.

Ips overwinter in all stages in scattered single trees and recently cut logs and slash.

7

Black Turpentine Beetle

Until about 1949 the black turpentine beetle was considered relatively innocuous, rarely killing healthy pines (60, 92). Today it is recognized as one of the most serious pests of partially cut stands. Its attacks are not always lethal, but the risk of losing high-value trees is enough to warrant prompt control wherever infestations are heavy.

The black turpentine beetle is the largest southern pine bark beetle, being 5.0 to 8.0 mm. long (table 3). The elytral declivity is convex. Females have broader, stouter, and more compressed antennal clubs than males, narrower heads, and smaller mandibles (16). Additional diagnostic features are needed.

The species is active during most of the year in the southern part of its range, although somewhat restricted from December through March. Early in spring, large numbers of adults emerge and attack freshly cut stumps and the lower trunks of weakened trees. Occasionally stumps and apparently healthy trees are attacked simultaneously (5, 65).

The beetle has occasionally been observed in swarms (48, 52, 55). Greatest flight activity apparently occurs during late afternoon (98).

Where trees are attacked, the larger ones are preferred. Initially, entries are usually on the lower 18 inches of the trunk and are few in number. Eventually they may occur 10 feet or more up the stem and on the larger lateral roots (65, 98, 100, 102).

The insect is usually monogamous. Working in pairs, the adults bore through the bark to the soft phloem, at which point they excavate an egg gallery first above the entrance for a short distance, then downward in a general longitudinal direction. The gallery varies in length from 6 to more than 20 inches. It sometimes branches but usually is a simple tunnel with irregular widenings. At one or more of the widened areas the female deposits clusters of 50 to 200 eggs on a cushion of fine boring particles separated from the main gallery by a partition of similar material.

In the Gulf States the eggs hatch in about 10 days. Larvae feed gregariously in the soft inner bark for 5 to 7 weeks. The number of instars remains to be determined. Larvae from a single egg gallery may kill 2 square feet of bark. If several feeding areas join, the tree is girdled. The larvae pupate in individual cells beneath the bark, the pupal stage lasting 10-14 days. Callow adults feed beneath the bark until fully mature, then emerge through ventilating or exit holes.

In the Gulf States a generation may mature in 2½ to 4 months (65). There are two and part of a third generations per year, with a complex overlapping. The insect overwinters in all stages of development, the adult apparently predominating.

Populations may develop rapidly following outbreaks of other bark beetles or extensive stand disturbances (14, 55, 64, 65, 69, 100, 113, 117). Beetle activity and tree mortality usually begin the first year following such disturbances and generally subside after about 2 years; but in the naval stores region severe attacks may continue for 3 or more years (98). Infestations usually are worst on poorly drained sites, although upland areas are by no means imune. Smith (100) found that 20 percent of the trees remaining after logging, burning, or turpentining may be attacked in a single season.

Interrelationships of Bark Beetles

⌊A tree may be killed by the attacks of a single beetle species, but commonly two or more species are present. Quite typically the upper, central, and lower parts of a large tree may be attacked by the small, medium, and large Ips, respectively, or the southern pine beetle may be accompanied by one or more Ips. Similarly the black turpentine beetle may enter the bases of trees whose upper stems contain the southern pine beetle or Ips, or Ips may attack the upper stems of trees infested with the black turpentine beetle. Zones of occupancy often overlap completely, making it difficult to, determine the primary attacker, the role of the various species in destruction of the host, or the extent to which the species support or impede each other.⌋

The role of a species may vary from time to time. During epidemics, the southern pine beetle is typically the primary attacker (47), but in South Carolina during 1955 Ips calligraphus and the southern pine beetle were equally represented in the central areas of infestations and the proportion of Ips in individual trees increased with distance from the infestation center (73). Elsewhere in the Southeast these species have at times been equally abundant in individual trees (66, 78).

8

Fiske and Snyder observed that *I. avulsus* was at times more destructive than the southern pine beetle, and noted instances in which *calligraphus* and the southern pine beetle entered trees following primary attacks by *avulsus.*[a] In 1955 and 1956, *avulsus* was found working alone in tops of green trees around the periphery of southern pine beetle infestations in Alabama *(114, 117, 119).* It was not determined whether *avulsus* was the primary insect or whether populations built up in trees infested by the southern pine beetle and then, by virtue of a shorter life cycle and in the absence of preferred breeding material, preceded the latter insect into green trees.

Beal and Massey *(12)* found the southern pine beetle breeding occasionally in windfalls, larger pieces of slash, and trees attacked by other insects, particularly *Ips.* This tendency was most pronounced during years when the insect occurred in limited numbers.

Ips and black turpentine beetle populations increase considerably during and after southern pine beetle epidemics *(62, 108, 109),* for trees infested by the southern pine beetle evidently are favorable breeding sites *(12).* The large populations of *Ips* and turpentine beetle then spread to nearby uninfested trees as their preferred host material becomes exhausted. During population increases, intra- and interspecies competition for food is thought to occur between developing broods *(102).* Such competition may reduce not only population potential but also the vigor of current broods.

ENVIRONMENTAL INFLUENCES

Forest Types and Conditions

Ips and the black turpentine beetle exhibit no preference for timber type but seem to be attracted to any stand in which some disturbance has left fresh pine slash, stumps, or weakened or injured trees. Stands of large trees on flat, poorly drained sites are particularly susceptible to the turpentine beetle, although similar stands on upland sites are by no means immune.

Hopkins *(55)* reported that mature old-growth pine was very attractive to the southern pine beetle. Most of the southern pine forest is now second growth, and this beetle attacks trees of practically all sizes *(12, 36, 43, 62, 70, 80, 87, 110).* It prefers dense pure stands of pulpwood and pole size, especially during epidemics *(11, 23, 36).* Beal and Massey *(12),* as well as Balch *(7),* refer to mixed pine-hardwood stands of the Piedmont and southern Appalachians as relatively free from attack. Observations in the flatwoods of southeast Texas tend to confirm a preference for pure stands, but enough attacks occur in mixed stands to suggest that the topic needs more investigation.

In the southern Appalachians, outbreaks of the southern pine beetle usually originate on ridges or other dry sites with south or west exposures. Most of the pine in the area is on such sites *(26, 29, 62, 70, 80).*

All the bark beetles are troublesome in the poorly drained bottoms and flatwoods of the Gulf Coast. Here root systems are shallow, and prolonged drought or flooding may weaken the trees seriously. The hazards are exemplified by the heavy *Ips* activity on flatwoods sites in east Texas at the height of the 1952-1956 drought and black turpentine beetle attacks over extensive areas flooded in northwestern Louisiana during 1957-1958 *(117, 119).*

A number of soil types have been associated with beetle infestations. From 1924-1931, drought augmented by bark beetle attack caused heavy pine mortality on the gumbo or clay subsoils characteristic of many Coastal Plain sites, and on shallow soils overlying limestone and solid clay hardpans *(21).* Infestations in mountainous and rolling hill areas of Alabama in 1953-1954 *(62)* occurred on sand or sandy loam soils underlain by a clay pan, or on sandy, rocky, or silt loam soils.

Stand Disturbances

Natural disturbances and the management, harvest, and utilization of southern pine forests frequently contribute to fluctuations in beetle populations.

[a] Unpublished reports, copies of which are on file at the Forest Insect Laboratory, Southern Forest Experiment Station, Gulfport, Mississippi:

Fiske, W. F. The destructive pine bark beetle in the southern states—a report of investigations made in cooperation with work at the Southern Field Station, Tyron, N. C, during the years 1903, 1904, and 1905.

Snyder, T. E. Brief summary of conditions as observed in South and North Carolina during the fall and winter of the 3rd year of invasion by D. frontalis. Report is dated January 1912, and covers period 1909-1911.

Lightning strikes are often the centers for localized beetle activity *(12, 41, 59, 107)*. Windfalls and pines damaged by ice or hail, particularly over extensive areas, are attractive to beetles *(12, 74, 104)*.

Pruning, thinning, and harvesting leave fresh stumps and tops and wound residual trees. Road building and grading, ditch-digging, plowing of fire lanes, and right-of-way clearing may alter soil and moisture levels and expose or damage roots. These conditions favor *Ips* and black turpentine beetles and may induce southern pine beetle attacks if this species is in the area.

Harvests in southern pine forests often involve successive operations for ties, cooperage, poles and piling, saw logs, and pulpwood; hardwood and pine components are usually removed separately. Skidding and hauling during each operation may compact soils, alter soil levels in relation to root systems, injure residual trees either above or below ground, concentrate infested logs or bolts near previously uninfested stands, and accumulate large quantities of fresh-cut material. After the cut material is exhausted, beetle populations frequently spread into residual trees *(6, 112, 120)*.

Tractor operations leave more injured trees than horse or mule logging. Furthermore, the larger and more powerful machines of recent years require more space and tend to be handled more carelessly than older, lighter equipment. Convergence of skidding trails, multiple relocation of roads, and deep rutting during wet weather all damage pines which then become attractive to beetles, particularly the black turpentine beetle *(6, 64, 65, 113, 119, 120)*.

Hopkins *(55)*, as early as 1909, pointed to the desirability of continuous rather than intermittent logging. He reported that, where new slash and stumps were continuously available, *Ips* and black turpentine beetles confined themselves to this material. When logging was suspended, they shifted to live trees. Other workers *(11, 105)* have confirmed these observations, and continuous operation is widely recommended to minimize *Ips* damage, especially in dry seasons.

Winter logging has also been proposed. It would seem advantageous for small tracts where continuous operation is infeasible, provided that the slash deteriorates before beetles

begin their spring activity. On the other hand, winter logging on wet ground may compact soil and damage roots enough to create insect hazards which would offset possible advantages. Research on the possibilities is much needed.

Many wildfires and some prescribed burns damage main stems and surface roots and seriously defoliate groups of pine trees. Fires seem to be particularly harmful on sites where roots are close to the surface *(42, 116)*. Areas of concentrated fire damage often become starting points for *Ips* and southern pine beetle outbreaks *(109)*. This is particularly true where trees are weakened by fires but not severely defoliated *(12, 23, 30, 91)*.

St. George and Beal *(91)* found that trees severely defoliated by fire developed high inner-bark moisture contents which caused heavy mortality of southern pine beetle broods.

There are no reports of southern studies aimed at reducing bark beetle damage by silvicultural means, but it is widely recognized that forest management may greatly influence the activities of these insects. Management which exposes stands to minimum disturbance may minimize beetle losses. Many entomologists have indicated, however, that overstocked pure stands are prone to beetle epidemics, particularly in dry weather *(35, 62, 70, 116)*. Silvicultural systems that permit maximum forest production, recognize the capabilities of specific sites for such production, and keep insect losses at acceptable levels must be a goal of future research.

Moisture and Temperature

Observations throughout the South have related drought to increases in bark-beetle activity *(26, 42, 71, 115)*. Some workers propose that drought occasionally has been the primary cause of heavy pine mortality and that beetles merely assisted in killing the trees *(21, 27)*.

Others point out that excessive precipitation may weaken trees, making them attractive to bark beetles *(41, 42)*. At least three outbreaks of the southern pine beetle since 1890 have developed during excessively wet periods following drought *(26, 117, 119)*. On the other hand, heavy rains may kill beetles in flight *(8, 12, 26, 102)*.

Early research in the Southeast indicated that moisture content of trees has a marked

10

effect on establishment and development of broods *(13, 25, 29, 78, 88, 90)*. After 4 or 5 weeks, depending on severity of attack, there is a definite increase in moisture content of the sapwood at the base of the tree, a reverse situation from that in unattacked trees. This reversal was ascribed to interruption in conduction of water from the roots and to rapid drying of tops by continuing transpiration. Phloem moisture followed a pattern similar to that in the wood but usually was 10 to 20 percent higher. In severely defoliated or decapitated trees, increase in phloem moisture materially checked development of young broods *(91, 94)*.

R. W. Caird *(20)* found that the outer three rings of an attacked tree ceased to conduct moisture in 3 to 5 days, depending upon the severity of attack. Extensive tunneling in the phloem exposed the surface of the wood to the outer atmosphere through open entrance and ventilation holes. By stopping conduction, associated fungi apparently accelerated the rate at which the tree died.

Mild winters favor beetle populations by prolonging their active season—an example is the southern pine beetle activity in southeast Texas which continued throughout the winter 1959-1960 *(12, 52, 65, 70, 71, 123)*. St. George and Beal *(91)* determined that eggs and some pupae of the southern pine beetle could survive -5° F. In other studies, air temperatures from -5° to 10° F. damaged all stages except the egg *(8, 10)*. Mortality was heaviest in the moist inner bark *(81, 91, 107, 119)*. Bark has insulating value, and its thickness may affect brood survival during unusually cold periods.

No instances of lethal high temperatures in standing beetle-infested trees have been reported, but several workers have indicated that exposed sides of felled products reach temperatures fatal to *Ips* and southern pine beetles.

Host Physiology

Most research on host-insect relationships has been concerned with attacks on weakened or recently dead trees and cut products. While stand disturbances appear to be related to successful attack, the specific host conditions associated with such attacks, and the reasons why beetles select apparently healthy hosts, are little understood.

Early explanations of host-beetle relationships centered around the theory that "sap flow" helped to determine success of attacks by the southern pine beetle. Hopkins *(52)* suggested that by late July "sap flow" was less profuse and that, if southern pine beetles were numerous, they would attack living trees. He felt that preliminary attacks were concentrated in the central portion of the trunk because there was less "resistance" to injury in this zone than in the lower stem.

MacAndrews *(66)* supplemented Hopkins' assumptions as to the influence of moisture and resin on establishment of southern pine beetle broods. He reported that initial attacks drained resin supplies enough to permit later attacks to succeed. No measurements of resin flow were made. Lee and Smith *(65)* found that the quantity of gum produced by a tree had little effect on its resistance to the black turpentine beetle. In *Ips* species, which are polygamous, loss of considerable numbers of males in unsuccessful initial attacks would still leave enough to fertilize the entire female population *(37)*.

Bark thickness apparently influences the location of attacks and the survival of broods *(29, 37, 66, 79, 91)*. An outstanding example is the black turpentine beetle's selection of the thick-barked basal portion of the trunk and the main roots of trees. Attacks by the two larger *Ips* species and the southern pine beetle occur in the lower three-quarters of the main stem, where larger populations may successfully complete development than would be possible beneath the thinner bark of tops and small limbs. Because of its small size, *I. avulsus* is able to develop and multiply rapidly in thin-barked upper stems and branches.

ASSOCIATED FORMS AFFECTING BEETLE POPULATIONS

Fungi

The southern pine beetle and *Ips* beetles introduce staining fungi and yeasts into the trees they infest *(18, 19, 32, 77, 78, 84, 125)*. Associated mites also seem to disseminate the fungi *(41)*.

Nelson *(77)* believed that southern pine beetle broods would be unable to develop in the phloem were it not for the rapid establishment of staining fungi which, in his opinion, killed the tree. Bramble and Holst *(18, 19)* and

11

Holst *(45)*, on the other hand, found no evidence that the fungi generally associated with southern pine beetles are essential for beetle development from the egg stage. They indicated that the fungi do no more than assist in killing beetle-attacked trees.

Ceratocystis minor (Hedgc.) Hunt or *C. ips* (Rumbold) C. Moreau, *Pichia pini* (Holst) Phaff,[1] and an unnamed basidiomycete are the first forms to attack the sapwood following beetle entry *(18, 19, 44, 83, 84)*. *C. minor* is specifically associated with the southern pine beetle and *C. ips* with *Ips* engraver beetles. *Dacromyces* sp. and *P. pini* penetrate outer sapwood rings rapidly during the first week of beetle attack. During the second week, *C. minor* or *C. ips* penetrates as deeply as the primary forms; these two blue stain fungi are the prominent micro-organisms in the sapwood during the final stages of beetle attack.

Penetration by fungi is accompanied by a gradual drying of the sapwood—the result of continuing transpiration by the crown while the infected stem is losing its ability to transmit water from the roots. The result is the reversed moisture situation described by Beal and St. George *(13)*.

At least some of the fungi discussed above are capable of killing trees by themselves *(77, 78)*. However, they are disseminated mainly by insects, require some type of mechanical injury as an infection court in the host, and must encircle the stem before mortality ensues *(18)*. Death from blue stain following unsuccessful beetle attacks, if it occurs at all, is a slow process because of the limited number of beetle contacts with the sapwood *(32)*.

Limited observations indicate that other fungal forms sometimes influence the susceptibility of pines to beetles. Hetrick *(41, 42)* noted several instances where trees infested with the southern pine beetle also had rhizomorphs of the mushroom root rot *(Armillaria mellea* (Vahl.) Quel.) between the bark and sapwood near the groundline. Callus sapwood at points where the fungus mycelium was growing upward clearly indicated that fungus development had preceded beetle attack.

Hopkins *(51)* found evidence that disease reduced southern pine beetle populations in an outbreak area in the central Atlantic States

in the early 1890's. A fungus associated with the beetle was later placed in the Family Tuberculaniaceae and named *Cylindrocola dendroctoni* Peck *(52)*.

Snyder[2] observed a parasitic fungus common in the pupal cells of the southern pine beetle, *Ips avulsus*, and *I. calligraphus*. Later, Harrar and Ellis *(38)* and Hetrick *(40)* found an entomophagous fungus of the genus *Beauvaria* which was pathogenic to healthy southern pine beetle larvae and caused high mortality of overwintered broods.

Conditions under which pathogenic fungi and virus organisms develop and reduce beetle populations require considerable study. Research to determine pathogenic organisms other than those presently known is also needed.

Insects

Various insects are associated with all of the southern bark beetles. Many are parasites, hyperparasites, and predators (tables 4, 5). Others are scavengers or competitors for food, and still others are responsible for the initial deterioration of the host plant (table 6).

Most insect parasites are small wasps and flies.

A few species deposit their eggs in the host egg galleries or larval mines; the parasite larvae seek their host after hatching. Some oviposit through the bark, while micro-forms commonly enter the galleries of the host. The parasites usually spend their lives in or on the body of a single host, ultimately causing its death. Fiske *(34)* found that 45 percent of the southern pine beetle larvae in the upper thin-barked zone of the main stem were parasitized by braconids, whereas the same group was unable to parasitize larvae beneath the thicker bark of the lower stem.

The most important predators are beetles and piercing and sucking insects. Very little has been published on the habits and role of these forms, except for the clerids and ostomids, two predatory beetle families. As early as 1893, Hopkins *(49)* determined that *Clerus quadrisignatus* var. *nigripes* Say and *Thanasimus dubius* Fab. are predaceous on *Ips grandicollis* and that *T. dubius* also attacks *Ips calligraphus* and the southern pine beetle. He im-

---

[1] P. pini (Holst) Phaff was previously described as Zygosaccharomyces pini Holst.
[2] Snyder, T. E. 1912. Brief summary of conditions as observed in South and North Carolina during the fall and winter of the third year of invasion by Dendroctonus frontalis. Unpublished memo to files. U. S. Dept. Agr., Bur. Ent.

Table 4.—*Insect parasites of the southern pine bark beetles*

Parasite family and species	Host and stage parasitized
Braconidae	
Bracon pissodis Ashm. (49, 50, 52)	Southern pine beetle—larva and pupa
Coeloides brunneri Vier. (22)	Ips calligraphus
Coeloides pissodis (Ashm.) (22, 35, 39)	Southern pine beetle
Compyloneurus (Bracon) mavoritus (Cress.) (22)	Southern pine beetle
Dendrosoter sulcatus Meus. (39, 76)	Southern pine beetle I. avulsus
Doryctes sp. (22)	Southern pine beetle
Ecphylus (Sactopus) schwarzii (Ashm.) (22)	Southern pine beetle
Heydenia unica C. and D. (22, 39, 49, 50, 52)	Southern pine beetle—larva and pupa
Lochites sp. (49, 50, 52)	Southern pine beetle—larva and pupa I. grandicollis—larva and pupa I. calligraphus
Spathius canadensis Ashm. (22, 39, 49, 50)	Southern pine beetle I. grandicollis
Spathius pallidus Ashm. (22, 49, 50, 52)	I. grandicollis—larva
Dolichopodidae	
Medetera sp. (35)	Southern pine beetle
Eulophidae	
Tetrastichus thanasimi Ashm. (52)	Thanasimus dubius
Pteromalidae	
Cecidostiba dendroctoni Ashm. (22, 35, 39, 52)	Southern pine beetle I. grandicollis
Tomicobia tibialis Ashm. (22, 52)	I. grandicollis I. calligraphus—adult
Stratiomyidae	
Microchrysa polita (L.) (35)	Southern pine beetle
Tachinidae	
Tachina sp. (52)	Thanasimus dubius
Torymidae	
Roptrocerus (Pachyceras) eccoptogasteri Ratz. (22, 39, 52)	Southern pine beetle—larva and pupa I. grandicollis—larva and pupa I. calligraphus—larva and pupa

ported large numbers of a closely allied predator, *Thanasimus formicarius* (F.), from Europe for use in controlling the southern pine beetle *(46, 52)*, but an outbreak in the central Atlantic States (table 1) ended before the value of this predator could be determined.

Subsequent observations throughout the South indicated that larvae of predaceous clerids and ostomids feed on the eggs, larvae, pupae, and callow adults of *Ips* and the southern pine beetle in and beneath the bark. Adults of these predators also destroy large numbers of adult bark beetles as they attack green trees *(28)*. The effectiveness of these insects in widespread biological control is as yet undetermined, although they have been observed in great abundance in several beetle outbreak areas.

While little is known about the influence of environment on associated insects, clerid and ostomid larvae have been observed to survive temperature drops to 0° F. while bark beetle broods suffered heavy mortality *(107, 119)*. Low temperatures may thus favor biological control by increasing the predator-bark beetle ratio.

Insect competitors for food limit bark beetle populations, but their overall influence is un-

13

known. A possible exception is the relation of cerambycid larvae to bark-beetle development. Adults of *Monochamus titillator* (F.), *Acanthocinus nodusus* (F.), *Stenocorus lineatus* Oliv., and *Xylotrechus sagittatus* (Germ.) oviposit in the bark at or very soon after initial attack by the southern pine beetle and *Ips*. Oviposition may continue for 10 days. Larvae of these wood and bark borers develop rapidly and may mine so extensively that bark beetle broods are destroyed directly or starve because their phloem food supply has been consumed *(66, 73)*. If larvae of the southern pine beetle begin mining before or immediately after cerambycid larvae become active, however, they may subsist in outer layers of the bark in thick-barked trees where wood-borer larvae do not feed.

Smith and Lee (102) observed that competition for food with wood destroyers killed some black turpentine beetle larvae.

Despite these interrelationships, there is no record that bark beetle broods have ever been completely destroyed by predators, parasites, or competitors.

Table 5.—*Insect predators of the southern pine bark beetles*

Predator family and species	Host and role of predator
Anthocoridae	
Anthocoria sp. *(52)*	*Ips grandicollis*
	I. calligraphus
Lyctocoris elongatus (Reuter) *(35)*	Southern pine beetle. Nymphs and adults feed on eggs and larvae
Scoloposcelia flavicornis (Reuter) *(35)*	Southern pine beetle. Nymphs and adults feed on eggs and larvae
Cleridae	
Enoclerus quadriguttatus Oliv. *(22)*	Southern pine beetle
Enoclerus quadrisignatus var. *nigripes* Say *(22, 49, 52)*	*I. grandicollis*
Priocera castanea (Newman) *(17)*	Southern pine beetle
Thanasimus dubius (F.) *(17, 34, 35, 49, 52)*	Southern pine beetle and 3 *Ips*. Larvae feed on eggs and larvae, adults on adults
Elateridae	
Elaterid sp. *(22, 52)*	Southern pine beetle and black turpentine beetle —larvae feed on larvae, pupae, young adults
Histeridae	
Cylistix cylindrica (Payk.) *(22)*	*I. grandicollis*
	I. calligraphus
Hister cylindricus Payk. *(49, 52)*	*I. grandicollis*
	I. calligraphus
Ostomidae	
Temnochila virescens (F.) *(35)*	Southern pine beetle. Larvae feed on larvae and pupae, adults on adults
Staphylinidae	
Gryohypnus (Xantholinus) emmenus (Grav.) *(22)*	*I. calligraphus*
Tenebrionidae	
Hypophloeus parallelus Melsh. *(49)*	Southern pine beetle
	I. grandicollis
Hypophloeus tenuis Lec. *(22, 52)*	*I. calligraphus*
Tenebroides collaris (Strum) *(35)*	Southern pine beetle. Larvae feed on larvae and pupae, adults on adults

Nematodes and Mites

High mortality of southern pine beetle broods has been noted where nematode and mite species were associated with beetles in egg through adult stages *(35, 39, 67)*. The value of these associates for biological control has not been appraised. A list of the forms follows:

Nematodes

Genus *Anguillonema:* endoparasitic on southern pine beetle

Genus *Aphelenchoides*

Aphelenchulus barberus Massey: males nonparasitic, females parasitic on southern pine beetle

Aphelenchulus gradicollis Massey: associated with *Ips grandicollis*

Mites

Family Parasitidae, *Parasitus* sp.: feed on southern pine beetle larvae

Family Uropinae, *Uropoda* sp.: heavy infestations prevent southern pine beetle flight

Family Dameosmidae

Family Cheltidae, *Cheltia* sp.

Family Laelaptidae, *Dendrolaelaps* sp., *Zercoseius* sp.

Family Acaridae, *Histiogaster carpio* (K.): feed on southern pine beetle larvae

Family Oribatoidae

Woodpeckers

Woodpeckers are commonly observed on beetle-infested trees. In seeking larvae, pupae, and adults of the southern pine beetle, woodpeckers frequently remove so much outer bark that sawlog-size trees assume a distinguishing buckskin or reddish-brown appearance *(36)*. Some of the bark fragments that fall to the ground are so large that beetles in them can still complete their development. Osgood *(107)* found that 77 percent of the southern pine beetle larvae remaining in the bark of "woodpeckered" trees were killed by low winter temperatures as opposed to 44 percent in trees not worked by woodpeckers. Smith and Lee *(102)* observed that woodpeckers exercise no appreciable control in the thick-barked basal portion of trees or stumps occupied by the black turpentine beetle.

Woodpecker activity is usually seasonal, reaching its peak in winter, and limited to occasional trees. The birds have their greatest value when infested trees are so few that most of the broods can be destroyed.

CHEMICAL CONTROL

For many years, standard recommendations for controlling bark beetles were to utilize infested trees as rapidly as possible; burn the slabs, tops, and unmerchantable infested trees; and peel and burn bark from stumps and unused logs *(4)*. Chemicals have facilitated immediate control where such methods have proved too costly or slow for such aggressive insects as the southern pine beetle. In addition, it has been found that many trees infested with the black turpentine beetle can be saved by timely spraying.

Early researchers attempted to introduce poisons into the sap-stream, the object being a low-cost application that would destroy the insects regardless of the effect on the trees *(13)*. Sodium arsenite, mercuric chloride, ammonium fluoride, sodium fluoride, carbon disulphide, hydrocyanic acid gas, and ethyl monodichloroacetate all reduced or destroyed broods, but only when applied on newly attacked trees and before conduction ceased *(9, 13, 31, 91, 93)*. The saw-kerf or saw-cut injection method *(3)* proved most suitable.

Limited tests of sprays were undertaken by St. George *(89)* in 1932. Kerosene injured and often killed pines. Orthodichlorobenzene destroyed broods and prevented further attack, although infested trees were seldom saved.

Experiments by western forest entomologists led to the development of a mixture of orthodichlorobenzene and fuel oil (1:5). The formulation controlled the mountain pine beetle *(95)*, and was successfully used on the southern pine beetle during the 1940's.

In 1950, Morris *(75)* demonstrated that broods of the southern pine beetle can be destroyed and the insect's spread prevented by spraying infested trees with 0.25 percent gamma isomer of benzene hexachloride in No. 2 fuel oil. Later studies in western North Carolina *(122)* indicated that a 0.5 percent spray was even more effective in killing either broods beneath the

Table 6.—*Insect competitors and scavengers associated with the southern pine bark beetles*

Associated insect family and species	Primary insect	Role
Buprestidae		
Buprestis apricans Hbst. *(28)*	Southern pine beetle	Competitor for phloem food supply
Cerambycidae		
Acanthocinus nodosus (F.) *(29, 66, 73)*	Southern pine beetle	Do.
	Ips grandicollis	Do.
	I. calligraphus	Do.
Asemum moestum Hald. *(29)*	Southern pine beetle	Do.
Astylopsis (Leptostylus) guttata (29)	Southern pine beetle	Fungal spore feeder
Monochamus titillator (F.) *(13, 66, 73, 90)*	Southern pine beetle	Competitor for phloem food supply
	I. grandicollis	Do.
	I. calligraphus	Do.
Stenocorus lineatus Oliv. *(73)*	Southern pine beetle	Do.
	I. grandicollis	Do.
	I. calligraphus	Do.
Xylotrechus sagittatus (Germ.) *(29, 73)*	Southern pine beetle	Do.
	I. grandicollis	Do.
	I. calligraphus	Do.
Colydiidae		
Aulonium tuberculatum Lec. *(52)*	*I. grandicollis*	Scavenger
Cucujidae		
Laemophlaeus testaceus Fab. *(52)*	*I. grandicollis*	Scavenger
Curculionidae		
Cossonus corticola Say *(28)*	Southern pine beetle	Do.
	I. grandicollis	Do.
	I. calligraphus	Do.
Pachylobius picivorus Germ.	Black turpentine beetle	Competitor for phloem food supply
Pissodes nemorensis Germ.	*I. calligraphus*	Do.
Histeridae		
Hister lecontei Mars. *(52)*	*I. calligraphus*	Predator
Hister parallelus Say *(52)*	*I. calligraphus*	Do.
Plegaderus transversus Say *(28)*	*I. grandicollis*	Do.
	I. calligraphus	Do.
Lathridiidae		
Corticaria elongata Hum. *(49, 52)*	*I. calligraphus*	Unknown
Nitidulidae		
Colastus unicolor Say *(49)*	*I. calligraphus*	Feeds on decaying and fermenting juices beneath bark

16

Table 6.—(Continued)

Associated insect family and species	Primary insect	Role
Ostomidae		
Corticotomus cylindricus (Lec.) (28, 49, 52)	I. grandicollis	Predator on ambrosia beetles, Cossonids
Platypodidae		
Platypus flavicornis Fab.	Black turpentine beetle	Pinhole borer in sapwood
Rhinotermitidae		
Reticulitermes flavipes Kol.	Southern pine beetle	Wood feeder
	Black turpentine beetle	Do.
Scolytidae		
Crypturgus alutaceus Sz. (28, 73)	Southern pine beetle	Competitor for phloem food supply
	I. grandicollis	Do.
	I. calligraphus	Do.
Hylastes sp.	Black turpentine beetle	Do.
Hylurgops glabratus (47)	Black turpentine beetle	Do.
Orthotomicus caelatus Eichh. (15)	I. grandicollis	Do.
	I. calligraphus	Do.
	Black turpentine beetle	Do.
Pityogenes meridianus Blkm. (15)	I. avulsus	Do.
Pityogenes plagiatus Lec. (15)	I. avulsus	Do.
Pityophthorus annectens Lec. (15)	I. avulsus	Do.
Pityophthorus bellus Blkm. (28, 73)	Southern pine beetle	Competitor for phloem food supply
	I. grandicollis	Do.
	I. calligraphus	Do.
Pityophthorus granulatus Sw. (15)	I. avulsus	Do.
Pityophthorus lautus Eichh. (15)	I. avulsus	Do.
Pityophthorus nudus Sw. (15)	I. avulsus	Do.
Pityophthorus pulicarius Zimm. (15)	Southern pine beetle	Do.
	I. avulsus	Do.
	I. grandicollis	Do.
Pityophthorus pullus Zimm. (15)	I. avulsus	Do.
	I. grandicollis	Do.
Xyleborus confusus Eichh. (15)	Black turpentine beetle	Pinhole borer in wood
Staphylinidae		
Xantholinus emmesus Grav. (52)	I. calligraphus	Scavenger or predator
Tenebrionidae		
Corticeus glaber Lec. (28)	I. avulsus	Plant feeder
Corticeus parallelus Melsh. (28)	Southern pine beetle	Do.
Corticeus piliger Lec. (28)	I. calligraphus	Do.
Trogositidae		
Trogosita virescens Fab. (52)	I. calligraphus	Unknown

17

bark or emerging beetles. However, the lower concentration continues to yield acceptable results and is widely used throughout the South. The spray is applied until the bark is dripping wet or at the rate of approximately 1 gallon per 100 square feet of bark surface. The long residual life of the chemical permits control crews to treat infested trees over extensive areas ahead of salvage units or to leave treated logs in the woods during adverse weather or under other conditions which prohibit salvage.

Also in 1950, tests of BHC for control of the black turpentine beetle were undertaken by J. F. Coyne, as reported by Lee and Smith (65). As this insect occupies the thick-barked basal portion of trees and broods mature more slowly than those of the southern pine beetle, a stronger concentration with a long residual life was necessary. A spray of 0.5 percent gamma isomer of BHC in fuel oil proved highly effective when applied at the rate of 1 gallon to 40 or 50 square feet of bark. The addition of 3 pounds of ethylene dibromide to 5 gallons of spray improved control but not enough to justify the increased cost.

Stronger concentrations of BHC were more effective in killing the black turpentine beetle (96, 97). A 1.0 percent concentration reduced tree mortality from the turpentine beetle by as much as 90 percent, as compared with unsprayed check trees (101). Removal of duff and loose bark plates also aided in killing turpentine beetles inhabiting the thick bark of the lower stem and large roots.

In 1954 experimental spraying of the basal 20 to 25 feet of fire-scorched loblolly and shortleaf pines with BHC in fuel oil was found to reduce attacks by the large *Ips* species for several months (63). Because attacks by *I. avulsus* occur on the upper stem, it is difficult to control this group in standing trees, but the treatment has been effective in cut logs or slash and is sometimes used where large populations develop in logging debris and threaten residual trees.

BARK-BEETLE RESEARCH NEEDS IN THE SOUTH

Necessary research on bark beetles that attack southern pines falls into two broad categories:

1. Basic research, primarily in insect and plant physiology and in insect biology and ecology, aimed at securing fundamental knowledge of the immediate environmental factors affecting bark beetles and their interrelationships.

2. Applied research into chemical, biological, and silvicultural means of dealing with the bark beetles.

Past study of forest insects has amply justified itself by the practical controls that have been developed, but the present lack of basic information sharply handicaps further applied research.

The following analysis of research needs has been prepared chiefly from the standpoint of the Southern Forest Experiment Station and its area of responsibility, but no single organization is likely to have the resources to cope with the job in its entirety. Much that is contemplated in the following paragraphs can and should be accomplished by Federal, State, and private research agencies, educational institutions, specialized laboratories, and other groups within the range of the southern pine bark beetles. The proposals stress the importance of basic knowledge from which practical controls can be developed. Often both basic and applied research are described or implied under the same subject heading.

Insect Biology and Physiology

Basic to progress in beetle control is thorough knowledge of the insects. Although more is known about the southern pine beetle than the other species, detailed research on all 5 beetles is needed, specifically:

Each species' habits of mating, gallery excavation, oviposition, and brood development.

Effects on all beetle stages of variations in temperature, humidity, resin production, moisture and nutrient content of the phloem, and other environmental factors.

Techniques for rearing the southern pine beetle artifically, to facilitate detailed biological and physiological research.

Flight and dispersal habits of the 5 species. Techniques for rearing and handling large populations, and for

18

using radioactive tracers and other aids.

Variations in life histories which may be related to climatic differences and locations. Such studies are particularly needed in the Gulf South.

Possible genetic variations which may be related to population fluctuations, especially of the southern pine beetle.

Host Physiological Relationships

Research in plant physiology as it relates to bark beetle populations should include the following basic studies:

Conditions or processes in the host which predispose a tree or stand to initial or continuing attack and favor or oppose successful brood development. Examples are the effect of resin and sap flow, physical and chemical characteristics of sap and resin, presence of fungi and bacteria, growth rate, bark thickness, and possibly other measurable factors of host physiology.

Root development and possible relationships between condition of roots and beetle attack. Many initial buildups may be associated with root deterioration caused by adverse weather, site, nematodes, or root-rot fungi.

Morphological and physiological features of host which influence effectiveness of associated forms as control agents.

Effect of seasonal variations in rainfall and temperature on host resistance.

Associated Forms Affecting Bark Beetles

Appraisal of the control value of pathogenic fungi, parasites, and predators should include the following studies:

Isolation and identification of entomophagous fungi.

Pathogenicity of entomophagous fungi to various beetle stages.

Conditions necessary for optimum development and effectiveness of pathogenic fungi.

Isolation and identification of predators and parasites capable of materially affecting beetle populations, and detailed study of their life histories and environmental requirements to determine their utility as substitutes for chemicals.

Relationships between and within bark beetle species and associated inner bark forms during epidemic and endemic periods.

Usefulness of woodpeckers in direct control or in altering the beetles' environment until they succumb to other environmental influences.

Silvicultural-Management Relationships

Research on silvicultural means for reducing losses from bark beetles should include:

Stand density or basal area as it relates to beetle populations. Long-term studies should be undertaken in areas where bark beetles have frequently been a problem.

Consideration of a beetle risk-class system for southern pine forests. The tree-age classes that are most susceptible in the West are lacking in the South, and the possibilities for a southern system have hardly been explored.

Merits of a single continuous operation for harvesting all wood products, as opposed to separate operations for individual products.

Logging techniques that minimize insect damage to residual stands. E. g., tree-length versus log-length skidding, need for follow-up sanitation cuttings, relation of beetle attack to season of cut on upland and flatwood sites, damage to residual stands as related to type of logging equipment, and preventive spraying of injured residuals.

Effect of cutting systems—seed tree, shelterwood, and clear-cutting in

19

strips—on susceptibility of residual stands under various weather conditions.

Relation of beetle damage to density and proportion of hardwoods in mixed stands.

Chemical Control

In the absence of more complete knowledge, chemicals are frequently the only means for combating beetles. Research should include:

Continued screening of insecticides to secure economical control with minimum damage to other organisms.

Continuing study to improve formulations, application methods, equipment, and timing. The importance of treating certain portions of beetle-infested trees has recently been questioned, particularly in the case of the black turpentine beetle. Refined criteria are urgently needed for selecting trees to be sprayed or salvaged.

Confirmation of recommended dosages for both preventive and remedial control.

Effect of insecticides on parasites and predators, and ways of modifying control procedures to favor these forms.

Biological Appraisals and Economic Evaluations

Research on appraisal survey techniques should seek to develop:

Systematic and quantitative techniques for evaluating trends in bark beetle populations.

A technique for appraising effectiveness and population trends of known parasites, predators, and other natural control agents.

A system for determining effectiveness of chemical control and the need to continue direct control—i.e., a sampling procedure for measuring mortality of existing beetle broods and rate at which new infestations occur.

LITERATURE CITED

(1) ANONYMOUS.
1924. BEETLE WORKING DAMAGE TO YELLOW PINE IN SOUTH. Natl. Lumberman 73(1025):10.

(2) ——
1927. THE RELATION OF INSECTS TO SLASH DISPOSAL. U. S. Dept. Agr. Dept. Cir. 411, 12 pp.

(3) ——
1933. REPORT OF STUDIES CONDUCTED AT ASHEVILLE, NORTH CAROLINA, 1933. U. S. Dept. Agr. Bur. Ent. and Plant Quar., Asheville. [Unpublished.]

(4) ——
1935. A NAVAL STORES HANDBOOK DEALING WITH THE PRODUCTION OF PINE GUM OR OLEORESIN. U. S. Dept. Agr. Misc. Pub. 209, 201 pp., illus.

(5) ——
1952. INSECTS AND DISEASES THREATEN FORESTS. Tex. Forest News 31(1):5-8.

(6) ——
1958. WHAT YOU SHOULD KNOW ABOUT THE BLACK TURPENTINE BEETLE. Forest Farmer 18(3): 8, 16-18, illus.

(7) BALCH, R. E.
1928. THE INFLUENCE OF THE SOUTHERN PINE BEETLE ON FOREST COMPOSITION IN WESTERN NORTH CAROLINA. Master's thesis, N. Y. State Col. Forestry. [Unpublished.]

(8) BEAL, J. A.
1927. WEATHER AS A FACTOR IN SOUTHERN PINE BEETLE CONTROL. Jour. Forestry 25:741-742.

(9) ——
1929. TREE INJECTION. U. S. Dept. Agr. Bur. Ent. and Plant Quar., Asheville, N. C. [Unpublished.]

(10) ——
1933. TEMPERATURE EXTREMES AS A FACTOR IN THE ECOLOGY OF THE SOUTHERN PINE BEETLE. Jour. Forestry 31:329-336.

(11) —— HALIBURTON, W., and KNIGHT, F. B.
1952. FOREST INSECTS OF THE SOUTHEAST: WITH SPECIAL REFERENCE TO SPECIES OCCURRING IN THE PIEDMONT PLATEAU OF NORTH CAROLINA. Duke Univ. School Forestry Bul. 14, 168 pp., illus.

(12) —— and MASSEY, C. L.
1945. BARK BEETLES AND AMBROSIA BEETLES (COLEOPTERA: SCOLYTOIDEA): WITH SPECIAL REFERENCE TO SPECIES OCCURRING IN NORTH CAROLINA. Duke Univ. School Forestry Bul. 10, 178 pp., illus.

(13) —— and ST. GEORGE, R. A.
1926. PROGRESS REPORT ON THE SOUTHERN PINE BEETLE. SUMMARY OF OBSERVATIONS AND EXPERIMENTS—1926. U. S. Dept. Agr. Bur. Ent. and Plant Quar., Asheville, N. C. [Unpublished.]

(14) BENNETT, W. H., CHELLMAN, C. W., and HOLT, W. R.
1958. INSECT ENEMIES OF SOUTHERN PINES. U. S. Forest Serv. South. Forest Expt. Sta. Occas. Paper 164, 35 pp., illus.

(15) BLACKMAN, M. W.
1922. MISSISSIPPI BARK BEETLES. Miss. Agr. Expt. Sta. Tech. Bul. 11, 130 pp., illus.

(16) BLATCHLEY, W. S. and LENG, C. W.
1916. RHYNCOPHORA OR WEEVILS OF NORTHEASTERN AMERICA. 682 pp., illus. Indianapolis.

(17) BOVING, A. G., and CHAMPLAIN, A. B.
1921. LARVAE OF NORTH AMERICAN BEETLES OF THE FAMILY CLERIDAE. Proc. U. S. Natl. Mus. 57:575-649, illus.

(18) BRAMBLE, W. C., and HOLST, E. C.
1935. MICROORGANISMS INFECTING PINES ATTACKED BY *Dendroctonus frontalis*. Phytopath. 25:7.

(19) —— and HOLST, E. C.
1940. FUNGI ASSOCIATED WITH *Dendroctonus frontalis* IN KILLING SHORTLEAF PINES AND THEIR EFFECT ON CONDUCTION. Phytopath. 30:881-899, illus.

(20) CAIRD, R. W.
1935. PHYSIOLOGY OF PINES INFESTED WITH BARK BEETLES. Bot. Gaz. 96:709-733, illus.

(21) CARY, A.
1932. ON THE RECENT DROUGHT AND ITS EFFECTS. Naval Stores Rev. 17:14-15; 18:14-15, 20; 19:14-15, 18.

(22) CHAMBERLIN, W. J.
1939. BARK AND TIMBER BEETLES OF NORTH AMERICA. Oreg. State Col. Coop. Assoc., 513 pp., illus. Corvallis.

(23) CHAPMAN, H. H.
1942. MANAGEMENT OF LOBLOLLY PINE IN THE PINE-HARDWOOD REGION OF ARKANSAS AND IN LOUISIANA WEST OF THE MISSISSIPPI RIVER. Yale Univ. School Forestry Bul. 49, pp. 143-146.

(24) CHITTENDEN, F. H.
1897. INSECT INJURY TO CHESTNUT AND PINE TREES IN VIRGINIA AND NEIGHBORING STATES. U. S. Dept. Agr. Bur. Ent. Bul. 7, n. s., pp. 67-75, illus.

(25) CRAIGHEAD, F. C.
1925. THE *Dendroctonus* PROBLEMS. Jour. Forestry 23:340-354.

21

(26) CRAIGHEAD, F. C.
1925. BARK BEETLE EPIDEMICS AND RAINFALL DE-
FICIENCY. Jour. Econ. Ent. 18:577-586.

(27) ————
1941. THE INFLUENCE OF INSECTS ON THE DEVELOP-
MENT OF FOREST PROTECTION AND FOREST
MANAGEMENT. Ann. Rpt. Smithsonian Inst.,
pp. 367-392, illus.

(28) ————
1950. INSECT ENEMIES OF EASTERN FORESTS. U. S.
Dept. Agr. Misc. Pub. 657, 679 pp., illus.

(29) ————and ST. GEORGE, R. A.
1925. PROGRESS REPORT ON FOREST INSECT INVESTI-
GATIONS CONDUCTED AT ASHEVILLE, N. C.,
APRIL TO OCTOBER, 1925. U. S. Dept. Agr.
Bur. Ent., Asheville, N. C. [Unpublished.]

(30) ———— and ST. GEORGE, R. A.
1928. SOME EFFECTS OF FIRE AND INSECT ATTACK
ON SHORTLEAF PINE. U. S. Forest Serv.
Forest Worker 4(2):11-12.

(31) ———— and ST. GEORGE, R. A.
1938. EXPERIMENTAL WORK WITH THE INTRODUC-
TION OF CHEMICALS INTO THE SAP STREAM
OF TREES FOR THE CONTROL OF INSECTS.
Jour. Forestry 36: 26-34.

(32) ———— and ST. GEORGE, R. A.
1940. FIELD OBSERVATIONS ON THE DYING OF PINES
INFECTED WITH THE BLUE-STAIN FUNGUS,
Ceratostomella pini MUNCH. Phytopath.
30:976-979.

(33) DeBACH, P.
1958. THE ROLE OF WEATHER AND ENTOMOPHAGOUS
SPECIES IN THE NATURAL CONTROL OF INSECT
POPULATIONS. Jour. Econ. Ent. 51:474.

(34) FISKE, W. F.
1908. NOTES ON INSECT ENEMIES OF WOOD BORING
COLEOPTERA. Ent. Soc. Wash. Proc. 9:24-
26.

(35) FRONK, W. D.
1947. THE SOUTHERN PINE BEETLE—ITS LIFE HIS-
TORY. Va. Agr. Expt. Sta. Tech. Bul. 108,
12 pp., illus.

(36) GERHART, G. A., and AHLER, E. E.
1949. SOUTHERN PINE BEETLE CONTROL ON NORRIS
RESERVOIR LANDS. Jour. Forestry 47:636-
639.

(37) HALIBURTON, W.
1943. SOME FACTORS IN THE ENVIRONMENTAL RE-
SISTANCE OF *Ips* DeGEER. Master's thesis,
Duke Univ. School Forestry. [Unpub-
lished.]

(38) HARRAR, J. G., and ELLIS, R. P.
1940. THE BIOLOGY OF A SPECIES OF *Beauvaria*
FROM THE SOUTHERN PINE BARK BEETLE.
Va. Acad. Sci. Proc. 1:211.

(39) HETRICK, L. A.
1940. SOME FACTORS IN NATURAL CONTROL OF THE
SOUTHERN PINE BEETLE, *Dendroctonus frontalis* ZIMM. Jour. Econ. Ent. 33:554-556.

(40) ————
1941. FOREST INSECT INVESTIGATIONS OF THE VIR-
GINIA AGRICULTURAL EXPERIMENT STATION.
Ent. Soc. Wash. Proc. 43:168.

(41) ————
1949. SOME OVERLOOKED RELATIONSHIPS OF
SOUTHERN PINE BEETLE. Jour. Econ. Ent.
42:466-469.

(42) ————
1949. SUSCEPTIBILITY OF PINE TREES TO BARK
BEETLE ATTACK. Arborist's News 14:149-
151.

(43) HOFFMAN, C. H., and ANDERSON, R. F.
1945. EFFECT OF SOUTHERN PINE BEETLE ON
TIMBER LOSSES AND NATURAL RESTOCKING.
Jour. Forestry 43:436-439.

(44) HOLST, E. C.
1936. *Zygosaccharomyces pini*, A NEW SPECIES
OF YEAST ASSOCIATED WITH BARK BEETLES
IN PINES. Jour. Agr. Res. 53:513-518, illus.

(45) ————
1937. ASEPTIC REARING OF BARK BEETLES. Jour.
Econ. Ent. 30:676-677.

(46) HOPKINS, A. D.
1891. REPORT OF ENTOMOLOGIST. Fourth Ann.
Rpt. W. Va. Agr. Expt. Sta., pp. 29-48.

(47) ————
1892. NOTES ON A DESTRUCTIVE FOREST TREE SCO-
LYTID. Sci. 20:64.

(48) ————
1893. DESTRUCTIVE SCOLYTIDS AND THEIR IMPORT-
ED ENEMY. Insect Life 6:123-130.

(49) ————
1893. CATALOGUE OF WEST VIRGINIA SCOLYTIDAE
AND THEIR ENEMIES WITH LIST OF TREES
AND SHRUBS ATTACKED. W. Va. Agr. Expt.
Sta. Bul. 31, pp. 121-168.

(50) ————
1893. CATALOGUE OF WEST VIRGINIA FOREST AND
SHADE TREE INSECTS. W. Va. Agr. Expt. Sta.
Bul. 32, pp. 171-251.

(51) ————
1896. SOME NOTES ON INSECT ENEMIES OF TREES.
Canad. Ent. 28:245-250.

(52) ————
1899. REPORT ON INVESTIGATIONS TO DETERMINE
THE CAUSE OF UNHEALTY CONDITIONS OF THE
SPRUCE AND PINE FROM 1880-1893. W. Va.
Agr. Expt. Sta. Bul. 56, 461 pp., illus.

(53) HOPKINS, A. D.
    1903. SOME OF THE PRINCIPAL INSECT ENEMIES OF
        CONIFEROUS FORESTS IN THE UNITED STATES.
        U. S. Dept. Agr. Yrbk. 1902, pp. 265-282,
        illus.

(54) ————
    1903. FOREST INSECT EXPLORATIONS IN THE SUM-
        MER OF 1902. Canad. Ent. 35:59-61.

(55) ————
    1909. PRACTICAL INFORMATION ON THE SCOLYTID
        BEETLES 'OF NORTH AMERICAN FORESTS. I.
        BARK BEETLES OF THE GENUS Dendroctonus.
        U. S. Dept. Agr. Bur. Ent. Bul. 83, pp.
        56-72, 146-153.

(56) ————
    1909. CONTRIBUTIONS TOWARD A MONOGRAPH OF
        THE SCOLYTID BEETLES. U. S. Dept. Agr.
        Bur. Ent. Tech. Ser. 17, Part 1, pp. 94-95,
        illus.

(57) ————
    1911. THE DYING OF PINE IN THE SOUTHERN
        STATES: CAUSE, EXTENT, AND REMEDY. U. S.
        Dept. Agr. Farmers' Bul. 476, 15 pp., illus.

(58) ————
    1921. THE SOUTHERN PINE BEETLE: A MENACE TO
        THE PINE TIMBER OF THE SOUTHERN STATES.
        U. S. Dept. Agr. Farmers' Bul. 1188, 15 pp.

(59) KNULL, J. W.
    1934. THE SOUTHERN PINE BEETLE IN PENNSYL-
        VANIA (Dendroctonus frontalis ZIMM.).
        Jour. Econ. Ent. 27:716-718.

(60) KOWAL, R. J., and COYNE, J. F.
    1951. THE BLACK TURPENTINE BEETLE CAN KILL
        TREES. AT-FA Jour. 13(9):7-8.

(61) LEE, R. E.
    1954. MUCH EAST TEXAS DAMAGE CAUSED BY
        FOREST INSECTS IN RECENT YEARS. Tex.
        Forest News 33(4):5-6.

(62) ————
    1955. A STUDY OF THE SOUTHERN PINE BEETLE IN
        EPIDEMIC STATUS. U. S. Forest Serv. South.
        Forest Expt. Sta., 33 pp. [Unpublished.]

(63) ————
    1955. INVESTIGATIONS OF Ips CONTROL IN FIRE-
        SCORCHED PINES. Office report. U. S.
        Forest Serv. South. Forest Expt. Sta. 7
        pp. [Unpublished.]

(64) ———— and COYNE, J. F.
    1955. SUGGESTED GUIDES FOR DETECTING THE
        BLACK TURPENTINE BEETLE. Tex. Forest
        News 34(6):4-5.

(65) ———— and SMITH, R. H.
    1955. THE BLACK TURPENTINE BEETLE, ITS HABITS
        AND CONTROL. U. S. Forest Serv. South.
        Forest Expt. Sta. Occas. Paper 138, 14 pp.,
        illus.

(66) MACANDREWS, A. H.
    1926. THE BIOLOGY OF THE SOUTHERN PINE BEETLE.
        Master's thesis, N. Y. State Col. Forestry.
        [Unpublished.]

(67) MASSEY, C. L.
    1957. FOUR NEW SPECIES OF Aphelenchulus (NE-
        MATODA) PARASITIC IN BARK BEETLES IN THE
        UNITED STATES. Helminthol Soc. Wash.
        Proc. 24:29-34, illus.

(68) MCCAMBRIDGE, W. F., and KOWAL, R. J.
    1957. FOREST INSECT CONDITIONS IN THE SOUTH-
        EAST DURING 1956. U. S. Forest Serv.
        Southeast. Forest Expt. Sta. Sta. Paper 76,
        7 pp., illus.

(69) MERKEL, E. P.
    1952. THE BLACK TURPENTINE BEETLE. NORTHEAST
        FLORIDA. U. S. Forest Serv. Southeast.
        Forest Expt. Sta., Asheville, N. C. [Un-
        published.]

(70) ————
    1954. SOUTHERN PINE BEETLE CONDITIONS ON THE
        CHEROKEE NATIONAL FOREST AND ADJOINING
        PRIVATE LANDS. U. S. Forest Serv. South-
        east. Forest Expt. Sta., Forest Pest Survey
        Rpt. 2, 4 pp.

(71) ————
    1956. RAINFALL DEFICIENCY AND BARK BEETLE EPI-
        DEMICS IN THE SOUTH. Assoc. South. Agr.
        Workers Proc. 53.

(72) ———— and KOWAL, R. J.
    1956. FOREST INSECT CONDITIONS IN THE SOUTH-
        EAST DURING 1955. U. S. Forest Serv.
        Southeast. Forest Expt. Sta. Sta. Paper 67,
        pp. 2-5.

(73) ———— and KULMAN, H. M.
    1955. SOUTHERN PINE BEETLE AND PINE ENGRAVER
        BEETLE CONDITIONS IN NORTH-CENTRAL
        SOUTH CAROLINA. U. S. Forest Serv. South-
        east. Forest Expt. Sta. Forest Insect Sur-
        vey Rpt. 4, 4 pp., illus.

(74) MILLER, J. M.
    1929. THE RELATION OF WINDFALLS TO BARK
        BEETLE EPIDEMICS. Fourth Internatl. Cong.
        Ent. Trans. 2:992-1002.

(75) MORRIS, R. C.
    1951. THE SOUTHERN PINE BEETLE IN EAST TEXAS.
        U. S. Dept. Agr. Bur. Ent. and Plant Quar.,
        Gulfport, Miss. [Unpublished.]

(76) MUESEBECK, C. F. W.
    1938. THE GENUS Dendrosoter WESMAEL IN THE
        UNITED STATES (Hymenoptera: Braconi-
        dae). Ent. Soc. Wash. Proc. 40:281-287,
        illus.

(77) NELSON, R. M.
    1934. EFFECT OF BLUESTAIN FUNGI IN SOUTHERN
        PINES ATTACKED BY BARK BEETLES Phyto-
        path. Ztschr. 7:327-353.

23

(78) NELSON, R. M., and BEAL, J. A.
   1929. EXPERIMENTS WITH BLUESTAIN FUNGI IN SOUTHERN PINES. Phytopath. 19:1101-1102, 1105-1106.

(79) OSGOOD, E. A.
   1958. THE SOUTHERN PINE BEETLES: A REVIEW OF PRESENT KNOWLEDGE. U. S. Forest Serv. Southeast. Forest Expt. Sta., Asheville, N. C., 24 pp. [Unpublished.]

(80) ————
   1958. A STUDY OF SITE AND STAND CONDITIONS OF SOUTHERN PINE BEETLE INFESTATIONS. U. S. Forest Serv. Southeast. Forest Expt. Sta., Asheville, N. C., 5 pp. [Unpublished.]

(81) ————
   1958. MORTALITY OF THE SOUTHERN PINE BEETLE DUE TO LOW TEMPERATURE IN THE SOUTHERN APPALACHIANS. U. S. Forest Serv. Southeast. Forest Expt. Sta., Asheville, N. C., 13 pp. [Unpublished.]

(82) ———— and CARTER, W. A.
   1958. TECHNIQUES USED IN THE PRELIMINARY ATTEMPTS TO REAR THE SOUTHERN PINE BEETLE, Dendroctonus frontalis ZIMM. U. S. Forest Serv. Southeast. Forest Expt. Sta., Asheville, N. C., 10 pp. [Unpublished.]

(83) RUMBOLD, C. T.
   1929. BLUE-STAINING FUNGI FOUND IN THE UNITED STATES. Phytopath. 19:597-599.

(84) ————
   1931. TWO BLUE-STAINING FUNGI ASSOCIATED WITH BARK-BEETLE INFESTATION OF PINES. Jour. Agr. Res. 43:847-873, illus.

(85) ST. GEORGE, R. A.
   1925. THE RECENT DEATH OF LARGE QUANTITIES OF SOUTHERN PINE. Amer. Lumberman 2607: 50-51.

(86) ————
   1926. PROGRESS REPORT ON TRAP TREE EXPERIMENTS. U. S. Dept. Agr. Bur. Ent. and Plant Quar., Asheville, N. C., 12 pp. [Unpublished.]

(87) ————
   1930. DROUGHT-AFFECTED AND INJURED TREES ATTRACTIVE TO BARK BEETLES. Jour. Econ. Ent. 23:825-828.

(88) ————
   1931. AN INSTANCE OF NATURAL CONTROL OF THE SOUTHERN PINE BEETLE. U. S. Forest Serv. Forest Worker 7(6):16-17.

(89) ————
   1932. PROGRESS REPORT ON EXPERIMENTS TO CONTROL THE SOUTHERN PINE BEETLE UNDER SHADE TREE CONDITIONS. U. S. Dept. Agr. Bur. Ent. and Plant Quar., Asheville, N. C., 11 pp. [Unpublished.]

(90) ST. GEORGE, R. A., and BEAL, J. A.
   1926. SOUTHERN PINE BEETLE STUDIES — 1926. U. S. Dept. Agr. Bur. Ent. and Plant Quar., Asheville, N. C. [Unpublished.]

(91) ———— and BEAL, J. A.
   1927. PROGRESS REPORT ON STUDIES ON THE SOUTHERN PINE BEETLE (Dendroctonus frontalis ZIMM.)—1927. U. S. Dept. Agr. Bur. Ent. and Plant Quar., Asheville, N. C., 40 pp. [Unpublished.]

(92) ———— and BEAL, J. A.
   1929. THE SOUTHERN PINE BEETLE: A SERIOUS ENEMY OF PINES IN THE SOUTH. U. S. Dept. Agr. Farmers' Bul. 1586, 18 pp., illus.

(93) ———— and CRAIGHEAD, F. C.
   1930. A NEW TECHNIQUE IN TREE MEDICATION FOR THE CONTROL OF BARK BEETLES. Sci. 72 (1869):433-435.

(94) ———— and HUCKENPAHLER, B. J.
   1934. DISTRIBUTION OF MOISTURE IN PINES. Jour. Forestry 32:885.

(95) SALMAN, K. A.
   1938. RECENT EXPERIMENTS WITH PENETRATING OIL SPRAYS FOR THE CONTROL OF BARK BEETLES Jour. Econ. Ent. 31:118-123.

(96) SMITH, R. H.
   1954. BENZENE HEXACHLORIDE CONTROLS BLACK TURPENTINE BEETLE. South. Lumberman 189(2369):155-157.

(97) ————
   1955. CONTROL OF THE BLACK TURPENTINE BEETLE (Dendroctonus terebrans) WITH A BENZENE HEXACHLORIDE (BHC) POST-ATTACK SPRAY. Assoc. South. Agr. Workers Proc. 52:99-100.

(98) ————
   1956. STUDIES OF THE BLACK TURPENTINE BEETLE (Dendroctonus terebrans Oliv.) IN 1952-1955. U. S. Forest Serv. Southeast. For. Expt. Sta. Asheville, N. C., 77 pp., illus. [Unpublished.]

(99) ————
   1956. DEATH OF A PINE. Forest Farmer 15(12):7, illus.

(100) ————
   1957. HABITS OF ATTACK BY THE BLACK TURPENTINE BEETLE ON SLASH AND LONGLEAF PINE IN NORTH FLORIDA. Jour. Econ. Ent. 50: 241-244, illus.

(101) ————
   1958. CONTROL OF THE TURPENTINE BEETLE IN NAVAL STORES STANDS BY SPRAYING ATTACKED TREES WITH BENZENE HEXACHLORIDE. Jour. Forestry 56:190-194, illus.

24

(102) SMITH, R. H., and LEE, R. E.
    1957. BLACK TURPENTINE BEETLE. U. S. Dept.
    Agr. Forest Serv. Forest Pest Leaflet 12,
    7 pp., illus.

(103) SMITH, V. K.
    1954. SUMMARY OF ATTEMPTS TO REAR *Dendroc-tonus frontalis* DURING THE SUMMER OF
    1954. Master's research project, Miss.
    State Col. [Unpublished.]

(104) SNYDER, T. E.
    1935. THE *Ips* ENGRAVER BEETLES IN THE SOUTH.
    Naval Stores Rev. 45(32):15.

(105) ———
    1936. BARK BEETLES IN RELATION TO SELECTIVE
    LOGGING. Naval Stores Rev. 46(27):19.

(106) SOUTHEASTERN FOREST EXPERIMENT STATION.
    1946. ANNIVERSARY REPORT 1921-1946. U. S.
    Forest Serv. P. 32.

(107) ———
    1958. Southeastern Forest Insect and Disease
    Newsletter No. 5. U. S. Forest Serv. Pp.
    1-2.

(108) ———
    1958. Southeastern Forest Insect and Disease
    Newsletter No. 6. U. S. Forest Serv. P. 2.

(109) SOUTHERN FOREST EXPERIMENT STATION.
    1953. FOREST INSECT CONDITIONS—ALABAMA, AR-
    KANSAS, LOUISIANA, MISSISSIPPI, OKLAHOMA,
    TEXAS. U. S. Forest Serv., Gulfport. 4 pp.

(110) ———
    1955. SUMMARY OF INSECT CONDITIONS IN 1954.
    Southern Forest Pest Reporter 6, 5 pp.
    U. S. Forest Serv., New Orleans.

(111) ———
    1955. Southern Forest Pest Reporter 8, 5 pp.
    U. S. Forest Serv.

(112) ———
    1955. GENERAL SUMMARY OF INSECT CONDITIONS
    IN 1955. Southern Forest Pest Reporter 9,
    8 pp. U. S. Forest Serv.

(113) ———
    1956. Southern Forest Pest Reporter 11, 7 pp.
    U. S. Forest Serv.

(114) ———
    1956. Southern Forest Pest Reporter 12, 6 pp.
    U. S. Forest Serv.

(115) ———
    1956. Southern Forest Pest Reporter 13, 5 pp.
    U. S. Forest Serv.

(116) ———
    1957. Southern Forest Pest Reporter 15, 7 pp.
    U. S. Forest Serv.

(117) ———
    1957. Southern Forest Pest Reporter 16, 7 pp.
    U. S. Forest Serv.

(118) ———
    1958. SUMMARY OF MIDSOUTH PEST CONDITIONS
    IN 1957. Southern Forest Pest Reporter
    20, 10 pp. U. S. Forest Serv.

(119) ———
    1958. Southern Forest Pest Reporter 22, 8 pp.
    U. S. Forest Serv.

(120) ———
    1959. SUMMARY OF MIDSOUTH PEST CONDITIONS
    IN 1958. Southern Forest Pest Reporter
    25, 6 pp. U. S. Forest Serv.

(121) SPEERS, C. F.
    1956. RADIOISOTOPES IN FOREST INSECT STUDIES.
    Assoc. South. Agr. Workers Proc. 53:130.

(122) ———MERKEL, E. P., and EBEL, B.
    1955. TESTS OF INSECTICIDES FOR THE CONTROL OF
    THE SOUTHERN PINE BEETLE IN NORTH CARO-
    LINA. Assoc. South. Agr. Workers Proc.
    52:100.

(123) SWAINE, J. W.
    1925. THE FACTORS DETERMINING THE DISTRIBU-
    TION OF NORTH AMERICAN BARK BEETLES.
    Canad. Ent. 57:261-266.

(124) U. S. FOREST SERVICE.
    1958. TIMBER RESOURCES FOR AMERICA'S FUTURE.
    U. S. Dept. Agr. Forest Res. Rpt. 14, 713
    pp., illus.

(125) VERRALL, A. F.
    1941. DISSEMINATION OF FUNGI THAT STAIN LOGS
    AND LUMBER. Jour. Agr. Res. 63:549-558.

1960

OCCASIONAL
PAPER 180

SOUTHERN FOREST EXPERIMENT STATION
Philip A. Briegleb, Director
FOREST SERVICE
U. S. DEPARTMENT OF AGRICULTURE

FOMES ANNOSUS:

A BIBLIOGRAPHY
with
SUBJECT INDEX

JEROME W. KOENIGS

SOUTHERN FOREST EXPERIMENT STATION
PHILIP A. BRIEGLEB, DIRECTOR
Forest Service, U. S. Department of Agriculture

Fomes annosus: A Bibliography with Subject Index

Jerome W. Koenigs

SOUTHERN FOREST EXPERIMENT STATION

Fomes annosus (Fr.) Cke. has damaged many plantations and forests in Europe and Asia and threatens to become increasingly important in the United States as forest management intensifies. .A considerable literature has accumulated on the fungus and the disease it causes. To facilitate use of this literature a relatively complete bibliography, preceded by a subject index, is presented here. 1/

Some publications were cited from abstracts: these are identified with asterisks immediately before the titles. Sources of abstracts for these publications, as well as for some read in the original, are in parentheses following the citations. Chief abstract sources were Biological Abstracts (BA), the Boyce Index (BI), Forestry Abstracts (FA), and the Review of Applied Mycology (RAM). Regardless of source, all citations are in the bibliographic style of the U.S. Department of Agriculture.

Numbers following each division of the subject index denote numbered items in the bibliography. Contents of most entries in the bibliography are summarized by references to the subject index. For example, the symbol A1 following a citation indicates a discussion of Fomes annosus attacking species of the genus Pinus, B1 indicates a report of the fungus occurring in the United States, C1 indicates a description of the cultural characteristics of F. annosus.

Because of the difficulty of classifying information and the possible incompleteness of information obtained from abstracts, the list of reference numbers after any division of the subject index is unlikely to be all-inclusive. Articles of a general or speculative nature can seldom be classified precisely. Finally, occasional errors were doubtlessly introduced, particularly where the original literature was not obtained. The author hopes that these limitations will not seriously affect the usefulness of the bibliography and index.

1/ This paper was largely completed while the author was a Research Fellow at the College of Forestry, State University of New York, Syracuse, New York. The author wishes to thank Dr. R.A. Zabel, Chairman, Department of Forest Botany and Forest Pathology, for his continued interest and suggestions during the preparation of this publication.

3. British Isles: 15, 16, 18, 20, 22, 28, 29, 35, 51, 65, 77, 79, 107, 108, 109, 110, 111, 112, 113, 114, 115, 116, 117, 118, 119, 136, 141, 171, 189, 202, 206, 239, 253, 258, 260, 269, 270, 297, 301, 314, 340, 341, 342, 343, 344, 346, 348, 349, 381, 408, 409, 424, 425.

4. Germany: 78, 133, 141, 144, 161, 177, 194, 206, 233, 243, 244, 253, 276, 308, 310, 311, 336, 357, 372, 381, 402, 408, 426.

5. Scandinavian countries: 23, 24, 59, 65, 159, 164, 170, 192, 206, 212, 213, 214, 215, 218, 220, 222, 238, 246, 251, 253, 274, 275, 283, 291, 306, 318, 324, 325, 326, 328, 329, 330, 355, 358, 359, 381, 391, 431, 432.

6. Other European countries: 5, 7, 9, 11, 12, 27, 30, 57, 61, 69, 75, 76, 93, 121, 122, 140, 151, 156, 160, 166, 167, 201, 206, 208, 211, 221, 225, 226, 227, 234, 235, 248, 263, 264, 273, 280, 282, 290, 294, 307, 309, 362, 378, 381, 389, 404, 406, 435.

7. Other countries of the world: 8, 10, 26, 31, 34, 37, 83, 84, 90, 91, 190, 191, 205, 223, 229, 365, 366, 390, 433, 434.

C. The fungus in culture (including growth on media, wood, soil)
   1. Cultural characteristics: 35, 46, 74, 89, 90, 129, 130, 149, 160, 189, 200, 262, 264, 285, 358.

   2. Effect of chemical factors:
      a. Nutrients: 41, 43, 50, 72, 81, 106, 148, 149, 150, 194, 209, 212, 232, 286, 287, 288, 322, 325, 397, 437.

      b. Toxicants: 40, 41, 42, 120, 123, 129, 137, 138, 139, 153, 154, 224, 287, 289, 301, 302, 315, 319, 321, 323, 328, 331, 334, 361, 370, 410, 416, 428.

      c. pH: 41, 90, 130, 163, 212, 261, 304, 328, 332, 354, 392, 396, 397, 416.

      d. Other: 41, 72, 126, 127, 148, 150, 212, 222, 224, 274, 283, 287, 303, 322, 325, 326, 329, 332, 340, 341, 387, 396, 397, 408, 437.

   3. Effects of physical factors:
      a. Temperature: 41, 88, 90, 130, 150, 204, 209, 223, 224, 242, 292, 332, 340, 341, 343, 358, 392, 408.

      b. Moisture content, relative humidity, miscellaneous: 44, 150, 163, 194, 232, 241, 283, 320, 343, 437.

   4. Physiological products: 49, 149, 154, 209, 247, 272, 286, 287, 288, 304, 316, 332, 422, 423, 437.

   5. Effect of the fungus on wood and wood products:
      a. On physical properties: 36, 59, 90, 130, 135, 152, 160, 222, 260, 301, 302, 320, 321, 386, 405, 438.

      b. On chemical properties: 59, 90, 132, 133, 134, 135, 152, 252, 267, 287, 385.

c. On anatomical properties: 198, 263, 292, 313, 438.

d. On other properties: 59, 87, 90, 222, 326, 385, 411.

6. Production of sporophores in culture: 36, 90, 189, 232, 242, 358.

7. Nomenclature:
   a. Synonyms: 7, 13, 31, 35, 36, 45, 74, 243, 256, 263, 292, 296, 378, 391, 394, 395, 407, 427.

   b. Madison 517[2/]: 86, 96, 97, 98, 99, 100, 101, 105, 180, 181, 204, 259, 335, 337, 338, 339, 356, 371, 410.

8. Detection of F. annosus: 165, 184, 189, 222, 313, 324, 326, 353, 358, 431.

D. Fungus in nature
   1. Sporophore description: 22, 45, 67, 68, 89, 90, 124, 146, 189, 199, 216, 231, 249, 254, 255, 256, 263, 296, 377, 380.

   2. Location of sporophores: 22, 37, 67, 68, 70, 85, 123, 136, 142, 197, 218, 238, 245, 253, 264, 268, 270, 272, 280, 296, 317, 358, 379, 407, 414, 418, 426.

   3. Attack on forest products:
      a. Mine props: 45, 79, 90, 159, 171, 203, 273, 296, 301, 307, 364.

      b. Pulp: 145, 152.

      c. Other: 38, 90, 241, 263, 296.

   4. Role as a forest saprophyte: 4, 22, 28, 34, 45, 66, 69, 72, 80, 81, 85, 127, 133, 142, 158, 238, 253, 264, 296, 298, 307, 324, 407, 414, 417, 436.

   5. Conidial production: 35, 36, 69, 124, 127, 199, 218, 238, 253, 280, 408.

   6. F. annosus, general: 7, 17, 21, 22, 23, 28, 29, 47, 64, 69, 70, 90, 107, 119, 194, 199, 206, 214, 216, 231, 253, 297, 317, 324, 325, 329, 330, 380, 408.

E. Disease in trees and in stands
   1. Points of entry into host:
      a. Roots, general: 55, 73, 82, 112, 123, 127, 133, 142, 158, 168, 251, 253, 275, 317, 329, 340, 365, 408.

      b. Root grafts or root contacts: 13, 15, 16, 22, 70, 72, 194, 201, 206, 237, 253, 268, 274, 292, 329, 336, 343, 346, 348, 380, 407, 426.

      c. Dead roots: 30, 37, 59, 69, 90, 141, 186, 189, 194, 212, 213, 218, 238, 275, 283, 284, 324, 344, 380, 425, 426.

[2/] This category includes references concerning a culture initially believed to be Fomes annosus but later proven to be Polyporus tulipiferus. (See Darley and Christensen, 1945.)

- 4 -

d. Live roots--injured: 22, 28, 61, 90, 113, 189, 194, 201, 233, 237, 238, 266, 380, 404, 407, 425, 426, 433.

e. Live roots--uninjured: 113, 161, 194, 275, 292, 340, 408, 426.

f. Stumps: 13, 15, 16, 18, 19, 22, 29, 34, 186, 253, 292, 329, 341, 343, 349, 406, 408, 409, 431.

g. Trunk wounds: 22, 55, 73, 82, 118, 127, 128, 133, 142, 237, 253, 317, 333, 349, 404, 429, 430, 433.

h. Sunscald injuries and broken tops: 333, 414, 429, 430.

i. Inoculation: 8, 10, 13, 212, 275, 336, 343, 344, 358, 399, 408.

j. Fence posts: 22, 164, 206, 215, 253.

k. Soil: 58, 186, 283, 380, 435.

2. Means of spread--also see points of entry, e.g., root contacts:
a. Spores: 22, 28, 60, 69, 70, 72, 123, 133, 194, 201, 206, 207, 233, 238, 253, 268, 269, 270, 340, 343, 344, 345, 346, 349, 350, 351, 353, 380.

b. Rhizomorphs: 69, 127.

c. Mycelial strands: 28, 69, 272, 317, 341, 374, 380.

3. Symptoms:
a. Gross tree symptoms:
(1) Needles: 13, 26, 210, 341, 343, 407.

(2) Crown: 13, 26, 144, 210, 308, 311, 336 343, 379.

(3) Stem: 7, 13, 26, 29, 31, 67, 68, 144, 185, 201, 233, 248, 268, 292, 296, 308, 357, 380, 407.

(4) Roots: 13, 20, 26, 37, 47, 85, 110, 124, 197, 201, 233, 245, 248, 292, 336, 341, 342, 343, 360, 374, 393, 407, 418.

(5) Other: 63, 70, 125, 133, 167, 184, 210, 218, 279, 292, 308, 336, 374, 380, 407.

(6) Absence of symptoms: 54, 201, 221, 260, 407.

b. Description of rot:
(1) Incipient: 22, 67, 69, 70, 90, 124, 127, 189, 198, 199, 268, 296, 317, 405, 414, 430.

(2) Advanced: 22, 67, 68, 69, 70, 90, 124, 127, 186, 189, 197, 198, 199, 268, 296, 317, 342, 380, 391, 407, 414, 430.

c. Degree of infection before symptoms appear: 144, 201, 218, 346.

d. Symptoms in stand:
    (1) Circular patches of dying trees: 7, 9, 15, 29, 54, 70, 194, 216, 233, 336, 407.

    (2) Windthrown trees: 22, 24, 45, 53, 70, 85, 168, 189, 197, 208, 221, 253, 305, 311, 344, 380, 418, 419, 434.

    (3) Other: 229.

4. Seriousness of F. annosus attack:
  a. Extent of rot in tree: 5, 22, 55, 67, 68, 80, 82, 123, 125, 127, 142, 169, 201, 212, 253, 282, 306, 308, 324, 333, 336, 366, 391, 408, 435.

  b. Intensity of infection in stand: 5, 12, 22, 24, 55, 56, 59, 61, 68, 70, 80, 82, 91, 125, 127, 140, 142, 143, 144, 151, 156, 161, 170, 185, 197, 201, 206, 208, 210, 211, 218, 221, 223, 253, 276, 282, 290, 309, 318, 324, 326, 347, 349, 365, 366, 391, 408, 430, 434, 435.

  c. Economic loss: 21, 22, 55, 56, 123, 133, 142, 143, 192, 201, 212, 231, 246, 253, 283, 306, 318, 328, 330, 359, 362, 430.

  d. Rate of spread: 212, 238, 253, 292, 326, 344, 349, 379.

5. Soil factors affecting F. annosus attack:
  a. Chemical nature of soil: 7, 15, 16, 22, 25, 28, 29, 93, 110, 111, 123, 141, 179, 194, 206, 210, 213, 251, 253, 276, 291, 324, 325, 329, 336, 340, 341, 342, 343, 344, 349, 407, 418.

  b. Physical and structural nature of soil: 20, 22, 25, 30, 70, 71, 93, 110, 111, 112, 115, 116, 140, 141, 191, 194, 206, 212, 233, 239, 253, 260, 266, 275, 276, 279, 310, 324, 325, 329, 362, 380, 399, 407, 408, 409.

  c. Drainage or moisture relations of soil: 12, 18, 26, 29, 30, 31, 34, 108, 110, 112, 113, 114, 115, 116, 117, 125, 127, 136, 141, 191, 194, 201, 206, 229, 237, 251, 266, 291, 308, 310, 311, 325, 326, 329, 362, 391, 418.

  d. Soil aeration: 37, 114, 117, 191, 194, 237, 362.

  e. Soil, general: 21, 28, 107, 111, 119, 133, 151, 201, 292, 324, 358, 372, 421.

6. Effect of site, site quality, host range, and geographical location: 22, 34, 37, 91, 107, 117, 127, 151, 186, 206, 220, 229, 253, 298, 309, 324, 329, 358, 407.

7. Effect of climate: 21, 22, 26, 185, 253, 298, 309, 336, 355, 358.

8. Effect of aspect, slope, or elevation: 12, 34, 37, 91, 116, 133, 201, 251, 309.

3. F. annosus and fungus competition:
   a. In soil: 58, 189, 274, 284, 329, 343, 344, 396.

   b. On cultural media: 126, 283, 284, 327, 332, 340, 341, 422, 423.

   c. On stump surfaces: 22, 157, 269, 270, 343, 346, 347, 352.

4. F. annosus and insects: 35, 70, 125, 144, 167, 218, 245, 340, 343, 344, 425, 435.

G. Control
   1. Chemical methods (includes creosoting, painting): 19, 22, 34, 37, 70, 145, 153, 157, 166, 189, 201, 203, 205, 206, 212, 213, 253, 270, 295, 299, 343, 347, 352.

   2. Physical methods (stump extraction, soil trenching, etc.): 7, 22, 26, 28, 158, 166, 189, 201, 206, 234, 299, 336, 343, 346, 406, 408.

   3. Biological methods: 58, 157, 283, 284, 346, 408.

   4. Planting on correct site or in natural range: 22, 28, 29, 30, 34, 37, 107, 191, 357.

   5. Planting trees in mixed stands: 5, 12, 22, 24, 26, 29, 30, 37, 71, 140, 189, 191, 201, 212, 221, 230, 233, 234, 275, 305, 310, 311, 324, 336, 346, 358, 380, 408, 421.

   6. Thinning: 22, 28, 71, 168, 212, 221, 266, 345, 380.

   7. Other: 7, 22, 29, 34, 71, 93, 107, 144, 189, 201, 203, 212, 218, 221, 230, 233, 234, 266, 275, 311, 346, 357, 359, 362, 366, 380, 388, 416, 421.

   8. General: 21, 64, 72, 76, 231, 264, 325.

BIBLIOGRAPHY

1. Anonymous.
   1887.*ÜBER BESCHÄDIGUNGEN DURCH PILZE IM WALDE. Forstwiss. Centbl. 9: 379. (BI)

2. _____
   1901.*LE POURRITURE ROUGE. Jour. Forest. Suisse 52: 68-70. (BI)

3. _____
   1910.*CHARACTER, EXTENT AND MANUFACTURE OF THE WHITE CEDAR OF NEW JERSEY. Amer. Lumberman 1851: 40-41. (BI) A6.

4. _____
   1911. USE OF WHITE CEDAR AND ENEMIES. Forestry Quart. 9: 149. (BI) (Abs. from Amer. Lumberman No. 1851, pp. 40-41. Nov. 12, 1910.) A6, B1, D4.

5. _____
   1924.*LA POURRITURE ROUGE DE L'EPICÉA EN BELGIQUE. [THE RED ROT OF FIR IN BELGIUM.] Soc. Cent. Forest. de Belg. Bul. 31: 653-657. (Bot. Abs. 15: 1111.) A2, B6, E4a, b, G5.

6. _____
   1928.* MASSENSTERBEN DER KIEFERNKULTUR. Deut. Forst. Ztg. 43: 230-231. (BI) A1.

7. _____
   1930.*CHRONIQUE FORESTIÈRE. LA MALADIE DU ROND. [FORESTRY NOTES. THE RING DISEASE.] Soc. Cent. Forest. de Belg. Bul. 37: 522-526. (RAM 10: 355.) A1,2,3,4,7, B6, C7a, D6, E3a(3), d(1), 5a, 10a, 13b, 16a,b, G2,7.

8. _____
   1936.* FOREST RESEARCH IN INDIA, 1935-36. Part I. Forest Res. Inst. and Col., Dehra Dun. 91 pp. (RAM 16: 146.) A1,6, B7, E1i.

9. _____
   1936.* OBSERVATIONS EN MATIÈRE FORESTIÈRE EN 1934. [OBSERVATIONS ON FOREST MATTERS IN 1934.] Soc. Cent. Forest. de Belg. Bul. 43: 23-31. (RAM 15: 473.) B6, E3d(1), F1.

10. _____
    1937.* FOREST RESEARCH IN INDIA, 1936-37. Part I. Forest Res. Inst. and Col., Dehra Dun. 92 pp. (RAM 17: 278.) A6, B7, E1i.

11. _____
    1937.*PĀRSKATS PAR KAITĒKLU UN SLIMĪBU IZPLATĪBU LATVIJAS VALSTSMEŽOS 1935/36 G. [A SUMMARY OF THE INCIDENCE OF TREE PESTS AND DISEASES IN THE SILVICULTURAL PROPERTIES OF LATVIA IN 1935-36.] Reprinted from Latv. Mežu Statist. [Statist. Forest.] 9, 11 pp. (RAM 17: 214.) A1,2, B6.

12. _____
    1939.*FRÉQUENCE DU CHAMPIGNON PROVOQUANT LA POURRITURE 'ROUGE TENDRE' DU SAPIN DANS LE CANTON DE RHODES EXTÉRIEURES. [INCIDENCE OF THE FUNGUS CAUSING 'PALE RED' ROT OF FIRS IN THE CANTON OF OUTER RHODES.] Jour. Forest. Suisse 90: 15-16. (RAM 18: 357.) A4, B6, E4b, 5c, 8, 10a, 16a, G5.

13. _____
    1942. ROOT DISEASE OF PINE SAPLINGS. Amer. Nurseryman 76(9): 22-23. (FA 4: 247.) A1, B1, C7a, E1b,f,i, 3a(1),(2),(3),(4), 10b, 13b.

14. _____
    1942.*TWENTY-FIRST ANNUAL REPORT OF THE CANADIAN PLANT DISEASE SURVEY 1941. Canada Dept. Agr., Div. Bot. and Plant Path., 102 pp. (FA 4: 246-247.) A5,6, B2.

15. _____
    1948.*FOMES ANNOSUS INFECTION OF PINE IN EAST ANGLIA. Gt. Brit. Forestry Comn. Rpt. 1947: 39. (FA 10: 2239.) A1, B3, E1b,f, 3d(1), 5a.

16. _____
    1948.* TWENTY-EIGHTH ANNUAL REPORT OF THE FORESTRY COMMISSIONERS FOR THE YEAR ENDING SEPTEMBER 30TH, 1947. Gt. Brit. Forestry Commrs. Ann. Rpt., 68 pp. (RAM 27: 591.) A1, B3, E1b,f, 5a, 12.

17. _____
    1950. THIRTIETH ANNUAL REPORT OF THE FORESTRY COMMISSIONERS FOR THE YEAR ENDING SEPTEMBER 30TH, 1949. Gt. Brit. Forestry Commrs. Ann. Rpt., 148 pp. (RAM 30: 203.) D6.

18. _____
    1951. REPORT ON FOREST RESEARCH FOR THE YEAR ENDING MARCH, 1950. Gt. Brit., 126 pp. (RAM 30: 590-591.) A6, B3, E1f, 5c.

19. Anonymous.
1951. THIRTY-FIRST ANNUAL REPORT OF
THE FORESTRY COMMISSIONERS FOR THE
YEAR ENDING SEPTEMBER 30TH, 1950.
Gt. Brit. Forestry Commrs. Ann.
Rpt., 75 pp. (RAM 30: 552.) E1f,
G1.

20. _____
1956.* THIRTY-FIRST ANNUAL REPORT OF
THE IMPERIAL FORESTRY INSTITUTE,
1954-5. Oxford Univ., 32 pp. (RAM
35: 643.) A5, B3, E3a(4), 5b, 11b.

21. _____
1957.* [FOMES ANNOSUS.] Norsk.
Skogbr. 3(23/24): 623...632. (FA
19: 1942.) D6, E4c, 5e, 7, G8.

22. _____
1957. FOMES ANNOSUS: A FUNGUS CAUS-
ING BUTT ROT AND DEATH OF CONI-
FERS. (Previous versions published
in 1921, 1925, 1933, 1946, and
1948.) Gt. Brit. Forestry Comm.
Leaflet 5, 10 pp. A1,2,3,4,5,6,7,
B3, D1,2,4,6, E1b,d,f,g,j, 2a,
3b(1),(2), d(2), 4a,b,c, 5a,b, 6,
7,9, 10a,b,c, 12, 13a, 14, F3c,
G1,2,4,5,6,7.

23. _____
1959.* [ROT IN NORWAY SPRUCE.] Dansk
Skovfor. Tidsskr. 44: 78-125. (FA
20: 4780.) A2, B5, D6.

24. Abell, J.
1938.* BØG EFTER RØDGRAN. NOGLE
IAGTTAGELSER PAA HVIDKILDE SKOV-
DISTRIKT. [BEECH SUCCEEDING NORWAY
SPRUCE. SOME OBSERVATIONS ON
HVIDKILDE FOREST DISTRICT.] Dansk
Skovfor. Tidsskr. 23: 11-16. (BA
14: 7485.) A2, B5, E3d(2), 4b, G5.

25. _____
1940.* RØDGRAN PAA HVIDKILDE. EN SAM-
MENLIGNING MELLEM TILVAEKSTOVER-
SIGT OG BOGFØRT MASSE. [NORWAY
SPRUCE AT HVIDKILDE. A COMPARISON
OF INCREMENT TABLES WITH RECORDED
VOLUME.] Dansk Skovfor. Tidsskr.
25: 617-633. (FA 8: 745.) E5a,b,
10a.

26. Aggarwal, K.L.
1933. FOMES ANNOSUS ON DEODAR.
Indian Forester 59: 239-242. (RAM
12: 605-606.) A6, B7, E3a(1),(2),
(3),(4), 5c, 7, 10a, 16a, G2, 5.

27. Am. C.
1926.* LA POURRITURE ROUGE DE
L'ÉPICÉA EN BELGIQUE. Soc. Cent.
Forest. de Belg. Bul. 29: 263.
(BI) B6.

28. Anderson, M.L.
1921. SOIL CONDITIONS AFFECTING THE
PREVALENCE OF FOMES ANNOSUS
(TRAMETES RADICIPERDA). Roy. Scot.
Arbor. Soc. Trans. 35: 112-117.
(RAM 1: 402-404.) A1,5, B3, D4,6,
E1d, 2a,c, 5a,e, 10c, 13a, 14,
G2,4,6.

29. _____
1924. HEART ROT IN CONIFERS. Roy.
Scot. Arbor. Soc. Trans. 38: 37-45.
(RAM 3: 494-495.) A1,3,5, B3, D6,
E1f, 3a(3), d(1), 5a,c, 10a, 13a,
14, 16a, G4,5,7.

30. Ankudinov, A.M.
1950.* USYHANIE SOSNOVYH KULJTUR NA
STARYH PAŠNJAH. [DEATH OF PINE
PLANTATIONS ON FORMER ARABLE
LAND.] Lesn. Hoz. 3(9): 46-49. (FA
13: 3096.) A1, B6, E1c, 5b,c, 10a,
b, 13a, 16a, G4,5.

31. Aoshima, K.
1952.* [BUTT-ROT OF ABIES MARIESII AND
A. VEITCHII CAUSED BY TYROMYCES
BALSAMEUS AND FOMITOPSIS ANNOSA.]
Jap. Forestry Soc. Jour. 34: 305-
307. (RAM 33: 391.) A4, B7, C7a,
E3a(3), 5c.

32. Arvidson, B.
1954.* EN STUDIE AV GRANROTRÖTANS
(POLYPORUS ANNOSUS FR.) EKONOMISKA
KONSEKVENSER. Svenska Skogsvårds-
för. Tidskr. 52: 381-412. (From
Low and Gladman, 1960.)

33. Aytoun, R.S.C.
1953. THE GENUS TRICHODERMA: ITS
RELATIONSHIP WITH ARMILLARIA
MELLEA (VAHL. EX FRIES) QUEL. AND
POLYPORUS SCHWEINITZII FR., TO-
GETHER WITH PRELIMINARY OBSERV-
ATIONS ON ITS ECOLOGY IN WOODLAND
SOILS. Bot. Soc. Edinb. Trans. and
Proc. 36, (Part II): 99-114. (RAM
32: 497-498.) F2.

34. Bagchee, K.
1952. A REVIEW OF WORK ON INDIAN
TREE DISEASES AND DECAY OF TIMBER
AND METHODS OF CONTROL. Indian
Forester 78: 540-546. (RAM 32:
158.) A6, B7, D4, E1f, 5c, 6, 8,
12, 15, G1, 4, 7.

35. Bakshi, B.K.
1950. FUNGI ASSOCIATED WITH AMBROSIA BEETLES IN GREAT BRITAIN. Brit. Mycol. Soc. Trans. 33: 111-120. A3, B3, C1, 7a, D5, F2, 4.

36. ⸻
1952. OEDOCEPHALUM LINEATUM IS A CONIDIAL STAGE OF FOMES ANNOSUS. Brit. Mycol. Soc. Trans. 35: 195. (RAM 32: 341.) C5a, 6, 7a, D5.

37. ⸻
1955. DISEASES AND DECAYS OF CONIFERS IN THE HIMALAYAS. Indian Forester 81: 779-797. (RAM 35: 405-406.) A6, B7, D2, E1c, 3a(4), 5d, 6, 8, G1,4,5.

38. Ballman, D.K., and Smith, F.B.
1943. FUNGICIDES AND GERMICIDES IN THE PULP AND PAPER INDUSTRY. Paper Indus. 25: 143-148. (RAM 22: 413-414.) D3c.

39. Baraban.
1881.*RECHERCHES DES CAUSES DE DÉPÉRISSEMENT DES PINS MARITIMES DANS CERTAINES DUNES DE LA VENDÉE. MALADIE DU ROND. Rev. des Eaux et Forêts 20: 72-79. (BI)

40. Barr, H.T.
1930. LABORATORY STUDIES ON TOXIC CHEMICAL CONTROL OF WOOD DESTROYING FUNGI. Agr. Engin. 11: 161-163. (RAM 9: 692-693.) C2b.

41. Bateman, E.
1929. STUDIES IN TOXICITY. (Abstract.) Amer. Jour. Bot. 16: 845-846. (BI) C2a,b,c,d, 3a,

42. ⸻ and Baechler, R.
1927. THEORY OF THE MECHANISM OF PROTECTION OF WOOD BY PRESERVATIVE. Part VII: SOME EXPERIMENTS ON THE TOXICITY OF INORGANIC SALTS. Amer. Wood Preservers' Assoc. Proc. 1927: 41-48. (RAM 6: 707-708.) C2b.

43. Bavendamm, W.
1928.*NEUE UNTERSUCHUNGEN ÜBER DIE LEBENSBEDINGUNGEN HOLZZERSTÖRENDER PILZE. EIN BEITRAG ZUR FRAGE DER KRANKHEITSEMPFÄNGLICHKEIT UNSERER HOLZPFLANZEN. II. MITTEILUNG: GERBSTOFFVERSUCHE. [NEW INVESTIGATIONS OF THE CONDITIONS GOVERNING THE EXISTENCE OF WOOD-DESTROYING FUNGI. A CONTRIBUTION TO THE PROBLEM OF THE SUSCEPTIBILITY TO DISEASE OF OUR WOODY PLANTS. NOTE II: TANNIN EXPERIMENTS.] Zentbl. f. Bakt., Abt. 2, 76(8-14): 172-227. (RAM 8: 281.) C2a.

44. ⸻ and Reichelt, H.
1938.*DIE ABHÄNGIGKEIT DES WACHSTUMS HOLZZERSETZENDER PILZE VOM WASSERGEHALT DES NÄHRSUBSTRATES. [THE DEPENDENCE OF THE GROWTH OF WOOD-DECOMPOSING FUNGI ON THE WATER CONTENT OF THE NUTRIENT MEDIUM.] Arch. f. Mikrobiol. 9: 486-544. (RAM 18: 360.) C3b.

45. Baxter, D.V.
1940. SOME RESUPINATE POLYPORES OF THE REGION OF THE GREAT LAKES. XII. Mich. Acad. Sci., Arts, and Letters Papers 26: 107-121. C7a, D1, 3a, 4, E3d(2).

46. ⸻
1943. SOME RESUPINATE POLYPORES FROM THE REGION OF THE GREAT LAKES. XV. Mich. Acad. Sci., Arts, and Letters Papers 29: 85-109. C1.

47. ⸻
1952. PATHOLOGY IN FOREST PRACTICE. John Wiley and Sons, Inc., New York. 601 pp. A1,6, B1,2, D6, E3a(4).

48. ⸻
1953.*RELATION OF CULTURAL PRACTICES TO DISEASE IN AMERICAN FOREST PLANTATION. In Proceedings of the Seventh International Botanical Congress, Stockholm 1950. Chronica Botanica Co., Waltham, Mass., pp. 319-320. (RAM 35: 84.) E16a.

49. Bazzigher, G.
1957.*TANNIN- UND PHENOLSPALTENDE FERMENTE DREIER PARASITISCHER PILZE. [TANNIN- AND PHENOL-SPLITTING ENZYMES OF THREE PARASITIC FUNGI.] Phytopath. Ztschr. 29: 299-304. (RAM 36: 796.) A2, C4.

50. ⸻
1958.*WUCHSSTOFFBEDARF ZWEIER PHYTOPATHOGENER PILZE. [THE GROWTH-SUBSTANCE-REQUIREMENTS OF TWO PHYTOPATHOGENIC FUNGI.] Phytopath. Ztschr. 32: 352-358. (FA 21: 634.) C2a.

51. Beaumont, A.
1954.*DISEASES OF RHODODENDRON. Gard. Chron. Ser. 3, 136(3522): 15. (RAM 33: 605.) A7, B3.

52. Beliaev, I.A.
1939.*KORNEVAIA GUBKA I MERY BORBY
S NEIU. [ROOT FUNGUS AND MEASURES
TO COMBAT IT.] Lesnoe Khoziaistvo
6: 57-61. (BI)

53. Bertog, H.
1929.*STURMSICHERHEIT D.R.P. 435552.
Deut. Forst. Ztg. 44: 70. (BI)
E3d(2).

54. Bier, J.E.
1942. FOREST PATHOLOGY IN BRITISH
COLUMBIA. Pulp and Paper Mag.
Canada 43: 528, 530. (RAM 21:
543-544.) A6, B2, E3a(6), d(1),
16b.

55. _____ Foster, R.E., and
Salisbury, P.J.
1946. STUDIES IN FOREST PATHOLOGY.
IV. DECAY OF SITKA SPRUCE ON THE
QUEEN CHARLOTTE ISLANDS. Canada
Dept. Agr. Tech. Bul. 56, 35 pp.
A2, B2, E1a,g, 4a,b,c.

56. _____ Salisbury, P.J., and
Waldie, R.A.
1948. DECAY IN FIR, ABIES LASIOCARPA
AND A. AMABILIS, IN THE UPPER
FRASER REGION OF BRITISH COLUMBIA.
Canada Dept. Agr. Tech. Bul. 66,
28 pp. A4, B2, E4b,c.

57. Biraghi, A.
1949.*IL DISSECCAMENTO DEGLI ABETI
DI VALLOMBROSA. [THE WITHERING OF
THE FIRS OF VALLOMBROSA.] Ital.
Forest. Mont. 4(3): 1-11. (RAM 29:
184-185.) A4, B6, F1.

58. Bjorkman, E.
1949. SOIL ANTIBIOTICS ACTING
AGAINST THE ROOT-ROT FUNGUS
(POLYPORUS ANNOSUS FR.). Physiol.
Plant. 2: 1-10. E1k, F2, 3a, G3.

59. _____ Samuelson, O.,
Ringstrom, E., et al.
1949. OM ROTSKADOR I GRANDSKOG OCH
DERAS BEYDELSE VID FRAMSTALLNING
AV KEMISK PAPPERSMASSA OCH SIL-
KAMASSA. [DECAY INJURIES IN SPRUCE
FORESTS AND THEIR IMPORTANCE FOR
THE PRODUCTION OF CHEMICAL PAPER
PULP AND RAYON PULP.] Roy. School
Forest. Bul. 4. Stockholm, 73 pp.
A2, B5, C5a,b,d, E1c, 4b.

60. Bjørnekaer, K.
1938.*UNDERSØGELSER OVER NOGLE
DANSKE PORESVAMPES BIOLOGI MED
SAERLIGT HENSYN TIL DERES SPORE-
FAELDNING. [STUDIES ON THE BIOLOGY
OF SOME DANISH POLYPORACEAE WITH
SPECIAL REFERENCE TO THEIR SPORE
DISCHARGE.] Friesia 2: 1-41. (RAM
18: 215.) E2a.

61. Blokhuis, J.L.W.
1938.*BASTBESCHADIGINGEN AAN JAPAN-
SCHEN LARIKS EN EIK. [CORTICAL IN-
JURIES ON JAPANESE LARCH AND OAK.]
Nederland. Boschbouw Tijdschr. 11:
352-354. (RAM 18: 74.) A3, B6,
E1d, 4b, 11b, 13a, 16a.

62. Booth, J.
1907.*DAS VERHALTEN DER DOUGLAS-
FICHTE GEGEN WURZELFÄULE. Deut.
Dendrol. Gesell. Mitt. 16: 183-
186. (BI) A5.

63. Bornebusch, C.H., and Holm, F.
1934. KULTUR PAA TRAMETESINFICERET
BUND MED FORSKELLIGE TRAEARTER.
[REPLANTING OF AREAS INFECTED WITH
POLYPORUS (FOMES) ANNOSUS.]
Forstl. Forsøgsv. i Danmark Beret.
13: 225-264. (From Peace, 1938.)
E3a(5).

64. Boyce, J.S.
1926.*DISEASES OF COMMERCIALLY IM-
PORTANT CONIFERS IN THE PACIFIC
NORTHWEST. Off. Invest. Forest
Path. Bur. Plant Indus., 37 pp.
(reissued). (RAM 6: 449-450.) A1,
B1, D6, G8.

65. _____
1927. OBSERVATIONS ON FOREST PATH-
OLOGY IN GREAT BRITAIN AND DEN-
MARK. Phytopath. 17: 1-18. (RAM
6: 446-447.) A2,3,4,5, B3, 5,
E16a,b.

66. _____
1929. DETERIORATION OF WIND-THROWN
TIMBER ON THE OLYMPIC PENINSULA,
WASH. U.S. Dept. Agr. Tech. Bul.
104, 28 pp. A2,4,5,6, B1, D4.

67. _____
1930. DECAY IN PACIFIC NORTHWEST
CONIFERS. Yale Univ. Osborn Bot.
Lab. Bul. 1, 51 pp. A1, B1, D1,2,
E3a(3), b(1),(2), 4a.

68. _____
1932. DECAY AND OTHER LOSSES IN
FIR IN WESTERN OREGON AND WASHING-
TON. U.S. Dept. Agr. Tech. Bul.
286, 60 pp. A5, B1, D1,2, E3a(3),
b(2), E4a,b.

69. Boyce, J.S.
1948. FOREST PATHOLOGY. McGraw-Hill
Book Co., Inc. New York, 550 pp.
A2,4,6,7, B1,6, D4,5,6, E1c, 2a,
b,c, 3b(1),(2), 10a, 11a.

70. Boyce, J.S., Jr.
1959. ROOT ROT IN PINE PLANTATIONS.
Forest Farmer 19(3): 8, 17-18.
A1,6, B1, D2,6, E1b, 2a, 3a(5),
b(1),(2), d(1),(2), 4b, 5b, 12,
16a,b, F4, G1.

71. Brachfeld, K.
1935.*ZTRÁTY NA HODNOTĚ U POROSTŮ
SMRKOVÝCH V DŮSLEDKU LESNIHO
POLAŘENÍ. [DETERIORATION OF SPRUCE
STANDS FOLLOWING CULTIVATION OF
THE SITE.] Lesnická Práce 14
(9/10): 460-466. (BA 10: 11661.)
E5b, G5,6,7.

72. Braun, H.J.
1958.*UNTERSUCHUNGEN ÜBER DEN
WURZELSCHWAMM FOMES ANNOSUS (FR.)
COOKE. [INVESTIGATIONS ON F.
ANNOSUS.] Forstwiss.Centbl. 77:
65-88. (FA 20: 710.) C2a,d, D4,
E1b, 2a, G8.

73. ―――――――
1960.*ZUR FRAGE DER INFEKTION VON
SCHÄL- UND SCHÜRFWUNDEN DURCH DEN
WURZELSCHWAMM FOMES ANNOSUS (FR.)
COOKE (TRAMETES RADICIPERDA
HARTIG). [DOES F. ANNOSUS INFECT
WOUNDS CAUSED THROUGH BARKING BY
DEER OR LOGGING?] Allg. Forst u.
Jagd Ztg. 131: 67-68. (FA 21:
3353.) E1a,g.

74. Brefeld, O.
1889.*UNTERSUCHUNGEN AUS DEM GES-
AMTGEBIETE DER MYKOLOGIE. BASIDIO-
MYCETEN III. AUTOBASIDIOMYCETEN
UND DIE BEGRUNDING EINES NATUR-
LICHEN SYSTEMES DER PILZE. Heft 8.
Leipzig. 305 pp. (From Hiley,
1919.) C1, 7a.

75. Bronchi, P.
1956.*ORIGINE DELL' ABETINA PURA
ARTIFICIALE NELLA FORESTA DEMAN-
IALE DI BADIA PRATAGLIA IN RELA-
ZIONE AI RECENTI DANNI DA FOMES
ANNOSUS SU ABIES ALBA. [THE ORIGIN
OF THE PURE,ARTIFICIALLY PLANTED
FIR STAND IN THE STATE FOREST OF
BADIA PRATAGLIA IN RELATION TO
RECENT INJURY BY 'FOMES ANNOSUS' TO
ABIES ALBA.] Monti e Boschi 7:
368-373. (RAM 36: 363-364.) A4,
B6, E10a, 13a,b, 16a.

76. ―――――――
1957.*MORIE CAUSATE DA FOMES ANNOSUS
SU NOVELLETI DI ABIES ALBA NELLA
FORESTA DEMANIALE DI BADIA PRATA-
GLIA. [LOSSES CAUSED BY F. ANNOSUS
IN YOUNG PLANTATIONS OF A. ALBA IN
THE STATE FOREST OF BADIA PRATA-
GLIA.] Ital. Forest. Mont. 12:
287-294. (FA 19: 3159.) A4, B6,
E13a, 16a, G8.

77. Brown, J.M.B.
1953. STUDIES ON BRITISH BEECHWOODS.
Gt. Brit. Forestry Comn. Bul. 20,
100 pp. (RAM 32: 347-348.) A7, B3,
E9, 13b.

78. Bruggisser.
1940.*DIE REINEN FICHTENBESTÄNDE IM
FÜNFTEN AARGAUISCHEN FORSTKREISE.
[THE PURE SPRUCE STANDS OF THE
FIFTH AARGAU FOREST DISTRICT.]
Schweiz. Ztschr. f. Forstw. 91:
64-70. (FA 2: 19.) A2, B4, E13a,
16a.

79. Bryan, J., and Richardson, N.A.
1935.*EXPERIMENTS ON THE PRESERVA-
TION OF MINE TIMBER. Progress
Report No. 1. Gt. Brit. Forest
Prod. Res. Rec. 3, 10 pp. (RAM
15: 186-187.) B3, D3a.

80. Buchanan, T.S.
1940. FUNGI CAUSING DECAY IN WIND-
THROWN NORTHWEST CONIFERS. Jour.
Forestry 38: 276-281. D4, E4a,b.

81. Buckland, D.C.
1946. INVESTIGATIONS OF DECAY IN
WESTERN RED CEDAR IN BRITISH
COLUMBIA. Canad. Jour. Res. Sect.
C, 24: 158-181. (RAM 26: 272-273.)
A6, B2, C2a, D4, E10a.

82. ―――――― Foster, R.E., and
Nordin, V.J.
1949. STUDIES IN FOREST PATHOLOGY
VII. DECAY IN WESTERN HEMLOCK AND
FIR IN THE FRANKLIN RIVER AREA,
BRITISH COLUMBIA. Canad. Jour.
Res. Sect. C, 27: 312-331. A4,6,
B2, E1a,g, 4a,b.

83. Butler, E.J.
1903.*A DEODAR DISEASE IN JAUNSAR.
Calcutta. (BI) A6, B7.

84. ―――――――
1906.*A DEODAR DISEASE IN JAUNSAR.
Ztschr. f. Pflanzenkrank.16: 33.
(BI) A6, B7.

- 13 -

85. Campbell, W.A., and Hepting, G.H.
   1954. *FOMES ANNOSUS* ON SLASH PINE.
   Plant Dis. Rptr. 38: 217. (RAM
   33: 512.) A1,6, B1, D2,4, E3a(4),
   d(2), 10a, 12, 16a,b.

86. Carter, D.G., Barr, H.T., and
   Wood, J.B.
   1933. DURABILITY OF POSTS, AND RE-
   SULTS OF PRESERVATIVE TREATMENT.
   Ark. Agr. Expt. Sta. Bul. 287, 16
   pp. (RAM 12: 740.) C7b.

87. Cartwright, K. St. G.
   1942. THE VARIABILITY IN RESISTANCE
   TO DECAY OF THE HEARTWOOD OF HOME-
   GROWN EUROPEAN LARCH, *LARIX
   DECIDUA*, MILL. *(L. EUROPAEA)* AND
   ITS RELATION TO POSITION IN THE
   LOG. Forestry 16: 49-51. (RAM
   22: 189.) C5d.

88. _____and Findlay, W.P.K.
   1934. STUDIES IN THE PHYSIOLOGY OF
   WOOD-DESTROYING FUNGI. II. TEMPER-
   ATURE AND RATE OF GROWTH. Ann.
   Bot. 48: 481-496. C3a.

89. _____and Findlay, W.P.K.
   1938. PRINCIPAL DECAYS OF SOFTWOODS
   USED IN GREAT BRITAIN. H.M.
   Stationery Office, Lond. 106 pp.
   (RAM 18: 361-362.) C1, D1.

90. _____and Findlay, W.P.K.
   1950. DECAY OF TIMBER AND ITS PRE-
   VENTION. Chemical Publishing Co.,
   Inc., Brooklyn, N.Y., 294 pp. B7,
   C1, 2c, 3a, 5a,b,d, 6, D1, 3a,c,
   6, E1c,d, 3b(1),(2).

91. Ch'ên, L.-P., and Ch'iu, T.-H.
   1959.*[FUNGI OF ABIES STANDS IN THE
   MA-ERH-K'ANG LESKHOZ, SZECHWAN
   PROVINCE.] Forest Sci., Peking (2):
   134-142. (FA 21: 1993.) A4, B7,
   E4b, 6, 8, 10a.

92. Christa.
   1928.*BEHANDLUNG ROTFÄULER FICHTEN-
   BESTÄNDE. Deut. Forst. Ztg. 43:
   879. (BI) A2.

93. Čomić, B.
   1957.* NEKA ZAPAŽANJA O POJAVI
   DASYSCYPHA WILLKOMMII (HART.)
   REHM. NA ARIŠU I *TRAMETES RADI-
   CIPERDA* HARTIG NA SMRČI U ŠUMAMA
   MOJSTRANE. [*D. WILLKOMMII* ON
   LARCH AND *FOMES ANNOSUS* ON SPRUCE
   IN THE MOJSTRANA FORESTS.] Šumar-
   stvo 10(9/10): 629-631. (FA 19:
   3160.) A2, B6, E5a,b, G7.

94. Commonwealth Mycological Institute.
   1953.*DISTRIBUTION MAPS OF PLANT
   DISEASES. Map 271. (RAM 33: 654.)
   A6, 7.

95. Cooke, W.B., and Shaw, C.G.
   1952. NOTES ON ALASKAN FUNGI. State
   Col. Wash. Res. Stud. 20: 15-19.
   (RAM 31: 401.) A6, B2.

96. Curtin, L.P.
   1927. EXPERIMENTS IN WOOD PRESER-
   VATION. I. PRODUCTION OF ACID BY
   WOOD-ROTTING FUNGI. Indus. and
   Engin. Chem. 19: 878-881. (RAM 7:
   130.) C7b.

97. _____
   1927. EXPERIMENTS IN WOOD PRESER-
   VATION. II. ARSENITES OF COPPER
   AND ZINC. Indus. and Engin. Chem.
   19: 993-999. (RAM 7: 213.) C7b.

98. _____
   1927. EXPERIMENTS IN WOOD PRESER-
   VATION. III. PRESERVATIVE PROPER-
   TIES OF BASIC SUBSTANCES. Indus.
   and Engin. Chem. 19: 1159-1161.
   (RAM 7: 293.) C7b.

99. _____and Bogert, M.T.
   1927. EXPERIMENTS IN WOOD PRESER-
   VATION. IV. PRESERVATIVE PROPER-
   TIES OF CHLORINATED COAL-TAR DE-
   RIVATIVES. Indus. and Engin. Chem.
   19: 1231-1240. (RAM 7: 294.) C7b.

100. _____and Thordarson, W.
   1928. EXPERIMENTS IN WOOD PRESER-
   VATION. VI. RECENT LABORATORY
   WORK. Indus. and Engin. Chem. 20:
   28-30. (RAM 7: 484-485.) C7b.

101. _____ Kline, B.L., and
   Thordarson, W.
   1927. EXPERIMENTS IN WOOD PRESER-
   VATION. V. WEATHERING TESTS ON
   TREATED WOOD. Indus. and Engin.
   Chem. 19: 1340-1343. (RAM 7: 294.)
   C7b.

102. d'Arbois de Jubainville.
   1875.*LE *TRAMETES RADICIPERDA*. Rev.
   des Eaux et Forêts 14: 105-108.
   (BI)

103. _____
   1877.*LA MALADIE DU ROND. Rev. des
   Eaux et Forêts 16: 296. (BI)

104. _____
   1878.*LA MALADIE DU ROND. Rev. des
   Eaux et Forêts 17: 368. (BI)

105. Darley, E.F., and Christensen, C.M.
1945. THE CULTURE DESIGNATED MADISON
517 IDENTIFIED AS *POLYPORUS TULI-
PIFERUS*. Phytopath. 35: 220-222.
(RAM 24: 299.) C7b.

106. Davidson, R.W., Campbell, W.A., and
Blaisdell, Dorothy J.
1938. DIFFERENTIATION OF WOOD-DECAY-
ING FUNGI BY THEIR REACTION ON
GALLIC OR TANNIC ACID MEDIUM.
Jour. Agr. Res. 57: 683-695.
C2a.

107. Day, W.R.
1929. THE HEART ROT OF TIMBER IN
RELATION TO FOREST MANAGEMENT.
Quart. Jour., Forestry 23: 242-251.
(RAM 9: 74.) A2,3, B1,3, D6, E5e,
6, 16a, G4, 7.

108. ―――――
1941.*FOREST PATHOLOGY. Imp. Forestry
Inst. Rpt., Oxford, 1940-41:
11-13. (RAM 21: 234.) A2,3, B3,
E5c.

109. ―――――
1946.*FOREST PATHOLOGY. Imp. Forestry
Inst. Rpt., Oxford, 1944-45: 8-10.
(RAM 25: 482-483.) A1, B3, E16a.

110. ―――――
1946. ROOT DISEASES IN CONIFERS.
Nature, Lond. 158: 57. B3, E3a(4),
5a,b,c, 10c.

111. ―――――
1946. THE PATHOLOGY OF BEECH ON
CHALK SOILS. Quart. Jour. Forestry
40: 72-82. A1,3, B3, E5a,b,e, 9.

112. ―――――
1948.*FOREST PATHOLOGY. Imp. Forestry
Inst. Rpt., Oxford, 1946-47:
8-12. (RAM 27: 500-501.) A5, B3,
E1a, 5b,c, 16a.

113. ―――――
1948.*ROOT DISEASE AND BUTT-ROT OF
CONIFERS. Imp. Forestry Inst.
Rpt., Oxford, 1946-47: 9. (FA
10: 765.) A1, B3, E1d,e, 5c.

114. ―――――
1948. THE PENETRATION OF CONIFER
ROOTS BY *FOMES ANNOSUS*. Quart.
Jour. Forestry 42: 99-101. A5,
B3, E5c,d.

115. ―――――
1952. DEATH, DIE-BACK AND CANKER OF
PINUS CONTORTA (LODGEPOLE PINE).

Imp. Forestry Inst. Rpt., Oxford,
1950-51: 15. (FA 13: 3947.) A1,
B3, E5b,c.

116. ―――――
1952. ROOT DISEASE OF CONIFERS IN
RELATION TO SOIL CONDITIONS. (A)
DEVELOPMENT OF BUTT-ROT IN CONI-
FERS IN RELATION TO SOIL DEPTH.
(B) THE DYING OF SITKA SPRUCE.
Imp. Forestry Inst. Rpt., Oxford,
1950-51: 13-14. (FA 13: 3946.) A2,
3,5,6, B3, E5b,c, 8.

117. ―――――
1953. THE GROWTH OF SITKA SPRUCE ON
SHALLOW SOILS IN RELATION TO ROOT-
DISEASE AND WIND-THROW. Forestry
26: 81-95. (RAM 33: 190.) A2, B3,
E5c,d, 6.

118. ―――――
1954.*DROUGHT CRACK OF CONIFERS. Gt.
Brit. Forestry Comn. Forest Rec.
26, 40 pp. (RAM 33: 570.) A2, B3, E1g.

119. ―――――― and Peace, T.R.
1935. BUTT ROT OF CONIFERS. Forestry
9: 60-61. (RAM 14: 803.) A1,2,3,
B3, D6, E5e, 9.

120. Dehnst.
1928.*ÜBER DEN MECHANISMUS DES
HOLZSCHUTZES DURCH KONSERVIERUNGS-
MITTEL. [ON THE MECHANISM OF TIM-
BER PROTECTION BY PRESERVATIVES.]
Ztschr. f. Angew. Chem. 41: 355-
358. (RAM 7: 687-688.) C2b.

121. Delevoy, G.
1946.*À PROPOS D'UN CAS DE VIRU-
LENCE EXCEPTIONELLE *D'ARMILLARIA
MELLEA* (VAHL) QUÉL. [ON A CASE OF
EXCEPTIONAL VIRULENCE OF *ARMIL-
LARIA MELLEA* (VAHL) QUÉL.] Soc.
Cent. Forest. de Belg. Bul. 53:
104-114. (RAM 25: 482-483.) A2,
B6, F1.

122. Domański, S.
1952.*ZGNILIZNY ODZIOMKOWE SOSNY
ZWYCZAJNEJ I PRÓBA OCENY ICH WAR-
UNKÓW ROZWOJOWYCH. [BUTT ROTS OF
SCOTS PINE AND AN ATTEMPT TO ESTI-
MATE THEIR DEVELOPMENTAL CON-
DITIONS.] Sylwan 96: 5-30. (RAM
32: 44.) A1, B6.

123. Dwyer, W.W., Jr.
1951. *FOMES ANNOSUS* ON EASTERN RED
CEDAR IN TWO PIEDMONT FORESTS.
Jour. Forestry 49: 259-262. A6,
B1, C2b, D2, E1a, 2a, 4a,c, 5a.

124. Eades, H.W.
      1932. BRITISH COLUMBIA SOFTWOODS:
      THEIR DECAYS AND NATURAL DEFECTS.
      Canada Dept. Int., Forest Serv.
      Bul. 80, 126 pp. A6, B2, D1,5,
      E3a(4), b(1),(2), 10c.

125. Ehrlich, J.
      1939. A PRELIMINARY STUDY OF ROOT
      DISEASES IN WESTERN WHITE PINE.
      U.S. Forest Serv. Northern Rocky
      Mountain Forest and Range Expt.
      Sta. Sta. Paper 1, 11 pp. A1, B1,
      E3a(5), 4a,b, 5c, F4.

126. Enebo, L.
      1949. EXPERIMENTS WITH CLAVIFORMIN
      AS AN ANTIBIOTIC AGAINST POLYPORUS
      ANNOSUS, FR. Physiol. Plant. 2:
      56-60. (BA 23: 2499.) C2d, F3b.

127. Englerth, G.H.
      1942. DECAY OF WESTERN HEMLOCK IN
      WESTERN OREGON AND WASHINGTON.
      Yale Univ., School Forestry Bul.
      50, 53 pp. A6, B1, C2d, D4,5, E1a,
      g, 2b, 3b(1),(2), 4a,b, 5c, 6,
      10a,b, 15, F1.

128. _____ and Isaac, L.A.
      1944. DECAY OF WESTERN HEMLOCK FOL-
      LOWING LOGGING INJURY. Timberman
      45(8): 34-35, 56. (FA 6: 114.)
      A6, B1, E1g.

129. Erdtman, H., and Rennerfelt, E.
      1949. FUNGICIDAL PROPERTIES OF SOME
      CONSTITUENTS OF THE HEARTWOOD OF
      TETRACLINIS ARTICULATA (VAHL)
      MASTERS. Acta Chem. Scand. 3:
      906-911. (RAM 29: 447-448.) C1,2b.

130. Etheridge, D.E.
      1955. COMPARATIVE STUDIES OF NORTH
      AMERICAN AND EUROPEAN CULTURES OF
      THE ROOT ROT FUNGUS, FOMES ANNOSUS
      (FR.) COOKE. Canada. Jour. Bot.
      33: 416-428. C1, 2c, 3a, 5a.

131. Falck, R.
      1927.* SECHS MERKBLÄTTER ZUR HOLZ-
      SCHUTZFRAGE. [SIX LEAFLETS ON THE
      QUESTION OF WOOD PRESERVATION.]
      Hausschwammforsch. 8, 71 pp. (RAM
      7: 292-293.)

132. _____
      1927.* ÜBER KORROSIVE UND DESTRUKTIVE
      HOLZZERSETZUNG UND IHRE BIOL-
      OGISCHE BEDEUTUNG. Deut. Bot.
      Gesell. Ber. 44: 652-664. (BA 3:
      17606.) C5b.

133. _____
      1930.*NEUE MITTEILUNGEN ÜBER DIE
      ROTFÄULE. [NEW NOTES ON RED ROT.]
      Reprinted from Mitt. aus Forstw.
      u. Forstwiss. 1930, 42 pp. (RAM 10:
      354-355.) A1, B4, C5b, D4, E1a,g,
      2a, 3a(5), 4c, 5e, 8, 11b, F1.

134. _____ and Coordt, W.
      1928.*DER METHOXYL-GEHALT BEIM
      LIGNIN- UND CELLULOSE-ABBAU DES
      HOLZES. [THE METHOXYL CONTENT IN
      THE LIGNIN AND CELLULOSE DECOMPO-
      SITION OF WOOD.] Deut. Chem.
      Gesell. Ber. 61B(9): 2101-2106.
      (RAM 9: 150.) C5b.

135. _____ and Haag, W.
      1927.*DER LIGNIN- UND DER CELLULOSE-
      ABBAU DES HOLZES. ZWEI VERSCHIE-
      DENE ZERSETZUNGSPROZESSE DURCH
      HOLZ-BEWOHNENDE FADENPILZE. [DE-
      COMPOSITION OF LIGNIN AND CELLU-
      LOSE: TWO DISTINCT DISINTEGRATION
      PROCESSES BY WOOD-INHABITING
      HYPHOMYCETES.] Deut. Chem. Gesell.
      Ber. 60: 225-232. (RAM 6: 453.)
      C5a, b.

136. Fenton, E.W.
      1943. SOME OBSERVATIONS ON HEART ROT
      IN CONIFERS FROM AN ECOLOGICAL
      POINT OF VIEW. Forestry 17: 55-60.
      (RAM 23: 199-200.) A2, B3, D2,
      E5c, 9, 10a,d.

137. Findlay, W.P.K.
      1943. WOOD TAR AS A PRESERVATIVE
      FOR TIMBER. Empire Forestry Jour.
      20: 151-153. (RAM 23: 282-283.)
      C2b.

138. _____ and Vernon, J.W.
      1951. A SIMPLE METHOD FOR TESTING
      THE TOXICITY OF VOLATILE ANTI-
      SEPTICS TO WOOD-ROTTING FUNGI.
      Ann. Appl. Biol. 38: 876-880.
      (RAM 31: 465-466.) C2b.

139. Flerov, B.C., and Popov, C.A.
      1933.*METHODE ZUR UNTERSUCHUNG DER
      WIRKUNG VON ANTISEPTISCHEN MITTELN
      AUF HOLZZERSTÖRENDE PILZE. [METHODS
      FOR THE INVESTIGATION OF THE
      ACTION OF ANTISEPTIC PREPARATIONS
      ON WOOD-DESTROYING FUNGI.] Angew.
      Bot. 15: 386-406. (RAM 13: 70.)
      C2b.

140. Flury, P.
      1926.*ÜBER ZUWACHS UND ERTRAG REINER
      UND GEMISCHTER BESTÄNDE. Schweiz.

Ztschr. f. Forstw. 77: 337-342.
(From Wagener and Davidson, 1954.)
A2, 7, B6, E4b, 5b, 16a, G5.

141. F. [Forbes], A.C.
1907. ROOT ROT IN SCOTCH PINE.
Quart. Jour. Forestry 1: 32-38.
(BI) A1, B3,4, E1c, 5a,b,c, 10a,b,
13a.

142. Foster, R.E., and Foster, A.T.
1951. STUDIES IN FOREST PATHOLOGY.
VIII. DECAY OF WESTERN HEMLOCK ON
THE QUEEN CHARLOTTE ISLANDS, BRIT-
ISH COLUMBIA. Canad. Jour. Bot.
29: 479-521. A6, B2, D2,4, E1a,g,
4a,b,c.

143. _____ and Foster, A.T.
1953. ESTIMATING DECAY IN WESTERN
HEMLOCK. (II.) SUGGESTED AIDS TO
THE INVENTORY IN THE QUEEN CHAR-
LOTTE ISLANDS. Brit. Columbia
Lumberman 37(4): 40-41, 56, 58,
102. A6, B2, E4b,c.

144. Francke-Grosmann,Helene.
1948.*ROTFÄULE UND RIESENBASTKÄFER,
EINE GEFAHR FÜR DIE SITKAFICHTE
AUF ÖD- UND ACKERLANDAUFFORSTUNGEN
SCHLESWIG-HOLSTEINS. [RED ROT AND
GIANT BARK BEETLE, A THREAT TO THE
SITKA SPRUCE IN AFFORESTATIONS ON
WASTE AND ARABLE LAND IN SCHLES-
WIG-HOLSTEIN.] Forst u. Holz 3:
232-235. (RAM 29: 67.) A2, B4,
E3a(2),(3), c, 4b, 9, 13a, 16a,
F4, G7.

145. Freyschuss, S.K.L.
1958.*BEKÄMPNING AV SVAMPANGREPP I
SLIPMASSA. [CONTROL OF FUNGAL IN-
FECTION IN MECHANICAL PULP.] Norsk
Skogindus. 12(3): 104-113. (RAM
37: 610.) D3b, G1.

146. Fries, E.
1821. SYSTEMA MYCOLOGICUM, SISTENS
FUNGORUM ORDINES, GENERA ET
SPECIES, HUC USQUE COGNITAS QUAS
AD NORMAM METHODI NATURALIS DE-
TERMINAVIT, DISPOSUIT ATQUE
DESCRIPSIT. Vol. 1. Sumptibus
Ernesti Mauritii. Gryphiswaldie,
520 pp. D1.

147. Fries, N.
1938.*UBER DIE BEDEUTUNG VON WUCHSS-
TOFFEN FÜR DAS WACHSTUM VERSCHIE-
DENER PILZE. [ON THE IMPORTANCE
OF GROWTH SUBSTANCES FOR THE
GROWTH OF VARIOUS FUNGI.] Symb.
Bot. Upsaliens. 3(2), 188 pp. (RAM
18: 335.)

148. _____
1950.*GROWTH FACTOR REQUIREMENTS OF
SOME HIGHER FUNGI. Svensk Bot.
Tidskr. 44: 379-386. (RAM 30:
65.) C2a,d.

149. _____
1951. EFFECT OF CERTAIN NUCLEIC ACID
CONSTITUENTS ON THE GROWTH OF
SOME HIGHER FUNGI. Nature, Lond.
168: 1045-1046. (FA 13: 1858.)
C1, 2a, 4.

150. _____
1954.*THE RESPONSE OF SOME HYMEN-
OMYCETES TO CONSTITUENTS OF
NUCLEIC ACIDS. Svensk Bot. Tidskr.
48: 559-578. (RAM 33: 749.) C2a,d,
3a,b.

151. Fröhlich, J.
1931.*DIE WICHTIGSTEN KRANKHEITEN
DER BÄUME UND FEHLER DES HOLZES
IM SÜDOSTEUROPÄISCHEN URWALDE.
[THE PRINCIPAL DISEASES OF TREES
AND DEFECTS OF TIMBER IN THE
PRIMEVAL FORESTS OF SOUTH-EASTERN
EUROPE.] Forstwiss. Centbl. 53:
277-285. (RAM 10: 631-632.) A2,4,
B6, E4b, 5e, 6, 10a, 16b.

152. Gadd, G.O.
1949. FUNGAL DAMAGES IN GROUNDWOOD
PULP. Pulp and Paper Mag. Canada
50(11): 98-99. (RAM 29: 325.)
C5a,b, D3b.

153. _____
1951.*ON THE MICROBIOLOGICAL PROB-
LEMS OF THE PULP AND PAPER INDUS-
TRIES. Paperi ja Puu [Paper &
Timber] 33(3): 49-52. (RAM 3¹:
155.) C2b, G1.

154. _____ and Wartiovaara, V.
1954.*ON THE CHEMICAL REACTION CAUS-
ING ROT STAINS IN WET PULP AND IN
WOOD. Paperi ja Puu [Paper &
Timber] 36: 291-295. (RAM 34:
560.) C2b, 4.

155. Galloy, A.
1925.*DE LA POURRITURE ROUGE CON-
SECUTIVE AUX DEGATS DE CERF DANS
CERTAINES PESSIERES DE L'HERTOGEN-
WALD. Soc. Cent. Forest. Belg.
Bul.32: 400-405. (BI) A2.

156. Garbowski, L.
1926.*CHOROBY ROŚLIN UPRAWNYCH W
WIELKOPOLSCE, NA POMORZU I NA
ŚLĄSKU W R. 1924 I 1925. [DISEASES
OF CULTIVATED PLANTS IN GREAT

POLAND, POMERANIA, AND SILESIA IN 1924 AND 1925.] Pam., Publishing Inst. 'Bibljoteka Polska,' Bydgoszcz, 47 pp. (RAM 5: 713-714.) A1, 7, B6, E4b.

157. Garrett, S.D.
1951. *In* REPORT ON FOREST RESEARCH FOR THE YEAR ENDING MARCH, 1950. Gt. Brit., p. 124. (RAM 30: 591.) F3c, G1,3.

158. ―――――――
1956. BIOLOGY OF ROOT-INFECTING FUNGI. University Press, Cambridge, England, 293 pp. D4, E1a, F2, G2.

159. Gertz, O.
1946.*EINIGE BEMERKENSWERTE PILZFORMEN AUS DEN KOHLENGRUBEN SCHONENS. [SOME REMARKABLE FUNGUS FORMS FROM THE COAL MINES OF SCANIA.] K. Fysiogr. Sällsk. Lund Förh. 16 (11): 88-101. (RAM 27: 206.) B5, D3a.

160. Glaser, T., and Sosna, Z.
1956.* BADANIA PORÓWNAWCZE HUBY KORZENIOWEJ *(FOMES ANNOSUS FR.)* POCHODĄZCEJ Z SOSNY ŚWIERKA I BROZOZY NA SZTUCZNYCH POZYWKACH. [COMPARATIVE STUDIES ON *FOMES ANNOSUS* FROM PINE, SPRUCE, AND BIRCH GROWN IN CULTURE.] Soc. Bot. Polon. Acta 25: 285-303. (FA 18: 574.) A1,2,7, B6, C1, 5a.

161. Gothe, H.
1957.*BEOBACHTUNGEN ÜBER STOCKFÄULE IN SCHLITZER LÄRCHENBESTÄNDEN. 2. MITTEILUNG. [OBSERVATIONS ON BUTT ROT IN THE LARCH STANDS OF SCHLITZ, NOTE 2.] Forst u. Holz 12(5): 70-74. (RAM 37: 253.) A3, B4, E1e, 4b, 10a, F1.

162. Graham, J.E.
1948.*THE ANTAGONISTIC ACTION OF *TRICHODERMA VIRIDE* ON *FOMES ANNOSUS* AND OTHER SOIL FUNGI. Unpublished Thesis, Edinburgh Univ. (From Aytoun, 1953.) F2.

163. Grainger, J.
1946. ECOLOGY OF THE LARGER FUNGI. Brit. Mycol. Soc. Trans. 29: 52-63. (RAM 25: 512-513.) C2c, 3b.

164. Gram, E., and Rostrup, Sofie.
1922.*OVERSIGT OVER SYGDOMME HOS LANDBRUGETS OG HAVEBRUGETS KULTURPLANTER I 1921. [SURVEY OF THE DISEASES OF CULTIVATED AGRICULTURAL AND HORTICULTURAL PLANTS IN 1921.] Tidsskr. for Planteavl 28: 185-246. (RAM 1: 369-371.) A7, B5, E1j.

165. Gram, K., and Jørgensen, E.
1953. AN EASY, RAPID AND EFFICIENT METHOD OF COUNTER-STAINING PLANT TISSUES AND HYPHAE IN WOODSECTIONS BY MEANS OF FAST GREEN OR LIGHT GREEN AND SAFRANIN. Friesia 4: 262-266. C8.

166. Guyot, R.
1933.*DE LA MALADIE DU ROND: DE L'INFLUENCE DES FOYERS OU DES FOYERS D'INCENDIE DANS SA PROPAGATION. [ON THE RING DISEASE AND ON THE INFLUENCE OF FIRES OR CONFLAGRATIONS ON ITS SPREAD.] Rev. Gén. des Sci. Pures et Appl. 44: 239-247. (RAM 12: 798-799.) A1, B6, E15, F1, G1,2.

167. Györfi, J.
1943-44.*A *FOMES ANNOSUS* FRIES KÁROSÍTÁSA A SOPRONI BOTANIKUS KERTBEN. [DAMAGE BY *FOMES ANNOSUS* IN THE SOPRON BOTANIC GARDEN.] Erdészeti Kisérletek 45(1/4): 71-86. (FA 8: 1412.) A2, B6, E3a(5), 10a, 13a, F4.

168. Haasis, F.W.
1923. ROOT ROT AS A FACTOR IN SURVIVAL. Jour. Forestry 21: 506. A1, B1, E1a, 3d(2), G6.

169. Haig, I.T., Davis, K.P., and Weidman, R.H.
1941. NATURAL REGENERATION IN THE WESTERN WHITE PINE TYPE. U.S. Dept. Agr. Tech. Bul. 767, 98 pp. (RAM 20: 435-436.) A1, B1, E4a.

170. Hansen, V.
1928.* FREMMENDE NAALETRAEER I LANGESØ SKOVE. [FOREIGN CONIFERS IN LANGESØ FOREST.] Dansk Skovfor. Tidsskr. 13: 413-483. (BA 5: 8782.) A5, B5, E4b.

171. Hardy, E.
1940.*PIT-PROP FUNGI. Colliery Engin. 17(195): 116-117. (RAM 19: 633.) B3, D3a.

172. Hartig, R.
1874.*WICHTIGE KRANKHEITEN DER WALDBÄUME. Berlin. Julius Springer, 127 pp.

173. Hartig, R.
    1877.*DIE ROTFÄULE DER FICHTE.
    Monatschr. f. das Forst u. Jagdw.
    21: 97-113. (BI) A2.

174. ──────
    1878.*TRAMETES RADICIPERDA. Zie
    Zersetzungs, des Holzes, 14-31.
    (BI)

175. ──────
    1878.*ZERSETZUNGSERSCHEINUNGEN DES
    HOLZES. Berlin, 127 pp. (From
    Baxter, 1940.)

176. ──────
    1889.*ZUR KENNTNIS DES WURZELSCH-
    WAMMES, (TRAMETES RADICIPERDA).
    Ztschr. f. Forst u. Jagdw. 21:
    428-432. (BI)

177. ──────
    1894.*THE DISEASE OF TREES (TRANS-
    LATED BY W. SOMERVILLE AND H.
    MARSHALL WARD). Lond. (From
    Wilson, 1927.) A1,6,7, B4.

178. Hartley, Carl.
    1910. FOMES ANNOSUS AND TWO SPECIES
    OF GYMNOSPORANGIUM ON JUNIPERUS
    VIRGINIANA, Science (N.S.) 31:
    639. (BI) A1,6, B1.

179. ──────
    1930.*RELATION BETWEEN SOIL ACIDITY
    AND ROOT DISEASES OF FOREST TREES.
    Forest Worker 6(5): 15. (BI) E5a.

180. Hatfield, I.
    1931. RECENT EXPERIMENTS WITH CHEMI-
    CALS SUGGESTED FOR WOOD PRESERVA-
    TION. Amer. Wood Preservers'
    Assoc. Proc. 1931: 304-315. (RAM
    10: 765-766.) C7b.

181. ──────
    1935. TOXICITY IN RELATION TO THE
    POSITION AND NUMBER OF CHLORINE
    ATOMS IN CERTAIN CHLORINATED BEN-
    ZENE DERIVATIVES. Amer. Wood
    Preservers' Assoc. Proc. 1935:
    57-66. (RAM 15: 69-70.) C7b.

182. Havelik, K.
    1924.*KERNFÄULE FICHTE. Centbl. f.
    das Gesam. Forstw. 50: 348-357.
    (From Peace, 1938.) E10b, 13a, 16a.

183. Hawley, L.F., Fleck, L.C., and
    Richards, C.A.
    1924. THE RELATION BETWEEN DURABIL-
    ITY AND CHEMICAL COMPOSITION IN
    WOOD. Indus. and Engin. Chem. 16:
    699-700.

184. Henriksen, H.A.
    1951. RØNTGENFOTOGRAFERING SOM DI-
    AGNOSTISK HJAELPEMIDDEL VED UNDER-
    SØGELSE AF TRAEER. [X-RAY PHOTO-
    GRAPHY AS AN AID TO DIAGNOSIS IN
    INVESTIGATING TREES.] Dansk
    Skovfor. Tidsskr. 36: 515-520.
    (FA 14: 430.) C8, E3a(5).

185. ────── and Jørgensen, E.
    1953.*RODFORDAERVERANGREB I RELATION
    TIL UDHUGNINGSGRAD: EN UNDER-
    SØGELSE PÅ EKSPERIMENTELT GRUND-
    LAG. [FOMES ANNOSUS ATTACK IN
    RELATION TO GRADE OF THINNING: AN
    INVESTIGATION ON THE BASIS OF EX-
    PERIMENTS.] Forstl. Forsøgsv. i
    Danmark Beret. 21: 215-251. (FA
    15: 3728.) A1,2, E3a(3), 4b, 7,
    12, 16a.

186. Hepting, G.H., and Downs, A.A.
    1944. ROOT AND BUTT ROT IN PLANTED
    WHITE PINE AT BILTMORE, N.C. Jour.
    Forestry 42: 119-123. A1, B1, E1c,
    f,k, 3b(2), 6, 9, 12.

187. ────── and Toole, E.R.
    1950. SOME SOUTHEASTERN TREE DIS-
    EASES--1948 AND 1949. Plant Dis.
    Rptr. 34: 135-137. (RAM 29: 589.)
    A6, B1.

188. Hermann, F.
    1900.*ÜBER BEKÄMPFUNG UND VERBREIT-
    UNGSWEISE DES TRAMETES RADIC-
    IPERDA. Tharandter Forstl. Jahrb.
    50: 195-199. (BI)

189. Hiley, W.E.
    1919. FUNGAL DISEASES OF THE COMMON
    LARCH. Clarendon Press. Oxford.
    204 pp. A1,2,3,4,5,6, B3, C1,6,8,
    D1, E1c,d, 3b(1),(2), d(2), 9,
    10a, 11b, 13a, 14, F3a, G1,2,5,7.

190. Hole, R.S.
    1927.*MORTALITY OF SPRUCE IN THE
    JAUNSAR FORESTS, UNITED PROVINCES.
    Indian Forester 53: 434-443,
    483-493. (BI) A2, B7.

191. ──────
    1933.*PLANT PATHOLOGY IN THE FORESTS
    OF INDIA. Part II. Indian Forester
    59: 500-507. (BI) A6, B7, E5b,c,d,
    13a, 16a, G4,5.

192. Holmsgaard, E.
    1957.*FORSØG PÅ EN OPGØRELSE OVER
    TRAMETES-SKADERNES ØKONOMISKE BE-
    TYDNING. [CALCULATIONS OF THE ECO-
    NOMIC IMPORTANCE OF DAMAGE BY

FOMES ANNOSUS.] Dansk Skovfor. Tidsskr. 42: 237-343. (FA 19: 1943.) B5, E4c.

193. Holmsgaard, E.
[n.d.]*OVERSIGT OVER IGANGVAERENDE UNDERSØGELSER UNDER TRAMETESUD-VALGET. [SURVEY OF CURRENT IN-VESTIGATIONS BY THE TRAMETES COM-MITTEE.] (RAM 39: 198.)

194. Hopffgarten, E.H. von.
1933.*BEITRÄGE ZUR KENNTNIS DER STOCKFÄULE *(TRAMETES RADICIPERDA.)* [CONTRIBUTIONS TO THE KNOWLEDGE OF THE BUTT ROT *(TRAMETES RADI-CIPERDA).*] Phytopath. Ztschr. 6: 1-48. (RAM 12: 738-739.) A1,2, B4, C2a, 3b, D6, E1b,c,d,e, 2a, 3d(1), 5a,b,c,d, 13a.

195. Hord, H.H.V., and Quirke, D.A.
1956. ANNUAL REPORT OF THE FOREST INSECT AND DISEASE SURVEY, CANADA DEPARTMENT OF AGRICULTURE, 1955: 56-69. (RAM 36: 70.) A1, B2, E12, 16a.

196. Howe, P.J.
1928. WEATHERING AND FIELD TESTS ON TREATED WOOD. Amer. Wood Pre-servers' Assoc. Proc. 1928: 192-209. (RAM 7: 756.)

197. Hubert, E.E.
1918. FUNGI AS CONTRIBUTORY CAUSES OF WINDFALL IN THE NORTHWEST. Jour. Forestry 16: 696-714. A1,2, B1, D2, E3a(4), b(2), d(2), 4b, 10a.

198. ————
1924. THE DIAGNOSIS OF DECAY IN WOOD. Jour. Agr. Res. 29: 523-567. C5c, E3b(1),(2).

199. ————
1931. AN OUTLINE OF FOREST PATHOL-OGY. John Wiley & Sons, Inc., New York, 543 pp. A6,7, B1, D1,5,6, E3b(1),(2).

200. ————
1950.*ROOTROTS OF THE WESTERN WHITE PINE TYPE. Northwest Sci. 24(1): 5-17. (RAM 30: 131.) A1, B1, C1.

201. Huet, M.
1936.*LA MALADIE DU ROND *(POLYPORUS ANNOSUS).* [THE RING DISEASE *(POLYPORUS ANNOSUS).*] Soc. Cent. Forest. de Belg. Bul. 43: 349-71. (RAM 16: 145.) A1,2, B6, E1b,d,

2a, 3a(3),(4),(6), c, 4a,b,c, 5c, e, 8, 10a,b, 13a, G1,2,5,7.

202. Hummel, F.C.
1950. INTERIM NOTE ON A THINNING STUDY IN YOUNG PINE IN EAST ANGLIA. Forestry 23: 78-89. (FA 12: 2941.) A1, B3, E12.

203. Humphrey, C.J.
1922. DECAY OF MINE TIMBER. Amer. Wood Preservers' Assoc. Proc. 1922: 213-222. (RAM 4: 4-5.) B1, D3a, G1,7.

204. ———— and Siggers, P.V.
1933. TEMPERATURE RELATIONS OF WOOD-DESTROYING FUNGI. Jour. Agr. Res. 47: 997-1008. C3a, 7b.

205. Hussain, S.M.
1952.*FOMES ANNOSUS* (FR.) CKE. A COMMON ROOT-ROT. Pakistan Jour. Forestry 2: 216-220. (FA 14: 1317.) A1, 7, B7, G1.

206. International Union of Forest Re-search Organizations.
1954. SPECIAL CONFERENCE ON ROOT AND BUTT ROTS OF FOREST TREES BY *FOMES ANNOSUS.* Wageningen, July 22-26, 1954, 30 pp. A1,2,3,5,7, B1,3,4, 5,6, D6, E1b,j, 2a, 4b, 5a,b,c, 6, 10a,b, 12, 13a, G1,2.

207. Iversen, A.
1955.*OM JORDVANDETS BEVAEGELSER OG DETS EVT. BETYDNING SOM SMITTEVEJ FOR RODFORDAERVEREN *FOMES ANNOSUS.* [ON THE MOVEMENTS OF SOIL WATER AND ITS POSSIBLE SIGNIFICANCE AS A CHANNEL OF INFECTION FOR ROOT ROT, *FOMES ANNOSUS.*] Dansk Skovfor. Tidsskr. 40: 432-437. (RAM 36: 797.) E2a.

208. Jaczewski, A.A.
1926.* [BREAKAGE AND UPROOTING OF FOREST TREES IN RELATION TO PARA-SITIC FUNGI ATTACKING THEM.] (Re-printed from Materials for My-cology and Phytopathology.) Len-ingrad, Part I, 18 pp. (RAM 6: 200-201.) A2, B6, E3d(2), 4b, F2.

209. Jennison, M.W., Newcomb, M.D., and Henderson, R.
1955. PHYSIOLOGY OF THE WOOD-ROTTING BASIDIOMYCETES. I. GROWTH AND NUTRITION IN SUBMERGED CULTURE IN SYNTHETIC MEDIA. Mycologia 47: 275-304. C2a, 3a, 4.

210. Jones, T.W., and Bretz, T.W.
1958. FIRST REPORT OF TREE MORTALITY FROM *FOMES ANNOSUS* ROOT ROT IN MISSOURI. Plant Dis. Rptr. 42: 988. (RAM 39: 59.) A1, B1, E3a(1), (2),(5), 4b, 5a, 12.

211. Jordan, H.
1935.*ZTRÁTY NA HODNOTĚ U POROSTŮ SMRKOVÝCH V DŮSLEDKU LESNÍHO POLÁRENÍ. [DETERIORATION OF SPRUCE STANDS FOLLOWING CULTIVATION OF THE SITE.] Lesnicka Prace 14(6): 277-289. (BA 10: 11669.) A2, B6, E4b, 10a, 13a.

212. Jørgensen, C.A., Lund, A., and Treschow, C.
1939.*UNDERSØGELSER OVER RODFORDA-ERVEREN, *FOMES ANNOSUS* (FR.) CKE. [STUDIES OF THE ROOT-DESTROYER *FOMES ANNOSUS* (FR.) CKE.] K. Vet-Højsk. Aarsskr. 1939: 71-128. (RAM 18: 772-773.) A1,2,4,5, B5, C2a,c,d, E1c,i, 4a,c,d, 5b, 9, 10a, 14, 16a,c, G1,5,6,7.

213. _____and Treschow, C.
1948.*OM BEKAEMPELSE AF RODFORDAER-VEREN (*FOMES ANNOSUS* (FR.) CKE.) VED FLADRODPLANTNING OG VED KALK-OG FOSFATTILSKUD. [ON THE CONTROL OF THE AGENT OF ROOT ROT (*FOMES ANNOSUS* (FR.) CKE.) BY SUPERFICIAL PLANTING AND THE APPLICATION OF LIME AND PHOSPHATE.] Forstl. Forsøgsv. i Danmark, Beret. 19: 253-284. (RAM 29: 391-392.) A2, B5, E1c, 5a, 11b, 16a, G1.

214. Jørgensen, E.
1954.*TRAMETESINFEKTION. [TRAMETES INFECTION.] Dansk Skovfor. Tidsskr. 39: 583-611. (RAM 35: 565.) A7, B5, D6.

215. _____
1955.*TRAMETESANGREB I LAEHEGN. [TRAMETES INFECTION IN SHELTER BELTS.] Dansk Skovfor. Tidsskr. 40: 279-285. (RAM 35: 731.) A2, 6, B5, E1j.

216. _____
1956. *FOMES ANNOSUS* (FR.) CKE. ON RED PINE IN ONTARIO. Forestry Chron. 32: 86-88. A1, B2, D1,6, E3d(1), 11b.

217. _____
1956.*NOTE ON THE DISTRIBUTION OF *FOMES ANNOSUS* (FR.) CKE. IN PLANTATIONS IN ONTARIO. Bi-mo. Prog. Rpt. Div. Forest Biol. Dept. Agr. Canada 12(6): 2. (FA 18: 3008.) A1, B2, E16a.

218. _____ and Petersen, B.B.
1951.*ANGREB AF *FOMES ANNOSUS* (FR.) CKE. OG *HYLESINUS PINIPERDA* L. PÅ *PINUS SILVESTRIS* I DJURSLANDS PLANTAGER. [ATTACK OF *FOMES ANNOSUS* (FR.) CKE.AND *HYLESINUS PINIPERDA* L. ON *PINUS SYLVESTRIS* IN THE DJURSLAND PLANTATIONS.] Dansk Skovfor. Tidsskr. 36: 453-479. (RAM 31: 412.) A1, B5, D2,5, E1c, 3a(5), c, 4b, 10a, 12, 13a, F4, G7.

219. Jørstad, I.
1948.*STORSOPPER PÅ FRUKTTRAER OG BAERBUSKER I NORGE. VEDOG BARK-BOENDE HETEROBASIDIOMYCTEN OG APHYLLOPHORACÉER. Friesia 3: 352-376. (From Wagener and Davidson, 1954.)

220. _____ and Roll-Hansen, F.
1943.*MELDING OM SYKDOMMER PÅ SKOG-TRAER I ÅRENE 1936-1941. [THE REPORT ON FOREST TREE DISEASES IN 1936-1941.] Oslo, Nasjonal Samlings Rikstrykkeri, 25 pp. (RAM 25: 17-18.) A1,2,7, B5, E6.

221. Josifović, M.
1952.*[*TRAMETES RADICIPERDA* AND *DASYCYPHA WILLKOMMII* IN SOME FORESTS OF SLOVENIA.]Bul. Forest. Fac., Beograd 5: 209-219. (RAM 32: 598-599.) A2, B6, E3a(6), d(2), 4b, G5,6,7.

222. Käärik, A., and Rennerfelt, E.
1957.*INVESTIGATIONS ON THE FUNGAL FLORA OF SPRUCE AND PINE STUMPS. Statens SkogsforsknInst. [Sweden], Meddel. 47, 88 pp. (FA 19: 1939.) A1,2, B5, C2d, 5a,d, 8, E10c.

223. Kamei, S., and Hoshi, S.
1948.*ON THE BROWN ROOT AND BUTT ROT OF CONIFERS IN THE NATIONAL FOREST OF AKAN, HOKKAIDO. Hokkaido Imp. Univ., Expt. Forests Res. Bul. 14(1): 144-176. (FA 11: 1459.) A2,4, B7, C3a, E4b.

224. Kamesam, S.
1933. TESTING AND SELECTION OF COMMERCIAL WOOD PRESERVATIVES. Forest Res. Inst. and Col., Dehra Dun, Forest Bul. 81 (Econ. Ser.), 40 pp. (RAM 13: 284.). C2b,d, 3a.

- 21 -

225. Kangas, E.
1952.*MAANNOUSEMASIENEN (POLYPORUS ANNOSUS FR.) ESIINTYMISESTA TARTUNNASTA JA TUHOISTA SUOMESSA. [FOMES ANNOSUS IN FINLAND: APPEARANCE, INFECTION AND DAMAGE.] Inst. Forest Fenniae Commun. 40(33), 34 pp. (FA 16: 634.) A2,B6.

226. ――――――
1952.* ÜBER AUFTRETEN, INFEKTION UND SCHADEN DES WURZELSCHWAMMS (POLYPORUS ANNOSUS FR.) IN FINNLAND. Finland. Metsätieteell. Tutkimuslaitoksen Julkaisu. 40(33): 1-34. (From Wagener and Davidson, 1954.) B6.

227. ――――――
1954.*MAANNOUSEMASIENEN ESIINTYMISESTÄ METSISSÄMME. [FOMES ANNOSUS IN FINNISH FORESTS.] Metsätaloudellinen Aikakausk. 1954 (5): 175-177. (FA 15: 3727.) B6.

228. Kauffman, C.H.
1917. UNREPORTED MICHIGAN FUNGI FOR 1915 AND 1916, WITH AN INDEX TO THE HOSTS AND SUBSTRATA OF BASIDIOMYCETES. Mich. Acad. Sci., Arts, and Letters Ann. Rpt. 19: 145-157. A6, B1.

229. Khan, A.A.
1948. THE IMPORTANCE OF THE METHOD OF APPROACH TO PROBLEMS IN FOREST HYGIENE WITH PARTICULAR REFERENCE TO THE EXPERIENCE IN THE PUNJAB. Indian Forester 74: 102-104. A6, B7, E3d(3), 5c, 6.

230. Kilias, G.
1959.*WAS IST BEI DER AUFFORSTUNG VON ÖDLAND MIT KIEFER ZU BEACHTEN? [WHAT SHOULD BE TAKEN INTO CONSIDERATION WHEN AFFORESTING NON-FOREST SOILS WITH PINE?] Deut. Landw. 10: 43-47. (FA 20: 3334.) A1, E16a, G5,7.

231. Kljušnyk, P.I.
1955.*KORENEVA GUBKA FOMES ANNOSUS (FR.) CKE. [F. ANNOSUS.] Botaničnij Žurnal, Kyjiv [Kiev] 12: 97-105. (FA 20: 2003.) A1, D1,6, E4c, G8.

232. Koch, W.
1958.*UNTERSUCHUNGEN ÜBER MYCELWACHSTUM UND FRUCHTKÖRPERBILDUNG BEI EINIGEN BASIDIOMYCETEN (POLYSTICTUS VERSICOLOR, POLYPORUS ANNOSUS, PLEUROTUS OSTREATUS UND PSALLIOTA BISPORA). [Studies on MYCELIAL GROWTH AND FRUITBODY FORMATION IN SOME BASIDIOMYCETES (P. VERSICOLOR, FOMES ANNOSUS, PLEUROTUS OSTREATUS, AND AGARICUS BISPORUS).] Arch. f. Mikrobiol. 30: 409-432. (RAM 39: 9.) C2a, 3b, 6.

233. König.
1923.*ÜBER ROTFÄULEBESTÄNDE UND DEREN BEHANDLUNG. [STANDS INFECTED WITH RED ROT AND THEIR TREATMENT.] Tharandter Forstl. Jahrb. 74(2): 63-74. (RAM 2: 482.) A4, B4, E1d, 2a, 3a(3),(4),d(1), 5b, 13a, G5,7.

234. Koning, M. De.
1923.*EEN NIEUW BESTRIJDINGSMIDDEL TEGEN DE WORTELZWAM. [A NEW MEASURE FOR THE CONTROL OF THE ROOT FUNGUS.] Tijdschr. over Plantenziekten 29: 1-4. (RAM 2: 430.) A1, B6, G2,5,7.

235. ――――――
1928.*ZIEKE DOUGLASDENNEN. [DISEASED DOUGLAS FIRS.] Tijdschr. over Plantenziekten 34: 109-110. (RAM 7: 609.) A1, B6, E9.

236. Korstian, C.F., and Brush, W.D.
1931. SOUTHERN WHITE CEDAR. U.S. Dept. Agr. Tech. Bul. 251, 75 pp. (RAM 11: 140.) A6, B1.

237. Ladefoged, K.
1959.*UNDERSØGELSER OVER FOSBINDELSEN MELLOM HUGSTSTYRKE, RODDØD OG RÅDDANNELSER I RØDGRAN. [RESEARCH ON THE RELATIONS BETWEEN FELLING GRADE, ROOT DEATH, AND ROT IN NORWAY SPRUCE.] Dansk Skovfor. Tidsskr. 44: 5-53. (FA 20: 3335.) A2, E1b,d,g, 5c,d, 12.

238. Lagerberg, T.
1936.*NÅGRA SYNPUNKTER PÅ BESTÅNDSVÅRD OCH-VIRKESVÅRD. [SOME ASPECTS OF CARE OF STANDING TIMBER AND OF WOOD.] Svenska Skogsvardsfor. Tidskr. 34: 396-406. (RAM 16: 145-146.) A2,7, B5, D2,4,5, E1c,d, 2a, 4d.

239. Leslie, P.
1915. THE PLANTING OF THE SAND DUNES AT CULBIN. Roy. Scot. Arbor. Soc. Trans. 29: 19-28. A5, B3, E5b.

240. Liese.
1950.*NEUERE SCHWEDISCHE ARBEITEN ÜBER DEN WURZELSCHWAMM. Forst u. Holz 4: 233-234. (BI)

241. Liese, J.
1928.*VERHALTEN HOLZZERSTÖRENDER
PILZE GEGENÜBER VERSCHIEDENEN
HOLZARTEN UND GIFTSTOFFE. [RE-
ACTION OF WOOD-DESTROYING FUNGI
TOWARDS THE VARIOUS KINDS OF TIM-
BER AND TOXIC SUBSTANCES.] Angew.
Bot. 10: 156-170. (RAM 7: 689-
690.) C3b, D3c.

242. ─────
1931.*BEOBACHTUNGEN ÜBER DIE BIOLO-
GIE HOLZZERSTÖRENDER PILZE. [OB-
SERVATIONS ON THE BIOLOGY OF WOOD-
DESTROYING FUNGI.] Angew. Bot.
13: 138-150.. (RAM 10: 572-573.)
C3a, 6.

243. ─────
1931.*ZUM KIEFERNSTERBEN IN NORD-
WESTDEUTSCHLAND. [ON THE DYING-OFF
OF PINES IN NORTH-WEST GERMANY.]
Forstarchiv 7: 333-334. (RAM 11:
82.) A1, B4, C7a.

244. ─────
1931.*ZUR RHABDOCLINEKRANKHEIT DER
DOUGLASIE. [ON THE RHABDOCLINE
DISEASE OF THE DOUGLAS FIR.]
Forstarchiv 7: 341-346. (RAM 11:
141-142.) A5, B4.

245. Lightle, P.C.
1960. FOMES ANNOSUS ROOT ROT OF
LOBLOLLY PINE. Plant Dis. Rptr.
44: 423. A1, B1, D2, E3a(4), 12,
16a, F4.

246. Lind, J.
1913.*DANISH FUNGI. Glydendalske
Boghandel-Nordisk Forlag. Copen-
hagen. (From Wilson, 1927, and
Baxter, 1940.) A4,7, B5, E4c.

247. Lindberg, G.
1948. SOME PROPERTIES OF THE CATE-.
CHOLASES OF LITTER-DECOMPOSING
AND PARASITIC HYMENOMYCETES.
Physiol. Plant. 1: 401-409. (RAM
29: 45.) C4.

248. Liubarski, L.V.
1936.* [FUNGAL DISEASES OF FOREST
TREES IN THE ZEYA AND RUKHLOVO
DISTRICTS OF THE RUSSIAN FAR
EAST.] Bul. Far East. Br. Acad.
Sci. U.S.S.R. 1936(17): 79-85.
(RAM 16: 357-358.) A3, B6, E3a(3),
(4).

249. Lloyd, C.G.
1915. SYNOPSIS OF THE GENUS FOMES.
Mycological Writings of C.G.
Lloyd 4: 209-288. D1.

250. Løfting, E.C.L.
1937.*HEDESKOVENES FORYNGELSE. V.
RODFORD AERVERANGREBENES BETYD-
NING FOR SITKAGRANS ANVEDLIGHED
I KLITTER OG HEDER. [REPRODUCTION
OF HEATH FORESTS. V. THE SIGNIFI-
CANCE OF THE ATTACKS OF POLYPORUS
ANNOSUS ON THE SUITABILITY OF
SITKA SPRUCE FOR DUNES AND
HEATHS.] Forstl. Forsøgsv. i
Danmark, Beret. 14: 133-157. (BI)
A2.

251. ─────
1937.*RODFORDAERVERANGREBENES BE-
TYDNING FOR SITKAGRANS ANVENDE-
LIGHED I KLITTER OG HEDER. [THE
SIGNIFICANCE OF THE ATTACK OF
POLYPORUS ANNOSUS TO THE SUIT-
ABILITY OF SITKA SPRUCE FOR DUNES
AND HEATHS.] Forstl. Forsøgsv.
i Danmark, Beret. 14: 133-160.
(From Wagener and Davidson, 1954.)
A2, B5, E1a, 5a,c, 8, 13a,b, 14.

252. Lohwag, K.
1955. ZUR ABBAUINTENSITÄT HOLZZER-
STÖRENDER PILZE. [ON THE INTENSITY
OF DECOMPOSITION BY WOOD-DESTROY-
ING FUNGI.] Sydowia 9: 359-366.
(RAM 35: 857.) C5b.

253. Low, J.D., and Gladman, R.J.
1960. FOMES ANNOSUS IN GREAT BRIT-
AIN. AN ASSESSMENT OF THE SITU-
ATION IN 1959. Gt. Brit. Forestry
Comm. Forest Rec. 41, 22 pp. A1,2,
3,4,5,6,7, B3,4,5, D2,4,5,6, E1a,
b,f,g,j, 2a, 3d(2), 4a,b,c,d, 5a,
b, 6, 7, 9, 10a,b, 12, 13a,b, 14,
16a,b, F1, G1.

254. Lowe, J.L.
1934. THE POLYPORACEAE OF NEW YORK
STATE (PILEATE SPECIES). N.Y.
State Col.   Forestry Tech. Pub.
41, 142 pp. D1.

255. ─────
1942. THE POLYPORACEAE OF NEW YORK
STATE (EXCEPT PORIA). N.Y. State
Col. Forestry Tech. Pub. 60, 128
pp. D1.

256. ─────
1955. PERENNIAL POLYPORES OF NORTH
AMERICA. III. FOMES WITH CONTEXT
WHITE TO ROSE. Mycologia 47:
213-224. C7a, D1.

257. Lyr, H.
1956.*ZUR FRAGE DER WIDERSTANDS-
FÄHIGKEIT DES KERNHOLZES ERKRANK-

TER UND GESUNDER DOUGLASIEN GEGEN-
ÜBER HOLZZERSTÖRENDEN PILZEN. [ON
THE QUESTION OF THE RESISTANCE OF
DISEASED AND HEALTHY DOUGLAS FIR
HEARTWOOD TO WOOD-DESTROYING
FUNGI.] Arch. Forstw. 5: 96-103.
(RAM 36: 149-150.) E9, F2.

258. MacDonald, J.
1939. THETFORD CHASE, WITH NOTES ON
SWAFFAM FOREST AND THE KING'S
FOREST. Forestry 13: 1-18. A2,3,7,
B3, E9, 10a, 13b.

259. McFarland, W.H.
1946. THE FUNGICIDAL PROPERTIES OF
DDT. South. Lumberman 178(2163):
48. (RAM 25: 589.) C7b.

260. M'Hardy, J.
1929. HEART ROT IN CONIFERS. Scot.
Forestry Jour. 43: 18-19. (RAM
9: 149.) A3,5, B3, C5a, E3a(6),
5b, 10a, 13a.

261. McLachlan, T.
1936. INFLUENCE OF CALCIUM IN THE
DECAY OF WOOD. Jour. Soc. Chem.
Indus. Lond. 55: 329. (RAM 15:
622.) C2c.

262. McNabb, H.S.
1954.*VARIATIONS AMONG ISOLATES OF
FOMES ANNOSUS (FR.) CKE. OF DIF-
FERENT GEOGRAPHICAL AND HOST
ORIGIN. Cong. Internatl. de Bot.
Rap. et Commun. 8(sect. 18/20):
133. (Citation from Bibliog. of
Agr. 20: 10927; abstract inform-
ation from RAM 37: 441-442.) C1.

263. Mangin, L., and Patouillard, N.
1922.*SUR LA DESTRUCTION DE CHAR-
PENTES AU CHÂTEAU DE VERSAILLES
PAR LE PHELLINUS CRYPTARUM KARST.
[ON THE ROTTING OF THE TIMBERWORK
IN THE PALACE OF VERSAILLES BY
PHELLINUS CRYPTARUM KARST.] Acad.
des Sci. Colon. Paris, Compt.
Rend. 175: 389-394. (RAM 2: 97-
98.) B6, C5c, 7a, D1, 3c.

264. Martínez, J.B.
1943.*EL FOMES ANNOSUS FR. (TRAMETES
RADICIPERDA HART.) EN ESPAÑA.
[FOMES ANNOSUS FR. (TRAMETES RADI-
CIPERDA HART.) IN SPAIN.] Re-
printed from An. Jard. Bot. Madrid
3, 49 pp. (RAM 25: 52.) A1, B6,
C1, D2,4, G8.

265. Mathes, M.T.
1911.*MITTEILUNGEN ÜBER BAU UND
LEBEN DER FICHTENWURZELN UND

UNTERSUCHUNGEN ÜBER DIE BEEIN-
FLUSSUNG DES WURZELWACHSTUMS DURCH
WIRTSCHAFTLICHE EINWIRKUNGEN.
Allg. Forst u. Jagd. Ztg. _:_.
(From Hiley, 1919.)

266. Mayer, K.
1919.*DIE ROTFÄULE. Forstwiss.
Centbl. 41: 121-127, 185-195.
(Bot. Abs. 4: 67-68.) A2, E1d,
5b,c, G6,7.

267. Meier, H.
1955.*ÜBER DEN ZELLWANDABBAU DURCH
HOLZVERMORSCHUNGSPILZE UND DIE
SUBMIKROSKOPISCHE STRUKTUR VON
FICHTENTRACHEIDEN UND BIRKENHOLZ-
FASERN. [ON CELL WALL DEGRADATION
BY WOOD-ROTTING FUNGI AND THE SUB-
MICROSCOPIC STRUCTURE OF SPRUCE
TRACHEIDS AND BIRCH WOOD FIBRES.]
Holz Roh- u. Werkstoff 13: 323-
338. (RAM 35: 563.) A2,7, C5b.

268. Meineke, E.P.
1914. FOREST TREE DISEASES COMMON
IN CALIFORNIA AND NEVADA. U.S.
Dept. Agr. Forest Serv., 67 pp.
A6, B1, D2, E1b, 2a, 3a(3), b(1),
(2), 10c, 16b.

269. Meredith, D.S.
1957.*ECOLOGY OF FUNGI COLONISING
CONIFEROUS STUMPS IN EAST ANGLIA.
Gt. Brit. Forestry Comn. Rpt.
1956/57: 99-100. (FA 20: 707.)
B3, E2a, F3c.

270. _____
1959.*THE INFECTION OF PINE STUMPS
BY FOMES ANNOSUS AND OTHER FUNGI.
Ann. Bot., Lond. (N.S.) 23:
455-476. (FA 21: 1992.) A1, B3,
D2, E2a, 10c, F3c, G1.

271. Meulen, J.E. van der.
1932.*DE BESTRIJDING VAN DEN 'DEN-
NENMOORDER', FOMES ANNOSUS.
(TRAMETES RADICIPERDA.) Nederland.
Heidemaatsch. Tijdschr. 44: 267-
270. (BI)

272. Miller, J.K.
1943. FOMES ANNOSUS AND RED CEDAR.
Jour. Forestry 41: 37-40. A6, B1,
C4, D2, E2c, 10b.

273. Moesz, G. von.
1941.*DIE PILZE DER BERGWERKE UND
HÖHLEN IN UNGARN. [MINE AND CAVE
FUNGI IN HUNGARY.] Bot. Közlem.
38(1-2): 4-11. (RAM 20: 505.)
B6, D3a.

274. Molin, N.
1957.*OM *FOMES ANNOSUS* SPRIDNINGS-
BIOLOGI. [THE INFECTION BIOLOGY
OF *F. ANNOSUS*.] Statens SkogforsknInst. [Sweden], Meddel.
47(3), 36 pp. (FA 18: 4228.) A1,
2, B5, C2d, E1b, F3a.

275. Møller, C.M.
1939.*NYE DANSKE UNDERSØGELSER OVER
RODFORDAERVEREN. [FRESH INVESTI-
GATIONS IN DENMARK ON *FOMES
(POLYPORUS) ANNOSUS*.] Dansk
Skovfor. Tidsskr. 1939: 433-454.
(FA 1: 294.) B5, E1a,c,e,i, 5b,
12, 13a, 16a,b, G5,7.

276. Mörmann, P.
1953.*DIE EUROPÄISCHE LÄRCHE IN
BADEN: HERKUNFT, ENTWICKLUNG UND
ANBAUAUSSICHTEN. [EUROPEAN LARCH
IN BADEN: PROVENANCE, DEVELOPMENT,
AND PROSPECTS FOR ITS CULTI-
VATION.] Forstwiss. Forsch. 2,
71 pp. (FA 15: 1267.) A3, B4, E4b,
5a,b, 10a.

277. Morogues, Baron de.
1877.*LA MALADIE DU ROND. Rev. des
Eaux et Forêts 16: 186-192. (BI)

278. _____
1878.*LA MALADIE DU ROND. Rev. des
Eaux et Forêts 17: 318-319. (BI)

279. Morville, K.
1958.*TRAMETES I EN SLANGEGRAN-
BEVOKSNING. [*FOMES ANNOSUS* IN A
PLANTATION OF 'SNAKE' SPRUCE.]
Dansk Skovfor. Tidsskr. 43: 221-
230. (FA 19: 4408.) A2, E3a(5),
5b, 10d, 16a.

280. Nechleba, A.
1927.*NOTIZEN ÜBER DAS VORKOMMEN
EINIGER FORSTLICH BEMERKENSWERTER
PATHOGENER PILZE IN BÖHMEN. [NOTES
ON THE OCCURRENCE IN BOHEMIA OF
SOME SILVICULTURALLY REMARKABLE
PATHOGENIC FUNGI.] Ztschr. f.
Pflanzenkrank. 37(9-10):267-270.
(RAM 7: 205.) A7, B6, D2, 5.

281. Neger, F.W.
1917.*BEITRÄGE ZUR KENNTNIS DES
ROTFÄULEPILZER (*TRAMETES RADICI-
PERDA* HARTIG). Naturw. Ztschr. f.
Forst-u. Landw. 15: 52-68. (BI)

282. Nestertschuk, G.I.
1930.* [FORESTS OF THE KARELIA-MURMAN
REGION AND THEIR ENEMIES.] Morbi

Plant., Leningrad 19(3-4): 159-
182. (RAM 10: 416.) A1,2, B6,
E4a,b, 10a.

283. Nissen, T.V.
1956. ACTINOMYCETES ANTAGONISTIC TO
POLYPORUS ANNOSUS FR. Experimentia
12: 229-230. (RAM 35: 732.) A2,
B5, C2d, 3b, E1c,k, 4c, F3b, G3.

284. _____
1956. SOIL ACTINOMYCETES ANTAGON-
ISTIC TO *POLYPORUS ANNOSUS* FR.
Friesia 5: 332-339. (RAM 36: 221.)
A2,6, E1c, F3a,b, G3.

285. Nobles, Mildred K.
1948. STUDIES IN FOREST PATHOLOGY.
VI. IDENTIFICATION OF CULTURES OF
WOOD-ROTTING FUNGI. Canad. Jour.
Res. Sect. C, 26: 281-431. C1.

286. Nord, F.F., and Vitucci, J.C.
1947. ENZYME STUDIES ON THE MECHAN-
ISM OF WOOD DECAY. Nature, Lond.
160(4059): 224-225. (FA 9: 1622.)
C2a, 4.

287. _____ and Vitucci, J.C.
1947.*ON THE MECHANISM OF ENZYME
ACTION. XXIX. THE ACETATE METABO-
LISM OF CERTAIN WOOD-DESTROYING
MOLDS AND THE MECHANISM OF WOOD
DECAY. Arch. Biochem. 14(1-2):
229-241. (RAM 26: 517.) C2a,b,d,
4, 5b.

288. _____ Sciarini, L.J.,
Vitucci, J.C., and Pallares, E.S.
1946. ALCOHOLIC FERMENTATION OF
CARBOHYDRATES AND DEHYDROGENATION
OF ALCOHOLS BY CERTAIN WOOD-
DESTROYING FUNGI. Nature, Lond.
157(3985): 335-336. (FA 8: 303.)
C2a, 4.

289. Nowotny, R.
1924.*ÜBER DIE BEDEUTUNG DER WASSER-
LOSLICHEN BESTANDTEILE IN IMPRÄG-
NIERTEERÖLEN. [THE IMPORTANCE OF
THE WATER-SOLUBLE CONSTITUENTS IN
COAL-TAR OILS FOR IMPREGNATION.]
Ztschr. f. Angew. Chem. 37(5):
59-61. (RAM 3: 617.) C2b.

290. Oechslin, M.
1957.*SCHÄDIGUNGEN IN AUFFORSTUNGEN
IM HOCHGEBIRGE. [PATHOGENIC
AGENCIES IN AFFORESTATIONS IN THE
HIGH MOUNTAINS.] Schweiz. Ztschr.
f. Forstw. 108: 93-101. (RAM 37:
560.) B6, E4b.

291. Oksbjerg, O., and West-Nielsen, G.
1953.*OM RODFORDAERVERANGREB. [DAM-
AGE [TO SPRUCE] BY *FOMES ANNOSUS*.]
Hedeselsk. Tidsskr. 74: 319-334.
(FA 15: 3729.) A2, B5, F5a,c, 13a.

292. Olson, A.J.
1941. A ROOT DISEASE OF JEFFREY AND
PONDEROSA PINE REPRODUCTION.
Phytopath. 31: 1063-1077. A1, B1,
C3a, 5c, 7a, E1b,e,f, 3a(3),(4),
(5), 4d, 5e, 10a, 16b.

293. Oort, A.J.P.
1950.*DENNENMOORDER EN ZWAVELKOPJE
ALS CONCURRENTEN. [THE PINE-
DESTROYER AND SULPHUR TUFT AS
COMPETITORS.] Fungus, Wageningen
20(1): 2-4. (RAM 29: 546.)

294. Orłoś, H.
1935.*SPRAWOZDANIE Z DZIALALNOSCI
INSTYTUTU BADAWCZEGO W DZIEDZINIE
FITOPATOLOGJI ZA ROK 1933. [REPORT
ON THE PHYTOPATHOLOGICAL ACTIVITY
OF THE RESEARCH INSTITUTE IN
1933.] Trav. Inst. Rech. Forest.
Doman. Varsovie, Ser. A(11): 7-19.
(RAM 14: 663.) B6.

295. _____ and Brennejzen, B.
1957.*BADANIA NAD ZWALCZANIEM HUB
DRZEWNYCH ZA POMOCĄ ZASTRZYKOW
ŚRODKÓW GRZYBOBÓJCZYCH. [INVESTI-
GATIONS INTO METHODS OF CONTROL-
LING DECAY BY INJECTING FUNGI-
CIDES INTO STANDING TREES.] Rocz.
Nauk Rolnicz. i Leśnych 19: 3-42.
(FA 20: 713.) A1, G1.

296. Overholts, L.O.
1953. THE POLYPORACEAE OF THE UNITED
STATES. Univ. Mich. Press, Ann
Arbor, 466 pp. A1,2,4,5,6,7, B1,
C7a, D1,2,3a,c, 4, E3a(3), b(1),
(2).

297. Peace, T.R.
1938. BUTT ROT OF CONIFERS IN GREAT
BRITAIN. Quart. Jour. Forestry 32:
81-104. A1,2,3, B3, D6, E9, 10a,
13a.

298. _____
1939. FOREST PATHOLOGY IN NORTH
AMERICA. Forestry 13: 36-45. (RAM
18: 827-828.) B1, D4, E6,7, 11a.

299. _____
1957. THE CONTROL OF DISEASES IN
THE FOREST. (Abstract.) Brit.
Mycol. Soc. Trans. 40: 166. (RAM
36: 626.) G1,2.

300. Pearson, G.A.
1950. MANAGEMENT OF PONDEROSA PINE
IN THE SOUTHWEST. U.S. Dept. Agr.
Agr. Monog. 6v. 218 pp. A1, B1,
E10a, 16b.

301. Pearson, R.S.
1930.*REPORT OF THE DIRECTOR OF
FOREST PRODUCTS RESEARCH FOR THE
PERIOD OCTOBER, 1928, TO 31ST
DECEMBER, 1929. Gt. Brit. Forest
Prod. Res. Bd. Rpt. 1929: 11-50.
(RAM 10: 141-143.) B3, C2b, 5a,
D3a.

302. _____
1932.*REPORT OF THE DIRECTOR OF
FOREST PRODUCTS RESEARCH FOR THE
YEAR 1930. Gt. Brit. Forest
Prod. Res. Bd. Rpt. 1930: 5-52.
(RAM 11: 487-488.) C2b, 5a.

303. Pehrson, S.O.
1949. FUNGICIDAL EFFECTS OF CULTURE
FILTRATES OF A COLIFORM BACTERIUM-
TYPE. Physiol. Plant. 2: 149-156.
(RAM 31: 155-156.) C2d.

304. Persson, E.
1957.*ÜBER DEN STOFFWECHSEL UND EINE
ANTIBIOTISCH WIRKSAME SUBSTANZ VON
POLYPORUS ANNOSUS FR. [THE METABO-
LISM AND AN ANTIBIOTIC SUBSTANCE
OF *FOMES ANNOSUS*.] Phytopath.
Ztschr. 30: 45-86. (FA 19: 1941.)
C2c, 4.

305. Petrini, S.
1926.*SPRIDDA DRAG FRÅN SKÖGSSKÖT-
SELN PÅ FRIJSENBORG. Skogen 13(6):
176-196. (BA 1: 10287.) E3d(2),
G5.

306. _____
1946.*OM GRANRÖTANS INVERKAN PÅ
AVVERKNINGENS ROT VÄRDE. [ON THE
INFLUENCE OF SPRUCE ROOT ROT ON
THE YIELD FROM CLEAR-CUTTING.]
Statens Skogsforsoksanst. [Sweden],
Meddel. 34: 327-340. (RAM 26:
367.) A2, B5, E4a,c.

307. Pinto-Lopes, J.
1950.*POLIPOROSES E FUNGOS DA DE-
COMPOSIÇÃO DA MADEIRA EM PORTUGAL.
[POLYPOROSES AND FUNGI CAUSING
DECOMPOSITION OF WOOD IN PORTUGAL.]
Rev. Fac. Ciênc. Lisb., Sér. 2,
C, 1: 53-108. (RAM 31: 92-93.) B6,
D3a, 4.

- 26 -

308. Pollich.
1958.*BEOBACHTUNGEN ÜBER ROTFÄULE
AUF JURATROCKENBODEN. [OBSERVA-
TIONS ON RED ROT ON DRY SITES IN
THE [FRANCONIAN] JURA.] Allg.
Forstzeitschr. 13: 312-313. (FA
19: 4407.) A2, B4, E3a(2),(3),(5),
4a, 5c.

309. Populer, C.
1956.*LA POURRITURE ROUGE DU COEUR
DES RÉSINEUX (FOMES ANNOSUS (FR.)
COOKE). [RED HEART ROT OF RESINOUS
TREES (FOMES ANNOSUS (FR.) COOKE.)]
Soc. Cent. Forest. de Belg. Bul.
63: 297-329. (RAM 36: 221.) A2,
B6, E4b, 6,7,8.

310. Priehäusser, G.
1935.*BEITRAG ZUR FRAGE DER ENTSTE-
HUNG DER FICHTENROTFÄULE. [A CON-
TRIBUTION TO THE PROBLEM OF THE
DEVELOPMENT OF RED ROT OF SPRUCE.]
Forstwiss. Centbl. 57: 649-655.
(RAM 15: 184-185.) A2, B4, E5b,c,
G5.

311. ───────
1943.*ÜBER FICHTENWURZELFÄULE, KRON-
ENFORM UND STANDORT. BEITRAG ZUR
KENNTNIS DER FICHTENROTFÄULE. [ON
SPRUCE ROOT ROT, CROWN SHAPE, AND
HABITAT. A CONTRIBUTION TO THE
KNOWLEDGE OF SPRUCE RED ROT.]
Forstwiss. Centbl. 65: 259-273.
(RAM 23: 417-418.) A2, B4, E3a(2),
d(2), 5c, 12, G5,7.

312. Prillieux, E.
1895.*MALADIES DES PLANTES AGRI-
CALES. Paris. (From Wilson, 1927.)
A7.

313. Proctor, P.
1941. PENETRATION OF THE WALLS OF
WOOD CELLS BY THE HYPHAE OF WOOD-
DESTROYING FUNGI. Yale Univ.,
School Forestry Bul. 47, 31 pp.
(RAM 21: 110-111.) C5c, 8.

314. Quirke, D.A.
1946.*FOREST PATHOLOGY: ITS SIGNIFI-
CANCE IN RELATION TO IRISH
FORESTRY PRACTICE. Irish Forestry
3: 10-25. (FA 8: 1445.) B3.

315. Rabanus, A.
1931.*DIE TOXIMETRISCHE PRÜFUNG VON
HOLZKONSERVIERUNGSMITTELN. [THE
TOXIMETRIC TESTING OF WOOD PRESER-
VATIVES.] Angew. Bot. 13: 352-371.
(RAM 11: 83-84.) C2b.

316. ───────
1939.*ÜBER DIE SÄURE-PRODUKTION VON
PILZEN UND DEREN EINFLUSS AUF DIE
WIRKUNG VON HOLZSCHUTZMITTELN. [ON
THE ACID PRODUCTION OF FUNGI AND
ITS INFLUENCE ON THE ACTION OF
WOOD PRESERVATIVES.] Mitt. Deut.
Forstver. 23: 77-89. (RAM 18:
426.) C4.

317. Rankin, W.H.
1918. MANUAL OF TREE DISEASES. Mac-
millan Co., New York, 398 pp. A1,
2,4, B1, D2,6, E1a,g, 2c, E3b(1),
(2), 10c.

318. Rattsjö, H., and Rennerfelt, E.
1955.*VÄRDEFÖRLUSTEN PÅ VIRKESUT-
BYTET TILL FÖLJD AV RÖDROTA.
[DEPRECIATION OF SAW TIMBER IN
CONSEQUENCE OF ROOT ROT.] Norr-
lands SkogsvFörb. Tidskr. 1955(3):
279-298. (RAM 35: 565.) A2, B5,
E4b,c.

319. Reeve, C.S.
1928. THE DETERMINATION OF THE
TOXICITY OF WOOD PRESERVATIVES.
Amer. Wood Preservers' Assoc.
Proc. 1928: 42-52. (RAM 7: 755.)
C2b.

320. Rennerfelt, E.
1942.*DAS WACHSTUM EINIGER FÄULNIS-
PILZE AUF HOLZSCHLIFF. [THE GROWTH
OF SOME ROT FUNGI ON MECHANICAL
PULP.] Svensk Bot. Tidskr. 36:
301-311. (RAM 21: 357.) C3b, 5a.

321. ───────
1943.*DIE TOXIZITÄT DER PHENOLISCHEN
INHALTSSTOFFE DES KIEFERNKERN-
HOLZES GEGENÜBER EINIGEN FÄULNIS-
PILZEN. [THE TOXICITY OF THE PHEN-
OLIC INGREDIENTS OF PINE HEARTWOOD
TO SOME ROT FUNGI.] Svensk Bot.
Tidskr. 37: 83-93. (RAM 22: 282-
283.) C2b, 5a.

322. ───────
1944.*DIE ENTWICKLUNG VON FOMES
ANNOSUS FR. BEI ZUSATZ VON ANEURIN
UND VERSCHIEDENEN EXTRAKTEN. [THE
DEVELOPMENT OF FOMES ANNOSUS FR.
WITH THE ADDITION OF ANEURIN AND
VARIOUS EXTRACTS.] Svensk Bot.
Tidskr. 38: 153-162. (RAM 23:
464.) C2a,d.

323. ───────
1944.*UNDERSÖKNINGAR ÖVER TOXICITE-
TEN EMOT ROTSVAMPAR HOS TALLKÄRN-

VEDENS FENOLISKA BESTANDSDELAR.
[INVESTIGATIONS ON THE TOXICITY
TO ROT FUNGI OF THE PHENOLIC COM-
PONENTS OF PINE HEARTWOOD.]
Statens Skogförsöksanst. [Sweden],
Meddel. 33: 331-364. (RAM 23:
465.) C2b.

324. Rennerfelt, E.
1945.*OM GRANENS ROTRÖTA, DESS FÖRE-
KOMST OCH UTBREDNING. [THE OCCUR-
RENCE AND DISTRIBUTION OF SPRUCE
BUTT ROT.] Svenska Skogsvårdsför.
Tidskr. 43: 316-334. (RAM 25: 374.)
A1,2,3, B5, C8, D4,6, E1c, 4a,b,
5a,b,e, 6, 9, 10a, 13a, G5.

325. ⸻
1946.*OM ROTRÖTAN (POLYPORUS ANNOSUS
FR.) I SVERIGE. DESS UTBREDNING
OCH SÄTT ATT UPPTRÄDA. [ON BUTT
ROT CAUSED BY POLYPORUS (FOMES)
ANNOSUS IN SWEDEN. ITS DISTRIBU-
TION AND MODE OF OCCURRENCE.]
Statens SkogforsknInst. [Sweden],
Meddel. 35(8): 1-88. (FA 8: 2097.)
A2, B5, C2a,d, D6, E5a,b,c, G8.

326. ⸻
1947.*NÅGRA UNDERSÖKNINGAR ÖVER
OLIKA RÖTSVAMPARS FÖRMÅGA ATT
ANGRIPA SPLINT- OCH KÄRNVED HOS
TALL. [SOME INVESTIGATIONS ON THE
APTITUDE OF DIFFERENT ROT FUNGI
FOR THE INFECTION OF SAP AND
HEARTWOOD OF PINE.] Statens Skogs-
forskInst. [Sweden],Meddel. 36(9):
1-24. (RAM 27: 397-398.) A1, B5,
C2d, 5d, 8, E4b,d, 5c, F2.

327. ⸻
1949.*THE EFFECT OF SOIL ORGANISMS
ON THE DEVELOPMENT OF POLYPORUS
ANNOSUS FR., THE ROOT ROT FUNGUS.
Oikos 1: 65-78. (RAM 29: 595-596.)
F3b.

328. ⸻
1949.*THE EFFECT OF SOME ANTIBIOTIC
SUBSTANCES ON THE GERMINATION OF
THE CONIDIA OF POLYPORUS ANNOSUS
FR. Acta Chem. Scand. 3: 1343-
1349. (RAM 29: 524.) A1,2, B5,
C2b,c, E4c.

329. ⸻
1952. OM ANGREPP AV ROTRÖTA PÅ TALL.
[ON THE INFECTION OF SCOTS PINE
BY ROOT ROT.] Statens Skogsforskn-
Inst. [Sweden], Meddel. 41(9)
1-39. (RAM 33: 190.) A1,2,3, B5,
C2d, D6, E1a,b,f, 5a,b,c, 6, 9,
10a, 12, 13a, 14, 16b, F3a.

330. ⸻
1956.*UNTERSUCHUNGEN ÜBER DIE WUR-
ZELFÄULE AUF FICHTE UND KIEFER IN
SCHWEDEN. [ROOT ROT OF SPRUCE AND
PINE IN SWEDEN.] Phytopath.Ztschr.
28: 259-274. (FA 18: 4227.) A1,2,
B5, D6, E4c.

331. ⸻ and Nacht, Gertrud.
1955.*THE FUNGICIDAL ACTIVITY OF
SOME CONSTITUENTS FROM HEARTWOOD
OF CONIFERS. Svensk Bot. Tidskr.
49: 419-432. (RAM 35: 58.) C2b.

332. ⸻ and Paris, Sheila K.
1953.*SOME PHYSIOLOGICAL AND ECO-
LOGICAL EXPERIMENTS WITH POLYPORUS
ANNOSUS FR. Oikos 4: 58-76. (RAM
33: 271.) C2c,d, 3a, 4, F3b.

333. Rhoads, A.S., and Wright, E.
1946. FOMES ANNOSUS COMMONLY A WOUND
PATHOGEN RATHER THAN A ROOT PARA-
SITE OF WESTERN HEMLOCK IN WESTERN
OREGON AND WASHINGTON. Jour.
Forestry 44: 1091-1092. A2,6, B1,
E1g,h, 4a.

334. Rhodes, F.H., and Erickson, I.
1933. EFFICIENCIES OF TAR OIL COM-
PONENTS AS PRESERVATIVE FOR TIMBER.
Indus. and Engin. Chem. 25: 989-
991. (RAM 13: 137.) C2b.

335. ⸻ and Gardner, F.T.
1930. COMPARATIVE EFFICIENCIES OF
THE COMPONENTS OF CREOSOTE OIL AS
PRESERVATIVES FOR TIMBER. Indus.
and Engin. Chem. 22: 167-171. (RAM
9: 619-620.) C7b.

336. Ribbentrop, B.
1908. ROOT DISEASE IN SCOTS PINE ON
FARM LANDS. Roy. Scot. Arbor. Soc.
Trans. 21: 143-149. A1,7, B4, E1b,
i, 3a(2),(4),(5), d(1), 4a, 5a, 7,
10a, 13a, 14, G2, 5.

337. Richards, C. Audrey.
1924. THE COMPARATIVE RESISTANCE OF
17 SPECIES OF WOOD-DESTROYING
FUNGI TO SODIUM FLUORIDE. Amer.
Wood Preservers' Assoc. Proc.
1924: 37-44. (RAM 4: 579.) C7b.

338. ⸻.
1925. THE COMPARATIVE RESISTANCE OF
EIGHTEEN SPECIES OF WOOD-DESTROY-
ING FUNGI TO ZINC CHLORIDE. Amer.
Wood Preservers' Assoc. Proc.
1925: 18-22. (RAM 5: 397.) C7b.

339. Richards. C. Audrey.
    1937. THE DOUBTFUL IDENTITY OF
    FUNGUS NO. 517. Amer. Wood Pre-
    servers' Assoc. Proc. 1937: 104-
    106. (RAM 17: 5.) C7b.

340. Rishbeth, J.
    1949. *FOMES ANNOSUS* FR. ON PINES IN
    EAST ANGLIA. Forestry 22: 174-183.
    A1, B3, C2d, 3a, E1a,e, 2a, 5a,
    10a, 12, 13a, F1, 3b, 4.

341. _____
    1950. OBSERVATIONS ON THE BIOLOGY
    OF *FOMES ANNOSUS*, WITH PARTICULAR
    REFERENCE TO EAST ANGLIAN PINE
    PLANTATIONS. I. THE OUTBREAK OF
    DISEASE AND ECOLOGICAL STATUS OF
    THE FUNGUS. Ann. Bot. (N.S.) 14:
    365-383. A1,7, B3, C2d, 3a, E1f,
    2c, 3a(1),(4), 5a, 10a,b, 12, 13a,
    F2, 3b.

342. _____
    1951. BUTT ROT BY *FOMES ANNOSUS* FR.
    IN EAST ANGLIAN CONIFER PLANTA-
    TIONS AND ITS RELATION TO TREE
    KILLING. Forestry 24: 114-120.
    (FA 13: 2256.) A1,2,3,5,6, B3,
    E3a(4), b(2), 5a, 9, 10a, 12, 13a.

343. _____
    1951. OBSERVATIONS ON THE BIOLOGY OF
    FOMES ANNOSUS, WITH PARTICULAR
    REFERENCE TO EAST ANGLIAN PINE
    PLANTATIONS. II. SPORE PRODUCTION,
    STUMP INFECTION, AND SAPROPHYTIC
    ACTIVITY IN STUMPS. Ann. Bot.
    (N.S.) 15: 1-22. A1,2,3,5,7, B3,
    C3a,b, E1b,f,i, 2a, 3a(1),(2),(4),
    5a, 13a, F2, 3a,c, 4, G1,2.

344. _____
    1951. OBSERVATIONS ON THE BIOLOGY
    OF *FOMES ANNOSUS* WITH PARTICULAR
    REFERENCE TO EAST ANGLIAN PINE
    PLANTATIONS. III. NATURAL AND
    EXPERIMENTAL INFECTION OF PINES,
    AND SOME FACTORS AFFECTING SEVER-
    ITY OF THE DISEASE. Ann. Bot.
    (N.S.) 15: 221-246. A1, B3, E1c,i,
    2a, 3d(2), 4d, 5a, 10a,b,c, 12,
    13a, F3a, 4.

345. _____
    1951. *In* REPORT ON FOREST RESEARCH
    FOR THE YEAR ENDING MARCH, 1950.
    Gt. Brit., p. 77. (RAM 30: 591.)
    E2a, G6.

346. _____
    1952. CONTROL OF *FOMES ANNOSUS* FR.
    Forestry 25: 41-50. (FA 13: 3095.)

    A1, B3, E1b, 2a, 3c, F3c, G2,3,5,
    7.

347. _____
    1957. *FOMES ANNOSUS* ON STUMPS.
    (Abstract.) Brit. Mycol. Soc.
    Trans. 40: 167. (RAM 36: 626.)
    E4b, 16a, F3c, G1.

348. _____
    1957.*REPORT ON FOREST RESEARCH FOR
    THE YEAR ENDED MARCH 1956. Gt.
    Brit., pp. 87-88. (RAM 36: 794-
    795.) A1, 2,3, B3, E1b, 13a,b, 14,
    16a.

349. _____
    1957. SOME FURTHER OBSERVATIONS ON
    FOMES ANNOSUS FR. Forestry 30:
    69-89. A1, B3, E1f,g, 2a, 4b,d,
    5a, 10a,b, 12.

350. _____
    1958. DETECTION OF VIABLE AIR-BORNE
    SPORES IN AIR. Nature, Lond. 181
    (4622): 1549. (FA 20: 709.) E2a.

351. _____
    1959.*DISPERSAL OF *FOMES ANNOSUS* FR.
    AND *PENIOPHORA GIGANTEA* (FR.)
    MASSE. Brit. Mycol. Soc. Trans.
    42: 243-260. (FA 21: 632.) E2a.

352. _____
    1959.*STUMP PROTECTION AGAINST *FOMES
    ANNOSUS*. I. TREATMENT WITH CREO-
    SOTE. II. TREATMENT WITH SUB-
    STANCES OTHER THAN CREOSOTE. Ann.
    Appl. Biol. 47: 519-528, 529-541.
    (RAM 39: 251.) I: G1, II: F3c, G1.

353. _____ and Meredith, D.S.
    1957. SURFACE MICROFLORA OF PINE
    NEEDLES. Nature, Lond. 179(4561):
    682-683. C8, E2a.

354. Robak, H.
    1933.*ON THE GROWTH OF THREE WOOD-
    DESTROYING POLYPOREAE IN RELATION
    TO THE HYDROGEN-ION CONCENTRATION
    OF THE SUBSTRATUM. Svensk Bot.
    Tidskr. 27: 56-76. (RAM 12: 543-
    544.) C2c.

355. _____
    1951.*NOEN IAKTTAKELSER TIL BE-
    LYSNING AV FORHOLDET MELLOM KLIM-
    ATISKE SKADER OG SOPPANGREP PÅ
    NÅLETRAER. [SOME OBSERVATIONS TO
    ELUCIDATE THE CONNECTION BETWEEN
    CLIMATIC INJURIES AND FUNGAL IN-
    FECTION OF CONIFERS.] Vestland

Forstl. Forsøkssta. Meddel. 27
(8,2), 43 pp. (RAM 31: 92.) A1,2,
3,5, B5, E7,9, 14, 16a.

356. Robertson, W.A.
1936.*REPORT OF THE DIRECTOR OF
FOREST PRODUCTS RESEARCH FOR THE
YEAR 1935. Gt. Brit. Forest Prod.
Res. Bd. Rpt. 1935: 3-55. (RAM 16:
290.) C7b.

357. Rohmeder, E.
1937.*DIE STAMMFÄULE (WURZELFÄULE
UND WUNDFÄULE) DER FICHTENBESTOCK-
UNG. [STEM ROT (ROOT ROT AND WOUND
ROT) OF STANDING SPRUCES.] Mitt.
LandesForstverw. Bayerns, 23, 166
pp. (RAM 17: 86.) A2, B4, E3a(3),
G4,7.

358. Roll-Hansen, F.
1940. UNDERSOKELSER OVER POLYPORUS
ANNOSUS FR., SAERLIG.MED HENBLIKK
PÅ DENS FOREKOMST I DET SONNAFJEL-
SKE NORGE. [STUDIES IN POLYPORUS
ANNOSUS FR., ESPECIALLY IN RESPECT
OF ITS OCCURRENCE IN NORWAY SOUTH
OF THE DOVRE FELL.] Norske Skogs-
forsoksv. Meddel. NR. 24, 7(1):
1-100. (RAM 25: 193-194.) A1,2,3,
4,5,6,7, B5, C1, 3a, 6,8, D2, E1i,
5e, 6,7, 10a,c, 11a,b, G5.

359. ─────
1942.*LITT OM ROTKJUKEN. [NOTES ON
POLYPORUS ANNOSUS.] Tidsskr. for
Skogbruk. 50(7/8): 208-212. (FA
5: 60.) A1,2, B5, E4c, 9, G7.

360. Roth, E.R.
1952. ROOTS OF LIVING PINUS RIGIDA
DECAYED BY FOMES ANNOSUS. Plant
Dis. Rptr. 36: 330. A1,6, B1,
E3a(4).

361. Russell, P.
1956. A SELECTIVE MEDIUM FOR THE
ISOLATION OF BASIDIOMYCETES.
Nature, Lond. 177(4518): 1038-
1039. (RAM 35: 698.) C2b.

362. Růžička, J.
1928.*OHNILOBĚ LESNÍCH STROMŮ. [ON
THE DECAY OF FOREST TREES.]
Czechoslovak Acad. Agr. Bul. 4(1):
8-9. (RAM 7: 551-552.) A1, B6,
E4c, 5b,c,d, 11b, G7.

363. Samofal, S.A.
1926.*[THE PARASITIC FUNGI ARMILLARIA
MELLEA QUÉLET AND POLYPORUS
ANNOSUS FRIES IN PINE FORESTS AND
THEIR IMPORTANCE IN FOREST CUL-

TURE.] [Russian.] Mater. po Mikol.
i Fitopat. 5(2): 93-116. (BI) A1.

364. Šarić-Sabadoš, Ana.
1957.*PRILOG POZNAVANJU MIKOFLORE
NEKIH JUGOSLAVENSKIH RUDNIKA
UGLJENA. [CONTRIBUTION TO THE
STUDY OF THE FUNGAL FLORA IN
CERTAIN COAL MINES IN YUGOSLAVIA.]
Acta Bot. Croat. 16: 113-127. (RAM
37: 688.) D3a.

365. Sasaki, T., and Yokota, S.
1955.*[WOOD DECAY OF ABIES SACHALIN-
ENSIS FOREST IN TOKYO UNIVERSITY
FOREST IN HOKKAIDO.] Misc. Inform.
Tokyo Univ. Forestry 10: 15-21.
(RAM 35: 251.) A4, B7, E1a, 4b, F1.

366. ───── and Yokota, S.
1956.*[WOOD DECAY OF ABIES SACHALIN-
ENSIS FOREST IN TOKYO UNIVERSITY
FOREST IN HOKKAIDO. II.] Bul.
Tokyo Univ. Forests 52: 75-87.
(FA 19: 3154.) A4, B7, E4a,b, G7.

367. Sauer, F.
1917.*DIE ROTFÄULE. Forstwiss.
Centbl. 39: 26. (BI)

368. ─────
1918.*DIE ROTFÄULE. Ztschr. f.
Pflanzenkrank.28: 68. (BI)

369. Schmitschek.
1929.*WALDHYGIENISCHE BEOBACHTUNGEN
ANLÄSSLICH DER SCHWEIZER LEHR-
WANDERUNG DES ÖSTERREICHISCHEN
REICHSFORSTVEREINS 1929. Österr.
Vrtljschr. f. Forstw. 47: 347-356.
(BI) A2.

370. Schmitz, H.
1933. THE TOXICITY TO WOOD-DESTROY-
ING FUNGI OF COAL-TAR CREOSOTE-
PETROLEUM AND COAL-TAR CREOSOTE-
COAL-TAR MIXTURES. Amer. Wood
Preservers' Assoc. Proc. 1933:
125-139. (RAM 13: 69.) C2b.

371. ───── and Buckman, S.
1932. TOXIC ACTION OF COAL-TAR
CREOSOTE WITH SPECIAL REFERENCE
TO THE EXISTENCE OF A BARREN NON-
TOXIC OIL. Indus. and Engin. Chem.
24: 772-777. (RAM 11: 758.) C7b.

372. Schober, R., and Zycha, H.
1948.*BEOBACHTUNGEN ÜBER STOCKFÄULE
IN NORDWESTDEUTSCHEN LÄRCHENBEST-
ÄNDEN. Forstwiss. Centbl. 67: 119-
128. (From Wagener and Davidson,
1954.) A3, B4, E5e.

373. Schoenwald, R.
1931.*WAHRNEHMUNGEN ÜBER DAS TRIEBS-
CHWINDEN DER KIEFER (CENANGIUM
ABIETIS [PERS.]) IN DEN JAHREN
1926-28. [OBSERVATIONS ON THE DIE-
BACK OF PINE SHOOTS (CENANGIUM
ABIETIS [PERS.]) DURING THE YEARS
1926-28.] Deut. Forst. Ztg. 46:
484-485. (RAM 10: 699.) F1,2.

374. Schrenk, H. von.
1900. SOME DISEASES OF NEW ENGLAND
CONIFERS: A PRELIMINARY REPORT.
U.S. Dept. Agr. Div.   Veg.
Physiol. and Path. Bul. 25, 56 pp.
A2, B1, E2c, 3a(4),(5).

375. Schwarz.
1938.*SCHÄDEN AN DER FICHTE IN
WIENERWALD. Wien. Allg. Forst. u.
Jagd. Ztg. 56: 288-289. (BI) A2.

376. Schwerin, Graf von.
1929.*SCHLECHTE ERFAHRUNGEN MIT
PINUS INOPS (= CONTORTA) UND P.
RIGIDA. Deut. Dendrol. Gesell.
Mitt. p. 167. (BI) A1.

377. Shope, P.F.
1931. THE POLYPORACEAE OF COLORADO.
Mo. Bot. Gard. Ann. 18: 287-456.
A2, B1, D1.

378. Siemaszko, W.
1933.*QUELQUES OBSERVATIONS SUR LES
MALADIES DES PLANTES EN POLOGNE.
[SOME NOTES ON PLANT DISEASES IN
POLAND.] Rev. Path. Vég. et Ent.
Agr. 20: 139-147. (RAM 12: 550.)
A1, B6, C7a.

379. Siggers, P.V.
1938. FOMES ANNOSUS ON PINUS PAL-
USTRIS. Plant Dis. Rptr. 22: 140.
A1, B1, D2, E3a(2), 4d, 16a.

380. Spaulding, P.
1952. ROOT ROTS OF CONIFERS. In
Important tree pests of the North-
east. New England Sect. Soc. Amer.
Foresters. Evans Printing Co.,
Concord, N.H., pp. 138-140. A6,7,
B1, D1,6, E1b,c,d,k, 2a,c, 3a(3),
(5), b(2), d(2), 5b, 10a, 16a,b,
G5,6,7.

381. _____
1956. DISEASES OF NORTH AMERICAN
FOREST TREES PLANTED ABROAD. U.S.
Dept. Agr. Agr. Handb. 100, 144 pp.
A1,2,4,5,6, B3,4,5,6.

382. Speidel, G.
1949.*DIE SCHNEIDERSCHE KONSTANTE.
EINE UNTERSUCHUNG ÜBER DIE BRAUCH-
BARKEIT DER SCHNEIDERSCHEN FORMEL
ZUR BESTIMMUNG DES MASSENZUWACHS-
PROZENTES IM STEHENDEN HOLZ AN
HAND VON 70 STAMMANALYSEN DER
EUROPÄISCHEN LÄRCHE. Forstwiss.
Centbl. 68: 161-183. (BI) A3.

383. Stock, P.
1929.*STURMSICHERHEIT D.R.P. 435552.
EINE ERWIDERUNG. Deut. Forstw.
11: 303. (BI)

384. Stoddard, E.M., McDonnell, A.D., and
Hicock, H.W.
1939. FOMES ANNOSUS ON CONIFERS IN
CONNECTICUT. Plant Dis. Rptr. 23:
385-386. A1,2,4, B1.

385. Storch, K.
1937.*ÜBER DEN ABBAU DES FICHTEN-
HOLZES DURCH DEN ROTFÄULEPILZ
(POLYPORUS ANNOSUS). [THE DE-
GRADATION OF SPRUCE WOOD BY THE
RED ROT FUNGUS (POLYPORUS AN-
NOSUS).] Papier Fabrik. 35: 485-
492. (RAM 17: 361.) C5b,d.

386. Suolahti, O.
1948.*INVERKAN AV TALLENS KVALITET
PÅ DESS RÖTHÄRDIGHET. [THE IN-
FLUENCE OF THE QUALITY OF SCOTS
PINE ON ITS RESISTANCE TO DECAY.]
Papp. Travarutidskr. Finland 30
(23): 421-425. (FA 10: 2641.) C5a.

387. _____
1951.*ÜBER EINE DAS WACHSTUM VON
FÄULNISPILZEN BESCHLEUNIGENDE
CHEMISCHE FERNWIRKUNG VON HOLZ.
[ON A REMOTE CHEMICAL ACTION OF
WOOD ACCELERATING THE GROWTH OF
ROTTING FUNGI.] Publ. Tech.
Forschungsanst. Finland 21, 95 pp.
(RAM 31: 93.) C2d.

388. Sylvén, N.
1941.*SKOGSTRÄDENS FÖRÄDLING. II.
[IMPROVEMENT OF FOREST TREES. II.]
Skogen 28: 81-83. (RAM 20: 387.)
E10d, G7.

389. Szulczewski, J.W.
1930.*PRZYCZYNEK DO ZIMOWEJ MYKO-
FLORY POZNANIA I OKOLICY. [CON-
TRIBUTION TO THE WINTER FUNGUS
FLORA OF POSEN AND ITS ENVIRONS.]
Kosmos Lwow 55(1-2): 232-248. (RAM
10: 271.) A1,2, B6.

390. Teng, S.C.
    1940.*STUDIES OF CHINESE TIMBER
    TREES IN REFERENCE TO FOREST MAN-
    AGEMENT, I. Sinensia 10(5-6):
    363-395. (RAM 22: 233.) A2,4, B7.

391. Tikka, P.S.
    1934.*ÜBER DIE STOCKFÄULE DER NADEL-
    WALDER NORD-SUOMIS (-FINNLANDS).
    [ON THE BUTT ROT OF THE CONIFER
    WOODS OF NORTH FINLAND.] Acta
    Forest. Fenn. 40: 293-308. (RAM
    13: 738.) A1,4, B5, C7a, E3b(2),
    4a,b, 5c.

392. Tilford, P.E.
    1936. THE RELATION OF TEMPERATURE
    TO THE EFFECT OF HYDROGEN- AND
    HYDROXYL-ION CONCENTRATION ON
    SCLEROTINIA FRUCTICOLA AND FOMES
    ANNOSUS. SPORE GERMINATION AND
    GROWTH. Ohio Agr. Expt. Sta. Bul.
    567, 25 pp. (RAM 15: 677.) C2c,
    3a.

393. Toole, E.R., and Boyce, J.S., Jr.
    1952. FOMES ANNOSUS ON ATLANTIC
    WHITE CEDAR. Plant Dis. Rptr. 36:
    330. A6, B1, E3a(4).

394. Trenél, M.
    1931.*BEITRAG ZUM KIEFERNSTERBEN IN
    NORDWEST-DEUTSCHLAND. Forstarchiv
    7: 285-294. (BI) C7a.

395. _____
    1931.*'ZUM KIEFERNSTERBEN IN NORD-
    WEST-DEUTSCHLAND'. ERWIDERUNG AUF
    DIE BEMERKUNGEN VON PROFESSOR
    LIESE UND PROFESSOR ALBERT. Forst-
    archiv 7: 390-391. (BI) C7a.

396. Treschow, C.
    1941.*ZUR KULTUR VON TRAMETES AUF
    STERILISIERTEM WALDHUMUS. [ON THE
    CULTURE OF TRAMETES ON STERILIZED
    FOREST SOIL.] Zentbl. f. Bakt.
    Abt. 2, 104(8-10): 186-188. (RAM
    22: 120.) C2c,d, F3a.

397. _____
    1943.*UNDERSØGELSER OVER BRINTJON-
    KONCENTRATIONENS INDFLYDELSE PAA
    VAEKSTEN AF SVAMPEN POLYPORUS
    ANNOSUS. [STUDIES ON THE INFLUENCE
    OF THE HYDROGEN-ION CONCENTRATION
    ON THE GROWTH OF THE FUNGUS
    POLYPORUS ANNOSUS.] Forstl.
    Forsøgsv. i Danmark, Beret. 15:
    17-32. (RAM 25: 374.) C2a,c,d.

398. _____
    1958.*FORSØG MED RØDGRANRACERS RE-
    SISTENS OVERFOR ANGREB AF FOMES
    ANNOSUS (FR.) CKE. [STUDIES ON THE
    RESISTANCE OF RACES OF NORWAY
    SPRUCE TO ATTACK BY F. ANNOSUS.]
    Forstl. Forsøgsv. i Danmark,
    Beret. 25: 1-23. (FA 20: 711.)
    A2, E10d.

399. _____
    1958.*FORSØG OVER JORDBEHANDLINGENS
    INDFLYDELSE PA RØDGRANBEVOKSNIN-
    GERS RESISTENS OVERFOR ANGREB AF
    FOMES ANNOSUS. [STUDIES ON THE
    EFFECT OF SITE TREATMENT ON THE
    RESISTANCE OF NORWAY SPRUCE PLAN-
    TATIONS TO ATTACK BY F. ANNOSUS.]
    Forstl. Forsøgsv. i Danmark,
    Beret. 25: 25-34. (FA 20: 712.)
    A2, E1i, 5b.

400. Tristan, Marquis de.
    1892.*LA MALADIE DES PINERAIES DITE
    'DU ROND'. Rev. des Eaux et Forêts
    31: 258-264. (BI)

401. Tubeuf, C. von.
    1897.*DISEASES OF PLANTS. (Trans-
    lated by W.G. Smith, London.)
    (From Wilson, 1927.) A4.

402. _____
    1933.*STUDIEN ÜBER SYMBIOSE UND
    DISPOSITION FÜR PARASITENBEFALL
    SOWIE ÜBER VERERBUNG PATHOLOGIS-
    CHER EIGENSCHAFTEN UNSERER HOLZ-
    PFLANZEN. II. DISPOSITIONSFRAGEN
    FÜR DEN BEFALL DER BÄUME DURCH
    PILZE UND KÄFER. III. UNTERSUCH-
    UNGEN ÜBER ZUWACHSGANG, WASSERGE-
    HALT, HOLZQUALITAT, ERKRANKUNG UND
    ENTWERTUNG GEHARZTER FICHTEN.
    [STUDIES ON SYMBIOSIS AND TEN-
    DENCY TO PARASITIC INFECTION AND
    ON THE INHERITANCE OF PATHOLOGICAL
    CHARACTERS IN OUR WOODY PLANTS.
    II. QUESTIONS ON THE LIABILITY OF
    TREES TO FUNGUS AND BEETLE ATTACK.
    III. INVESTIGATIONS ON INCREMENTAL
    GROWTH, WATER CONTENT, WOOD QUAL-
    ITY, DISEASE, AND DEGENERATION OF
    SPRUCES DENUDED OF RESIN.] Ztschr.
    f. Pflanzenkrank. 43: 257-357,
    369-417. (RAM 12: 737.) A2, B4.

403. Twarowski, Z.
    1937.*HUBA KORZENIOWA--TRAMETES
    RADICIPERDA. Las Polski 17(5):
    207-218. (BI)

404. Vakin, A.T.
1927.*DIE HERZFÄULE DER FICHTE IN
DEN REVIEREN DES RSHEVSKY FORSTES
IN GOUVERNEMENT TVER. [HEART ROT
OF SPRUCE IN THE RSHEVSKY FOREST
DOMAINS IN THE TVER GOVERNMENT.]
Mitt. Leningrad Forstinst. 35:
105-154. (RAM 7: 813.) A2, B6,
E1d, g, F2.

405. Vanine, S.I., and Andreyeff, I.E.
1935.*[PHYSICAL AND MECHANICAL
PROPERTIES OF FIR TIMBER IN THE
INITIAL STAGE OF THE ROT CAUSED BY
FOMES ANNOSUS.] Mitt. Forsttech.
Akad. Leningrad 1935(6): 9-21.
(RAM 15: 68.) C5a, E3b(1).

406. Vloten, H. van.
1942.*FOMES ANNOSUS FR. IN ONDER-
PLANTINGEN. [FOMES ANNOSUS IN UN-
DERPLANTED STANDS.] Nederland.
Boschbouw Tijdschr. 15: 337-338.
(FA 9: 537.) A3,5, B6, E1f, G2.

407. Wagener, W.W., and Cave, M.S.
1946. PINE KILLING BY THE ROOT
FUNGUS, FOMES ANNOSUS, IN CALI-
FORNIA. Jour. Forestry 44: 47-54.
A1,4, B1, C7a, D2,4, E1b,d, 3a(1),
(3),(4),(5),(6), b(2), d(1), 5a,
b, 6, 10a, F1.

408. ———— and Davidson, R.W.
1954. HEART ROTS IN LIVING TREES.
Bot. Rev. 20: 61-134. A2,3,6, B1,
3,4, C2d, 3a, D5,6, E1a,e,f,i, 4a,
b, 5b, F2, G2,3,5.

409. Wass, J.G.
1952-54.*FOMES ANNOSUS IN EAST
ANGLIAN PINE SAMPLE PLOTS. Gt.
Brit. Forestry Comn. Jour. 23:
75-81. (RAM 35: 133.) A1, B3, E1f,
5b.

410. Waterman, R.E., Koch, F.C., and
McMahon, W.
1934. CHEMICAL STUDIES OF WOOD PRES-
ERVATION. III. ANALYSIS OF PRE-
SERVED TIMBER. Indus. and Engin.
Chem., Analyt. Ed. 6: 409-413.
(RAM 14: 276.) C2b.

411. Wegelius, T.
1938.*OM RÖTA I SULFITVED OCH DESS
INVERKAN PÅ FABRIKATIONSPROCESSEN
OCH MASSAUTBYTET. [SULPHITE WOOD
DECAY AND ITS INFLUENCE ON THE
MANUFACTURING PROCESS AND PULP
YIELD.] Finsk Papp. Tidskr. 1938
(15a): 125-126, 128-130; (15):
594, 595-598. (RAM 18: 564.) C5d.

412. Weir, J.R.
1914. NOTES ON WOOD DESTROYING FUNGI
WHICH GROW ON BOTH CONIFEROUS AND
DECIDUOUS TREES. I. Phytopath. 4:
271-276. A6,7, B1.

413. ————
1917. MONTANA FOREST TREE FUNGI. I.
POLYPORACEAE. Mycologia 9: 129-
137. A1,3, B1.

414. ————
1923. THE EFFECT OF BROADCAST BURN-
ING OF SALE AREAS ON THE GROWTH
OF CULL-PRODUCING FUNGI. Jour.
Forestry 21: 183-184. (RAM 2:
531.) A1,3,4, B1, D2,4, E1h,
3b(1),(2), 15.

415. ———— and Hubert, E.E.
1919. A STUDY OF THE ROTS OF WESTERN
WHITE PINE. U.S. Dept. Agr. Bul.
799, 24 pp. A1, B1.

416. Weis, F., and Nielsen, N.
1927.*NOGLE UNDERSØGELSER OVER ROD-
FORDAERVERSVAMPEN (POLYPORUS RADI-
CIPERDA). [SOME INVESTIGATIONS OF
THE ROOT-DESTROYING FUNGUS (POLY-
PORUS RADICIPERDA).] Dansk Skov-
for. Tidsskr. 12: 233-246. (RAM 7:
551.) C2b,c, G7.

417. Weiss, F., and O'Brien, M.J.
1950-53. INDEX OF PLANT DISEASES IN
THE U.S. U.S. Dept. Agr. Plant
Dis. Surv. Spec. Pub., Parts 1-5,
1263 pp. A1,2,3,4,5,6,7, B1, D4.

418. Welch, D.S., and Stone, E.L.
1953. FOMES ANNOSUS (FR.) CKE. IN
CONIFEROUS PLANTATIONS IN NEW YORK
STATE. Plant Dis. Rptr. 37: 247-
248. (RAM 32: 651.) A1, B1, D2,
E3a(4), d(2), 5a,c, 10a, 12, 16a.

419. Wense, H. von der.
1929.*FICHTENWACHSTUM AUF ALTEN
FELD- UND WALDBODEN DER SACHSIS-
CHEN STAATSFORSTEN. [THE GROWTH
OF SPRUCE ON OLD-FIELD AND FOREST
SOILS IN THE SAXON STATE FORESTS.]
Ztschr. f. Forst u. Jagdw. 61(1):
7-31, (2): 65-95. (BA 5: 2070.)
E3d(2), 13a.

420. Wiedemann.
1929.*BEITRÄGE ZUR KENNTNIS VON
WALDKRANKHEITEN. IV. DER EINFLUSS
VON RINDENBESCHÄDIGUNGEN DIE ROT-
WILDSCHÄLUNG UND HARZNUTZUNG AUF
ROTFÄULE DER FICHTE. Silva 17:
139-140. (BI) A2.

421. Wiedemann.
1929.*HALLIMASCH UND WURZELSCHWAMM,
ZWEI GEFAHRLICHE WALDFEINDE. [THE
HONEY AGARIC AND ROOT-ROT, TWO
DANGEROUS FOREST ENEMIES.] Biol.
Reichsanst. f. Land u. Forstw.
Flugbl. 22, 4 pp. (Abs. in Jour.
Forestry 28: 998-999.) A1,2, E5e,
13a, 16a, G5,7.

422. Wilkins, W.H.
1946.*INVESTIGATIONS INTO THE PRO-
DUCTION OF BACTERIOSTATIC SUB-
STANCES BY FUNGI. PRELIMINARY EX-
AMINATION OF THE FIFTH 100 SPE-
CIES, ALL BASIDIOMYCETES, MOSTLY
OF THE WOOD-DESTROYING TYPE. Brit.
Jour. Expt. Path. 27: 140-142.
(RAM 26: 504.) C4, F3b.

423. ─────
1952.*INVESTIGATIONS INTO THE PRO-
DUCTION OF BACTERIOSTATIC SUB-
STANCES BY FUNGI. PRELIMINARY EX-
AMINATION OF THE ELEVENTH 100
SPECIES, ALL BASIDIOMYCETES. Brit.
Jour. Expt. Path. 33: 46-47. (RAM
31: 569.) C4, F3b.

424. Wilson, M.
1927. THE HOST PLANTS OF FOMES
ANNOSUS. Brit. Mycol. Soc. Trans.
12: 147-149. (RAM 6: 763.) A1,2,
3,4,5,6,7, B3.

425. ─────
1928. SUCCESSIONAL DISEASE IN THE
SCOTS PINE. Brit. Mycol. Soc.
Trans. 13: 81-85. (RAM 7: 607.)
A1, B3, E1c,d, 16a, F2,4.

426. Woeste, U.
1956.*ANATOMISCHE UNTERSUCHUNGEN
ÜBER DIE INFEKTIONSWEGE EINIGER
WURZELPILZE. [ANATOMICAL STUDIES
ON THE CHANNELS OF INFECTION OF
SOME ROOT FUNGI.] Phytopath.
Ztschr. 26: 225-272. (RAM 35: 800.)
A2, B4, D2, E1b,c,d,e.

427. Wollenweber, H.W.
1931.*ZUM KIEFERNSTERBEN IN NORD-
WEST-DEUTSCHLAND. OEDOCEPHALUM-
POLYPORUS ANNOSUS. [ON THE DYING-
OFF OF PINES IN NORTH-WEST
GERMANY. OEDOCEPHALUM-POLYPORUS
ANNOSUS.] Forstarchiv 7: 391. (RAM
11: 145.) C7a.

428. Wolman, K.H., and Pflug, H.
1929. ZINC META-ARSENITE--A (PRO-
POSED) NEW AMERICAN WOOD PRESERV-
ATIVE. Indus. and Engin. Chem.
21: 705-707. (RAM 9: 80.) C2b.

429. Wright, E., and Isaac, L.A.
1956. DECAY FOLLOWING LOGGING INJURY
TO WESTERN HEMLOCK, SITKA SPRUCE,
AND TRUE FIRS. U.S. Dept. Agr.
Tech. Bul. 1148, 34 pp. (RAM 36:
291.) A2,4,6, B1, E1g,h.

430. ───── Rhoads, A.S., and
Isaac, L.A.
1947. DECAY LOSSES FOLLOWING LOGGING
INJURY IN PARTIALLY CUT STANDS OF
WESTERN HEMLOCK AND SITKA SPRUCE.
Timberman 48(10): 52-54, 72-76.
(RAM 27: 105.) A2,6, B1, E1g,h,
3b(1),(2), 4b,c.

431. Yde-Andersen, A.
1958.*KAERNERÅD I RØDGRAN FORÅRSAGET
AF HONNINGSVAMPEN. (ARMILLARIA
MELLEA (VAHL) QUÉL.) [BUTT ROT OF
NORWAY SPRUCE CAUSED BY A.
MELLEA.] Forstl. Forsøgsv. i Dan-
mark, Beret. 25: 79-91. (FA 20:
705.) A2, B5, C8, E1f.

432. ─────
1959.*KAERNERÅD I RØDGRAN. [HEART
ROT IN NORWAY SPRUCE.] Dansk
Skovfor. Tidsskr. 44: 78-80, 81-
110. (RAM 39: 198.) A2, B5.

433. Yokota, S.
1956.*OBSERVATIONS ON THE BUTT ROT
OF SAKHALIN FIR (ABIES SACHALIN-
ENSIS MAST.) IN THE TOKYO UNIVER-
SITY FOREST, HOKKAIDO, WITH
SPECIAL REFERENCE TO INFECTION
AND PROPAGATION OF DECAY. Tokyo
Univ. Forest Bul. 52: 165-171.
(FA 19: 3153.) A4, B7, E1d,g,
F1,2.

434. ─────
1957.*WOOD DECAY OF ABIES SACHALIN-
ENSIS IN THE TOKYO UNIVERSITY
FOREST, HOKKAIDO. III. ON WOOD
DECAY OF ONI-TODO. Tokyo Univ.
Forest Bul. 53: 139-148. (FA 19:
3155.) A4, B7, E3d(2), 4b.

435. Younitzky, A.A.
1927.*[FUNGI ATTACKING HEALTHY AND
SCORCHED TREES IN THE FORESTS OF
THE MARI REGION, AND THE DAMAGE
THEY CAUSE TO YOUNG STANDS ARISING
ON AREAS DEVASTATED BY FIRE OR BARK
INSECTS, ACCORDING TO THE OBSER-
VATIONS OF THE 1926 EXPEDITION.]
Reprinted from Kazan Inst. of Agr.
and Silvic. News 3(1), 21 pp.
(RAM 6: 700.) A2,4, B6, E1k, 4a,b,
F4.

436. Zeller, S.M.
    1935. SOME MISCELLANEOUS FUNGI OF
    THE PACIFIC NORTHWEST. Mycologia
    27: 449-466. (RAM 15: 117.) D4.   438.

437. Zycha, H.
    1937. *ÜBER DAS WACHSTUM ZWEIER
    HOLZZERSTORENDER PILZE UND IHR
    VERHALTNIS ZUR KOHLENSÄURE. [ON
    THE GROWTH OF TWO WOOD-DESTROYING
    FUNGI AND THEIR RELATION TO CARBON
    DIOXIDE.] Zentbl. f. Bakt. Abt. 2,

EXPLORATORY RELATIONS OF STAND

GROWTH TO MEASURABLE ELEMENTS

OF STAND STRUCTURE

Clement Mesavage

SOUTHERN FOREST EXPERIMENT STATION
PHILIP A. BRIEGLEB, DIRECTOR
Forest Service, U. S. Department of Agriculture

An exploratory study with shortleaf pine (*Pinus echinata* Mill.) in north Arkansas indicates that variations in basal area growth may be strongly correlated with measurable elements of stand structure. This possibility was studied to reduce the time needed to assess the desirability of alternative forest cutting practices, to make possible growth predictions based on data normally collected by forest inventories, to provide timber markers with guides to future tree behavior, and, ultimately, to permit linear programming aimed at predicting the structure best calculated to achieve

a specified objective given various cost-price assumptions and an initial structure.

PLAN OF STUDY

Twenty-seven one-acre plots installed in 1956 provided a controlled range in sawtimber stocking, tree diameter, and space occupied by pines of sawtimber size. Other variables included age in several forms, data pertaining to the density and size of various stand components (such as growing stock, ingrowth reservoir, etc.) competition, and other factors (table 1).

Table 1.—*Independent variables available for regression analysis*

X_1 Number of residual pines per acre, larger than 3.5 inches d.b.h.

X_2 do.   , larger than 7.5 inches

X_3 do.   , from 6.6 to 7.5 inches

X_4 Sum of residual diameters (inches per acre), pines 0.6 to 3.5 inches

X_5 do.   , pines larger than 3.5 inches

X_6 do.   , pines 3.6 to 6.5 inches

X_7 do.   , pines 3.6 to 7.5 inches

X_8 Sum of residual basal areas (square feet per acre), all species, 0.6 to 3.5 inches

X_9 do.   , pines 3.6 to 7.5 inches

X_{10} do.   , pines larger than 3.5 inches

X_{11} do.   , pines larger than 7.5 inches

X_{12} Squared sum of basal areas of residual pines larger than 7.5 inches

X_{13} Mean age of pine dominants

X_{14} Reciprocal of mean age of pine dominants

X_{15} Mean age of pines larger than 7.5 inches

X_{16} Coefficient of variation about mean age, pines larger than 7.5 inches

X_{17} Mean diameter of residual pines larger than 3.5 inches

X_{18} Coefficient of variation about mean diameter, pines larger than 7.5 inches

X_{19} Coefficient of variation of basal-area spatial distribution (7-diopter point samples)

X_{20} Percent of live crown length, residual pines larger than 7.5 inches

X_{21} Index to recent cutting: residual pines larger than 3.5 inches after recent cutting divided by total basal area (all species 0.6 inch and larger) present prior to recent cutting

X_{22} Index to recent cutting: 100 times the reciprocal of 1 plus the ratio of basal area of residual pines and hardwoods to basal area of cut pines and hardwoods (in each case only pines larger than 7.5 inches and hardwoods larger than 6.5 inches are included)

X_{23} Basal area removed in recent cutting

X_{24} Mean height of pine dominants divided by mean age in years

X_{25} Site index (mean height of dominants at age 50 years)

X_{26} 10-year radial growth of pine dominants, in inches

This study indicates that the following types f independent variables are more or less corre- ated with basal-area growth of shortleaf pine 1 the Arkansas Ozarks:

Some function of stand age.

Variables describing distribution in size and space of growing stock component including N, D, D², coefficient of varia- tion of diameter, and coefficient of vari- ation of basal-area spatial distribution.

Similar variables describing potential in- growth components.

Similar variables describing competitive components (undesirable stems and de- sirable stems not contributing to sur- vivor growth or ingrowth).

Variables describing severity of recent drastic reduction in tree population (due to cutting, TSI, windthrow, etc.).

Past growth.

Some specific findings in regard to choice f variables were as follows:

1. Age of dominant trees was a more useful variable than the reciprocal of age. For sawtimber growth, it was better than the mean age of sawtimber-size trees. The coefficient of variation of mean age im- proved the regression, but not significant- ly. Possibly, age of dominants may be best for use in predicting the growth of even-aged stands, and mean age of the growing stock components and the co- efficient of variation of mean age may be best for uneven-aged stands (i.e., where larger coefficients of variation of age pre- vail).

2. Site index did not appear important in the presence of age, but did appear im- portant in the absence of age. It is un- fortunate that through accident there was a fairly strong nonsense correlation (nega- tive) between site and age.

3. A curvilinear function of basal area appeared somewhat better in general than the simple linear form for explaining growth differences.

4. Number of trees per acre, or the sum of tree diameters, can under some circum- stances be more important than basal area, and hence should be included as an expres- sion of density. These terms seem to be particularly important for introducing the effect of ingrowth and competition, where the range of sizes is not great.

5. Probably because the stands were essentially even-aged, the coefficient of variation of diameter did not show up as an important element.

6. The regression outputs indicate that ingrowth tends to increase *directly* with coefficient of variation of growing space. When ingrowth is not included in growth estimates, growth of survivors appears to be *inversely* proportional to the same vari- able.

7. Competition was not important in the present study, because hardwoods larger than 3 inches d.b.h. had been killed on all plots before the measured growth period.

8. Effects of recent cuttings may be quite important in predicting growth, but the effect should lessen with the length of time since cutting.

9. Past radial growth may be a useful variable, but exploratory work is needed to ascertain whether some non-linear func- tion of it might not be preferable, as well as to learn whether growth of dominants will suffice or whether the term should be broad enough to include past ingrowth.

In designing studies for predicting growth by regression analysis, it seems best to express growth in terms of basal area, since this meas- ure will not be affected much by site variation, unless extreme. When predictions are in terms of volume growth, tree height is introduced as a variable that will fluctuate with site index, making the regression analyses more complex. Ultimately, when site-prediction regressions based on soil variables have been worked out, volume predictions based on both site and stand structure may be developed, but progress will be more rapid initially if each is studied separ- ately.

4

The "best" regressions for predicting two-year basal area growth in square feet per acre were:

Pine cordwood and sawtimber, survivors plus ingrowth (first output)

$$= 0.272066\ X_8 - 0.220255\ X_{13} + 8.79020\ X_{21} + 9.65455$$

Pine cordwood and sawtimber, survivors plus ingrowth (second output)

$$= 0.0112359\ X_1 - 0.176182\ X_{13} + 11.9865$$

Pine sawtimber, survivors plus ingrowth (first output)

$$= 0.0297886\ X_2 - 0.190111\ X_{13} + 13.4249$$

Pine sawtimber, survivors plus ingrowth (second output)

$$= 0.030790\ X_2 - 0.200788\ X_{15} + 13.3904$$

Pine sawtimber, survivors only

$$= 0.0587584\ X_{11} - 0.137340\ X_{13} + 7.81012$$

The importance of age in predicting growth on the study plots was unexpected. Average ages of dominant trees on a given plot ranged from 39 to 67 years Since a restricted age range of 39 to 48 years was present on 19 of the 27 plots, a separate regression output involving pine sawtimber (survivors plus ingrowth) was obtained for this group. Value of R^2 (the squared coefficient of multiple correlation) for the 9-variable regression was .8026 for the restricted range in age, compared with R^2 of .8362 for the corresponding regression involving all 27 plots. This difference supports the inference that age is important in accounting for growth differences on these plots even when oldest trees are excluded. The "best"

regression for the 19 plots with a narrow range in ages also included mean age of dominant pines (X_{13}) and number of pines 7.6 inches d.b.h. and larger (X_2). The 19-plot R^2 involving X_{13} and X_2 was .707, as compared with an R^2 of .736 for the 27-plot regression involving the same two independent variables.

Unless age or some function of age was included with the independent variables, none of the regressions was significant at the .01 level. Several of the sawtimber growth regressions that lacked age, however, were significant at the .05 level, and might be of interest when it is impracticable to determine age. These were:

2-year basal-area growth in pine sawtimber, survivors plus ingrowth

$$= .101121\ X_2 - .00127480\ X_{12} + 4.74338\ X_{26} - 1.74492$$

2-year basal-area growth in pine sawtimber, survivors only

$$= 0.0607037\ X_2 - .00186244\ X_7 + .0596870\ X_{11} + 2.76410$$

DISCUSSION

Examination of the amount of variation that each independent variable accounted for, individually and in combination with others, shows that basal-area growth variations between stands can be satisfactorily attributed to measurable elements of stand structure.

Further research is needed to determine whether other easily measured important independent variables can be discovered. In addition, it may be fruitful to investigate whether the accuracy of estimates can be improved by changing the functions of the variables used.

3

Gross basal-area growth of sawtimber and cordwood, including mortality, was determined by stand remeasurement after two growing seasons.

ANALYSIS

The Southern Forest Experiment Station's IBM 704 Regression Program was employed in the analysis. Regression program outputs, each yielding regression coefficients and the variation accounted for by 511 regressions (one for every possible linear combination of the 9 or fewer independent variables), were obtained for two-year basal-area growth of the following:

(a) Pine cordwood and sawtimber component (survivors plus ingrowth), 3.6 inches d.b.h., threshold diameter.

(b) Pine sawtimber component (survivors plus ingrowth), 7.6 inches d.b.h., threshold diameter.

(c) Pine sawtimber component (survivors only).

Several exploratory selections of independent variables were made, and separate regression outputs were obtained for each selection.

Dependent and independent variables selected for each output are shown in table 2.

Table 2.—*Squared multiple correlation coefficients (R^2) for several regression analyses*

Dependent variable: two-year basal-area growth in square feet per acre	Independent variables selected for analyses	R^2 for 9 variables	Independent variables in "best" regression	R^2
Pine cordwood and sawtimber, survivors plus ingrowth (first output)	X_5 X_8 X_9 X_{11} X_{13} X_{17} X_{19} X_{20} X_{21}	.647	X_8 X_{13} X_{21}	.564
Pine cordwood and sawtimber, survivors plus ingrowth (second output)	X_1 X_4 X_5 X_{10} X_{13} X_{14} X_{19} X_{21} X_{24}	.635	X_1 X_{13}	.475
Pine sawtimber, survivors plus ingrowth (first output)	X_2 X_7 X_8 X_{11} X_{13} X_{18} X_{19} X_{23} X_{25}	.836	X_2 X_{13}	.795
Pine sawtimber, survivors plus ingrowth (second output)	X_2 X_3 X_8 X_{11} X_{12} X_{15} X_{16} X_{22} X_{26}	.824	X_2 X_{15}	.721
Pine sawtimber, survivors only	X_2 X_7 X_8 X_{11} X_{13} X_{18} X_{19} X_{23} X_{25}	.893	X_{11} X_{13}	.837

RESULTS

As table 2 indicates, the 9-variable regressions accounted for 65 percent of the variation in cordwood basal-area growth, 84 percent of the variation in sawtimber basal-area growth including ingrowth, and 89 percent of the variation in sawtimber basal-area growth excluding ingrowth. The most worthwhile regressions with fewer than 9 independent variables were easily screened from the remainder of the IBM 704 outputs. Residual mean squares from the 9-variable regressions were used as rough error terms to screen the difference in variation accounted for by the "best" 1-variable regression, the "best" 2-variable regression, etc., up to the full 9-variable regression. Value of F_{05} for degrees of freedom 1 and 17 (27 sets of observed values, less 10 degrees for data-derived constants) is 4.45, and any difference in sums of squares attributable to regression that was 4.45 times as large as the residual mean square seemed unlikely to be chance-caused. Sums of squares attributable to regression were given directly as a part of the IBM 704 program outputs.

2

HEAT EFFECTS
ON
LIVING PLANTS

Robert C. Hare

Southern Forest Experiment Station
Philip A. Briegleb, Director
FOREST SERVICE
U. S. Department of Agriculture

HEAT EFFECTS
ON
LIVING PLANTS

Southern Forest Experiment Station
Philip A. Briegleb, Director
FOREST SERVICE
U. S. Department of Agriculture

CONTENTS

INTRODUCTION

This review of knowledge concerning the effects of high temperatures on plants was undertaken in preparation for research aimed at determining how forest fires affect physiological processes in woody species. Major subjects discussed include morphological and physiological responses to high temperatures, external and internal factors governing these responses, recognition and assessment of fire damage, and ecological effects of fire, including benefits from prescribed burning. Consideration is given also to techniques for measuring high temperatures outside and inside the plant, and for reproducing these temperatures artificially in controlled experiments. Some of the fire effects reviewed here are not physiological, but a cursory survey of literature on them was included to round out the treatment, since they all constitute ways in which excessive heat influences plants.

A major conclusion from this literature survey is that we know little about the physiological effects of fire. Even such prerequisite information as that on internal temperatures during fires seems completely lacking. Investigations of heat-induced changes in physiological processes like respiration, translocation, and auxin or enzyme reactions should lead to improved ability to appraise wildfire damage, and to produce desired results by prescribed burning. Physiological research may also provide methods for increasing the fire resistance of desirable trees through genetics or chemistry. The closing section of this paper is thus devoted to present research needs in physiology, and to possible experimental approaches.

No geographical limits have been placed on this review; any preponderance of data from the southern United States merely reflects the greater use and occurrence of fire in this region. Other aspects of fire research in the South have been analyzed by Bruce (36)[1], and Nelson and Bruce (160).

TEMPERATURES ENCOUNTERED IN FOREST FIRES

The temperatures to which a plant is subjected depend on its distance from the flames as well as on the intensity and duration of the fire. Intensity and duration are determined by such factors as the fuel (type, moisture content, size, spatial distribution) (42), the general slope of the ground, and external atmospheric influences like wind speed and relative humidity.

In Air

Air temperatures during fires in various types of fuel vary greatly. Convection columns reached 1,100° F.[2] 45 feet above a pile of burning railroad ties (214). Flame temperature (measured with an optical pyrometer) averaged 1,600°, with a maximum of 2,000°. In a running brush fire the convection column reached 915° at 15 feet above the ground. In fires in Appalachian hardwoods (161) maximum temperatures near the ground varied from 1,112° to 1,832°. At 5 feet the maximum was 392°, at 10 feet, 212°. Uggla (209) reported maxima of more than 2,100° during slash fires in pine and spruce stands in Sweden.

During experimental fires in a longleaf pine stand with a large accumulation of needle litter (8-year rough) maximum temperatures approached 1,600° (64). Maxima were somewhat higher immediately adjacent to tree trunks (1,560°) than in the open (1,300°). Radiation from heated bark surfaces and induced convection currents close to the boles presumably accounted for the difference. In the open, temperature decreased consistently with height above ground, but next to tree trunks highest readings occurred 3 feet above ground on the lee side.

Both temperature and duration of exposure are greatly influenced by the wind. Headfires develop considerably more heat than backfires because the flames are fanned by the wind to ignite new fuel ahead of the front, more fuel burns per unit of time, and more aerial fuels are consumed. Therefore, headfires usually do more crown damage than backfires. In backfires, where the heat is blown into the burned area, progress of the flame front is very much slower, and parts near the ground are exposed to high temperatures for a longer time.

---

[1] Italic numbers in parentheses refer to Literature Cited, page 24.

[2] Unless otherwise indicated, all temperatures are in Fahrenheit.

In South Carolina, Lindenmuth and Byram *(127)* measured heating at several levels with heavy-gauge thermocouples having approximately the heat capacity of buds of longleaf pine seedlings. The "temperature factor," representing both temperature and its duration, was greatest 5 inches above the ground in both headfires and backfires. Measured in this way, backfires were consistently hotter below 18 inches, and headfires were hotter above this level. The fuel included much grass, which burns with the base of the flames at a higher elevation than in unsupported pine litter. Byram *(43)* suggests that headfires in grassy fuels may do less damage close to the ground than backfires.

Measured with fine thermocouples, headfires in homogeneous pine litter in southern Mississippi were generally hotter at all levels than backfires *(64)*. Maximum air temperatures adjacent to tree trunks at ground level (for both lee and windward sides of the tree) averaged 1,144° in headfires versus 974° in backfires. Peaks were at 1,520° and 1,325°, respectively. At the 1-foot level, maxima averaged 1,058° and 819° but ranged to 1,460° for headfires and to 1,240° for backfires. Headfire maxima showed little change up to 3 feet (average at 3 feet was 1,023°), whereas backfire maxima dropped rapidly with height (average at 3 feet was 375°). In the open air, away from tree trunks, air maxima at the litter surface were 1,300° in a backfire, 1,215° in headfires. At 5 inches the backfire maximum had dropped to 670°, and at 10 inches to 350°, as compared with 1,135° and 800°, respectively, for headfires. Backfire temperatures continued to drop more rapidly than headfire temperatures with height. Thus in these fuels, backfires may be hotter than headfires, if at all, only at the surface. Radiation from the approaching flame front and slow movement of the front may make backfires more damaging at points close to the ground.

In gallberry-palmetto roughs of Georgia a maximum of 1,600° was measured in headfires at the 1-foot level, the temperature falling off with height in a sloping curve *(56)*. Backfires at one foot reached only 250° to 600°, but maintained this level for several minutes. At 4 feet, headfires reached 500°, backfires 125°. Again headfires did not appear to be cooler near the ground, unless within a few inches.

Wind and convection currents also affect heat damage through the so-called chimney effect. Almost invariably bark charring is highest on the leeward side of the trees. As the wind blows the flames around the bole a convection column rises on the protected side, carrying the heat and flames up as in a chimney. This occurs in both headfires and backfires. It is more pronounced in headfires because the leeward fuel has already burned when the flame reaches the windward side in backfires. In the experimental burns mentioned above *(64)*, air maxima averaged 1,330° at 3 feet above ground on the lee side, and 716° on the windward side. Backfire maxima averaged 468° on the lee and 282° to windward. At one foot and above, leeward maxima were up to 4 times as high as windward maxima, high temperatures were maintained longer, and cambium kill was considerably greater.

In Soil

During 44 experimental fires in a diversity of natural fuels in longleaf pine stands soil temperatures at a depth of ⅛- to ¼-inch reached 274°, but most readings at this depth were less than 175° *(104)*. Below ½ inch there was usually little or no rise. Thus the fires probably had little direct effect on soil or underground plant organs.

Under natural burning conditions in Australia, surface temperatures ranged from 178° to 416° *(17)*. A maximum of 153° was recorded 1 inch below the surface. Beneath a pile of burning slash the soil reached 238° at 1 inch and 153° at 3 inches. Dryness favored the penetration of heat into the soil.

The humus layer had a strong insulating effect during a very hot fire in Sweden *(209)*. Temperatures reached 2,100° in the air, 1,000° at the litter surface, but only 250° 1¼ inches below the surface. In grass fuels in California, maximum temperatures were 250° at the surface and 180°, 165°, 145°, and 135°, respectively, at depths of 1, 2, 3, and 4 inches *(21)*. With heavy brush fuels soil temperatures ranged about 3 times as high as with grass.

In Plant Tissues

Published data on internal plant temperatures during forest fires are lacking. Some unpublished records have been obtained of

2

cambium temperatures during both actual and simulated forest fires. During natural-fuel burns in the longleaf pine region of Mississippi, maximum cambium temperatures varied from 85° to 500° at the 1-foot level on the leeward side *(64)*. Maximum external temperatures at this position were 550° to 1,460°. Bark thickness averaged 0.62 inch.

Both pines and hardwoods were heated by igniting an oil-saturated asbestos rope that had been wrapped around the base of the bole *(188)*. Maxima on the bark surface 1 to 2 feet above the rope ranged from 612 to 1,530°, indicating fairly close approximation to a natural forest fire. Cambium temperatures directly beneath the external measuring points, varied from 80° to 520°. The average external temperature in 40 tests was 1,054°, the average cambium temperature 155°, and the average bark thickness 0.66 inch. In general, cambium temperature was related more to bark thickness than to maximum external temperature or species.

GENERAL EFFECTS OF HIGH TEMPERATURE

Fire Effects

Fire injures trees physically by burning off bark or causing it to slough off later, and by killing leaves, buds, branches, roots, or portions of cambium of the main stem. Loss of growth frequently follows such injuries. If the damage is great enough, such as complete defoliation or girdling of the bole, the tree may die. Even if death is not immediate, decay, insects, or disease may enter through the fire wounds or otherwise attack and ultimately kill the weakened tree. In addition to such physical manifestations of heat injury there may be less obvious effects on the physiology of the plant.

Fire scars.—Wounds may be either open or hidden under the bark, in which case callus may eventually bulge out and split the bark, exposing the sapwood *(121, 122)*. Thirty-three years after a fire in a lodgepole pine stand in Alberta, 86 percent of the trees examined had basal fire scars, averaging 4.7 feet in length *(163)*. Of 2,703 felled loblolly pines in Alabama, 16 percent had one or more fire scars *(80)*. Hardwoods in plots burned every fifth year had more fire scars than those in annually burned plots—34 percent vs. 27 percent *(170)*.

Scarring from single fires in the South is usually more serious in hardwood stands than in pines. For various reasons southern pine stands are burned more frequently than hardwoods, so that fuel accumulations in pine types are often too low to support very hot fires. Resin flow in pines also helps prevent the entry of decay; and they have relatively thick bark, though bark thickness may be reduced slightly by repeated fires *(145)*.

Growth loss.—Loss of growth as a result of fire damage varies considerably. For several years following a fire, annual rings in western yellow pine were severely reduced or missing, depending on the amount of defoliation *(54)*. Growth is, of course, slowed by loss of leaves for manufacturing food, but apparently basal fire wounds have little effect on hardwood growth *(115)*. Even severe wounding of yellow-poplar and white oak stems did not decrease diameter growth, although growth of scarlet oak on a poor site was reduced somewhat. Injured trees were not significantly lower in moisture content, ash, nitrogen, or carbohydrates, except that in scarlet oak foliar nitrogen tended to be low in trees with large wounds. Phloem and xylem near fire wounds quickly became oriented in such a direction as to favor passage around the wounds. Thus, translocation of water, minerals, or food was not seriously hampered.

In ponderosa pine a single fire reduced height growth but not diameter growth *(156)*. In comparison with unburned controls, longleaf pine saplings exposed to 5 years of annual burning lost 20 percent in diameter growth and 25 percent in height growth; larger trees were little affected *(223)*. In another study of longleaf pine *(146)* three annual fires slowed both diameter and height growth, especially in younger trees. According to Wahlenberg *(222)*, a single fire causing heavy defoliation in sapling or pole-sized longleaf commonly results in a loss equivalent to one full year's height growth, the loss being distributed over about 3 years.

In southern Mississippi and western Louisiana, Stone *(197)* compared the annual radial growth of 1,200 longleaf pines subjected to numerous fires. Decrease during the first year following a fire ranged from 0 to 65 percent of the expected growth. Recovery was rapid and usually complete in two to three years.

3

Winter backfires in grass or litter fuels did not affect height or diameter growth of slash pine. Headfires reduced both types of growth, particularly of trees under 12 feet high *(89, 149)*. Heat from backfires did not reach high enough to defoliate the trees.

In slash pine, as in ponderosa and longleaf, height growth seems more sensitive to fire than diameter growth *(149)*. Slash pines up to 7 inches d.b.h. lost height growth where no needle scorch was apparent, whereas diameter growth was not affected even in 3-inch saplings with 1/3 of the crown scorched. (It would be interesting to know what factors reduce height growth in the absence of apparent foliar injury). In trees less than 3 inches d.b.h. diameter growth was lost even without scorching. Crown scorch greater than 1/3 decreased both height and diameter growth of all trees in proportion to degree of scorching. Within three years after injury diameter growth, but not height growth, had returned to normal, except in severely scorched small trees.

A single severe April fire in North Carolina seemed not to retard diameter growth of surviving 30-year-old shortleaf pines, even where crowns had been 100 percent scorched *(114)*.

In the Plains of New Jersey dwarf forests of pitch pine, scrub oak, and blackjack oak may average only 4 to 6 feet in height, though up to 60 years old. Andresen *(7)* showed that frequent fires are the cause of this dwarfing, and not toxic levels of aluminum, as often suggested. Trees on similar soils, but protected from fire, grew normally.

An anomalous effect on diameter growth may be the development of an enlarged bole near ground level. Such buttressing has been reported in loblolly pine *(49)*, longleaf pine *(6)*, and in hardwoods *(206)*. In pine it is claimed to be a protective reaction *(49)*, although it is not clear whether the increased diameter is due to thicker bark, which would be necessary for increased protection of the cambium. Stone *(198)* questions the buttressing effect in longleaf pine because he found that fire drastically reduced radial growth in the lower trunk, reducing rather than increasing the taper.

Mortality.—Mortality is a more important type of damage than growth loss, particularly

with hardwoods. Immediate appraisal of kill in the Northeast proved unreliable since mortality did not reach a peak until the second year *(192, 193, 194)*. Oaks appeared only scorched after a surface fire, but more than 60 percent of the survivors showed later effects, such as death, open scars, or attacks by insects or fungi. In order to avoid serious losses from delayed effects a conservative policy would be to cut severely all scorched hardwoods as soon as possible after a fire *(194)*.

Of 829 hardwoods on 15 burned plots in New York and New England 65 percent were killed outright by fire, more than half of these being in the 1- and 2-inch d.b.h. classes *(193)*. Only 4 percent of the remaining trees escaped basal scorching. After 6 years about one-third of the surviving scorched trees had recovered, a third had died, and the remainder showed fire scars and insect and fungal attacks. White pine followed a similar course of delayed mortality and disease and insect infestation.

With southern pines there have been many attempts to predict fire mortality, with varying degrees of error. The extremes of damage are easily recognized but recovery from moderate wounding is affected by many variables. In severely burned loblolly and shortleaf pine *(151)*, percent of crown scorch and extent of cambium kill at groundline were better mortality indicators than height of bark charring, presence of bark beetles, or pitch bleeding. Needle scorch was the best indicator, especially if combined with "100 percent" cambium kill, i.e., cambium found dead at 4 sampled points around the circumference. Any lesser degree of cambium kill had little effect, and even with "100 percent" kill less than 50 percent crown scorch was seldom fatal. About 11 percent of the injured trees died within two years.

Degree of crown scorch seems to be the best indicator of mortality in longleaf and slash pines also *(199)*. In a severe March headfire even 100 percent needle scorch caused no mortality, presumably because of the low initial temperature (45°); where needles were actually consumed many trees were killed. Ninety percent of the pines died when half the needles or more were consumed, 40 percent when less than half. Height of bark char in relation to tree height was also correlated with mortality. Few trees with less than 60 percent

4

stem char died, whereas 90 percent of those with over 80 percent char succumbed. Species or diameter did not seem to affect results.

Ferguson (68) states that the pines most likely to die after a fire are first, those with all foliage consumed, second, those with complete crown scorch plus severe bark burn, and third, those with complete crown scorch or severe basal damage alone. Of 975 fire-damaged trees, 15 percent died. Summer fires were twice as damaging as winter fires. Mc-Culley (149) found that less than 70 percent crown scorch is seldom fatal to slash pine over 5 feet tall, but that if part of the crown is consumed mortality is much greater. He developed a prediction equation for slash pine mortality based on d.b.h., percent foliage scorched, and percent foliage consumed.

Most healthy loblolly pines survived a 5-acre hot spot in a prescribed summer burn in Virginia (4), despite severe needle kill. Only the smaller trees (87 percent scorch) were seriously affected (48 percent mortality in trees 5 inches d.b.h. vs. 2 percent in 8-inch or larger diameters).

Mortality in 30- to 40-year-old ponderosa pines was correlated with crown scorch (143). All trees with scorch exceeding 90 percent died within two years, but little mortality occurred with less than 80 percent crown scorch. Bark scorch caused no mortality in trees of more than 6 inches d.b.h. unless accompanied by more than 80 percent crown scorch. On smaller trees mortality was correlated with bark scorch. Survival of fire-damaged ponderosa pine is also discussed by Herman (100).

On all reports thus far cited, mortality rates were determined from selected injured trees, hence the apparently high losses for large trees. Bruce (34) summarized data on all exposed trees on 479 plots in 188 wildfires, a total of 69,000 southern pines. No deaths were recorded in trees larger than 9 inches d.b.h.; 10 percent died in the 6-inch class, and 40 percent were lost from the 1-inch class. Among seedlings between ½ and 2 feet in height, the fires killed 98 percent of the slash and loblolly, and 48 percent of the longleaf. Loblolly was generally most susceptible, longleaf least. Contrasted to the relatively low average mortality of southern pines in most fires is the killing of nearly all trees by very severe fires (24).

According to Wahlenberg (222) it is necessary to wait until the end of the growing season following the fire to predict mortality in longleaf pine. Even the apparent intensity of a fire can be misleading. Six months after a slow fire in a Texas loblolly-shortleaf stand, there was no apparent damage to crowns or trunks. But 12 months later many trees were dying, and eventually about 10 percent succumbed. Enough fuel had accumulated at the base of large trees to permit the fire to burn deeply into the bark in the lower foot of the trunk (71).

Seedlings of most species, being tender and succulent, are very suspectible to fire. Longleaf pine in the grass stage is an exception because of certain adaptations, including a stout taproot, thick bark, and protection of the growing tip by heavy foliage and a position below the zone of flames. When height growth is beginning longleaf is more vulnerable than in the grass stage, but once well out of the grass it excels all other southern pines in fire resistance (222). Bruce (33) observed the effects of winter fires on longleaf seedlings. All vigorous yearling seedlings and about ¾ of those in fair vigor survived. Mortality was correlated with groundline diameter, all seedlings 0.20 inch or more in diameter surviving. The tolerance of seedlings of other pine species to artificial heat has been found (12, 213) to vary more among individual plants than among species.

Root damage from fire has received little attention. Heat penetration in moist soils is very limited; dry soils provide less protection (17). Heyward (101) reported that a very hot fire in Georgia killed all pine feeding roots to a depth of one inch. Even though the greatest concentration of pine roots is usually in the top inch, he believed that little harm results even from such exceptional fires, since the roots were quickly regenerated.

In dried swamps the high organic matter may allow ground fires to burn, consuming even large tree roots and killing the trees (101). In Alaska, on sites where roots are shallow and humus deep, ground fires may burn off roots up to 9 inches in diameter (139).

Insects and decay.—Following fire, insects and decay are responsible for much loss of timber (95). Stickel (191) points out that in appraising fire damage little attention is paid

5

to trees with slight basal scorching if they remain green. But more than half of the fire-scorched hardwoods examined six months after a fire were infested with beetles. It has been estimated that 97 percent of basal wounds are caused by fire *(99)* and that 90 percent of butt rots enter through these wounds *(93)*.

In the Northeast, insects attack hardwoods within a year after fire injury, but fungal decay may not be evident until the third year or even later *(193, 194)*. Of 30 species of wood-rotting fungi identified in hardwoods of the Mississippi Delta, 5 were responsible for half the decay. Within 4 years the bark had sloughed off most wounds and decay fungi had become well established. Wounds less than 2 inches wide led to no serious decay *(206, 207)*.

Hepting and Blaisdell *(97)* reported that sweetgum and persimmon were resistant to decay infection through fire wounds. This resistance was ascribed to the formation on the wound surface of a hard zone of sapwood cells, heavily infiltrated with gum. Blocks of this tissue, inoculated with decay fungi and incubated in closed tubes, were able to resist decay for a year. Copious flows of resin tend to keep fungi out of wounds in pine. Intense heat per se also promotes resin flow (personal observation). Resin has no toxic effect but prevents the entrance of fungi by its waterproofing action *(217)*.

Because fire wounds do not lead to decay as frequently in southern pines as in hardwoods, a scar, by itself, is a very uncertain indication of rot. In contrast to the many species of fungi which cause decay in hardwoods and enter mainly through fire wounds, most rot in shortleaf and loblolly pines in Arkansas and Texas was red heart *(Fomes pini)*, which usually entered through branch stubs *(98)*. *Polyporus schweinitzii* caused some cull in the butts, gaining entrance largely through fire wounds. Lodgepole pine seems less resistant to infection than southern pines; 45 percent of fire-scarred trees in Alberta had infected wounds *(163)*. However, there was considerable resistance to rot, since 33 years after the fire the wood evidenced no advanced decay, only firm red stain.

Disease.—Diseases (other than decays) may be influenced by fire, both positively and negatively. Fire aids in controlling the brown-spot

needle blight of longleaf pine seedlings, but brown spot increases fire mortality of the seedlings by decreasing their vigor and by adding diseased needles to the fuel *(35)*.

The fusiform rust disease on slash pine is also influenced by fire. Siggers *(185)* prescribe-burned in an attempt to reduce rust infection, primarily by killing infected branches. However, the end result was increased infection, presumably because the fires stimulated susceptible new growth in early spring when weather was favorable to spore germination and growth, and when production of sporidia was at a peak. The effect of early spring growth on rust susceptibility is also shown where slash pine is cultivated and fertilized *(14, 27)*.

Like brown spot, fusiform rust infection increases vulnerability of the tree to fire. The disease not only reduces plant vigor, but also causes pitch to flow on and below the canker which adds fuel *(14)*.

Physiological effects.—Fire effects on plant tissues are not well understood. Little is known about effects of near-lethal high temperatures on plant functions, or, in fact, on how heat kills cells. Belehradek lists 5 general theories, any or all of which may explain the mechanism of heat injury to protoplasm. These are: coagulation, heat destruction of enzymes, asphyxiation, intoxication, and lipoid liberation.

Coagulation of the proteins in protoplasm is the oldest and most widely accepted theory *(20)*. This process seems to progress from an increase in permeability to a visible coagulation of the protoplast *(39)*. Two common objections are that proteins usually require higher than lethal temperatures for coagulation, and that coagulative changes in the beginning are reversible in protoplasm but irreversible in proteins.

Heilbrunn *(94)* advances the idea that coagulation depends primarily on the action of heat on fats and lipoids which are emulsified in all living matter. These fats are easily liquefied at lethal temperatures and their liquefaction, or solution, generally results in coagulation of the protoplasm. Small quantities of fat solvents such as ether promote heat coagulation of both plant and animal protoplasm. Like heat, ether in dilute solution increases the fluidity of protoplasm, whereas at slightly higher concentrations it causes coagulation. In both animals and plants there seems to be a correlation between lethal temperatures and fat melting points, the less heat-resistant organisms having endogenous fats with lower melting points.

Fire may influence some physiological functions indirectly. In hardwoods basal wounds had little effect on translocation, since nearby conductive elements became quickly reoriented to maintain transport around the wound (115). In pines, defoliation by fire increased the moisture content of the upper stems (179) and appeared thereby to lessen the attractiveness of the trees to beetles immediately after the fire. Defoliated trees averaged 91 percent moisture content above the base, as compared to 64 percent in normal trees. Apparently, transpiration in the foliated trees reduced moisture content in the upper stem. Another indirect physiological effect of severe fires may be to reduce the incidence of mycorrhizae, known to be important in tree nutrition, on roots in the upper soil layer (240).

Loss of food production may not be the only factor retarding the growth of fire-defoliated trees. Oland (164) quotes Murneek to the effect that prior to natural abscission some 40 to 50 percent of the total nitrogen of the leaves is reabsorbed by the tree. This nitrogen is an important source of reserves for use the following season. Thus premature defoliation, at least of deciduous trees, may result in a loss of nitrogen to the plant.

Other possible physiological effects of fire on such life processes as respiration and enzyme action have not been reported.

Insolation Effects

Not all heat injury is caused by fire. The direct heat of the sun occasionally wounds plants, e.g., sunscald of tree trunks in winter and the "white spot" lesions of tree seedlings at groundline (134). The latter effect is increased by anything which raises the soil surface temperature, such as dryness, duff, and litter. The temperature in a sawdust mulch may be as much as 17° higher than in bare soil (150). Surface soil temperatures up to 160° in the sun were recorded by Baker (12).

Conifer seedlings were killed at these temperatures, but were able to survive surface temperatures of 140° to 150° with little injury, because the plants were generally 15° to 20° cooler than the soil surface.

When insolation raises cambium temperatures, less heat is required from a fire to bring the tissue to a lethal level. Eggert (60) measured over 80° in the cambium of peach trees on the south side while cambium on the north side and air temperature were below 32°; Bergstrom (22) reports a difference of 13°. A fire under these conditions would be expected to cause more injury on the south side, other factors being equal. Internal leaf temperatures in sunlight may exceed air temperature by 25° or more (8, 39, 51, 119).

EFFECTS OF FIRE ON SOILS

Although fire effects on soil as such are beyond the scope of this review, soil changes by heat do affect the growth of plants, hence constitute an indirect fire effect.

Probably because many factors influence the results, authorities differ as to whether fire is detrimental to forest soils. On some points there is general agreement. The ash deposit from a fire increases available phosphorus, potassium, calcium, and magnesium (2, 11, 40, 74, 102, 106, 139, 209, 218). The alkaline ash decreases soil acidity, thereby stimulating nitrification (5, 13, 15, 200, 239). Thus soil is generally improved chemically by fire. While consumption of organic matter may decrease total nitrogen in the upper inch (5, 11, 15, 74), the sharp increase in nitrification is reflected in more luxuriant growth of vegetation, particularly grasses and herbs (13). This fact has given to the southern stockman his strongest argument for frequent burning of forest lands. Most forest trees do not seem to be significantly affected by chemical soil changes brought about by fire (200), but growth of seedlings may be stimulated. In a greenhouse study slash pine seedlings grew better on burned-over than on unburned soil (221); and growth of loblolly pine seedlings in Louisiana was much better for the first three years on plots where hardwood slash had been burned than in an unburned clearing (9). Phosphorus, potassium, and magnesium were all much higher on burned plots, and remained higher for at least two years. In Alaska forest soils are said to be benefited by fire, both chemically and physically (138, 139).

Ahlgren (2) found that, while soil nutrients were at maximum right after fire, they remained high up to 5 years. Many herbaceous species grew rapidly and displayed marked lushness in size, color, and leaf thickness the first few years (especially the first year) after a fire. Sunflower and oats grown in a greenhouse on burned-over field soils were heavier and more vigorous than those on similar soils that had not been burned over.

Wahlenberg (221) reports that 10 years of protection from fire improved the physical but not the chemical properties of soil from the longleaf pine region. By removing litter and exposing soil to rain, fire can reduce porosity and infiltration rates. Protection from fire soon changes the A_1 horizon from a dense structure to one that is easily penetrable and porous (103). This effect is ascribed both to the puddling effect of rain and to the action of soil faunas which are greatly reduced in frequently burned-over soils (107). In the Northwest soil bacteria and actinomycetes were found to increase after severe burning (239), but fungi decreased.

Sometimes organic matter is increased by burning, owing to stimulation of grass growth and incorporation of roots into the soil. After 8 years of annual grass fires, Mississippi soils had 60 percent more organic matter and 50 percent more nitrogen than similar soils in unburned areas. Forage growth was doubled and soil moisture was not decreased (86).

Alway and Rost (5) likewise found no effect on moisture equivalent, but Austin and Baisinger (11) report lower waterholding capacity just after a fire. An immediate effect may be to reduce soil moisture near the surface, but by removal of shallow-rooted plants and formation of loose mulch fire may also increase soil moisture (105).

Soil texture and structure were not appreciably altered by fire in Alaska, since changes require fusion or baking of mineral particles into larger units, which rarely occurred (139). In most undisturbed mineral soils the low organic content was not conducive to aggregate formation so burning had little effect on soil aggregates.

In some western soils fire seems to increase porosity. Brush burning markedly improved permeability of surface layers, degree of aggregation, and infiltration rates (181). In the ponderosa pine region both percolation rate and macroscopic pore volume were increased (201); the fire was moderate and no incorporated humus was consumed, but the effect may have partially resulted from the burning of dead roots a few inches into the soil. Improved aggregation resulting from the release of basic ash material may also have contributed to the increased volume of macroscopic pores.

Bruce (31) found no significant difference between soils of south Mississippi that had not burned for 13 years and those burned over 3 times in the interval, and Heyward (102) concludes that fire neither definitely harms nor benefits soils of the longleaf pine region.

EFFECTS OF FIRE ON PLANT ASSOCIATIONS

Fire profoundly influences the flora and fauna of a community. The changes in plant ecology depend on such factors as the intensity and frequency of the burns, how many of each species survive, and the capacity of each species to regenerate. Chemical and physical changes in the soil, and exposure to erosion, may also influence the end result. Benefits from prescribed fires, such as release of pines from hardwood competition, promotion of grass for grazing, and improving conditions for wildlife, all depend on ecological changes brought about by fire.

Most ecologists recognize the existence of a fire subclimax, in which certain timber types, notably pines, owe their existence to periodic fires that prevent taking-over by the climax type. Where the climax type is less desirable man may use fire to maintain the subclimax stage. Little and Moore (130) cite references which indicate that fire may have had an important role in maintaining such types as Douglas-fir, paper birch, and various pines (pitch, shortleaf, longleaf, loblolly, eastern and western white, lodgepole, and ponderosa). Slash pine should no doubt be included also. The frequency of burning makes fire a major ecological factor in southern pine forests. Garren (81) states that longleaf pine, and possibly scrub oak, require occasional winter fires for their survival, although annual burning is detrimental.

8

Fire Ecology

Two principal grasses, Curtis dropseed and pineland threeawn, may make up half the herbaceous ground cover in the flatwoods of Georgia, since they are adapted to survival by having their meristems 1.5 inches underground (125). In the western portion of the longleaf belt species of *Andropogon* (bluestems) usually predominate (222). These grasses are important for maintaining structure and organic matter in the soil, and for furnishing fuel. Like longleaf pine, they are well adapted to fire. The "fire-followers" include a large number of species abundant mainly the first year after fire. Most of the forbs in this group are composites and various legumes (110). Ahlgren (2) lists a number of species which he found only on burned sites.

The fire succession pattern in ungrazed upland southern pine forests is forbs-to-perennial-grasses-to-perennial-woody-species a n d depends on the seeding and sprouting habits of the species (110). In the first growing season after burning, the cover of forbs increased and grass and shrubs decreased. After 2½ growing seasons grass recovered completely, and sprout growth more than replaced hardwood cover under 6 feet. Burning of Ozark hardwoods increased both the number of species and the number of individual plants of most species of grasses, forbs, and mosses (170).

In northeastern Minnesota jack pine, black spruce, quaking aspen, and paper birch reproduced vigorously on burned-over land (1). Seedbed conditions were generally improved except where burning was slight. Similar effects are reported from Alaska (138, 139), where climax stands of white and black spruce are being replaced by shorter-lived hardwoods (paper birch, quaking aspen, balsam poplar) as a result of fires, largely man-made. These hardwoods are able to invade fire-killed areas by virtue of their prolific sprouting and small seed, easily dispersed by wind. The semiserotinous cones of black spruce, however, are opened by fire, resulting in pure, even-aged stands of this species in some areas following fire.

In boreal forests fire may raise soil temperatures by burning off the heavy layer of insulating duff, by blackening from charcoal, and by removing foliar shade, thus increasing absorption of solar radiation. The result is a downward retreat of the permafrost, which may greatly stimulate later tree growth (138).

On upland sites in New Jersey fire eliminated or greatly reduced shade-tolerant species and those reproducing by seed (29). Hemlock, beech, birch, and white pine were replaced by intolerant sprouting species like white, scarlet, and black oak, and pitch pine.

After a fire in California killed all aboveground plant parts, manzanita, gooseberry, and deerbrush (173) took over. Seeds of these firetype species are very heat resistant, surviving for 20 minutes or more in boiling water.

Fire exclusion in areas previously subject to periodic fires also has profound ecological effects. In northern Arizona (53) and on the Pacific slope (230, 234), the forests up until the present century were open and parklike. As a result of overgrazing and fire protection, a dense understory has developed, grass has disappeared, and erosion increased. Competition for moisture seems to have enhanced susceptibility to bark-beetle attack. Prescribed fires have been suggested to prevent stagnation and reduce fuel hazard. Similar results in some portions of the longleaf-slash pine belt following complete exclusion of fire led to the present acceptance of prescribed burning.

Beneficial Fire Effects—Prescribed Burning

The use of fire for various silvicultural purposes, called prescribed burning, was approved by the U. S. Forest Service about 1942, some 13 years after the Southern Forest Experiment Station had initiated studies on the effects of fire on longleaf pine (92). The concept of prescribed burning has been explained by likening the forest manager to a physician who must examine his patient, analyze the findings, and prescribe what, in his opinion, is the remedy (52). It has been defined as: "Skillful application of natural fuels under conditions of weather, fuel moisture, soil moisture, etc., that will allow confinement of the fire to a predetermined area and at the same time will produce the intensity of heat and rate of spread required to accomplish certain planned benefits. . . . Its objective is to employ fire scientifically to realize maximum net benefits at minimum damage and acceptable cost." (212). Most or all of the benefits of prescribed burning could be obtained by other means, but the advantages of fire is its low cost (70).

In the South fire is frequently employed for seedbed preparation, control of brown-spot disease, release of longleaf seedlings to promote height growth, control of brush competition, reduction of hazardous fuel, and preparation for planting (23, 24, 25, 28, 37, 48, 69, 70). Stoddard (192) discusses uses of fire in wildlife management. Fire is also widely employed for improvement of grazing, often to the detriment of the forest (92). As has been noted, either complete exclusion or too frequent burning may be undesirable (57).

Control of brown-spot disease (Scirrhia acicola) on longleaf pine seedlings is one of the most important uses of fire in the South. Seedlings annually defoliated by this disease do not make height growth and eventually succumb. Wakeley (224) states that, to control this disease, "Prescribed burns should be thorough enough to reach practically all infected seedlings, and hot enough to brown, though preferably not hot enough to consume, all needles as high up as infection extends on the seedlings." Verrall (216) has shown that temperatures lethal to leaf tissue are also lethal to the fungus, even though not hot enough to consume or char the needles.

Burns properly made before infection has sapped vitality will greatly reduce the disease without killing the plants. By reducing the number of spores available to infect new needles the following spring, the burns permit seedlings to retain a full crown of healthy needles (32). Fire is an effective preventive because brown-spot spores under usual conditions are disseminated in appreciable numbers only for short distances. As annual defoliation by either fire or disease prevents height growth (224), Siggers recommends burning at three-year intervals (184). Wakeley and Muntz (225) compared 11-year-old longleaf pines on a plot burned twice with unburned controls of the same age. On burned plots 64 percent of the seedlings were above 4½ feet tall, as compared to only 22 percent on the unburned plots. At the time of the first burn brown spot had killed 37 percent of the foliage; the unburned stand continued to be heavily infected.

Because it is large and firmly attached to its wing, longleaf seed will not easily sift through vegetative ground cover. It germinates promptly and may do so precociously if temporarily prevented from reaching mineral soil. Burning in advance of seedfall is therefore common practice in longleaf silviculture.

Prescribed burns are frequently made in the South to control undesirable hardwoods, since these are generally more vulnerable to fire than the pines. Ferguson (69, 70), in Texas, reports temporary control of hardwoods less than 1.5 inches d.b.h. and substantial control of larger ones by single headfires in summer. Successive burns at 1- to 5-year intervals can check competing hardwoods at low cost. One burn may suffice to improve seedbeds. Growing-season headfires are generally most effective.

Prescribed burning has a definite place in the management of even-aged loblolly pine on the Coastal Plain (136, 137). An initial dormant season fire to reduce rough is followed by three annual light summer fires to kill hardwoods.

Little (128) reports successful applications of fire in the Northeast. In the pine-oak forests of southern New Jersey fire is necessary to maintain or create the subclimax pine stage (129, 130). To completely kill small hardwoods, prescribed burns must be started as soon as the pines are large enough, and repeated every 5 years. LeBarron (124) recommends burning to maintain and regenerate timber types in northeastern Washington. As mentioned above, Weaver (230, 231, 232, 233, 234) makes a strong case for prescribed burning in the ponderosa pine forests of the Pacific Slope, both to thin young stands and to control fuel accumulation.

Morris and Mowat (156), in a study of one of Weaver's burns, found that competition on potential crop trees (selected individuals) had been reduced from 2,410 trees to 895 trees per acre. Forty-six percent of the crown was scorched, and 20 percent of the trees developed fire scars, but in 6 years the crop trees grew 36 percent more in diameter and 7 percent more in height than those on unburned plots. Cause of the accelerated growth in excess of benefits from thinning is unknown, but improved soil characteristics may have contributed. They conclude that fire may be an effective thinning tool in ponderosa stands under the right conditions. Decay following fire is not a problem

10

with this species since wounds seldom become infected.

In northern Michigan, prescribed burning promotes regeneration of jack pine following harvest of mature stands *(18)*. Temperatures of over 122° are needed to melt the resin which seals the cone scales together; without fire the seeds remain bound in the cone indefinitely.

According to Uggla *(210)* fire is being used to an increasing extent in silviculture in northern Sweden. Low temperatures inhibit chemical weathering and soil organism activity which normally promote incorporation of humus into mineral soil. Controlled burning when soil is not too dry is the most efficient method of activating the humus, and of reducing the labor of planting and sowing on such land. On this basis and others, Lutz *(139)* believes that prescribed burning may also have a place in Alaska.

LETHAL TEMPERATURES

Much of the research on heat tolerance and lethal temperatures in plants has been in relation to insolation damage, but the data should be applicable to fire effects. The external temperature which may be lethal for a given plant tissue depends on many factors—the initial temperature of the tissue, insulating qualities of dead tissue such as bark which separates the living cells from the heat source, physiological condition of the protoplasm, and length of exposure.

The relationship between time and temperature is exponential (within the biokinetic, or "living temperature" zone), so that as the temperature is raised the critical time moves from infinity slowly, then approaches zero very rapidly. Thus a fairly high temperature may cause no apparent injury during comparatively long exposures, whereas a few degrees higher will kill in a brief time. Baker *(12)* explained this phenomenon on the basis that coagulation of the protoplasm causing death is an exothermic process, causing a kind of chain reaction like an explosion. Therefore, its rate does not conform to the van't Hoff-Arrhenius law that the speed of chemical reaction is doubled with every 10° C. rise in temperature. The effect of temperature on reaction time is called the "temperature coefficient" or "Q" value. When the reaction speed is doubled with a 10° C. rise in temperature, the coefficient is 2 for 10°, or $Q_{10}=2$.

Lorenz *(134)* obtained Q_{10} values between 3.6 and 360 in 5 tree species. These unusually high coefficients are also associated with the coagulation of proteins, a fact considered by many to lend support to the coagulation theory of heat injury. However, certain other chemical reactions yield a similarly high temperature coefficient, e.g., the action of hot water on starch grains, with a Q_{10} between 57 and 83,900 *(20)*.

It is apparent from the above discussion that the term "lethal temperature" has little meaning unless the time factor is also indicated. The time required for killing bacteria by heat increased in a geometrical progression as the temperature was lowered arithmetically *(26)*.

According to a number of workers the thermal death point at the cellular level for average mesophytic plants lies between 122° and 131° F.; 140° is frequently given as lethal for the plant as a whole. Baker *(12)* includes a table on the influence of high temperatures on different plants, compiled from the data of a number of investigators. Minimum lethal temperatures for some 20 species varied from 113° to 139°. Only cacti could survive over 140°

Seedlings

Seedlings have been used most frequently in studying lethal temperatures.

Baker *(12)*, Lorenz *(134)*, and Shirley *(183)* investigated the lethal temperature-time curves of tree tissues by heating seedlings in a water bath. Baker studied stem injury in conifers by heating the tops only, the roots being protected in soil or water. Monterey pine was killed in 2 minutes at 130° or in 5 minutes at 125°. Fifteen minutes at 120° caused little injury. Lorenz used a neutral red stain to identify living cortical parenchyma cells of 5 tree species after heat treatment. Thirty minutes at 135° or 1 minute at 152° was lethal, with no marked difference between species. His "lethal temperatures" were much higher than Baker's, because the two workers were measuring different things. Even though the stain indicated that cells were still alive after exposure to 135° or more, it is doubtful if a plant so treated

11

would survive if planted out. Shirley, working with 4 species of conifers, found that heat tolerance increased with age and mass and that tops were more resistant than roots. The external killing temperature was approximately the same for all species.

Dry heat gave results similar to those obtained in water baths. Baker (12) measured both internal and external stem temperatures of several conifers planted in soil and exposed to artificial radiant heat plus sunshine. Seedlings were killed quickly at 131° but withstood a few degrees lower for some time. Although no specific differences were found in internal lethal temperatures, species varied somewhat in their tolerance to external heat. Tolerance increased with age but not on a cellular level (12). Seedlings of western conifers were killed when the tops were exposed to 141° for 1 minute (16). Resistance to hot sand sprinkled over the tops of 4 species of conifer seedlings increased with age, presumably a result of increased lignification (178). Temperatures up to 120° caused little injury. Above this temperature heat tolerance varied with species, depending on anatomical and transpirational factors.

Ursic (213) heated entire loblolly pine seedlings by placing an electric light in a bundle of seedlings and moist moss. He concluded that seedlings from bales that have been heated to over 122°, even for a short time, should not be planted. Two hours at 130° was lethal.

Stems and Roots

Stems and roots of mature plants have apparently received little study in regard to lethal temperatures. Ursic (213) immersed roots of loblolly pine seedlings in hot water; 129° for 5 minutes was generally lethal, as was 122° for 30 minutes, or 118° for 2 hours. Tolerance of individual seedlings varied considerably. In a similar study, 125 ° for 17 minutes was lethal for both slash pine and sand pine (82), while 120° was mostly lethal to sand pine but only slightly so to slash. Neither species was affected by 116° for 25 minutes.

Leaves

Leaves, being thin and unprotected, are easily killed by fire. Nelson (159) immersed needles of southern pines in hot water, and observed yellowing as a symptom of death. Average lethal temperatures for the 3 species were 147° for 3 seconds, 142° for 5 seconds, 140° for 31 seconds, and 126° for 11 minutes. Species differences were small.

Konis (119), Kurtz (120), and MacDougal (144) measured the internal temperatures of various xerophytic plants under intense insolation. Cactus continued growing even when the internal temperature reached 137°, and it could tolerate 144° without injury (120, 144). The mechanism permitting such heat tolerance is not known, but Konis explains it on the basis of dehydration of the protoplasm. During the warm season in Palestine leaves of heat-resistant plants contain relatively small amounts of water and have consequently high osmotic values. Plants with the highest osmotic values are generally the most heat-resistant, and vice versa. Younger leaves have lower heat resistance and lower osmotic values. Konis placed leaves of several species of maquis plants in blackened bottles in the sunshine. The lethal temperature varied between species (127 to 138°), but was always several degrees higher than the maximum observed in nature. Thus the plants should never be damaged by extreme solar heat alone, although desiccation plus high temperatures may cause injury. Young leaves, more sensitive to heat, are not produced in the dry season.

Seeds

Seeds are apt to be the most heat-resistant stage in the life cycle of the plant. Frequently the embryo is protected by a tough seed coat and the seed itself may be insulated by a hard woody fruit. If it becomes buried under even a shallow layer of earth, it is further protected from fire.

Fire promotes the germination of many Australian tree seeds by drying up and cracking open the fruit (17). Dry seeds of several native species withstood 230° for 4 hours. In water, soft seeds were killed in 5 minutes at 140° to 180°, but some hard seeds withstood 70 minutes in boiling water.

Carmichael (44) also found that heat resistance of seeds was inversely correlated with moisture content. At 10 percent relative humidity red pine, jack pine, and black spruce

12

ls were scarcely injured by 180° for 70
rs. At 20 percent relative humidity, 50
rs was the limit, and at 30 percent more
1 10 hours greatly reduced germination.
iperatures lethal to the seeds of 7 weed
:ies from 5 families ranged from 185° to
' with 15 minutes of exposure *(112)*. Per-
. of germination diminished rapidly as the
al point for all seeds was neared, indicating
proteins may have been coagulated or
ymes inactivated at these temperatures.
ording to Sampson *(180)* most dry seeds
killed by 5 minutes' exposure at 250° to
'.

1 contrast to the low heat resistance of most
st seeds, ceanothus seeds survived 25 min-
in boiling water *(173)*.

eaufait *(18)* found that jack pine seeds are
emely heat resistant; when cones contain-
seed were heated to 900° for 30 seconds
e was no adverse effect on germination,
60 seconds at this temperature ignited the
:s and was lethal to the seeds. Three min-
at 700° was required to kill the seeds,
:s being ashed under this treatment. As
cribed fires do not normally ash the cones
:anding trees, Beaufait concludes that they
iot markedly affect seed viability. When
s unprotected by cone scales were sub-
:d to temperatures up to 1,000°, viability
not decrease significantly until the wings
d and the seed coats cracked. Lethal ex-
res for 700° ranged between 10 and 15
nds; for 1,000° between 0 and 5 seconds.

'ARIABLES AFFECTING HEAT INJURY

:mperature and its duration, the two prin-
factors outside of the plant that control
injury, have already been discussed. Wind,
affects both of these factors, has likewise
mentioned. A number of internal vari-
; also influence fire resistance.

ical Factors in Heat Resistance

:tial *temperatures and season.*—Byram
43) emphasizes the importance of initial
e temperature on fire resistance. If 140°
thal, plants at 50° can endure twice as
1 heat as those at 95°. The difference in
il temperature is probably the most im-
int reason why greater damage results
summer than from winter fires, particu-

larly with evergreen species. Thus Cary *(45)*
states that whereas summer fires often kill
large trees and seriously reduce growth, dor-
mant-season burns tend to cause little damage.
More trees died in loblolly-shortleaf plantings
burned in August than in those burned in
January *(110)*. In east Texas summer fires
killed twice as many pines as winter fires *(68)*,
and headfires in summer were most effective
in controlling hardwoods *(69)*.

Direct radiation from the sun may increase
plant temperature above that of the air and
thus accentuate fire damage, as already mentioned. Another factor with deciduous plants
is that they have no foliage to be injured or
to provide aerial fuel during the dormant
season.

Transpiration, thermal emissivity.—Theoretically transpiration should cool the leaf by
removing the latent heat of vaporization, but
the practical importance of this process has
long been debated. Shirley *(183)* found the
heat resistance of conifer seedlings to be higher
in air than in water, and highest in dry air.
This difference he ascribed to the cooling effect
of transpiration. However, transpiration in loblolly pine seems to be more a function of available soil water and insolation than of atmospheric humidity *(204)*. Transpiration continued
even in a saturated atmosphere. The accelerating effect of radiation on transpiration seems
to depend on temperature differences between
the air and the leaf. But no evidence was obtained to indicate cooling by transpiration,
since actively transpiring leaves were not significantly cooler than those reduced to the
wilting point.

Reynolds *(175)* suggests that the evaporative
cooling effect of transpiration may extend into
the interior of the bole. He kept continuous
records for 4 years of air, cambium, and center
temperatures of a cottonwood tree. Under
certain environmental conditions he observed
a distinct thermostatic action controlling internal temperatures. He ascribed this to transpiration, since it was apparent only when the
tree was in foliage. When the air temperature
rose rapidly in summer the center temperature
began dropping. He theorizes that tension in
the water columns resulting from rapid transpiration causes water to evaporate, thus cooling the tree and keeping the cambium temperature below that of the air.

13

Thermal emissivity of a leaf has been defined as the number of calories of heat given off per minute from a square centimeter of leaf surface for each degree of temperature difference between the leaf and the air (229). It is thus a measure of the radiation properties of a surface. According to Watson (228) emissivity rather than transpiration is the chief agent in preventing solar overheating of plant tissue; the proportion of available energy absorbed in transpiration does not indicate its true cooling value. Clum (51) found no consistent correlation between transpiration and leaf-air temperature difference, although leaves coated with vaseline were from 2° to 4° C. higher than transpiring leaves. Leaf temperature depended on insolation and not on water content, for a turgid leaf varied over as great a range as a dried one. He concluded that radiation and convection are more important than transpiration in controlling leaf temperatures. The two or three degrees that transpiration may cool the leaf are probably not important in protecting it from intense sunlight. Ansari and Loomis (8) essentially agree and conclude that leaf temperatures are controlled primarily by air temperature, radiation, air movement, and leaf mass, and only to a smaller and frequently insignificant extent by transpiration. In daylight leaf temperatures were always higher than air temperatures, and some leaves rose 20° above air temperature in 60 seconds when exposed to direct sunlight. Wilted leaves showed temperature-time curves similar to those of turgid leaves, with only a 2° difference accounted for by transpiration.

Thus thermal emissivity, and to a lesser extent, transpiration and other factors, may effect fire injury by their influence on initial temperature. Thermal emissivity may also play a direct part in fire damage. Radiation, particularly from a slow-moving backfire on the leeward side of the tree, raised the temperature of bark (and no doubt low foliage) considerably before the flame front arrived (64). This heat would be transmitted through the bark by conduction and raise the temperature of the cambium. The increase in initial temperature of living tissue from preliminary radiation may result in more injury as the flame passes the tree. The effect was especially evident from one to three feet above ground, where air temperatures on the trunk commonly reached several hundred degrees minutes before the flame front arrived.

Natural insulation.—Living cells in woody plants are insulated from excessive heat in various ways. Bark, with its numerous air cells and abundance of cork, is an excellent insulator (47), its efficiency varying with thickness, composition, structure, density, and moisture content (55). Cracks and fissures may be weak spots in the armor (76), but tests with longleaf pine indicate that the dead air space may act as an insulator (64). During fires air temperatures in fissures were as much as 500° lower than the air above adjacent bark plates.

Bark thickness has often been linked with fire resistance (190), but other factors, mainly percentage of cork or outer bark, may override the effect of thickness (195). More than 1,000 tests on living trees of 14 species indicated that, for the same thickness, the bark of southern conifers (pines, baldcypress) was twice as good an insulator as that of cherry, holly, or sweetgum (91). Other hardwoods were intermediate in cambial fire resistance for a given bark thickness, except that the magnolias were relatively resistant.

Thermal conductivity of wood increases with moisture content (202); this is in contrast to the situation in soils, where moisture decreases heat penetration (17). Thus, if bark behaves as wood does, high moisture content may reduce its protection to the cambium. Amount of water in bark and wood fluctuates seasonally, being highest in spring and lowest in fall for most species (83). The obvious inference is that bark affords the best protection to trees in fall and winter, the least in spring. If the xylem acts as an effective heat sink, fluctuation in wood moisture content also increases fire resistance in fall and winter.

Bark characteristics are much more important in fire resistance than is indicated by their brief mention here. A forthcoming publication by Spalt and Reifsnyder (189) reviews knowledge on this subject comprehensively.

Examples of insulating tissues other than bark include seed coats, fruits, and bud scales. In some instances the position of the sensitive growing tip offers protection. Chapman (48) wrapped tissue paper around the buds of longleaf seedlings 1 to 3 feet high and found it unscorched after a hot fire. Apparently, insula-

14

tion was provided by dense surrounding foliage, which was seared to within 3 inches of the paper. Little and Somes (131) point out that sprouting of pitch and shortleaf pine after a fire depends on dormant buds being protected by the basal crook of the seedlings, as well as by relatively thick bark.

Intermediate Factors in Heat Resistance

Species.—Specific differences in heat tolerance apparently stem more from external factors such as insulation than from any differences on the cellular level. Baker (13) states: "There is no evidence that the protoplasm of one species of vascular plant has a higher thermal tolerance than that of another when the protoplasm is well-hydrated and in an actively functional state." The importance of "well-hydrated" protoplasm must be stressed, for dehydration increases both heat and cold resistance (117). Since polar or xerophytic plants have few, if any, morphological features enabling them to withstand extremes of temperature, it is obvious that their heat and cold resistance must depend almost entirely on the composition or condition of the protoplasm (144). The protoplasm of many xerophytes contains large amounts of mucilages or pentosans that are unharmed by boiling and have great water-holding capacity.

Baker (12), Lorenz (134), and Shirley (183) found no significant differences between species of tree seedlings in relation to lethal temperatures. But Weddell and Ware (235) obtained large species differences in the survival of southern pine seedlings burned two years after planting: loblolly 18 percent survival, slash 32 percent, shortleaf (including sprouts) 56 percent, and longleaf 58 percent.

Variables between species that may affect relative fire resistance include bark thickness and composition, growth form, sprouting ability, typical growing site, and fuel accumulation in a typical site (190). Various attempts have been made to classify United States trees on the basis of their fire tolerance (55, 73, 190). In the eastern United States longleaf pine is rated highest, followed by various other southern pines. These species occur in fairly open stands and have a relatively thick bark, a high open crown, and deep roots. Least resistant are certain hardwoods, firs, cedars, and spruces which grow in dense stands, and have thin bark, low dense crowns, and shallow roots. Allen (4) found hardwoods, especially the oaks and holly, less resistant than loblolly pine. Blackgum seemed more resistant than the other hardwoods. Jameson (113) found pinyon and juniper tissue much more resistant to heat and desiccation than the tissue of various grasses. Nakamura (157) rated 74 Japanese tree species according to the relative inflammability of their leaves and twigs.

Age and size.—The fire resistance of any tree increases with lignification, diameter, bark thickness, and elevation of the crown, all commonly associated with age (12, 33, 170, 178, 222). Longleaf pine is a partial exception to this general rule because seedlings in the grass stage are much more resistant than those between 1 and 4½ feet in height (222). This is an effect of height more than of age, because other factors as well as age influence longleaf height growth. Bruce (33), however, found a correlation between age and fire mortality in longleaf pine seedlings.

Diseases, insects.—Although trees infested with insects and disease may be less resistant to fire injury than healthy trees on the basis of reduced vigor alone, other effects of pests are probably more important. Slash pines infected with fusiform rust are killed more readily by fire than are healthy trees, mostly because pitch from the cankers catches fire (185). Bruce (35) showed that brown-spot infected longleaf seedlings were much more susceptible to fire-kill than healthy seedlings, especially where the plant is more than two-thirds defoliated by the disease. He attributed this susceptibility more to the change of foliage from green insulation to dead fuel than to reduced plant vigor. Insects and rot following fire may also predispose the tree to more damage by enlarging the wound and exposing more area to later fires, which may eventually girdle or topple the tree.

Physiological Factors in Heat Resistance

Succulence, hardening.—Degree of succulence in mesophytic plants seems inversely associated with both dormancy and resistance to heat (or cold). Fast-growing, succulent tissues are very susceptible, whereas such hard and desiccated tissues as seeds, dormant twigs, and in lower forms spores, are heat and cold resistant. "In the dry state the protoplasm of seeds and spores has been found to withstand quite long exposures to temperatures less than 1°K. (-458°F.) or more than 120°C. (248° F.), while vigorously growing tissues tend to have little or no hardiness." (63). The effect of moisture content on heat resistance of seeds is well illustrated by Carmichael (44).

Even among actively growing plants, resistance is influenced by water content. Watered bluestem grass was killed in 4 hours by the same degree of heat that required 16 hours to kill drought-hardened bluestem (117). Hardening against heat is analogous to frost hardening, and the two effects seem to be reciprocal, i.e., hardening for frost resistance may increase heat resistance, and vice versa, indicating a common mechanism (126).

Konis (119) states that individual maquis plants are inured to heat by growing in a habitat which is consistently warm during the day. Such adjustment may simply be the product of increased osmotic values due to an increase in sugars and a decrease in water in the cells. Bukharin (39) proposes a unique mechanism to explain the increased heat resistance of plants held at 86° for a short time. At this temperature protective hydrophilic colloids are at a maximum, and the coagulation temperature of protoplasm reaches a peak. Heat resistance decreases in plants held above 86° because of a decline in the amount of hydrophilic colloids, as well as in the coagulation threshold of protoplasm. Thus at high temperatures the protective action of the hydrophilic colloids is lost and protoplasm coagulates at a lower temperature, with resultant loss of heat resistance.

The essential change in hardening of plants seems to be an increase in the ability of the proteins to absorb water (hydrophily) (63). Since this effect is common to all types of hardiness, one of the best ways to increase heat tolerance is to harden plants at very low temperatures. Low temperatures reduce the growth rate and salts and sugars accumulate in the cells. The result is an increase in osmotic pressure of the cell vacuoles and the withdrawal of water from the protoplasm. This in turn increases hydrophily in the plant.

The coagulation threshold of protoplasm may also be affected by the presence of auxins. In-doleacetic acid or 2, 4-D applied to sections of pea stems greatly reduced the amount of protein coagulated by heat from extracts of these tissues (78, 79). Total protein content was not altered, only the coagulation threshold. As auxin analogs that do not promote growth had little or no effect on coagulation, a physiological relationship was suggested, although the effect also occurred in roots where auxin inhibits growth. Auxins influenced stem protein coagulability most where auxin-induced growth was greatest and were ineffective where auxin did not influence growth. Gibberellic acid, which also promotes stem growth, enhanced the auxin effect on proteins. These data indicate that growth substances probably play a part in heat hardening.

Heat resistance of peas of both a heat-sensitive and a heat-resistant variety was markedly increased by vernalizing the seed for 25 days at 39° (109). Growing the plants at high temperature devernalized them with respect to flowering but not with respect to heat resistance.

Phenology, dormancy, food reserves.— Season of burning may influence not only direct fire damage, but also the ability of the plant to recover from injury by sprouting or refoliation. Foresters have observed that the best time to eradicate deciduous woody plants by cutting or burning usually is in spring, before the food reserves depleted by spring growth have been restored by the expanded leaves (237). Both shoot and root reserves in most deciduous trees peak in late summer, decrease slowly after leaf fall, and are depleted rapidly when active growth is resumed (172). Root reserves in Florida oaks reached a minimum in late April and early May, and a maximum in July (238). In evergreens the cycle may be reversed, as food accumulates in winter. Hepting (96) found a minimum of shoot and root reserves in shortleaf pine during fall, and a maximum in spring. On this basis a spring fire should cause greatest injury to deciduous trees with least loss to evergreens.

A burn during late April increased the number of buckbrush sprouts, a May burn decreased them (3). Starch reserves had been nearly depleted in the 23 days between the two burns. Sumac produced fewest sprouts when cut in June, when starch in this species was at a

16

minimum. In the South, Chaiken (46) found summer fires more effective than winter fires in killing rootstocks and reducing size and vigor of sprouts from surviving rootstocks. Oak stumps in California sprouted less when cut in summer than in winter or early spring (133). In the southern Appalachians, dogwoods cut in early summer sent up fewer and less vigorous sprouts than those cut at any other time. Stumps from late-summer cuts had the most and longest sprouts (38). Similar results were obtained with oaks (50, 84): quickest kill, least sprouting, and poorest survival of sprouts occurred when trees were girdled in May or June.

Food reserves seem to have a direct effect on heat resistance as well as on sprouting capacity. Julander (117) showed that hardening by drought under conditions favorable for food accumulation increased heat resistance of 5 grass species; in fact, any treatment that increased food reserves improved the resistance of the plant to heat.

Dormancy, particularly in deciduous trees, denotes lack of foliage to be injured by fire as well as the presence of dormant buds, which are presumably more heat-resistant than actively growing terminal buds. It is also conceivable that dormant cambium may be more tolerant of high temperatures than active cambium. If so, then any of the external or internal factors which, according to Wareing (227), control and modify cambial activity, may also influence fire resistance. Evidence indicates that growing buds produce auxin which initiates cambial activity. The presence of this auxin in itself may modify the heat resistance of the protoplasm (78).

Chemical factors.—Chemical reactions unrelated to auxins and food reserves also influence heat resistance. Heat effects sometimes can be alleviated chemically by supplying a deficiency or removing a toxin produced at high temperatures. Mitchell and Houlahan (153) studied a temperature-sensitive mutant of the red bread mold (Neurospora) which grows normally up to 77° but ceases to grow above 82°; the normal parent grows well at 95° to 104°. The mutant was unable to produce the essential nutrient riboflavin at elevated temperatures, but addition of this vitamin restored high-temperature growth. Other temperature-sensitive *Neurospora* mutants were cured by the addition of adenine and pyrimidines.

Results similar to those with molds have been obtained with higher plants. Peas, for example, turn yellow and die in a few days at 95° even when water and mineral supplies are adequate. Galston and Hand (77) showed that this response has a chemical basis in that adenine, an essential growth factor, becomes deficient at high temperatures. Supplying adenine through the roots largely prevented yellowing and death. Peas of a heat-sensitive variety contained equal amounts of adenine at both high and low temperatures, but in a heat-resistant strain the adenine content doubled when temperatures were increased from 57° to 78° (108), indicating increased requirements at higher temperatures. Addition of adenine for protection against high temperature has also been reported for duckweed (120), bean, grape, and peach leaves (118). Heat lesions in mouse-ear cress were alleviated by supplying thiamine, adenine, pantothenic acid, biotin, and similar compounds (123). In fact, one characteristic of mutants that are sensitive to high temperature is the frequency with which they are reparable by single diffusable substances (10). Chemical control of climatic diseases may have practical value in extending the range of economic plants (120).

Although enzymes are easily inactivated by heat (152, pp. 466-467), their role in heat injury is unknown. By one theory, heat injury is initially due to the denaturation of specific thermolabile enzymes. The chief difficulty here is the relatively low temperature at which heat injury occurs in some plants, but it may be that enzymes are more thermolabile *in vivo* than *in vitro* (63). Support for this theory comes from numerous cases, as those cited above, in which heat injury is reparable by single compounds that presumably replace the heat-inactivated part of the enzyme. However, there is no evidence that inactivation of the enzyme peroxidase is accomplished at a lower temperature *in vivo*, since it remains active even after the cells have been killed by heat (personal observation).

Some strains of *Neurospora* apparently have more stable enzymes and hence are able to withstand more heat than others (63). Several enzymes are known to exist in forms that vary in thermostability. Possibly breeding for heat resistance could be accomplished by selecting genes that provide thermostable enzymes.

17

Desert plants are remarkably tolerant of high temperature, as has already been shown. Roots of the creosote bush grow ten times as fast at 86 to 95° as they do at 68 to 77°, the optimum temperature range for mesophytic plants. Mesquite roots grow rapidly at 106° *(120)*. The mechanism permitting xerophytic plants to withstand such temperatures is not known. Petinov and Molotkovsky *(171)* propose that the reparative capacity of heat-resistant cells is based on the production of the necessary organic acids, from which amides are synthesized. These amides eliminate the toxic effect of ammonia produced at high temperatures. Other theories of heat resistance are reviewed by Levitt *(126)*.

Sprouting ability.—Because many hardwoods sprout from the base after the top has been killed *(133)*, a single prescribed fire frequently results in many more stems than there were originally *(69, 170)*. Most pines lack this sprouting ability, or lose it beyond the seedling stage. Thus, loblolly seedlings will not sprout after 7 or 8 years *(132)*. In a severe fire which kills all tops, hardwoods therefore have the advantage over the typically more fire-resistant pines.

Notable exceptions to this general rule include pitch pine and shortleaf pine, which sprout from axillary buds or dormant buds under the bark. Shortleaf tops are less fire-resistant than other southern pines but the species' sprouting ability gives it an advantage in severe fires. Basal sprouts have been reported from pitch pines up to 79 years old and shortleaf up to 70 years *(131)*. Pitch pine in New Jersey's Plains areas, subject to frequent fires, forms characteristic large clumps which may have as many as 249 living 1-year-old sprouts on a single stool.

Recovery processes.—The physiological processes accompanying recovery from fire damage apparently have received little attention. Defoliation may be followed by growth of new leaves if the tree or buds have not been killed. As long as a leaf is healthy it exerts apical dominance, so that the axillary leaf bud is prevented from growing. In the South, refoliation following fire is seen most frequently in pines, for in hardwoods the tops, twigs, or buds are likely to be killed if the fire is hot enough to kill the leaves.

Wound healing is accomplished by callus tissue which grows in from all sides, eventually closing the wound if it is not too large and is not attacked by insects or fungi. Fingers of callus (and presumably cambium) can often be seen within the wound. The origin of callus tissue seems debatable. Usually it is assumed to arise from the surrounding cambium *(170)*, but Soe *(186)* found that the cambium took very little part in callus formation in hardwoods following scoring to the wood. Callus originated from ray cells or phloem parenchyma on both sides of the wound. About a week after joining, this tissue gave rise to a new vascular cambium. In the species studied, cork cambium was always formed ahead of vascular cambium.

EXPERIMENTAL METHODS, INSTRUMENTATION

External Evidence of Heat Injury

Color changes.—Color provides a convenient and rapid method for diagnosing heat injury in those species where browning or yellowing occurs soon after the plant has lost its ability to recover *(168)*. Nelson *(159)* used yellowing of southern pine needles as an identification of heat injury following immersion in a water bath.

Subsequent growth.—Measurement of subsequent growth is the most reliable method of assaying physiological heat injury and often the most practical, but sufficient time must be allowed to assure that delayed effects will not be missed. Ursic *(213)* found that many pine seedlings appeared normal for two months before they died of heat treatment.

Bark and crown scorch.—Scorch is the most commonly accepted diagnostic criterion of injury after a fire. Many attempts have been made to assay damage on this basis, with varying success. Degree of crown scorch seems the best indicator *(68, 69, 151, 220)*. Adding an estimate of cambium injury to estimates of defoliation may improve the accuracy of mortality predictions *(68, 151)*. Nelson et al. *(162)*, maintain that the area of a wound can be predicted in the first growing season after a fire from such measurements as the height and width of the discolored area of bark and d.b.h. (as correlated with bark thickness), but Stickel *(194)* believes it necessary to wait several years to predict damage accurately.

18

Pitch flow.—Obvious pitch flow is a good indication of cambium injury in pines, although it may not occur in all species or at all seasons. Several weeks after prescribed burning of longleaf pine in April the cambium under areas of pitch flow was examined, either visually or electrically *(64)*. Discoloration, or an increase in electrical resistance *(90)*, showed that the cambium had been killed in all of these areas. Dogwood and some other hardwoods also exude gum from fire wounds under the bark (personal observation).

Internal Evidence of Heat Injury

Various changes, e.g., in the appearance of internal tissues, response of cells to dyes, tissue fluorescence, cytoplasmic streaming, electrical resistance, gas exchange, and enzyme activity may be used as indications of plant injury. The method of diagnosis used is determined by the species, tissue, and specific problem *(168)*.

Appearance of cambium.—Cambial fire injury is usually hidden by the bark, which may remain attached for several years before being split off by the swelling callus *(122)*. Diagnosis by direct cambium examination therefore requires removal of the bark *(151)*, a time-consuming and injurious process.

Electrical resistance in the cambium.—Tests in south Mississippi have indicated a relationship between electrical resistance and heat injury in the cambium *(90)*. Resistance was measured with a modified lumber moisture meter having long probes sensitive only at the tips. Readings in the cambial region dropped sharply within a week after heat-killing, indicating an increase in resistance, presumably due to loss of moisture. Resistance readings may thus provide a rapid and non-injurious method for assaying cambial damage. Moisture-meter indications corresponded well with direct examination *(64)*.

Most workers report a decrease, rather than an increase, in electrical resistance following death *(58, 72, 87, 140, 165)*. Osterhout *(165)* was the first to demonstrate that resistance to low-frequency alternating current decreased with injury, then fell to a low level at death. This resistance drop preceded visible signs of death by several days. The tissue to be measured was immersed in water of high electrolyte content. Greenham et al. *(87, 88)* found that,

when measurements were made *in situ* with a lower electrolyte content, loss of moisture following death increased the resistance. Thus a dead and partially desiccated root had the same low-frequency resistance as a healthy root. This may be the effect observed in tree cambium following death. The cambial region is high in moisture and low in electrolytes, so that desiccation following death would increase the electrical resistance.

In order to avoid the effect of desiccation Greenham *(58, 88)* used a ratio of low-frequency resistance to high-frequency resistance. This ratio is not affected by water content and is approximately 1 in dead tissue. The ratio is very high in healthy tissue, may increase with initial injury, but decreases with further injury from such causes as poisons, cold, heat, or drought.

The drop in low-frequency resistance at death where desiccation is not a factor is believed due to the action of the plasmalemma, or cell membrane. This membrane effect has been questioned *(111)*, but Walker *(226)* demonstrated its existence with direct-current measurements. Luyet *(140)* observed that with high frequencies resistance in both living and dead tissues was low, whereas with low frequencies resistance was much higher in living tissues. The drop in low-frequency resistance provided an instantaneous measure of death. The plasmalemma seems to act like a capacitance in living cells, imposing a high impedance on low-frequency current *(58)*. At death this capacitance effect breaks down. Resistance in healthy tissue would then be the sum of electrolyte resistance plus the capacitive impedance of the plasmalemma. With high frequencies death has no effect, because capacitive impedance is very low; with low frequencies the impedance is great until destroyed by death.

Filinger and Cardwell *(72)* used electrical-resistance measurements to detect killing of raspberry canes by freezing or boiling. Electrodes were inserted 10 inches apart, and were connected to a resistance bridge and source of 1000-cycle alternating current. Resistance increased from 72 to 90 percent following death of the stems.

There is very little literature regarding electrical resistance measurements in tree cambium. Fensom *(67)* used silver nails set in the cambium to measure resistance in maple branches. The resistance decreased with declining temperature and with the onset of phenological stages such as sap flow, budding, flowering, and leaf opening.

Russian work (241) indicates that the moisture content, thickness, pH, and electrical properties of pine phloem may be changed by fungus infections. In addition, the catalase activity of the inner bark and needles and the starch content of phloem parenchyma show differences between healthy trees and those attacked by Fomes annosus and other fungi. If heat also affects some of these properties, measurement of them could be used in assaying fire injury.

Another Russian paper (158) describes four instruments for determining cambial moisture differences between normal and diseased trees. The instruments make use of cobalt chloride paper, expressed sap volume, or galvanomic output from bimetallic electrodes pressed against the cambium. All four are said to be highly reliable. Tests on oak, pine, chestnut, ash, and other species showed a consistently lower cambial moisture content in diseased trees.

Cytological examination. — Lorenz (134) tried various means of assessing cell injury in cortical parenchyma. These included (1) direct observation of the plant material, which may require 2 days to 2 weeks before lethal effects become apparent; (2) use of ultraviolet absorption, in which living cells appear black in an ultraviolet photograph and dead cells appear white; and (3) staining with neutral red and methyl blue, so that living cells show up red and dead cells blue.

Lorenz decided on a simple, neutral red stain; at death the cell membrane loses its permeability and does not absorb this dye. Monselise (154) used sodium selenite and indigo carmine to determine viability in citrus seed. Living cells were stained red by reduction of selenite to red selenium by enzyme action, while dead cells were stained blue by indigo. Much work has been done recently with tetrazolium chloride (TTC) as a vital stain (30, 85, 113, 166, 167, 177). This compound is reduced to an insoluble red formazan by enzymes in living cells, making visible numerous cell structures that contain the en-

zymes. The value of tetrazolium chloride for pine studies is questionable, because resin also reduces it (167).

Observation of cytoplasmic streaming constitutes an easy visual method of studying heat effects in tissues where streaming occurs, although streaming may stop before the cell is killed. Thimann and Kaufman (205) found that rate of streaming in cambial cells of white pine was proportional to temperature up to 93°. At higher temperatures the rate decreased. All streaming stopped at 110°. This happens to be the temperature at which Bukharin (39) found that protoplasm reached its maximum viscosity. If irreversible coagulation occurs at 110°, this would be the lethal temperature of the protoplasm, although it seems low. Thimann and Kaufman's data do not indicate that brief exposure to this temperature is lethal. Some damage occurred, however, for when cells were returned to lower temperatures streaming was resumed at a reduced rate.

Luyet and Gehenio (141) used ultraviolet absorption to differentiate between living and dead cells in onion epidermis. A microscope with quartz lenses was used to transmit the ultraviolet. Living cells absorbed ultraviolet and photographed black, whereas dead cells showed up white. Cells lost the power of absorption when heated, poisoned, frozen, or injured. Apparently some living cells contain a natural pigment that absorbs ultraviolet and is lost at death (142). The effect could be simulated in cells lacking the pigment by the use of neutral red stain and green light, in which case living cells again appeared black and became transparent at death.

Enzyme detection and respiration measurements.—Colorimetric enzyme tests, similar to those used for peroxidase in blanching vegetables (155), may possibly be useful for assaying fire damage. However, most enzymes have inactivation temperatures higher than the general lethal temperature of plant tissue. Measurement of gas exchange is another physiological test which would determine viability, by indicating whether respiration was taking place.

Methods of Heat Application

Of many different methods of applying controlled heat to plants, immersion in a water

20

bath (12, 82, 134, 183, 213) has been the most popular. Uniform temperatures are easily maintained, and conduction of heat into plant tissue is rapid. Other heat sources used include ovens (12, 16), radiant electric heaters (12, 16, 59), a hot plate (195), solar heating in a blackened bottle (119), sprinkling hot sand over seedlings planted in soil (178), electric heating in a synthetic bale (213), slash burning (240), and a propane torch (91), kerosene wick or hot air blower (187, 188). Lorenz (134) used a heated microscope stage, thermostatically controlled, by which he could observe cellular heat effects directly.

MacLean (147) points out that the rate of heat movement through a body is affected by the method of heating as well as by the temperature difference between the heat source and the body. For a given temperature at the source he found steam to be the most effective, followed by water, creosote, and hot plates. Differences in heat source efficiency may be ascribed to surface resistance or intimacy of contact. Changes in bark properties with charring is another variable that must be considered.

Techniques For Measuring Temperature

The problems connected with measurement of temperature, both external and internal, involve mainly considerations of accuracy, fast response, sufficient range, and ability to place the sensitive element within the desired tissue with a minimum disturbance to the physical structure. The thermocouple appears to meet these requirements best. Eggert (61) discusses the construction and installation of thermocouples for biological research. He describes a method for inserting thermocouples in tree trunks, and emphasizes the use of fine wire to insure rapid response to quick changes in temperature. Further applications in agricultural research are discussed by Lorenzen (135).

Considerable information is available on thermocouple fundamentals, applications, and sources of error (65, 169, 174, 176, 203, 219). The construction of micro-thermocouples, necessary for rapid response and minimum disturbance of tissue, has been approached in several ingenious ways (135, 215, 236). The National Bureau of Standards has published two lists of references on temperature measurement (75, 211).

Some specific applications of the thermocouple in studies of heat effects in trees might be mentioned. Devet (59) used 24-gage wire for bark-surface temperatures and 36-gage for the cambium, the latter being inserted in a hole made by a needle. Vehrencamp (214) measured air temperatures during fires with 24-gage iron-constantan couples. Radiation shields were unsatisfactory. Leads were insulated with asbestos and glass. Protection of leads exposed to flame is a major problem; Davis and Martin (56) used fiberglass-stainless steel mesh insulation. Some sort of metallic armor seems to be the only flexible insulation capable of withstanding repeated exposure to flame. In south Mississippi (64) extension wire leads insulated with asbestos were carried through flexible steel conduit to a buried junction box containing a common reference junction. At the tree the exposed leads were protected by ceramic insulators. External thermocouples were 22-gage iron constantan and internal couples were 28-gage IC enclosed in stainless steel for insertion under the bark. Temperatures were recorded automatically at 2-second intervals on a 16-point Brown recorder, or manually on a portable potentiometer (64).

Shcherbakov (182) described an electric thermometer, possibly a thermistor, for measuring tree temperatures. Uggla (209) used resistance bridges to obtain air and soil temperatures during fires. Thermistors are adapted to precise measurement of a narrow range of temperatures (19, 116, 208); thermocouples have a wider range, and are much cheaper.

Non-electric methods of temperature measurement often make use of the melting points of various substances. The fusible compounds indicate only minimum temperatures, i.e., whether the melting point of each compound has been reached. Nelson and Sims (161) employed Seger cones and metal alloy ribbons for determining maximum temperatures at various levels in a forest fire, while Beadle (17) made use of the melting points of various organic compounds placed in buried vials to measure soil temperatures during a fire. Fenner and Bentley (66) painted solutions of different compounds in strips on sheets of mica. When the solvent had evaporated the crystals were left and could be observed for fusion. The

21

sheets of mica were buried in the soil vertically so that depth of each fusion temperature could be observed. These methods obviously are unsuited to measurement of internal temperatures of living organisms.

SUMMARY OF RESEARCH NEEDS

Although many things related to the problem of fire tolerance in trees have been mentioned in this review, it is clear that very little is known about the subject. The ensuing discussion considers, in the approximate sequence that it should be developed, the information that seems most important to an understanding of the subject. Each section indicates the status of knowledge as uncovered in the literature review, and thus serves as a summary.

Temperature Measurement During Fires

Basic to further study of fire injuries to trees are records of temperatures and their durations both immediately external to plants and in the tissues themselves. The records should be obtained from fires that burn in natural fuels and are hot enough to kill or wound. Then, with readily controlled heat sources, simulated forest fires could be designed for further studies. This approach would eliminate waiting for the right weather conditions; remove worry about causing excessive timber loss; and facilitate replications of conditions of exposure.

Thermal Characteristics of Bark

Most fire damage to trees is stem injury or defoliation, although buds can be killed and roots injured. Thus the protection afforded the stem by bark is an important factor in resistance. It is apparent and often reported that thick barks are better insulators than thin barks, and fire resistance ratings of the various species are largely assigned on the basis of bark thickness.

Such generalizations do not tell how much fire a given tree can stand, or help predict damage to individual trees. Laboratory studies, now under way or contemplated, can determine the physical constants involved—thermal conductivity and diffusivity, specific heat, density, and moisture content of inner and outer bark—and thus explain species differences and provide means for predicting damage from fires of known intensities. There also is

room for empirical field tests to uncover interspecific differences other than bark thickness, and help in the interpretation of laboratory findings.

Identification of Internal Heat Injury

Before high-temperature effects on cells or tissues can be studied, before lethal temperatures can be determined, a technique is needed for differentiating between living and dead material. At present the most reliable method for assaying damage to tissue is by observing subsequent growth, but this sometimes takes too much time.

Foliage injury and cambium browning indicate localized death of plant parts but not necessarily death of the tree. The cambium may discolor slowly and examination of it further injures the tree. A rapid, reliable, and relatively non-injurious assay method is needed. Even methods dealing with individual cells or small groups of cells have not been entirely satisfactory. Microscopic observation of vital staining, cytoplasmic streaming, or plasmolysis is tedious and interpretation in terms of damage to living trees is uncertain.

The rapid identification of injured tissue in the field is therefore an important goal. At present, electrical-resistance measurements seem promising, but more work is needed on factors other than death that affect resistance in the cambium. Stains and other reactions of living tissue that can be observed in the field should be investigated. There may be a chemical response to wounding that could be made the basis of a diagnostic test (148).

Lethal Time-Temperature Curves

Some data are now available on how long foliage, seeds, and seedlings can endure various high temperatures. This kind of information is needed for different parts of trees. Controlled heat sources and accurate measurement of internal temperatures are necessary. The effect of such factors as moisture content, age, and species should be studied.

Physiological Effects of High Temperature

There is little information on the effect of near-lethal temperatures on physiological functions, yet such data might reveal how cells or tissues are injured by heat. Among the many

22

possibilities are changes in respiration, in translocation of food, water or growth substances, or in enzyme reactions.

Secondary physiological effects caused by partial or complete girdling of stems have received some attention. Changes in moisture content of leaves are apparently slight, but variations in sprouting have been described for fires of different intensities and in different seasons. Some of these effects may be explained by destruction of basal (dormant) buds and the effect of current food reserves.

The effect of temperature on respiration in plants is well known (152) but forest fires usually pass too swiftly to have much permanent direct effect on plant respiration. Translocation of foods and other metabolites might very well be influenced if phloem were injured. Sub-injurious temperatures affect phloem transport (62) but the same objections of short duration hold here. Enzymes are easily inactivated by heat but usually only at temperatures above those which would be lethal for the cell itself. Thus, translocation may be the chief physiological function disrupted by damaging high temperatures, and this only until uninjured conductive tissue becomes adapted to bypass the wound. Research to determine if translocation is an important factor in heat injury would require radioactive or other types of tracers. Active enzymes could be identified chemically after heat treatment.

Importance of Various Factors in Fire Resistance

Besides the obvious external factors that affect fire injury, such as temperature and duration, there are several internal conditions which alter high temperature effects. Species differ in bark and growth habit, e.g., succulent plants are more susceptible than hardened ones. Age, vigor, degree of dormancy, and food reserves also affect heat tolerance.

The initial approach to the study of these factors as they affect high temperature tolerance will require greenhouse studies on seedlings, perhaps with field observations on mature trees to follow. Season, as it affects moisture content of bark, as well as succulence in living tissue, may be important. The relationship between chemistry of the plant (adenine content, e.g.) and heat resistance needs to be studied, as does the possibility of hardening for heat resistance. Moisture content must be known or controlled, not only to standardize results but to determine its effect on heat resistance.

Recovery Processes

The processes of recovery in fire-damaged tree tissues have received little attention. When a spot of cambium is killed callus tissue forms, whether from cambium, ray cells, or phloem parenchyma, and eventually covers the lesion if it is not too large. But what physiological processes accompany this growth? Knowledge of the part played by growth substances, enzymes, food, minerals, and other metabolites might lead to means of accelerating the healing process itself.

23

LITERATURE CITED

(1) AHLGREN, CLIFFORD E.
1959. SOME EFFECTS OF FIRE ON FOREST REPRO-
DUCTION IN NORTHEASTERN MINNESOTA.
Jour. Forestry 57:194-200, illus.

(2) ———
1960. SOME EFFECTS OF FIRE ON REPRODUCTION
AND GROWTH OF VEGETATION IN NORTHEAST-
ERN MINNESOTA. Ecol. 41:431-445, illus.

(3) ALDOUS, A. E.
1929. THE ERADICATION OF BRUSH AND WEEDS
FROM PASTURE LANDS. Jour. Amer. Soc.
Agron. 21:660-666.

(4) ALLEN, PETER H.
1960. SCORCH AND MORTALITY AFTER A SUMMER
BURN IN LOBLOLLY PINE. U. S. Forest Serv.
Fire Control Notes 21: 124-125.

(5) ALWAY, F. J., and ROST, C. C.
1928. EFFECT OF FOREST FIRES UPON THE COM-
POSITION AND PRODUCTIVITY OF THE SOIL.
Internatl. Cong. Soil Sci. Proc. 3:546-576.

(6) ANDERSON, D. A., and BALTHIS, R. F.
1944. EFFECT OF ANNUAL FALL FIRES ON THE
TAPER OF LONGLEAF PINE. Jour. Forestry
42:518.

(7) ANDRESEN, JOHN W.
1959. A STUDY OF PSEUDO-NANISM IN Pinus rigida
MILL. Ecol. Monog. 29:309-332, illus.

(8) ANSARI, A. Q., and LOOMIS, W. E.
1959. LEAF TEMPERATURES. Amer. Jour. Bot.
46:713-717, illus.

(9) APPLEQUIST, M. B.
1960. EFFECTS OF CLEARED-AND-BURNED HARD-
WOOD SLASH ON GROWTH OF PLANTED LOB-
LOLLY PINE IN LIVINGSTON PARISH, LOUISI-
ANA. Jour. Forestry 58:899-900.

(10) ATWOOD, K. C., and MUKAI, F.
1953. INDISPENSABLE GENE FUNCTIONS IN NEURO-
SPORA. Natl. Acad. Sci. Proc. 39:1027-
1035.

(11) AUSTIN, R. C., and BAISINGER, D. H.
1955. SOME EFFECTS OF BURNING ON FOREST SOILS
OF WESTERN OREGON AND WASHINGTON.
Jour. Forestry 53:275-280, illus.

(12) BAKER, F. S.
1929. EFFECT OF EXCESSIVELY HIGH TEMPERATURES
ON CONIFEROUS REPRODUCTION. Jour. Forestry 27:949-975, illus.

(13) ———
1950. PRINCIPLES OF SILVICULTURE. 414 pp., illus.
New York.

(14) BALTHIS, R. F., and ANDERSON, D. A.
1944. EFFECT OF CULTIVATION IN A YOUNG SLASH
PINE PLANTATION ON THE DEVELOPMENT OF
CRONARTIUM CANKERS AND FORKED TREES.
Jour. Forestry 42:926-927.

(15) BARNETTE, R. M., and HESTER, J. B.
1930. EFFECT OF BURNING UPON THE ACCUMULA-
TION OF ORGANIC MATTER IN FOREST SOILS.
Soil Sci. 29:281-284, illus.

(16) BATES, C. G., and ROESER, J., JR.
1924. RELATIVE RESISTANCE OF TREE SEEDLINGS
TO EXCESSIVE HEAT. U. S. Dept. Agr. Bul.
1263, 16 pp., illus.

(17) BEADLE, N. C. W.
1940. SOIL TEMPERATURES DURING FOREST FIRES
AND THEIR EFFECT ON THE SURVIVAL OF
VEGETATION. Jour. Ecol. 28:180-192, illus.

(18) BEAUFAIT, WILLIAM R.
1960. SOME EFFECTS OF HIGH TEMPERATURES ON
THE CONES AND SEEDS OF JACK PINE. Forest
Sci. 6:194-199, illus.

(19) BECKER, J., GREEN, C., and PEARSON, G.
1946. PROPERTIES AND USES OF THERMISTORS-
THERMALLY SENSITIVE RESISTORS. Amer.
Inst. Elec. Engin. Trans. 65:711-725, illus.

(20) BELEHRADEK, J.
1935. TEMPERATURE AND LIVING MATTER. Proto-
plasma Monog. 8, 277 pp., illus.

(21) BENTLEY, J. R., and FENNER, R. L.
1958. SOIL TEMPERATURES DURING BURNING RE-
LATED TO POSTFIRE SEEDBEDS ON WOODLAND
RANGE. Jour. Forestry 56:737-740, illus.

(22) BERGSTROM, H.
1958. TEMPERATURES IN THE TRUNK OF LIVING
TREES. Svensk PappTidn. 61 (20):902,
illus.

(23) BICKFORD, C. A.
1942. THE USE OF FIRE IN THE FLATWOODS OF THE
SOUTHEAST. Jour. Forestry 40:132-133.

(24) ——— and BULL, HENRY.
1935. A DESTRUCTIVE FOREST FIRE AND SOME OF
ITS IMPLICATIONS. U. S. Forest Serv.
South. Forest Expt. Sta. Occas. Paper 46,
4 pp.

(25) ——— and CURRY, J. R.
1943. THE USE OF FIRE IN THE PROTECTION OF
LONGLEAF AND SLASH PINE FORESTS. U. S.
Forest Serv. South. Forest Expt. Sta.
Occas. Paper 105, 22 pp., illus.

(26) BIGELOW, W. D.
1921. THE LOGARITHMIC NATURE OF THERMAL
DEATH CURVES. Jour. Infectious Diseases
29:528-536, illus.

(27) BOGGESS, W. R., and STAHELIN, R.
1948. THE INCIDENCE OF FUSIFORM RUST IN SLASH
PINE PLANTATIONS RECEIVING CULTURAL
TREATMENTS. Jour. Forestry 46:683-685.

(28) BOYD, HELEN.
1952. BURNING FOR CONTROL OF BRUSH AND BROWN
SPOT DISEASE: SELECTED REFERENCES. U. S.
Dept. Agr. Library, (Louisiana Branch,
New Orleans).

(29) BROWN, JAMES H., JR.
1960. THE ROLE OF FIRE IN ALTERING THE SPECIES
COMPOSITION OF FORESTS IN RHODE ISLAND.
Ecol. 41:310-316, illus.

(30) BROWN, WALTER.
1954. A PRELIMINARY STUDY OF THE STAINING OF
PLANT CELLS BY TETRAZOLIUM CHLORIDE.
Bul. Torrey Bot. Club 81:127-136, illus.

(31) BRUCE, DAVID.
1949. SOIL ANALYSIS OF H-2 PLOTS. U. S. Forest Serv. South. Forest Expt. Sta. Office
Rpt. [Unpublished.]

(32) ———
1951. FIRE, SITE, AND LONGLEAF HEIGHT GROWTH.
Jour. Forestry 49: 25-28, illus.

(33) ———
1951. FIRE RESISTANCE OF LONGLEAF PINE SEED-
LINGS. Jour. Forestry 49:739-740.

(34) ———
1951. A STUDY OF AVERAGE PINE MORTALITY
CAUSED BY FIRE. U. S. Forest Serv. South.
Forest Expt. Sta. Office Rpt., 21 pp., illus.
[Unpublished.]

(35) ———
1954. MORTALITY OF LONGLEAF PINE SEEDLINGS
AFTER A WINTER FIRE. Jour. Forestry 52:
442-443, illus.

(36) ———
1957. FOREST FIRE RESEARCH NEEDS IN THE SOUTH.
U. S. Forest Serv. South. Forest Expt. Sta.
Problem Analysis, 28 pp., illus.

(37) ——— and NELSON, RALPH M.
1957. USE AND EFFECTS OF FIRE IN SOUTHERN
FORESTS: ABSTRACTS OF PUBLICATIONS BY
THE SOUTHERN AND SOUTHEASTERN FOREST
EXPERIMENT STATIONS, 1921-55. U. S. Fo-
rest Serv. Fire Control Notes 18:67-96.

(38) BUELL, J. H.
1940. EFFECT OF SEASON OF CUTTING ON SPROUT-
ING OF DOGWOOD. Jour. Forestry 38:649-
650.

(39) BUKHARIN, P. D.
1958. LEAF TEMPERATURE AND HEAT RESISTANCE
IN CERTAIN CULTIVATED PLANTS. Fiziol.
Rast. (English transl.) 5(2):117-124, illus.

(40) BURNS, P. Y.
1952. EFFECT OF FIRE ON FOREST SOILS IN THE
PINE BARREN REGION OF NEW JERSEY. Yale
Univ. School Forestry Bul. 57, 50 pp.,
illus.

(41) BYRAM, GEORGE M.
1948. VEGETATION TEMPERATURE AND FIRE DAM-
AGE IN THE SOUTHERN PINES. U. S. Forest
Serv. Fire Control Notes 9(4):34-36, illus.

(42) ———
1957. SOME PRINCIPLES OF COMBUSTION AND THEIR
SIGNIFICANCE IN FOREST FIRE BEHAVIOR.
U. S. Forest Serv. Fire Control Notes 18:
47-57, illus.

(43) ———
1958. SOME BASIC THERMAL PROCESSES CONTROL-
LING THE EFFECTS OF FIRE ON LIVING VEGE-
TATION. U. S. Forest Serv. Southeast. Forest Expt. Sta. Res. Note 114, 2 pp., illus.

(44) CARMICHAEL, ALAN J.
1958. DETERMINATION OF MAXIMUM AIR TEMPER-
ATURE TOLERATED BY . . . SEEDS AT LOW
RELATIVE HUMIDITIES. Forestry Chron. 34:
387-392, illus.

(45) CARY, AUSTIN.
1932. SOME RELATIONS OF FIRE TO LONGLEAF PINE.
Jour. Forestry 30:594-601, illus.

(46) CHAIKEN, L. E.
1952. ANNUAL SUMMER FIRES KILL HARDWOOD
ROOT STOCKS. U. S. Forest Serv. Southeast. Forest Expt. Sta. Res. Note 19, 1 p.

(47) CHANG, YING PE.
1954. BARK STRUCTURE OF NORTH AMERICAN CONI-
FERS. U. S. Dept. Agr. Tech. Bul. 1095,
86 pp., illus.

(48) CHAPMAN, H. H.
1936. EFFECT OF FIRE IN PREPARATION OF SEEDBED
FOR LONGLEAF PINE SEEDLINGS. Jour. Forestry 34:852-854.

(49) ———
1942. EFFECT OF ANNUAL SPRING FIRES ON STUMP
TAPER OF LOBLOLLY PINE. Jour. Forestry
40:962-963.

(50) CLARK, F. B., and LIMING, F. G.
1953. SPROUTING OF BLACKJACK OAKS IN THE
MISSOURI OZARKS. U. S. Forest Serv. Cent.
States Forest Expt. Sta. Tech. Paper 137,
22 pp., illus.

(51) CLUM, H. H.
1926. THE EFFECT OF TRANSPIRATION AND ENVIRON-
MENTAL FACTORS ON LEAF TEMPERATURES.
I. TRANSPIRATION. II. LIGHT INTENSITY.
Amer. Jour. Bot. 13:194-230, illus.

(52) CONARRO, RAYMOND M.
1942. THE PLACE OF FIRE IN SOUTHERN FORESTRY.
Jour. Forestry 40: 129-131.

(53) COOPER, CHARLES F.
1960. CHANGES IN VEGETATION, STRUCTURE, AND
GROWTH OF SOUTHWESTERN PINE FORESTS
SINCE WHITE SETTLEMENT. Ecol. Monog.
30:129-164, illus.

(54) CRAIGHEAD, F. C.
1927. ABNORMALITIES IN ANNUAL RINGS RESULT-
ING FROM FIRES. Jour. Forestry 25:840-
842, illus.

25

(55) Davis, Kenneth P.
1959. FOREST FIRE: CONTROL AND USE. 584 pp.,
illus. N. Y.

(56) Davis, L. S., and Martin, R. E.
1960. TIME-TEMPERATURE RELATIONSHIPS OF TEST
HEAD FIRES AND BACKFIRES. U. S Forest
Serv. Southeast. Forest Expt. Sta. Res.
Note 148, 2 pp., illus.

(57) Demmon, E. L.
1935. THE SILVICULTURAL ASPECTS OF THE FOREST-
FIRE PROBLEM IN THE LONGLEAF PINE RE-
GION. Jour. Forestry 33:323-331.

(58) De Plater, C. V., and Greenham, C. G.
1959. A WIDE-RANGE BRIDGE FOR DETERMINING
INJURY AND DEATH. Plant Physiol. 34:661-
667, illus.

(59) Devet, David D.
1940. HEAT CONDUCTION OF BARK IN CERTAIN SE-
LECTED SPECIES. Unpublished thesis on
file N. Y. State Col. Forestry Library,
Syracuse. Illus.

(60) Eggert, Russell
1944. CAMBIUM TEMPERATURES OF PEACH AND
APPLE TREES IN WINTER. Amer. Soc. Hort.
Sci. Proc. 45:33-36.

(61) ———
1946. THE CONSTRUCTION AND INSTALLATION OF
THERMOCOUPLES FOR BIOLOGICAL RESEARCH.
Jour. Agr. Res. 72:341-355, illus.

(62) Esau, Katherine, Currier, H. B., and
Cheadle, V. I.
1957. PHYSIOLOGY OF PHLOEM. Ann. Rev. Plant
Physiol. 8:349-374.

(63) Evans, L. T.
1959. THE CHEMICAL BASIS OF CLIMATIC RESPONSE
IN PLANTS. Roy. Austral. Chem. Inst. Proc.
26:222-224.

(64) Fahnestock, George R., and Hare, Robert C.
1961. TEMPERATURES OF TREE TRUNK SURFACES
AND SURROUNDING AIR IN FOREST FIRES. U. S.
Forest Serv. South. Forest Expt. Sta. Progress Rpt. [Unpublished.]

(65) Farrar, G. L., and Platt, A. M.
1949. SOME FUNDAMENTALS OF TEMPERATURE
MEASUREMENT WITH THERMOCOUPLES. Petroleum Engin 21:5-10, illus.

(66) Fenner, R. L., and Bentley, J. R.
1959. A FUSION PYROMETER TO MEASURE SOIL
TEMPERATURES DURING WILDLAND FIRES.
U. S. Forest Serv. Fire Control Notes 20:
124-125.

(67) Fensom, D. S.
1960. A NOTE ON ELECTRICAL RESISTANCE MEAS-
UREMENTS IN *Acer saccharum.* Canad.
Jour. Bot. 38:263-265, illus.

(68) Ferguson, E. R.
1955. FIRE SCORCHED TREES—WILL THEY LIVE OR
DIE? La. State Univ. School Forestry, 4th
Ann Forestry Symp Proc., pp 102-112.
illus.

(69) ———
1957. STEM-KILL AND SPROUTING FOLLOWING PRE-
SCRIBED FIRES IN A PINE-HARDWOOD STAND
IN TEXAS. Jour. Forestry 55:426-429, illus.

(70) ———
1958. PRESCRIBED BURNING AS AN AID IN REGENER-
ATING DIFFICULT AREAS. Soc. Amer. Foresters Gulf States Sect. Proc. 1958 Ann.
Meeting, pp. 35-41.

(71) ———, Gibbs, C. B., and Thatcher, R. C.
1960. "COOL" BURNS AND PINE MORTALITY. U. S.
Forest Serv. Fire Control Notes 21:27-29,
illus.

(72) Filinger, G. A, and Cardwell, A. B.
1941. A RAPID METHOD OF DETERMINING WHEN A
PLANT IS KILLED BY EXTREMES OF TEMPERA-
TURES. Amer. Soc. Hort. Sci. Proc. 39:85-
86, illus.

(73) Flint, H. R.
1925. FIRE RESISTANCE OF NORTHERN ROCKY
MOUNTAIN CONIFERS. Idaho Forester 7:7-10,
41-43.

(74) Fowells, H. A., and Stephenson, R. E.
1934. EFFECT OF BURNING ON FOREST SOILS. Soil
Sci. 38:175-181.

(75) Freeze, Paul D.
1951. BIBLIOGRAPHY ON THE MEASUREMENT OF GAS
TEMPERATURE. U. S. Dept. Com., Natl.
Bur. Standards Cir. 513, 14 pp.

(76) Fritz, Emanuel.
1932. THE ROLE OF FIRE IN THE REDWOOD REGION.
Calif. Agr. Expt. Sta. Cir. 323, 23 pp., illus.

(77) Galston, Arthur W., and Hand, M. E.
1949. ADENINE AS A GROWTH FACTOR FOR ETIO-
LATED PEAS AND ITS RELATION TO THE THER-
MAL INACTIVATION OF GROWTH. Arch. Biochem. 22:434-443, illus.

(78) ——— and Kaur, R.
1959. AN EFFECT OF AUXINS ON THE HEAT COAGU-
LABILITY OF THE PROTEINS OF GROWING
PLANT CELLS. Natl. Acad. Sci. Proc. 45:
1587-1590.

(79) ———, Kaur, R., Maheshwari, N., and
Maheshwari, S. C.
1960. FURTHER EXPERIMENTS ON AUXIN-INDUCED
ALTERATION OF THE HEAT COAGULABILITY OF
PEA STEM PROTEINS. Plant Physiol. Suppl.
35:xxvii. (Abstract.)

(80) Garren, K. H.
1941. FIRE WOUNDS ON LOBLOLLY PINE AND THEIR
RELATION TO DECAY AND OTHER CULL. Jour.
Forestry 39:16-22, illus.

(81) GARREN, K. H.
1943. EFFECTS OF FIRE ON VEGETATION OF THE SOUTHEASTERN UNITED STATES. Bot. Rev. 9:617-654, illus.

(82) GENTILE, A. C., and JOHANSEN, R. W.
1956. HEAT TOLERANCE OF SLASH AND SAND PINE SEEDLINGS. U. S. Forest Serv. Southeast. Forest Expt. Sta. Res. Note 95, 1 p.

(83) GIBBS, R. DARNLEY.
1958. PATTERNS IN THE SEASONAL WATER CONTENT OF TREES. The Physiology of Forest Trees, pp 43-69, illus N. Y

(84) GRANO, CHARLES X.
1955. BEHAVIOR OF SOUTH ARKANSAS OAKS GIRDLED IN DIFFERENT SEASONS. Jour. Forestry 53: 886-888, illus.

(85) ————
1958. TETRAZOLIUM CHLORIDE TO TEST LOBLOLLY PINE SEED VIABILITY. Forest Sci. 4:50-53, illus.

(86) GREENE, S. W.
1935. EFFECT OF ANNUAL GRASS FIRES ON ORGANIC MATTER AND OTHER CONSTITUENTS OF VIRGIN LONGLEAF PINE SOILS. Jour. Agr. Res. 50: 809-822.

(87) GREENHAM, C. G., and COLE, D. J.
1950. STUDIES ON THE DETERMINATION OF DEAD OR DISEASED TISSUES. I. INVESTIGATIONS ON DEAD PLANT TISSUES. Austral. Jour. Agr. Res. 1:103-117, illus.

(88) ———— and DADAY, H.
1957. ELECTRICAL DETERMINATION OF COLD HARDINESS IN Trifolium repens L. AND Medicago sativa L. Nature 180 (4585):541-543.

(89) GRUSCHOW, G. F.
1952. EFFECT OF WINTER BURNING ON GROWTH OF SLASH PINE IN THE FLATWOODS. Jour. Forestry 50:515-517, illus.

(90) HARE, ROBERT C.
1960. DETECTING DEAD CAMBIUM WITH A MOISTURE METER. Jour. Forestry 58:815-817, illus.

(91) ————
1961. RELATION OF BARK THICKNESS AND SPECIES TO CAMBIAL FIRE RESISTANCE. U. S. Forest Serv. South. Forest Expt. Sta. Office Rpt., 16 pp., illus. [Unpublished.]

(92) HARTMAN, ARTHUR W.
1949. FIRE AS A TOOL IN SOUTHERN PINE. U. S. Dept. Agr. Yearbook 1949:517-527, illus.

(93) HEDGCOCK, G. G.
1926. FIRE-SCAR DAMAGE IN WOODLANDS HEAVY. U. S. Dept. Agr. Yearbook 1926:363-364.

(94) HEILBRUNN, L. V.
1924. THE COLLOIDAL CHEMISTRY OF PROTOPLASM. IV. THE HEAT COAGULATION OF PROTOPLASM. Amer. Jour. Physiol. 69:190-199, illus.

(95) HEPTING, GEORGE H.
1935. DECAY FOLLOWING FIRE IN YOUNG MISSISSIPPI DELTA HARDWOODS. U. S. Dept. Agr. Tech. Bul. 494, 32 pp., illus.

(96) ————
1945. RESERVE FOOD STORAGE IN SHORTLEAF PINE IN RELATION TO LITTLE-LEAF DISEASE. Phytopath. 35:106-119, illus.

(97) ———— and BLAISDELL, DOROTHY J.
1936. A PROTECTIVE ZONE IN RED GUM FIRE SCARS. Phytopath. 26:62-67, illus.

(98) ———— and CHAPMAN, A. D.
1938. LOSSES FROM HEART ROT IN TWO SHORTLEAF AND LOBLOLLY PINE STANDS. Jour. Forestry 36.1193-1201.

(99) ———— and HEDGCOCK, G. G.
1937. DECAY IN MERCHANTABLE OAK, YELLOW-POPLAR, AND BASSWOOD IN THE APPALACHIAN REGION. U. S. Dept. Agr. Tech. Bul. 570, 29 pp., illus.

(100) HERMAN, F. R.
1950. SURVIVAL OF FIRE-DAMAGED PONDEROSA PINE; A PROGRESS REPORT. U. S. Forest Serv. Southwest. Forest and Range Expt. Sta. Res. Note 119, 3 pp.

(101) HEYWARD, FRANK D.
1934. COMMENTS ON THE EFFECT OF FIRE ON FEEDING ROOTS OF PINE. Naval Stores Rev. 44(19):4.

(102) ————
1936. SOIL CHANGES ASSOCIATED WITH FOREST FIRES IN THE LONGLEAF PINE REGION OF THE SOUTH. Amer. Soil Survey Assoc. Bul. 17:41-42.

(103) ————
1937. THE EFFECT OF FREQUENT FIRES ON PROFILE DEVELOPMENT OF LONGLEAF PINE FOREST SOILS. Jour. Forestry 35:23-27, illus.

(104) ————
1938. SOIL TEMPERATURES DURING FOREST FIRES IN THE LONGLEAF PINE REGION. Jour. Forestry 36:478-491, illus.

(105) ————
1939. SOME MOISTURE RELATIONS OF SOILS FROM BURNED AND UNBURNED LONGLEAF PINE FORESTS. Soil Sci. 47:313-324, illus.

(106) ———— and BARNETTE, R. M.
1934. EFFECT OF FREQUENT FIRES ON CHEMICAL COMPOSITION OF FOREST SOILS IN THE LONGLEAF PINE REGION. Fla. Agr. Expt Sta. Bul. 265, 39 pp., illus.

(107) ———— and TISSOT, A. N.
1936. SOME CHANGES IN THE SOIL FAUNA ASSOCIATED WITH FOREST FIRES IN THE LONGLEAF PINE REGION Ecol. 17:659-666, illus

(108) HIGHKIN. H R.
1957   THE RELATIONSHIP BETWEEN TEMPERATURE
        RESISTANCE AND PURINE AND PYRIMIDINE
        COMPOSITION IN PEAS. Plant Physiol.
        Suppl 32 1 (Abstract)

(109) ————
1959.   EFFECT OF VERNALIZATION ON HEAT RESIST-
        ANCE IN TWO VARIETIES OF PEAS. Plant
        Physiol. 34:643-644.

(110) HODGKINS, E. J.
1958.   EFFECTS OF FIRE ON UNDERGROWTH VEGETA-
        TION IN UPLAND SOUTHERN PINE FORESTS.
        Ecol 39.38-46, illus

(111) HOPE. A. B , and ROBERTSON, R N.
1953   BIOELECTRIC EXPERIMENTS AND THE PROP-
        ERTIES OF PLANT PROTOPLASM. Austral.
        Jour. Sci 15:197-203, illus

(112) HOPKINS, C. Y.
1936   THERMAL DEATH POINT OF CERTAIN WEED
        SEEDS. Canad. Jour. Res. 14:178-183, illus.

(113) JAMESON, DONALD A.
1961.   HEAT AND DESICCATION RESISTANCE OF IM-
        PORTANT TREES AND GRASSES OF THE PINYON-
        JUNIPER TYPE. Bot. Gaz. 122: 174-179,
        illus

(114) JEMISON, G M.
1943   EFFECT OF SINGLE FIRES ON THE DIAMETER
        GROWTH OF SHORTLEAF PINE IN THE
        SOUTHERN APPALACHIANS. Jour. Forestry
        41· 574-576.

(115) ————
1944.   THE EFFECT OF BASAL WOUNDING BY FOREST
        FIRES ON THE DIAMETER GROWTH OF SOME
        SOUTHERN APPALACHIAN HARDWOODS. Duke
        Univ. School Forestry Bul. 9, 63 pp., illus.

(116) JOHNSON, J. C.
1945.   THERMISTOR TECHNICS. Electronic Indus.
        4:74-77, illus.

(117) JULANDER, O.
1945.   DROUGHT RESISTANCE IN RANGE AND PASTURE
        GRASSES. Plant Physiol. 20:573-599, illus.

(118) KESSLER, B.
1959.   NUCLEIC ACIDS AS FACTORS IN DROUGHT RE-
        SISTANCE OF PLANTS. IX Internatl. Bot.
        Cong Proc II:190

(119) KONIS, E.
1949.   THE RESISTANCE OF MAQUIS PLANTS TO
        SUPRAMAXIMAL TEMPERATURES. Ecol. 30:
        425-429.

(120) KURTZ, EDWIN B., JR.
1958.   CHEMICAL BASIS FOR ADAPTATION IN PLANTS.
        Science 128:1115-1117.

(121) LACHMUND, H. G.
1921.   SOME PHASES IN THE FORMATION OF FIRE
        SCARS. Jour. Forestry 19:638-640.

(122) ————
1923.   BOLE INJURY IN FOREST FIRES. Jour. Fo-
        restry 21:723-731, illus.

(123) LANGRIDGE, J., and GRIFFING, B.
1959.   A STUDY OF HIGH TEMPERATURE LESIONS IN
        Arabidopsis thaliana. Austral. Jour. Biol.
        Sci. 12:117-135.

(124) LEBARRON, RUSSELL K.
1957.   SILVICULTURAL POSSIBILITIES OF FIRE IN
        NORTHEASTERN WASHINGTON. Jour. Forestry
        55:627-630.

(125) LEMON, P. C.
1949   SUCCESSIONAL RESPONSES OF HERBS IN THE
        LONGLEAF-SLASH PINE FORESTS AFTER FIRE.
        Ecol 30:135-145.

(126) LEVITT, J.
1951.   FROST, DROUGHT AND HEAT RESISTANCE. Ann.
        Rev. Plant Physiol. 2:245-268.

(127) LINDENMUTH, A. W., JR., and BYRAM,
      GEORGE M.
1948.   HEADFIRES ARE COOLER NEAR THE GROUND
        THAN BACKFIRES. U. S. Forest Serv. Fire
        Control Notes 9(4): 8-9, illus.

(128) LITTLE, S.
1953.   PRESCRIBED BURNING AS A TOOL OF FOREST
        MANAGEMENT IN THE NORTHEASTERN STATES.
        Jour. Forestry 51:496-500.

(129) ———— ALLEN, J. P., and MOORE, E. B.
1948.   CONTROLLED BURNING AS A DUAL-PURPOSE
        TOOL OF FOREST MANAGEMENT IN NEW
        JERSEY'S PINE REGION. Jour. Forestry 46:
        810-819, illus.

(130) ———— and MOORE, E. B.
1949.   THE ECOLOGICAL ROLE OF PRESCRIBED BURNS
        IN THE PINE-OAK FORESTS OF SOUTHERN NEW
        JERSEY. Ecol. 30:223-233, illus.

(131) ———— and SOMES, H. A.
1956.   BUDS ENABLE PITCH AND SHORTLEAF PINES TO
        RECOVER FROM INJURY. U. S. Forest Serv.
        Northeast. Forest Expt. Sta. Sta. Paper 81,
        14 pp.

(132) ———— and SOMES, H. A.
1960.   SPROUTING OF LOBLOLLY PINE. Jour. Fo-
        restry 58:195-197, illus.

(133) LONGHURST, WILLIAM M.
1956.   STUMP SPROUTING OF OAKS IN RESPONSE TO
        SEASONAL CUTTING. Jour. Range Mangt.
        9:194-196.

(134) LORENZ, RALPH W.
1939.   HIGH TEMPERATURE TOLERANCE OF FOREST
        TREES. Univ. Minn. Agr. Expt. Sta. Tech.
        Bul. 141, 25 pp., illus.

(135) LORENZEN, C., JR.
1949.   THE THERMOCOUPLE IN AGRICULTURAL RE-
        SEARCH. Agr. Engin. 30:275-279, illus.

(136) LOTTI, THOMAS.
1956. ELIMINATING UNDERSTORY HARDWOODS WITH SUMMER PRESCRIBED FIRES IN COASTAL PLAIN LOBLOLLY PINE STANDS. Jour. Forestry 54:191-192, illus.

(137) ————
1960. THE USE OF FIRE IN THE MANAGEMENT OF COASTAL PLAIN LOBLOLLY PINE. Soc. Amer. Foresters Proc. 1959: 18-20, illus.

(138) LUTZ, H. J.
1956. ECOLOGICAL EFFECTS OF FOREST FIRES IN THE INTERIOR OF ALASKA. U. S. Dept. Agr. Tech. Bul. 1133, 121 pp., illus.

(139) ————
1960. FIRE AS AN ECOLOGICAL FACTOR IN THE BOREAL FOREST OF ALASKA. Jour. Forestry 58:454-460, illus.

(140) LUYET. B. J.
1932. VARIATION OF THE ELECTRICAL RESISTANCE OF PLANT TISSUES FOR ALTERNATING CURRENTS OF DIFFERENT FREQUENCIES DURING DEATH. Jour. Gen. Physiol. 15:283-287, illus.

(141) ———— and GEHENIO, P. M.
1936. ULTRAVIOLET ABSORPTION IN LIVING AND DEAD CELLS. Biodynamica 1(11):1-8, illus.

(142) ———— and GEHENIO, P. M.
1936. CELLULAR PIGMENTS VERSUS VITAL STAINS IN THE SPECTRAL ABSORPTION OF LIVING AND DEAD MATTER. Biodynamica 1(24):1-4, illus.

(143) LYNCH, D. W.
1959. EFFECTS OF A WILDFIRE ON MORTALITY AND GROWTH OF YOUNG PONDEROSA PINE TREES. U. S. Forest Serv. Intermountain Forest and Range Expt. Sta. Res. Note 66, 8 pp., illus.

(144) MacDOUGAL, D. T.
1922. HOW PLANTS ENDURE HEAT AND COLD. Gard. Mag. and Homebuilder 36:152-154, illus.

(145) MacKINNEY, A. L.
1934. SOME FACTORS AFFECTING THE BARK THICKNESS OF SECOND-GROWTH LONGLEAF PINE. Jour. Forestry 32:470-474.

(146) ————
1934. SOME EFFECTS OF THREE ANNUAL FIRES ON GROWTH OF LONGLEAF PINE. Jour. Forestry 32:879-881.

(147) MacLEAN, J. D.
1940. RELATION OF WOOD DENSITY TO RATE OF TEMPERATURE CHANGE IN WOOD IN DIFFERENT HEATING MEDIUMS. Amer. Wood Preservers' Assoc. Proc. 36:220-248, illus.

(148) McCLURE, T. T.
1960. CHLOROGENIC ACID ·ACCUMULATION AND WOUND HEALING IN SWEET POTATO ROOTS. Amer. Jour. Bot. 47:277-280.

(149)
1950.

(150)
1955.

(151)
1960.

(152)
1939.

(153)
1946.

(154)
1953.

(155)
1958.

(156)
1958.

(157)
1959.

(158)
1959.

(159)
1952.

(160)
1958.

(161)
1934.

(162)
1933.

(163) Nordin, V. J.
1958. basal fire scars and the occurrence of
       decay in lodgepole pine. Forestry Chron.
       34:257-265, illus.

(164) Oland, K.
1960. nitrogen feeding of apple trees by post-
       harvest urea sprays. Nature 185(4716)·
       857.

(165) Osterhout, W. J. V.
1922. injury, recovery and death in relation
       to conductivity and permeability 259
       pp., illus. Philadelphia.

(166) Parker, Johnson.
1953. some applications and limitations of
       tetrazolium chloride. Sci. 118:77-79,
       illus.

(167) ————
1955. effects of vital staining in Pinus pon-
       derosa. Plant Physiol. Suppl. 30:x (Abs.)

(168) ————
1956. drought resistance in woody plants.
       Bot. Rev. 22·241-289.

(169) Parmelee, George V., and Huebscher,
       Richard G.
1946. the shielding of thermocouples from
       the effects of radiation. Heating, Piping
       and Air Cond., Feb., 144-146, illus.

(170) Paulsell, Lee K.
1957. effects of burning on ozark hardwood
       timberlands. Mo. Agr. Expt Sta. Res.
       Bul. 640, 24 pp., illus.

(171) Petinov, N. S, and Molotkovsky, Y. G.
1957. protective reactions in heat-resistant
       plants induced by high temperatures.
       Fiziol. Rastenii (Transl.) 4930:221-228.

(172) Preston, J. F., and Phillips, F. J.
1911. seasonal variation in the food reserves
       of trees. Forestry Quart. 9:232-243.

(173) Quick, C. R.
1959. ceanothus seeds and seedlings on burns.
       Madrono 15:79-81.

(174) Quiggle, D., Tonberg, C. O., and Fenske,
       M. R.
1937. reliability of common types of thermo-
       couples. Ind. Engin. Chem. 29.827-830,
       illus.

(175) Reynolds, E. S.
1939. tree temperatures and thermostasy. Mo.
       Bot. Gard. Ann. 26:165-255, illus.

(176) Roberts, C. C., and Vogelsang, C. A.
1949. some basic concepts of thermoelectric
       pyrometry. Instrumentation 4(1):25-27,
       illus.

(177) Roberts, L. W.
1951. survey of factors responsible for re-
       duction of 2, 3, 5- triphenyltetrazolium
       chloride in plant meristems. Sci. 113:
       692-693.

(178) Roeser, J., Jr.
1932. transpiration capacity of coniferous
       seedlings and the problem of heat in-
       jury. Jour. Forestry 30:381-395, illus.

(179) St.George, R. A., and Beal, J. A.
1927. studies on the southern pine beetle.
       U S. Forest Serv. Appalachian Forest
       Expt Sta Prog. Rpt., 37 pp, illus. [Un-
       published.]

(180) Sampson, Arthur W.
1944. plant succession on burned chaparral
       lands in northern california. Calif. Agr.
       Expt. Sta. Bul. 685, 144 pp., illus

(181) Scott, V. H, and Burgy, R. H.
1956   effects of heat and brush burning on
       the physical properties of certain up-
       land soils that influence infiltration.
       Soil Sci. 82:63-70, illus.

(182) Shcherbakov, I. N.
1956. [use of a semi-conducting electric ther-
       mometer for temperature measure-
       ments in tree tissue.] (Russian.) Re-
       ferat. Zhur., Biol. 1956:71653. (Transl.)

(183) Shirley, H. C.
1936. lethal high temperatures for conifers,
       and the cooling effect of transpiration.
       Jour. Agr. Res. 53:239-258, illus.

(184) Siggers, P. V.
1934. observations on the influence of fire on
       the brown-spot needle blight of long-
       leaf pine seedlings. Jour. Forestry 32:
       556-562, illus.

(185) ————
1949. fire and the southern fusiform rust.
       Forest Farmer 8(5): 16, 21, illus.

(186) Soe, K.
1959. anatomical studies of bark regenera-
       tion following scoring. Jour. Arnold Ar-
       boretum 40:260-267, illus.

(187) Southern Forest Experiment Station.
1959. 1958 at the southern forest experiment
       station. U. S. Forest Serv. South. Forest
       Expt. Sta. 1958 Ann. Rpt., 72 pp., illus.

(188) ————
1960. 1959 at the southern forest experiment
       station. U. S. Forest Serv. South. Forest
       Expt. Sta. 1959 Ann. Rpt., 77 pp., illus.

(189) Spalt, Karl, and Reifsnyder, W. E.
1961. bark characteristics and fire resist-
       ance: a literature survey. U. S. Forest
       Serv. South. Forest Expt. Sta. Occas.
       Paper [In press.]

(190) Starker, T. J.
1934. fire resistance in the forest. Jour. Fo-
       restry 32:462-467.

(191) STICKEL, PAUL W.
1934. FOREST FIRE DAMAGE STUDIES IN THE NORTHEAST. *I.* BARK-BEETLES AND FIRE DAMAGED HARDWOODS. Jour. Forestry 32:701-703.

(192) ————
1935. FOREST FIRE DAMAGE STUDIES IN THE NORTHEAST. *II.* FIRST-YEAR MORTALITY IN BURNED-OVER OAK STANDS. Jour. Forestry 33: 595-598.

(193) ————
1940. THE BASAL-WOUNDING OF TREES BY FIRE—A PROGRESS REPORT. U. S. Forest Serv. Northeast. Forest Expt. Sta., 14 pp., illus.

(194) ————
1940. THE EFFECT OF BASAL-WOUNDING BY FIRE ON TREES IN THE NORTHEAST. U. S Forest Serv. Northeast. Forest Expt. Sta. Tech. Note 30, 2 pp.

(195) ————
1941. ON THE RELATION BETWEEN BARK CHARACTER AND RESISTANCE TO FIRE. U. S. Forest Serv. Northeast. Forest Expt. Sta. Tech. Note 39, 2 pp.

(196) STODDARD, H. L.
1936. RELATION OF BURNING TO TIMBER AND WILDLIFE. North Amer. Wildlife Conf. Proc. 1:399-403.

(197) STONE, E. L., JR.
1940. PROGRESS REPORT ON THE EFFECT OF FIRE ON THE RADIAL GROWTH OF LONGLEAF PINE. U. S. Forest Serv. South. Forest Expt. Sta., 26 pp., illus. [Unpublished.]

(198) ————
1944. EFFECT OF FIRE ON TAPER OF LONGLEAF PINE. Jour. Forestry 42:607.

(199) STOREY, T. G., and MERKEL, E. P.
1960. MORTALITY IN A LONGLEAF-SLASH PINE STAND FOLLOWING A WINTER WILDFIRE. Jour. Forestry 58:206-210, illus.

(200) TARRANT, ROBERT F.
1954. EFFECT OF SLASH BURNING ON SOIL pH. U.S. Forest Serv. Pacific Northwest Forest and Range Expt. Sta. Res. Note 102, 5 pp.

(201) ————
1956. CHANGES IN SOME PHYSICAL SOIL PROPERTIES AFTER A PRESCRIBED BURN IN YOUNG PONDEROSA PINE. Jour. Forestry 54:439-441, illus.

(202) TEESDALE, L. V.
1955. THERMAL INSULATION MADE OF WOOD-BASE MATERIALS. U. S. Forest Serv. Forest Prod. Lab. Rpt. 1740, 46 pp., illus. (Rev. 1958.)

(203) TERRY, R. A.
1951. HOW TO CONSERVE THERMOCOUPLE EXTENSION WIRE. Instrumentation 5(5):24, illus.

(204) THAMES, J. L.
1959 THE EFFECT OF SOME ENVIRONMENTAL FACTORS ON TRANSPIRATION OF LOBLOLLY PINE. U. S. Forest Serv. South. Forest Expt. Sta. Prog. Rpt.

(205) THIMANN, K. V., and KAUFMAN, DAVID.
1958. CYTOPLASMIC STREAMING IN THE CAMBIUM OF WHITE PINE. The Physiology of Forest Trees, pp. 479-492, illus. N. Y.

(206) TOOLE, E. RICHARD.
1959 DECAY AFTER FIRE INJURY TO SOUTHERN BOTTOM-LAND HARDWOODS. U. S. Dept. Agr. Tech. Bul. 1189, 25 pp., illus.

(207) ———— and McKNIGHT, J. S.
1956. FIRE EFFECTS IN SOUTHERN HARDWOODS. U S Forest Serv Fire Control Notes 17(3): 1-4, illus

(208) TWEEDDALE, J. E.
1945. THERMISTORS. Western Electric Oscillator 2:3-5, 34-37, illus.

(209) UGGLA, EVALD.
1957. [TEMPERATURES DURING CONTROLLED BURNING. THE EFFECT OF THE FIRE ON THE VEGETATION AND THE HUMUS COVER.] (Swedish.) Norrlands Skogsvardsfor. Tidskr. 1957 (4):443-500.

(210) ————
1958. ECOLOGICAL EFFECTS OF FIRE ON NORTH SWEDISH FORESTS. Almqvist and Wiksells, Upsalla, 18 pp.

(211) U. S. DEPT. COMMERCE.
1955. TEMPERATURE MEASUREMENTS—A LIST OF PUBLICATIONS. Natl. Bur. Standards Publ. LP 32.

(212) U. S. FOREST SERVICE.
1956. GLOSSARY OF TERMS USED IN FOREST FIRE CONTROL. U. S. Dept. Agr. Agr. Handb. 104, 24 pp.

(213) URSIC, S. J.
1961. LETHAL ROOT TEMPERATURE OF 1-0 LOBLOLLY PINE SEEDLINGS. U. S. Forest Serv. Tree Planters' Notes. (In press.)

(214) VEHRENCAMP, JOHN E.
1956. AN INVESTIGATION OF FIRE BEHAVIOUR IN A NATURAL ATMOSPHERIC ENVIRONMENT. Univ. Calif. Dept. Engin. Tech. Rpt. 1, 85 pp., illus.

(215) VERE, D. W.
1958. HEAT TRANSFER MEASUREMENT IN LIVING SKIN. Jour. Physiol. (London) 140:359-380, illus.

(216) VERRALL, ARTHUR F.
1936. THE DISSEMINATION OF *Septoria acicola* AND THE EFFECT OF GRASS FIRES ON IT IN PINE NEEDLES. Phytopath. 26: 1021-1024.

(217) VERRALL. ARTHUR F.
1938. THE PROBABLE MECHANISM OF THE PROTEC-
TIVE ACTION OF RESIN IN FIRE WOUNDS ON
RED PINE. Jour. Forestry 36:1231-1233,
illus.

(218) VLAMIS, J , BISWELL, H. H., and SCHULTZ,
A. M.
1955 EFFECTS OF PRESCRIBED BURNING ON SOIL
FERTILITY IN SECOND GROWTH PONDEROSA
PINE. Jour. Forestry 53:905-909, illus.

(219) VOGELSANG, C A , and SINE, J. D
1953. PYROMETRIC MIDGETS. Instrumentation
6(4):33-36, illus.

(220) WAGENER, WILLIS W.
1955. PRELIMINARY GUIDELINES FOR ESTIMATING
THE SURVIVAL OF FIRE-DAMAGED TREES.
U. S. Forest Serv. Calif. Forest and Range
Expt. Sta. Forest Res. Note 98, 9 pp.

(221) WAHLENBERG, W. G
1935. EFFECT OF FIRE AND GRAZING ON SOIL PROP-
ERTIES AND THE NATURAL REPRODUCTION OF
LONGLEAF PINE. Jour. Forestry 33:331-337.

(222) ————
1946. LONGLEAF PINE. 429 pp., illus. Wash., D. C.

(223) ———— GREENE, S. W., and REED, H. R.
1939. EFFECTS OF FIRE AND CATTLE GRAZING ON
LONGLEAF PINE LANDS AS STUDIED AT MC-
NEILL, MISSISSIPPI. U. S. Dept. Agr. Tech.
Bul. 683, 52 pp., illus.

(224) WAKELEY, P. C.
1954. PLANTING THE SOUTHERN PINES. U. S. Forest
Serv. Agr. Monog. 18, 233 pp., illus.

(225) ———— and MUNTZ, H. H.
1947. EFFECT OF PRESCRIBED BURNING ON HEIGHT
GROWTH OF LONGLEAF PINE. Jour. Forestry
45:503-508, illus.

(226) WALKER, N. A.
1958. ION PERMEABILITY OF THE PLASMALEMMA
OF THE PLANT CELL. Nature 181(4618):
1288-1289.

(227) WAREING, P. F.
1958. THE PHYSIOLOGY OF CAMBIAL ACTIVITY.
Inst. Wood Sci. Jour. 1:34-42.

(228) WATSON, A. N.
1933. PRELIMINARY STUDY ON THE RELATION BE-
TWEEN THERMAL EMISSIVITY AND PLANT
TEMPERATURES. Ohio Jour. Sci. 33:435-
450.

(229) ————
1934. FURTHER STUDIES ON THE RELATION BETWEEN
THERMAL EMISSIVITY AND PLANT TEMPERA-
TURES. Amer. Jour. Bot. 21:605-609.

(230) WEAVER, HAROLD.
1943. FIRE AS AN ECOLOGICAL AND SILVICULTURAL
FACTOR IN THE PONDEROSA PINE REGION OF
THE PACIFIC SLOPE. Jour. Forestry 41:7-15,
illus.

(231) ————
1947. FIRE—NATURE'S THINNING AGENT IN PONDER-
OSA PINE STANDS. Jour. Forestry 45:437-
444, illus.

(232) ————
1955. FIRE AS AN ENEMY, FRIEND, AND TOOL IN
FOREST MANAGEMENT. Jour. Forestry 53:
499-504, illus.

(233) ————
1957. EFFECTS OF PRESCRIBED BURNING IN SECOND
GROWTH PONDEROSA PINE. Jour. Forestry
55:823-826, illus.

(234) ————
1959. ECOLOGICAL CHANGES IN THE PONDEROSA
PINE FORESTS OF THE WARM SPRINGS INDIAN
RESERVATION IN OREGON. Jour. Forestry
57:15-20, illus.

(235) WEDDELL, D. J., and WARE, L. M.
1936. THE EFFECT OF FIRES OF DIFFERENT FRE-
QUENCIES ON THE SURVIVAL OF DIFFERENT
SPECIES OF PINE. Ala. Agr. Expt. Sta. 47th.
Ann Rpt., pp 28-29

(236) WHITAKER, D. M.
1929. CONSTRUCTION OF MICRO-THERMOCOUPLES.
Sci. 70:263-266, illus.

(237) WOODS, FRANK W.
1955. CONTROL OF WOODY WEEDS, SOME PHYSI-
OLOGICAL ASPECTS. U. S. Forest Serv.
South. Forest Expt. Sta. Occas. Paper 143,
50 pp.

(238) ————HARRIS, H. C., and CALDWELL, R. E.
1959. MONTHLY VARIATIONS OF CARBOHYDRATES
AND NITROGEN IN ROOTS OF SANDHILL OAKS
AND WIREGRASS. Ecol. 40:292-295, illus.

(239) WRIGHT, ERNEST, and TARRANT, ROBERT F.
1957. MICROBIOLOGICAL SOIL PROPERTIES AFTER
LOGGING AND SLASH BURNING. U. S. Forest
Serv. Pacific Northwest Forest and Range
Expt. Sta. Res. Note 57, 5 pp.

(240) ———— and TARRANT, ROBERT F.
1958. OCCURRENCE OF MYCORRHIZAE AFTER LOG-
GING AND SLASH BURNING IN THE DOUGLAS-
FIR FOREST TYPE. U. S. Forest Serv. Pa-
cific Northwest Forest and Range Expt.
Sta. Res. Note 160, 7 pp., illus.

(241) ZDRAJKOVSKIJ, D. I.
1958. [DETERMINATION OF THE RESISTANCE OF
PINE IN FOCI OF *Fomes annosus* INFECTION.]
(In Russian.) Lesn. Hoz. 11(12):40-42.
Forestry Abs. 21(2):1912. 1960.

MEASURING

BRANCH CHARACTERS

of

LONGLEAF PINES

E. B. Snyder

SOUTHERN FOREST EXPERIMENT STATION
PHILIP A. BRIEGLEB, DIRECTOR
Forest Service, U. S. Department of Agriculture

The aim of the investigation reported here was to develop methods of obtaining quantitative values of branch sizes and angles for scoring plus-tree selections and inheritance studies. Measurements were made of all mature branches on 48 widely spaced longleaf pines in southern Mississippi, at the Southern Institute of Forest Genetics. The relations of branch diameter and angle effects to knot size, and of branch angle to natural pruning, were also examined.

LITERATURE

Most investigators have used a specific sampling point in the crown for branch measurement. For example, Eklund and Huss (1946) chose the largest branch nearest the point one-fourth of the way up the crown. Squillace and Bingham (1954) used average results from the ninth, tenth, and eleventh whorls from the top, corresponding to the ninth, tenth, and eleventh years of most recent growth. Many workers, including Toda (1958), Veen (1953), Miegroet (1956), and Squillace and Bingham (1954), have expressed branch diameter relative to bole diameter. Miegroet used a function of the square of the diameter of the branch and divided this by the stem diameter at mid-height. Some of these methods have been adapted in this study; others are inapplicable because of the irregular growth habit of southern pines.

METHODS

The 48 trees are in a square-mile area on the Harrison Experimental Forest. They are widely spaced, have from 16 to 29 rings at breast height, and range from 8.5 to 13.0 inches in d.b.h.

The uppermost measurement was at the fourth whorl from the top of the tree. This was the first mature whorl, i.e., where limbs branched, and corresponded to a safe climbing height. The following measurements were recorded on it and lower branches: bole diameter just above each whorl, to 0.1 inch; mean branch diameter 3 inches from the bole, to 0.1 inch; mean angle of attachment from the vertical (Busgen and Munch, 1929), to the nearest 5°; the average crown radius at the whorl, to the nearest 6 inches; and the distance from the whorl immediately above, to 1.0 inch. Branches less than 1 inch in diameter, old dead branches, and single-branched whorls were not included. Other measurements were total tree height, d.b.h., specific gravity, age, height to the living crown, and radius to 1.0 foot as sighted from the ground and derived by averaging the distances of the outer edge of crown from the trunk in the four cardinal directions. Three branches on each of 20 trees were cut as near vertical and as close to the bole as possible. Their cross-sectional outlines were measured to 0.01 square inch with a dot grid.

DETERMINING THE PLACE TO SAMPLE

Branch Sizes and Angles

Before a particular place in a tree can be specified as the sampling zone, tree architecture must be examined. An initial step was to express mean limb diameter as a ratio of stem diameter at each whorl. Data for five trees selected at random are in table 1. For the 48 trees the following zones were distinguished:

Zone 1.—Mean branch diameters for the top whorl measured were 65 percent of the stem diameters. Here branches are competing with the leader and some are almost as large as the leader. Stem diameters increased below each whorl in a stepwise pattern. The average branch angle was 55°. Typically, the relative size of the branches decreased rapidly and progressively for 5 to 10 whorls below.

Zone 2.—Still farther down, the ratio and the angles became more constant; branch dia-

1

SUMMARY

To find an appropriate place to sample branch diameters, lengths, and angles for genetic purposes, all the mature branches on 48 wide-spaced longleaf pines, varying from 8.5 to 13.0 inches in d.b.h., were measured.

Three types of branch growth were noted. At the top, branches are almost as thick as the leader and competing with it; their attachment angles are acute. Next comes a series of 2 to 7 whorls where there is an equilibrium in growth among the branches and between them and the main stem. Branches tend to thicken progressively toward the ground but in proportion to the thickening of the main stem; angles are less sharp. This zone of growth equilibrium is an appropriate place to sample for branch characters. Below it is a senescence zone where branches are smaller and are not growing in proportion to the main stem; here branch angles approach 90°.

On-the-ground readings for crown radius compared favorably to those taken in the tree. It is suggested that on-the-ground data be used but that the radii be transformed to branch lengths by multiplying them by the cosecant of the average branch angle. The effect of the sine of the angle on height to first live branch was not demonstrated even though regression adjustments were made for height, age, d.b.h., competition, specific gravity, branch diameter, and branch length. Observed values for knot size measured from 60 severed branches were, for a constant branch size, proportional to the cosecants of the angles.

LITERATURE CITED

BUSGEN, M., and MUNCH, E.
　1929. THE STRUCTURE AND LIFE OF FOREST TREES. 436 pp. London.

EKLUND, B., and HUSS, E.
　1946. [INVESTIGATIONS OF OLD FOREST CULTIVATIONS IN NORTHERN SWEDEN]. Statens SkogsforsknInst. [Sweden], Meddel. 35-(6):1-104.

GROSENBAUGH, L. R.
　1958. THE ELUSIVE FORMULA OF BEST FIT: A COMPREHENSIVE NEW MACHINE PROGRAM. U. S. Forest Serv. South. Forest Expt. Sta. Occas. Paper 158, 9 pp.

MIEGROET, M. VAN.
　1958. DIE BESTIMMUNG DER AESTIGKEIT IN DICKUNGEN. [EVALUATION OF BRANCHINESS IN THICKET-STAGE STANDS]. Twelfth Cong. Int. Union Forest Res. Organ. Papers 2(23): 56-62.

MILLER, V. J.
　1959. CROTCH INFLUENCE ON STRENGTH AND BREAKING POINT OF APPLE TREE BRANCHES. Amer. Soc. Hort. Sci. Proc. 73: 27-32.

SQUILLACE, A. E., and BINGHAM, R. T.
　1954. BREEDING FOR IMPROVED GROWTH RATE AND TIMBER QUALITY IN WESTERN WHITE PINE. Jour. Forestry 52: 656-665.

TODA, R.
　1958. VARIATION AND HERITABILITY OF SOME QUANTITATIVE CHARACTERS IN *Cryptomeria*. Silvae Genetica 7: 87-93.

VEEN, B.
　1954. REPORT ON THE TEST AREAS OF THE INTERNATIONAL PROVENANCE TESTS WITH LARCH, PINE AND SPRUCE OF 1938-39 AND 1944-45, AND SUGGESTIONS FOR FUTURE TREATMENT AND ASSESSMENTS. Eleventh Cong. Int. Forest Res. Organ. 1953: 536-551.

4

Also encouraging is the fact that this equilibrium-zone method appeared reasonable when tried on a few larger trees in another stand. It approximates a method subsequently used by J. Barber (personal communication) for a slash pine plantation wherein sampled whorls were in the zone beginning at a point 65 percent of total height and ending at 85 percent of total height.

Crown Radius

Measuring crown radius with a pole extended horizontally in a tree proved tedious, but the mean aerial radius of the whorl with the longest branches corresponded reasonably well with the radius as measured by sighting from the ground. For the 48 trees the mean aerial radius was 9.7 feet; the mean ground radius was 9.9 feet. The ground measurements underestimated the aerial ones 14 times, overestimated them 19 times, and were the same 15 times.

Crown radius is of no great importance *per se;* a crown can be narrow either because the branches are short or their angles are small. As photosynthetic efficiency is more closely related to branch length than to crown radius, the radius should be converted by the formula:

Branch length = crown radius x cosecant angle

BRANCH SIZE AND ANGLE EFFECTS

Deviations from a 90° attachment will produce elliptical scars whose areas are functions of the cosecant angle. Table 2 shows theoretical knot-size values for various angles. To obtain experimental indications, the regression adjustments of branch diameter on knot size were first made. The basic formula calculated was: $y = -0.865 + 0.971x$, where y is the area of the knot and x is the square of the branch diameter, both in square inches. Knot sizes, calculated on the basis of mean branch diameter, follow theoretical values satisfactorily (table 2). Observed values also appear in figure 1.

Branch angles are supposed to influence natural pruning: the more horizontal the branch, the more leverage its own weight adds toward breaking it. This natural pruning force is a function of the sine of the attachment angle, theoretical values of which are shown in table 2. The data failed to demonstrate this relation, but the mathematical procedure may be of interest. It consisted of finding how much

Table 2. *Relations between branch angles, knot size, and natural pruning force*

| Branch angle | Relative knot size | | Relative natural pruning force— theoretical |
	Theoretical	Actual	
	Cosecant x 100	*Percent*	*Sine x 100*
90	100	. . .	100
85	100	. . .	100
80	102	. . .	98
75	104	105	97
70	106	106	94
65	110	. . .	91
60	115	109	87
55	122	108	82
50	130	112	77
45	141	130	71
40	156	140	64

of the variation in height to first live limb could be explained by possible factors. With the 704 Regression Program (Grosenbaugh, 1958), an index of determination (R^2) of 0.58 was obtained from the combination of age, height, d.b.h., an arbitrary index of tree competition, specific gravity, branch diameter, branch length, and branch angle. The most important factors were d.b.h., tree height, age, and competition, which together resulted in an R^2 = 0.49. The difference between 0.49 and 0.58 was divided among the small effects of the other factors, including sine angle. Further studies should be made to refine measurements, to consider other variables including the cube of the branch diameter (Miller, 1959), and to expand the range and amount of material.

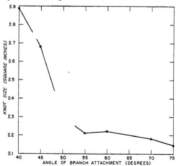

Figure 1. *Observed mean knot sizes (adjusted to the mean branch diameter) for 60 branches with various angles of attachment.*

3

meter stabilized to average 30 percent that of the bole, and angles were about 68°. This zone of stabilization included 2 to 7 whorls, depending on the tree. Limbs continued to thicken but in proportion to the thickening of the main stem. Competition apparently causes an equilibrium in growth among the branches and between them and the main stem.

Some objective way of locating this appropriate sampling zone was sought, but specifying a certain bole diameter or distance from top of tree failed to demark it. Fortunately, the zone can be recognized satisfactorily by eye. It starts at the whorl having branches of the greatest diameter and extends upward to include the first whorl from the top in which bole diameter does not change perceptibly from above the whorl to below the whorl. Four consecutive whorls in the equilibrium zone and including the whorl having the largest branches

are suggested as a sample. If the zone contains fewer than four whorls, a lesser number should be used in preference to taking readings in another zone. The mean branch-to-stem ratio and the mean branch angle of these four whorls are the values to be compared to those from other trees in genetic studies.

Zone 3.—Below the largest branches of the tree, which in this group occurred one-fourth to one-third of the way up the crown, is the zone of branch senescence. Branches become smaller while the trunk becomes larger. They are doomed to die as the tree ages. The average angle of the lowest limb was 81° and in several trees the branch-to-stem ratio attained a value of 15 percent.

The means from readings within the equilibrium zone (Zone 2) reveal a frequency distribution adequate for genetic selection:

Ratio (percent)	25	26	27	28	29	30	31	32	33	35	36	37	38	39
Trees (number)	2	3	5	5	3	4	4	9	4	3	1	1	3	1

Angle (degrees)	56	57	59	62	63	64	65	66	67	68	69	70	71	74	76	78	79	81
Trees (number)	1	1	2	4	2	1	7	3	2	4	3	7	2	3	1	2	2	1

Table 1. *Branch-to-stem diameter ratios and branch angles for 5 trees chosen at random from the 48 sampled. Lines bound zones of equilibrium*

Whorl number	Tree 1		Tree 2		Tree 3		Tree 4		Tree 5	
	Ratio	Angle	Ratio	Angle	Ratio	Angle	Ratio	Angle	Ratio	Angle
	Percent	Degrees	Percent	Degrees	Percent	Degrees	Percent	Degrees	Percent	Degrees
1	75	50	55	70	89	50	69	60	50	55
2	54	60	50	70	53	60	67	55	52	50
3	48	65	53	70	47	60	68	60	47	55
4	37	70	39	70	46	60	56	60	41	60
5	38	60	46	70	36	60	44	55	35	65
6	33	65	26	80	28	65	52	55	30	70
7	34	70	40	75	29	70	46	55	27	70
8	30	75	21	90	25	65	41	80	22	70
9	33	70	30	75	19	90	33	60	21	75
10	21	80	27	75	17	90	36	60	22	70
11	21	90	25	80	16	90	27	70	21	80
12	19	90	25	75			32	60		
13	16	90	22	80			24	60		
14	15	90	25	80			26	65		
15	16	90					18	70		
16							25	65		
17							20	75		
18							22	75		
Means from zone of equilibrium	32	70	27	76	30	65	32	62	31	68

2

MULATING WOODLAND MANAGEMENT
IN NORTH MISSISSIPPI:
AN APPRAISAL

Alfred Pleasonton & Sam Guttenberg

Acknowledgement

The Yazoo-Little Tallahatchie Flood Prevention Project of the Southern Region, U. S. Forest Service, cooperated in planning and carrying out this study, and four members of the Project staff made all the interviews. They were Don L. Gerred, George J. Parish, Jr., Stanley D. Pulliam, and Edmond I. Swenson.

The U. S. Soil Conservation Service participated in the planning and furnished information from its records.

The eroded Yazoo-Little Tallahatchie watershed of Mississippi is the setting for the largest land rehabilitation project in the Nation. Appraisal of the results so far shows that the program has had considerable success in encouraging landowners to improve their woodlands. Owners with above-average assets responded best, but low-income owners also participated substantially.

Major reasons for this achievement are:

- *All public agricultural agencies are co-operating.*
- *Land-use improvements are carefully planned to the owner's needs and the capabilities of his soils.*
- *Public cost-sharing programs are available, and landowners are encouraged to use them.*
- *Trained men from the cooperating agencies visit owners to provide technical advice.*

The same approach seems applicable to other problem areas.

Figure 1.—*Yazoo-Little Tallahatchie Project area.*

How to improve management of small woodlands is a question often studied but seldom resolved. One effective system of dealing with this ageless problem is being used in the Yazoo-Little Talla-hatchie watershed of Mississippi (fig. 1). A principle of the solution is close cooperation among State and Federal agencies and local civic groups interested in land use—a pooling of resources to bring about improved landowner attitudes and resource management in community after community.

This report is based on a 1960 study of a sample of the area's landowners. Participants and non-participants in the Yazoo-Little Tallahatchie (Y-LT) Flood Prevention Project were interviewed to obtain information for assessing the current system of promoting land-use adjustments, and to indicate its applicability in other areas. Though the Project deals with all forms of land use, the woodland aspects are stressed in this analysis.

THE Y-LT PROGRAM

The project was jointly undertaken in 1946 by the U. S. Forest Service and Soil Conservation Service, with local leadership from the Soil Conservation District commissioners. The four major objectives were: (1) reduction of flood water and sedimentation damage, (2) proper land use, (3) channel stabilization, and (4) improvement of the local economy. The Project, whose area of responsibility comprises 4.2 million acres of undulating and hilly land in 19 counties of north Mississippi, is the largest individual land and water management program in the Nation.

Over many decades, exploitive agriculture on highly erosive soils has made the region a depressed rural area. Forest resources suffered too. Timber stands average one thousand board feet per acre, of which 70 percent is hardwood—farm woodlands are even more depleted. The hardwoods are predominantly small, defective trees of low value. Current growth is barely one-fifth of the soil's potential.

As opportunities diminished, farm families moved out. Since 1940 the total population has dropped 20 percent, to 356,000, and the number of farms fell from 76,000 to 36,000, while average farm acreage rose from 70 to 135. While emigration has reduced population pressure on the land, the region is still characterized by low per-capita income (about $600) and fragmented holdings. The effects of severe soil erosion are widely evident.

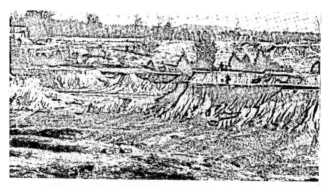

Figure 2.—*Restoring land like this is the mission of the Yazoo-Little Talla-hatchie Project.*

To make effective use of pooled agency resources, the Y-LT Project area was divided into 54 subwatersheds. The agencies, in consultation with the Soil Conservation District (SCD) commission-ers, decide which subwatersheds are to be activated each year. Land-owners in the activated watersheds are then urged to cooperate with the local SCD. Each landowner is assisted by a Soil Conservation Service technician in preparing a farm conservation plan outlining desirable land-use adjustments. The technician also explains the various assistance programs and encourages the owner to use them.

Land-use adjustment based on soil capabilities is the central theme of the Project. In the plan, cultivated crops are usually restricted to fertile bottom lands, terraces, and wide, level ridge tops. Recommended treatments are intended to reduce runoff, ero-sion, and sedimentation, and to increase productivity. Equal empha-sis is given treatment of crop, pasture, and forest land.

Planting pines on eroded and abandoned hillside cropland, and converting upper slopes and ridge tops from low-grade hardwood to pine, together with some interplanting, are needed on nearly one million acres. Erosion from a very few properties will provide the material for downstream siltation and thereby nullify costly soil stabilization measures. For this reason success requires that virtually all owners in a subwatershed be persuaded to cooperate. To protect the public's investments in water control structures and soil stabiliza-tion practices, the agencies have found it beneficial to offset the costs of land-use adjustments, particularly for owners of limited means.

Figure 3.—*Sterile sand and silt from the gully . . . .*

have buried the fertile soil of this bottom-land field.

Two types of financial assistance are available, the choice depending upon severity of erosion.

1. *Land is designated as a "critical area" if the soil is exposed, the slope is over 8 percent, active erosion is present, and downstream damage is occurring. When the owner signs a farm plan that includes a critical area, the entire cost of stabilizing the eroded area is paid from Federal funds. Stabilization is usually accomplished by plugging the gully and planting pines.*

2. *Upper slopes and ridges occupied by virtually worthless hardwoods are a source of severe sheet erosion. Where planting will aid in flood prevention, the land qualifies for free planting stock. The cost of deadening hardwoods and planting can be shared by the owner and the Agricultural Conservation Program (ACP). Though owners are encouraged to plant, they typically hire contractors whose crews will plant pine and deaden hardwood for a standard fee, of which about two-thirds is paid by the ACP and one-third by the landowner.*

Some idea of the effectiveness of the Y-LT Program is provided by table 1. The data are from 6,134 participants. In the aggregate, these holdings amount to 1.3 million acres—one-third of the Project region. The tabulation is not a complete statement of accomplishments, for on another 2,000 properties not owned by individuals—estates, partnerships, and corporations—a substantial acreage of woodlands has been planted or improved.

Table 1.—*Forest practices of 6,134 landowners participating in the Y-LT Project*

Owner's annual income (dollars)	Proportion of owners	Tract size	Wood-lands fenced	Cull timber removed	Trees planted
	Percent	– – – – Average acreage – – – –			
Less than 1,500	17	113	7	2	20
1,500 — 2,999	23	136	8	4	19
3,000 — 4,499	29	185	12	7	25
4,500 +	31	364	24	22	57

In general, owners with greatest assets and income have been the most likely to invest in timber growing. Business and professional owners responded best to the Project. Forest investment also varied with owners' age, sex, race, and residence, but the differences were fundamentally related to level of assets.

Administrative costs for influencing landowners in the 2 lowest income strata have been high, yet the Project has succeeded in getting these people to plant an average of 20 acres apiece to pine.

STUDY METHOD

Cluster sampling was used to obtain a representative cross section of owners in the various Y-LT subwatersheds. Odd-numbered sections were randomly drawn within townships randomly picked from detailed maps. The odd section plus the following even one constituted the cluster. Clusters lying wholly or partially outside the Y-LT were rejected, as were those falling entirely on public lands, industrial forest holdings, and towns. Tracts of less than 10 acres were omitted, the purpose being to exclude most of the properties held for residence or commercial purposes.

The sample consisted of 308 owners having more than half their acreage inside the 2-section clusters. Data were obtained by personal interview (for the questionnaire, see page 17). Homogeneity of the responses, question by question, was evaluated by Chi-square tests. Among the attributes tested were income group, type of farm, residence, race, and ownership motivation. Differences in such variables as acreage and age were tested by analysis of variance.

ASSETS FACILITATE LAND-USE IMPROVEMENT

Participation in the ACP, tree planting, intention to plant, and cull timber removal were the chief indicators that owners were interested in improving land use.

Participation was greatest among landowners in the highest income group. This group also had the largest average holdings and the greatest proportion of individuals with investments in assets other than land and improvements (table 2). The overriding effects of income are further indicated by the fact that, of the 6,134 owners reached by the Project so far, 31 percent earned more than $4,500 annually. In the general population, 23 percent of the owners are in this income category. These findings as to assets conform with those of other studies (1, 4, 5).[1]

That 42 percent of the owners receive less than $1,500 annually underscores the prevalence of low-income families in the region.

---

[1] Numbers in italics refer to Literature Cited, page 16.

Though the point was beyond the scope of the study, it seems reasonable to assume that the sizable response from low-income owners was related to the availability of public programs that pay almost all of the costs of land rehabilitation on critical areas.

Table 2.—*Owners' assets and participation in the Y-LT program*

Owner's annual income (dollars)	Proportion of owners [1]	Tract size	Proportion of owners with investments	Program participators
	Percent	*Acres*	*Percent*	*Percent*
Less than 1,500	42	122	16	50
1,500 — 2,999	23	217	40	57
3,000 — 4,499	12	273	49	54
4,500 +	23	805	89	78

[1] Information from 308 respondents representing 18,500 owners.

The owners with less than $1,500 of annual income were older and included a higher percentage of women than did any other income class. Negroes comprised 16 percent of the sample. Virtually all of them earned less than $3,000 annually and more than three-fourths were in the lowest income group.

Of the 261 farmers interviewed, 102 had invested capital in assets other than land and improvements. Among the investing farmers, 28 percent had also put at least $5,000 into their farms over the last three years. Among non-investing farmers, 9 percent had put this amount into their farms during the same period. As will be seen, improving the farm does not necessarily lead to improved woodlands.

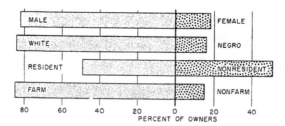

Figure 4.—*Owner characteristics.*

SCD PLANS HELP PROGRAM

Of the sampled owners, 156 had cooperated with their Soil Conservation Districts in drawing up plans for their tracts. Participation did not vary with income class, but degree of application did. Owners in the watersheds that had been activated earliest had the greatest proportion of plans and also the best record of having put plans into action: an indication of the benefits of sustained effort.

The proportion of owners who had adopted one or more parts of their SCD plans averaged 87 percent. Planting pine was the favored practice. Nearly 90 percent of the nonfarmers had planted trees, and even among the farmers, tree planting was as popular as all other practices combined.

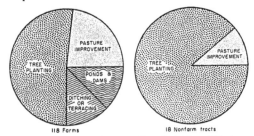

118 Farms   18 Nonfarm tracts

Figure 5.—*Distribution of primary practices adopted from SCD plans.*

Thirteen percent of the owners had not used their plans. Some cited financial reasons for not having done so, but most were indifferent.

Owners of more than two-thirds of the planned tracts had received ACP payments for forestry or agricultural practices. Payments for forest improvements had been made to 76 owners. Nearly half the owners in the top income group had received forestry payments, as contrasted to one-seventh of those in the lowest group. More low-income owners would probably have participated if they could have paid their share of the costs in labor.

Owners of 100 tracts received payments for practices other than forestry; of these, about two-thirds were for pasture improvement. Dairy farmers, nonfarmers, and cattlemen, in that order, were the chief pasture improvers.

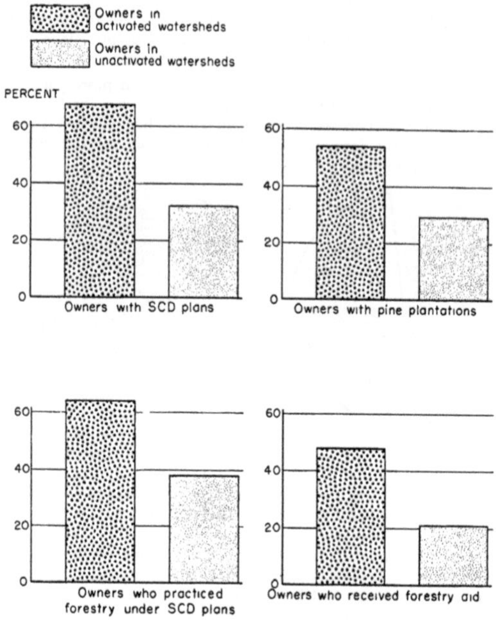

Figure 6.—*Program effects.*

FACTORS AFFECTING IMPROVEMENT OF WOODLANDS

The forestry portion of the program is affected by how e owner views his woodlands and by his intentions and expectati regarding their future. In justifying forest investments, the likelih of long-term ownership is especially beneficial.

Owners' Outlook and Tenure Problems

Most owners considered their tracts a place to live, and virtually all of them planned to retain their holdings for at least the next ten years. Half of those who planned to keep their tracts dwelt on them. Investment was the other principal reason stressed for holding land; it was given as the primary motive by 31 percent of the nonfarmers and 5 percent of the farmers.

The seemingly stable tenure implied by the responses is dubious in view of the well-developed trend toward fewer and larger farms. About 3 out of 10 tracts changed hands within the last 10 years. Further changes are foreshadowed by the general age of the owners—about half are in their 60's or above. Frequent land trading, combined with the generally modest circumstances of an elderly population, poses two problems for the Y-LT

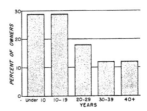

Figure 7.—*Duration of tenure: land trading is common.*

program. The first is how to create interest in land-use adjustments and the second is how to retain beneficial changes when tracts change hands. These problems are of immediate concern because, in the long run, aggregation of presently fragmented land holdings should contribute towards improved use.

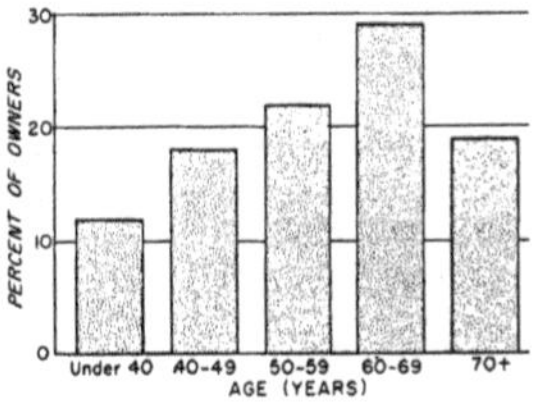

Figure 8.—*Seven out of ten owners are above 50 years of age.*

Farm Characteristics Significant

Cotton was the main cash crop for more than half the owners. Operators of the 167 cotton farms were predominantly poor, whether they were owners or, more typically, tenants. Their holdings have largely been producing at the subsistence level. Though every second owner had an SCD plan, the combination of tenancy and poverty made forest investments difficult for them.

At the other extreme were the cattle and dairy farmers, typically in the highest income group. About 38 percent of these progressive farmers had SCD plans, and a substantial portion of the rest had made plans of their own.

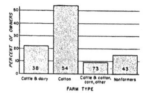

Figure 9.—*Most owners are cotton farmers. Numbers on bars indicate percentage of tracts with SCD plans.*

Virtually all the dairymen owned and operated their farms, and 83 percent of them lived on their tracts. Many of these enterprises are being expanded and require considerable additional capital. Land unsuited for pasture and requiring cash outlays to be productive of timber will have to take second priority for funds. Where total acreage is less than 200, demand for improved pasture will probably reduce forest acreage. From the Project standpoint, the problem is how to encourage landowners to maintain the sod during droughts.

Nonfarm woodlands averaged about 100 acres, twice that of all tracts. The owners' eagerness to receive ACP payments both for forest and pasture improvements and their active demand for other tree-planting assistance made them good Project cooperators. Though they have fewer plans than the farmers, they have generally adopted forestry recommendations more completely.

Owners of the cattle-and-cotton, corn, and miscellaneous farm types were uniformly high participators in SCD planning. Having moderate capital to work with, they were commonly eager for assistance in planning and making land-use adjustments.

Owners' Planting Intentions

Forty-three percent of the owners sampled expected to plant pines. Those already having plantations were twice as likely to plant as those with none. Visits from representatives of the forestry agencies also doubled the inclination to plant—the personal contact is a stimulus.

Figure 10.—*Owners of upland scrub hardwoods think they have timber. But trees like these produce no income and control erosion less well than a good stand of pine.*

The respondents' chief reason for not desiring to plant trees was lack of suitable land. This was the opinion of 109 owners or 62 percent of the non-planters. Most of the others objected because of their advanced age, concepts of costs, lack of information, and the feeling that land in trees was unproductive. The amount of planting would increase if the opportunities for stand conversion were understood by the owners, including the cattle and dairy farmers who will convert some of their woodland to pasture.

Owners' Forestry Experience Limited

Not only did a high proportion of the owners in the highest income group receive forestry assistance, but they were active in requesting it from the various agencies. Among low-income owners, the agencies often found it necessary to stimulate a demand for tree planting.

As table 3 shows, two-thirds of the owners had not yet had technical forestry assistance; most of these were in subwatersheds awaiting activation. Regardless of tract location, cotton, cattle, and dairy farmers were the least common users of forestry assistance. In contrast, almost half the owners of nonfarm tracts had been helped.

Table 3.—*Owners' sources of technical forestry assistance*

Source	Proportion of owners
	Percent
Forest Service only	23
SCS only	3
Forest Service and SCS	6
Other	3
None	65
Total	100

As program emphasis is on planting and cull timber removal, it is not surprising to find that technical assistance was not widely used by owners in marketing their timber. About half had sold timber. Four percent of the sellers had had their stumpage marked by a forester, almost a third had sold to a minimum diameter limit, and almost two-thirds had sold all their merchantable timber "by the boundary."

Only 7 percent of the owners had sold cut products. Great as is the need for marketing assistance today, it will become more acute as the supply of merchantable timber increases. On the erosive soils of this region, special timber marking and harvesting practices will likely be needed to protect the watershed.

What Landowners Wanted From Public Agencies

At the close of the interview, the owners were asked to suggest what the SCS or Forest Service could do for them. Two out of every three expressed an interest in receiving particular kinds of assistance from the public agencies. Within the broad groupings of farm versus nonfarm owners the responses were consistent. Proportionately the nonfarmers were twice as interested in forestry help as the farmers. Owners retaining their land for investment wanted help with agricultural and forestry practices. The sentimental, who wished to retain the old "homeplace," were primarily interested in advice rather than action. An encouraging third of all owners were ready to accept forest management. Even with allowance for the imprecision of questionnaire surveys, it seems likely that many owners are ready to cooperate in the Project if properly approached.

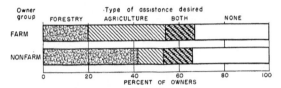

Figure 11.—*Kind of help the owners wanted.*

CONCLUSIONS

The Y-LT program has made considerable progress in encouraging land-use improvements. This study indicates some possibilities for further strengthening the program. In view of its success in a very difficult area, the same general approach seems suitable for other regions.

Strengthening the Y-LT Approach

Additional effort to visit landowners would be worth while. Reactions of the people interviewed disclosed that many owners must be visited and revisited before they will make land-use adjustments. The initial visit is often crucial. Currently it is made by a farm planner, but a specialist in the owner's main crop might have the advantage in gaining confidence. Once interest is created, other workers should follow up promptly.

ACP payments would be more readily taken by the prevalent low-income owners if they could pay their share of the cost in labor. Outlays for forest improvements are beyond the resources of many owners. Project workers could probably arrange for contractors of tree planting and cull-timber removal to offer landowners sufficient employment to meet their ACP requirements.

Special efforts are needed to encourage cooperation from the

Figure 12.—*Visits stimulate landowners who cannot be motivated by radio, television, brochures, or demonstrations.*

high proportion of aged landowners. It seems possible to convince these owners that estate values can be markedly increased at little cost to them. Long-term management plans acceptable to both owner and heir might also be developed.

Budget analyses of individual operating units could improve upon traditional SCD planning by showing the costs and returns associated with various shifts in resources. Such budgets might be an additional stimulus to improve soil management and thereby income.

Implications for Programs in Other Areas

A landholder's level of assets is the best clue to his probable response to forestry programs. This fact has been so clearly established here and in other studies that any public or private agency interested in improving woodlands can use it advantageously.

At county seats, tax assessors, sheriffs, bankers, and credit bureaus know the economic status of most landowners. Federal and

State agricultural workers can provide evaluations of individual farms and their special problems. They have or can make land capability maps for each ownership. Comparisons of present and potential land uses will indicate where forest investments might pay. From such convenient and inexpensive sources public groups can get information helpful in stimulating local action (2, 3), and consulting and industrial foresters can identify owners likely to hire professional services or lease their woodlands.

As acreage held is related to assets, State estimates of woodland owners, stratified by size of holding, would be invaluable for anticipating differential response to public and private forestry efforts, and for checking on program results. The Forest Survey is the ideal organization for providing such information. Not only in the Y-LT area, but in the southern Coastal Plain generally, other characteristics of landowners are decidedly secondary to assets. It appears that ownership research in the Midsouth should be directed towards techniques for improving public and private programs.

A strengthened Y-LT approach seems eminently suitable for areas that qualify for assistance under Public Law 566, the Watershed Protection and Flood Prevention Act. In eligible watersheds, landowners have already recognized that land-use adjustments are needed and public help is available—the first step to success under the Y-LT approach.

LITERATURE CITED

(1) MIGNERY, A. L.
   1956. FACTORS AFFECTING SMALL-WOODLAND MAN-
        AGEMENT IN NACOGDOCHES COUNTY, TEXAS.
        Jour. Forestry 54: 102-105.

(2) MILLER, R. L., and SOUTHERN, J. H.
   1960. MANAGEMENT INTENT OF SMALL TIMBERLAND
        OWNERS IN EAST TEXAS. Texas Agr. Expt. Sta.
        MP-439, 7 pp., illus.

(3) MITCHELL, J.
   1960. INFLUENCE OF WOODLAND AND OWNER CHAR-
        ACTERISTICS ON FOREST MANAGEMENT IN THE
        TENNESSEE VALLEY. The Unit, News Letter 85,
        pp. 12-14.

(4) PERRY, J. D., and GUTTENBERG, S.
   1959. SOUTHWEST ARKANSAS' SMALL WOODLAND OWN-
        ERS. U. S. Forest Serv. South. Forest Expt.
        Sta. Occas. Paper 170, 14 pp., illus.

(5) WEBSTER, H. H., and STOLTENBERG, C. H.
   1959. WHAT OWNERSHIP CHARACTERISTICS ARE USE-
        FUL IN PREDICTING RESPONSE TO FORESTRY
        PROGRAMS? Land Economics 35: 292-295.

1. Name of owner: _____
2. Mail address of owner: _____
3. Ownership sample code number. _____
4. County _____ Township _____ Range _____ Section _____
5. Code class for years in which program started. _____
6. Sample tract has or doesn't have SCD farm plan.
7. Code class for percent range of minor watershed area covered by farm plans.
8. (a) Acreage of tract in sampling unit.
   (b) Acreage of woodlands in sampling unit.
   (c) How much land do you own in the United States?
   (d) How much land do you own in the Y-LT?
   (e) Do you have investments other than those in land and improvements, such as bonds, stocks, and insurance?
9. How old are you?
10. Please tell me in which of those groups your net taxable 1958 income fell?
    (a) Less than $1,500
    (b) between $1,500 and $2,999
    (c) between $3,000 and $4,499
    (d) over $4,500.
11. How many people do you earn a living for?
12. (a) Is the tract by which we located you being farmed?
    IF YES,
    (b) (1) Do you farm yourself? or (2) by rental?
    (c) IF BY RENTAL, does renter object to tree planting?
    (d) Has farming required additional capital investment exceeding $5,000 in the past 3 years?
    (e) What is your main cash crop?
    IF NO,
    (f) Was this tract farmed in the past 5 years?
13. Do you live on this tract?

14. (a) When did you last sell any timber?
    (b) Was the timber sold as (1) stumpage or (2) cut products?
    (c) Was the timber marked by or according to the instructions of a forester or technician?
    (d) IF TIMBER WAS NOT MARKED, which way did you sell: (1) To a stump or tree diameter limit? or (2) by the boundary?
15. OWNERSHIPS EQUIPPED WITH SOIL CONSERVATION DISTRICT FARM PLANS.
    Have you done anything under your Soil Conservation District farm plan?
    (a) IF NOT, Why not?
    (b) IF YES, What?

    FOR OWNERSHIPS WITH NO RECORDED S.C.D. PLAN.
    (c) Have you ever talked with an S.C.S. man about planning your farm?
    (d) IF YES, Why wasn't the farm plan made?
16. (a) Which of the following people, if any, have you given you technical forestry assistance on any of your properties? (1) none; (2) consulting forester; (3) industrial service forester; (4) state forester; (5) SCS forester; (6) SCS technician, (7) Y-LT forester, (8) Y-LT technician; (9) other (specify).

    IF FORESTER OR TECHNICIAN EMPLOYED:
    (b) (1) Did you seek this service? or (2) was initial contact made by the technician?
    (c) IF SERVICE REQUESTED, How did you happen to know it was available? (1) County agent, (2) ASC committee man; (3) SCS personnel, (4) neighbor's recommendation; (5) public demonstrations and meetings; (6) other (specify).

IF FORESTER OR TECHNICIAN WAS NEVER EMPLOYED—

(d) Why have you not used technical assistance? _____

17. (a) Have you obtained ACP forestry payments on any of your properties? _____

IF YES,

(b) How many acres were planted under ACP? _____

(c) How many acres were released from undesirable trees? _____

(d) How many acres of woodlands were fenced? _____

(e) Other payment practices (specify): _____

18. Have you Soil Banked any of your acreage with trees? IF YES, How many acres? _____

19. (a) Have you invested in forestry on any of your properties over that for which you received or will receive government payments? _____

IF YES,

(b) How many additional acres did you plant? _____

(c) How many additional acres did you release from undesirable trees? _____

(d) How many acres did you purchase to grow timber on? _____

(e) Other (specify): _____

20. To respondents with known plantings.

(a) Do you intend to plant more trees? _____

(b) IF NO, Why have you made this decision? _____

21. WHERE PLANTINGS NOT KNOWN. Do you have trees planted on your land? _____

(a) IF YES, Do you intend to plant more trees? _____

(b) IF NO, Why have you made this decision? _____

22. (a) Have you placed any of your forest properties under long-term lease or other type of permanent management contract? _____

IF YES,

(b) How much acreage is leased? _____

(c) What is the name and address of lessor or management firm? _____

23. How many years have you owned this tract? _____

24. Do you plan to keep this tract in the family another 10 years? _____

(a) IF YES, Why? _____

(b) IF NO, Why? _____

25. In what ways, if any, could the SCS or the Forest Service help you with your lands? _____

26. Owner race, white or colored? _____

27. _____

28. Remarks: _____

Recorder: _____

Date: _____

—18—

OCCASIONAL PAPER 185

Southern Forest Experiment Station
Philip A. Briegleb, Director
FOREST SERVICE, U. S. DEPT. OF AGRICULTURE

1961

—

SPROUT

nt on

TES

- **Frank W. Woods**
  John T. Cassady

- **Charles X Grano**

- **Robert L. Johnson**

SOUTHERN FOREST EXPERIMENT STATION
Philip A. Briegleb, Director
FOREST SERVICE
U. S. DEPARTMENT OF AGRICULTURE

Clearing forest land of undesirable vegetation, with a view to obtaining desirable trees, is becoming increasingly common in the South. Bulldozers and other heavy equipment are generally used in such efforts. Success is measured largely by the degree to which recovery of the unwanted plants is prevented or slowed.

This Occasional Paper contains three articles on the general topic of site-clearing. The first describes the response of scrub oaks cut and recut at varying intervals; the aim of the study was to secure information on the timing of stand-conversion operations in the sandhills of western Florida. The second article deals with the speed of hardwood resprouting in the understory of a pine forest in southern Arkansas. The third briefly describes a bull-dozing operation in the Mississippi Delta, where the intention was to encourage hardwoods of better species and quality than those already present.

HARDWOOD SPROUT DEVELOPMENT ON CLEARED SITES

- Frank W. Woods
  John T. Cassady

- Charles X Grano

- Robert L. Johnson

CONTENTS

SPROUTING OF SANDHILLS SCRUB OAKS
FOLLOWING CUTTING

Frank W. Woods [1] and John T. Cassady

SOUTHERN FOREST EXPERIMENT STATION

Turkey and bluejack oaks in the sandhills of western Florida were cut four inches above the ground in May, and rootstock sprouts were removed twice thereafter during the same growing season. Removals at 6 or 8 weeks apart were better than those at 4-week intervals.

This paper reports a study of periodic removal of oak stems and resulting sprouts at selected time intervals. The object was to determine the most effective intervals for site-preparation treatments aimed at controlling scrub oaks on west Florida sandhills. On these dry sites complete eradication of existing vegetation is essential to the establishment of pine forests.

METHODS

The study tract, on the Chipola Experimental Forest in northwest Florida, is representative of large areas in the sandhills. Turkey oak *(Quercus laevis* Walt.*)*, bluejack oak *(Q. incana* Bartr.*)*, and wiregrass *(Aristida stricta* Michx.*)* dominate in the scrubby vegetation. A few longleaf pine *(Pinus palustris* Mill.*)* seedlings, saplings, and flat-topped residual trees are scattered over most areas. The predominant soil series is Lakeland sand, deep phase, with excessive internal drainage.

The study design was a randomized complete block, with two blocks of 6 treatments applied to two oak species and replicated in time by similar studies begun in 1955 and 1956. Turkey oak and bluejack oak were studied separately within each block. Each species treatment was applied to 10 single-stemmed, healthy-looking trees from 1.5 to 3.0 inches in diameter, measured 4 inches above ground. Small trees were chosen because they sprout more vigorously than large trees.

Initially, each stem, except in the check treatments, was sawn off 4 inches aboveground. The resulting sprouts were counted, measured, and removed at specified times for two growing seasons, as described below:

Treatment

1. Stems cut off 4 inches aboveground at beginning of study; all sprouts removed one year later.

2. Stems cut at beginning of study; sprouts removed at 4-week intervals, i. e., 4 weeks and 8 weeks after initial cut. Third and final sprout removal one year after initial cut.

3. Same as treatment 2 except that first-year sprout removal was at 6-week intervals.

4. Same as 2 except that first-year sprout removal was at 7-week intervals.

[1] Field work was done while Dr Woods was on the staff of the Marianna Research Center, Southern Forest Experiment Station, Marianna, Florida He is now a member of the School of Forestry, Duke University, Durham, N C.

5. Same as 2 except that first-year sprout removal was at 8-week intervals.

Control. No treatment during the first year; stems were cut at a height of 4 inches in May of second year, at same time as final removal of sprouts in all other treatments.

A 2-week treatment was planned, but no sprout growth was produced within that interval.

The number and length of sprouts on each stump were recorded weekly during the first growing season, and monthly during the second. Sprouting ability was summarized by adding together the length of every sprout on a stump and then averaging all stumps in the treatment.

Stump and rootcollar samples were sectioned to determine the origin and development of sprouts.

RESULTS

Sprouting during the first season

Figure 1 illustrates the average sprout growth (total length of sprouts per stump) of turkey oak during the first growing season under selected treatments. Bluejack oak showed a similar pattern but greater sprout length in all cases.

Figure 1.—
Average total length of sprouts on turkey oaks.

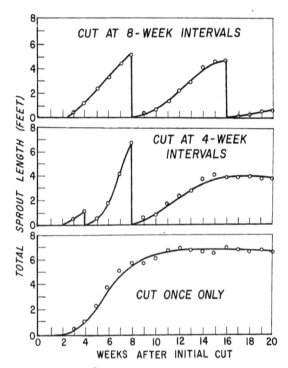

2

The initial cut for each treatment was made when leaves were fully developed—May 26, 1955, in the first study and May 15, 1956, in the second. Sprout growth immediately after the initial cut was the same under each treatment—there was no measurable growth during the first two weeks and only 12 to 15 inches during the second two weeks. Thus, in sprout removal at 4-week intervals, the first removal was wasted on a few small sprouts, and this removal came during the period of maximum sprout development, as illustrated by results of the cut-once-only plots. Removal after just 4 weeks increased the rate of sprout growth, so that at 8 weeks after the initial cut the stumps in the 4-week treatments had as much total sprout growth as the cut-once or 8-week treatments.

The first measure of treatment success was total sprout length at the end of the first growing season, which is represented by the twentieth week on the charts (fig. 1). The cut-once-only treatment resulted in about 6 feet of sprouts per stump; the 4-week intervals had about 4 feet; and the stumps cut at 8-week intervals averaged less than one foot of total sprout length.

The 6- and 7-week intervals gave results similar to 8-week intervals.

Variation in the total number of sprouts per stump (fig. 2) followed the same patterns as in total sprout length. At the end of the first season the treated stumps averaged about 14 sprouts if they had been cut once only, 17 sprouts if cut at 4-week intervals, and 3 sprouts if cut at 8-week intervals.

Sprouting during the second season

In May of the second year, sprouts were again removed from all plants cut the first year and oaks in the check treatment were cut for the first time.

These second-year measurements, with the check treatment for comparison, gave an indication of the effect on sprouting vigor caused by the first-year treatments. Total sprout growth in mid-July of the second season, two months after cutting or sprout removal in May, was selected to illustrate the final effects of first-year treatments; sprout growth was near maximum by mid-July.

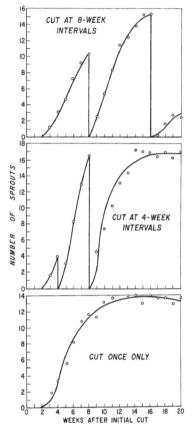

Figure 2.—*Average numbers of sprouts per stump, on turkey oaks.*

Figure 3 shows clearly that sprout removal at 6-, 7-, or 8-week intervals reduced sprouting considerably more than removal at 4-week intervals or cutting once only. Treatment differences for turkey oak were highly significant

3

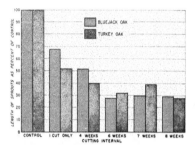

Figure 3.—*Relative total length of sprouts per stump in the second season following different cutting regimes (length of sprouts on controls taken as 100 percent).*

as tested by analysis of variance. Data for bluejack oak were not analyzed but were quite similar to those for turkey oak.

Stumps killed by cutting treatments

As might be expected, many tree stumps were killed by repeated sprout-removal treatments (table 1). Progressively higher mortality resulted from removal at increasing intervals.

Table 1 —*Dead stumps at end of second season*

First-year treatment	Bluejack oak	Turkey oak	Total
	Percent	Percent	Percent
Check—no first-year treatment	2.5	2.5	2.5
Tops only removed	5.0	12.5	8.8
Four-week intervals	5.0	25.0	15.0
Six-week intervals	17.5	25.0	21.2
Seven-week intervals	27.5	15.0	21.2
Eight-week intervals	22.5	35.0	28.8

Origin of sprouts

Cross-sections of treated oak stumps indicated that the first sprouts after initial cutting were from dormant buds. Development of the buds was evidenced by radial traces from the pith to the cambium. After the first sprouts were removed, a callus (primordial tissue) formed at the termination of bud trace over the injured wood and became the source of many new buds and sprouts. Resprouting from

the callus started quickly after sprout removal but at least two weeks were required for sprouting to develop from dormant buds in a freshly made stump.

DISCUSSION

There is abundant evidence that rootcollar sprouts, epicormic branches, and water sprouts originate from dormant buds. This is true for broadleaved woody species (Schreiner, 1933) as well as for conifers (Stone and Stone, 1954). These latent buds connect with the primary xylem and move outward to the same extent that the tree grows in radius each year (Roth and Hepting, 1943). Some bud traces divide at various points in their outward migration, so that the number of subsurface buds increases as the tree grows (Hahne, 1926). Terminal shoots cause these buds to remain dormant, apparently through the action of auxins which move basipetally. When the source of auxins is removed by cutting or some other action, dormant buds may start to grow (Doorenbos, 1953).

External factors, such as the loss of leaves, sudden exposure of stems to light, and increased bark temperatures, may interrupt the downward movement of auxins sufficiently to stimulate growth of dormant buds. Such effects occur more in some species than others. Adventitious buds, which do not connect with the primary xylem, develop only at the site of injuries (Voss, 1935). They originate on callus tissue which forms during the healing process (Burger, 1931). Burger asserted that rootcollar sprouts originate from adventitious buds, but this investigation indicates that the initial stump sprouts are entirely from dormant buds. Once the initial sprouts are removed, callus tissue forms and succeeding sprouts are nearly all from adventitious buds.

APPLICATION

This study was planned on the hypothesis that scrub oak stems and sprouts must be removed at least three times during a single season to obtain a satisfactory kill. Later work indicates that two removals may be adequate under certain conditions. Where three treatments are needed, the first may be accomplished quickly and cheaply by prescribed burning as soon as leaves are full grown in

4

Figure 4.—
*Sprouts always origina-
ted at or above the root-
collar, never on roots.*

spring, provided that there is enough fuel to defoliate the oaks and kill small stems. The second and third sprout-removals are best carried out by heavy doubledrum brush cutters that push over and chop woody plants into the ground. The same treatment destroys wiregrass and herbaceous vegetation. In this study, three top-removal treatments were made to represent experimentally the timing of three mechanical site-preparation treatments. However, the experimental techniques were much gentler

and much less destructive to scrub oaks than the heavy equipment, which usually uproots and partially buries the stumps.

Follow-up studies with chopping equipment have produced very satisfactory kill of scrub oaks with two cuts spaced 6 to 10 weeks apart during the main growing season. Prescribed burning 6 to 10 weeks before the first chop usually gives even better control.

5

LITERATURE CITED

BURGER, H.
1931. WASSERREISER AND WURZELBRUT. Schweiz. Ztschr. f. Forstw. 82: 305-308.

DOORENBOS, J.
1953. [REVIEW OF THE LITERATURE ON DORMANCY IN BUDS OF WOODY PLANTS.] Meded. Landbouwloogesch. Wageningen 53 (1): 1-24.

HAHNE, BRUNO.
1926. THE ORIGIN OF SECONDARY DORMANT BUDS IN DECIDUOUS FRUIT TREES. Univ. Calif. Publ. Bot. 13: 125-126.

ROTH, E. R., and HEPTING, G. H.
1943. ORIGIN AND DEVELOPMENT OF OAK STUMP SPROUTS AS AFFECTING THEIR LIKELIHOOD TO DECAY. Jour. Forestry 41: 27-36, illus.

SCHREINER, D.
1933. KLEBASTBILDUNG AN EICHEN. Forstwiss. Centbl. 55: 405-414.

STONE, E. L., JR., and STONE, M. H.
1954. ROOT COLLAR SPROUTS IN PINE. Jour. Forestry 52: 487-491, illus

VOSS, J.
1935. DIE NOTWENDIGKEIT UND MOGLICHKEIT DER WASSERREISERBILDUNG BEI EICHE VORZUBEUGEN. Forstarchiv. 11: 49-52.

HARDWOOD REOCCUPATION OF BULLDOZED SITES

Charles X Grano

SOUTHERN FOREST EXPERIMENT STATION

Hardwood thickets in south Arkansas were bulldozed and observed to study site reoccupation by sprouts. First-year sprouts were few, and the tallest averaged 1.8 feet. After 3 years one-fourth of the area was overtopped by sprouts; after 7 years half was overtopped by sprouts averaging 6 feet tall.

Very dense hardwood thickets in south Arkansas pine-hardwood stands were bulldozed clean, down to mineral soil, and observed for seven years thereafter to follow the rate of site reoccupation by sprouts (fig. 1).

Figure 1.—1953: *Cleared area immediately after it was bulldozed to remove dense hardwood thicket.*

When the site was bulldozed in 1953 there were approximately 24,000 hardwood stems per acre under 3.5 inches in diameter. Some of these were more than 15 feet tall. Species present included southern red oak, post oak, mulberry, witch hazel, red maple, sweetgum, blackgum, sassafras, dogwood, sumac, hickory, persimmon, elm, ash, wild plum, and Hercules-club. Thirty-one percent of the stems were mulberry and witch hazel, 17 percent were oaks, and 15 percent were gums. The oaks and gums were the largest trees present.

The soil is a sloping phase of Caddo silt loam. A 20-inch top layer of light brown silt loam grades into a very compact silty clay loam and silty clay. The clay layer impedes internal drainage, but a gently sloping topography provides good surface drainage.

Rainfall was less than normal and soil moisture in short supply during the 1954, 1955, and 1956 growing seasons. During the next three years soil moisture was very favorable, and in 1960 it was only slightly deficient.

A sparse growth of small sprouts appeared one year after treatment; the taller ones averaged 1.8 feet. At the end of the second year they were 3.0 feet. In 1956, 24 percent of the area was overtopped by hardwood sprouts, the tallest averaging 4.0 feet (fig. 2). By 1960, the sprouts had increased in number and size to

7

Figure 2.—1956: *About one-fourth of the area has been reoccupied by hardwoods. The tallest sprouts average 4 feet in height.*

Figure 3.—1960: *Fifty-two percent of the area has been reoccupied by hardwoods. Tallest stems are 15 feet, the average is 6 feet.*

such an extent that they overtopped 52 percent of the area. Some of the stems were 15 feet high, but they averaged 6 feet (fig. 3).

Less drastic mechanical treatment than bull-dozing clean resulted in much greater and more rapid hardwood reoccupation, as illustrated in figure 4. In 1953 this area, which is part of the same study reported above, was given a combination treatment—one pass with a brush cutter hooked ahead of a light disk. Three years later 58 percent of the area was once more overtopped by hardwoods and, by 1960, 92 percent was reoccupied. The disk used was too light; a larger one with an adequate tractor would have been more effective.

Figure 4.—1960: *Small hardwoods on this site were leveled in 1953 with a brush cutter and a light disk—a less thorough treatment than bulldozing. Ninety-two percent of the area is now reoccupied by hardwoods — the tallest are 25 feet in height, the average 10 feet.*

8

HARDWOOD SPROUTS DOMINATE BOTTOM-LAND CLEARINGS

Robert L. Johnson
SOUTHERN FOREST EXPERIMENT STATION

Five years after they had been cleared of all aboveground vegetation, openings in a stand of bottom-land hardwoods were dominated by sprout trees, mainly bitter pecan and green ash.

Six openings in a bottom-land hardwood forest near Stoneville, Mississippi, were bull-dozed clear of all vegetation in the fall of 1954. The openings, which averaged 1 by 1½ chains, had been created by selective logging and by deadening of all culls larger than 4 inches in d.b.h. The bulldozer cut off all remaining plants—vines and small cull trees—but left underground roots largely undisturbed.

One opening was on a well-drained ridge; the others were on poorly drained flats. The soil was Sharkey clay.

Two years after treatment, sprouts of bitter pecan and green ash were the most common trees, but were growing in association with annual weeds, vines, and briers. Other tree species included Nuttall oak, overcup oak, American elm, willow oak, hackberry, and persimmon, all of which were present in the surrounding overstory.

After five growing seasons, green ash and bitter pecan almost completely dominated four of the openings on the flats. In the fifth, trees were being suppressed by similax and trumpet-creeper vines. On the ridge, green ash sprouts were competing with seedlings of cedar elm and willow oak. Trees of desirable species and form numbered between 2,000 and 7,500 per acre. Dominants among the bitter pecan and green ash were about 1½ inches in d.b.h. and 15 feet tall.

From these observations, it appears that light bulldozing after logging in similar mixed hard-wood stands will stimulate reproduction by root sprouting. The composition of the new stand will be governed by the most prolifically sprouting species, not necessarily the most desirable; in this test, green ash and bitter pecan comprised 65 percent of the commercial species present after 5 years.

Figure 1.—
This area was scraped bare of all vegetation 5 years ago. It now has about 7,500 trees per acre, mostly green ash and bitter pecan sprouts. Dominant trees are about 1½ inches d b.h. and 15 feet tall.

FOREST

TAXATION

in

LOUISIANA

William C. Siegel
Joe D. Perry

HERN FOREST EXPERIMENT STATION
PHILIP A. BRIEGLEB, DIRECTOR
Service, U. S. Department of Agriculture

FOREST

TAXATION

in

LOUISIANA

William C. Siegel
Joe D. Perry

loxa

in L

FOREST TAXATION IN LOUISIANA

This report is a statistical summary of a 1960 study of forest taxation in Louisiana. The purposes were to determine trends during the preceding twenty years and to trace preliminary effects of the 1954 Forest Tax Law. Past and present legal bases for taxation are briefly reviewed and the sampling method is described.

LEGAL SETTING

Forest Tax Legislation

Prior to January 1, 1955, land and timber were assessed together in Louisiana. Act 759, adopted by the State Legislature on November 2, 1954, amended Section I of Article X of the State Constitution to provide that the land alone be subject to ad valorem taxation. [1]

A general severance tax also was formerly levied on timber. It ranged from 25 cents to $1.50 per MBF for sawtimber, depending on species, and was 15 cents per cord for pulpwood. The entire severance revenue was allocated to the State Forestry Commission.

The new law superseded the general severance tax and in principle placed Louisiana's woodlands on a yield tax basis. Nevertheless this mandatory levy on timber harvested is still officially called a severance tax. Under it sawtimber is taxed at 2¼ percent and pulpwood at 5 percent of current average market value for stumpage by species. Seventy-five percent of the receipts are returned to the parishes where the timber was cut and twenty-five percent to the State General Fund. Virgin timber, for practical purposes nonexistent, is still subject to the old law.

---

[1] *Acts of the Legislature, State of Louisiana, Regular Session 1954, Extraordinary Session 1953, and Constitutional Amendments Adopted 1952.* Baton Rouge, 1684 pp. 1954.

Not supplanted by the 1954 law was a reforestation contract severance tax enacted in 1922 by Legislative Act 90 of that year. The act and subsequent amendments permit landowners who reforest denuded land to enter into contract with the State and parish for a fixed assessment on both the land and the planted timber. A 6 percent severance tax is paid on products cut. After a maximum of 50 years from the date of contract, the land and any timber remaining thereon become subject to regular ad valorem taxation. Three-fourths of the severance revenue is returned to the parishes where the timber was cut, while one-fourth goes into the State General Fund. An amendment passed in 1926 provides that contracts entered into can be made retroactive.

In recent years acreage involved has been declining. The first contracts were let in 1933. The peak year was 1946, when 621 thousand acres were reported under contract. By 1959 only 450 thousand acres remained *(3, 5, 6, 7, 8)* [1].

The new law requires all woodlands, except those under reforestation contract, to be placed in one of four categories: tidewater cypress, hardwood, longleaf pine, and other pine. In most parishes no more than two of these types are found. Most of the State's timber is classified either as other pine or hardwood. The new classification system is far simpler than the old, which had numerous categories. Transition from one to the other, however, has not been easy. In 1956 only 9 percent of reported forest land was legally classified. By the end of 1959, the percentage had risen to 40 *(2)*. Although eight classifications were still being used in addition to "miscellaneous land," which may or may not be forest, there has evidently been a steady effort to apply the law.

Real Property Taxation in Louisiana

The State Constitution specifies that property be taxed in proportion to its actual cash value *(4)*. It defines taxable property to include real property, movable personal property, other personal property, and mixtures of the foregoing (Revised Statute 47: 1980). It further provides that real estate be assessed at actual market value and so listed on the tax rolls. Assessments are subject to annual approval by a board of review within each parish. After the approval each assessor must furnish the State Tax Commission an abstract by property class of all valuations within his parish. The State Homestead Exemption Act of 1934 provides that upon the owner's application, any homestead in the city or the country may be exempted from taxes on the first $2,000 of assessed valuation.

---

[1] Italic numbers in parentheses refer to Literature Cited, p. 12.

For war veterans, additional exemptions are provided. Veterans of either World War II or the Korean War receive a total exemption of $5,000 for five years. For veterans of both wars, the exemption is for ten years. In rural areas, parcels of land separate from the home tract may be included in the exemption, either to an aggregate of 160 acres or to the amount of the exemption. Exemptions apply to most State and local property taxes, but with some exceptions. City taxes are exempt only in New Orleans. Since August 1956, water, sewerage, and lighting district taxes are no longer exempt unless they are parish-wide.

Local units are reimbursed from the State property tax relief fund for the amount of the exempted taxes. This fund is supported by the State alcoholic beverage, income, and public utility taxes. In recent years the State has been returning more money to the parishes under this act than it has been receiving from its portion of ad valorem taxes.

Upon receipt of parish assessment abstracts, the Tax Commission can adjust group valuations within and among parishes. Ostensibly this is to achieve equalization, as provided for by law. Nevertheless assessments have been raised to help meet State budget requirements since the Louisiana ad valorem tax rate is fixed in the Constitution at 5¾ mills.

Though market value is required by law, most assessments are considerably lower and have been so for many years. Tax statutes permit parishes to levy on as little as 25 percent of the total assessment. To offset the prevalent under-valuations, however, most apply millage to the entire amount.

Unlike the State, parishes have wide latitude in setting rates. Therefore, as local revenue needs have increased, general practice has been to raise millage. Even so, local levies are often well below constitutional limits. Except in Jackson and Orleans Parishes the general parish tax may not rise above 4 mills. Limits on the parish-wide school maintenance and general municipal taxes are 5 and 7 mills respectively. The levy for a single public improvement cannot exceed 5 mills and the aggregate may not surpass 25. The Constitution sets no limit on local school taxes other than for maintenance purposes.

STUDY METHOD

The 1959 tax rolls for each parish were sampled for information on assessments, millage, and taxes. The State Constitution requires that duplicate copies of the rolls be submitted annually to the State auditor before November 15. After audit, the records, arranged by ward within parishes, are filed by the Tax Commission and made available for public inspection. Aggregate holdings within wards are usually listed alphabetically by ownership. Within holdings, assessments by type are usually given separately but with only the total tax recorded.

Holdings larger than 499 acres comprise more than half the State's forest land. The relatively few such ownerships made it feasible to control sampling error by taking data on all of them. The data included forest acreage, forest assessment, total assessment (all assets combined), forest protection tax, and total tax. Tracts of less than 500 acres were sampled by taking a random start from among the first thirty on a parish roll; complete data were taken from this entry and every thirtieth thereafter. To enhance accuracy of acreage estimates, the forested acreage of every fifteenth entry was also recorded.

To establish trends, the procedure used for the 1959 data was followed for nine selected parishes at 5-year intervals beginning with 1939. The parishes were Beauregard, Concordia, Iberville, Jackson, La Salle, Richland, Sabine, Washington, and Webster. These constitute a good geographic distribution, typify ownership conditions, and afford proportional representation of forest types throughout the State. They are the same parishes that Craig (1) studied earlier. Time and expense limitations precluded sampling by forest type and condition class as was done by him, but each of these parishes has a predominant timber type.

ASSESSMENT LEVELS AND TRENDS

The assessor and his approach to valuation are the foundation of the property tax system. Even for those who are well trained and experienced, judging the worth of property, particularly woodlands, is more art than science.

For a given millage, the amount of a tax bill is determined by the assessment, which is subject to examination by a parish board of review and appeal by the property owner. Even if all properties within a parish are assessed consistently, their values may still be set above or below similar properties in other parishes and thus contribute disproportionally to State revenues. From parish to parish, assessments tend to vary in direct proportion to per capita income.

Forest assessments in the 9 sample parishes varied widely between 1939 and 1959 (table 1). Iberville Parish has consistently had the lowest valuations—under two dollars per acre—with Concordia not far behind. Richland averaged highest with assessments of over seven dollars per acre except in 1954. Richland is only about

Table 1.—*Average assessment per forest acre for 9 sample parishes*

Parish	1939	1944	1949	1954	1959
			Dollars		
Beauregard	3.11	3.10	4.03	4.57	5.70
Concordia	2.22	1.92	1.98	2.29	3.59
Iberville	1.71	1.76	1.78	1.68	1.72
Jackson	3.68	3.81	3.84	4.19	5.11
La Salle	2.74	3.58	4.66	5.28	6.85
Richland	7.48	7.71	7.26	5.98	7.29
Sabine	3.62	3.70	3.73	3.61	4.92
Washington	4.12	4.01	4.11	4.29	4.33
Webster	5.79	5.91	5.82	5.96	6.22

40 percent forested *(7)* and has considerably more valuable agricultural acreage than Iberville or Concordia. The forests of all three
parishes are predominantly hardwood *(9)*, and provide only a small
portion of the tax base—in part because they are largely on lands
that are subject to overflow and thus receive a minimum of public
services.

In most parishes assessments fluctuated only slightly between
1939 and 1954 but rose in all between 1954 and 1959. Except in
Iberville and Washington, these increases were substantial. The
largest gains were 57 percent in Concordia, 36 percent in Sabine, and
30 percent in La Salle.

Figure 1 portrays average forest assessments for the entire

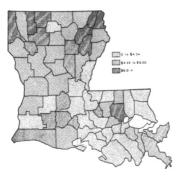

Figure 1.—*Average assessment per forest acre, by parishes, 1959.*

State. The ranges from which these averages were determined are shown in figure 2. For the State as a whole, 1959 valuations averaged $5.52 per acre (table 2). Parish averages varied from $1.63 for

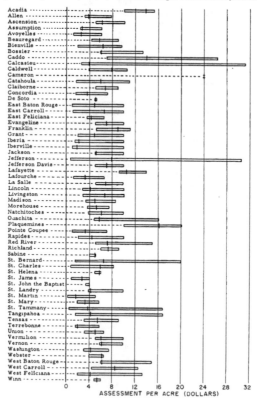

Figure 2.—Range in assessment by parishes. Short vertical lines through bars are the parish averages.

St. Martin to $20.00 for Cameron. Those falling in the middle one-third ($4.35 to $6.20) were chiefly "pine parishes" of north-central and northern Louisiana. The twenty-one parishes having average assessments of less than $4.35 were mostly in southern Louisiana's cutover cypress areas. Those in the highest bracket—exceeding $6.20 per acre—were scattered throughout the State. Four—Caddo, Lafayette, St. Bernard, and Jefferson—contain centers of high population density. Cameron Parish, which has the highest average assessment in the State, contains only a very small acreage of forest land, consisting mostly of one- and two-acre "islands." In general, the high-assessment parishes in southern Louisiana are not present or prospective sources of commercial timber.

TAX AND MILLAGE LEVELS AND TRENDS

Though millage fluctuated widely during the twenty-year period 1939-1959, the general trend in the sample parishes was upward (table 3).

The Statewide average (table 2) was 50 mills per dollar of

Table 2.—*Average assessments, millage, and taxes for forest land, 1959* [1]

Parish	Assessment per acre	Millage per dollar of assessment	Tax per acre
	Dollars	Mills [1]	Cents
Acadia	14.98	28	42
Allen	3.72	64	24
Ascension	6.19	46	29
Assumption	2.70	46	12
Avoyelles	2.56	76	19
Beauregard	5.70	47	27
Bienville	6.38	46	30
Bossier	6.06	35	21
Caddo	13.92	29	40
Calcasieu	3.92	51	20
Caldwell	7.89	45	35
Cameron	20.00	31	61
Catahoula	6.00	54	32
Claiborne	6.77	35	24
Concordia	3.59	57	21
De Soto	5.00	41	21
East Baton Rouge	4.84	38	18
East Carroll	6.51	45	30
East Feliciana	4.28	30	13
Evangeline	6.96	40	28
Franklin	8.89	57	51
Grant	4.79	64	31

Table 2.—*Continued*

Parish	Assessment per acre	Millage per dollar of assessment	Tax per acre
	Dollars	Mills [1]	Cents
Iberia	2.09	53	11
Iberville	1.72	49	8
Jackson	5.11	44	22
Jefferson	7.94	103	82
Jeff. Davis	7.03	37	26
Lafayette	10.49	43	45
Lafourche	3.25	57	18
La Salle	6.85	55	37
Lincoln	4.06	49	20
Livingston	6.65	64	43
Madison	4.89	39	19
Morehouse	5.10	38	19
Natchitoches	6.05	53	32
Ouachita	5.65	42	24
Plaquemines	16.14	54	86
Pointe Coupee	3.27	38	12
Rapides	4.43	61	26
Red River	7.12	38	27
Richland	7.29	40	29
Sabine	4.92	56	28
St. Bernard	6.47	66	43
St. Charles	5.89	44	26
St. Helena	5.73	43	25
St. James	2.72	48	13
St. John the Baptist	3.98	31	12
St. Landry	4.08	45	18
St. Martin	1.63	62	10
St. Mary	3.25	39	13
St. Tammany	3.70	59	22
Tangipahoa	4.19	66	28
Tensas	5.50	40	22
Terrebonne	2.02	57	12
Union	5.01	53	26
Vermilion	5.98	30	18
Vernon	6.08	73	44
Washington	4.33	47	21
Webster	6.22	40	25
West Baton Rouge	6.22	48	30
West Carroll	8.45	47	40
West Feliciana	4.22	22	9
Winn	5.42	51	28

[1] Orleans Parish is omitted, as it contains no forest land.
[2] A mill refers to a tax rate of one-tenth of a cent per dollar of assessment, or one dollar per thousand

assessment in 1959 ($50 per $1,000). Individual parishes varied from 22 mills for West Feliciana to 103 for Jefferson. Fifty parishes fell between 30 and 60 mills. Of the ten parishes exceeding 60 mills, most are in central Louisiana or among the "Florida Parishes." Only three—Acadia, Caddo, and West Feliciana—had levies lower than 30 mills.

The tax pattern was one of gradual rises between 1939 and 1954, followed by heavy increases in the subsequent five years (table 4). The largest spurts between 1954 and 1959 were in Concordia Parish, where taxes rose 90 percent, and in Sabine and Beauregard, where they went up approximately 50 percent. These increases are largely due to the rise in forest assessments in these parishes. Of the seven sample parishes with substantial increases in taxes between 1939 and 1959, La Salle had the largest overall gain (270 percent). Iberville and Richland experienced virtually no rise during the two decades.

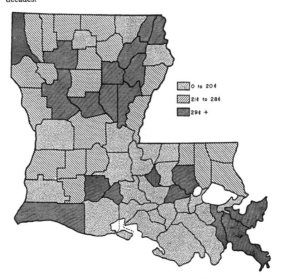

Figure 3.—*Average tax per forest acre, by parishes, 1959*

The average tax per acre on Louisiana woodlands in 1959 was 28 cents. Individual parishes (table 2) varied from 8 cents per acre for Iberville to 86 cents for Plaquemines. Figure 3 portrays parishes by tax brackets. The one-third with average taxes of 20 cents or less per acre are mostly in southern Louisiana's cutover cypress area.

Table 3.—*Average millage per dollar of assessment for 9 sample parishes*

Parish	1939	1944	1949	1954	1959
	---------- Mills ----------				
Beauregard	47	39	43	40	47
Concordia	44	44	48	46	57
Iberville	43	37	53	58	49
Jackson	42	41	37	38	44
La Salle	36	26	38	55	55
Richland	38	39	41	45	40
Sabine	55	49	40	50	56
Washington	29	27	28	35	47
Webster	26	25	30	34	40

Virtually all in the middle bracket (21 to 28 cents) are "pine parishes." Of those with taxes above 29 cents per acre, three—St. Bernard, Jefferson, and Lafayette—are not important timber producers. Their forest acreage is small and likely to diminish further.

Ad valorem receipts from Louisiana's forest lands in 1959 totaled 4 million dollars, comprising about 2.7 percent of all property taxes

collected. These do not represent total revenues to local and State governments from forest land. Severance taxes, of which 75 percent are returned to the parishes, yielded about 750 thousand dollars in 1959. Figure 4 shows how severance receipts varied from 1939 to

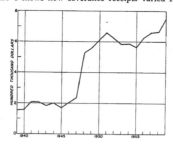

Figure 4.—*Statewide severance-tax receipts, 1939-1959.*

1959 *(6)*. The big rise after 1947 was largely due to postwar increases in stumpage values and pulpwood production.

The forest protection or acreage tax is collected in 33 parishes (fig. 5). In 21 parishes all forest land is subject to a levy of 2 cents

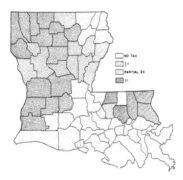

Figure 5.—*Protection tax per forest acre, by parishes, 1959.*

per acre. In 9 others, only some of the owners pay this tax. In 3 parishes the rate is ½ cent per acre. Of the parishes that do not collect this tax 29 are either in the southern cutover cypress belt or in the extreme northeast. The thirtieth is St. Helena, one of the Florida Parishes, which has continuously had the worst fire record in the State.

Table 4.—*Average taxes per forest acre for 9 sample parishes*

Parish	1939	1944	1949	1954	1959
			Cents		
Beauregard	14	12	17	18	27
Concordia	10	8	9	11	21
Iberville	7	7	9	10	8
Jackson	16	15	14	16	22
La Salle	10	9	18	26	37
Richland	29	30	30	27	29
Sabine	20	18	15	18	28
Washington	12	11	12	15	21
Webster	15	15	18	20	25

LITERATURE CITED

1. CRAIG, R. B.
   1942. TAXES ON FOREST PROPERTY IN NINE SELECTED
   PARISHES OF LOUISIANA, 1937-40, IN NINE
   COUNTIES OF ALABAMA, 1937-41, AND IN SEVEN
   COUNTIES OF MISSISSIPPI, 1936-41. U. S. Forest
   Serv. South. Forest Expt. Sta. Occas. Paper
   101, 23 pp., illus.

2. HAYES, R. W.
   1960. PROGRESS IN LAND CLASSIFICATION IN LOUISIANA
   UNDER THE 1954 FOREST TAX LAW. La. State
   Univ. School Forestry LSU Forestry Notes
   40, 3 pp.

3. LOUISIANA TAX COMMISSION.
   1940. TWENTY-THIRD ANNUAL REPORT OF THE LOUISI-
   ANA TAX COMMISSION FOR THE YEAR 1939.
   341 pp.

4. ————
   1942. PRINCIPAL LAWS GOVERNING ASSESSMENT FOR
   AD VALOREM TAX PURPOSES IN THE STATE OF
   LOUISIANA. 161 pp.

5. ————
   1946. THIRD BIENNIAL REPORT OF THE LOUISIANA TAX
   COMMISSION FOR THE YEARS 1944-1945. 261 pp.

6. ————
   1950. FOURTH BIENNIAL REPORT OF THE LOUISIANA
   TAX COMMISSION FOR THE YEARS 1948-1949.
   314 pp.

7. ————
   1956. SEVENTH BIENNIAL REPORT OF THE LOUISIANA
   TAX COMMISSION FOR THE YEARS 1954-1955.
   323 pp.

8. ————
   1960. NINTH BIENNIAL REPORT OF THE LOUISIANA TAX
   COMMISSION FOR THE YEARS 1958-1959. 355
   pp.

9. SOUTHERN FOREST EXPERIMENT STATION.
   1955. FORESTS OF LOUISIANA, 1953-54. U. S. Forest
   Serv. Forest Survey Release 75, 64 pp., illus.

THE FOREST TAXATION LAW

(Adopted November 2, 1954)

An amendment to Section I of Article X of the Constitution
of Louisiana levying a severance tax on timber, and classifying and providing for the assessment of forest lands and
timber.

Section 1 . . . .

Timber, other than virgin timber, shall be recognized as a growing
crop. A severance tax on trees and timber severed from the soil or
water is hereby levied at the rate of 2¼% on all forms of timber
except pulpwood, and 5% for pulpwood, of the then current average
stumpage market value of such timber, to be determined annually
on the second Monday of January by the Louisiana Forestry Commission and the Louisiana Tax Commission, such tax to be collected
in accordance with the laws for the collection of severance taxes
on natural resources, existing at the time of collection.

Commencing on July 1, 1956, seventy-five percentum of the proceeds
of the severance tax on timber severed in each parish shall be
remitted by the State Treasurer to the governing authority of the
parish from which the timber is severed. The remaining twenty-five
percentum of the proceeds of the severance tax on timber shall be
credited to the State General Fund.

After the effective date of this amendment, no additional value shall
be added to the assessment of timber in excess of such value as was
included in the assessment of said timber at the time of the adoption
of this amendment.

Forest lands are hereby classified for assessment purposes as follows:

1. TIDEWATER CYPRESS LAND—Forest land that is adjacent
   to tidewater and that is supporting a growth of trees which are
   predominantly cypress or that at some time in the past supported
   a growth of trees which were predominantly cypress, and which
   has not been captured or occupied predominantly by commercial
   species other than cypress.

2. HARDWOOD LAND—Forest land that is supporting a growth
   of trees or shrubs which are predominantly broadleaf species
   and that in the past supported a growth of predominantly broadleaf species, and which has not been captured or occupied by
   tidewater cypress or pine. Tidewater Cypress Land, Longleaf

Pine Land, and Other Pine Land on which broadleaf species of commercial importance have become established as predominant species is Hardwood Land.

3. LONGLEAF PINE LAND—Forest land that is supporting a growth of pine predominantly of the Longleaf pine species (Pinus palustris) or that at some time in the past supported a growth of longleaf pine and on which other pine species or broadleaf species of commercial importance have not become established as the predominant species.

4. OTHER PINE LAND—Forest land that is supporting a growth of pine predominantly of a species other than longleaf pine or that at some time in the past supported a growth of pine predominantly of a species other than longleaf pine and on which longleaf pine or broadleaf species of commercial importance have not become established as predominant species.

For the purpose of taxation, the assessed value of the above classifications of forest lands shall be determined and the assessment of such lands shall be made in the manner provided by law. After the effective date of this amendment, no additional value shall be added to the assessment of land by reason of the presence of timber thereon in excess of such value as was included in the assessment of said lands and timber thereon at the time of the adoption of this amendment; provided that standing timber shall be and remain liable equally with the land on which it stands for ad valorem taxes levied on said land.

Any provision of this constitution, and particularly of Section I (as amended by Acts Nos. 162 of 1926 and 81 of 1934) and 21 (as amended by Acts Nos. 51 of 1932, 395 of 1938, 392 of 1940 and 546 of 1948) of Article X thereof, and of any law of this state, in conflict with the provisions of this amendment, to the extent of such conflict only, is hereby repealed. Provided, that no contract heretofore entered into under the authority of Section I of Article X of the Constitution as amended and Act No. 90 of 1922, Act No. 71 of 1924 as amended, R. S. 56: 1471 through 1495, and Acts Nos. 120 and 121 of 1926 shall be held to have been impaired by the provisions of this amendment. This amendment shall be self-operative and no legislation shall be required to carry it into effect except as otherwise provided herein. The provisions of this amendment shall take effect on January 1, 1955.

[*Sections 2 and 3 omitted*]

Guidelines for

DIRECT – SEEDING

LOBLOLLY PINE

W. F. Mann, Jr.

H. J. Derr

Guidelines for

DIRECT – SEEDING

LOBLOLLY PINE

W. F. Mann, Jr.

H. J. Derr

The development of methods for direct seeding loblolly pine was greatly facilitated by the cooperation of the Louisiana Forestry Commission and many of Louisiana's industrial landowners, especially International Paper Company, Bodcaw Company, T. L. James & Company, Crosby Chemicals, Inc., Hillyer-Deutsch-Edwards, Inc., and Roy O. Martin Lumber Company. These organizations provided seed, equipment, labor, and sites for most of the tests.

Assistance in screening repellents and in appraising seed losses to birds and mammals was furnished by the Denver Wildlife Research Center, a unit of the Bureau of Sport Fisheries and Wildlife, Fish and Wildlife Service, U. S. Department of the Interior.

CONTENTS

Small mammals cause heavy seed losses on most sites unless endrin is used in the repellent coating.

The guidelines offered here were formulated from a large number of detailed studies on small plots, and are supported by observations on most of the commercial operations in the State. Enough trials have been made in neighboring states to show that the information is applicable to reasonably broad areas without change. It is anticipated, however, that adjustments in some of the prescriptions will be necessary to fit local conditions in more distant parts of the loblolly pine range. The most obvious example is the optimum date of sowing, which varies from 3 to 5 weeks throughout the broad range of the species. The possibility of other deviations is pointed out in appropriate sections.

As the southern pines differ in their response to the basic factors affecting germination and survival, no attempt should be made to apply the rules contained here to other species. Detailed guidelines for direct seeding longleaf pine were published by the authors in 1959, and interim recommendations for slash pine are available in several publications.

This paper is intended to cover all of the steps from selection of sites to evaluation of the newly established stands. Each phase is presented in sufficient detail to permit foresters inexperienced in seeding to plan and execute a commercial operation. No literature is cited in the text, but some references for further reading are listed at the end of the text.

PLANNING

should not be seeded if it cannot be planted with high survival (this statement does not necessarily apply to rocky sites where planting is impractical). The recommended procedure for starting a direct-seeding program is to restrict initial trials to average or better sites, and work toward more difficult ones as experience is gained.

Three situations should be avoided in any

direct seeding. First are steep, eroded sites where seeds are easily washed away. Second are upland soils with coarse, sandy surface layers that dry out and crust over within 4 to 8 hours after a rain. Rapid loss of moisture from the surface sharply reduces germination, although the sites may be quite productive otherwise. Furrow-seeding machines that bury seed ½ to 1 inch deep are being tested on such sites, but broadcast methods cannot be recommended. Third are sites subject to spring floods. Viability of loblolly seed is reduced by submergence for as little as 2 weeks, and still shorter periods lessen the effectiveness of the repellents.

Loblolly seeding has been successful under a wide variety of cover conditions—none have yet been found that limit applicability of the method. Generally, cover situations fall into two broad categories, depending on the amount of grass. The first includes open, cutover sites and old fields with dense grass (fig. 1). For consistent success on such areas, disking or other mechanical seedbed preparation is required to reduce competition for soil moisture during the critical first year and to prevent seedlings from being smothered by the grass.

The other category consists of upland sites dominated by low-grade hardwoods (fig. 2) and poorly stocked stands of loblolly-shortleaf and mixed pine-hardwoods. While these areas are the most costly to plant, they are the easiest and cheapest to seed. A burn to remove excessive litter ordinarily is adequate site prep-

Figure 1 —**Heavy grass on open areas competes severely with first-year seedlings.**

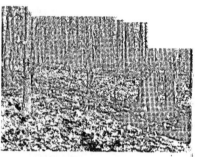

Figure 2 —**Areas with dense hardwoods are good seeding chances, because grass is never a problem.**
(Photo by Louisiana Forestry Commission.)

aration, because the native sod is too sparse to hamper survival or growth of pine seedlings.

The natural range of loblolly extends along the Coastal Plain from New Jersey to Florida and westward to the eastern part of Texas; it includes most of the Piedmont. Within this range loblolly grows vigorously on many types of soils, but excels on moist, well-drained sites. On extremely wet or dry sites other species usually fare better. Slash pine is preferred on the "flatwoods" soils of the lower Gulf Coastal Plain where a tight, impervious subsoil lies within 4 to 12 inches of the surface and the water table is high most of the winter. Deep coarse sands, such as those in western Florida, are also poor choices for loblolly, for growth is slow and tipmoth infestation is apt to be severe. Longleaf, and possibly sand pine, are the best species for droughty sands in the southern part of the range; in the northern extremes, shortleaf is often the best choice.

The chances are good that loblolly will grow satisfactorily wherever it occurred in virgin stands. If past performance is unknown, the vigor of young natural reproduction on the site, or on similar ones nearby, may serve as a guide.

Site inspection and protection

Sites should be chosen and inspected at least 8 months in advance, so that plans can be made for seedbed preparation, seed pro-

2

curement, and special protection. A map is needed for the examination, and aerial photographs are helpful, especially for tracts over 500 acres. Items to note or map include severe grazing by livestock; infestations of town ants, harvester ants, and pocket gophers; signs of unusual predators; areas with adequate natural reproduction; condition of the seedbed and need for burning; and advantageous ridges for flagging if aerial sowing is contemplated.

Light grazing by cattle is not usually a hazard, but in heavy concentrations animals cause damage by trampling as well as browsing. All forms of seedbed preparation—burning, furrowing, and disking—as well as hardwood control attract livestock from several miles about. The hazard from cattle is greatest on areas which are so small that the congregation of a few animals results in an overgrazing condition. Damage rarely is serious on tracts of 1,000 acres or more.

It is necessary, then, to appraise the number of livestock using nearby areas, as well as those on the area to be seeded, to estimate the severity of grazing after cultural treatments are initiated. Danger of overgrazing may be minimized by burning more acreage than will be sown, or by burning nearby tracts as a di-versionary measure. In severe situations temporary fencing may be needed until seedlings exceed 5 feet tall, when they are safe from grazing animals.

Town ants, found only in portions of Louisiana and Texas, destroy seed and seedlings. Colonies should be fumigated in the winter before sowing, and annually thereafter until the pines are no longer vulnerable. Harvester ants inhabit sandy sites throughout the South. If numerous, nests should be poisoned before sowing. Since these ants attack only seed, and not seedlings, follow-up treatments are unnecessary.

Pocket gophers, often called salamanders, feed on the roots of young pines. In a few years their inconspicuous damage can seriously deplete a pine stand. They should be killed (by placing poisoned grain in underground tunnels) prior to seeding, with annual retreatments if inspections indicate a resurgence of the population. When populations are high, large mammals such as deer or rabbits can heavily damage young seedling stands. Assistance of State game technicians should be sought when game animals are a problem.

Woods hogs occasionally harm loblolly seedlings, and will bear close watching.

SEEDBED PREPARATION

The choice of seedbed depends largely on cover and site conditions, and on probable distribution of summer rains.

As previously indicated, disking is unnecessary on areas where hardwood trees or brush shade out most of the grass. Burning is required only if the litter is deep enough to prevent seed from reaching mineral soil. Specific criteria on litter depth have not been developed, but a good rule-of-thumb is not to burn unless ground fuels are heavy and continuous enough to carry fire over the entire area.

The best time to burn is in the autumn when about half the leaves have fallen from the hardwoods and when the litter is dry. Freshly dropped leaves help carry the fire where the old litter is matted down. If the weather is wet at this time, burns can be made at any time during the winter.

Landowners who lack the necessary equipment for burning or are unwilling to risk spreading fire to adjacent land may resort to seed spotting, described in the section on hand sowing.

Open, treeless areas with a heavy sod should be disked for consistent success. Summer disking—anytime from July to October—is preferred because the best kill of grass roots is obtained if the sod is turned when the weather is hot. Moreover, allowing time for the soil to settle minimizes seed losses from silting, which have been as high as 50 percent on fresh disking.

Burning off the accumulation of dead grass facilitates pulverization of the soil by the disk

3

Figure 3 —**For best pulverization, heavy roughs should be burned before they are disked.** (Photo by Louisiana Forestry Commission)

(fig. 3). The burn can be made immediately before disking or during the preceding winter.

A heavy-duty offset disk, cutting about a 7½-foot swath, does a good job at a reasonable cost. It can be pulled by a light crawler tractor of the kind commonly used for planting or to pull fire plows. A single disking reduces the grass competition enough to facilitate pine establishment. Costs can be reduced if disking

is done in strips spaced 6 to 8 feet apart edge-to-edge (fig. 4). In commercial operations, expenses of strip disking have ranged from $1.50 to $2.00 per acre when light tractors such as John Deere models 420 and 440 were used.

Plowed furrows have not proved satisfactory, although they may have limited utility under special conditions. Their main drawbacks are that seed is washed away on sloping

Figure 4 —**In a light rough, a single pass with an offset disk prepares strips for seeding.**

ground or killed by flooding on flat, poorly drained sites. Furrowing has been effective in several operations on flat, well-drained, sandy sites where flooding and washing were minor. Furrow seeding, a technique entirely different from sowing in plowed furrows, will be discussed in the section on methods of sowing.

There is an intermediate condition between the open, grassy areas and those with a heavy cover of hardwoods. Frequently hardwoods grow as individuals or in small groups, and the grass is light beneath them but fairly dense in openings (fig. 5). Here the soil type

Figure 5.—Scattered hardwoods often have patchy stands of heavy grass that may need disking if the soil is droughty. (Photo by Louisiana Forestry Commission)

largely determines the kind of seedbed to prepare. Sandy or droughty soils should be disked. On soils with good moisture, disking is unnecessary but burning may be desirable to reduce grass and litter.

Open areas or those with a partial stand of hardwoods are often direct seeded with no more site preparation than a burn, even though disking is recommended. The chance for success, however, is substantially less than on disked sites. In a wet summer enough seedlings will survive and outgrow the grass to form a good stand. In dry years mortality is heavy and stocking is further depleted as grasses overtop and smother seedlings. Summer droughts of 4 to 6 weeks are common in Louisiana, and in adverse years dry periods may last for 2 or 3 months; satisfactory stands have nearly always been attained on disked strips, but seedings on fresh burns or light roughs have succeeded in only about 5 years out of 10. These odds may differ in other parts of the loblolly range, especially in the southerly and easterly portions where summer rains are more evenly distributed. Where droughts are uncommon, local tests may be advisable to verify the need for seedbed preparation.

Disking may be justified by improved growth even if not needed for protection against drought. In 9-year-old direct-seeded stands in Louisiana, dominant loblolly pines averaged 19.2 feet tall on disked strips, while those established on a light rough were 15.2 feet (fig. 6). The difference represents almost 2 years' growth—more than enough to offset the cost of disking.

Figure 6.—Disking for seedbed preparation not only protects against first-year drought but also improves growth. At age 9 years the trees at left, which were seeded on disked strips, are 4 feet taller than those at right, which were established on a light rough.

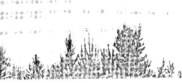

SEED PROCUREMENT

Procurement of seed should be arranged well in advance, preferably as soon as the site is selected and inspected. At that time, the amount of seed can be determined from the acreage and the indicated sowing rate.

Of the several ways to obtain seed, the easiest is to buy it from a commercial dealer. Prices have ranged from $2.50 to $4.50 per pound in recent years, depending on the abundance of seed and the quantity purchased.

Buying has several disadvantages. First, seed from a local source is difficult to obtain unless a commercial kiln is nearby; yet seed source probably is more important for loblolly than for any other southern pine. Loblolly from nonlocal sources may grow more slowly than the native race, have poorer form, or be more susceptible to diseases or insects. A second disadvantage of buying seed is the probability that it will be from trees with inferior form or growth rate. Ordinarily, commercial dealers buy cones from small collectors who pick largely from inferior trees removed in improvement cuttings or limby trees that are easy to climb (fig. 7).

When purchasing seed, minimum standards for viability, soundness, purity, and moisture content should be specified. Carefully handled seed, whether fresh or stored, should have at least 80 percent germinability on a sound seed basis. Lower viability suggests that the lot has been mishandled and its vigor has started to decline.

Seed should be cleaned until empties are 10 percent or less by number and impurities are under 2 percent by weight. Trash must be removed, because it may clog sowing machines and thus cause poor seed distribution.

A moisture content of 10 percent or less should be specified, both to get as nearly as possible the maximum number of seeds per pound and to avoid the need for drying the seed if it is to be stored.

When it is desired to have the dealer stratify the seed and treat it with repellents, costs for these treatments should be negotiated separately from the price of the seed. It is uneconomical to pay the same price per pound for stratified and repellent-coated seed as for untreated seed, because the treatments add great-

Figure 7.—Why gamble on seed from trees of poor form?

ly to the original weight of the seed and correspondingly decrease the number of seeds per pound when the seed is reweighed after treatment.

This may be illustrated as follows. Stratification adds about 25 percent to the weight of seed, and coating with repellents adds about 20 percent. The two combined increase weight by 45 percent, which means that 0.69 pound of untreated seed will weigh a full pound after treatment. At $4.00 per pound, 0.69 pound of untreated seed would cost $2.76. To pay $4.00 a pound for treated seed would be equivalent to paying $4.00 minus $2.76, or $1.24 for the treatments. Stratification usually costs about $0.10 per pound, or $0.07 for 0.69 pound, and repellent coating about $0.30, or $0.21 for 0.69 pound, or a total actual cost of only 28¢ instead of $1.24.

In summary, then, seed should be purchased dry, untreated, and with moisture content, purity percent, sound-seed percent, and viability specified. Stratification and repellent application should be priced separately.

Often the user can get better seed by collecting cones locally and having them processed in a commercial kiln than by buying extracted seed. By hiring and directing his own collecting crews, he can restrict collection, in any but poor seed years, to trees of better-than-average form and growth rate. Total cost of drying cones and dewinging and cleaning seed in commercial plants ranges from $0.50 to $1.00 per bushel.

It is also quite feasible for a landowner to process his own cones. Specialized equipment is required, but its cost can be recovered if a substantial acreage is to be sown. A small, forced-draft kiln now available for about $1,500 will efficiently handle 1,000 bushels of cones in a single season. Equipment for dewinging and cleaning costs an additional $400. Improvised facilities are usually unsatisfactory: they are seldom efficient, and are likely to damage the seed.

Loblolly seed can readily be kept for 5 years or more. High viability will be maintained if the seed is dried to 8 or 10 percent moisture content, placed in sealed containers, and stored at a temperature between 0°F. and 32°F. Four prerequisites for successful storage are: (1) collection of fully ripe cones, (2) careful storage of cones in a well-ventilated building to prevent molding before they go into the kiln, (3) processing of cones within 60 days after collection, and (4) placing the seed in cold storage immediately after processing.

The ease of storing loblolly seed makes possible substantial savings. Supplies collected in bumper years can be saved for use in lean years. Not only are cones cheapest when they are most abundant, but seed yields are greatest. Thus, in years of heavy cone crops, yields often average 1¼ pounds of seed per bushel of cones, as contrasted to ½ to ¾ pound when cones are relatively scarce.

SEED TREATMENT

Cold stratification

As loblolly seed invariably is dormant, cold stratification is needed to speed germination and thus reduce exposure to predators and adverse weather. Completeness as well as speed of germination is usually improved by cold stratification, though a small loss in total germination sometimes occurs. A reduction is most common with old, highly dormant seeds, which are in greatest need of stratification. But rapidity of germination is so important that stratification is essential even though it lessens viability.

Optimum length of stratification varies with seed lots. For this reason, comparative germination tests with sublots stratified for different periods are recommended. When this procedure is not feasible, the blanket prescription is to stratify for 60 days.

Cold stratification is simple and economical. There are several methods, but the most common is as follows:

Cut the top out of a 55-gallon steel drum and punch a number of holes in the bottom to permit drainage of surplus water (fig. 8).

7

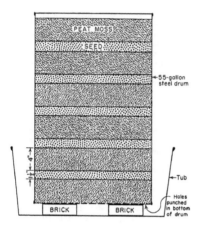

Figure 8.—Section of drum and tub used to stratify seed.

Set drum in a tub or pan and place three bricks under it (in the bottom of the tub) so that water can drain off freely.

Thoroughly soak granulated peat moss in water and pulverize all lumps.

Place 25-pound sublots of seed in large cotton sacks. Tie sacks with enough slack so the seed can be spread out to a uniform thickness in the drum.

Gently squeeze excess moisture from moss and place a 4-inch layer in the bottom of the steel drum. Tamp firmly.

Dip sack in water to wet the seed thoroughly and then place it on top of moss, spreading the seed inside the sack evenly in a layer 1 to 2 inches thick.

Add another 4-inch layer of moss to the drum, and tamp. Continue with alternating layers of seed and moss, and then cap off the drum with at least 4 inches of moss. Place drum in cold room at a constant temperature between 34° F. and 36° F.

Applying repellents

The process of coating seed with repellents is simple and fast. With inexpensive equipment, three men can treat 2,000 pounds of seed daily. Careful attention to details, however, is essential to obtain a coating durable enough to withstand repeated rains and wide fluctuations in temperature.

The equipment consists of a drum for dipping seed into the sticker, a tumbling drum, a fine-meshed heavy wire basket, scales, and heavy waterproof paper or tarpaulins. A shed or well-ventilated building must be available for drying seed if bad weather prevents sun drying.

The dipping drum and the tumbler can be made from 55-gallon steel drums (fig. 9). The dipping drum has the top removed. The tumbling drum, for applying the chemicals, is mounted on an axle attached to a frame and rotates end-over-end with a crank. It has a tight-fitting lid and a single set of baffles welded inside to help mix the seed and repellents.

The wire basket is about 20 inches deep and just small enough to be lowered into the dipping drum.

reating equipment. A small concrete mixer may be easier to

Fifty pounds (dry weight) of seed are treated in each charge. If seed has been stratified with 25 pounds to a sack, further weighing is unnecessary. Otherwise, the ratio of stratified to untreated weight must be determined so that each sublot can be weighed out accurately. For example, if 1 pound of dry seed weighs 1.25 pounds after stratification, 62.5 pounds of stratified seed should be used in each charge. Similarly, the blended chemicals, in quantities sufficient to treat 50-pound seed lots, should be preweighed and placed in paper bags.

The sticker is mixed with water directly in the dipping drum. It should be thoroughly stirred at the beginning and restirred between batches. (When mixing asphalt, stir until all lumps disappear.) Hard or dirty water should not be used because it will break the emulsion. The sticker should be discarded at the end of each day's work and a fresh batch mixed the next morning.

After the sticker is mixed, pour 50 pounds of seed, dry weight (2 of the original 25-pound lots stratified in separate sacks), into the wire basket and lower it into the sticker. Stir the seeds with a wooden paddle so that they are thoroughly wetted. In about 2 minutes, lift the basket and allow the surplus sticker to drain off for about 30 seconds. Next, pour seed into the mixing drum, add the weighed repellent, and stir it into the seed with a paddle. Then close the cover tightly and rotate the drum for about 2 minutes. Finally, remove the coated seed and spread it out to dry in a layer 2 or 3 inches thick on paper or canvas.

Aluminum powder can be added to the coating to hasten drying, reduce dusting, and lubricate the seed so that it will flow through airplane hoppers more freely. It has no repellent qualities. Half a cup suffices for 50 pounds of seed. It should be added to the treating drum after the repellents have been mixed with the seed, and the drum tumbled for another minute.

The repellent coating must be dried enough to permit free flow through hoppers or sowing machines. On bright, sunny days, seed can be dried outdoors in 5 or 6 hours. During inclement weather, it should be spread out in a well-ventilated building and stirred periodically with a rake. Fans blowing over it will hasten drying. Seed can also be sacked and dried in a forced-draft kiln operating below 100°F.

A small cement mixer will serve when the sticker is latex. Twenty-five pound batches of seed can be treated in mixers of 2¼ cubic-foot capacity, while 3¼ cubic-foot models will handle 50-pound lots. The seed is placed in the mixer with enough diluted sticker to wet it thoroughly. About 2 quarts of sticker are needed for 50-pound lots. The mixer is operated for about one minute and then the weighed repellents are added. The mixer is run again for another 2 minutes, after which either the aluminum powder is added or the seed is removed to dry. Excess tumbling should be avoided because it tends to rub off the repellents. This method is satisfactory only for latex, as the asphalt sticker does not weather well unless seeds are immersed in it for several minutes.

Small lots can be repellent-coated with a lard can, a small wire basket made of window screen, and heavy-weight paper bags. One-pound batches are best in this method. Seed is placed in the wire basket and dipped into the sticker in the lard can. It is stirred with a wooden paddle for about 2 minutes, lifted out and allowed to drain for 30 seconds, and poured into a paper bag. A weighed quantity of blended repellents is put into the bag, which is closed tightly and shaken vigorously for about 60 seconds. If it is desired to overcoat with aluminum, one or two teaspoons of the powder can be added and the bag shaken again for about 30 seconds. Finally, the seed is spread out to dry.

It is reassuring to check the potential durability of the repellent coating before sowing, especially when seed treatment is being attempted for the first time. This can be done after drying is completed by putting several hundred seeds in a small wire basket and running a full stream of cold water from a faucet over them for 2 minutes. If more than two-thirds of each seed remains coated, the repellents will weather satisfactorily in the field. A greater loss of repellents indicates improper application and the seed should be retreated.

Most of the seeding failures in recent years have been traced to improper handling of the sticker. Trouble usually stems from excessive delay in applying the chemical repellent after the seed has been removed from the sticker. Draining of surplus sticker should be restricted to about 30 seconds because if the sticker is given time to set much of the repellent can be washed off by rains. Careful storage of latex is also important. It should never be kept in a metal container or at temperatures above 110°F. or below 32°F. The emulsion is easily broken through improper storage and cannot be recovered.

Men treating seed with repellents are exposed to considerable chemical dust even when working outdoors. Some workers are highly allergic to Arasan, and nearly all are irritated by it. Endrin is a poison that can be absorbed through the skin. Consequently, workers exposed to it should wear protective respirators, eye shields, rubber gloves and aprons, and tight-fitting clothes. They should wash their hands and faces thoroughly before eating, bathe at the end of the day, and change clothes before going home.

Treated seed can be stored safely for periods up to 2 weeks if bad weather prevents sowing. Cold storage at 34°F. is preferable, but seed can also be kept in a well-ventilated, unheated building. The bags of seed should be stacked to permit free circulation of air around each one, including those in the bottom course.

SEASON OF SOWING

For Louisiana conditions, the optimum date of sowing on most sites is mid-February. Sowing at this time will result in the earliest possible germination with the least seed exposure. For other regions, a good rule is to sow 2 weeks prior to the average date of the last killing frost. Ordinarily, this will roughly coincide with flowering of early species such as redbud and maple.

When sowing cannot be completed at the optimum time, it is preferable to sow too early rather than too late. The danger of late sowing is the possible onset of an early spring drought that will reduce germination or kill the seedlings before their roots are well developed. The chances for adverse conditions usually increase as the season advances. On the other hand, sowing several weeks prior to the optimum date involves no special danger other than some unnecessary stress on the repellents, because seed will not germinate until maximum daily temperatures begin to reach 75°F. At that time, the risk of killing frosts is about over.

Special conditions may justify delays up to 45 days. For example, in southwest Louisiana several landowners sow in late March, when drying begins on flat, wet sites that have standing water most of the winter. Similarly, the likelihood of late winter floods in or adjacent to creek bottoms may dictate sowing later than normal.

Fall sowing of unstratified seed was recommended at one time for sites dominated by low-grade hardwoods. The seed, partially hidden by leaves, stratifies on the ground during the winter and germinates promptly in the spring. But it now seems safer to sow stratified seed in February, as overwinter exposure weakens the repellents. Stratified seed never should be sown in the fall because seedlings that might germinate would be winterkilled.

METHODS OF SOWING

Loblolly can be sown by hand, by hand-operated "cyclone" seeders, by airplane, by helicopter, and by tractor-drawn machines.

Hand sowing

Distribution by hand is efficient on small areas disked in strips. One man can cover 15 to 20 acres per day, and seed is conserved because it is cast only on the disked portions.

The "cyclone" hand-operated seeder (fig. 10) is useful on tracts up to 200 acres in size. Its greatest utility is on areas that are irregular in shape or that have scattered patches of established pines. Crews can quickly be trained to broadcast seed uniformly, and one

11

Figure 10.—

A hand "cyclone" seeder is economical on small tracts. (Photo by Louisiana Forestry Commission.)

man can sow 20 acres daily on open land with good terrain.

The chief disadvantage is exposure of workers to dust from the repellent coating. Use of anthraquinone instead of Arasan will eliminate skin irritations. Aluminum overcoating will reduce dusting and minimize the danger from endrin. Careful washing before eating and at the end of each day also is a necessary safety precaution.

Spotting is an old method that is being re-evaluated by many landowners. A spot about

1 foot square is raked or kicked free of leaves or grass, and 5 or 6 seeds are dropped on it and very lightly pressed into mineral soil. About 1,000 spots per acre are needed. It is estimated that one man can sow 2 to 4 acres daily if the underbrush is light. Although spotting appears impractical for large areas, it should be generally useful on small tracts.

A number of special tools have been developed for spotting. Most have a device for baring mineral soil and a mechanism for metering a predetermined number of seeds on the prepared spot (fig. 11). They sell for

Figure 11 —Three seed-spotting tools. A and B rake a clean spot, while C opens a small hole in the ground with 2 metal jaws.

$15 to $30. Each model has features that adapt it to special soil and cover conditions. A short-handled firerake and an apron for carrying seed probably are also adequate for most operations (fig. 12).

Figure 12.—A short-handled firerake is a practical tool for preparing spots on areas with heavy litter.

Rubber gloves should be worn for all hand seeding.

Airplane sowing

Fixed-wing aircraft, used extensively for direct seeding in the past 5 years, have con-sistently given excellent distribution and pre-cise showing rates (fig. 13). Their chief ad-vantage is the ability to broadcast large areas quickly when weather is optimum for prompt germination. Another advantage is that labor requirements are small. With a ground crew of 3 or 4 flagmen and 2 men to weigh and load seed, a light plane can cover 1,200 to 1,500 acres daily. Capital outlay for the landowner is negligible.

Airplanes also have drawbacks, some of which can be overcome by careful planning and reasonable precautions. Bad flying weather causes expensive delays and problems of stor-ing stratified, treated seed. The possibility of errors in sowing rates is always present, but can be minimized by screening seed before it is placed in the hopper, by methodical calibra-tion of the plane, and by limiting each flight to 100 acres or less. Seed is often wasted on hardwood bottoms or upland areas with ade-quate pine reproduction. This, too, can be largely avoided by careful site inspection, ac-curate maps, and close supervision of the pilot.

Any type of plane used in agricultural pest control can be adapted to direct seeding if slight modifications are made in the gate of the hopper. Most planes have long gates that can be opened wide for heavy applications of fertilizer or insecticide. When the gate is closed enough for pine seeding, the opening is so narrow that it often clogs. The solution is to set the opening wide enough to allow free flow of pine seed but to block off enough of the length to achieve the proper sowing rate.

Figure 14 shows an inexpensive method of converting the narrow slot into 4 wider, adjustable openings by blanking-off part of the gate with plates installed in the bottom of the hopper. The plates are wedge-shaped to help divert seed toward the openings.

Piper P18A planes have two openings between the hopper and distributor, each controlled by a separate gate about 10 inches long. Here again it is necessary to block off much of the gate length in order to have the seed pass through wider holes. This is accomplished by inserting, above each gate, a fixed plate having 2 holes, each 1 inch square. Flow through these openings is then adjusted by regular movement of the gate. A necessary preliminary to this modification is to synchro-

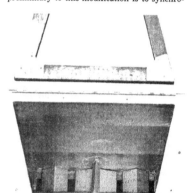

Figure 14.—Hopper with part of gate blanked off for loblolly seeding.

nize the two gates so that they open the same amount.

Costs of airplane sowing have ranged from $0.40 to $0.90 per acre, depending on the acreage seeded and the location of a landing strip. Construction of a temporary dirt strip on the seeded area has been profitable in several instances where other landing facilities were 8 or 10 miles away.

Helicopter seeding

Small helicopters, like the Bell 47G-2, have been used extensively for seeding, and with

Figure 15.—Helicopters can operate from small clearings and the landowner can ride with the pilot.

excellent success. Most landowners who have used different types of aircraft believe that helicopters distribute seed more uniformly than airplanes, although both are satisfactory.

In good weather a helicopter can sow 2,500 acres daily. The swath is 99 feet wide, as compared to 66 feet for airplanes. The craft can operate from small, level clearings; hence, little time is lost in ferrying. Because the seed is thrown out with a revolving slinger (fig. 16), altitude while sowing is not so important

Figure 16.—Seed from a helicopter is distributed through a slinger mechanism (at lower left in photo) over a 99-foot swath. (Photo by Elemore Morgan for T. L. James and Company.)

14

Figure 17.—Four furrow seeders that have been used in various parts of the South.

A.—Adjustable hillers (indicated by arrow) on the H-C seeder may be replaced with an agricultural sword.

B.—This seeder works on the same principle as the H-C, but the hillers are fixed in place.

C.—Front-end seeder with hopper in center of V-blade operates in heavy brush.

D.—Furrowing device is the same as in C, but sowing is on spoil after tracks have packed it down. (Photo courtesy Ernest Hinson.)

years, and new ones continue to appear. All have one feature in common: they prepare a seedbed and sow in rows at a single pass. Otherwise, they are so diverse and numerous that a full description of each is impractical.

Furrow seeders, the most common kind, are of 2 types. One has a middle-buster plow pulled by the tractor; the other has a plow mounted on the front end of the tractor.

Those pulled by a tractor scalp a shallow furrow and elevate a narrow mound within the furrow with a set of hillers (fig. 17A and B). Seeds are dropped from a hopper at predetermined intervals onto the mound and pressed by a packing wheel. Elevating the row reduces the chance of loss from prolonged flooding, and rolling the seed into contact with the soil improves germination. In another model the hillers are replaced by an agricultural sword. The sword opens a shallow trench for the seeds and the packing wheel covers them with soil. This modification is intended for light, sandy soils where the seed must be covered lightly to obtain complete germination.

as with airplanes. A big advantage of the helicopter is that the landowner can ride with the pilot and direct the entire operation.

Contract prices for the Bell helicopter vary with the acreage to be seeded. Usually they average $0.10 per acre more than the cost of an airplane. Greater daily production, however, results in enough savings on flagging to offset the higher rental.

Tractor seeding

At least 10 models of tractor-drawn seeding machines have been developed in the last 5

15

Front-end furrow seeders work best on sandy soils. They can be operated on brushy sites where the use of other types is limited. With one model (fig. 17C), seeds are dropped directly into the furrow and are pressed down by a packing wheel. Another model has a cutaway V-plow that pushes the soil directly into the path of the tractor tracks (fig. 17D). The weight of the tractor packs the loose soil and seeds are sown on each ridge from hoppers mounted on the rear of the tractor.

All types of furrow seeders will sow from 15 to 20 acres daily. Their main advantage is low cost per acre, resulting from combined seedbed preparation and sowing in a single operation, and from reduced seeding rates. The fact that they establish trees in rows may also be advantageous, but spacing within rows is not easily regulated, and this may retard growth. Disadvantages include: (1) high capital outlay for tractors and machines, with consequent temptation to sow beyond the optimum date in order to utilize machines fully; (2) rough condition of the ground after seeding; (3) displacement of topsoil (probably a serious drawback only on sites where fertility is low); and (4) limited utility—they perform best on sandy, level sites (some models are restricted to cleared or open sites).

Disk seeders were developed to sow two rows simultaneously with the same tractor power required for single-row furrow seeding (fig. 18A). They are also made in 1-row

models, for maneuverability in hardwood stands (fig. 18B). Two separate offset disk units, each 1½ feet wide, are mounted 4½ feet apart (edge-to-edge) on a tool bar behind the tractor. Behind each set of disks are packing wheels and seed funnels. A disk seeder can sow about 30 acres a day, and operates fairly well on a wide variety of soils. Sowing rates must be higher than with furrow seeders, because considerable seed is lost from silting on all soil types. These machines are too new for full appraisal, but disking in the cool, wet part of the year appears to be ineffective for reduction of grass competition. Many of the objections and advantages noted for furrow seeders also apply.

One of the earliest tractor-drawn row seeders deserves mention because it employed a rotatiller instead of a plow or disks. The rotatilled bed was 14 inches wide and 1½ inches deep. Seeds were dropped onto the bed from a hopper, and not covered or packed. Use of the machine was discontinued in 1955, after several years, because it could operate only on areas free of debris and roots.

Power-driven "cyclone" seeders are sometimes mounted on tractors to broadcast seed. They are useful where brush is too dense for crews with hand seeders or when it is necessary to avoid excessive exposure of personnel to the chemical dust from the seed. As a light tractor can cover from 30 to 50 acres daily, the cost is comparable to hand seeding.

Figure 18.—Disk seeders have offset disks for flat-breaking.

A.—The 2-row model covers 30 acres a day in open country.

B.—Single-row machine for operating among hardwoods. An innovation is that the disks are of graduated size. (Photo by Elemore Morgan for T. L. James and Company.)

RATE OF SOWING

Recommended sowing rates per acre are 1 pound when broadcast, ¾ pound for disk seeding, and ½ pound for furrow seeding. These weights are in terms of seed before stratification and repellent-coating, and at least 80 percent viable.

When well cleaned, loblolly seed numbers about 17,500 to the pound. Initial catches (stands in May before the start of hot, dry weather) in commercial operations over the last 4 years have averaged about 5,000 seedlings per acre from 1 pound of seed. This is not considered to be excessive, because first-summer mortality on experimental plots has often reached 80 percent in dry years, even on disked seedbeds. Therefore, consistent success in loblolly seeding is dependent on high

initial catches that can be achieved only by sowing the recommended rates.

Some landowners have reduced rates 30 to 50 percent to cut costs and to avoid overdense stocking in favorable years. Usually they have obtained satisfactory stands, because summer weather over much of the South has been generally good since commercial seeding of loblolly started in 1957. In Louisiana dry summers can be expected about 5 years in 10, however, and sowing rates should be cut only when it is clearly understood that the chances for success are lessened by doing so. The best plan for those starting to seed is to use recommended rates for several years and gradually reduce them if experience in specific areas shows that it can be done safely.

CALIBRATING SOWING EQUIPMENT

Any of the machines described will sow loblolly accurately and uniformly if the repellent coating is dry, and if trash and clumps of seed (stuck together with the repellents) have been screened out. Putting seed through ¼-inch hardware cloth immediately before it is placed in a hopper will insure against clogging.

Calibration of machines for broadcast sowing (aircraft and cyclone seeders) and subsequent checking are accomplished by area control. In other words, a predetermined quantity of seed is broadcast on an area of known size, with the assumption that distribution is equally good over the entire area. Procedures for calibrating a fixed-wing airplane are as follows:

Determine the ratio of dry seed to stratified repellent-treated seed. Ordinarily, the weight gain will average about 45 percent; that is, 1 pound of untreated seed will weigh 1.45 pounds after it has been stratified and coated.

Select three 20-acre areas with regular boundaries and measure off 1-chain flight strips on each end of the area to guide the flagmen. A 66-foot swath has given excellent seed distribution with all airplanes used so far.

Open the hopper gate ¼ inch. If the plane has twin gates, set both for the same opening. Check gate to be certain it opens the same width each time, because loose linkage is found with almost all airplanes.

Weigh seed needed for 20 acres. Add 20 pounds extra for a reserve in the hopper. Screen seed before it is loaded into the plane.

Sow the 20-acre test area crosswind at normal speed. Flying parallel to the wind results in varying ground speeds and differential sowing rates.

Weigh seed remaining in hopper to determine accuracy of sowing. Adjust as needed, and sow another 20-acre test area in the same manner. Three flights ordinarily will calibrate an airplane satisfactorily. A pilot experienced in direct-seeding often sets the hopper gate correctly on the first or second try.

Once the airplane is calibrated, gradually increase the area sown on each flight to 100 acres. Seeding more than 100 acres per flight is risky, because mistakes in the sowing rate are almost impossible to correct.

17

Calibration of helicopters and of hand or tractor-mounted "cyclone" seeders follows the same general pattern. Helicopters seed a 99-foot swath, hand seeders 16¼ feet, and tractor-mounted seeders about 40 feet. A calibration area of 1 acre is adequate for hand seeders; a strip ½-mile long is equivalent to 1 acre. For tractor-mounted cyclone seeders, 5 acres (a strip 5,450 feet long and 40 feet wide) are enough.

Small adjustments in hopper openings are usually required during the day as the relative humidity changes. Absorption and loss of moisture by the repellent seed coating influence the rate of flow.

Aerial seeding should not be attempted when winds are gusty or exceed 10 miles per hour. Crosswinds have little or no effect on the width of the seed swath, but they change the pattern, shortening the distribution upwind and extending it downwind. Sowing in gusty winds must be avoided because the aircraft flies an irregular course and differential drift of seed results in erratic distribution.

A plane's altitude has some effect on the width of the swath. Flying at heights of 80-125 feet will give good distribution if ridges are cleared by 60 feet. Below this level, strip width narrows excessively. Helicopters can operate at altitudes as low as 10 feet because the seed is thrown out the full width by the slinger mechanism.

Flagmen must be used to guide flights of aircraft. For accurate alignment, the pilot needs to see at least two flags, other than the one directly below the ship, after completing each turn. Usually three flagmen are sufficient, but more may be needed if the terrain is rolling or tall trees obstruct the pilot's view. Flags, mounted on long bamboo poles, should be a distinctive color and they should be kept in motion at all times when the plane is approaching.

It is best to measure and mark flagging points on the ground in advance. When flagmen pace off distances between strips, they

often get out of alignment and the pilot then has difficulty in determining the correct flight line.

A map showing flight lines and the acreage in each swath facilitates the entire operation (fig. 19). With this information the acreage

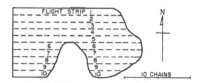

Specifications:
Flight strips: 1 chain wide (airplane sowing)
Sowing rate: 1 pound per acre (untreated, unstratified)
Weight ratio of treated to untreated seed: 1.4 pounds

Flight strip	Acres	Treated seed needed (pounds)
1	1.6	2.2
2	1.7	2.4
3	1.7	2.4
4	1.8	2.5
5	1.9	2.7
6	1.6	2.2
7	1.5	2.1
8	1.4	2.0
9	1.2	1.7
10	1.0	1.4

Figure 19.—Plans for aerial seeding should include a map of proposed flight strips, with acreage and seed requirements noted for each strip as shown on this small example.

to be sown for each takeoff and the seed needed are quickly determined, and the pilot can be told how many strips to fly before returning for more seed.

Tractor-drawn seeders are calibrated by checking the number of seeds dropped on 100-foot segments of prepared bed. For example, a rate of ½ pound per gross acre on plowed furrows spaced 8 feet apart (center-to-center) requires 320 seeds on a 100-foot segment if the lot contains 17,500 seeds per pound.

OBSERVATIONS AFTER SOWING

In initial trials it is quite important to inspect seeded areas systematically during the germination period. This is the only way to determine if unusual predators are present,

18

and to pinpoint the cause of failure when stocking is low. After several successful trials, these observations usually can be discontinued.

Because loblolly seed is difficult to find after a few rains, observation stations are helpful in checking the progress of germination and determining the extent and causes of seed and seedling losses. A station that has given satisfactory results consists of an identification stake, 50 extra seeds sown within 18 inches of the stake, and 2 seed spots screened to keep out predators. Screened spots should be several feet from the stake on level ground where the seeds cannot wash away. Window screening or hardware cloth with ¼-inch mesh makes satisfactory covers when fastened down firmly. The number of stations depends on the size of the area. If well distributed, 50 are sufficient to detect major depredations on areas up to several thousand acres. One man can inspect this number in a day.

Stations should be checked weekly until most seeds have germinated and shed their coats. Progress of germination, number of seeds and seed hulls found, and type of damage should be noted for each station during the weekly inspections.

Birds and other large predators take loblolly seed whole, leaving no remnants for identification. Tracks or droppings will sometimes afford a clue to their identity. Rodents and shrews characteristically crack the seed in half like clamshells, to get the endosperm, but the remnants are so much alike that they offer little clue as to the predatory species (fig. 20).

New seedlings are often clipped off near the groundline and the severed portions carried off or eaten. Clipping is most common in March, and the first seedlings to become estab-

Figure 20.—Rodents of all species split loblolly seed in a similar manner.

lished are hardest hit. However, total losses rarely exceed 10 or 15 percent. Unless seedlings on the observation stations are marked with pins immediately after germination these losses may go undetected. Rabbits, shrews, and crickets probably are responsible in most cases. If crickets are the culprits, pieces of the cotyledons can be found in the upper food chamber of their burrows. Rabbits and shrews will consume seedlings immediately after clipping them.

Ants also destroy seeds and seedlings. Harvester ants carry large numbers of seeds into their nests. Town ants take portions of the germinating seed and sections of seedlings to their colonies. Ants of several other species cause minor damage by feeding on endosperms after the seed cracks open for radicle emergence.

SEEDLING INVENTORIES

Two seedling inventories should be taken during the first year. The first is made in May to evaluate the efficiency of repellents against local predators and the effects of weather on germination, and to determine if release should begin from unwanted hardwoods.

Because first-summer mortality may be high a second inventory is required in the winter

following seeding. It measures the success or failure of the operation, for losses after the first year are negligible. It is preferable to use the same sample plots in both inventories.

The number of plots needed to estimate stocking depends on the accuracy desired and the plot-to-plot variation (expressed as the coefficient of variation) in numbers of seedlings. Size of area seeded and size of sample

19

plot influence the coefficient of variation. Experience indicates that, with plots of the size suggested here, a coefficient of variation of 100 percent may safely be assumed for areas up to several thousand acres. The formula for computing intensity of sampling with 67-percent reliability is:

$$\text{Sample plots needed} = \left(\frac{\text{coefficient of variation}}{\text{accuracy desired}} \right)^2.$$

If a landowner chooses to sample for $\pm$ 10 percent accuracy, the number of plots would be:

$$\left(\frac{100}{10} \right)^2 = 100.$$

When seeding rates, methods of sowing, or sites vary within an area, it is desirable to inventory homogeneous sub-blocks separately. Similarly, more intensive sampling is needed when accurate estimates for sub-units (i.e., by forties) are required.

For broadcast sowing, circular milacre plots equally spaced over the area are satisfactory. Average plot stocking multiplied by 1,000 provides an estimate of seedlings per acre. Distribution is expressed as the proportion of sample plots with one or more seedlings. These two statistics are closely related: adequate distribution is rarely obtained with less than 750 seedlings per acre.

Estimates on broadcast-sown disked strips require a modified technique. Two milacres—one on a disked strip and one on an undisked balk—are used at each sample location. The distance between disked strips (edge-to-edge) at each location is measured to determine the proportion of the area that is disked. To obtain overall stocking, average stocking on disked and undisked milacres is weighted by the area represented by each.

Where sowing is confined to rows, as on plowed furrows or on disked strips, inventories are made differently from those on broadcast areas. Sample plots, located mechanically over the area, consist of a 13.2-foot segment of a row or strip. This plot is divided into two 6.6-foot subplots and the number of seedlings on each is recorded separately. Distances from the center of the sample strip to the center of each adjoining strip are measured at each location to adjust average stocking to a gross acre. Seedlings per gross acre are estimated by multiplying the average stocking for 13.2-foot plots by

$$\frac{3,300}{\text{averaged distance between disked or furrowed strip centers}}.$$

Thus, if average stocking per 13.2-foot plot is 5 and rows are 10 feet apart:

$$5 \times \frac{3,300}{10} = 1,650 \text{ seedlings per acre.}$$

The constant, 3,300, is derived by dividing 43,560 (square feet per acre) by 13.2. If the size of the sample plot is changed, a new constant must be calculated.

Stocking percent based on 1,000 perfectly spaced seedlings per acre is obtained by multiplying the percent of stocked subplots (6.6-foot segments of strip) by

$$\frac{6.6}{\text{average distance between strip centers}}.$$

With this method, full plot stocking is less than 100 percent when the average distance between strips exceeds 6.6 feet. Maximum stocking obtainable with strips on 10-foot centers is:

$$100 \times \frac{6.6}{10.0} = 66 \text{ percent.}$$

The impact of strip spacing on subsequent seedling distribution should be carefully weighed when planning a seeding operation.

In seed-spot operations the simplest method of inventory is to determine the proportion of spots with at least one seedling. As more than one seedling per spot is excess stocking, it is unimportant to calculate the stand per acre. If the spots cannot be found readily, stocking can be estimated from mechanically spaced milacre plots.

SEEDLING RELEASE

On areas with overtopping hardwoods, pine seedlings must be released early in the first growing season. Delay until late in the first year or until the second year jeopardizes estab-

20

lishment of the stand and retards growth. The need for prompt release is most urgent on droughty sites and where dense, small hardwoods cast low shade.

The best procedure is to start hardwood control immediately after the May inventory, provided that there are sufficient seedlings to justify the work. If possible, all release should be completed before hot summer weather begins. Where a large area is to be treated, it is advisable to schedule the critical sites first, leaving work on better soils and in relatively open hardwood stands until last.

First-year release is advocated because studies by the Alexandria Research Center have consistently shown that delay lessens pine growth. Unreleased year-old loblolly pine seedlings typically average 3 inches tall, while those freed from hardwood competition before July average 9 to 18 inches (fig. 21). These studies also have shown that timely release markedly improves survival on dry sites, and on all sites in dry years. The most compelling purpose of early, first-year release is to prevent complete loss of seedlings in an adverse summer.

Any method of deadening hardwoods can be employed except foliar sprays that kill succulent yearling pines. As a general rule, it is best to use a chemical to inhibit hardwood sprouts that may resuppress pine seedlings.

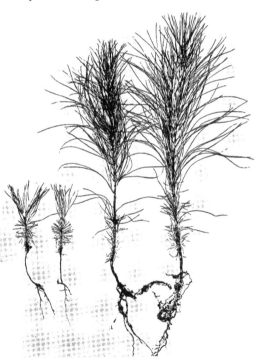

Figure 21.—

These 1-year-old seedlings demonstrate the need for early removal of overtopping hardwoods. Pair on right was released in June, other pair was unreleased.

21

COSTS

Costs, time requirements, and production estimates have been mentioned for many phases of the seeding job. The purpose of this section is to consolidate and summarize costs for the situations that are most often encountered. While the summaries will give realistic estimates of average costs, it must be recognized that size of the operation, individual efficiency, and price of seed introduce considerable variation.

Because a number of economies are possible in large-scale work, per-acre costs usually are lower for seeding large tracts that small ones, site and cover conditions being equal. Costs for burning, flying, and seed all decrease with increasing acreages. Data given here are for tracts 300 to 1,000 acres. Landowners seeding less than 100 acres should increase these estimates by 20 percent. On larger tracts, costs may be 10 to 15 percent less.

Seed is the largest single item of expense. Many landowners have been able to lower seed costs $1.00 to $2.00 per acre by collecting their own cones and having them processed in commercial kilns. This procedure also tends to stabilize costs if cone collections are confined to bumper years and seed is stored for use when cones are scarce. The price in the following estimates, $3.25 per pound, is the average for purchased seed in Louisiana during the past 4 years. Added to this is $0.10 per pound for cold stratification and $0.30 for repellents and the labor to apply them—for a total price of $3.65 per pound.

Labor rates are $1.00 per hour plus $0.25 per hour for insurance, social security, and the like. No allowance is included for supervision and overhead.

Broadcast sowing 1 pound of seed per acre on open areas disked in strips:

	Cost per acre
Burning	$ 0.10
Disking	2.00
Seed (treated)	3.65
Aerial sowing	.50
Flagging of aircraft	.15
Total	$ 6.40

Furrow seeding open areas with ½ pound of seed per acre, assuming daily production of 15 acres:

	Cost per acre
Burning	$ 0.10
Seed (treated)	·1.88
Furrowing and seeding	2.50
Total	$ 4.48

Broadcast sowing 1 pound of seed per acre on hardwood areas, with no allowance for hardwood removal:

	Cost per acre
Burning	$ 0.50
Seed (treated)	3.65
Aerial sowing	.50
Flagging	.20
Total	$4.85

Seed spotting on hardwood areas, 5 seeds on each of 1,000 spots, with no allowance for hardwood removal:

	Cost per acre
Seed (treated)	$ 1.22
Distributing seed (3 acres per man-day)	3.33
Total	$ 4.55

SELECTED REFERENCES

Barnes, O. L., and Nerney, N. J.
1953. the red harvester ant and how to subdue it. U. S. Dept. Agr. Farmers' Bul. 1668, 11 pp., illus.

Bennett, Wm. H.
1958. the texas leaf-cutting ant. U. S. Dept. Agr. Forest Pest Leaflet 23, 4 pp., illus.

Burns, R. M.
1961. seed sowing tool. U. S. Forest Serv Tree Planters' Notes 45, pp. 3-4, illus.

Cobb, H. C.
1959. seed collection and processing. direc seeding in the south—1959, a sympo sium, pp. 40-46. Duke Univ.

CROKER, T. C., JR.
1960. THE H-C FURROW SEEDER. U. S. Forest
Serv. Tree Planters' Notes 43, pp. 15-16,
illus.

DERR, H. J.
1959. TIME OF YEAR FOR DIRECT SEEDING. DIRECT
SEEDING IN THE SOUTH—1959, A SYMPO-
SIUM, pp. 114-118. Duke Univ.

———
1960. PREVENTING STICKER FAILURES IN DIRECT
SEEDING. U. S. Forest Serv. South. Forest
Expt. Sta. South. Forestry Notes 128.

——— and MANN, W. F., JR.
1959. GUIDELINES FOR DIRECT-SEEDING LONGLEAF
PINE. U. S. Forest Serv. South Forest
Expt. Sta. Occas. Paper 171, 22 pp., illus.

ERVIN, R. G.
1959. HELICOPTER APPLICATION TECHNIQUES FOR
DIRECT SEEDING. DIRECT SEEDING IN THE
SOUTH—1959, A SYMPOSIUM, pp. 147-150.
Duke Univ.

EVANS, T. C.
1959. FIELD TECHNIQUE FOR EVALUATING THE SUC-
CESS OF ESTABLISHMENT. DIRECT SEEDING
IN THE SOUTH—1959, A SYMPOSIUM, pp.
161-166. Duke Univ.

FERGUSON, E. R., and DUKE, W. B.
1956. COMPETITION AFFECTS FIRST-YEAR GROWTH.
U. S. Forest Serv. South. Forest Expt. Sta.
South. Forestry Notes 106.

HATCHELL, G. E.
1961. A LOOK AT 9-YEAR-OLD SEEDED LOBLOLLY
PINE. Forests and People 11(3):25, 44-45,
illus.

HOSNER, J. F., DICKSON, R. E., and KAHLER, LESLIE.
1959. STORING LOBLOLLY PINE SEED IN POLYETHY-
LENE BAGS AS A SUBSTITUTE FOR STRATIFI-
CATION. Jour. Forestry 57: 495-496, illus.

LEHTO, T. V.
1960. STRATIFYING PINE SEEDS IN PLASTIC BAGS.
Amer. Nurseryman 111(7): 15, illus.

McLEMORE, B. F.
1960. SMALL, FAST-DRYING CONE KILN. Forest
Farmer 19(13): 10-11, 15, illus.

——— and CZABATOR, F. J.
1961. LENGTH OF STRATIFICATION AND GERMINA-
TION OF LOBLOLLY PINE SEED. Jour Forestry
59: 267-269.

McLINTOCK, T. F.
1942. STRATIFICATION AS A MEANS OF IMPROVING
RESULTS OF DIRECT SEEDING OF PINES. Jour.
Forestry 40: 724-728.

McReynolds, R. D.
1960. MORTALITY OF NEWLY GERMINATED SOUTH-
ERN PINE SEEDLINGS FOLLOWING INUNDA-
TION. U. S. Forest Serv. Tree Planters'
Notes 43, pp. 23-25.

MALAC, B. F.
1960. MORE ON STRATIFICATION OF PINE SEED IN
POLYETHYLENE BAGS. U. S. Forest Serv.
Tree Planters' Notes 42, pp. 7-9.

MANN, W. F., JR.
1957. DIRECT SEEDING THE SOUTHERN PINES. Forest Farmer 17(2): 8-9, illus.

———
1959. INDUSTRY TESTS LOBLOLLY DIRECT SEEDING.
Forests and People 9(1): 22-23, 30-32,
illus.

———
1959. PREPARING SEED FOR DIRECT SEEDING. DI-
RECT SEEDING IN THE SOUTH—1959, A SYM-
POSIUM, pp. 52-59. Duke Univ.

——— and BURKHALTER, H. D.
1961. THE SOUTH'S LARGEST SUCCESSFUL DIRECT
SEEDING. Jour. Forestry 59: 83-87, illus.

——— and DERR, H. J.
1955. NOT FOR THE BIRDS. Forests and People
5(3): 32-33, illus.

——— DERR, H. J., and MEANLEY, BROOKE.
1956. BIRD REPELLENTS FOR DIRECT SEEDING LONG-
LEAF PINE. Forests and People 6(3):
16-17, 48.

MILLER, S. R.
1957. GERMINATION OF SLASH PINE SEED FOLLOW-
ING SUBMERGENCE IN WATER. Union Bag
and Paper Corp. Woodland Res. Notes 3,
2 pp.

RUSSELL, T. E.
1960. WHY GAMBLE ON PINE SEED? Forests and
People 10(3): 35, 42, 46-47, illus.

——— and MEANLEY, BROOKE.
1957. LISTEN FOR THE CRICKETS. U. S. Forest
Serv. South. Forest Expt. Sta. South. Forestry Notes 110.

SCOTT, LOUIS.
1959. FIXED WING AERIAL APPLICATION TECH-
NIQUES FOR DIRECT SEEDING. DIRECT SEED-
IN THE SOUTH—1959, A SYMPOSIUM, pp.
143-146, illus. Duke Univ.

WAKELEY, P. C.
1954. PLANTING THE SOUTHERN PINES. U. S. Dept.
Agr. Agr. Monog. 18, 233 pp., illus.

WOODS, J. B., JR.
1945. THE DIRECT-SEEDING GUN. Jour. Forestry
43: 39-40, illus.

23

SOUTHERN FOREST EXPERIMENT STATION
Philip A. Briegleb, Director
FOREST SERVICE
U. S. DEPARTMENT OF AGRICULTURE

GROWTH OF
LONGLEAF PINE SEEDLINGS
UNDER
LARGE PINES AND OAKS
IN
MISSISSIPPI

Lloyd F. Smith

SOUTHERN FOREST EXPERIMENT STATION
PHILIP A. BRIEGLEB, DIRECTOR
Forest Service, U. S. Department of Agriculture

When brown spot needle blight was controlled, longleaf pine seedlings survived and started height growth near large pines and oaks. Oaks were severer competitors than pines.

In 1949 a study was established in south Mississippi to measure the response of longleaf pine *(Pinus palustris* Mill.) seedlings to competition from overstory pines and oaks. An earlier publication [1] summarized results for the first 5 years after the seedlings were established—i. e., while they were mainly still in the grass. This article reports their development during the early stages of height growth.

THE STUDY

The competing trees were southern red oak *(Quercus falcata* Michx.), post oak *(Q. stellata* Wangenh.), and old- and second-growth longleaf pine seed trees. The old-growth pines had been suppressed in early life; their crowns averaged 18 feet in diameter, as compared to 22 feet for second-growth longleaf and 29 feet for oaks.

Overstory trees numbered 28: 12 pines and 4 oaks on the Harrison Experimental Forest in Harrison County, and 12 pines on the McNeill Experimental Forest in Pearl River County. (An oak from the original establishment died in 1953). Thus there were 84 plots near overstory trees, plus 12 check plots in the open.

A circle of 30-foot radius was drawn around each large tree and divided into 3 concentric circular zones 10 feet in width. A rectangular plot about 25 square feet in area was then located in each zone, and check plots of the same size were established nearby in the open. About half the plots had seedlings from the 1947 crop and half from the 1948 crop. Each age class was on a separate area that had been burned before seedfall.

Soils on both areas were upland fine sandy loams, well drained. Starting in 1949, seedlings were sprayed periodically to reduce defoliation by the brown spot needle disease.

RESULTS

When the plots were last examined, in January 1958, the 1948 seedlings were 9 years old and the 1947 seedlings 10 years old. To simplify comparisons, the data here presented are for an age of 9 years in both seedling classes. At this age the seedlings varied widely in size but most were making active height growth in the sense that they had attained a stem height of at least 3 inches.

At 9 years, average seedling survival was 86 to 100 percent (table 1). It was high on all plots except those with 1948 seedlings near three old-growth pines at McNeill, where, for reasons unknown, it ranged from 53 to 70 percent. Differences among the types of competition trees and among zones were not statistically significant.

A few seedlings had begun height growth at 4 years of age. By 9 years, 55 to 83 percent of the seedlings near large pines had started height growth, as compared with 89 percent of those on check plots (table 1). Near large oaks 24 to 68 percent of the living seedlings were making height growth; these percentages were significantly less than those for seedlings near large pines.

The proportion making height growth was consistently higher on check plots than near large trees (fig. 1).

Average heights ranged from 9 to 24 inches. In general, seedlings were smallest in the 0- to 10-foot zone and on check plots, but there were some exceptions near individual large trees. Differences in average seedling heights among zones were significant at the 1-percent level, but

[1] Smith, L F 1955 Development of longleaf pine seedlings near large trees. Jour Forestry 53: 289-290.

Table 1.—*Seedling data ata 9 years*

Type of large tree and competing zone (feet)	Living seedlings [1]	Seedlings making height growth	Seedling heights		
			Average of seedlings making height growth	Average of tallest seedling per plot [2]	Tallest individual in each treatment
	– – Percent – –		– – – – – – – Inches – – – – – – – –		
Old-Growth longleaf					
0-10	92	66	17	28	94
10-20	92	83	17	31	124
20-30	92	82	20	38	102
Second-Growth longleaf					
0-10	92	55	10	19	64
10-20	100	80	15	32	93
20-30	98	83	24	45	99
Oaks					
0-10	95	24	9	12	41
10-20	100	38	13	22	53
20-30	100	68	17	38	78
Check	97	89	21	38	86

[1] Basis: 10 seedlings per plot in 1952
[2] Means of tallest seedling per plot on 12 plots in each zone near pines and on 4 plots in each zone near oaks.

differences between the 20- to 30-foot zone and the check plots were not significant. Average seedling heights did not differ significantly by type of large tree.

One seedling per plot is considered adequate for restocking the stand. Height of the tallest individual per plot—i. e., the tree that will dominate plot population in the future—fol-

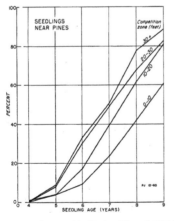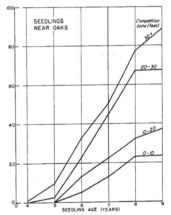

Figure 1.—*Percent of longleaf seedlings starting height growth, in competition zones near large pines and oaks.*

Guide for

EVALUATING

CHERRYBARK

OAK SITES

W. M. Broadfoot

ON

1961

Guide for

EVALUATING CHERRYBARK OAK SITES

W. M. Broadfoot

This booklet briefly describes three ways of estimating the capabilities of soils in the Midsouth for growing cherrybark oak (*Quercus falcata* var. *pagodaefolia* Ell.). The procedures were developed at the Stoneville Research Center[1] with data from 285 sample plots[2] in the area mapped in figure 1. The total height that a free-growing forest tree will reach at age 50 years was taken as the standard measure of site index, or site capability.

The purpose of the research was to find a way of evaluating sites in terms of the physical and chemical properties of the soil. Tests of 1,022 single and multiple regression equations indicated that site index can be estimated from depth of topsoil, depth to pan, and depth to mottling. When imbibitional water was substituted for depth to mottling the equation was slightly more accurate, but imbibitional water must be determined in the laboratory, while depth to mottling is easily measured in the field.

In the first of the 3 appraisal methods, depth of topsoil and depth to pan and mottling are sampled and then site index is read from a table constructed from the 3-variable equation.

The second method permits a rapid field estimate from observations of soil texture, internal drainage, presence or absence of pan, depth of topsoil, and inherent moisture of the site.

The third procedure requires identification of soil series and phase, after which site index can be read from a table of averages.

[1] Maintained at Stoneville, Mississippi, by the Southern Forest Experiment Station in cooperation with the Mississippi Agricultural Experiment Station and the Southern Hardwood Forest Research Group.
[2] Data for 26 plots were furnished by the Soil Conservation Service, U.S. Department of Agriculture.

Figure 2.—*Depth of topsoil is the most influential factor in the prediction of site quality for cherrybark oak. The plot shown at left has less than 6 inches of topsoil; that at the right has more than 6 inches. All other soil-site factors are approximately equal.*

3

oil-site description	Not eroded (more than 6 in. of topsoil)	Eroded (less than 6 in. of topsoil)
	– – – – *Site index* – – – –	
Fine texture		
A. Good internal drainage	95-104	80-89
B. Poor internal drainage		
1. Without pan		
a. Moist	80-89	65-74
b. Dry	90-99	75-84
2. With pan	75-84	60-69
Medium texture		
A. Good internal drainage		
1. Without pan		
a. Moist	110-119	95-104
b. Dry	100-109	85-94
2. With pan	85-94	70-79
B. Poor internal drainage		
1. Without pan		
a. Moist	90-99	75-84
b. Dry	95-104	80-89
2. With pan	80-89	65-74
I. Coarse texture		
A. Good internal drainage		
1. Without pan		
a. Moist	105-114	90-99
b. Dry	95-104	80-89
2. With pan	80-89	65-74
B. Poor internal drainage		
1. Without pan		
a. Moist	95-104	80-89
b. Dry	90-99	75-84
2. With pan	75-84	60-69

5

Table (soil series with particle-size / depth ranges and mean ± SD values; blank indicates less than 5 plots):

Soil series	Range	Mean ± SD	No.	Range	Mean ± SD	No.
Alligator	75-84	80 ± 3	10	90-99	95 ± 10	10
Alligator (eroded)	85-94	91 ± 5	17	75-84		
Bibb	100-109	93 ± 5	9	90-99		
Booker	90-99			100-109		
Brittain	80-89			75-84		
Buxin-Midland				105-114		
Carroll	75-84	115 ± 5	12	80-89		
Collins	110-119			100-109		
Daugherty (eroded)				95-104		
Dundee	95-104	98 ± 6	17	100-109	105 ± 5	16
Falaya	95-104			95-104	102 ± 7	11
Flint-Muskogee	85-94	89 ± 8	14	100-109		
Forestdale	70-79			95-104	98 ± 6	17
Gore (eroded)†	90-99	94 ± 1	6	70-79		
Hebert	80-89			80-89		
Hegary-Grenada (eroded)	95-104	100 ± 4	10	95-104	102 ± 6	5
Ina	110-119			95-104	98 ± 7	8
Iuka	110-119					
Lintonia	95-104	98 ± 3	8	95-104		
Mantachie				95-104		
Memphis-Loring	105-114			95-104	98 ± 3	8
Memphis-Loring (eroded)	90-99	111 ± 1	5	80-89	98 ± 5	17
Memphis-Loring-Natchez	80-89			80-89	83 ± 5	18
Mhoon-Waverly	75-84					
Olivier		86 ± 5	5	80-89	86 ± 5	5
Perry	80-89	82 ± 8	5	80-89		
Richland-Houlka-Gallion-Bowdre	85-94			95-104		
Scipio-Myatt	105-114			85-94		
Shannon	75-84			85-94		
Sharkey	80-89			75-84		
Tunica				80-89		
Urbo				90-99		
Yahola	95-104			90-99		

† Blank indicates less than 5 plots.

to cherrybark oak in the Midsouth.
them was obtained by felling trees
counting the rings at 8-foot intervals
stump to the top. These data were
height-age data from the study plots.
drawn by eye and the site index of

EXTRACTING, PROCESSING, AND STORING
SOUTHERN PINE POLLEN

E. BAYNE SNYDER

SOUTHERN FOREST EXPERIMENT STATION
PHILIP A. BRIEGLEB, DIRECTOR

Forest Service, U. S. Department of Agriculture

CONTENTS

EXTRACTING, PROCESSING, AND STORING
SOUTHERN PINE POLLEN

E. Bayne Snyder

Southern Forest Experiment Station

Four years of experiments at the Southern Institute of Forest Genetics have confirmed and amplified prescriptions of previous writers for successful handling of pine pollen. The warm, humid climate of southern Mississippi, conducive to rapid deterioration of pollen, afforded rigorous conditions for the Institute's work. The purpose of this paper is to report results of the tests and put them into form for practical application.

Current prescriptions for extraction, processing, and storage are summarized immediately below. In effect, they comprise the Institute's extensions and modifications of earlier and less comprehensive suggestions by Wakeley and Campbell (1954), Mergen *et al.* (1955), and others. Later pages discuss the experimental basis for recommending these procedures in preference to others and suggest possible refinements that await further research.

RECOMMENDATIONS IN BRIEF

Optimum stage for collection.—Ideally, strobili should be plucked just before they are ready to shed pollen. For any given tree the best indication of such maturity is actual pollen release by some strobili. Ripeness is also indicated when a pasty yellow juice instead of a clear one can be squeezed from the strobili.

Contaminating pollen may be floated off by immersing strobili in an overflowing container of water, after which the wet strobili can be partially dried with paper toweling.

Forcing.—Less mature strobili can be nursed into shedding if pollen nuclei have reached a sufficiently advanced stage. Branches bearing strobili that are nearly ready to shed need only be stored in a warm place for a few days, with stems in water. When shedding begins, the strobili are plucked for extraction.

If pollen is desired before natural shedding, very immature strobili may be forced. To avoid premature drying, clusters should be covered with plastic or sausage-casing bags until they begin to shed. Some viable pollen will develop from material collected in the tetrad stage, but germinability increases with maturity of the strobili.

Another way of forcing pollen is to cover the male strobili on the tree at the same time that the female flowers are isolated for pollination, and with the same type of sausage-casing

bags. This method is also useful in catching pollen from early maturing strobili on distant trees.

Extraction.—Both speed of extraction and quality of the pollen depend on exposing strobili to dry, warm (80° to 90° F.), moving air. They can be exposed either in closed kraft bags around which air is circulated briskly, or in screened funnels (covered with 10-oz. canvas) through which forced air is piped. In neither case should the strobili be piled more than one or two layers deep in the container. In damp, cold weather the circulating air requires artificial heating and dehumidification.

Before reuse, funnels and similar nondisposable extracting equipment should be decontaminated with rubbing alcohol, or by heating to 80° C. for 12 hours.

Drying.—For successful storage, pollen must be dry. It is dry if it pours smoothly like water, and falls freely from the walls of glass containers—i.e., is not sticky. It must also be free of sawfly larvae; these may be sieved out through voile cloth or 60-mesh screen, either during or after extraction. If relative humidity during extraction has been below 20 percent, the larvae will be automatically killed and dried up. Some drying of pollen can be accomplished during refrigeration, but this, even in combination with desiccants, may be insufficient.

Desiccation for 15 minutes at 5 mm. of vacuum will quickly reduce moisture content to a safe level. Silica gel (part tell-tale grade) is a convenient desiccant.

Storage.—Pollen keeps best in containers no bigger than 2-oz. pill bottles and filled no more than half way. These should be plugged loosely with cotton to avoid contamination, but not capped or sealed, and should be stored at freezing or slightly above. Accidental exposure to a humid atmosphere may be avoided by storing over a saturated solution of potassium acetate to maintain humidity at 22 percent. (This solution requires 2 to 3 weeks to saturate before it can be used.)

Dispensing.—When part or all of the pollen in a bottle is withdrawn for use, water of condensation must not be allowed to vitiate past good storage practices. It must be allowed to evaporate before the pollen is manipulated.

Testing.—Before use, stored pollen should be tested for germination.

EXTRACTING POLLEN FROM NORMALLY MATURED STROBILI

"It seems clear that standardization of humidity and temperature at which pollen is extracted must precede any careful work on pollen storage and barriers to species crosses" (Duffield, 1953).

Figure 1.—*Pollen extractor used for temperature-humidity tests.*

Agencies known to the writer use many types of extractors. Some enclose plucked strobili in sausage casings; others prefer wire cages in paper bags (Wakeley and Campbell, 1954). Some circulate dry air around extractors; others, including the Western Institute of Forest Genetics at Placerville, California, force dry filtered air through individual extractors by a blower and manifold system. The more primitive methods yield less pollen, and in damp weather increase the danger of spoilage.

When techniques for hastening the maturity of pine flowers become further advanced and specially designed batteries of environmentally controlled chambers become available, it will often be convenient to let strobili mature and shed while still attached to cut twigs (Barner and Christiansen, 1958; Worsley, 1959). The research to be described here, however, was concerned with the more general method of extracting pollen from plucked strobili that are placed in pollen-proof extractors through which filtered air is forced. This method produces dry, clean pollen, but to adapt it to the needs of the Southern Institute of Forest Genetics it was necessary to learn how various humidity-temperature combinations, and also the relative size of the strobili, affect extraction time, yield, moisture content, and insect pests of pollen from longleaf and slash pine *(Pinus palustris* Mill., *P. elliottii* var. *elliottii* Engelm.).

Methods.—Two series of tests were made, one in 1956 and one in 1957. Both measured the yield, moisture content, and germinability of pollen extracted at various combinations of temperature and relative humidity.

In 1956 two cabinets, each divided into 5 airtight compartments, were constructed in a refrigerator (fig. 1). One was heated to 20 and

2

the other to 25° C. Within the compartments, relative humidities of 25 to 65 percent were maintained with the aid of 1-liter dishes of sulfuric acid solutions of suitable concentrations (Wilson, 1921). Humidities were spotchecked with an electric psychrometer and found to be within 3 percent of expectation. The extractor in each compartment was covered with batiste, through which the appropriately conditioned air was pushed by a small electric fan. Each extractor was filled with 65 g. of strobili just beginning to shed pollen.

In 1957 both cabinets were kept at 25°, but a greater range of humidities was tested.

Pollen moisture was obtained from 1-gram samples oven-dried at 105° C. or above for 12 hours. Details of an improved method are given on page 6.

The medium used for pollen germination— 0.75 percent agar and 10 percent sucrose—was that developed by Johnson (1943). From a 10-ml. pipette, 0.25 ml. of the unsterilized medium liquified by heat was dropped near each end of a microscope slide. When the agar medium had solidified, it was dusted with pol-

len from a loop of wire. The slide was then set vertically in a staining rack and placed in a moist chamber for incubation at 28° C. for 72 hours (fig. 2). A pollen grain was counted as germinated when the tube growth was as great as the grain's short dimension. Counts were made of 50 grains on each of two drops on separate slides. Results were comparable to those from liquid culture, but the method was much faster. Processing, from preparing the agar through recording the data, was performed at the rate of 45 counts per hour. The coefficient of variation was 7 percent.

Results.—After a 36-hour extraction period, dry-weight yields for slash pine pollen were 3.4 g. at 20° C. and 5.4 g. at 25°; longleaf yields were 4.2 and 5.0 g. (table 1). Relative humidity (RH) did not influence yields appreciably in either year. In most trials extractions below 45 percent gave best yields, but exact conditions cannot be specified. They apparently vary with the maturity of the strobili. Probably because of their larger mass, longleaf strobili required about 5 percent lower RH to make them comparable to slash pine strobili in yield and in pollen moisture content (MC).

Figure 2.—

A moist chamber for testing pollen germination. The racks hold 140 microscope slides, each with 2 drops of agar that have been lightly dusted with pollen.

3

Table 1.—*Dry-weight yields, moisture contents, and germination of pollen extracted from 65-g. samples of strobili in 36 hours at various combinations of temperature and humidity* [1]

YIELDS

Mean relative humidity (percent)	1956				1957	
	Slash pine		Longleaf pine		Slash at 25° C.	Longleaf at 25° C.
	20° C.	25° C.	20° C.	25° C.		
	― ― ― ― ― ― ― ― ― ― ― ― ― ― ― ― Grams ― ― ― ― ― ― ― ― ― ― ― ― ― ― ― ―					
10				...	3.7	3.2
15			...	...	2.8	3.1
20	...	...	4.1	5.0	2.7	2.6
25	3.0	5.2	...	...	2.7	2.7
30	...	...	4.2	5.2	2.8	2.9
35	3.1	5.2	4.3	5.0	3.4	2.8
40	...	...	...	...	2.9	2.5
45	3.7	5.7	4.2	5.0	2.5	2.8
50	...	...	...	...	2.2	2.3
55	4.0	5.5			2.2	2.6
60	...	...	...	...	...	...
65	3.3	5.4	...	...	...	...

MOISTURE CONTENTS

Mean relative humidity (percent)	Slash pine 20° C.	Slash pine 25° C.	Longleaf pine 20° C.	Longleaf pine 25° C.	Slash at 25° C.	Longleaf at 25° C.
	― ― ― ― ― ― ― ― ― ― ― ― ― ― ― Percent ― ― ― ― ― ― ― ― ― ― ― ― ― ― ―					
10			...		11	13
15			...	...	12	14
20	...	...	17	12	14	19
25	11	11	...	...	16	20
30	...	...	15	13	17	22
35	14	11	18	14	24	24
40	...	...	...	...	29	28
45	14	13	29	15	35	36
50	...	...	...	...	36	38
55	14	13			40	43
60	...	...	...	...	...	...
65	22	15	...	...	...	...

GERMINATIONS

Mean relative humidity (percent)		After 10 weeks	After 6 weeks
10		97	95
15		95	95
20		97	95
25	At 3 days after extraction, samples composited over all humidities germinated 96 to 98 percent.	94	95
30		97	93
35		91	93
40		69	94
45		58	86
50		59	85
55		59	79

[1] Values in the table are means of pollen from 2 slash and 4 longleaf trees in 1956, and from 3 different slash and 4 different longleaf trees in 1957. Pollen from each tree was extracted separately.

In 1957 the decreased yields and increased MC may have been due to the fact that strobili of both species matured about a month earlier than usual.

After extraction, the 1957 pollen was put in sealed containers and kept at 5 to 10° C. until germination could be tested. The storage period for slash was 10 weeks; for longleaf, whose strobili generally mature about a month after slash, it was 6 weeks. Table 1 shows that serious deterioration may occur during even brief storage when extraction RH has been above 35 percent. The difference in storage periods may explain the greater loss in viability of slash pollen.

In 1957, a correlation was noted between the abundance of pollen sawfly larvae (Xyela sp.) and RH of the extractor. For example, at 20 percent RH (16 percent MC) there were only a few dried-up larvae, while at 55 percent RH the larvae were many and vigorous.

Extraction appeared to be more rapid in the forced-air extractors than in other types being tried at the same time. Because a gain of a few hours may permit crosses that otherwise would be impossible, this point was checked by filling kraft bags with the same quantities of strobili as forced-air extractors. Enough pollen for pollinations was produced in 12 hours by forced air, but not until after 24 hours in the closed kraft bags.

Wakeley and Campbell (personal correspondence) found that pollen extracted in sausage casing bags spoiled more easily than that extracted under similar conditions in kraft bags.

Everything considered, this research confirms that of Duffield (1953), who suggested extraction at 15 to 30 percent RH. Possibly 35 percent would be safe for southern pines under some conditions, but lower humidity affords insurance against damp weather or sawfly larvae.

ADJUSTING AND DETERMINING POLLEN MOISTURE

The work just discussed demonstrated that the quality of pollen is affected by moisture content. Information on pine pollen moisture content is meager. Ehrenberg (1961) reported

naturally shed *Pinus sylvestris* pollen to have 6 to 9 percent moisture. This is well below the 10 to 14 percent noted in this paper for "dry" extracted southern pine pollen. If the difference is a species characteristic, southern pine pollen may be the more difficult to store.

A simple and effective method is to dry pollen over silica gel for 15 minutes at 5 mm. of vacuum. This treatment has saved portions of wet southern pine pollen, other portions of which spoiled when placed over a desiccant in a refrigerator. In four successive annual tests, pollen vacuum-desiccated promptly after extraction has had consistently high germination after 1 year's storage.

Moisture contents best for storage can also be attained by regulating the humidity of the storage chamber, provided that the pollen is dry enough to keep until adjustment can occur. At the Southern Institute pollens placed in storage at MC's of greater or less than 12 percent have come to equilibrium at 12 percent in an atmosphere of 22 percent RH and 5 to 10° C.

Two new ways of determining pollen moisture contents have been devised. The first was suggested by the phenomenon that most pollen freshly extracted at 35 percent RH, and hence with MC of 22 percent or less, can easily be jarred loose from the walls of a glass container. While failure to stick to glass is a rough criterion, it may be reliable enough for practical purposes.

The second method is a revised oven-drying technique. Attempts to dry pollen by the standard method encountered difficulties similar to those reported by J. R. Hart[1] and coworkers (1959). Hart thereupon worked out a more accurate procedure with pollen sent him by the Southern Institute. It is a modification of techniques published by the U. S. Agricultural Marketing Service (1959).

For this technique, moisture dishes are necessary to protect the samples from losing or gaining moisture before and after the pollen is heated in the oven. Heavy aluminum dishes similar to those supplied by the Fisher Scientific Company as Special, Precision, No. 1631, are satisfactory. Before dishes are used, they should be dried for 1 hour at 100° C., cooled in a desiccator, and weighed. The desiccator

[1] Chemist, Field Crops and Animal Products Branch, Market Quality Research Division, Agricultural Marketing Service, U S. Department of Agriculture.

should be airtight and should contain activated alumina or "Molecular Sieves" (Linde Air Products Company).

The procedure is to place portions (duplicates at least) of approximately 1 to 2 g. of the well-mixed sample in the tared moisture dishes, cover the dishes immediately, and weigh. When weights of the samples have been recorded, the dishes are set, with covers beneath, in a convection oven regulated to 100° $\pm$ 1° C. All dishes should be on the same shelf, with the bulb of the oven thermometer as close as possible to them.

After 1 hour at 100°, the dishes are covered and transferred from oven to desiccator for cooling. They are weighed at room temperature. Replicate determinations of moisture should check within 0.2 percent.

With 6 samples varying from 10 to 14 percent in MC, Hart noted a maximum difference of 0.2 percent in MC between the Karl Fischer chemical method and the revised oven method. He found 130° C. unsuitable because pollen changed to a dark brown, which indicated loss of carbon dioxide in addition to water vapor (Hodge, 1953). Temperatures lower than 100° C. were not tested because of the likelihood of failure in driving off absorbed moisture. No change in weight occurred if drying was extended from 1 hour to 6 hours.

HASTENING POLLEN SHEDDING

A problem frequently confronting forest geneticists is how to obtain pollen from late-flowering trees for application to early-flowering trees of the same or other species. Often days or weeks separate the natural shedding of pollen on different trees.

Forcing may be regarded as a part of the extraction process; sometimes the extractor is also the forcing container. F. C. Cech, P. C. Wakeley, T. E. Campbell (personal communications), and the writer have forced pollen shedding as much as two weeks prematurely by covering the strobili on the tree with sausage-casing bags. This technique is also useful for catching uncontaminated pollen from early maturing strobili on trees that cannot be inspected frequently.

Mergen (1954) forced longleaf pollen shedding in the greenhouse by December grafting of scions bearing male strobili.

Cuttings with strobili may also be cultured with their bases in water or in nutrient solutions, and their tops exposed to one or another special environment. Thus, Santamour and Nienstaedt (1956) forced hemlock pollen shedding by liquid culture of twigs under 20 hours of light. Barner and Christiansen (1958) demonstrated the importance of maintaining a high humidity, which they attained by putting plastic bags over clusters of strobili on twigs in liquid culture. Worsley (1959) successfully forced shedding of pine pollen by exposing the strobili to either 600 watts at 1 m. for 18 to 22 hours with temperatures up to 27° C. or to 200 watts at 1.5 m. for 24 hours with temperatures up to 20° C. He used plastic bags to keep relative humidity at 80 to 100 percent for ripening and 60 to 70 percent for shedding.

The results reported here were obtained with cuttings in liquid cultures. Repetitions of elementary treatments previously described (Snyder, 1958), and included in the following discussion, have continued to save several days of ripening time, but no new treatments have been consistently worth while.

Methods and results.—Eleven trials were conducted in the greenhouse with shoots bearing male strobili: Slash and longleaf pine were studied in 1956; longleaf and loblolly in 1957; slash, longleaf, loblolly, and shortleaf in 1958; and slash, longleaf, and loblolly in 1959. "Plots" consisted of 1 shoot apiece from each of 6 to 8 trees, and treatments were applied in factorial design, with 2 replications. Maturities when treatment began varied with tree source, and ranged from early meiosis to immature pollen. Strobili that shed pollen in the greenhouse did so on an average of 3 weeks after collection of cuttings. Treatment effects were measured by strobilus growth. Maximum strobilus elongation resulted in shedding; less elongation was also considered as a valid measure of treatment effects, even when no pollen was released.

In 1956, statistically significant increases were found for 25° C. air temperature over 20° C.; continuous 40-watt fluorescent light 18 inches above the plants (probably· as a heat effect) over no supplemental light; sugars plus bioticidal control (either 5 percent sucrose plus 0.75 percent ferbam or Floralife cut-flower preservative) over tap water control;

6

1960). Cumming and Righter (1948) say that the chances of getting good pine pollen are improved by deferring the plucking of strobili until the first prothallial nucleus of the pollen grain is microscopically visible.

STORING POLLEN

Southern pine pollen is at present being stored in quantities ranging from a gram to a gallon, in sealed or unsealed containers, and wet or dry—with variable results as a consequence. Both in research and in large-scale tree improvement there is obvious need for reliable methods of maintaining pollen in highly viable condition for one or more years.

In addition to storage at temperatures which can be obtained in a household refrigerator, there are at least two other methods for enhancing preservation. One of these, surface sterilization, has been practiced by Helmers (1950), Sato and Muto (1955), and Tulecke (1954, 1960). Tulecke has stored ginkgo pollen successfully for 4 years. Another way is to deep-freeze or vacuum-store, as exemplified by the work of Barber and Stewart (1957), Duffield and Callaham (1959), and Ehrenberg (1961). The last two papers give evidence that pollen from deep-freeze storage sets more seed than equally viable pollen kept at ordinary refrigerator temperatures. The Southern Institute of Forest Genetics has adapted the freeze-drying methodology of King (1959, 1961), whose research was stimulated in part by Hesseltine and Snyder (1958). The equipment is expensive, however, and the expected benefits are not yet fully confirmed.

For storage of pollens of most western pines at ordinary refrigerator temperatures, investigators, including Duffield and Snow (1941), Johnson (1943), and Duffield (1954), have found optimum humidities varying from 10 to 50 percent depending on the species. In recent research with western pine, Fechner et al. (1960) reported 35 percent germination at 50 percent RH after 6 years, while Stanley et al. (1960) obtained approximately similar germination after 15 years at 10 percent RH. Worsley (1959) found no loss in germination of *Pinus sylvestris* during 3 years at 10 percent RH and 0° C. For prolonged storage, Stanley et al. stress the advantage of 0° over 5° C.

Research at the Southern Institute of Forest Genetics has been limited to pollens with different moisture contents stored at 5 to 10° C.

Sealed vs. unsealed containers.—It was hypothesized that an optimum storage RH might be indirectly detected by finding the pollen MC resulting in best germination when storage is in sealed tubes, and equating this value with the RH equivalent. Unsealed containers were considered controls.

Pollens with known initial MC's were derived by bulking samples from the 1956 extraction trial (table 1). For slash pine, four 1-g. aliquots from each MC were placed in separate 15-ml. shell vials. Two vials were scheduled to be tested for germination after 22 months and two after 32 months. Before storage, the mouth of one member of each pair was corked and coated with hot paraffin; the other member was left unsealed and exposed during storage to the atmosphere above a saturated solution of potassium acetate. This solution is listed (by Winston and Bates, 1960) as giving an RH of approximately 22 percent; it requires several weeks to saturate before it can be used. The pollens and the bottles were weighed both before and after storage to determine MC after storage.

Longleaf pollens were treated similarly except that storage in sealed tubes was limited to 22 months and MC was not read.

Percentage of germination for each treatment was determined by counting 300 grains (50 grains on each of 6 slides).

Germination and final MC are shown in table 2. In the sealed tubes most MC's remained constant or declined only slightly. The one exception was in the 22-percent initial MC, where the pollen fermented, broke the seal, and fell to a much lower final MC.

Table 2.—*Final moisture contents and germination of pine pollens collected in 1956 and stored at 5 to 10° C.*

STORAGE IN UNSEALED TUBES AT 22 PERCENT RELATIVE HUMIDITY

| Initial moisture content (percent) | Slash pine | | | | Longleaf pine | | |
| | Moisture at— | | Germination at— | | Moisture at 32 months | Germination at— | |
	22 months	32 months	22 months	32 months		22 months	32 months
	— — — — — — — — — — — — — — — Percent — — — — — — — — — — — — — — —						
9	...	...	...	...	11	84	78
10	...	...	...	...	12	87	79
11	11	11	89	83	12	85	72
12	...	...	...	...	12	82	79
13	12	12	88	83	...	...	...
14	11	11	84	86	13	82	84
15	12	12	88	88	13	80	83
22	15	12	88	91	...	...	...
29	...	...	...	...	13	65	67
STORAGE IN SEALED TUBES							
9	...	...	...	...	...	88	...
10	...	...	...	...	...	90	...
11	11	11	91	79	...	92	...
12	...	...	...	...	...	85	...
13	13	12	86	80	...	...	...
14	13	12	82	72	...	79	...
15	14	14	79	64	...	73	...
22	11	8	0	0	...	...	...
29	...	...	...	...	...	0	...

8

When stored at 22 percent RH, most of the pollen came to an equilibrium MC of about 12 percent by 22 months; some vials lost and some gained, according to whether they were originally greater or less than this value. Germination as high as 91 percent was obtained after 32 months.

Optimum MC for storage appeared to be determined by and to vary with storage conditions, as follows:

For 32 months of unsealed storage in 22 percent RH, initial MC's of 9 to 22 percent insured germination of at least 72 percent. MC for best germination appeared to vary with length of storage, being 9 to 13 percent for 22 months and 14 to 22 percent for 32 months.

For sealed storage the range from 9 to 13 percent produced germinations about equal to those in unsealed storage, but at higher MC deterioration was greater. The difference in response from unsealed pollen is reflected in a highly significant *storage method* × *MC* interaction term in the analysis of variance. Visser (1955) stated from his work with several fruit, vegetable, and flower species that "Storage at 2-4° C. in sealed tubes appears to have no or little advantage over storage with an optimal relative humidity."

In 1957, pollens at various MC's were stored both sealed and exposed to 22 percent RH; temperatures were 5 to 10° C. The initial yield, MC, and germination means from the extraction data appear in table 1, and germination percentages after 22 months are in table 3. The results confirm those of 1956 in that sealing was detrimental with high MC's. In this test, though, even unsealed pollen suffered some reduction in germination if placed in storage at an initial MC above 25 percent.

Seed-setting ability was tested by Campbell and Wakeley (1961) in west-central Louisiana. Results (table 4) indicated that pollen of the sealed series lacked the fertilizing ability of the unsealed series, even when germination percentages were equal. Roughly 15 percent as many full seeds per collected cone were obtained from the best of the 2-year-old pollen as from fresh pollen. This is comparable to the 13 percent obtained with 1-year-old pollen in interspecific pine crosses (Wright and Gabriel, 1958), but contrasts with the 68 percent obtained with intraspecific pine crosses (Wright, 1959). Some deterioration may have occurred when the pollen was shipped from Mississippi to Louisiana.

Amount per bottle.—That pollen germination is sometimes poor if large volumes are stored in a bottle was shown by Snyder (1958). Worsley (1959) noted reduced germination in samples drawn from the lower portion of a test tube filled more than 5 cm. deep. The re-

Table 3.—*Germination of pine pollens collected in 1957 and stored at 5 to 10° C. for 22 months*

Initial moisture content (percent)	Slash pine			Longleaf pine		
	Samples	Sealed	Unsealed [1]	Samples	Sealed	Unsealed [1]
	Number	*– – Percent – –*		*Number*	*– – Percent – –*	
9-10	4	47	62	3	72	67
11-15	9	33	64	6	29	59
16-20	5	0	52	7	0	61
21-25	2	0	52	8	0	64
26-30	2	0	65	4	0	56
31-35	3	0	42	1	0	61
36-40	0	. . .	. . .	5	0	25
41-45	2	0	0	3	0	29
46-50	1	0	0	1	0	16
51-55	2	0	0	0	. . .	. . .

[1] In atmosphere at 22 percent RH.

Table 4.—*Seeds recovered from controlled pollinations of longleaf pine with pollen of varying germinations* [1]

Germination of pollen when applied (percent)	Full seeds		Proportion full
	Per matured cone	Per strobilus pollinated	
	– Number –		Percent
Stored unsealed			
65	11	3	88
74	14	3	22
Stored sealed			
58	0	0	0
76	6	1	11
87	5	2	12
92	13	2	22
Fresh pollen (control)			
92	91	26	96

[1] The stored pollen was from a single Mississippi lot extracted and stored for 2 years in different ways; the fresh control was from two Louisiana trees

sults reported here extend observations of Snyder (1958) to 22 months.

Samples having 12, 29, and 51 percent MC were stored for 10 and 22 months in 24-ml. vials filled to varying heights (table 5). Storage was at 5 to 10° C. and 22 percent RH. Germination percentages were calculated by counting 300 grains (3 bottles per treatment times 2 slides per bottle times 50 grains per slide).

With wet pollen (51 percent MC), storage in small amounts offered some protection for 10 months. Germination was 73 percent for pollen stored in amounts of 4 ml. per 24-ml.

vial, but dropped to 47 percent when amount per vial was increased to 20 ml. (table 5). The explanation probably is that the smaller amounts dried more efficiently during storage. The differences for 10 months of storage are highly significant, but after 22 months all pollen stored at 51 percent MC was dead.

Amount per bottle did not significantly affect the keeping quality of pollen at 12 or 29 percent MC.

DISPENSING STORED POLLEN

Mergen et al. (1955) warned against the wetting of stored pollen by water condensing on the cold glass walls of a container removed from refrigeration. Common observations that pollen apparently deteriorates when refrigeration is interrupted to remove samples prompted a study of the problem at the Southern Institute. The results showed that a few minutes of mishandling during withdrawal of pollen for current use may vitiate all the good effects of years of otherwise perfect storage.

Five-gram samples were stored at 5 to 10° C. in 2-oz. pill bottles. No pollen was actually taken out, but withdrawals were simulated by shaking the bottles. Pollen was "dispensed" in this way on two successive days; rainy periods in spring were chosen in order to make the tests as severe as possible. Pollen of two species was represented—slash at 50 percent initial MC, and longleaf at 12 percent. Slash was tested for germination 10 months after it had been dispensed; longleaf was tested after storage for 22 months, during which time it had been dispensed in two successive springs. Germination was calculated from counts of

Table 5.—*Germination, after 10 and 22 months of storage, by quantity of pollen per container
and moisture content.*

Ml. of pollen per 24-ml. vial	51 percent moisture		29 percent moisture		12 percent moisture	
	10 months	22 months	10 months	22 months	10 months	22 months
	– – – – – – – – – – – – – – – – Percent – – – – – – – – – – – – – – – –					
4	73	0	78	69	94	90
8	58	0	76	67	95	87
12	54	0	77	69	90	87
16	49	0	80	66	89	88
20	47	0	79	70	91	87

10

: treatment (50 grains on each

.marizes and compares the vari-
s. Treatment 1 consisted of re-
sealed bottle from the refrigera-
it to reach room temperature,
ome pollen, and restoring it to
till unsealed. Treatment 2 sealed
:viously unsealed bottle before
t out of the refrigerator but un-
. upon return. Treatments 3 and
and 2, except that storage was
es both before and after dispens-
or treatment 5, a sealed control,
6, an unsealed control refriger-
cent RH, were never dispensed,

but were brought to room temperature and then refrigerated. Treatment 7 was an unsealed control that was never removed from the refrigerator.

For slash pollen there were duplicate bottles for each treatment. One of these was put back into the refrigerator at night; the other left out until the end of the second day of dispensing. Longleaf pollen, in triplicate bottles, had a third treatment during the 2-day dispensing periods, viz., putting the bottle back into the refrigerator immediately after the dispensing.

Results indicate the benefit of minimizing exposure to air temperature during the 2-day dispensing period. Losses were heavy, however,

mination of pine pollen (slash initially at 50 and longleaf at 12 percent moisture)
after dispensing and subsequent storage '

Treatment after removal from storage until dispensing [2]	Slash pollen		Longleaf pollen		
	Refrigerated at night	At room temperature continuously	Refrigerated immediately after dispensing	Refrigerated at night	At room temperature continuously
	— — — — — — — — — — Percent — — — — — — — — — —				
Unsealed	74	72	80	78	74
Sealed after removal from refrigerator until dispensed	72	70	82	77	77
Unsealed after removal from refrigerator until dispensed	36	41	58	1	9
Sealed until dispensed	44	43	86	11	7
Sealed—never dispensed	30	19	87	89	83
Exposed to 22 percent RH—never dispensed	73	74	82	74	76
	55	53	79	55	54
Never removed from refrigerator	75		80		

10 months for slash pollen, 22 months for longleaf.
dispensed until they had reached room temperature.

11

only for longleaf pollen that was sealed in storage but left out of the refrigerator for 2 days in each of the 2 seasons. Germination for these lots was from 1 to 11 percent, as compared to 58 and 86 percent for pollen returned to the refrigerator immediately after being dispensed.

Eliminating condensation water by sealing bottles when they were taken from the refrigerator was effective only with the sealed-storage lots (cf. treatments 3 and 4, table 6). The lack of benefit with unsealed storage is probably explained by the subsequent removal of the condensed water through the desiccating action of the refrigerator.

TECHNICAL SUMMARY

Results from 4 years of experiments show that pollen can be extracted several days earlier than normal if strobilus-bearing cuttings are cultured in liquid. Best germination has been obtained when cuttings were taken after meiotic division had reached the tetrad stage. Low relative humidities in the extraction chamber have speeded recovery from fully matured strobili.

Either the use of dry air during extraction or vacuum desiccation after extraction reduced pollen moisture to levels safe for storage.

Relative humidity and temperature of air forced over strobili during extraction determined several characteristics of recovered pollen. Yield was satisfactory between 10 and 45 percent RH and was better at 25° than at 20° C. Pollen sawfly larvae were dried up

HESSELTINE, C. W., and SNYDER, E. B.
1958. ATTEMPTS TO FREEZE-DRY PINE POLLEN FOR PROLONGED STORAGE. Bul. Torrey Bot. Club 85:134-135.

HODGE, J. E.
1953. CHEMISTRY OF BROWNING REACTIONS IN MODEL SYSTEMS. Jour. Agr. Food Chem. 1: 928.

JOHNSON, L. P. V.
1943. THE STORAGE AND ARTIFICIAL GERMINATION OF FOREST TREE POLLENS. Canad. Jour. Res., Sect. C. 21:332-342.

KING, J. R.
1959. THE FREEZE-DRYING OF PINE POLLEN. Bul. Torrey Bot. Club 86: 383-386.

———
1961. THE FREEZE-DRYING OF POLLENS. Econ. Bot. 15: 91-98.

MERGEN, F.
1954. IMPROVING THE EARLY GROWTH OF LONG-LEAF PINE. Forest Farmer 13: 8-9, 16, 17, 19.

——— ROSSOLL, H., and POMEROY, K. B.
1955. HOW TO CONTROL THE POLLINATION OF SLASH AND LONGLEAF PINE. U. S. Forest Serv. Southeast. Forest Expt. Sta. Sta. Paper 58, 14 pp.

SANTAMOUR, F. S., and NIENSTAEDT, H.
1956. THE EXTRACTION, STORAGE, AND GERMINA-TION OF EASTERN HEMLOCK POLLEN. Jour. Forestry 54: 269-270.

SATO, Y., and MUTO, K.
1955. ON THE VIABILITY OF FOREST TREE POLLEN. Hokkaido Univ. Forest Res. Bul. 17: 967-980.

SNYDER, E. B.
1957. POLLEN HANDLING. Fourth South. Forest Tree Impr. Conf. Proc., pp. 111-115.

STANLEY, R. G., PETERSEN, J., and MIROV, N. T.
1960. VIABILITY OF PINE POLLEN STORED 15 YEARS. U. S. Forest Serv. Pacific Southwest. Forest and Range Expt. Sta. Res. Note 173, 5 pp.

TULECKE, W. R.
1954. PRESERVATION AND GERMINATION OF THE POLLEN OF GINKGO UNDER STERILE CONDI-TIONS. Bul. Torrey Bot. Club 81: 509-512.

———
1960. ARGININE-REQUIRING STRAINS OF TISSUE OB-TAINED FROM GINKGO POLLEN. Plant Phy-siol. 35: 19-24.

U. S. AGRICULTURAL MARKETING SERVICE.
1959. METHODS FOR DETERMINING MOISTURE CON-TENT AS SPECIFIED IN THE OFFICIAL GRAIN STANDARDS OF THE UNITED STATES AND IN

THE UNITED STATES STANDARDS FOR BEANS, PEAS, LENTILS, AND RICE. U. S. Agr. Market. Serv. Serv. and Regulatory Announc. 147 (rev.), 3 pp.

VISSER, T.
1955. GERMINATION AND STORAGE OF POLLEN. Meded. Landbouwhoogesch. Wageningen 55: 1-68.

WAKELEY, P. C., and CAMPBELL, T. E.
1954. SOME NEW PINE POLLINATION TECHNIQUES. U. S. Forest Serv. South. Forest Expt. Sta. Occas. Paper 136, 13 pp.

WILSON, R. E.
1921. HUMIDITY CONTROL BY MEANS OF SULFURIC ACID SOLUTIONS WITH CRITICAL COMPILATIONS OF VAPOR PRESSURE DATA. Jour. Indus. and Engin. Chem. 13: 326-331.

WINSTON, P. W., and BATES, D. H.
1960. SATURATED SOLUTIONS FOR THE CONTROL OF HUMIDITY IN BIOLOGICAL RESEARCH. Ecol. 41: 232-237.

WORSLEY, R. G. F.
1959. THE PROCESSING OF POLLEN. Silvae Genetica 8: 143-148.

WRIGHT, J. W.
1959. SPECIES HYBRIDIZATION IN THE WHITE PINES. Forest Sci. 5: 210-222.

————— and GABRIEL, W. J.
1958. SPECIES HYBRIDIZATION IN THE HARD PINES, SERIES SYLVESTRES. Silvae Genetica 7: 109-115.

'OREST GENETICS PUBLICATIONS

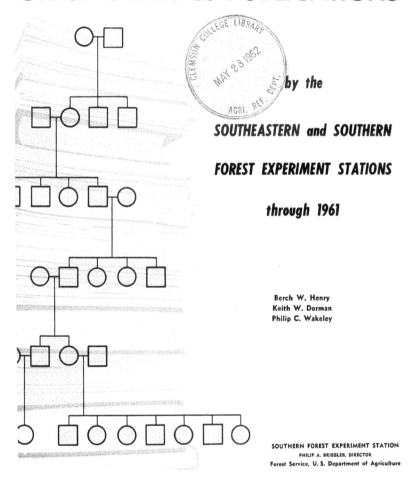

by the

SOUTHEASTERN and SOUTHERN

FOREST EXPERIMENT STATIONS

through 1961

Berch W. Henry
Keith W. Dorman
Philip C. Wakeley

SOUTHERN FOREST EXPERIMENT STATION
PHILIP A. BRIEGLEB, DIRECTOR
Forest Service, U. S. Department of Agriculture

FOREST GENETICS PUBLICATIONS BY THE SOUTHEASTERN AND SOUTHERN FOREST EXPERIMENT STATIONS THROUGH 1961

Berch W. Henry
Southern Forest Experiment Station

Keith W. Dorman
Southeastern Forest Experiment Station

Philip C. Wakeley
Southern Forest Experiment Station

The forest genetics and tree improvement programs of the South-eastern and Southern Forest Experiment Stations are closely coordinated and supplement or support each other at many points. Hitherto, however, the publications from them have been announced or listed separately by the issuing stations to separate mailing lists. As a result, many potential users of the genetics publications of both stations are acquainted with those of only one. The present unified list has been prepared to correct this situation.

The two stations published few genetics articles before 1940. During the 1940's there was a perceptible though still intermittent flow. After the middle 1950's the volume increased greatly as early long-time studies matured and new research programs got under way and began to yield results.

Most of the recent, and numbers of the earlier, releases and reprints are still available. Those marked SE may be requested from the South-eastern Forest Experiment Station, P. O. Box 2570, Asheville, North Carolina; and those marked SO, from the Southern Forest Experiment Station, T-10210 Federal Building, 701 Loyola Avenue, New Orleans 12, Louisiana.

This list is alphabetical by senior authors. An index of junior authors appears on page 27.

ALLEN, P. H.
1961. FLORIDA LONGLEAF PINE FAIL IN VIRGINIA.
Jour. Forestry 59: 453-454. SE
After five years, longleaf of local (Virginia) origin survived better (90 percent) than that from Louisiana (87 percent), Mississippi (81 percent), Georgia (76 percent), and southern Florida (48 percent), but was significantly taller only than Florida stock (7.7 vs. 2.5 feet). Florida longleaf was severely injured by temperatures between 12 and 26° F.

1961. NATURAL SELECTION IN LOBLOLLY PINE
STANDS. Jour. Forestry 59: 598-599. SE
On good sites in good seed years in the Virginia Coastal Plain a very large number of seedlings may become established, but only one of 60 seedlings may survive to maturity. Thus natural selection may be quite rigid for growth before artificial selection by forest tree breeders begins.

ALLEN, R. M.
1953. RELEASE AND FERTILIZATION STIMULATE
LONGLEAF PINE CONE CROP. Jour. Forestry
51: 827. SO
In the third and fourth years after treatment, released and fertilized pines produced several times as many cones as untreated trees.

1953. STIMULATION OF LONGLEAF PINE SEED PRODUCTION. Second South. Forest Tree Impr.
Conf. Proc. 1953, 3 pp. SO
Observations and designed studies in several places indicate substantial increases in cone production following release and some increase from fertilizing.

1960. CHANGES IN ACID GROWTH SUBSTANCES IN
TERMINAL BUDS OF LONGLEAF PINE SAPLINGS
DURING THE BREAKING OF WINTER DORMANCY. Physiologia Plant. 13: 555-558.
SO
Greatest changes were an increase in a promoter that chromatographs similarly to indoleacetic acid in isopropanol: ammonia: water and a decrease of an inhibitor found at Rf 0.6-0.7 with the same solvent.

1960. POLE STEPS FOR CLIMBING TREES. Jour.
Forestry 58: 563. SO
Telephone pole steps are useful on trees that are climbed repeatedly or are so far from roads that ladders must be carried considerable distances.

2

Forest Expt. Sta. Sta. Paper 126, 12 pp.
SE

After 4 years, heights of about 400 slash and loblolly pine seedlings in Georgia, selected in nursery beds for vigor, were 16 and 19 percent, respectively, taller than a similar number of controls from the same beds. Rust infection, survival, and tree form were about the same for selected seedlings as for controls. The tallest seedlings were over 14 feet.

——————— and ZOBEL, B. J.
1959. COMMENTS ON GENETIC VARIATION WITHIN GEOGRAPHIC ECOTYPES OF FOREST TREES AND ITS ROLE IN TREE IMPROVEMENT. Jour. Forestry 57: 439-441. SE

Describes factors in addition to clonal and one- or two-parent progeny tests that indicate intraspecific variation.

——————— DORMAN, K. W., and JORDAN, R. A.
1955. SLASH PINE CROWN WIDTH DIFFERENCES APPEAR AT EARLY AGE IN 1-PARENT PROGENY TESTS. U. S. Forest Serv. Southeast. Forest Expt. Sta. Res. Notes 86, 2 pp. SE

Crown width of 3-year-old trees in 1-parent progeny tests shows strong correlation with crown width of mother tree. This holds true for both wide-crown and narrow-crown trees.

BETHUNE, J. E., and ROTH, E. R.
1960. FIFTH YEAR RESULTS OF LOBLOLLY PINE SEED SOURCE PLANTING IN GEORGIA. U. S. Forest Serv. Southeast. Forest Expt. Sta. Res. Notes 145, 2 pp. SE

Seedlings of northern sources grew slower than those of southern origin. Infection by southern fusiform rust was related to seed origin but not to temperature zone.

——————— and ROTH, E. R.
1960. SOURCE OF SEED AFFECTS GROWTH OF LONGLEAF PINE—FIFTH YEAR RESULTS. U. S. Forest Serv. Southeast. Forest Expt. Sta. Res. Notes 146, 2 pp. SE

Seedling height, time in grass stage, percent of trees forked, and percent infected by brown spot needle blight, but not survival, exhibit significant differences.

BOURDEAU, P. F., and SCHOPMEYER, C. S.
1958. OLEORESIN EXUDATION PRESSURE IN SLASH PINE: ITS MEASUREMENT, HERITABILITY AND RELATION TO OLEORESIN YIELD. The Physiology of Forest Trees, pp. 313-319. New York. SE

Oleoresin exudation pressure is shown to be a variable trait that has high heritability and influences oleoresin yield.

3

Bower, D. R., and Smith, J. L.
1961. PARTIAL GIRDLING MULTIPLIES SHORTLEAF CONES. U. S. Forest Serv. South. Forest Expt. Sta. South. Forestry Notes 132, pp. 3-4. SO
Ouachita shortleaf seed trees tripled cone production the third year after treatment.

Campbell, T. E., and Wakeley, P. C.
1961. POSSIBLE REFINEMENTS IN CONTROLLED POLLINATION OF SOUTHERN PINES. Sixth South. Forest Tree Impr. Conf. Proc. 1961: 121-128. SO
Itemizes the "Placerville" stages of longleaf pine flowers for bagging, pollination, and debagging to attain certain degrees of seed set and of freedom from contamination, and evaluates laboratory germination of pollen in terms of fertilizing ability.

Campbell, W. A.
1959. LITTLELEAF DISEASE OF SHORTLEAF PINE (Pinus echinata Mill.): PRESENT STATUS AND FUTURE NEEDS. (Abstract.) Ninth Internatl. Bot. Cong. Proc. 2: 58-59. SE
Present research emphasizes soil improvement and selection and propagation of healthy shortleaf pines growing in severe littleleaf areas, and testing their progeny for resistance to the causal fungus Phytophthora cinnamomi.

Clapper, R. B.
1950. BREEDING NEW CHESTNUTS FOR SOUTHERN FORESTS. Forest Farmer 9(11): 8. SE
History of the chestnut blight, search for resistance among Oriental chestnuts, USDA breeding and hybridizing program, and problems of mass-producing resistant chestnuts.

———
1952. BREEDING AND ESTABLISHING NEW TREES RESISTANT TO DISEASE. Econ. Bot. 6: 271-293. SE.
USDA program of selecting, breeding, and testing blight-resistant chestnuts.

———
1952. RELATIVE BLIGHT RESISTANCE OF SOME CHESTNUT SPECIES AND HYBRIDS. Jour. Forestry 50: 453-455. SE
Summarizes 25 years of selecting and breeding.

——— and Miller, J. M.
1949. BREEDING AND SELECTING PEST-RESISTANT TREES. U. S. Dept. Agr. Yearbook 1949: 465-471. SE
Attempts to breed for resistance to tree diseases and insects in the United States.

Committee on Southern Forest Tree Improvement. (C. E. Ostrom, Chairman)
1952. SUGGESTED PROJECTS IN THE GENETIC IMPROVEMENT OF SOUTHERN FOREST TREES. U. S. Forest Serv. Southeast. Forest Expt. Sta. Sta. Paper 20, 12 pp. SE
Projects are listed in: (1) application of genetics to the collection of seed for planting, (2) geographic source of seed for forest planting, (3) improvement of southern forest trees through selection and breeding, (4) techniques and basic aspects of forest genetics such as selection, anatomical studies, breeding, methods for control of flowering and fruiting, methods of vegetative propagation, and equipment for tree improvement work.

Coyne, J. F.
1957. CONTROL OF CONE INSECTS IN SOUTHERN PINE. Fourth South. Forest Tree Impr. Conf. Proc. 1957: 64-66. SO
Chemicals may have to be used to prevent insects from chronically reducing the seed crop.

———
1957. MIST BLOWER FOR SPRAYING SEED TREES. U. S. Forest Serv. South. Forest Expt. Sta. South. Forestry Notes 111, p. 2. SO
A turbine mist blower, mounted on and powered by a jeep, successfully and economically sprayed 70-foot pines with benzene hexachloride for protecting cones against insects.

Curry, J. R.
1943. SELECTION, PROPAGATION, AND BREEDING OF HIGH-YIELDING SOUTHERN PINES FOR NAVAL STORES PRODUCTION. Jour. Forestry 41: 686-687. SO
Efficiency in naval stores production has been decreasing and competition is stronger. Development of a high-yielding strain is advanced as a means of increasing tree yields and efficiency of labor. Work is progressing along three lines: (1) selection of superior trees, (2) vegetative propagation experiments, and (3) controlled breeding.

Demmon, E. L.
1938. THE IMPORTANCE OF FOREST-GENETICS INVESTIGATIONS IN THE SOUTH. Cellulose Advisory Com. Perennial Crops, Natl. Farm Chemurg. Council, 4 pp. SO
Cites the few beginning experiments and observations made on southern species through 1937 and suggests a program of forest genetic studies to be carried out by the cellulose industry of the South.

4

Derr, H. J., and Dell, T. R.
1960. WHERE SHOULD WE GET SLASH PINE SEED
FOR LOUISIANA? Forests and People 10(2):
30-31. SO

A plantation in central Louisiana contains slash pines from seed collected in
South Carolina, Florida, and Georgia,
as well as from southern Mississippi and
eastern Louisiana. At age 22 years, trees
from the various sources do not differ
significantly in volume, size, or amount
of cankering from southern fusiform
rust.

———— and Enghardt, H.
1960. IS GEOGRAPHIC SEED SOURCE OF SLASH PINE
IMPORTANT? South. Lumberman 201
(2513): 95-96. SO

After 22 years' growth in western Louisiana, slash pines from 7 geographic
sources ranging from South Carolina to
northern Florida and west to eastern
Louisiana had developed no significant
differences in height, diameter, volume,
fusiform rust infection, or wood specific
gravity.

Doolittle, W. T.
1953. GROWTH AND SURVIVAL OF HYBRID POPLARS.
South. Lumberman 187(2345): 178-179.
SE

Growth of 12 clones planted in 1935 indicates that certain hybrid poplars on good
sites in the southern Appalachians grow
faster than the most rapid-growing native species such as white pine, yellow-
poplar, or northern red oaks.

Dorman, K. W.
1945. HIGH-YIELDING TURPENTINE ORCHARDS — A
FUTURE POSSIBILITY. Chemurg. Digest 4:
293, 295-299. SE

Development of a high-producing strain
is offered as a solution to many of the
problems of the naval stores industry.
Superior trees have been located, methods have been developed for vegetative
propagation of slash pine, and controlled
breeding with superior trees has been
carried out. It is estimated that yields
can be increased from the present average of 166 pounds per acre to 3,500
pounds by the use of superior trees
grown in well-managed, fully-stocked
stands.

1946. THE LIFE HISTORY OF SLASH PINE. Natl.
Container Digest 2(10): 1, 4-5. SE

Development of female flowers, seeds,
and slash pine trees for one life cycle
is discussed.

1947. BETTER PINES FOR TURPENTINING. Amer.
Forests 53: 498-500. SE

In the rubber industry production efficiency was greatly increased by the use
of superior trees obtained by controlled
breeding. On the other hand, the pine
gum industry in America is suffering
from decreasing efficiency. This article
is a popular account of selection and
breeding work, similar to that done with
the rubber tree, designed to increase the
efficiency of the gum industry by developing a strain of high-yielding trees
which will greatly increase yields per
acre with little additional labor.

1947. BREEDING BETTER SOUTHERN PINES FOR THE
FUTURE. South. Lumberman 175(2201):
147-150. SE

A popular account of the work in tree
selection, breeding, and vegetative propagation of southern pines. In a concluding section the author speculates on the
gum yields possible from a plantation
of cuttings from known superior trees.
The greater gum yield of these trees
and better stocking of the plantation
could yield 24 times as much gum per
acre as the present average acre of turpentine timber.

1947. LONGLEAF PINE CUTTINGS ROOTED IN GREEN-
HOUSE. Jour. Forestry 45: 594. SE

Longleaf pine cuttings from large trees
were rooted for the first time. The most
effective treatment consisted of soaking
the bases of the cuttings for 24 hours
in a water solution containing 15 p.p.m.
traumatic acid, 15 p.p.m. sodium penta-
chlorophenate, 10 p.p.m. vitamin B_1, 5
percent sucrose, and 0.4 percent of a
commercial plant food.

1947. PEDIGREED PINES FOR DIXIE'S FUTURE FOR-
ESTS. Forest Farmer 6(8): 7. SE

An outline of work already begun for
producing a better pine for southern
forests. This includes selection of superior breeding stock, vegetative propagation to preserve the valuable traits of
the stock, controlled breeding and further selection to combine the desirable
characteristics of two or more trees into
one tree or to increase some desirable
characteristic, and the checking of performance of the progeny.

5

DORMAN, K. W.

1947. PROGRESS IN BREEDING BETTER TURPENTINE
PINES. AT-FA Jour. 9(12): 10, 15. SE
*The controlled-breeding work of 1943
and 1944 with slash pine resulted in
enough seed to produce 600 seedlings.
These were set out in a plantation in
1946. Each of these seedlings has a carefully recorded pedigree. The plantation
includes crosses of high-yielding turpentine pines, average-yielding trees, and
some slash-loblolly and slash-longleaf
hybrids. When the seedlings are large
enough, the gum-yielding capacity of the
different groups will be compared by
small-scale chipping methods.*

1947. ROOTED PINE CUTTINGS MAKE RAPID GROWTH.
AT-FA Jour. 9(11): 8. SE
*Slash pine cuttings rooted in the green-
house and then planted in the field grow
rapidly. Within 3 or 4 years from the
parent tree they grow to be 6 feet or
more in height.*

1950. THE GENETICS OF SOUTHERN PINES (A PRE-
LIMINARY REPORT). U. S. Forest Serv.
Southeast. Forest Expt. Sta., 52 pp. SE
*Phytogeny of gymnosperms, classifica-
tion of pines, mechanism of pollination,
development of the seed, controlled-
breeding methods, and variation in wild
stands.*

1951. HYBRIDIZATION IN IMPROVING SOUTHERN
PINE. First South. Forest Tree Impr. Conf.
Proc. 1951, 10 pp. SE
*Résumé of interspecific hybridization
with non-southern and a few southern
pines, and a discussion of both inter- and
intraspecific hybridization of southern
pines, including slash pine in Australia.
Brief notes on induced mutation, and
comprehensive suggestions for tree improvement programs in the South.*

1951. WE NEED BETTER SEED COLLECTING EQUIP-
MENT. U. S. Forest Serv. Tree Planters'
Notes 5, : 2. SE
*The need for improved equipment for
tree climbing and cone picking.*

1952. DIRECTORY OF FOREST GENETICS ACTIVITIES
IN THE SOUTH. U. S. Forest Serv. Southeast. Forest Expt. Sta. Sta. Paper 17, 17 pp.
SE
*Lists by administrative agency work
now under way in tree introduction,
racial variation, selection and hybridization, vegetative propagation, cytology,
and stimulation of seed production.*

1952. HEREDITARY VARIATION AS THE BASIS FOR
SELECTING SUPERIOR FOREST TREES. U. S.
Forest Serv. Southeast. Forest Expt. Sta.
Sta. Paper 15, 88 pp. SE
*A comprehensive discussion of the basis
for heritable variation and selection in
tree improvement and silviculture.*

1953. A TAXONOMIC STUDY OF SLASH PINE. (Abstract.) Assoc. South. Agr. Workers Proc.
50: 116-117. SE
*Slash pine, one of the most valuable
southern pines, is a distinct species from
Caribbean pine, with which it has usually been united. The related pine of
southern Florida is now recognized as
a botanical variety.*

1955. PROGRESS IN TREE IMPROVEMENT RESEARCH
AT THE SOUTHEASTERN FOREST EXPERIMENT
STATION. Second Lake States Forest Tree
Impr. Conf. Proc. 1955: 28-33. U. S. Forest
Serv. Lake States Forest Expt. Sta. Misc.
Rpt. 40, 108 pp. SE
*The Station's research centers have veri-
fied some inheritance of gum yield, de-
veloped techniques for vegetative propa-
gation, and demonstrated mother-tree
heritability of crown form, growth rate,
and rust resistance in pines.*

1955. SHORT-TIME AND LONG-TIME POSSIBILITIES
OF SELECTION IN FOREST TREES. Third
South. Forest Tree Impr. Conf. Proc. 1955:
31-35. SE
*Selection of improved tree types should
be based on results of studies of inherent
variation within each species. Many
economically important plant varieties
have been obtained by selection, but the
process does not create new types—it
merely isolates those occurring naturally.*

1955. VEGETATIVE PROPAGATION PROBLEMS IN THE
SOUTH. Second Lake States Forest Tree
Impr. Conf. Proc. 1955: 56-57. U. S. Forest
Serv. Lake States Forest Expt. Sta. Misc.
Rpt. 40, 108 pp. SE
*". . . Much has been accomplished in
developing vegetative propagation methods to meet the needs in tree improvement research. Many problems remain,
but our current research is strong, and
it should not be long until the major
ones will be solved."*

6

DORMAN, K. W.

1956. GENETICS IN RELATION TO FOREST MANAGE-
MENT. Ia. State Col. School Forestry,
Ames Forester 43: 17-19. SE

Knowledge of variation and heredity in
trees can be applied whenever new
stands are established and when intermediate cuts are made.

1956. PROGRESS IN THE SELECTION OF SUPERIOR
STRAINS OF SOUTHERN PINES. (Abstract.)
Assoc. South. Agr. Workers Proc. 53:
151-152. SE

Variations in growth rate, fusiform rust
infection, and crown width among progeny of superior mother trees indicate
that important traits are strongly inherited and selection of superior types
is possible.

1956. PUBLICATIONS ON FOREST GENETICS, SOUTH-
EASTERN FOREST EXPERIMENT STATION. U. S.
Forest Serv. Southeast. Forest Expt. Sta.
Sta. Paper 63, 18 pp. SE

Annotated list, 1939 through 1955.

1957. BREEDING BETTER PINES. South. Planter
118(11): 20. SE

Describes progress of cooperative research in the South.

1959. FOREST GENETICS AND TREE IMPROVEMENT
RESEARCH AT THE SOUTHEASTERN FOREST
EXPERIMENT STATION. Sixth Meeting Com.
Forest Tree Breeding Canada Proc. 1958.
Pt. 2: Q1-Q2. SE

Outlines the program in applied tree
breeding through racial selection, single
tree selection, and intraspecific hybridization.

1959. THE STATUS OF WORK ON WOOD QUALITY IN
SOUTHERN FOREST TREE IMPROVEMENT RE-
SEARCH. Sixth Meeting Com. Forest Tree
Breeding Canada Proc. 1958. Pt. 2: S1-
S15. SE

Recent work in wood specific gravity,
tracheid length, and cellulose content
on the basis of correlation of mature
with juvenile traits, correlation of
branchwood with stemwood, and variation and inheritance.

1961. SELECTION AS A METHOD OF TREE BREEDING.
Sixth South. Forest Tree Impr. Conf. Proc.
1961: 65-72. SE

Though much research on variation and
inheritance within southern tree species
is still needed, utilization of the inherent
variation in these species seems to promise more rapid progress in tree breeding
than does species introduction or hybridization.

———— and BARBER, J. C.

1956. TIME OF FLOWERING AND SEED RIPENING IN
SOUTHERN PINES. U. S. Forest Serv. Southeast Forest Expt. Sta. Sta. Paper 72, 15
pp. SE

Approximate dates of pollen and seed
ripening for slash, longleaf, loblolly,
and shortleaf pines for many locations
throughout the natural ranges of the
species; similar data for minor southern
pines and the pines of the Appalachian
Mountains.

———— BAUER, E., and GREENE, J. T.

1953. TREE IMPROVEMENT MAKES A STEP AHEAD.
South. Lumberman 187 (2345): 170-171.
SE

History and progress of the tree improvement program at the Ida Cason
Callaway Foundation, Hamilton, Georgia. Reports variation in vigor of open-
pollinated progeny of slash and loblolly
pine maternal parents.

———— SCHOPMEYER, C. S., and SNOW, A. G., JR.

1944. TOP BRACING AND GUYING IN THE BREEDING
OF SOUTHERN PINES. Jour Forestry 42:
140-141. SO

Breeding or other work in the tops of
slash and longleaf pine can be made
safer and easier by reinforcing the upper
part of the central stem with 2- by 2-inch
splints and by the use of three guy
wires from the top of the tree to the
ground.

DOWNS, A. A.

1948. HOW PINE CUTTINGS ARE ROOTED. Forest
Farmer 7(5): 26. SE

Important factors in rooting cuttings of
slash and longleaf pine are treatment
with a growth regulator, such as traumatic acid, and a carefully controlled
environment. Cuttings must be sprayed
intermittently with water during the
daylight hours to prevent desiccation.

Downs, A. A.

1949. DEVELOPING BETTER PINES FOR GUM PRODUCTION. South. Lumberman 179(2249): 233-236. SE

Accomplishments of 8 years' work by the Lake City Branch of the Southeastern Forest Experiment Station toward the development of a high-yielding strain of naval stores pine are reported. A dozen trees have been found which produce at least twice as much gum as the average of the trees around them. One progeny test plantation of 600 trees is now 4 years old, and 800 one-year-old seedlings are available to establish another progeny test plantation. Methods of rooting pine cuttings have been developed. For trees of working size, 5 to 20 percent of the cuttings root. Cuttings from very young trees root more easily.

1949. LOW FORKING IN WHITE OAK SPROUTS MAY BE HEREDITARY. Jour. Forestry 47: 736. SE

In 30 clumps of sprouts in a 25-year-old stand in the Piedmont of Virginia in which the largest stem was forked, 53 percent of the next largest stems were also forked. In 102 clumps in which the largest stem was straight, all but 4 percent of the next largest stems were also straight. A chi-square test of the ratios showed that this difference was significant. Only stems definitely forked below 24 feet were classed as forked; all others were classed as straight or not forked.

1949. UNUSUAL TREE APPEARS IN BREEDING TESTS. Forest Farmer 9(2): 8. SE

During a dry period the needles of one tree in a slash pine gum-yield progeny test develop alternating rings of bright yellow and dull green. From a distance, this 4-year-old appears bright yellow. In drought periods the surrounding trees turn a uniform dull yellowish green. The unusual tree appears in no danger of dying. When a drought ends, the tree gradually regains a healthy green color.

Duffield, J. W., and Snyder, E. B.

1958. BENEFITS FROM HYBRIDIZING AMERICAN FOREST TREE SPECIES. Jour. Forestry 56: 809-815. SO

Reviews American work and concludes that, while successes have not yet been remarkable, hybridization has an important place among methods of improving adaptability and pest-resistance.

Echols, R. M.

1955. LINEAR RELATION OF FIBRILLAR ANGLE TO TRACHEID LENGTH, AND GENETIC CONTROL OF TRACHEID LENGTH IN SLASH PINE. Tropical Woods 102: 11-22. SE

Fibrillar angle bears a direct linear relation to tracheid angle, which appears to be under rigid genetic control.

1959. ESTIMATION OF PULP YIELD AND QUALITY OF LIVING TREES FROM PAIRED-CORE SAMPLES. TAPPI 42: 875-877. SO

To reduce the effect of variation from causes such as eccentricity and compression wood, pairs of samples for specific gravity and ring width are taken from opposite sides of trees, and include all growth rings. To derive wood quality index values, measurements are converted to estimated pulp yield.

1959. EVALUATING TREES AND STANDS FROM LARGE INCREMENT CORES. Soc. Amer. Foresters Proc. 1958: 145-147. SO

The Southern Institute of Forest Genetics is using 10-millimeter increment cores to study factors that influence wood quality.

1959. THE AMPLISCOPE—AN INSTRUMENT FOR WOOD-FIBER MEASUREMENTS. Jour Forestry 57: 43-44. SO

Construction details of a device for throwing a magnified image of small objects on a glass screen.

1960. EFFECTS OF GROWING SPACE ON WOOD SPECIFIC GRAVITY IN LOBLOLLY PINE. Soc. Amer. Foresters Proc. 1959: 140-143. SO

Trees were planted in central Louisiana at square spacings of 4, 6, 8, and 10 feet, thinned to 4 densities at age 20 years, and remeasured ten years later. For all degrees of thinning, trees at 6-foot spacing made the greatest gain in specific gravity between ages 20 and 30. The 8-foot spacing produced the most volume.

1960. THE IMPACT OF FOREST GENETICS ON FOREST UTILIZATION. (Abstract.) Assoc. South. Agr. Workers Proc. 57: 138-139. SO

Present results in forest genetics promise "The ultimate development of strains of trees with increased utilization values for sawlogs, poles, pilings, pulpwood, and other products . . . ."

GRANO, C. X.
1960. STRANGLING AND GIRDLING EFFECTS ON CONE
PRODUCTION AND GROWTH OF LOBLOLLY PINE.
Jour. Forestry 58: 897-898. SO
*Cone production was neither promoted
nor hindered. Diameter and height
growth were unimpaired. The trees were
3 to 15 inches in d.b.h. and showed no
sign of having borne cones previously.*

GREENE, J. T., DORMAN, K. W., and BAUER, E.
1957. DIFFERENTIAL GROWTH RATE OF YOUNG PRO-
GENY OF INDIVIDUAL SLASH PINE TREES.
Fourth South. Forest Tree Impr. Conf.
Proc. 1957: 47-50. SE
*Demonstrates growth differences in pro-
geny of different mother trees and indicates that the relationship between seed
size and seedling growth is not strong
when seed is kept separate by maternal
parent.*

GRIGSBY, H. C.
1959. TWO PROMISING PINE HYBRIDS FOR THE MID-
SOUTH. South. Lumberman 198(2466):
32-33. SO
*At Crossett, Arkansas, the cross of slash
and shortleaf pine is showing resistance
to tipmoth and is growing faster than
shortleaf pine. The hybrid of loblolly
and south Florida slash pine is also doing
well.*

GRUSCHOW, G. F.
1956. CURLY-PINE. South. Lumberman 193
(2417): 189-190. SE
*Twenty-seven percent of the lumber cut
from a 180-year-old shortleaf pine tree
in the Bigwoods Experimental Forest
had the rare and highly prized curly
grain.*

HARGREAVES, L. A., JR., and DORMAN, K. W.
1955. GEORGIA STARTS PINE SEED ORCHARDS. South.
Lumberman 191(2393): 189. SE
*Scions of superior phenotypes in lob-
lolly and slash pine will be grafted on
run-of-the-mill seedlings in establishing
500 acres of seed orchards.*

———— and DORMAN, K. W.
1957. ADMINISTRATIVE AND TECHNICAL ASPECTS
OF ESTABLISHING PINE SEED ORCHARDS. Soc.
Amer. Foresters Proc. 1956: 92, 93. SE
*Procedures and costs of establishing
three orchards in Georgia.*

HARRINGTON, T. A.
1953. HYBRID PINES FAIL TO GROW AS WELL AS
SHORTLEAF, LOBLOLLY. Miss. Farm. Res.
16(4): 8. SO
*Preliminary study utilizing hybrids pro-
duced in the arboretum at Placerville,
California.*

9

HENRY, B. W.
1955. SOUTHERN INSTITUTE OF FOREST GENETICS. Third South. Forest Tree Impr. Conf. Proc. 1955: 99-101. SO

Objectives and plans of the newly established Institute.

1955. THE TECHNIQUES OF TESTING FOR INSECT AND DISEASE RESISTANCE IN FOREST TREES. Second Lake States Forest Tree Impr. Conf. Proc. 1955: 85-87. U. S. Forest Serv. Lake States Forest Expt. Sta. Misc. Rpt. 40, 108 pp . SO

Purposes and general methods of testing for pest resistance.

1956. PROGRESS AT INSTITUTE OF FOREST GENETICS. Forest Farmer 16(3): 4-5, 18. SO

In 2 years, the Southern Institute of Forest Genetics has initiated or intensified more than 50 studies in 4 main categories: 1.—Variation between and within genetic groups or populations of pines. 2.—Mode or mechanism by which characters are inherited. 3.—Identification, preservation, and development of desirable plant material. 4.—Facilitating tchniques.

1957. BETTERING NATURE'S BEST. Forest Farmer 17(2): 10-11. SO

"Blessed with four native pine species that rank with the best in the world, are we a bit presumptuous to think that we can make them still better? Not at all. On the contrary, it is practically a sure bet .... Through selection and hybridization, differentiating genetic from environmental effects, and studying the physiology of the resultant tree, the Southern Institute of Forest Genetics, along with other research organizations, is embarked on a program to 'better the best'."

1959. DISEASES AND INSECTS IN THE SOUTHWIDE PINE SEED SOURCE STUDY PLANTATIONS DURING THE FIRST FIVE YEARS. Fifth South. Forest Tree Impr. Conf. Proc. 1959: 12-17. SO

Two pests have been of major importance. "Tip-moth injury was and is severe in most of the shortleaf and loblolly plantations, irrespective of seed source, and most certainly is impeding height growth. Fusiform rust is variable in intensity among the slash and loblolly plantations .... Incidence consistently showed significant differences between seed sources in the loblolly pine plantings, but in only one case with slash pine."

———— and BERCAW, T. E.
1956. SHORTLEAF-LOBLOLLY HYBRID PINES FREE OF FUSIFORM RUST AFTER 5 YEARS' EXPOSURE. Jour. Forestry 54: 779. SO

Five years after planting, none of the 31 surviving seedlings of the hybrid Pinus echinata Mill. × P. taeda L. had symptoms of the rust, while 67 percent of some adjacent slash pine seedings (P. elliottii elliottii (Engelm.) Little and Dorman) had typical fusiform cankers.

———— and COYNE, J. F.
1955. OCCURRENCE OF PESTS IN SOUTHWIDE PINE SEED SOURCE STUDY. Third South. Forest Tree Impr. Conf. Proc. 1955: 49-54. SO

Occurrence of fusiform rust, tip moth, and webworm by geographic sources of loblolly and slash pine in two-year-old plantations.

———— and HEPTING, G. H.
1957. PEST OCCURRENCES IN 35 OF THE SOUTHWIDE PINE SEED SOURCE STUDY PLANTATIONS DURING THE FIRST THREE YEARS. U. S. Forest Serv. South. Forest Expt. Sta., 7 pp. SE-SO

Drouth has caused most of the mortality so far. Fusiform rust is building up rapidly and may be expected to damage loblolly and slash pine plantings. The Nantucket tip moth is widespread in loblolly and shortleaf plantings, and may be retarding height growth appreciably. Brown-spot needle disease is being controlled in longleaf plantations with fungicides, but it and Hypoderma needle blight may be causing growth loss on loblolly. No other pests yet appear serious.

HEPTING, G. H.
1954. GUM FLOW AND PITCH SOAK IN VIRGINIA PINE FOLLOWING FUSARIUM INOCULATION. U. S. Forest Serv. Southeast. Forest Expt. Sta. Sta. Paper 40, 9 pp. SE

Describes gum yields and amount of pitch-soaking in Virginia pine following inoculations with the pitch canker fungus.

1955. LITTLELEAF. The Unit, News Letter 58, pp. 74-75. SE

Status of littleleaf and research on control through genetics and soil management. Forest management in littleleaf areas is discussed.

10

HEPTING, G. H., and TOOLE, E. R.
1948. WILT EPIDEMIOLOGY AND RESISTANCE IN THE
MIMOSA TREE. (Abstract.) Phytopath. 38:
13. SE
The wilt has spread from Maryland to
Florida in the 12 years since it was discovered in North Carolina. Occasional
seedlings have resisted the wilt following several severe inoculations. Twenty-
eight resistant clones are now available.
Cuttings from these are also highly resistant.

HESSELTINE, C. W., and SNYDER, E. B.
1958. ATTEMPTS TO FREEZE-DRY PINE POLLEN FOR
PROLONGED STORAGE. Bul. Torrey Bot. Club
85: 134-135. SO
Lyophilization techniques by which fungus spores have been stored successfully
for 15 years failed with longleaf pine
pollen.

HOEKSTRA, P. E.
1954. NEW BLOOD FOR SOUTHERN PINES. South.
Lumberman 189 (2369): 182-183. SE
Nonindigenous species and varieties of
pine are being established in Florida to
furnish material for tree improvement.

———— 1957. AIR-LAYERING OF SLASH PINE. Forest Sci.
3: 344-349. SE
Results were better in July than in September. Increased rooting followed an
increase from 0.4 to 0.8 to 1.2 percent
concentration of indolebutyric acid. A
1.2-percent concentration of naphthaleneacetic acid was not effective.

———— 1957. STIMULATION OF FLOWER AND SEED PRO-
DUCTION IN SLASH PINE. Fourth South.
Forest Tree Impr. Conf. Proc. 1957: 74-75.
SE
Root pruning, partial girdling, and fertilization induced 6-year-old saplings to
flower. The high nitrogen content of a
7-7-7 fertilizer was more effective than
the high phosphorus content of a 3-18-6
fertilizer.

———— and JOHANSEN, R. W.
1957. GROWTH OF PLANTED SLASH PINE AIR-LAYERS.
Jour. Forestry 55: 146. SE
During the first year after outplanting
air-layers from 6-year-old saplings grew
three and one-half times as much as did
air-layers from 23-year-old trees.

———— and MERGEN, F.
1957. EXPERIMENTAL INDUCTION OF FEMALE
FLOWERS ON YOUNG SLASH PINE. Jour.
Forestry 55: 827-831. SE

On 7-year-old trees root pruning, partial
girdling, strangulation, and application
of 5 pounds of 3-12-6 fertilizer per tree
increased the number of trees bearing
female flowers. On 21-year-old trees
partial girdling, 20 pounds of 7-7-7 fertilizer, and 40 pounds of 3-18-6 fertilizer
were effective.

HUCKENPAHLER, B. J.
1953. SOURCE OF SEED AFFECTS PINE SURVIVAL
AND GROWTH. Miss. Farm Res. 16(6): 6.
SO
In Lafayette County, Mississippi, marked
differences in survival and height growth
among loblolly pine seedlings from 8
geographic seed sources are apparent
after only 3 growing seasons.

———— 1955. AUXINS FAIL TO STIMULATE ROOTING OF
YELLOW-POPLAR CUTTINGS. Bot. Gaz. 117:
73-75. SO
The auxins were indolebutyric acid, in-
doleacetic acid, and naphthaleneacetic
acid, all applied in a variety of concentrations and immersion periods to cuttings made at several seasons from wood
of various ages.

JACKSON, L. W. R., and ZAK, B.
1949. GRAFTING METHODS USED IN STUDIES OF THE
LITTLELEAF DISEASE OF SHORTLEAF PINE.
Jour. Forestry 47: 904-908. SE
In transmission experiments with littleleaf disease both the aboveground parts
and the roots of shortleaf pines were
successfully grafted with seedlings, saplings, and adult trees serving as stock
trees. The bark-patch method proved
highly successful. The approach grafting
method, although not quite so successful
as the first method, nevertheless gave a
fair percentage of graft unions for both
stems and roots. Thus far, healthy trees
receiving the grafts have not developed
symptoms of the disease.

JEWELL, F. F.
1957. INOCULATION OF SEEDLINGS OF Pinus elliottii
var. elliottii WITH Cronartium fusiforme.
Phytopath. 47: 18. SO
Inoculation caused red needle spots and
subsequent gall formation.

———— 1957. INOCULATION TECHNIQUES IN STUDIES OF
RUST RESISTANCE. Fourth South. Forest
Tree Impr. Conf. Proc. 1957: 67-69. SO
Exploratory studies indicate that a satisfactory technique can be developed for
testing rust resistance in the southern
pines.

11

JEWELL, F. F.

1957. PREVENTING CONE RUST ON SLASH PINE BY POLLINATION TECHNIQUES USED IN BREEDING PROGRAMS. Phytopath. 47: 241-242. SO
Rust infection of first-year cones of slash pine was prevented by routine bagging of the conelets for controlled pollination; 27 percent of the non-bagged cones became infected. Infection of slash pine cones seems to coincide with the period of pollination.

1958. SOFTENING SLASH PINE TISSUES FOR SERIAL SECTIONING. Stain Technol. 33: 191-192. SO
A 10-percent aqueous solution of glycerol was found best for softening serial paraffin sections for anatomical studies of rust-infected slash pine.

1958. STAIN TECHNIQUE FOR RAPID DIAGNOSIS OF RUST IN SOUTHERN PINES. Forest Sci. 4: 42-44. SO
Two techniques, involving orseillin-BB and aniline blue, and safranin-O and aniline blue, have been used successfully for distinguishing the mycelium of Cronartium fusiforme in hand sections of slash and loblolly pines and of C. cerebrum in shortleaf pine.

1959. DISEASE RESISTANCE STUDIES IN TREE IMPROVEMENT RESEARCH. Fifth South. Forest Tree Impr. Conf. Proc. 1959: 18-20. SO
"The ultimate aim of disease resistance research is to be able to incorporate the factors for resistance . . . into trees possessing other superior traits as well."

1960. INOCULATION OF SLASH PINE SEEDLINGS WITH Cronartium fusiforme. Phytopath. 50: 48-51. SO
Cotyledonary seedlings were inoculated by placing telia-bearing oak leaves over them and maintaining high humidity for 72 hours. One-year-old seedlings were inoculated by wrapping the new growth in telia-bearing oak leaves and maintaining high humidity, and also by inserting telia into new stem tissue.

ARTIFICIAL TESTING OF INTRA- AND INTER-SPECIES SOUTHERN PINE HYBRIDS FOR RUST RESISTANCE. Sixth South. Forest Tree Impr. Conf. Proc. 1961: 105-109. SO
Crossing slash or loblolly with shortleaf will not consistently yield resistant progenies. Resistance in shortleaf hybrids

appears more complicated than inheritance of a simple dominant factor.

1961. INFECTION OF ARTIFICIALLY INOCULATED SHORTLEAF PINE HYBRIDS WITH FUSIFORM RUST. U. S. Dept. Agr. Plant Dis. Rptr. 45:639-640. SO
Characteristic rust galls developed on at least a few progenies from each of five crosses of shortleaf × slash pine and one cross of shortleaf × loblolly. Differences in number of galled individuals from the various crosses appeared traceable to particular shortleaf parents.

———— and HENRY, B. W.

1959. BREEDING FOR RESISTANCE TO SOUTHERN FUSIFORM RUST. (Abstract.) Ninth Internatl. Bot. Cong. Proc. 2: 181-182. SO
Data so far appear to justify initial hypotheses on possible sources of resistance, i. e., natural resistance in susceptible pine species and inherited resistance in hybrid progenies having shortleaf as a parent. The resistance of shortleaf appears to be transmitted as a dominant factor to the F_1 hybrids from crosses of shortleaf × slash and shortleaf × loblolly.

———— and HENRY, B. W.

1961. BREEDING FOR RESISTANCE TO SOUTHERN FUSIFORM RUST. Recent Advances in Botany, pp. 1694-1695. Toronto. SO
Text of paper read in 1959 by same authors and under same title; see entry above.

JOHANSEN, R. W.

1957. WHAT WE KNOW ABOUT AIR-LAYERING. Fourth South. Forest Tree Impr. Conf. Proc. 1957: 126-131. SE
Summarizes experiences in air-layering, with particular reference to the effects of tree age and use of growth regulators on slash, loblolly, and shortleaf pine.

———— and ARLINE, L.

1958. AN IDEA IN TRUCK-MOUNTED LADDERS. Jour. Forestry 56: 852-853. SE
Description of truck-mounted ladder for use in seed orchards and seed production areas.

———— and KRAUS, J. F.

1958. PROPAGATION TECHNIQUES APPLICABLE TO LONGLEAF PINE. Jour. Forestry 56: 664. SE
Longleaf pine can be vegetatively propagated by cuttings, grafting, and air-layers, with the same techniques that are used for other southern pines.

12

Percentage of summerwood is the best single criterion for estimating specific gravity. Within a tree cross-section, it is largely controlled by age. Between locations the best estimate of summerwood percentage was from total rainfall during June and July in combination with depth to a fine-textured horizon.

LIGHTLE, P. C.
1959. CONE RUST ON SLASH PINE CONTROLLED BY FERBAM. (Abstract.) Phytopath. 49: 318. SO
Sprays containing 2 pounds of ferbam per 100 gallons of water were effective, especially when the strobilus scales had opened or just after they had closed.

LINDGREN, R. M.
1951. THE DISEASE PROBLEM IN RELATION TO TREE IMPROVEMENT. First South. Forest Tree Impr. Conf. Proc. 1951, 5 pp. SO
Analysis of tree-improvement problems in general, and of breeding for disease resistance in particular, against the whole background of forest pathology.

LITTLE, E. L., JR., and DORMAN, K. W.
1952. GEOGRAPHIC DIFFERENCES IN CONE OPENING IN SAND PINE. Jour. Forestry 50: 204-205. SE
Suggests that typical sand pine with closed cones be called Ocala sand pine or Ocala race, whereas that occurring in western Florida with open cones be called Choctawhatchee sand pine or Choctawhatchee race.

———— and DORMAN, K. W.
1952. SLASH PINE *(Pinus elliottii)*, ITS NOMENCLATURE AND VARIETIES. Jour. Forestry 50: 918-923. SE
Recommends that the pine in the United States be separated from the Caribbean pine and that a new variety, South Florida slash pine, be recognized.

———— and DORMAN, K. W.
1954. SLASH PINE *(Pinus elliottii)* INCLUDING SOUTH FLORIDA SLASH PINE, NOMENCLATURE AND DESCRIPTION. U. S. Forest Serv. Southeast. Forest Expt. Sta. Sta. Paper 36, 82 pp. SE
A report on the botanical basis for a recent change in scientific nomenclature.

LOTTI, T.
1955. YELLOW- POPLAR HEIGHT GROWTH AFFECTED BY SEED SOURCE. U. S. Forest Serv. Tree Planters' Notes 22, p. 3. SE
At the end of the third growing season the mountain strain averaged 4.4 feet in height and that from the Coastal Plain 7.9 feet.

13

MCALPINE, R. G.
1957. AGE OF TREE AND ROOT DEVELOPMENT BY
AIR-LAYERS IN LOBLOLLY PINE. Fourth
South. Forst Tree Impr. Conf. Proc. 1957:
59-63. SE
*Rooting was best in the youngest trees,
and decreased sharply with increasing
age. All living air-layers on 2-year-old
trees rooted, but none rooted in trees 17
years or older.*

————— and JACKSON, L. W. R.
1959. EFFECT OF AGE ON ROOTING OF LOBLOLLY
PINE AIR-LAYERS. Jour. Forestry 57: 565-
566. SE
*Rooting was best in the youngest age
classes and declined sharply with increasing age. None of the air-layers
rooted on trees 17 and 20 years old.*

MCGREGOR, W. H. D., and KRAMER, P. J.
1957. EFFECT OF PHOTOPERIOD ON PHOTOSYNTHE-
SIS, RESPIRATION, AND GROWTH OF LOBLOLLY
PINE SEEDLINGS FROM TWO SOURCES. (Abstract.) Plant Physiol. 32: 10-11. SE
*The higher photosynthesis rates of larger
seedlings are a result of greater needle
area. Longer photoperiods increase the
needle area, but do not alter the basic
rate of photosynthesis.*

————— ALLEN, R. M., and KRAMER, P. J.
1961. THE EFFECT OF PHOTOPERIOD ON GROWTH,
PHOTOSYNTHESIS, AND RESPIRATION OF LOB-
LOLLY PINE SEEDLINGS FROM TWO GEO-
GRAPHIC SOURCES. Forest Sci. 7: 342-348.
SE-SO
*Long-day (15 hours) treatment stimu-
lated height growth significantly more
in Florida than in Georgia seedlings.
Georgia seedlings carried on photosynthesis at a significantly higher rate than
did Florida seedlings; the rate of long-
day seedlings was higher than that of
short-day (9.5 hours) seedlings, but the
difference was not significant. On the
basis of unit-fascicle length, there were
no significant source or treatment differences in photosynthesis, nor were
respiration differences significant.*

MCKNIGHT, J. S., and BONNER, F. T.
1961. POTENTIALS AND PROBLEMS OF HARDWOOD
TREE IMPROVEMENT. Sixth South. Forest
Tree Impr. Conf. Proc. 1961: 164-178. SO
*Literature references and tabular sum-
maries of information useful in tree-improvement programs for the southern
hardwoods.*

MCLEMORE, B. F,. CROW, A. B., and WAKELEY, P. C.
1951. DRY-MATTER CONTENT OF LOBLOLLY PINE
NEEDLES APPEARS UNRELATED TO GEOGRAPHIC
SEED SOURCE. Forest Sci. 7: 373-375. SO

*Samples from 25 sources representing
extremes in the species' range showed
no relation between dry-matter content
and latitude, longitude, or climate.*

MAISENHELDER, L. C.
1953. ROOTING ASH CUTTINGS WITH HORMONES.
U. S. Forest Serv. South. Forest Expt. Sta.
South. Forestry Notes 87, pp. 2-3. SO
*Forty-seven percent of treated cuttings
rooted, as compared to 20 percent of
untreated. Treatments were either naphthaleneacetic, indoleacetic, or indolebutyric acid.*

—————
1957. PROPAGATION OF SOME DELTA HARDWOODS
BY ROOTING. Fourth South. Forest Tree
Impr. Conf. Proc. 1957: 55-58. SO
*"So far all of our work . . . has been
directed toward finding a simple . . .
means of using dormant unrooted cuttings for field planting . . . . Cottonwood
and black willow have reproduced satisfactorily both in the nursery and in plantations. Sycamore and green ash have
done very well in nursery tests . . . . The
oaks will require more intensive testing
. . . . Sweetgum is the only species tested
that has failed to produce some rooting."*

—————
1961. SELECTION OF POPULUS CLONES FOR SOUTH-
ERN BOTTOM LANDS. Sixth South. Forest
Tree Impr. Conf. Proc. 1961: 110-115. SO
*In hardwood tree improvement work
at Stoneville, Mississippi, five clones of
native cottonwood and one Euramerican
hybrid have thus far emerged as the
best Populus planting stock. Some other
hybrids grow more slowly than cottonwood but have attributes worth per-
petuating.*

MANN, W. F., JR., and RUSSELL, T. E.
1956. RINGING STIMULATES LONGLEAF CONE PRO-
DUCTION. U. S. Forest Serv. South. Forest
Expt. Sta. South. Forestry Notes 103, pp.
3-4. SO
*Three years after partial girdling, cone
production on treated trees was more
than double that on untreated trees.*

————— and RUSSELL, T. E.
1957. LONGLEAF CONE PRODUCTION DOUBLED BY
RINGING. U. S. Forest Serv. Tree Planters'
Notes 28, pp. 6-7. SO
*Ringing was done by cutting two half-
circles through the cambium on opposite
sides of the tree, slightly above stump
height. Trees smaller than 10 inches in
d.b.h. did not respond, probably because
they were too small to bear cones abun-
dantly.*

14

1954. ANATOMICAL STUDY OF SLASH PINE GRAFT
UNIONS. Quart. Jour. Fla. Acad. Sci. 17:
237-245. SE
*Parenchymatous cells of medullary rays,
phloem, cortex, and cambium participated in bridging the space between stock
and scion tissues. The stock contributed
the greatest part of the wound tissue,
but the scion took part in callus formation. A continuous bridge between re-
spective anatomical parts of the graft
partners was apparent after 6 weeks.*

1954. GRAFTING SUCCULENT SLASH PINE SCIONS.
U. S. Forest Serv. Southeast. Forest Expt.
Sta. Res. Notes 59, 2 pp. SE
*The discovery that scions can be grafted
in the succulent stage promises to pro-
long the grafting season by several
months.*

1954. HETEROPLASTIC MICROGRAFTING OF SLASH
PINE. U. S. Forest Serv. Southeast. Forest
Expt. Sta. Sta. Paper 47, 17 pp. SE
*A project in grafting 1- to 6-month-old
slash pine seedlings onto other coniferous
species such as white spruce, white pine,
and ponderosa pine.*

1954. IMPROVING THE EARLY GROWTH OF LONGLEAF
PINE. Naval Stores Rev. 64(3): 12-13, 21.
Also in Forest Farmer 13(11): 8-9, 16-17.
SE
*Some 261 slash-longleaf pine hybrids
have been produced for possible use in
reforestation of dry sites.*

1954. INHERITANCE OF OLEORESIN YIELD IN SLASH
PINE. AT-FA Jour. 17(2): 16-18. *Also in*
Naval Stores Rev. 64(9): 8-9, 20. SE
*A test of the progeny from parent trees
selected for high-gum production showed
that gum-yielding ability is inherited.*

1954. SELF-FERTILIZATION IN SLASH PINE REDUCES
HEIGHT GROWTH. U. S. Forest Serv. Southeast. Forest Expt. Sta. Res. Notes 67, 2 pp.
SE
*Self-pollination tends toward poor seed
set, low germination, reduced vigor, deformed growth, retarded flowering, or
some degree of albinism.*

1954. VARIATION IN 2-YEAR-OLD SLASH PINE (*P.
elliottii* var. *elliottii*) SEEDLINGS. U. S.
Forest Serv. Southeast. Forest Expt. Sta.
Res. Notes 62, 2 pp. SE
*Survival of seedlings from all five geo-
graphic seed sources in Florida was high,
but the growth of one from Polk County
was low.*

15

MERGEN, F.
  1954. VEGETATIVE PROPAGATION TECHNIQUES FOR
        GENETICS STUDIES OF SLASH PINE (*Pinus
        elliottii* Engelm.). Amer. Soc. Plant Phy-
        siol. Program for 29th Ann. Mtg., pp. 6-7.
        SE
        Brief review of techniques.

  1955. AIR-LAYERING OF SLASH PINES. Jour. For-
        estry 53: 265-270. SE
        *The feasibility of air-layering as a tech-
        nique in asexual propagation of slash
        pine is demonstrated.*

  1955. GRAFTING SLASH PINE IN THE FIELD AND IN
        THE GREENHOUSE. Jour. Forestry 53: 836-
        842. SE
        *Summarizes experiments with cleft, ve-
        neer or side-slit, and bottle grafts in the
        greenhouse and field.*

  1955. INHERITANCE OF DEFORMITIES IN SLASH PINE.
        South. Lumberman 190(2370): 30-32. SE
        *Progeny after open pollination of a
        crooked slash pine were 76 percent
        crooked; those of the same tree crossed
        with a straight tree were 68 percent
        crooked; those of the straight tree used
        as a female parent in other crosses were
        41 percent crooked.*

  1955. ROOTING AND GRAFTING OF SLASH PINE. Third
        South. Forest Tree Impr. Conf. Proc. 1955:
        88-94. SE
        *Describes successful techniques for root-
        ing, grafting, and air-layering.*

  1955. VEGETATIVE PROPAGATION OF SLASH PINE.
        U. S. Forest Serv. Southeast. Forest Expt.
        Sta. Sta. Paper 54, 63 pp. SE
        *Details of many experiments in asexual
        propagation.*

  ———— and HOEKSTRA, P. E.
  1954. GERMINATION DIFFERENCES IN SLASH PINE
        FROM VARIOUS SOURCES. South. Lumber-
        man 189(2364): 62, 64, 66. SE
        *Real differences are indicated in seed
        characteristics from collections in differ-
        ent locations.*

  ———— and POMEROY, K. B.
  1953. SOME PRACTICAL SUGGESTIONS FOR BETTER
        SLASH PINE SEED. South. Lumber Jour.
        57(11): 88-89. SE
        *Organizations with extensive reforesta-
        tion programs might improve seed qual-
        ity in slash pine by improving selected
        natu...l stands of vigorous, even-aged,
        cone-bearing trees. Method of improve-
        ment and hints for seed collection are
        discussed.*

  ———— and POMEROY, K. B.
  1954. SUGGESTIONS FOR BETTER SLASH PINE SEED.
        Forest Farmer 13(5): 6-7, 15. SE
        *Directions for selection and reservation
        of trees capable of producing superior
        seeds in quantity.*

  ———— and POMEROY, K. B.
  1954. TREE IMPROVEMENT RESEARCH AT THE LAKE
        CITY, FLORIDA, RESEARCH CENTER, A PROJECT
        ANALYSIS. U. S. Forest Serv. Southeast.
        Forest Expt. Sta. Sta. Paper 45, 59 pp. SE
        *Superior attributes sought are rapid
        growth, disease resistance, better stem
        form, and improved grain or density of
        wood.*

  ———— and ROSSOLL, H.
  1954. HOW TO ROOT AND GRAFT SLASH PINE. U. S.
        Forest Serv. Southeast. Forest Expt. Sta.
        Sta. Paper 46, 22 pp. SE
        *A graphic exposition of new techniques
        for asexual propagation of pines useful
        as breeding stock (45 drawings).*

  ———— HOEKSTRA, P. E., and ECHOLS, R. M.
  1955. GENETIC CONTROL OF OLEORESIN YIELD AND
        VISCOSITY IN SLASH PINE. Forest Sci. 1:
        19-30. SE
        *Gum yield and viscosity were highly
        controlled genetically, while number and
        size of resin ducts were not.*

  ———— ROSSOLL, H., and POMEROY, K. B.
  1955. HOW TO CONTROL THE POLLINATION OF SLASH
        AND LONGLEAF PINE. U. S. Forest Serv.
        Southeast. Forest Expt. Sta. Paper 58,
        14 pp. SE
        *Latest techniques are presented in true-
        to-life drawings.*

MERKEL, E. P., BEERS, W. L., and HOEKSTRA, P. E.
  1959. PROBLEMS INVOLVED IN THE CONTROL OF
        CONE INSECTS BY AERIAL SPRAYING. Fifth
        South. Forest Tree Impr. Conf. Proc. 1959:
        77-81. SE
        *Evaluates problems brought to light in
        an inconclusive attempt to control, with
        BHC, Dioryctria and other cone insects
        on seed production areas 25 to 56 acres
        in size. Stresses importance of flower
        and cone counts at various stages, and
        need for knowledge of cone insect bi-
        ology.*

MINCKLER, L. S.
  1939. GENETICS IN FORESTRY. Jour. Forestry 37:
        559-564. SE
        *Considerable confusion exists regarding
        the application of genetics to forestry
        practice in America. It is emphasized
        that we should apply all that is known
        about genetics until research establishes
        further facts.*

16

MINCKLER, L. S.
1942. ONE-PARENT HEREDITY TESTS WITH LOBLOLLY
PINE. Jour. Forestry 40: 505-506. SE
*One hundred and five lots of 1-0 loblolly
seedlings grown from the seed of widely
differing parent trees were planted in
a randomized block. Fifth-year survival
and growth measurements showed no
significant relation with any observable
characteristics of adult mother trees. The
data did show significant differences in
both growth and survival of progenies
from different mother trees.*

1945. SEED SOURCE. IS IT TAKEN SERIOUSLY? Jour.
Forestry 43: 749-750. SE
*Data collected on shortleaf and loblolly
seed source for forest nurseries of 12
States show a lack of progress in obtaining a satisfactory seed source. Absence
of a sound policy is attributed to lack
of conviction that source is of real importance and to the conflict between
technical considerations and administrative efficiency.*

MITCHELL, H. L.
1942. BETTER TREE STRAIN SOUGHT IN TESTS AT
EXPERIMENT STATION. Forest Farmer 1(11):
1, 3. SO
*Trees of exceptionally high gum yield
are being identified and their vegetative
propagation attempted.*

1942. DEVELOPMENT OF A HIGH-YIELDING STRAIN
OF NAVAL STORES PINE. U. S. Forest Serv.
South. Forest Expt. Sta. South. Forestry
Notes 45, p. 3. SO
*Objectives and accomplishments of the
project after about 6 months of work.
Reports successful rooting of cuttings
from very young trees.*

1942. THE DEVELOPMENT OF A HIGH-YIELDING
STRAIN OF NAVAL STORES PINE. Naval Stores
Rev. 52(7): 10, 12. *Also as* VEGETATIVE
METHODS OFFER PROMISING SHORT CUTS IN
PROPAGATING THE HIGH-YIELDING PINE TREES.
AT-FA Jour. 4(7): 8-9. SO
*Announces establishment and objectives
of the project to develop a high-yielding
strain of pine for naval stores use and
gives progress for the first 6 months of
work. Reports successful rooting of cut-
tings from very young trees.*

———— and WHEELER, P. R.
1959. THE SEARCH FOR WOOD QUALITY. Two parts.
Forest Farmer 18(4): 4-6 and 18(5):
10-12. *Also as* WOOD QUALITY OF MISSIS-
SIPPI'S PINE RESOURCES. U. S. Forest Serv.
Forest Prod. Lab. Rpt. 2143, 20 pp. SO
*Highlights of wood-density research in
southern pines, carried on in connection
with the third Forest Survey of Mississippi.*

———— and WHEELER, P. R.
1960. SPECIFIC GRAVITY—A MEASURE OF INTRINSIC
WOOD QUALITY. Soc. Amer. Foresters Proc.
1959: 53-57. SO
*Relationships of specific gravity to age
of wood, species, and latitude and longitude of the growing site were investigated by extensive sampling of the major
southern pine species in Mississippi.*

———— SCHOPMEYER, C. S., and DORMAN, K. W.
1942. PEDIGREED PINE FOR NAVAL STORES PRODUC-
TION. Sci. 96: 559-560. SO
*Describes work on the project and ac-
complishments in selection where trees
producing from two to three times as
much gum as average trees were located.
Also reports on experiments in vegetative propagation and details of method
used to root cuttings from mature trees.*

———— SCHOPMEYER, C. S., and DORMAN, K. W.
1942. RECENT DEVELOPMENTS IN THE SELECTION
AND PROPAGATION OF HIGH-YIELDING NAVAL
STORES PINE. U. S. Forest Serv. South.
Forest Expt. Sta. South. Forestry Notes
46, pp. 3-4. SO
*Progress and accomplishments after a-
bout the first year of work. Superior
trees producing from two to three times
the yield of gum from average trees were
located, and cuttings from mature slash
pine trees were successfully rooted.*

NAMKOONG, G.
1960. FEMALE FLOWERS ON ONE-YEAR-OLD PITCH
PINE. Forest Sci. 6: 163. SO
*A new degree of female flowering pre-
cocity for pines.*

NEELANDS, R. W., and JEWELL, F. F.
1961. THE SEARCH FOR PEST-RESISTANT TREES.
Forest Farmer 21(1): 15, 26, 28. SO
*Work on fusiform-rust resistance at the
Southern Institute of Forest Genetics
exemplifies the possibilities of breeding
for pest resistance.*

NELSON, T. C.
1957. A METHOD FOR VEGETATIVELY PROPAGATING
YELLOW-POPLAR. Jour. Forestry 55: 589.
SE
*Entire seedlings were split longitudinal-
ly, the exposed tissues coated with lano-
lin, and the upper half of the stem
clipped off. All seedlings so treated in
December and January callused over and
grew.*

17

NELSON, T. C.
1957. ROOTING AND AIR-LAYERING SOME SOUTHERN HARDWOODS. Fourth South. Forest Tree Impr. Conf. Proc. 1957: 51-54. SE
Successful rooting of cuttings from eastern cottonwood, sycamore, and yellow-poplar, and successful air-layering of sycamore, green ash, sweetgum, and eastern cottonwood are reported.

———— and MARTINDALE, D. L.
1957. ROOTING AMERICAN SYCAMORE CUTTINGS. Jour. Forestry 55: 532. SE
Cuttings 20 inches long from 1-year-old sprouts were made in October, kept in cold storage, and planted in November and in March. Survival and growth were best for large-diameter cuttings.

NIENSTAEDT, H., CECH, F. C., MERGEN, F., AND OTHERS.
1958. VEGETATIVE PROPAGATION IN GENETICS RESEARCH AND PRACTICE. Jour. Forestry 56: 826-839. SE
Factors affecting success of vegetative propagation and details of methods—grafting, rooting, and air-layering—that seem to offer most promise with American species.

OSTROM, C. E.
1953. MORE AND BETTER TREES: THE ACTIVITIES OF THE COMMITTEE ON SOUTHERN FOREST TREE IMPROVEMENT. South. Lumberman 186 (2326): 35-36. *Also as* ACCOMPLISHMENTS OF THE COMMITTEE ON SOUTHERN FOREST TREE IMPROVEMENT. Naval Stores Rev. 62(51): 14-15, 26-28. *Also as* RECENT DEVELOPMENTS IN THE SOUTHERN FOREST TREE IMPROVEMENT PROGRAM. (Abstract.) Assoc. South. Agr. Workers Proc. 50: 115-116. SE
Function, accomplishments, and plans of the Committee on Southern Forest Tree Improvement.

1953. THE ACTIVITIES OF THE COMMITTEE ON SOUTHERN FOREST TREE IMPROVEMENT. Second South. Forest Tree Impr. Conf. Proc. 1953, 7 pp. SE
Origin, objectives, organization, and first 2 years' activities of the widely representative regional Committee.

1955. THE TREE IMPROVEMENT RESEARCH PROGRAM AT THE SOUTHEASTERN FOREST EXPERIMENT STATION. Third South. Forest Tree Impr. Conf. Proc. 1955: 101-104. SE
Studies in variation and inheritance, project work in selective breeding, and many facilitating studies are being conducted concurrently at several research centers.

PESSIN, L. J.
1934. EFFECT OF FLOWER PRODUCTION ON RATE OF GROWTH OF VEGETATIVE SHOOTS OF LONGLEAF PINE. Sci. 80: 363-364. SO
Does the production of staminate strobili reduce the growth of the shoots on which they occur, or does weakening of the shoots by other influences favor the development of staminate rather than pistillate strobili?

1936. UNUSUAL LONGLEAF PINE SEEDLINGS. Jour. Forestry 34: 817-818. SO
Natural seedlings produced pistillate cones when 1-4 feet high and in the sixteenth growing season.

POMEROY, K. B.
1953. BETTER TREES FOR TOMORROW. Naval Stores Rev. 63(20): 19, 21-22. *Also in* AT-FA Jour. 16(2): 18. SE
Propagation and controlled breeding, proven tools of the horticulturist and agronomist, are now being used in developing superior strains of longleaf and slash pine.

1953. RESEARCH IN TREE IMPROVEMENT AT LAKE CITY. TAPPI 36(11): 147a-150a. SE
Forest managers who remove undesirable trees, leave only the best trees for regeneration, and plant seedlings from the best available local parentage can reap the benefits of eugenic forestry while waiting for the deferred benefits of controlled breeding.

1953. TREE IMPROVEMENT—ITS POTENTIALITIES. Forest Farmer 12(11): 8-9, 11. *Also in* The Unit, News Letter 48, pp. 25-27. *Also in* Paper Trade Jour. 137(6): 18-19. SE
Preliminary results show that the value of forest trees can be increased by genetic control of inherited characteristics. Best returns in forest-tree improvement will probably be achieved by combined efforts of silviculturists working with environmental factors and geneticists working with inherited factors.

1954. BETTER TREES FOR TOMORROW. Fla. Grower and Rancher 17(2): 12, 34. SE
General review of the possibilities of improvement of southern pine trees through genetic research.

1954. LOOKING AHEAD WITH NAVAL STORES. Forest Farmer 13(12): 14, 18. SE
Discussion of future trends in the naval stores industry, describing the part to be played by high-yielding strains of pine.

POMEROY, K. B.
1955. SELECTING SLASH PINE FOR GREATER YIELDS OF TURPENTINE. Third South. Forest Tree Impr. Conf. Proc. 1955: 47-49. SE
Gives evidence that gum-yielding ability is strongly inherited in slash pine and that it is possible to select and breed genetically superior trees.

————. 1955. UP-GRADING SLASH PINE SEED SOURCES. Soc. Amer. Foresters Proc. 1954: 74-75. *Also as* HOW WE GET GOOD PINE SEED. Prog. Farmer 70(10): 34D. SE
Recommends selection of genetically superior trees and establishment of clonal seed orchards.

———— and MERGEN, F.
1955. BETTER SLASH PINE SEED. Forest Farmer 14(6): 11. *Also as* BETTER FORESTS A REALITY. Natl. Container Digest 8(4): 5. 1954. SE
An 86-acre seed producing area was created by removing undesirable phenotypes from a 20-year-old slash pine plantation.

PUTNAM, J. A.
1955. POSSIBILITIES OF GENETICS RESEARCH IN SOUTHERN HARDWOODS. Third South. Forest Tree Impr. Conf. Proc. 1955: 44-47. SO
A little work has been done on artificial regeneration and on genetic selection of cottonwood, but virtually nothing on numerous other valuable hardwood species. Specific suggestions are offered.

REINES, M., and McALPINE, R. G.
1960. THE MORPHOLOGY OF NORMAL, CALLUSED, AND ROOTED DWARF SHOOTS OF SLASH PINE. Bot. Gaz. 121: 118-124. SE
Individual needles are capable of callus formation and root development. Cortex and pith contribute largely to callus formation but cambial cells and parenchyma can also proliferate.

RUSSELL, T. E.
1960. WHY GAMBLE ON PINE SEED? Forests and People 10(3): 35, 42, 46-47. SO
"The time has come . . . when steps must be taken to improve the quality of Louisiana's pine seed, and to put seed procurement on the same high level as other forest practices."

SCHOENIKE, R. E.
1955. WHY PINE SEED CROPS FAIL. Forest Farmer 14(10): 10. SO
In March 1955, loblolly and shortleaf pines near Crossett, Arkansas, bore abundant flowers, but heavy spring rains washed the loblolly pollen out of the air, and a late freeze ruined the shortleaf flowers. In consequence, a very poor cone crop may be expected in 1956.

————. 1956. PLASTIC TUBES FOR CONTROLLED POLLINATION OF PINE. Jour. Forestry 54: 135. SO
Small plastic tubes have a slightly higher initial cost than most other bagging materials, but they can be used for years. They are light in weight, and their stiffness protects the flowers.

SCHOPMEYER, C. S.
1953. THE CHARACTERISTICS OF A HIGH GUM-YIELDING TREE. Naval Stores Rev. 63(12): 12-13. *Also in* AT-FA Jour. 15(10): 4. *Also as* U. S. Forest Serv. Southeast. Forest Expt. Sta. Res. Notes 39, 2 pp. SE
The factors controlling gum flow in slash pine appear to be size of resin ducts exposed by chipping, number of ducts per square inch of fresh face, viscosity of gum, and exudation pressure. If these factors are inheritable, trees rating high on all four can be developed by controlled breeding.

————. MERGEN, F., and EVANS, T. C.
1954. APPLICABILITY OF POISEUILLE'S LAW TO EXUDATION OF OLEORESIN FROM WOUNDS ON SLASH PINE. Plant Physiol. 29: 82-87. SE
The variables in a modification of the equation for Poiseuille's Law for the flow of liquids through capillaries were measured in the resin duct system of 12 slash pine trees (Pinus elliottii Engelm. var. elliottii). The modified equation is given.

SHOULDERS, E.
1961. EFFECT OF SEED SIZE ON GERMINATION, GROWTH, AND SURVIVAL OF SLASH PINE. Jour. Forestry 59: 363-365. SO
Small seeds yielded smaller seedlings and fewer of plantable grade than medium and large seeds, but growth during the first year in the field eliminated much of the height difference present in the nursery. Nursery germination and field survival were not related to seed size.

SLUDER, E. R.
1960. EARLY RESULTS FROM A GEOGRAPHIC SEED SOURCE STUDY OF YELLOW-POPLAR. U. S. Forest Serv. Southeast. Forest Expt. Sta. Res. Notes 150, 2 pp. SE
Seedlings of local source had significantly higher survival but not faster growth than others. Time of height growth initiation was correlated with length of growing season, date of last killing frost, and latitude of the source of seed.

19

SMITH, R. H., and MERGEN, F.
1954. A BARK BEETLE ATTACKING SCIONS OF GRAFT-
ED SLASH PINES. Jour. Forestry 52: 864-
865. *Also as Pityophthorus pulicarius*
(Zimm.), A BARK BEETLE ATTACKING SCIONS
OF GRAFTED PINES. U. S. Forest Serv. Southeast. Forest Expt. Sta. Res. Notes 64, 2 pp.
SE
In March and April, the beetle extensive-
ly damaged slash pines newly grafted
for seed orchards. It usually attacked
old growth, above the unions. Dusting
with BHC is suggested.

SNOW, A. G., JR., DORMAN, K. W., and SCHOPMEYER,
C. S.
1943. BREEDING BLUEBLOOD PINES. AT-FA Jour.
5(6): 8-10. SO
Flowering characteristics of slash pine
and the importance of using good breed-
ing stock in the development of superior
pine trees are given.

————— DORMAN, K. W., and SCHOPMEYER, C. S.
1943. DEVELOPMENTAL STAGES OF FEMALE STRO-
BILI IN SLASH PINE. Jour. Forestry 41: 922-
923. SO
Early growth and development of the
female flower is divided into four stages:
(1) suitable for placing pollination bags;
(2) latest stage for bagging; (3) optimum
for pollinating; (4) beyond receptive
stage, and bags may be removed.

SNOW, G. A.
1958. CULTURAL DIFFERENCES IN ISOLATES OF
Scirrhia acicola FROM *Pinus palustris* AND
P. taeda. (Abstract.) Phytopath. 48: 398.
SO
Considerable variation occurs in cultural
characteristics of isolates of the brown-
spot fungus. Differences are not corre-
lated with host species.

1961. ARTIFICIAL INOCULATION OF LONGLEAF PINE
WITH *Scirrhia acicola.* Phytopath. 51:
186-188. SO
Longleaf and loblolly seedlings were
inoculated with isolates from loblolly
as well as longleaf trees. Infection oc-
curred only on immature longleaf
needles, not on loblolly. Cultural char-
acters varied widely from isolate to iso-
late, and could not be correlated with
infectious characteristics. Isolates from
longleaf were more infective than those
from loblolly.

SNYDER, E. B.
1957. POLLEN HANDLING. Fourth South. Forest
Tree Impr. Conf. Proc. 1957: 111-115. SO
Means of hastening the shedding of pol-
len, and of extracting and storing pollen.

1959. COMMENTS ON "THE DIVERGENT POINTS OF
VIEW OF FOREST GENETICISTS AND OF AGRON-
OMIC AND HORTICULTURAL CROP BREEDERS."
Jour. Forestry 57: 666-668. SO
Rebuttal to an earlier article by L. I.
Inman.

SNYDER, E. B. (Editor)
1959. GLOSSARY FOR FOREST TREE IMPROVEMENT
WORKERS. U. S. Forest Serv. South. Forest
Expt. Sta. for Soc. Amer. Foresters, 22 pp.
SO
Simplified definitions of about 160 terms
that are in general use by tree breeders
but may not be familiar to persons with
only a slight botanical background.

SNYDER, E. B.
1960. A FOREST-GENETICS LITERATURE CLASSIFICA-
TION BASED ON THE OXFORD DECIMAL CLASSI-
FICATION (ODC). Silvae Genetica 9: 167-
168. SO
Adaptation of the ODC developed and
used at the Southern Institute of Forest
Genetics.

1961. EXTRACTING, PROCESSING, AND STORING
SOUTHERN PINE POLLEN. U. S. Forest Serv.
South. Forest Expt. Sta. Occas. Paper 191.
14 pp. SO
Results from four years' experimentation
at the Southern Institute of Forest Ge-
netics. Recommends extracting pollen
from ripe strobili in dry, warm, moving
air and storing it at 22 percent relative
humidity and 32° F.

1961. MEASURING BRANCH CHARACTERS OF LONG-
LEAF PINES. U. S. Forest Serv. South.
Forest Expt. Sta. Occas. Paper 184, 4 pp.
SO
From measurements of mature branches
on 48 longleaf trees it was deduced that
the best place to determine inherent
branch angles and diameters was a "zone
of equilibrium" in the middle crown
where diameters of successive branches
down the bole increased in proportion
to bole diameter.

1961. RACIAL VARIATION IN ROOT FORM OF LONG-
LEAF PINE SEEDLINGS. Sixth South. Forest
Tree Impr. Conf. Proc. 1961: 53-59. SO
Roots of 1-year-old longleaf pines from
seed sources in southeastern Georgia are
more fibrous than those of seedlings rep-
resenting sources in Alabama, Missis-
sippi, and Louisiana.

———— and DORMAN, K. W.

1961. SELECTIVE BREEDING OF SLASH PINE FOR HIGH OLEORESIN YIELD AND OTHER CHARACTERS. Recent Advances in Botany, pp. 1616-1621. Toronto. SE

Eleven-year-old progeny were micro-chipped. Crosses among high-yielding parents produced 238 grams; high yielders crossed with average yielders 140 grams; average yielders crossed with average yielders 109 grams. Heritability of yield computed by various methods was "selection experiment" 45 percent; correlation of offspring on mean yield of parents after control-pollination 56 percent; correlation of offspring on female parent after wind pollination 62 percent; and components-of-variance method with wind-pollinated progenies 90 percent.

———— and KRAUS, J. F.

1959. EARLY RESULTS OF A SEED SOURCE STUDY OF SLASH PINE IN GEORGIA AND FLORIDA. Fifth South. Forest Tree Impr. Conf. Proc. 1959: 21-34. SE

Seed collected from an apparently optimum climatic zone seems to be moderately superior even when planted in other climates within the range of the species.

TOOLE, E. R.

1948. ROOTABILITY OF CUTTINGS. Amer. Nurseryman 88(2): 72. SE

Rooting tests with the mimosa tree showed that in the case of stem cuttings the nearer the root system the cuttings were taken the better they rooted, indicating increased content of rooting hormone as one progresses from branch tip to branch-to-stem and down the stem.

1949. SELECTION AND PROPAGATION OF WILT-RESISTANT MIMOSA TREES. Trees 9 (4): 10, 12, 16. SE

Describes the wilt resistance found in the mimosa tree, and gives directions for rooting cuttings of root pieces for propagation of resistant clones.

1952. TWO RACES OF *Fusarium oxysporum f. perniciosum* CAUSING WILT OF *Albizzia* spp. Phytopath. 42: 694. SE

One race attacks A. julibrissin and one attacks A. procera (Puerto Rico).

1955. PERFORMANCE OF WILT-RESISTANT MIMOSA TREES IN HIGH-HAZARD AREAS. U. S. Dept. Agr. Plant Dis. Rptr. 39: 874. SE-SO

Ten resistant clones have survived and grown for 5 years in localities where native trees had been killed by the wilt.

TOOLE, E. R., and HEPTING, G. H.
1949. SELECTION AND PROPAGATION OF *Albizzia* FOR RESISTANCE TO FUSARIUM WILT. Phytopath. 39: 63-70. SE

> *In testing certain species of Albizzia, mainly A. julibrissin, for resistance to Fusarium wilt, 1,437 seedlings have been grown from seed collected at various locations from Maryland to Louisiana, and their roots inoculated. Twenty of these trees have survived the disease as long as 8 years, despite repeated inoculations, and in the more recent experiments many more have survived for shorter periods. Fifty-six percent of the seedlings grown from seed resulting from uncontrolled pollination of the resistant selections were wilt-resistant.*
>
> *All cuttings rooted from the resistant selections have thus far appeared immune to the wilt despite successive inoculations, while rooted cuttings from neighboring nonresistant wildings became diseased and died following inoculation.*

VANHAVERBEKE, D. F., and BARBER, J. C.
1961. LESS GROWTH AND NO INCREASED FLOWERING FROM CHANGING SLASH PINE BRANCH ANGLE. U. S. Forest Serv. Southeast. Forest Expt. Sta. Res. Notes 167, 2 pp. SE

> *Branches fixed at 90° from the vertical or 120° downward on 5-year-old grafted seed orchard trees showed no positive increase in flowering. Branch elongation decreased as branch angle increased with branches in upper whorls growing more than those in lower whorls.*

WAHLGREN, H. E., and FASSNACHT, D. L.
1959. ESTIMATING TREE SPECIFIC GRAVITY FROM A SINGLE INCREMENT CORE. U. S. Dept. Agr. Forest Prod. Lab. Rpt. 2146, 24 pp. SO

> *Method of estimating average specific gravity of the merchantable volume in a southern yellow pine tree from a single increment core.*

WAKELEY, P. C.
1927. THE SINS OF THE FATHERS. U. S. Forest Serv. Serv. Bul. 11(17): 3-4. SO

> *Sonderegger pine (longleaf × loblolly) is susceptible to forms of injury that affect one or the other parent species, but not both. Reports high incidence of brown spot (erroneously called "rust" in 1927) and rabbit damage on hybrids 5 months after they were planted as 1-0 stock.*

1937. RECOMMENDATIONS FOR IMPROVEMENT OF FOREST TREES. U. S. Dept. Agr. Yearbook 1937: 1266. SO

> *Urges study of climatic and edaphic races and of single- and double-parent inheritance of both pines and hardwoods; development of disease-, insect-, and wind-resistant pines and high-naval-stores-yielding pines; and, in particular, selection for superior height growth.*

1944. GEOGRAPHIC SOURCE OF LOBLOLLY PINE SEED. Jour. Forestry 42: 23-32. SO

> *The 15-year results of a provenance test of local (Louisiana), Texas, Georgia, and Arkansas loblolly pines established at Bogalusa, Louisiana, with seed of the 1925 crop. Differences in height, diameter, volume, and degree of fusiform rust infection were highly significant. The local stock excelled on all counts, with Texas stock next. Georgia stock was far more heavily infected with rust than the other 3. Survival did not vary significantly.*

1950. PLANT LOBLOLLY PINES FROM LOCAL SEED. U. S Forest Serv. South. Forest Expt. Sta. South. Forestry Notes 66, p. 1. *Also in* Jour. Forestry 48: 348; *and in* The Unit, News Letter 31, p. 18. SO

> *Loblolly pines from local (Louisiana), Texas, Georgia, and Arkansas seed, planted at Bogalusa, Louisiana, produced 41.8, 22.7, 17.7, and 15.4 cords per acre, respectively, in 22 years. Corresponding average heights were 46, 41, 38, and 36 feet; diameters b.h. were 6.7, 5.2, 5.2, and 4.7 inches. The Georgia stock had 37 percent of stems with fusiform rust cankers; the other 3 stocks, only 4 to 6 percent.*

1951. IMPORTANCE OF GEOGRAPHIC STRAINS. First South. Forest Tree Impr. Conf. Proc. 1951, 9 pp. SO

> *Touches briefly on the history of provenance tests. Enunciates the principle of selecting and hybridizing within the framework of geographic strains. Summarizes American findings with loblolly pine of the 1925 and 1935 crops and South African with the 1935 crop. Cites U. S. Department of Agriculture Forest Seed Policy, and proposes a new south-wide pine seed source study. A separate includes also 2 tables and 4 pages of references on provenance tests.*

1954. THE RELATION OF GEOGRAPHIC RACE TO
FOREST TREE IMPROVEMENT. Jour. Forestry
52: 653. SO

*Provenance tests do not of themselves
constitute tree improvement, as their
immediate function is to keep planted
stands from falling below the productive
level of indigenous natural stands. The
techniques they require, however, are
essentially those of progeny tests for tree
improvement, and in the broadest sense
provenance tests are basic to all tree
improvement, which must be carried
out within the framework of geographic
races.*

1955. SET-BACKS AND ADVANCES IN THE SOUTH-
WIDE PINE SEED SOURCE STUDY. Third
South. Forest Tree Impr. Conf. Proc. 1955:
10-13. SO

*Notes on racial variations in the nursery
and early plantation phases. Losses to
drought in western part of study territory necessitate additional longleaf and
shortleaf pine plantations.*

1957. FOREST TREE-IMPROVEMENT WORK IN THE
SOUTH. South. Lumberman 195(2441):
126-129. SO

*Work being done by educational insti-
tutions, Federal agencies, State departments of forestry, industrial organizations, and the Committee on Southern
Forest Tree Improvement.*

1958. SUMMARY OF FOREST TREE IMPROVEMENT
WORK IN THE SOUTH. Fifth Northeast. For-
est Tree Impr. Conf. Proc. 1957: 14-19.
Also in Third Lake States Forest Tree
Impr. Conf. Proc. 1957: 65-71. U. S. Forest
Serv. Lake States Forest Expt. Sta. Sta.
Paper 58, 87 pp. SO

*Past and current activities of educational
institutions, Federal agencies, State
forestry departments and commissions,
industry, and the Committee on Southern
Forest Tree Improvement.*

1959. FIVE-YEAR RESULTS OF THE SOUTHWIDE PINE
SEED SOURCE STUDY. Fifth. South. Forest
Tree Impr. Conf. Proc. 1959: 5-11. SO

*Preliminary analyses have shown sta-
tistically significant variations, attributable to seed source, in the survival and
average height of all four major southern
pines, and in the rust-susceptibility of
loblolly pine.*

3

WAKELEY, P. C.
1961. RESULTS OF THE SOUTHWIDE PINE SEED
SOURCE STUDY THROUGH 1960-61. Sixth
South. Forest Tree Impr. Conf. Proc 1961:
10-24. SO
*Significant variations in survival and
height appear among different geographic sources of both loblolly and shortleaf pine, especially from north to south.
In longleaf they appear almost as much
from east to west as from north to south.
Loblolly varies significantly in fusiform
rust infection, especially from east to
west. Slash pine occurring north and
west of mid-Florida exhibits relatively
less variation than these species.*

———— and CAMPBELL, T. E.
1954. SOME NEW PINE POLLINATION TECHNIQUES.
U. S. Forest Serv. South. Forest Expt. Sta.
Occas. Paper 136, 13 pp. SO
*Practical pointers on sausage-casing pol-
lination bags and on inexpensive pollen
extractors and pollenizers. Of greatest
value are close-up photographs of longleaf pine female strobili at "Placerville"
stages 2-6.*

———— and CAMPBELL, T. E.
1960. SEEDLESS LONGLEAF CONES CAN MATURE AND
OPEN. U. S. Forest Serv. South. Forest
Expt. Sta. South. Forestry Notes 127, pp.
3-4. SO
*An artificially pollinated longleaf flower
produced a cone with no seeds, either
filled or empty.*

———— and COSSITT, F. M.
1950. WHAT ABOUT OUR TREE SEED SOURCE? Forest
Farmer 9(7): 7, 13 SO
*The 22-year results of the 1925 loblolly
seed-source study at Bogalusa, Louisiana; interprets the findings in terms of
20-acre plantations from which wood
might be sold at $2.00 a cord; and ad-
vises concerning geographic sources of
seed for southern pine plantations in
general.*

———— and HENRY, B. W.
1955. PROGRESS IN TREE IMPROVEMENT RESEARCH
AT THE SOUTHERN FOREST EXPERIMENT STA-
TION. Second Lake States Forest Tree
Impr. Conf. Proc. 1955: 33-37. U. S Forest
Serv. Lake States Forest Expt. Sta. Misc.
Rpt. 40, 108 pp. SO
Scope, objectives, and results.

———— ANDERSON, D. A, BERCAW, T. E., AND
OTHERS.
1951. PROPOSAL FOR A COOPERATIVE STUDY OF
GEOGRAPHIC SOURCES OF SOUTHERN PINE
SEED. U. S. Forest Serv. South. Forest
Expt. Sta., 16 pp. SO
*The first document governing the de-
sign, establishment, and conduct of what
has since become the Southwide Pine*
*Seed Source Study. History of under-
taking, commitments involved in participation, objectives, errors to be avoided, hypotheses to be tested and means
of testing them, details of design, pertinent literature references, and specifications for seed collection.*

———— ANDERSON, D. A., BERCAW, T. E., AND
OTHERS.
1951. STANDARDIZED WORKING PLAN FOR LOCAL
TESTS OF SEED SOURCE. U. S. Forest Serv.
South. Forest Expt. Sta., 11 pp. SO
*" . . . Prepared at the request of . . .
planters who wish to test forest tree
seed from several different geographic
sources for suitability in some particular
planting locality. [It] is designed to . . .
save trouble and get dependable results
and . . . insure comparability among tests
by different planters."*

———— ANDERSON, D. A., BERCAW, T. E., AND
OTHERS.
1952. WORKING PLAN FOR COOPERATIVE STUDY OF
GEOGRAPHIC SOURCES OF SOUTHERN PINE
SEED. U. S. Forest Serv. South. Forest
Expt. Sta., 35 pp. SO
*Details the execution of the Southwide
Pine Seed Source Study up to first dis-
tribution of nursery stock in winter of
1952-53. Specifies planting methods, re-
porting, and early plantation care.*

———— ANDERSON, D. A., BERCAW, T. E., AND
OTHERS.
1956. SUPPLEMENT NO. 1 TO THE ORIGINAL WORK-
ING PLAN OF SEPTEMBER 12, 1952, FOR THE
SOUTHWIDE PINE SEED SOURCE STUDY. U. S.
Forest Serv. South. Forest Expt. Sta., 110
pp. SO
*Information furnished to cooperating
nurserymen and planters, and confirmed
or corrected by them, through the establishment from 1952 until 1954 of certain
initial series of longleaf, slash, loblolly,
and shortleaf plantations in 16 States.
Largely tabular, but with 13 pages of
additions to or amendments of the 1952
plan.*

————ZOBEL, B. J., GODDARD, R. E., AND OTHERS.
1960. MINIMUM STANDARDS FOR PROGENY-TESTING
SOUTHERN FOREST TREES FOR SEED-CERTIFI-
CATION PURPOSES. U. S. Forest Serv. South.
Forest Expt. Sta., 19 pp. SO
*Twenty-one standards, with explanatory
text, specifying the plant material, experimental design, field techniques, records, statistical analyses, and reporting
proposed by a special Subcommittee of
the Committee on Southern Forest Tree
Improvement as the minimum basis for
certifying genetic improvement of forest
tree seed.*

24

WENGER, K. F.
1953. THE EFFECT OF FERTILIZATION AND INJURY ON THE CONE AND SEED PRODUCTION OF LOBLOLLY PINE SEED TREES. Jour. Forestry 51: 570-573. SE

Application of fertilizer at the rate of 25 and 50 pounds per tree significantly increased cone production of 25-year-old loblolly pines. Forty-year-old trees did not respond. Half-girdling with a knife produced no increase in cone crop. Treatments did not significantly affect percentage of defective cones, number of seeds per cone, or percentage of defective seed per cone.

WHEELER, P. R.
1959. SPECIFIC GRAVITY VARIATION IN MISSISSIPPI PINES. Fifth South. Forest Tree Impr. Conf. Proc. 1959: 87-96. SO

Of the single variables tested to predict core specific gravity, the most important was the reciprocal of age. It was also found that the four southern pines show true variation in core specific gravity according to geographic location.

WRIGHT, J. W., BINGHAM, R. T., and DORMAN, K. W.
1958. GENETIC VARIATION WITHIN GEOGRAPHIC ECOTYPES OF FOREST TREES AND ITS ROLE IN TREE IMPROVEMENT. Jour. Forestry 56: 803-808. SE

Review of philosophy and results of work in individual tree variation and its utilization in establishing seed orchards.

ZAHNER, R.
1956. GENETICALLY SIMILAR SEEDLINGS FOR PHYSIOLOGY EXPERIMENTS. Jour. Forestry 54: 190. SO

Seedlings of different ancestry may respond differently to treatment, and may thus introduce error into otherwise carefully controlled experiments.

ZAK, B.
1953. DEVELOPING LITTLELEAF-RESISTANT SHORTLEAF PINE. South. Lumberman 187(2345): 147-149. SE

Healthy and vigorous individual trees have been found surrounded by dead and dying trees. Potted seedlings show variable susceptibility to fungus attack when inoculated. Open-pollinated seed has been collected from apparently healthy trees. Also, these trees have been cross-pollinated. Seed from more than a dozen localities over the range of shortleaf pine has been planted on severe littleleaf areas in Virginia, South Carolina, and Georgia in a test of racial variation in disease resistance. A number of selected trees have been propa-

gated by grafting. A method of testing potted seedlings against Phytophthora cinnamomi within 2 years has been developed; also, a shorter method using seedlings growing in liquid solutions.

1953. ROOTING AND GRAFTING IN A FOREST TREE IMPROVEMENT PROGRAM. Second South. Forest Tree Impr. Conf. Proc. 1953, 8 pp. SE

Techniques and relative feasibility and costs of rooting and grafting various southern pines.

1955. GRAFTING TECHNIQUES USED IN PROPAGATING SPECIES OF PINE IN THE SOUTHEAST FOR EXPERIMENTAL AND SEED ORCHARD USE. Third South. Forest Tree Impr. Conf. Proc. 1955: 83-88. SE

Purposes, possibilities, treatments tested, and results attained to date.

1955. INHERITANCE OF RESISTANCE TO LITTLELEAF IN SHORTLEAF PINES. U. S. Forest Serv. Southeast. Forest Expt. Sta. Res. Notes 88, 2 pp. SE

In growth and resistance to Phytophthora root rot, open-pollinated progeny from littleleaf trees were inferior to open-pollinated progeny from associated healthy trees.

1955. THE GRAFTING OF SHORTLEAF AND OTHER PINE SPECIES. U. S. Forest Serv. Southeast. Forest Expt. Sta. Sta. Paper 59, 13 pp. SE

Describes the use of cleft, bottle, side, veneer, and "soft-tissue" grafts, both indoors and out. Factors affecting the success of grafting are discussed. Soft-tissue grafts were especially successful, both intraspecific and interspecific, and are recommended wherever feasible.

1956. EXPERIMENTAL AIR-LAYERING OF SHORTLEAF AND LOBLOLLY PINE. U. S. Forest Serv. Southeast. Forest Expt. Sta. Sta. Paper 69, 12 pp. SE

Methods of air-layering stems and needle fascicles to obtain rooted cuttings.

1956. SEED ORCHARDS. Forest Farmer 15(12): 8-9, 16-17. SE

Factors to be considered in the establishment of seed orchards, and the advantages to be gained from seed orchards.

1957. RESISTANCE TO LITTLELÆAF IN SHORTLEAF PINE. Fourth South. Forest Tree Impr. Conf. Proc. 1957: 41-43. SE
Shortleaf pines on severe littleleaf sites are propagated by seeds and grafts for tests of resistance to Phytophthora cinnamomi.

———— and McALPINE, R. G.
1957. ROOTING OF SHORTLEAF AND SLASH PINE NEEDLE BUNDLES. U. S. Forest Serv. Southeast. Forest Expt. Sta. Res. Notes 112, 2 pp. SE
Needle bundles treated with indolebutyric acid were rooted in a 50-50 mixture of sand and peat moss.

ZOBEL, B., DORMAN, K. W., PERRY T., AND OTHERS.
1954. THE ROLE OF GENETICS IN SOUTHERN FOREST MANAGEMENT. Forest Farmer 14(1): 4-6, 14-15; 14(2): 8-9, 14-19; 14(3): 8-9, 14-15. SE
I.—Environment is the most important factor in tree development only within definite genetic limits. II.—Seed collection for forest nurseries must be from the most favorable geographic origin. III.—In preserving seed trees, select superior individuals insofar as possible.

———— BARBER, J., BROWN, C. L., and PERRY, T. O.
1958. SEED ORCHARDS—THEIR CONCEPT AND MANAGEMENT. Jour. Forestry 56: 815-825. SE
Pertinent information on American seed orchards: their objectives, establishment, and care.

INDEX OF JUNIOR AUTHORS